Washington, DC

"All you've got to do is decide to go
and the hardest part is over.

So go!"

TONY WHEELER, COFOUNDER – LONELY PLANET

THIS EDITION WRITTEN AND RESEARCHED BY

Karla Zimmerman

Regis St Louis

Contents

Plan Your Trip 4

Explore Washington, DC 52

Understand Washington, DC 237

Survival Guide 267

Washington, DC, Maps 292

(left) **Georgetown p94** Georgetown University

(above) **Southeast DC p112** Marine Corps War Memorial, by sculptor Felix de Weldon

(right) **Capitol Building p106** *Statue of Freedom*

Welcome to Washington, DC

The USA's capital teems with iconic monuments, vast museums and the corridors of power, where visionaries and demagogues roam.

Museums & Monuments

Thanks, James Smithson, you eccentric antimonarchist Englishman. That $508,318 gift you bequeathed to the USA back in 1829 to create a 'diffusion of knowledge' paid off big time. There's nothing quite like the Smithsonian Institution, a collection of 19 behemoth, artifact-stuffed museums, many lined up in a row along the National Mall. The National Air and Space Museum, National Museum of Natural History, National Museum of American History, Freer-Sackler Museums of Asian Art – all here, all free, always.

Alongside the museums, Washington's monuments bear tribute to both the beauty and the horror of years past. They're potent symbols of the American narrative, from the awe-inspiring Lincoln Memorial to the powerful Vietnam Veterans Memorial to the stirring Martin Luther King Jr Memorial.

Arts & Culture

Washington is the showcase of American arts, home to such prestigious venues as the National Theatre, the Kennedy Center and the Folger Theatre. Jazz music has a storied history here. In the early 20th century, locals such as Duke Ellington climbed on stages along U St NW, where atmospheric clubs still operate.

Political Life

The president, Congress and the Supreme Court are here – the three pillars of US government. In their orbit float the Pentagon, State Department, World Bank and embassies from most corners of the globe. If you hadn't got the idea, *power* is why Washington exerts such a palpable buzz.

As a visitor, there's a thrill in seeing the action up close – to walk inside the White House, to sit in the Capitol chamber while senators argue about Arctic drilling, and to drink in a bar alongside congresspeople likely determining your newest tax hike over their single-malt Scotch.

History

A lot of history is concentrated within DC's relatively small confines. In a single day, you could gawp at the Declaration of Independence, the real, live parchment with John Hancock's, er, John Hancock scrawled across it at the National Archives; stand where Martin Luther King Jr gave his 'I Have a Dream' speech on the Lincoln Memorial's steps; prowl around the Watergate building that got Nixon into trouble; see the flag that inspired the 'Star Spangled Banner' at the National Museum of American History; and be an arm's length from where Lincoln was assassinated in Ford's Theatre.

ANAGLIC / SHUTTERSTOCK ©

Why I Love Washington, DC

By Karla Zimmerman, Author

It begins with the Mall. How sweet is it to have a walkable strip of museums where you can see nuclear missiles, cursed diamonds and exquisite Asian ceramics in cool underground galleries – for *free?* Further down the path the notes and photos people leave at the Vietnam Veterans Memorial will break your heart, and the Lincoln Memorial just kills with its grandness and sweeping view. Shaw wins my affection for its neighborhoody beer halls and cafes. Most of all, I love how Ben's Chili Bowl makes you feel like a local even if you're not.

For more about our authors, see p320.

Top: The Reflecting Pool (p70) and Washington Monument (p59)

Washington, DC's Top 10

Lincoln Memorial *(p58)*

1 There's something extraordinary about climbing the steps of Abe Lincoln's Doric-columned temple, staring into his dignified eyes, and reading about the 'new birth of freedom' in the Gettysburg Address chiseled beside him. Then to stand where Martin Luther King Jr gave his 'Dream' speech and take in the sweeping view – it's a defining DC moment. At dawn, nowhere in the city is as serene and lovely, which is why the Lincoln Memorial is a popular place for proposals.

National Mall

Washington Monument *(p59)*

2 Tall, phallic and imbued with shadowy Masonic lore, the 555ft obelisk is DC's tallest structure. Workers set the pyramid on top in 1884 after stacking up some 36,000 blocks of granite and marble over the preceding 36 years. A 70-second elevator ride whisks you to the observation deck at the top for the city's best views. Recent renovations have freshened up the monument (and made it earthquake proof).

National Mall

TUPUNGATO / GETTY IMAGES ©

2

JOHN HUDSON PHOTOGRAPHY / GETTY IMAGES ©

Vietnam Veterans Memorial *(p60)*

3 The opposite of DC's white, gleaming marble, the black, low-lying Vietnam memorial cuts into the earth, just as the Vietnam War cut into the national psyche. The monument shows the names of the war's 58,272 casualties – listed in the order they died – along a dark, reflective wall. It's a subtle but remarkably profound monument, where visitors leave poignant mementos, such as photos of babies and notes ('I wish you could have met him, Dad').

National Mall

White House *(p78)*

4 Thomas Jefferson groused it was 'big enough for two emperors, one Pope and the grand Lama,' but when you tour the White House you get the feeling – despite all the spectacle – that it really is just a *house*, where a family lives. Admittedly, that family gets to hang out in Jefferson's green dining room and Lincoln's old office where his ghost supposedly roams. If you don't get in (tours require serious pre-planning), the visitor center provides the scoop on presidential pets and favorite foods.

White House Area & Foggy Bottom

National Gallery of Art *(p61)*

5 It takes two massive buildings to hold the National Gallery's free-to-see trove of paintings, sculptures and decorative arts from the Middle Ages to the present. The East Building gets the modern stuff – Calder mobiles, Matisse collages. The West Building hangs works from earlier eras – El Greco, Monet and North America's only Leonardo da Vinci. Free films and concerts, a sweet cafe with 19 gelato flavors and an adjoining garden studded with whimsical sculptures add to the awesomeness.

National Mall

3

4

Capitol Hill (p106)

6 City planner Pierre L'Enfant called it 'a pedestal waiting for a monument.' So that's how the Capitol came to sit atop the hill that rises above the city. You're welcome to go inside the mighty, white-domed edifice and count the statues, ogle the frescoes and visit the chambers of the folks who run the country. Afterward, call on the neighbors. The Supreme Court and Library of Congress also reside up here, across the street from the Capitol.

Capitol Hill & Southeast DC

Smithsonian Institution (p72)

7 If America was a quirky grandfather, the Smithsonian Institution would be his attic. Rockets, dinosaurs, Rodin sculptures, Tibetan *thangkas* (silk paintings) – even the 45-carat Hope Diamond lights up a room here. The Smithsonian is actually a collection of 19 museums and they're all free, baby. The National Air and Space, Natural History and National American History museums are the group's rock stars, while the National Museum of the American Indian, Freer-Sackler Museums of Asian Art and Reynolds Center for American Art & Portraiture provide quieter spaces for contemplation. RIGHT: NATIONAL AIR AND SPACE MUSEUM (P62)

National Mall

6

VACLAV / SHUTTERSTOCK ©

SIRI STAFFORD / GETTY IMAGES ©

Arlington National Cemetery *(p198)*

8 Soldiers from every war since the Revolution are buried in the 624-acre grounds here. Simple white headstones cover the green hills in a seemingly endless procession. Many US leaders and notable civilians are also buried here. An eternal flame flickers over the grave of John F Kennedy. Flowers pile at the marker for the space shuttle *Challenger* crew. Rifle-toting military guards maintain a 24-hour vigil at the Tomb of the Unknowns, affecting in its solemnity.

Northern Virginia

Ben's Chili Bowl & U Street Corridor *(p173)*

9 The U St Corridor has had quite a life. It was the 'Black Broadway' where Duke Ellington got his jazz on in the early 1900s. It was the smoldering epicenter of the 1968 race riots. There was a troubled descent, then a vibrant rebirth as an entertainment district. And Ben's Chili Bowl has stood there through most of it. Despite visits by presidents and movie stars, Ben's remains a real neighborhood spot, with locals downing half-smokes and gossiping over sweet iced tea. It's quintessential DC.

Logan Circle, U Street & Columbia Heights

WIM WISKERKE / ALAMY ©

RIVERNORTHPHOTOGRAPHY / GETTY IMAGES ©

National Archives *(p129)*

10 You're in line with all of the school groups, annoyed, thinking maybe your time would be better spent at a local watering hole. Then you enter the dim rotunda and see them – the Declaration of Independence, the Constitution and the Bill of Rights – the USA's founding documents. The National Archives has the real, yellowing, spidery-handwriting-scrawled parchments. And your jaw drops. There's John Hancock's signature, and Ben Franklin's, and Thomas Jefferson's! The archives also display the Magna Carta, George Washington's old letters and Charles 'Pa' Ingalls' homesteading paperwork.

Downtown & Penn Quarter

What's New

National Zoo's Panda

Bao Bao, the giant panda cub born in 2013, is the zoo's big star. Enjoy her while you can, as she'll be sent to China when she turns four. (p188)

National Museum of African American History and Culture

The Smithsonian's newest museum, opening in 2016 on the Mall, has everything from Louis Armstrong's trumpet to Emmett Till's casket to Nat Turner's bible. (p69)

National Mall Circulator

At long last: the Mall has a public transportation option. The Mall Circulator bus began running in 2015 on a route that loops by the main museums and memorials. (www.nationalmall.dccirculator.com)

White House Visitor Center

The visitor center is all spiffed up after a $12.6 million renovation, with cool artifacts (Roosevelt's fireside chat desk, Lincoln's cabinet chair) and multimedia exhibits. (p79)

DC Brew Tours

Hop in the Brew Tour van and get ready for tastings galore at local suds-makers such as Chocolate City, 3 Stars, Bluejacket and Atlas, most of which started pouring in the last few years. (p37)

Petworth

The northwest neighborhood is gentrifying fast, with indie shops and funky bars moving in to share sidewalks with long-time Caribbean, Ethiopian and soul-food joints. (p182)

Textile Museum

The grand new building for exquisite fabrics and carpets opened in 2015 and now shares space with a bonus trove of historic DC maps, drawings and ephemera. (p86)

Navy Yard

Hip eateries, impressive breweries and a mod, playful park have cropped up around the Navy Yard, joining the Nationals' ballpark in making this area a bona fide destination. (p112)

American Veterans Disabled for Life Memorial

Dedicated to the four-million-plus soldiers who've returned home with disabilities, the memorial features a star-shaped fountain, glass-etched walls and benches for contemplation. (p117)

Union Market

The market isn't so new (it opened in 2012), but fresh food and drink vendors and pop-up restaurants emerge all the time. It's a great place to get the pulse of DC's foodie scene. (p174)

Funk Parade

Locals in the U St neighborhood started the Funk Parade in 2014, a street festival that celebrates the area's musical heritage with groovy bands, live art and food. (www.funkparade.com)

For more recommendations and reviews, see **lonelyplanet.com/washington-dc**

Need to Know

For more information, see Survival Guide (p267)

Currency
US dollar ($)

Language
English

Visas
Visitors from Canada, the UK, Australia, New Zealand, Japan and many EU countries do not need a visa for stays under 90 days. Other visitors might (see www.travel.state.gov).

Money
ATMs widely available. Credit cards accepted at most hotels, restaurants and shops.

Cell Phones
Europe and Asia's GSM 900/1800 standard does not work in the USA. Consider buying a cheap local phone with a pay-as-you-go plan.

Time
Eastern Standard Time (GMT/UTC minus five hours)

Tourist Information
See www.washington.org or visit the DC Chamber of Commerce Tourist Information Center (Map p302; ☎202-347-7201; www.dcchamber.org; 506 9th St NW; ⏲8:30am-5:30pm Mon-Fri; Ⓜ Gallery Pl).

Daily Costs

Budget: Less than $125
- Dorm bed: $25–50
- Lunchtime specials for food and happy-hour drinks: $15–$30
- Metro day pass: $14.50
- Nationals baseball ticket: $15

Midrange: $125–350
- Hotel or B&B double room: $150–275
- Dinner in a casual restaurant: $25–50
- Bicycle tour: $40
- Capitol Steps theater ticket: $40.50

Top End: More than $350
- Luxury hotel double room: $400
- Dinner at Minibar: $250
- Washington National Opera ticket: $100–200

Advance Planning

Three months before Book your hotel, request a White House tour.

One month before Reserve tickets online for the National Archives, United States Holocaust Memorial Museum, Washington Monument, Ford's Theatre and Capitol tour.

Two weeks before Reserve ahead at your must-eat restaurants.

One week before Check www.washingtoncitypaper.com to see what's on for entertainment and make bookings.

Useful Websites

- **Lonely Planet** (www.lonelyplanet.com/washington-dc) Destination information, hotel bookings, travel forum and photos.
- **Destination DC** (www.washington.org) Official tourism site packed with sightseeing and event info.
- **Cultural Tourism DC** (www.culturaltourismdc.org) Neighborhood-oriented events and tours.
- **DCist** (www.dcist.com) Hip blog about all things DC.
- **Washingtonian** (www.washingtonian.com) Features on dining, entertainment and local luminaries.

WHEN TO GO

Peak season is late March to May. June and July are crowded and hot. August is steamy, but cheap. December is festive.

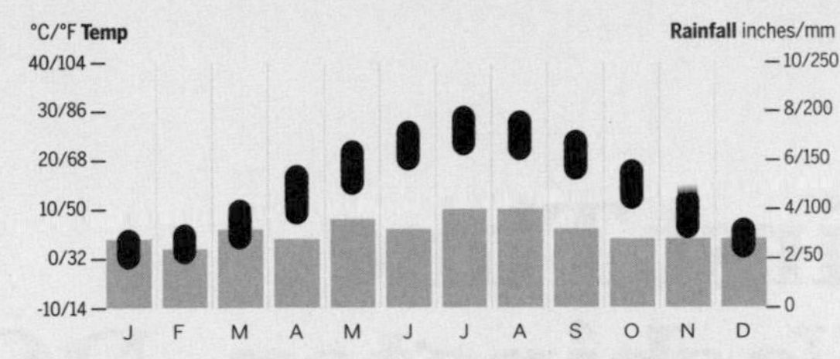

Arriving in Washington, DC

Ronald Reagan Washington National Airport Metro trains (around $2.50) depart every 10 minutes or so between 5am and midnight (to 3am Friday and Saturday); they reach the city center in 20 minutes. A taxi is $13 to $22.

Washington Dulles International Airport The Silver Line Express bus runs every 15 to 20 minutes from Dulles to Wiehle-Reston East Metro between 6am and 10:40pm (from 7:45am weekends). Total time to the city center is 60 to 75 minutes, total cost around $11. A taxi is $62 to $73.

Union Station All trains and many buses arrive at this huge station near the Capitol. There's a Metro stop inside for easy onward transport. Taxis queue outside the main entrance.

For much more on **arrival**, see p268

Getting Around

The Metro is the main way to move around the city. Buy a rechargeable SmarTrip card at any Metro station. You must use the card to enter *and* exit station turnstiles.

➡ **Metro** Fast, frequent, ubiquitous (except during weekend track maintenance). It operates between 5am and midnight (3am on Friday and Saturday). Fares from $1.75 to $5.90 depending on distance traveled. A day pass costs $14.50.

➡ **DC Circulator bus** Useful for the Mall, Georgetown, Adams Morgan and other areas with limited Metro service.

➡ **Bicycle** Capital Bikeshare stations are everywhere; a day pass costs $7.

➡ **Taxi** Relatively easy to find (less so at night), but costly. The rideshare company Uber is used more in the District.

For much more on **getting around**, see p269

Sleeping

Accommodations will likely be your biggest expense in DC. The best digs are monuments of Victorian and jazz-era opulence. Chain hotels, B&Bs and apartments blanket the cityscape, too. Several hostels are sprinkled around, typically in locations that are a bit far-flung. Groovy boutique hotels abound in the core neighborhoods, as do uber-luxury hotels catering to presidents, prime ministers and other heads of state. DC's atmospheric B&Bs (also called guesthouses) are often cheaper than hotels.

Useful Websites

➡ **Lonely Planet** (www.lonelyplanet.com/hotels) Author-recommended reviews and online booking.

➡ **Bed & Breakfast DC** (www.bedandbreakfastdc.com) One-stop shop to book B&Bs and apartments.

➡ **Destination DC** (www.washington.org) Options from the tourism office's website.

➡ **WDCA Hotels** (www.wdcahotels.com) Discounter that sorts by neighborhood, price or ecofriendliness.

For much more on **sleeping**, see p224

First Time Washington, DC

For more information, see Survival Guide (p267)

Checklist

➡ Check the airline baggage restrictions.

➡ Inform your debit-/credit-card company of your travel.

➡ Arrange for appropriate travel insurance (p274).

➡ International visitors: make sure your passport is valid for at least six months past your arrival date.

What to Pack

➡ Good walking shoes. You'll be on your feet a lot, especially around the Mall's museums and monuments.

➡ A small day pack or purse (the smaller the better to avoid lengthy searches by security staff when visiting museums).

➡ Easy-to-carry sweater or sweatshirt. In summer it's sweltering outside but chilly in the air-conditioned museums.

➡ Umbrella, because it can be rainy.

Top Tips for Your Trip

➡ Buy a rechargeable Metro SmarTrip card as soon as you arrive at the airport or Union Station. It's way more convenient than disposable fare cards and saves $1 per ride.

➡ Stock up on snacks before visiting the Mall. Few good dining options are there. Typically the museums allow you to bring in food, though you can't eat it in the galleries. The Capitol is an exception; no food is allowed inside.

➡ Prioritize your top museum or monument each day, and go there first to beat the crowds. Queues can be lengthy as everyone has to go through security (sometimes a metal detector, sometimes it's staff checking bags by hand).

➡ Make dinner reservations for restaurants in the midrange and upper price bracket. For hot spots that don't take reservations, arrive an hour before opening time to get in line.

What to Wear

DC has a reputation for having no style or fashion savvy. That's an outdated characterization, though no one would laud the city for its sartorial flair.

Don't worry about dressing up. It's a business suit kind of town by day, but it's perfectly fine to wear jeans and casual clothes to dinner or the theater at night.

Be Forewarned

➡ The Metro stops running at midnight (3am on weekends). Allow more time for travel during weekends, as track maintenance work slows down trains.

➡ Taxis can be hard to find. Many locals use Uber instead.

➡ While DC isn't dangerous, it does have typical big-city crime issues (mostly theft). Use common sense and be aware of your surroundings, especially around H St NE, Southeast DC and Anacostia.

➡ In the summer months DC boils. The humidity is outrageous. Be prepared to sweat buckets (and then freeze when you go into an air-conditioned museum).

Pre-Booking

Many of Washington's top sights require that you plan ahead. Foremost is the White House, for which you should make your tour request three to six months in advance. Sights that need two to three months' leeway include the Pentagon and Marine Barracks parade. Pre-booking one month in advance is useful (though not required) for the Washington Monument, National Archives, Ford's Theatre, Holocaust Memorial Museum and Capitol.

Taxes & Refunds

A tax is levied on most goods and services. In DC it is 14.5% for lodgings, 10% in restaurants and bars, and 5.75% for other items. In general it's less in Virginia and Maryland. The tax typically is not included in the price, but added when you pay.

Tipping

Tipping is not optional. Only withhold tips in cases of outrageously bad service.

➡ **Airport & hotel porters** $2 per bag, minimum $5 per cart.

➡ **Bartenders** 15% per round, minimum $1 per drink.

➡ **Hotel maids** $2 to $5 per night.

➡ **Restaurant servers** 15% to 20%, unless a gratuity is already charged on the bill.

➡ **Taxi drivers** 10% to 15%, rounded up to the next dollar.

➡ **Valet parking attendants** At least $2 when you're handed back the keys.

LISSANDRA MELO / SHUTTERSTOCK ©

Transportation options in Washington, DC

Etiquette

➡ **Smoking** Don't smoke in restaurants or bars: DC is smoke-free by law in those venues.

➡ **Dining** People eat dinner early in Washington, often by 6pm.

➡ **On the Metro** Stand to the right on the escalators; walk on the left.

➡ **Conversation** It's OK to ask locals you've just met, 'What do you do for work?' Most people in DC have an intriguing job that they're happy to discuss.

Tours

The following tours provide a good introduction to Washington, particularly if you're short on time:

➡ **DC by Foot** (p272) Offers a slew of pay-what-you-can walking tours that cover the Mall, Georgetown, U St and more.

➡ **Bike & Roll** (p272) Easy three-hour spins by the museums and monuments. The nighttime rides are particularly atmospheric.

➡ **Old Town Trolley Tours** (p272) Hop-on, hop-off bus that loops around the Mall, Arlington National Cemetery and beyond.

Top Itineraries

Day One

National Mall (p56)

You might as well dive right into the good stuff, and the **Lincoln Memorial** is about as iconically DC as it gets. It's also a convenient starting point, since Abe sits at the far end of the Mall. Next up as you walk east is the powerful **Vietnam Veterans Memorial**. Then comes the **Washington Monument**, which is pretty hard to miss, being DC's tallest structure and all.

Lunch Munch sandwiches by an artsy waterfall at the Cascade Cafe (p70).

National Mall (p56)

After lunch, it's time to explore the **National Gallery of Art**. Pick a side: East, for modern; or West, for Leonardo da Vinci, impressionists and other classics. Afterward, mosey across the lawn to the **National Air and Space Museum** and gape at the stuff hanging from the ceiling. The missiles and Wright brothers' original plane are incomparably cool.

Dinner Hop the Metro to Duke's Grocery (p148) in Dupont Circle.

Dupont (p142)

Dupont parties in the evening. Sip cocktails at **Firefly Bar** or **Bar Charley**. Casual types can hoist brews at **Bier Baron**.

Day Two

Capitol Hill (p106)

Do the government thing today. Start in the **Capitol** and tour the statue-cluttered halls. Then walk across the street and up the grand steps to the **Supreme Court**; hopefully you'll get to hear a case argument. The **Library of Congress** and its 500 miles of books blow minds next door.

Lunch Have a burger amid politicos at the Old Ebbitt Grill (p87).

White House Area (p76)

Hopefully you planned ahead and booked a **White House** tour. If not, make do at the **White House Visitor Center**. Pop into the **Round Robin** to see if any bigwigs and lobbyists are clinking glasses. Zip over to the **Kennedy Center** to watch the free 6pm show.

Dinner Go for French in laid-back elegance at Chez Billy Sud (p99).

Georgetown (p92)

After dinner, sink a pint in a friendly pub like **J Paul's**. On warm nights the outdoor cafes and boating action make **Georgetown Waterfront Park** a hot spot. And check if anyone groovy is playing at **Blues Alley**.

Day Three

Arlington (p199)

Walking around **Arlington National Cemetery** you can't help but be moved, from the Tomb of the Unknowns' dignified guards to John F Kennedy's eternal flame. One Metro stop south, the **Pentagon** offers another affecting memorial to those who died in the September 11, 2001, attacks.

Lunch Follow the smoked meat smell to Hill Country Barbecue (p135).

Downtown (p127)

It's an abundance of riches downtown. See the Declaration of Independence at the **National Archives**, and the seat where Lincoln was shot at **Ford's Theatre**. The **Reynolds Center for American Art & Portraiture** hangs sublime paintings. The **Newseum** has the Unabomber's cabin. You'll have to make some hard choices about which sights to visit.

Dinner Seek out Compass Rose (p174) for a romantic global taste-trip.

Logan Circle, U Street & Columbia Heights (p164)

There's nightlife galore. Soak up the neighborhood's jazzy vibe at **Bohemian Caverns**, split your eardrums at the rock-and-roll **Black Cat**, or grab a beer at neighborhood favorite **Right Proper Brewing Co**.

Day Four

Upper Northwest DC (p185)

If you have kids, get to the **National Zoo** now. Even without kids, the zoo entertains thanks to its giant pandas and brainy orangutans. Earmark some quality time for the **Washington National Cathedral** and its Darth Vader gargoyle, moon rock and Helen Keller's ashes, among other esoteric offerings.

Lunch 2 Amys (p190) serves excellent pizzas, antipasti and craft brews.

Adams Morgan (p155)

Adams Morgan is Washington's party zone, but during the day **Meeps** and **Crooked Beat Records** provide plenty to do. Plus you're well situated for happy hour at **Millie & Al's**, a classic dive bar.

Dinner Stroll into the Diner (p157) any time: it's open round the clock.

National Mall (p56)

End in the 'hood where you began your Washington trip, but experience it from a different perspective. Walk along Constitution Ave from east to west. The dramatically lit monuments glow ethereally at night. Climb the steps of the **Lincoln Memorial** and turn around for one last, long fantastic view. That'll do it, until you and DC meet again.

If You Like...

Famous Monuments

Lincoln Memorial Abraham Lincoln gazes peacefully across the Mall from his hallowed Doric-columned temple. (p58)

Vietnam Veterans Memorial Simple and moving, the black wall reflects the names of the Vietnam War's 58,272 Americans who gave their lives. (p60)

Tomb of the Unknowns Military guards maintain a somber, round-the-clock vigil at this crypt in Arlington National Cemetery. (p198)

Martin Luther King Jr Memorial Dr King's 30ft-tall likeness emerges from a mountain of granite. (p63)

Washington Monument The iconic obelisk, DC's tallest structure, offers unparalled views from the top. (p59)

National WWII Memorial Soaring columns and stirring quotes mark this memorial smack in the Mall's midst. (p69)

Franklin Delano Roosevelt Memorial FDR's monument sprawls across 7.5 acres, an oasis of alcoves, fountains and contemplative inscriptions. (p69)

Jefferson Memorial Thomas Jefferson's round shrine, set amid a grove of gorgeous cherry trees, represents his famously shaped library. (p69)

Not-So-Famous Monuments

Korean War Veterans Memorial The haunting tribute depicts

ELAN FLEISHER / GETTY IMAGES ©

Inside the greenhouse of the United States Botanic Garden (p67)

ghostly steel soldiers marching by a wall of etched faces. (p70)

George Mason Memorial The statesman who wrote the Bill of Rights' prototype gets his due via an oasis of flowers and fountains. (p69)

Women's Titanic Memorial The waterside figure honors the men who sacrificed their lives for the women and children aboard the sinking ship. (p117)

National Japanese American Memorial Two cranes bound with barbed wire represent Japanese American citizens held in internment camps during WWII. (p112)

Navy Memorial A large plaza of flags and masts surrounds the lone sailor with his duffel bag. (p132)

National Law Enforcement Officers Memorial Its walls show the names of all US police officers killed in the line of duty since 1794. (p133)

African American Civil War Memorial Rifle-bearing troops who fought in the Union Army are immortalized in bronze. (p166)

Green Spaces

United States National Arboretum Learn your state tree amid 450 acres of meadowlands and wooded groves. (p167)

Rock Creek Park It's twice the size of New York's Central Park and wild enough to house coyotes. (p188)

Dumbarton Oaks The Georgetown mansion features sprawling, fountain-dotted gardens; big bonus if you visit during spring. (p94)

United States Botanic Garden Exotic flowers bloom in a glassy Mall greenhouse that looks like London's Crystal Palace. (p67)

Theodore Roosevelt Island Car- and bike-free, this Potomac River isle floats woodlands, trails and tranquillity. (p199)

Georgetown Waterfront Park Sip an alfresco drink, ogle the yachts and watch rowing teams ply the Potomac. (p94)

East Potomac Park Walk, fish and smell the cherry blossoms in this lovely spot a hop and skip from the Mall. (p116)

Black History

Frederick Douglass National Historic Site The hilltop home of the escaped slave and statesman impresses almost as much as the man himself. (p112)

National Museum of African American History and Culture The Smithsonian's newest museum, open in 2016, has everything from Harriet Tubman's hymnal to Emmett Till's casket. (p68)

Anacostia Museum This small, Smithsonian neighborhood outpost rotates exhibits on African American history and culture. (p116)

African American Civil War Museum It goes beyond the war, following black history through the Civil Rights movement. (p166)

Howard Theatre It was the first major theater built to feature black entertainers performing for a predominantly black clientele. (p181)

Mt Zion Cemetery The crumbling headstones belong to free black residents who lived here in the 19th century. (p98)

Freedom House Museum Learn about America's darkest era in this former slave-holding quarters in Alexandria. (p201)

For more top Washington, DC, spots, see the following:

- Eating (p31)
- Drinking & Nightlife (p36)
- Entertainment (p40)
- Shopping (p42)
- Sports & Activities (p44)
- With Kids (p46)

Off-the-Beaten-Path Museums

National Postal Museum A whopping stamp collection and poignant old letters lift this museum beyond its humdrum name. (p111)

Textile Museum The nation's only textile museum unfurls exquisite fabrics and carpets from 3000 BC to the present. (p86)

National Museum of Health and Medicine Home to a giant hairball, Lincoln's assassination bullet and more macabre exhibits. (p170)

Hillwood Museum & Gardens Stunning works from Russian and French royal collections, plus pretty gardens and a charming cafe. (p189)

DEA Museum Showcase of America's war on drugs, with Nancy Reagan commercials and relics from old opium dens. (p199)

Woodrow Wilson House See how genteel Washingtonians lived and socialized in this 1920s-preserved home on Embassy Row. (p145)

Carlyle House The grand manor packs historic treasures and teaches about the lives of Alexandria's 18th-century gentry. (p200)

Art

Reynolds Center for American Art & Portraiture Portraits on one side, O'Keeffe, Hopper and more of America's best on the other. (p130)

National Gallery of Art It takes two massive buildings to hold the trove of paintings, sculptures and decorative arts from the Middle Ages to the present. (p61)

Phillips Collection The country's oldest modern-art museum is a cozy house that puts you face-to-face with Renoirs and Rothkos. (p145)

Freer-Sackler Museums of Asian Art An incredible ensemble of ancient ceramics and temple sculptures spreads across two tunnel-connected galleries. (p66)

Hirshhorn Museum Rodin and Brancusi sculptures mingle with Miró and Warhol canvases in the Mall's cylindrical modern-art house. (p66)

Torpedo Factory Art Center The former arms factory has morphed into three floors of artists' studios offering ceramics, glassworks and jewelry. (p201)

Kid-Friendly Activities

National Zoo Bamboo-nibbling pandas, roaring lions, swinging orangutans, frolicking otters and many more critters roam the 163 acres. (p188)

National Museum of Natural History Mummies! Henry the giant elephant! Insect zoo to watch tarantulas get fed! (p67)

Discovery Theater Cultural plays, puppet shows and storytelling are all part of the repertoire at the Smithsonian children's theater. (p71)

National Air and Space Museum It's a blast, with moon rocks, spaceships, starry films and wild simulator rides. (p62)

Albert Einstein Memorial Einstein's bemused, chubby bronze likeness is a magnet for climbing kids. (p86)

Newseum Junior journalists report 'live from the White House' via the TV studio (and get the take-home video to prove it). (p131)

International Spy Museum Budding James Bonds get to crawl through ductwork, peek through vents and find hidden recording devices. (p131)

Seeing Politics in Action

Capitol Sit in on committee hearings to see how bills start winding their way toward laws. (p106)

White House The protester-fueled political theater outside the building is where to observe democracy at its finest. (p78)

Round Robin Since 1850 bigwigs and lobbyists have swirled Scotch and cut deals in the gilded bar. (p89)

Le Diplomate Bustling French restaurant where politcos cozy up for coq au vin. (p173)

Pop-Culture Icons

Watergate Complex The chichi apartment-hotel complex is synonymous with political scandal, thanks to Richard Nixon and his wiretaps. (p87)

Lincoln Memorial Steps Where MLK gave his 'Dream' speech, and Owen Wilson and Vince Vaughn discussed girls in *Wedding Crashers*. (p58)

Washington Monument Tall, phallic and imbued with shadowy lore, it's also a frequent target of Hollywood destruction (think *2012* and *Mars Attacks*). (p59)

Exorcist Stairs Demonically possessed, head-spinning Reagan from *The Exorcist* sent victims to their screaming deaths in Georgetown. (p94)

Ben's Chili Bowl Everyone who's anyone – rock stars, actors, presidents – takes a counter seat at Ben's for the obligatory photo op. (p173)

Mayflower Renaissance Hotel J Edgar Hoover famously dined here; New York governor Eliot Spitzer infamously trysted with a call girl here. (p228)

Romantic Spots

Lincoln Memorial At dawn, nowhere in DC is as serene and lovely, which is why it's a popular place for proposals. (p58)

Constitution Gardens The shady grove, small pool and old stone cottage form a hidden oasis on the Mall. (p70)

National Sculpture Garden In summer, jazz concerts set the mood; in winter, the ice rink gets hearts racing. (p67)

Kennedy Center Terrace Grab a glass of wine and watch the city sparkling in every direction. (p90)

United States National Arboretum Take your sweetie to the Capital Columns Garden, and it's like you're walking amid Greek ruins. (p167)

Bishop's Garden Stroll hand-in-hand along the winding, rosebush-strewn paths in the National Cathedral's Gothic shadow. (p187)

Month by Month

TOP EVENTS

National Cherry Blossom Festival, March

White House Easter Egg Roll, April

Passport DC, May

Smithsonian Folklife Festival, June

Marine Corps Marathon, October

January

January is quiet – unless it's an inauguration year. Then it's madness. Crisp, clear days alternate with gray, frigid days. Every once in a while it will snow, shutting the city down.

Martin Luther King Jr's Birthday

On the third Monday in January and the weekend just prior, the city celebrates MLK's legacy with concerts, films and the recitation of his famous 'I Have a Dream' speech on the Lincoln Memorial steps.

Inauguration Day

Every four years, on January 20, DC is *the* place to be as the new president is sworn in. Dance cards' worth of inaugural balls accompany the peaceful power transition.

February

The weekend around President's Day (the third Monday) brings crowds, but otherwise it's time for low-season bargains. Several events brighten up the gloomy days.

DC Fashion Week

The five-day event (www.dcfashionweek.org) brings out an array of emerging talent and lesser-known international designers for runway shows and networking parties. Most events are open to the public, though some require tickets. It's also held in September.

March

Cherry-blossom season – DC's tourism apex – ramps up mid-month, culminating in the famed festival. The trees are gorgeous, but boy, are you gonna pay for it.

St Patrick's Day

Dancers, pipers, marching bands and assorted merrymakers share the Irish love along Constitution Ave NW (from 7th to 17th Sts) at this big annual event (www.dcstpatsparade.com). The parade is on the Sunday of or preceding March 17.

Blossom Kite Festival

On the last Saturday of March, the skies near the Washington Monument come alive with color as kite lovers swoop on the Mall. It's part of the National Cherry Blossom Festival.

National Cherry Blossom Festival

The star of DC's annual calendar celebrates spring's arrival with boat rides in the Tidal Basin, evening walks by lantern light, cultural fairs and a parade. The three-week event (www.nationalcherryblossomfestival.org), from late March to mid-April, also commemorates Japan's gift of 3000 cherry trees in 1912.

April

Cherry-blossom season continues to bring mega-crowds. April 4 is the average 'peak bloom,' so if you want to see the trees at their shimmery pink best, this is it.

White House Easter Egg Roll

A tradition since 1878, some 30,000 families from around the US descend on the South Lawn on Easter Monday for storytelling, games, music and dance. The big event is the massive egg hunt (www.whitehouse.gov/eastereggroll), featuring 13,000 wooden eggs.

FilmFest DC

Featuring over 70 films from across the globe, this 10-day, mid-month fest (www.filmfestdc.org) showcases new and avant-garde cinema at venues around the city. In addition to film screenings, there are guest appearances by directors and other special events.

May

It rains more in May than other months, but the temperature is comfy. It's a busy time for conventions, school groups and university graduations, so prices bump up and hotels are often full.

Passport DC

Passport DC (www.culturaltourismdc.org) offers the chance to peer inside some of the city's grandest embassies when they throw open their doors to the public throughout the month. Expect music, crafts, dancing and cuisine from each country hosting.

Rolling Thunder Ride for Freedom

Motorcycle-riding Vietnam vets commemorate Memorial Day (last Monday of May) with a ride (www.rollingthunder1.com) along the National Mall to draw attention to the POWs and MIAs who were left behind. The route goes from the Pentagon to the Vietnam Veterans Memorial.

June

Early June is a good time to visit, sort of post-school-group crowds and pre-summer-holiday crowds. The temperature steams up as the weeks go on.

Capital Pride

Some 250,000 people attend the gay pride party (www.capitalpride.org) held in early to mid-June. The parade along Pennsylvania Ave to the Mall is the focal point, although there are also film screenings as well as performances. Many bars and clubs host special events.

Barbecue Battle

Who makes the best barbecue? Teams compete (www.bbqdc.com) in late June for $40,000 in prizes. In addition to tender ribs, chicken and sausage, you'll find live bands, cooking demonstrations, celebrity chefs and kiddie toys.

Smithsonian Folklife Festival

For 10 days around Independence Day, this extravaganza (www.festival.si.edu) celebrates international and US cultures on the Mall by the Smithsonian Castle. The fest features folk music, dance, crafts, storytelling and ethnic fare, and it highlights a diverse mix of countries.

July

The days are exceptionally hot and humid, but that doesn't stop droves of vacationers from touring the sights. Temperatures regularly crack 90°F (32°C).

Independence Day

On July 4, huge crowds gather on the Mall to watch marching bands parade and hear the Declaration of Independence read from the National Archives' steps. Later, the National Symphony Orchestra plays a concert on the Capitol's steps, followed by mega-fireworks.

Capital Fringe Festival

The mid-month, 2½-week festival (www.capfringe.org) offers 500 wild and wacky performances of theater, dance, music, poetry and puppetry, performed by local and international artists at 30 venues around town.

September

The heat breaks. Kids go back to school. Everyone is refreshed after August's congressional break. Hotel rates start to creep up again.

National Book Festival

The Library of Congress brings big-name authors, literary events and, of course, books to the Convention Center for a page-packed day. It's the nation's largest reading fest (www.loc.gov/bookfest), and it's all free.

(Top) Independence Day fireworks
(Bottom) Dancers at the National Cherry Blossom Festival

HISHAM IBRAHIM / GETTY IMAGES ©

RICHARD GUNION / GETTY IMAGES ©

October

October is another banner month with lovely weather and fewer tourists, but business travelers keep hotel rates propped up.

Marine Corps Marathon

This popular road race (www.marinemarathon.com) routes through iconic DC scenery on the last Sunday in October. The course winds along the Potomac and takes in Georgetown, the length of the Mall, the Tidal Basin and Arlington National Cemetery.

High Heel Drag Race

Outrageously dressed divas strut their stuff before large crowds, then line up for a no-holds-barred sprint down 17th St. An informal block party, with more colorful mayhem, ensues. Traditionally held on the Tuesday before Halloween (October 31) in Dupont.

December

'Tis the holiday season, and the city twinkles with good cheer – there's Zoo Lights, candlelight tours of historic homes and free holiday concerts. Rates are reasonable.

National Christmas Tree & Menorah Lighting

In early December, the president switches on the lights to the national Christmas Tree (www.thenationaltree.org). Then he does the honors for the National Menorah. Live bands and choral groups play holiday music.

Like a Local

When in Washington, do as the Washingtonians do. Seek out beer gardens and bountiful happy hours. Make brunch plans and chase down epicurean food trucks. Cheer on the Nationals. Get on your bike. Get in line for late-night chow. Romantic strolls are always a fine option, too.

STEPHEN J BOITANO / GETTY IMAGES ©

Outdoor cafes at Eastern Market (p125)

Drinking

Hangouts

Neighborhood bars are all around the city, but the best batch for the local vibe are in Capitol Hill (particularly along H St NE and 8th St SE, aka Barracks Row), Shaw, Logan Circle and Columbia Heights. The hangouts come in many guises: some are watering holes for an older crowd, some are frat-boy-style keg-o-ramas, and some are mod gastropubs with sophisticated drink and comfort-food menus.

Alfresco

Rooftop terraces, backyard beer gardens, sidewalk patios – alfresco drinking by any name makes local tipplers happy. The relatively temperate climate means Washingtonians have much of the year to head outdoors and hoist their craft libations. Columbia Heights' nighthawk joints, U St's trendy bars, Georgetown's waterfront and the White House area's hotel bars are all good spots to get out with a glass in hand.

Happy Hour

Work hard, play hard – and that means hitting the bar right after the office. Washington is a big happy-hour town. Practically all bars (and restaurants that double as bars) have some sort of drink and/or food special for a few hours between 4pm and 7pm. Interns and staffers on a budget pile in to take advantage of half-price burgers and two-for-one mojitos and to decompress over the senator's latest appropriations bill. Downtown, Capitol Hill and Dupont Circle see lots of happy-hour action.

Check out www.dchappyhours.com.

Post-Bar Bites

While DC isn't known as a late-night town, it must be admitted that sometimes citizens do stay out carousing until 2am or so, and then they need something to soak up the booze. Mini-chain **Julia's Empanadas** (www.juliasempanadas.com) is often there to meet the need. Post-partiers also make their way to Adams Morgan or Dupont Circle, where 24-hour establishments like the Diner (p157) and Afterwords Cafe (p148) sling awesome hash in the wee hours.

Eating

Brunch

This meal is taken seriously on weekends, especially Sunday. Meeting up with friends at midday and lingering over bottomless Bloody Marys and a hulking pile of eggs and potatoes is de rigueur. Many restaurants offer boozy specials around Adams Morgan, Dupont Circle and Eastern Market. There are even blogs devoted to the subject. Check out the **Bitches who Brunch** (www.bitcheswhobrunch.com).

Food Trucks

It's official: locals are obsessed with food trucks. They stalk them via **Food Truck Fiesta** (www.foodtruckfiesta.com) and chase them around Farragut Sq, Foggy Bottom and L'Enfant Plaza at lunchtime, then Dupont Circle, Georgetown and Adams Morgan toward evening. New vehicles seem to roll out every week, including trucks by big-name chefs selling everything from Iberico pork sandwiches to gourmet mac 'n' cheese.

Markets

Eastern Market, near Capitol Hill, is the city's main bazaar and a great place to soak up local flavor. Families shop, browsers browse, friends laugh – oh, and there are good eats (mmm, fried oyster sandwiches), too. The time to go is on the weekend, when a lively craft market and adjoining flea market surround the area.

Hipsters and hipster families make an afternoon of it at Union Market, a sort of chowhound's food court. Vendors sell jerk chicken empanadas, craft kombucha, French pastries and more that folks nibble at sunlit tables in an urban-cool renovated warehouse.

Most neighborhoods also have their own farmers market one day per week from May through October. Residents flock to these to buy produce, eggs, cheese, honey and cider from nearby small farms.

Pastimes

Spectator Sports

Washingtonians support a full slate of pro sports teams – the Redskins (football), Nationals (baseball), Wizards (basketball), Capitals (hockey) and DC United (soccer) – and all have rabid fans. The surest way to feel like a local is to catch a Redskins game at a city pub and join in the grumbling when they lose. DC's transients and natives bond over the Nationals, too; games are good fun and tickets can be cheap (around $15). Imbibing in the park's outdoor beer garden is a pre-game ritual.

Cycling

The Capital Bikeshare program (p270) prompts many citizens to make short-haul trips on two wheels, and the District's terrific array of long-haul trails brings out droves of weekend cyclists. The 18.5-mile river-clasping Mount Vernon Trail (p207) is a particular favorite with locals, along with the Capital Crescent Trail and C&O Canal Towpath (p103). Bike-rental companies make it easy to join the action.

Mall Activities

Yes, tourists throng the Mall, but so do locals. Joggers, Ultimate teams and volleyball players are among those hanging out on the scrubby green grass.

Odds & Ends

Romantic Places

If you're looking for places that bestow a 'kiss me' vibe, follow locals to their favorites. Constitution Gardens (p70), the Lincoln Memorial (p58) and the National Sculpture Garden (p67) win smooching points on the Mall; being there at sunrise or sunset ups the ante. A Mall stroll at night past the dramatically lit monuments is another sure thing. And what lips can resist their beloved's in the Capitol Columns Garden (p167) at the National Arboretum or the Bishop's Garden (p187) at Washington National Cathedral?

Airplane Spotting

There are a couple of well-known sites where residents go for fun views of planes taking off and landing. Hains Point (p116), at the southern tip of East Potomac Park in southwest DC, is one with picnicking opportunities. Gravelly Point (p207) in Arlington, VA, is another.

For Free

Washington, DC, has a mind-blowing array of freebies. From the Smithsonian Institution's multiple museums, to gratis theater and concerts, to jaunts through the White House and Capitol, you can be entertained for weeks without spending a dime.

DANITA DELIMONT / GETTY IMAGES ©

Main Reading Room, Library of Congress (p108)

Smithsonian Museums

Top Draws

➡ **National Museum of Natural History** Gems, minerals, mummies and a giant squid. (p67)

➡ **National Air and Space Museum** Rockets, missiles and the Wright brothers' biplane. (p66)

➡ **National Museum of American History** Everything from the Star-Spangled Banner flag to Dorothy's ruby slippers. (p68)

➡ **National Zoo** Home to the famed, bamboo-lovin' giant pandas. (p188)

Less-Packed Troves

➡ **Reynolds Center for American Art & Portraiture** Part portrait gallery, part who's who of big-name US artists. (p131)

➡ **Freer-Sackler Museums of Asian Art** Ancient ceramics and temple sculptures spread across two tunnel-connected galleries. (p66)

➡ **National Museum of the American Indian** Creation stories, costumes, videos and audio recordings from tribes of the Americas. (p67)

➡ **Hirshhorn Museum and Sculpture Garden** Head-scratching, cutting-edge, provocative modern art. (p66)

➡ **National Museum of African American History and Culture** The Smithsonian's newest building, open in 2016, with items like Louis Armstrong's trumpet. (p69)

➡ **Steven F Udvar-Hazy Center** All the space stuff that doesn't fit into the Mall's National Air and Space Museum? It's in giant hangars by Washington Dulles International Airport. (p200)

Oft-Overlooked Gems

➡ **Renwick Gallery** Superb collection of American crafts and decorative art pieces. (p82)

➡ **National Museum of African Art** Masks, textiles, paintings, ceramics and ritual objects from sub-Saharan Africa. (p66)

➡ **National Postal Museum** Antique mail planes, historic letters and the world's largest stamp collection. (p111)

➡ **Anacostia Museum** Neighborhood outpost with rotating exhibits on African American culture. (p116)

Other Free Museums

National Gallery of Art

It splits into two massive buildings to show its trove of paintings, sculptures and decorative arts. (p61)

United States Holocaust Memorial Museum

The museum haunts with brutal and impassioned exhibits about the millions murdered by the Nazis. (p109)

Art Museum of the Americas

This hidden gallery features cool exhibits from its 20th-century collection. (p84)

African American Civil War Museum

It goes beyond the war between the states and follows black history through the Civil Rights movement. (p166)

National Archives

Really – we'd pay to see the Declaration of Independence with John Hancock's, er, John Hancock scrawled across the bottom. (p129)

Capitol

Guided excursions through the mighty, white-domed sanctum of Congress, cluttered with busts, statues, frescoes and gardens, cost zilch. (p106)

Bureau of Engraving & Printing

Though the Treasury tour is about money, it won't be taking any of yours. Watch millions of dollars as they're printed, cut and inspected. (p116)

Library of Congress

The world's largest library is more than a stack of books. It's a museum with 500-year-old world maps, historic photographs, concerts and film screenings – all free. (p108)

Free Days at Paid Museums

Phillips Collection

The permanent collection, aglow with Renoir, Gauguin, Matisse and other big names, is free every Tuesday through Friday. (p145)

National Museum of Women in the Arts

See works by Frida Kahlo, Georgia O'Keeffe and 700 more female artists for free the first Sunday each month. (p132)

National Museum of Natural History Butterfly Pavilion

The separate-admission area of fluttering beasties is free on Tuesday. (p67)

Government in Action

White House

Unlike many palaces around the globe, the US Presidential Palace (as it was once known) is free to tour. Heck, you might even run into the First Lady or First Dog. (p78)

Show Time

Kennedy Center

The show could star the National Symphony, a gospel group or an Indian dance troupe, but whatever it is, count on it happening at 6pm for free at the Kennedy's Millennium Stage. (p90)

Busboys & Poets

OK, the Tuesday-night open-mike costs $5. But that's nothing for the rollicking, two-hour show of seasoned performers, spoken-word rookies and jammin' musicians. (p137)

Politics & Prose Bookstore

Rock stars, past presidents, Pulitzer winners – if they've written a book, they'll do a free reading at Politics & Prose. Events take place almost daily. (p192)

National Theatre

Puppets, magic, ballet and music are all on tap for the free, family-oriented Saturday shows at 9:30am and 11am. (p138)

BARRY WINIKER / GETTY IMAGES ©

The Red Room, inside the White House (p78)

Shakespeare Theatre Company

'Free for All' is an annual end-of-summer tradition: the company picks a Bard classic and performs it gratis for two weeks. (p138)

Museum Concerts

The National Gallery of Art offers free choral and classical concerts at 6:30pm Sunday, which take place in the West Building. It also sponsors Jazz in the Garden outdoors amid the sculptures from 5pm to 8:30pm on summer Fridays. (p61)

History Highlights

Ford's Theatre

The theater where John Wilkes Booth shot Abraham Lincoln provides free tours exploring what happened that fateful night in April 1865. The basement museum shows artifacts such as the murder weapon. Petersen House, where Lincoln died, sits across the street and is included as part of the ticket. (p131)

Frederick Douglass National Historic Site

The hilltop home of revered abolitionist Frederick Douglass provides a compelling look into his life via original furnishings, books and personal belongings. (p137)

Tours

DC by Foot

Knowledgeable guides working on a tip-only basis share history and lore along routes covering the National Mall, U St and Lincoln's assassination. (p272)

Cultural Tourism DC

The tours are DIY using free maps, apps and audio provided by Cultural Tourism DC. More than 10 neighborhoods have in-depth heritage trails; the tours reveal civil-rights sites, espionage hot spots and more. (p272)

National Public Radio

Wave to your favorite correspondents as you peek into the newsroom and studios of the venerable news organization. (p111)

Cooked Chesapeake Bay crabs

Eating

A homegrown foodie revolution has transformed the once buttoned-up DC dining scene. Driving it is the bounty of farms at the city's doorstep, along with the booming local economy and influx of worldly younger residents. The result? Washington's restaurants have doubled in number over the past decade, with small, independent, local-chef-helmed spots leading the way.

Global Influence

Washington, DC, is one of the most diverse cities of its size in America, heavily populated by immigrants, expats and diplomats from around the world, so there's a glut of good ethnic eating. Salvadoran, Ethiopian, Vietnamese, French, Spanish, West African – they've all become Washingtonian.

Local Bounty

The city's unique geography puts it between two of the best food-production areas in America: Chesapeake Bay and the Virginia Piedmont. From the former comes crabs, oysters and rockfish; the latter provides game, pork, wine and peanuts. Chefs take advantage of this delicious abundance.

Southern Influence

Keep in mind that DC also occupies the fault line between two of America's greatest culinary regions: the northeast and the South. The South exerts a tremendous pull, with heaps of soul food and its high-class incarnations, so

NEED TO KNOW

Price Ranges

In our listings we've used the following price codes to represent the cost of a main dish at dinner:

$ less than $10

$$ $10 to $20

$$$ more than $20

Opening Hours

Most restaurants serve breakfast 8am to 11am, lunch 11:30am to 2:30pm and dinner 6pm to 10pm, or to 11pm Friday and Saturday.

Reservations

➡ Make dinner reservations for eateries in the midrange and upper price bracket, especially on weekends. A phone call the day before is usually sufficient.

➡ Many restaurants let you book online through **OpenTable** (www.opentable.com).

➡ For no-reservations hot spots, arrive an hour before opening time and be ready to wait. Monday and Tuesday are least crowded. Make sure your cell phone is charged; once the host takes your name, many restaurants will let you wait elsewhere (ie a nearby bar) and will text when your table is ready.

Tipping

Tipping 15% of the total bill is the accepted minimum. If service is good, 20% is a decent average tip; tip more if service is exceptional.

Credit Cards Versus Cash

Almost all restaurants accept credit cards, aside from a smattering of budget places.

Saving Money

Restaurants in downtown and the Kennedy Center often have pre-theater menus. This generally means a three-course meal for $35 or so, offered before 6:30pm.

get ready to loosen the belt for fried chicken, catfish, collard greens, sweet-potato hash and butter-smothered grits – all washed down with sweet iced tea, of course.

Half-Smokes

DC's claim to native culinary fame is the half-smoke, a bigger, coarser, spicier and better version of the hot dog. There's little agreement on where the name comes from. But there is general consensus as to what goes on a half-smoke: chili, mustard and chopped onions.

Food Trucks

As in most other US cities, the food-truck frenzy has hit Washington. Empanadas, chocolate pie, crab cakes, cupcakes – you name it and there's a truck driving around selling it out the window. Trucks generally prowl office-worker-rich hot spots like Farragut Sq, Foggy Bottom and L'Enfant Plaza around lunchtime, and then Dupont Circle, Georgetown and Adams Morgan toward evening. **Food Truck Fiesta** (www.foodtruckfiesta.com) tracks their real-time locations.

Supper Clubs

Underground supper clubs are having a moment in DC. Some are hoity-toity, but many offer great value if you're adventurous and don't mind hanging out with strangers around a communal table. Top picks:

Chez Le Commis (www.chezlecommis.com) The foodie chef makes wildly creative dishes incorporating unusual ingredients. The 15-seat club pops up sporadically, sometimes in a cafe, sometimes in the chef's apartment. It costs around $60 per person.

Glen's Garden Market (www.glensgardenmarket.com) Fork into seven or so courses in this Dupont grocery store while folks shop around you. The chef (who trained at Copenhagen's revered Noma restaurant) uses ingredients from the market for meals served at the 10-person tasting table. Dinners usually take place the last Thursday and Friday of the month. It costs $75 to $100 per person.

Feastly (www.eatfeastly.com) Locals cook a meal for you in their home. Feastly is in multiple cities, but it started in DC and has an active scene here. Dinners occur at least weekly. Price varies, but the average is around $40 per person.

Tours

DC Metro Food Tours (p272) These walking tours explore various neighborhoods, stopping for multiple bites along the way. Areas covered include Eastern Market, U St, Little Ethiopia, Georgetown and Alexandria, VA.

DC by Foot (p272) Among the company's many free, themed walking tours are food-oriented jaunts around Eastern Market and U St. Guides provide lots of history; they work on a tip basis.

Eating by Neighborhood

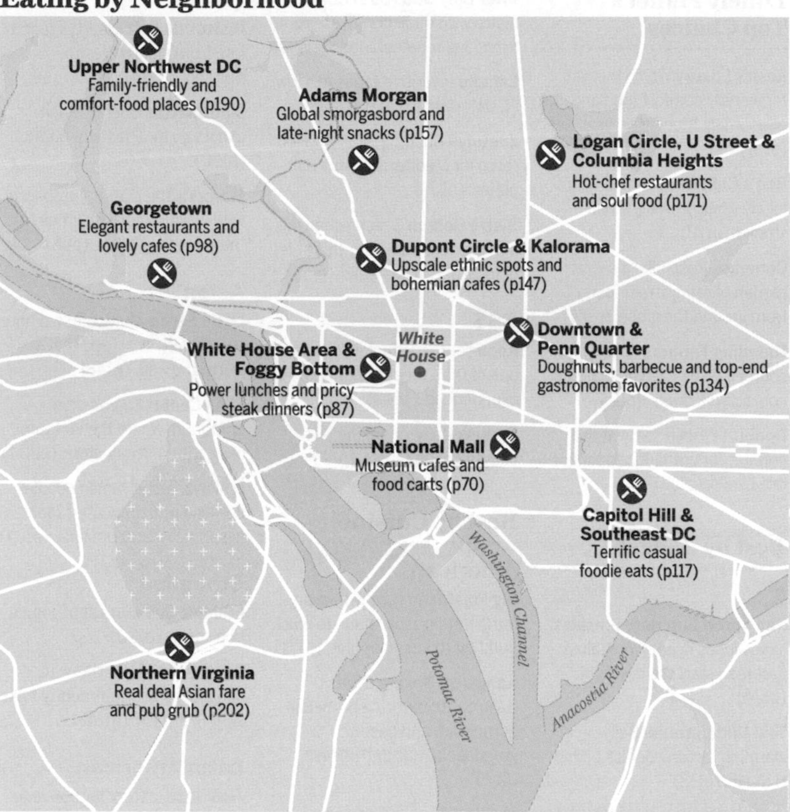

Festivals

Taste of DC (www.thetasteofdc.org) Forty restaurants sell mini portions of their wares downtown during a mid-October weekend. Includes the Ben's Chili Bowl Eating Championship.

National Capital Barbecue Battle (www.bbqdc.com) This meaty battle takes place during late June, with bands and celebrity chefs.

DC Restaurant Week (www.ramw.org/restaurantweek) For one week in January, 200 eateries serve affordable, three-course, fixed-price meals.

Foodie Blogs & Review Sites

Yelp (www.yelp.com/dc) Everyday eaters give their restaurant opinions.

Eater DC (www.dc.eater.com) News and reviews on the local dining scene.

Bitches Who Brunch (www.bitcheswhobrunch.com) These ladies have been at it for a while.

Hungry Lobbyist (www.hungrylobbyist.com) Restaurant reviews, chef interviews and event info by a group of locals.

Girl Meets Food (www.girlmeetsfood.com) Offbeat restaurant guides.

Eat Streets

- **14th St NW (Logan Circle)** DC's most happening road: an explosion of hot-chef bites and bars.
- **18th St NW (Adams Morgan)** Korean, West African, Japanese and Latin mash-up, plus late-night snacks.
- **11th St NW (Columbia Heights)** Ever-growing scene of hipster cafes and edgy gastropubs.
- **8th St SE (Capitol Hill)** Known as Barracks Row, it's the locals' favorite for comfort food.
- **H St NE (Capitol Hill)** Hip strip of pie cafes, noodle shops and foodie pubs.
- **9th St NW (Shaw)** Aka 'Little Ethiopia,' it has all the *wats* and *injera* you can handle.

Lonely Planet's Top Choices

Rose's Luxury Worth the wait for worldly comfort food and awesomely friendly service. (p121)

Ben's Chili Bowl Gossip with locals while downing a half-smoke. (p173)

Compass Rose Like a secret garden offering street foods from around the globe. (p174)

Founding Farmers Locally sourced dishes served in rustic-cool surroundings. (p87)

Donburi Fifteen seats at the counter for authentic Japanese rice bowls. (p157)

Chez Billy Sud (p99) Charming bistro with duck confit, *steak-frites* and mustachioed servers.

Estadio Inventive tapas in a low-lit, date-night space. (p171)

Zaytinya Bustling, glass-walled room for Mediterranean small plates. (p135)

Bistro Bohem Czech schnitzels and pilsners, served with a side of local art on the walls. (p175)

Best by Budget

$

Red Apron Butchery Breakfast sandwiches heaped on Italian flatbread start the day right. (p134)

Toki Underground Belly-warming ramen noodles on hip H St NE. (p118)

Tryst Delicious cafe for omelet and waffle breakfasts and creative sandwiches. (p157)

Bub & Pop's This fine dining chef turned sandwich fashioner even makes his own condiments. (p147)

BreadLine Locals' hangout to chomp sandwiches stacked high with chowhound ingredients. (p87)

$$

Duke's Grocery Cozy cafe where the chalkboard menu changes daily. (p148)

Mintwood Place Twinkling room for escargot hush puppies and other French-American mash-ups. (p160)

$$$

Komi Fantastic fusion fare and one of DC's most dazzling dining experiences. (p148)

Obelisk Daily-changing, set-course Italian feasts. (p149)

Best by Cuisine

American

Pig Porktastic spot with everything from crispy shank to black pudding to bacon apples. (p171)

Kangaroo Boxing Club Gastropub featuring barbecue, cornbread, and bacon gorgonzola mac and cheese. (p176)

Martin's Tavern Georgetown's oldest saloon has ambiance (JFK proposed to Jackie here) and dandy burgers. (p99)

Southern

Macon Creative blend of French and Southern fare in a buzzing part of Upper Northwest DC. (p191)

Bayou A jazzy taste of New Orleans that includes fiery spice and cooling Hurricanes. (p88)

Oohh's & Aahh's No-frills joint where locals go for collard greens and hummingbird cake. (p175)

Hitching Post Fried chicken and catfish with the neighbors in Petworth. (p182)

French

Bistrot du Coin Hearty French fare from *steak-frites* to mussels. (p148)

Montmartre Where French expats go for a taste of home. (p120)

Marcel's The classics prepared with class, along with limos to the Kennedy Center. (p88)

Asian

Little Serow Multicourse dinner of Northern Thai food that's worth the wait. (p148)

Eden Center Saigon-style emporium where the Vietnamese community clusters. (p204)

Daikaya Casual ramen noodles downstairs, fish-focused Japanese small plates upstairs. (p134)

Ethiopian

Ethiopic Superior list of veggie-rich stews. (p120)

Zenebech Hole-in-the-wall hangout where community folks stuff their face. (p174)

Latin American

Tico Buzzy eatery for nouveau tacos, small plates and 140 tequilas. (p175)

El Chucho Badass staff, cheap Mexican fare and magaritas on tap. (p176)

Best for Foodies

Atlas Room Quirky seasonal American plates in a shimmering ambiance. (p120)

Central Michel Richard Four-star bistro redefines comfort food. (p136)

Minibar Twelve-seat restaurant to experience Jose Andres' molecular gastronomy. (p136)

Union Market Korean tacos, jerk chicken empanadas and more from epicurean entrepreneurs. (p174)

Best Brunch

Ted's Bulletin Sink into a retro booth for beer biscuits and house-made pop tarts. (p120)

Tabard Inn Restaurant Poached eggs, chocolate waffles and oysters in English-manor environs. (p149)

Perrys The drag queen brunch packs the place every Sunday. (p160)

Best Seafood

Maine Avenue Fish Market Shrimp, crabs and oysters fried, broiled or steamed wharfside. (p122)

Fiola Mare Georgetown's sceney, river-view hot spot delivers the goods with an Italian twist. (p100)

BlackSalt Superb preparations of fish and crustaceans using globe-spanning flavors. (p100)

Best Vegetarian

Rasika Avant-garde Indian food served in a mod Jaipur palace. (p135)

Amsterdam Falafelshop Fried chickpea patties with DIY toppings. (p157)

Sticky Fingers Retro vegan bakery also makes meat-free burgers, burritos and breakfasts. (p175)

Best Sweets

Baked & Wired This sunny cafe serves DCs' biggest, bestest cupcakes. (p98)

Dolcezza Spoon into offbeat flavors like strawberry tarragon. (p147)

CakeRoom Date cupcakes and banana-toffee pie rock the old-timey shop. (p160)

Pie Sisters Three siblings bake 'em big and small, sweet and savory. (p99)

Best Late Night

Afterwords Cafe Browse the stacks and feed your face at this bookstore-bistro combo. (p148)

Diner Stuffed pancakes at 4am never tasted so good. (p157)

Julia's Empanadas This local chain fries plump, meat-filled turnovers into the wee hours. (p160)

Best Neighborhood Gems

Maple Tiny Columbia Heights spot for rich pastas and house-made *limoncello*. (p173)

Veranda on P Homey Mediterranean restaurant with genial alfresco dining. (p171)

Best for Romance

Unum A cozy, gold-glimmering room to share wine and modern American small plates. (p99)

La Chaumiere Classical French food, an intimate dining room and stone fireplace woo lovers. (p100)

Best Politician Spotting

Le Diplomate DC's political glitterati flock here for a Parisian-style night out. (p173)

Old Ebbitt Grill Play spot the senator while cracking open an oyster. (p87)

Cafe Milano Famed place to twirl spaghetti and spy big shots in Georgetown. (p101)

Best Pizza

2 Amys The pizzas that emerge from the wood-burning oven can barely keep up with neighborhood masses. (p190)

Seventh Hill Addictive pie joint with offbeat ingredients and killer crust. (p120)

Matchbox Blistered, thin-crust goodness accompanied by lots of craft beers. (p137)

&pizza Booming mini-chain that bakes high quality fast-food pies. (p173)

Best Burgers

Good Stuff Eatery Terrific fat farmhouse burgers made with sustainable ingredients. (p118)

Shake Shack The sweet and tangy sauce topping sets these griddled patties apart. (p135)

Ray's to the Third Juicy, cheese-loaded burgers in Arlington. (p203)

Best Steakhouses

Prime Rib Don a tie and jacket for this dark wood, power-player house of meat. (p88)

Occidental Grill Bigwigs roll up their pinstripes for the chops and steaks. (p89)

JASON COLSTON / GETTY IMAGES ©

Bar at the Red Derby (p181)

Drinking & Nightlife

When Andrew Jackson swore the oath of office in 1800, the self-proclaimed populist dispensed with pomp and circumstance and, quite literally, threw a raging kegger. Folks got so gone they started looting art from the White House. The historical lesson: DC loves a drink, and these days it enjoys said tipples in many incarnations besides executive-mansion-trashing throwdowns.

Beer

The city is serious about beer. It even brews much its own delicious stuff. That trend started in 2011, when DC Brau became the District's first brewery to launch in more than 50 years. Several more beer makers followed. As you drink around town, keep an eye out for local concoctions from Chocolate City, 3 Stars, Atlas Brew Works, Hellbender and Lost Rhino (from northern Virginia).

TASTING ROOMS & BEER GARDENS

Many breweries have no-frills tasting rooms where you can get pints or growlers of the house beers, and they usually offer free tours on Saturday (p177). DC Brau and Atlas Brew Works are heady ones to sample. The city also has a handful of brewpubs, such as Right Proper Brewing Co (p177) and Bluejacket Brewery (p122), where you can slurp the wares in a more refined ambience and get a meal.

Beer gardens are popular, especially in Shaw, Columbia Heights, Petworth and the H St Corridor. Dacha Beer Garden (p180), Bardo

Brewpub (p177) and DC Reynolds (p182) are exemplars of the genre.

TOURS

DC Brew Tours (☎202-759-8687; www.dcbrew-tours.com; tours $85; ⊙noon & 5pm Thu & Fri, 11am & 5pm Sat & Sun) offers five-hour jaunts by van that take in four breweries. Routes vary, but could include DC Brau, Right Proper Brewing, Chocolate City, 3 Stars and Atlas Brew Works, among others. Tastings of 15-plus beers and a beer-focused meal are part of the package. Departure is from downtown at 710 12th St NW, by the Metro Center station.

FESTIVALS

Snallygaster (www.snallygasterdc.com; tickets $30) Beloved by beer geeks, this outdoor fest by Nationals Park features a terrific selection of 250 brews (some quite rare), dance punk bands and food trucks. Held on a Saturday in mid-September.

Brew at the Zoo (www.nationalzoo.si.edu; tickets $65) The National Zoo fundraiser in mid-July brings out 46 breweries, including many small ones from Virginia that you don't often see in DC.

Savor (www.savorcraftbeer.com; tickets $135) The National Building Museum hosts the two-day fest in early June, described as the 'prom of the beer world.'

Cocktails

The craft-cocktail craze is in full swing. Mixologists do their thing using small-batch liqueurs, fresh-squeezed juices and hand-chipped ice. It may sound pretentious, but most of the bars are actually pretty cool.

And get this: DC has an official cocktail – the Rickey. It's a mix of bourbon or gin, lime juice and soda water over ice. Drinkers describe it as air-conditioning in a glass, and it's perfect on a summer day. It was invented in 1883 at a downtown (now defunct) bar popular with politicos and journalists. Colonel Joseph K Rickey, a Democratic lobbyist known to toss back a drink or 10 at the venue, lent his name to it. Daikaya (p134), Tryst (p157) and Room 11 (p181) make good Rickeys.

Wine

Virginia ranks fifth in number of wineries among US states, and many of the local varietals make their way to DC's tables. Particularly notable is the Virginia Viognier, an exotic white grape that becomes a lightly fruity wine that pairs well with seafood. Blue Duck Tavern (p149) and Marcel's (p88) both have robust lists of Virginia wines. Several wineries can be visited on a day trip from DC (p220).

Coffee

DC has been getting its caffeine on. Local mini-chains such as Filter (p152) and

NEED TO KNOW

Opening Hours

- **Bars** 5pm to 1am or 2am weekdays, 3am on weekends.
- **Nightclubs** 9pm to 1am or 2am weekdays, 3am on weekends.
- **Places that double as restaurants** open around 11:30am.

Taxes

Drink tax is 10%.

Tipping

Tipping 15% per round, minimum per drink $1.

Door Policies

- The drinking age is 21 years. Take your driver's license or passport out at night: you will be asked for ID.
- No dress code typically, though some clubs require closed-toe shoes and long pants, and occasionally no jeans or hats.

Resources & Websites

- **Washington City Paper** (www.washingtoncitypaper.com) Alternative publication with entertainment coverage.
- **DC Beer** (www.dcbeer.com) Info and events on the local craft brew scene.
- **Washington Blade** (www.washingtonblade.com) Gay and lesbian happenings.
- **On Tap** (www.ontaponline.com) Nightlife and entertainment listings.
- **Brightest Young Things** (www.brightestyoungthings.com) Web magazine of cultural and clubby events for 20-somethings.
- **DC Cool** (www.dccool.com) Tourism-bureau-affiliated site with info on the scene and deals.

Drinking & Nightlife by Neighborhood

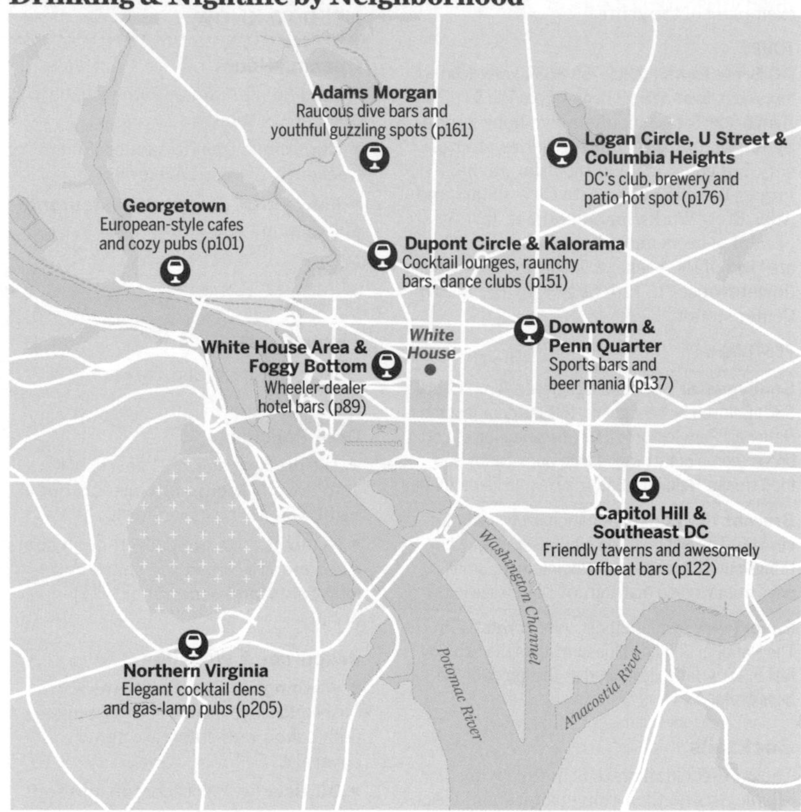

Peregrine Espresso (p123) use beans from small-batch roasters and get hard-core with their brewing techniques. Peregrine pays the knowledge forward by offering DIY brewing classes. Petworth's Qualia Coffee (p182)roasts its own beans and offers bimonthly tasting sessions. The city's Ethiopian community shows how it's done, too. Sidamo Coffee & Tea (p123) is one of several family-run shops that roasts beans and puts on traditional Ethiopian coffee ceremonies.

Boozy Cupcakes

Here's a trend you don't see often enough: crunk cakes, as in alcohol-infused cupcakes. A roving vendor sells them in bars around the city. Have a few Irish Car Bombs (Guinness, Jameson, Baileys and chocolate cake), but remember that each confection contains roughly a shot of liquor. Find the vendor's location via Twitter (@crunkcakesdc).

Clubs

Washington's club scene is pretty casual. Dupont Circle and U St host much of the action. Some places have a dress code that requires closed-toe shoes and long pants, and occasionally no jeans or hats, but usually you can come as you are. Many bars that are low-key drinking holes during the week turn clubby on weekends when they bring in DJs.

Happy Hour

Washington is a big happy-hour town. Practically all bars have some sort of drink and/or food special for a few hours between 4pm and 7pm. This is particularly welcome at restaurants that double as bars – which many do – because often they'll sell affordable, small-plate versions of menu items during happy hour.

Lonely Planet's Top Choices

Right Proper Brewing Co House-made ales flow in Duke Ellington's old pool hall. (p177)

Little Miss Whiskey's Golden Dollar Sip killer beer and whiskey amid hallucinogenic decor. (p122)

Dan's Cafe A great dive, like an evil Elks Club with massive pours of booze. (p161)

Room 11 Cute coffee slinger by day and wine pourer by night. (p181)

Bluejacket Brewery Genre-spanning suds made on-site, from sour blonds to barley wines. (p122)

Best Cocktails

PX Beautiful, speakeasy-style drinking den serving refined craft cocktails. (p205)

Firefly Bar Take a seat under the magical glowing tree and swirl a chai-tea Manhattan or boozy cream soda. (p151)

Bar Charley Friendly Dupont spot that mixes the gingery Suffering Bastard in vintage glassware. (p151)

A&D Bar Artsy neighborhood tavern gets creative with local spirits. (p177)

Best Beer

Churchkey The hulking menu has 500 different beers, including 50 craft brews on tap. (p176)

RFD Washington Tons of beers in a slick bar near downtown's Verizon Center. (p137)

City Tap House Lodge-like gastropub with 40 taps and upscale pub grub. (p138)

Best Wine

Cork Wine Bar Great reds, whites and nibbles; especially appealing for happy hour. (p176)

Dickson Wine Bar Cozy, candlelit and covert date-night spot. (p180)

Mockingbird Hill Sherry flights and ham turn this Shaw cafe into an Andalusian tapas bar. (p180)

Best Coffee

The Coffee Bar Beloved neighborhood cafe where folks hang out all day. (p177)

Sidamo Coffee & Tea Ethiopian family-run spot with traditional coffee ceremonies and organic beans. (p123)

Qualia Coffee Java heads get jacked up over this shop with tasting sessions. (p182)

Best Outdoor Terraces

Tabard Inn Bar Tip back Manhattans, Sidecars and other classics on the ivy-clad patio. (p151)

Dacha Beer Garden German brews in glass boots make their way around the picnic tables. (p180)

Best Local Scene

Wonderland Ballroom Edgy and eccentric, with oddball folk art and outdoor picnic tables for mingling. (p172)

H Street Country Club Booze while playing shuffleboard and DC-themed minigolf. (p122)

Board Room Knock back draft beers and crush your opponent at Battleship, Operation and other games. (p150)

Best Gay & Lesbian

JR's Dupont pub where a young, well-dressed crowd kicks back and sings show tunes. (p152)

Nellie's Drinkers amass for sports-tuned TVs and the sweet roof deck. (p180)

Phase 1 Four-decade-old lesbian bar with Jell-O wrestling and frisky dancing. (p124)

Cobalt Venerable gay club with wild dance parties throughout the week. (p152)

Best Clubs

U Street Music Hall Casual, DJ-owned spot to get your dance on. (p180)

Flash Deep house, techno and dubstep DJs spin in the intimate upstairs room. (p180)

18th Street Lounge Sexy young things groove in a Dupont mansion. (p152)

Best Dives

Raven Locals, lovers, neon and the finest jukebox in Washington. (p181)

Tune Inn Ah, beer under mounted deer heads and antler chandelier. (p118)

Red Derby Cash-only, hipster-punk lounge where everyone looks good under the crimson light. (p181)

Best Politico Bars

Round Robin Since 1850 bigwigs and lobbyists have swirled drinks and cut deals in the gilded bar. (p89)

Off the Record Where Very Important People drink martinis, steps from the White House. (p90)

Entertainment

From the evening-wear elegance of the Kennedy Center to punk stripping the paint at an H St club, the nation's capital has an envious slate of performances. It caters to Shakespeare, jazz, classical-music and poetry-slam fans particularly well. Best of all, many shows are free.

Music

JAZZ

Washington's jazz affair started in the early 20th century, when U St NW was known as 'Black Broadway' for its many music theaters. Relics from that era, such as Bohemian Caverns, still host sweet notes.

ROCK

DC's rock scene thrives, and the city is a great place to catch a show. Clubs like the Black Cat are typical: intimate, something indie-cool always going on, and nights of DJ music in the mix.

CLASSICAL

The Kennedy Center is the hub for symphony, opera and other classical fare. But for all its high-falutin' ways, it's also surprisingly accessible to the masses, with free performances nightly at 6pm.

MILITARY

Military music is big here. The Marine Corps, Air Force, Army and Navy bands alternate performing at 8pm most weeknights on the Capitol's steps and at the Mall's Sylvan Theater in summer.

Theater

Washington has many adventurous small stages and multifaceted arts centers that do intriguing work. Keep an eye out for Atlas, Studio and Source theaters.

Spoken Word

DC has hundreds of author readings, poetry slams, story slams and open-mike nights. Busboys & Poets anchors the scene.

Entertainment by Neighborhood

- **National Mall** Free jazz in the sculpture garden, free films on the lawn. (p71)
- **White House Area & Foggy Bottom** The Kennedy Center runs the show. (p90)
- **Georgetown** Dizzy Gillespie's old stomping grounds are the main draw. (p101)
- **Capitol Hill & Southeast DC** Rock, Shakespeare and avant-garde theater make this 'hood top of the heap. (p124)
- **Downtown & Penn Quarter** The majority of theaters, from opulent to comic to experimental, are concentrated here. (p138)
- **Dupont Circle & Kalorama** Improv, Jewish theater and artsy chamber music play. (p153)
- **Adams Morgan** Rowdy live music, deep reggae and cozy jazz fill the nights. (p162)
- **Logan Circle, U Street & Columbia Heights** Splendid mix of historic jazz venues, thrashing rock clubs and poetry slams. (p181)
- **Upper Northwest DC** A groovy cinema, starry outdoor amphitheater and literary events are on tap. (p192)
- **Northern Virginia** Fiddlin' pubs and a sleek, worldly art space make it worth the trip. (p206)

Lonely Planet's Top Choices

Kennedy Center DC's performing-arts king of the hill, home to the symphony, opera and more. (p90)

Black Cat Intimate, beer-splattered stalwart of DC's rock and indie scene. (p181)

Rock & Roll Hotel There's thrashing rock but also hip-hop, punk and metal in this down-and-dirty club. (p124)

Busboys & Poets Nerve center for open-mike poetry readings and story slams. (p137)

9:30 Club Where the Sleater-Kinney and New Pornographer–type bands of the world come to rock. (p181)

Best Jazz

Bohemian Caverns Seasoned veterans still play this cool-cat club where Duke and Coltrane bopped. (p182)

Blues Alley The sophisticated icon has been bringing in top names since Dizzy Gillespie's day. (p101)

Jazz in the Garden Tune in amid whimsical artworks in the National Sculpture Garden. (p71)

Best Rock, Funk & Blues

DC9 Up-and-coming local bands beat it at this snug, tri-level venue. (p183)

Hamilton Alt-rock and funk bands plug in a stone's throw from the White House. (p90)

Madam's Organ Prepare for yee-hawin' wild times in Adams Morgan's bluesy hot spot. (p162)

Best World & Folk Music

Bukom Cafe Join the West African crowd getting their groove on to reggae beats. (p162)

Birchmere Mural-splashed music hall for folk, country, R & B and even the odd burlesque show. (p206)

Best Theater

Shakespeare Theatre Company The nation's top troupe does the Bard proud. (p138)

Studio Theatre Award-winning venue for contemporary plays, known for its powerhouse premieres. (p183)

Best for Free

Kennedy Center The Millennium Stage hosts a free music or dance performance daily at 6pm. (p90)

Library of Congress Events daily, from swing bands to documentary films to poetry lectures. (p108)

Best Cinema

Avalon Theatre Much-loved local cinema that shows indie and mainstream films and hosts family events. (p193)

E Street Cinema Downtown theater where neighborhood urbanites drink craft beer and watch indie movies. (p138)

Best Comedy

Capitol Steps They take corny jabs at Congress in musical sketches à la 'Fiscal Shades of Gray.' (p138)

DC Improv National stand-up comics yuck it up alongside local amateurs. (p153)

NEED TO KNOW

Ticketplace

Ticketplace (www.ticketplace.org) sells discounted tickets – up to 50% off – to regional theater, dance, symphony and opera performances. All tickets are sold online. Some are for the day of a show, others are for shows up to a month in advance. Search by date or by venue.

Saving Money

- Patrons aged 18 to 30 years can get deep discounts – even free tickets – to all opera, ballet, symphony and other Kennedy Center performances via MyTix (p90).
- Arena Stage (p124) puts half-price tickets on sale at the box office 30 minutes before show time.
- Many theaters, such as Source (p183) and Woolly Mammoth (p138), offer 'pay what you can' admission during preview shows.

Websites

- **Gold Star** (www.goldstar.com/washington-dc) Half-price offers from a national ticket broker.
- **Destination DC** (www.washington.org/calendar) Full events listings.
- **Culture Capital** (www.culturecapital.com) Arts-specific listings.
- **Pink Line Project** (www.pinklineproject.com) Weekly newsletter about the coolest cultural things to do in DC.

Shopping

Shopping in DC means many things, from browsing funky antique shops to perusing rare titles at secondhand booksellers. Temptations abound for lovers of vinyl, vintage wares and one-of-a-kind jewelry, art and handicrafts. And, of course, that Abe Lincoln pencil sharpener and Uncle Sam bobblehead you've been wanting await...

Specialties

No surprise: politically oriented souvenirs are Washington's specialty, from stars-and-stripes boxer shorts to rubber Nixon masks to White House snow globes. Museum shops contain iconic gifts like stuffed pandas from the National Zoo and balsa-wood airplanes from the National Air and Space Museum, as well as more unusual items like weavings from indigenous tribes at the National Museum of the American Indian and Kenyan handicrafts from the National Museum of African Art.

Fashion

Don't be fooled by all the blue suits and khakis you see those government people wearing. This is a city where you'll find an assortment of funky vintage shops, fashion-forward boutiques, couture-loving consignment stores and specialty shops dealing in African robes, hats, lingerie, urban gear and stylish footwear.

Markets

Eastern Market, near Capitol Hill, is the city's main bazaar. It's a splendid place to pick up fresh fruits, vegetables and other foods. The time to go is weekends, when a lively craft market and flea market surround the area. Union Market, northeast in the NoMa neighborhood, is an old warehouse converted to a mod court of artisanal oils, smoked meats, herbed cheeses and microbrews. It has become quite the hot spot since opening in 2012.

Shopping by Neighborhood

- ➡ **National Mall** It's all about museum shops. (p68)
- ➡ **White House Area & Foggy Bottom** Gems hide in office buildings, but mostly souvenir shops dot the streets. (p91)
- ➡ **Georgetown** DC's top corridor for upscale brand-name stores, peppered with antique shops. (p102)
- ➡ **Capitol Hill & Southeast DC** Eastern Market is the core, along with homewares shops. (p124)
- ➡ **Downtown & Penn Quarter** It's mostly generic chains, though galleries and museum shops add character. (p139)
- ➡ **Dupont Circle & Kalorama** A big, quirky variety of bookstores, hats, homewares and artsy stuff. (p153)
- ➡ **Adams Morgan** Indie record shops, doorknob shops, bong shops and ethnic handicrafts scatter along 18th St. (p162)
- ➡ **Logan Circle, U Street & Columbia Heights** Distinctive antiques and homewares line 14th and U Sts; big-box retailers throng the Columbia Heights Metro. (p183)
- ➡ **Upper Northwest DC** Lots of family-friendly shops, plus a famed bookstore; malls toward Friendship Heights. (p193)
- ➡ **Northern Virginia** Galleries in Alexandria; malls in Arlington and beyond. (p206)

Lonely Planet's Top Choices

Eastern Market Butcher, baker and blue crab maker on weekdays, plus artisans and farmers on weekends. (p125)

National Archives Shop For when you need a Declaration-inscribed ruler or John Adams stuffed toy. (p139)

Capitol Hill Books So many volumes they're even for sale in the bathroom. (p124)

Miss Pixie's A trove of timeworn curiosities to sort through. (p183)

Old Print Gallery Vintage maps and prints, from pioneer land charts to Audubon lithographs. (p102)

Best Souvenirs

White House Historical Association Museum Shop Sells the president's official ornaments, artwork and classy tchotchkes. (p91)

White House Gifts Presidential golf balls, T-shirts, snow globes: a quintessential spot for goofy DC trinkets. (p91)

Best Books

Politics & Prose Bookstore Iconic, brain-food bookstore that hosts readings, open-mike nights and a comfy cafe. (p193)

Second Story Books Antiquarian books and old sheet music, plus cheap sidewalk bins to rummage through. (p153)

Kramerbooks New books on the shelves, hearty food in the cafe, happening round-the-clock on weekends. (p153)

Idle Time Books Great political and history stacks among the three creaky floors of used tomes. (p162)

Best Music

Crooked Beat Records Laid-back all-vinyl shop with crates of rock, punk and soul. (p162)

Red Onion Records Flick through the $1 bin after perusing the disco, funk and jazz. (p154)

Best Antiques

Book Hill Galleries, interior design stores and antique shops all in a row in Georgetown. (p93)

Brass Knob Salvaged lamps, mirrors, mantelpieces and heaps of doorknobs from old buildings. (p162)

Best Vintage

Meeps Cowboy shirts, Jackie O sunglasses and magnificent duds from past eras. (p162)

Treasury Well-curated selection from flapper dresses to tweed vests. (p184)

Best Homewares

Hill's Kitchen Groovy pots, pans, whisks and US state-shaped cookie cutters. (p125)

Hunted House Mid-century modern wares to make your pad look like Don Draper's on *Mad Men*. (p125)

Best Arts & Crafts

Torpedo Factory Art Center Three floors of artists' studios fill an old munitions factory. (p206)

Claude Taylor Photography Travel pictures from around the globe, including cool DC scenes. (p150)

NEED TO KNOW

Opening Hours

- **Malls** 10am to 8pm or 9pm Monday to Saturday, 11am to 6pm Sunday
- **Shops** 10am to 7pm Monday to Saturday, noon to 6pm Sunday

Taxes

Sales tax is 5.75% in DC, 6% in both Virginia and Maryland.

Websites

- **Washingtonian** (www.washingtonian.com) Upscale lifestyle magazine covering chic shops.
- **Capitol Hill Style** (www.caphillstyle.com) Fashion blog for professional women.
- **The Houndstooth** (www.thehoundstoothblog.com) Blog offering a male perspective on DC's fashion.

Best Museum Shops

International Spy Museum Shop The place to get that mustache disguise or hidden recording device. (p139)

National Air and Space Museum The only place to buy astronaut ice cream and a NASA spacesuit. (p62)

Best Markets

Flea Market Weekend browser for cool art, furniture, clothing, global wares and bric-a-brac. (p125)

Union Market Hipster entrepreneurs sell their lotions, cheeses and Korean tacos in a revamped warehouse. (p174)

Sports & Activities

The nation's capital comes together in ways unexpected and touching when sports are at stake. It's about the only thing that gets citizens as pumped as politics, and it's more accessible, if not quite as cutthroat. But the city doesn't just watch sports, it plays them too, from Ultimate games on the Mall to bocce ball in Capitol Hill.

Spectator Sports

The football-playing Redskins are the most watched team (though their fortunes have waned recently). The other ties that bind are the Capitals on ice; the Wizards pro basketball team; DC United, one of Major League Soccer's most popular and successful clubs; and the Nationals, with their shiny baseball stadium and 'Racing Presidents' tradition. The Howard Bisons, Georgetown Hoyas and other university teams have rabid student-body fans.

Cycling

DC has a savvy and ever-growing cycling population. The Capital Bikeshare (p270) program facilitates it. The network has 2500-plus bicycles at some 300 stations scattered around the region, including many that fringe the Mall. The flat green landscape is a great place to start rolling, and from there you can wheel onward to the Tidal Basin and beyond.

Acres of parkland along the Potomac River also make for great bike touring around DC. The miles and miles of off-road bike paths up the ante. Areas with sweet trails include Georgetown, Upper Northwest DC and Northern Virginia.

Hiking & Running

Everyone jogs on the Mall. Rock Creek Park has 15 miles of unpaved trails. A good map is *Map N: Trails in the Rock Creek Park Area,* published by the Potomac Appalachian Trail Club (www.patc.net).

Paddling

Kayaks and canoes cruise the waters of both the Potomac River and the C&O Canal. The canal is ideal for canoeing between Georgetown and Violettes Lock (mile 22). The Potomac has a great vantage point from which to admire the city skyline, but it also has some dangerous currents.

Sports & Activities by Neighborhood

- **National Mall** Join the locals tossing Frisbees, jogging and otherwise recreating. (p71)
- **Georgetown** Top 'hood for cycling trails and paddling options. (p103)
- **Capitol Hill & Southeast DC** Pro baseball, soccer and football, plus bicycle rentals and tours. (p125)
- **Downtown & Penn Quarter** Pro basketball and hockey. (p139)
- **Logan Circle, U Street & Columbia Heights** Golf and far-flung natural areas for hikes. (p184)
- **Upper Northwest DC** Horseback riding and sweet trails in Rock Creek Park. (p194)
- **Northern Virginia** Laced with hiking and biking paths like the Mount Vernon Trail. (p207)

Lonely Planet's Top Choices

Rock Creek Park Trails Amazingly wild paths for cycling and hiking crisscross a stone's throw from civilization. (p188)

Washington Nationals Cheap tickets, the Racing Presidents, and hip eats and drinks make a fun evening. (p125)

National Mall Nothing inspires a jog like this big green lawn studded with monuments. (p57)

Mount Vernon Trail Ride to George Washington's estate past Arlington Cemetery, airplanes, marshes and birds. (p207)

Theodore Roosevelt Island The Potomac River isle floats boardwalks and trails through tranquil woodlands. (p199)

Best Websites

Bike Washington (www.bikewashington.org) Trail information.

Running Report (www.run-washington.com) Information on races and training.

DC Front Runners (www.dc-frontrunners.org) Club for GLBT runners and walkers.

Best Spectator Sports

DC United Big tailgating scene, Latin American food and crazing-cheering fans. (p126)

Washington Capitals A hockey team that knows how to fight. (p139)

Best Walking & Jogging

Georgetown Waterfront Park Riverside path to watch yachts and take a break at outdoor cafes. (p94)

East Potomac Park A 5-mile paved trail bestows airplane-spotting, fishing holes and cherry blossoms. (p116)

Dumbarton Oaks Park Escape the crowds on wooded, bridge-crossed trails. (p94)

Yards Park Amble the boardwalk along the Anacostia River. (p112)

Best Cycling

C&O Canal Towpath Bucolic trail a few steps from Georgetown's shopping frenzy. (p103)

Capital Crescent Trail Converted rail bed that runs by Potomac River outlooks and woodsy scenes. (p103)

Big Wheel Bikes Convenient rental shop near three ace cycling trails. (p103)

Best Paddling

Key Bridge Boathouse Rents canoes, kayaks and stand-up paddleboards for Potomac River gliding. (p103)

Tidal Basin Boathouse Easy-breezy paddleboats offer sweet views of the MLK and Jefferson memorials. (p71)

Thompson Boat Center Georgetown hot spot for canoes, kayaks and rowing classes, plus bicycles for landlubbers. (p103)

Best Guided Jaunts

Key Bridge Boathouse Paddle by monuments on twilight kayaking tours. (p103)

DC by Foot Excellent pay-what-you-want walks by theme or by neighborhood. (p272)

Bike & Roll The nighttime cycling rides around the illuminated Mall impress. (p126)

NEED TO KNOW

Pro Teams

- **DC United** (MLS; www.dcunited.com)
- **Washington Capitals** (NHL; http://capitals.nhl.com)
- **Washington Nationals** (MLB; www.nationals.com)
- **Washington Redskins** (NFL; www.redskins.com)
- **Washington Wizards** (NBA; www.nba.com/wizards)

Tickets

You can buy tickets to games direct from teams' websites or stadiums, or from scalpers outside the venues. Or you can try online providers. Some charge a 'convenience' fee.

- **StubHub!** (www.stubhub.com)
- **Dream Tix** (www.dreamtix.com)
- **TicketExchange by Ticketmaster** (www.ticketexchangebyticketmaster.com)
- **Craigslist** (http://washingtondc.craigslist.org) No fee; the site serves as an online scalping service.

Recreational Leagues

- **DC Bocce League** (www.dcbocce.com) Lawn bowling league with the motto 'Our balls are hard-er.'
- **DC Kickball** (www.dckickball.org) League for the soccer-meets-baseball activity.

Best Golf

East Potomac Park Golf Course Eighteen holes plus a driving range and mini-golf course. (p126)

Displays at the Smithsonian Institution (p72)

With Kids

Washington bursts with kid-friendly attractions. Not only do they hold the nation's best collection of dinosaur bones, rockets and one-of-a kind historical artifacts, but just about everything is free. Another bonus: green space surrounds all the sights, so young ones can burn off energy to their hearts' content.

National Museum of the American Indian (p67)

Sights & Museums for Kids

The top-draw museums and National Zoo are geared to children, with free family guide booklets and hands-on activities to enhance young ones' experience. Ask at the information desk for any age-appropriate materials on offer. For instance, the zoo offers a 'Zoo Crew Training Manual' and various scavenger hunts. The National Gallery of Art has booklets with games and puzzles kids can do on-site, plus a children's audio tour. The National Air and Space Museum has a How Things Fly gallery that whooshes with interactive gadgets to play with.

As of early 2015, the **National Children's Museum** (Map p300; ☎301-686-0225; www.ncm.museum) is homeless, but looking for a new space to open in DC. Check the website for updates.

Attractions Out of Town

Glen Echo Park (☎301-634-2222; www.glenechopark.org; 7300 MacArthur Blvd, Glen Echo, MD; ⏰6am-1am) This beautiful park 9 miles northwest of downtown has a huge **carousel** (per ride $1.25; operating May through September) and children's shows by the **Puppet Company** (www.thepuppetco.org; tickets $10; ⏰Thu-Sun) and **Adventure Theatre MTC** (www.adventuretheatre-mtc.org; tickets $19).

Six Flags America (☎301-249-1500; www.sixflags.com/america; 13710 Central Ave, Upper Marlboro, MD; adult/child $60/40; ⏰May-Oct, hours vary) The park offers a full array of roller coasters and tamer kiddie rides. It's located about 15 miles east of downtown DC in Maryland.

NEED TO KNOW

Advance Reservations

You'll need to make reservations several weeks in advance for the White House, the Marine Barracks drill parade and for House and Senate chamber visits. For the following sights, it pays to go online and reserve tickets a month in advance during spring and summer (there's usually a small fee):

- International Spy Museum
- National Archives
- Washington Monument
- Ford's Theatre
- Capitol tours
- Washington National Cathedral tours

Saving Money

The Newseum, International Spy Museum and Crime Museum run money-saving promotions on their websites and offer coupons in visitor publications. The ticket broker **Goldstar** (www.goldstar.com/washington-dc) often has half-price tickets available, as well.

Films

- In *Night at the Museum 2: Battle of the Smithsonian* (2009), museum exhibits come to life for Ben Stiller in the National Air and Space Museum and National Gallery of Art. (FYI, the first film was set in the Smithsonian's New York City history museum, and the third film takes place at London's British Museum.)
- In *National Treasure* (2004) Nicolas Cage finds a coded map on the back of the Declaration of Independence that leads to – that's right – national treasure! The sequel came out in 2007, and the third installment supposedly is in the works.

Tours

Bike & Roll (p126) Among the company's offerings is an all-ages, 4-mile cycling tour around the Mall and Tidal Basin. Children's bikes are provided.

DC by Foot (p272) While not specifically geared to kids, its pay-what-you-want walking tours are popular with families. The Mall tour takes two hours and covers a mile; the route is stroller-friendly.

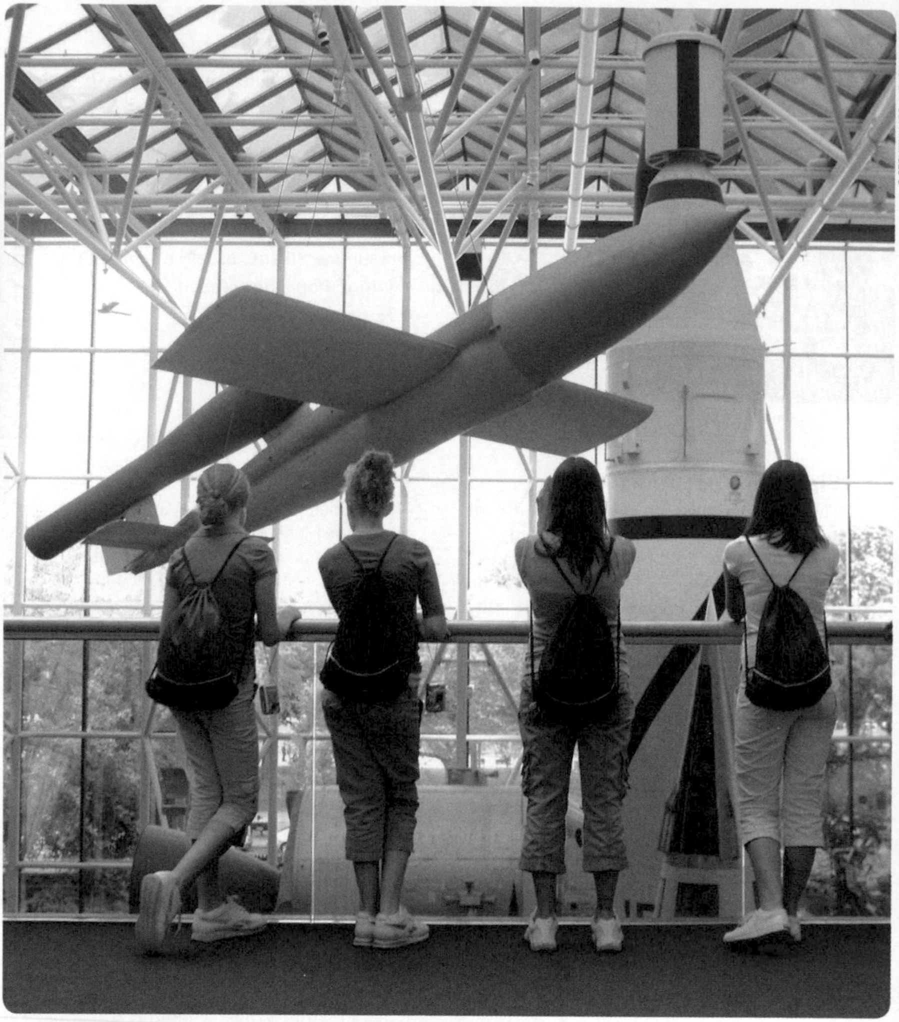

ELAN FLEISHER / GETTY IMAGES ©

DON MASON / GETTY IMAGES ©

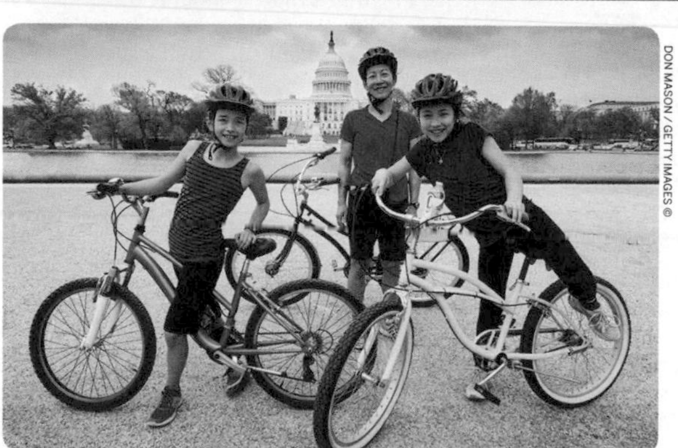

Above: National Air and Space Museum (p62)

Left: Family riding bicycles (p126) near the Capitol

Kids by Neighborhood

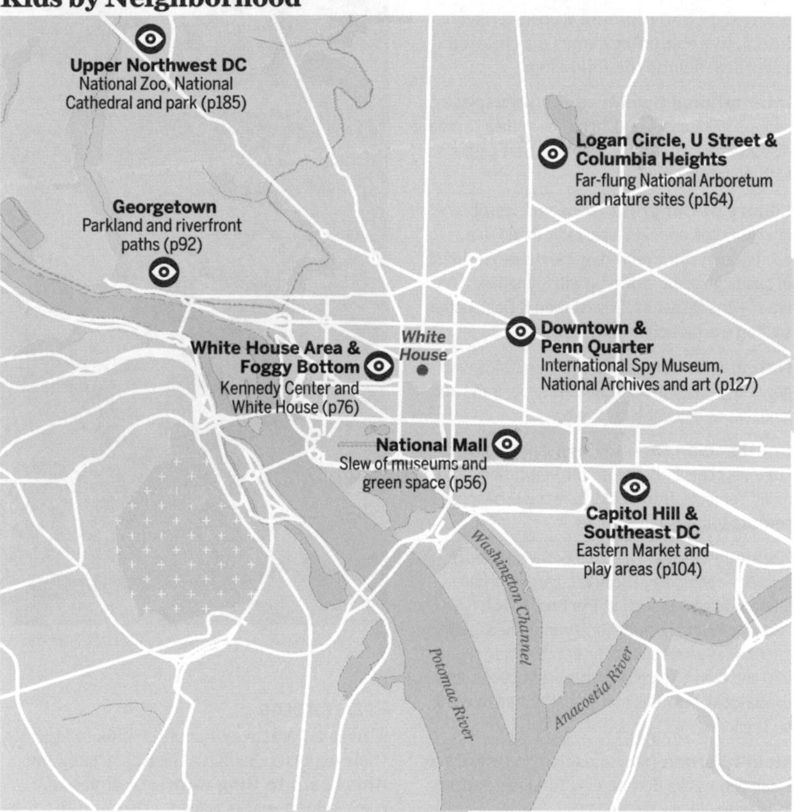

Rainy-Day Options

IMAX The Smithsonian (p72) has two IMAX theaters on the Mall: one in the National Museum of Natural History, and the other in the National Air and Space Museum. The latter also holds the Einstein Planetarium. Schedules are amalgamated at www.si.edu/imax.

Playseum (Map p300; ☎888-575-2973; www.playseum.com; 545 8th St SE; admission $7; ⏲9am-4pm Mon-Thu, 9am-7pm Fri & Sat, 1-6pm Sun) At this play facility by Eastern Market, the main level has a market room with pretend produce kids collect in baskets and 'buy' at the cash register. A beauty salon provides fingernail painting. Pirate's Cove offers sand, shells and a ship to climb. The lower level has a Chinatown room with woks to stir and Asian instruments to play.

Boogie Babes (www.boogiebabes.com; per child $5) They get the preschool-age crowd rockin' at Union Market every Wednesday, at Eastern Market on Thursday and at Atlas Performing Arts Center on Friday, all at 10:30am.

Eat Streets for Kids

➡ **7th St NW** Located by the International Spy Museum and National Archives, this street and its environs have quite a few kid-friendly burger and pizza places, such as Matchbox Pizza. (p137)

➡ **7th and 8th Sts NE** 7th St has Eastern Market (p125) for sandwiches and picnic supplies, plus gelaterias; 8th St has fast-food, bakeries and kid-friendly restaurants like Ted's Bulletin (p120).

➡ **Mall** The National Museum of the American Indian's Mitsitam Cafe (p71) offers unique options. The National Gallery of Art's Cascade Cafe (p70) has pizza, pasta and a gelato bar.

➡ **Zoo area** The areas north and south of the Connecticut Ave entrance have heaps of restaurants, such as Lebanese Taverna (p192).

Games for Kids

Many sight and museum websites have interactive computer games for children. Favorites include the following:

International Spy Museum (www.spymuseum.org/kidspy) Loud, booming games to create disguises and to 'diffuse robotic covert pigeons with explosive birdseed.'

Library of Congress (www.americaslibrary.gov) Kids can animate a cartoon, listen to a jukebox of historic recordings and see old videos of buildings being blown up with dynamite. The latter – the Disasters, Devastation & Destruction section – is particularly impressive.

National Gallery of Art (Map p294; www.nga.gov/kids) Young artists can create portraits and landscapes using interactive tools.

Smithsonian (www.smithsonianeducation.org/students) Lets kids peruse the institution's 140 million objects, from rocks to rockets, baseball cards to brontosaurus bones.

Kennedy Center (Map p296; www.artsedge.kennedy-center.org) The Arts Edge portal has interactive games such as **Perfect Pitch** (www.artsedge.kennedy-center.org/interactives/perfect-pitch), where kids choose an era (baroque, modern etc) and then a 'team' of instruments strolls onto the baseball field. Click on an instrument to see it and hear it.

Mount Vernon (www.mountvernon.org) Offers video games like Bombarding Yorktown and an interactive jigsaw puzzle.

Other Fun Projects

WRITE A LETTER TO THE PRESIDENT

There's something pretty cool about writing to the prez while you're in the neighborhood. White House staff respond to every letter, so make sure your child includes a return address both on the letter and on the envelope. Here are some writing tips:

➡ Introduce yourself to the president in one sentence (how old you are, where you live etc).

➡ Explain why you're writing. To ask for help with a certain issue? To approve or disapprove of a decision he made? To ask the president a personal question? Explain the action you'd like him to take, ie propose legislation, visit your town, send you a photo.

➡ Address it to: President, The White House, 1600 Pennsylvania Ave NW, Washington, DC 20500.

➡ Wait for his response!

'Junior journalists' at the highly interactive Newseum (p131)

CREATE A BLOG

This is a great way for older kids to share their experiences with friends. Check out **Kids Learn to Blog** (www.kidslearntoblog.com), which walks parents through the process of setting up a blog for youngsters, including information on safety and monitoring the blog. Kids also can sign up for blogs on monitored sites like **Kidzworld** (www.kidzworld.com).

Resources for Parents

DC Urban Mom (www.dcurbanmom.com) Has forums to post your DC questions; look for the Travel Discussion and Food & Restaurant threads.

DC Cool Kids (www.washington.org/dc-cool-kids) Features activity guides, insider tips from local youngsters on things to do, and museum info.

Smithsonian Kids (www.si.edu/kids) Has educational games and projects, plus the lowdown on pint-sized activities at the museums.

Kid Friendly DC (www.kidfriendlydc.com) A local mom's blog with good events listings.

Our Kids (www.our-kids.com) Local website listing kid-centric events, restaurants and activities.

Lonely Planet's Top Choices

National Zoo Pandas play, orangutans swing and lions roar at DC's top family attraction. (p188)

National Museum of Natural History The mummified kitty, T. rex skull and tarantula feedings generate big squeals. (p67)

National Air and Space Museum Touch moon rocks and walk through space capsules. (p62)

National Museum of American History Gawp at the Star-Spangled Banner flag, George Washington's sword and a 23-room doll house. (p68)

Best Sights for Preschoolers

Carousel Take a spin on the old-fashioned merry-go-round on the Mall. (p71)

National Building Museum Seek out the hands-on Building Zone where kids stack block towers and drive toy bulldozers. (p133)

Georgetown Waterfront Park Splash in the fountains and curlicue through the maze. (p94)

Best Sights for Grade-Schoolers

National Gallery of Art Stay busy with activity booklets and a ride on the underground walkway. (p61)

National Archives The Declaration of Independence and George Washington's letters make for a cool history lesson. (p129)

Washington National Cathedral Check out unusual gargoyles and the enchanted garden. (p187)

Best Sights for Teens

Newseum Junior journalists report 'live from the White House' via the TV studio. (p131)

Crime Museum Crack a safe, get fingerprinted and sit in a prison cell. (p132)

Capitol See government in action, plus magic tricks in the Hall of Statues. (p106)

Best Restaurants

Diner Drawing materials for kids, booze for parents, 24-hour service and American food classics for all. (p157)

Ted's Bulletin Retro spot serving smiley-face pancakes and peanut butter and jelly sandwiches. (p120)

Best Entertainment

National Theatre Free Saturday morning performances, from puppet shows to tap dancers. (p138)

Discovery Theater The Smithsonian's kids' theater features cultural plays and storytelling. (p71)

Best Shops

International Spy Museum The shop carries everything from mustache disguises to voice-changing gadgets. (p139)

Sullivan's Toy Store Inventive crafts, puzzles and games line the shelves of DC's oldest, family-run toy shop. (p193)

Best Lodging

Embassy Suites Washington DC Big rooms, an indoor pool and evening wine for mom and dad. (p233)

Hotel Monaco Cribs, safety kits and pet goldfish for rooms, plus a convenient downtown location. (p231)

Omni Shoreham Hotel Treats kids right with milk, cookies, toys and games a stone's throw from the zoo. (p236)

STEVEN HEAP / GETTY IMAGES ©

Explore Washington, DC

WASHINGTON, DC'S TOP SIGHTS

Neighborhoods at a Glance

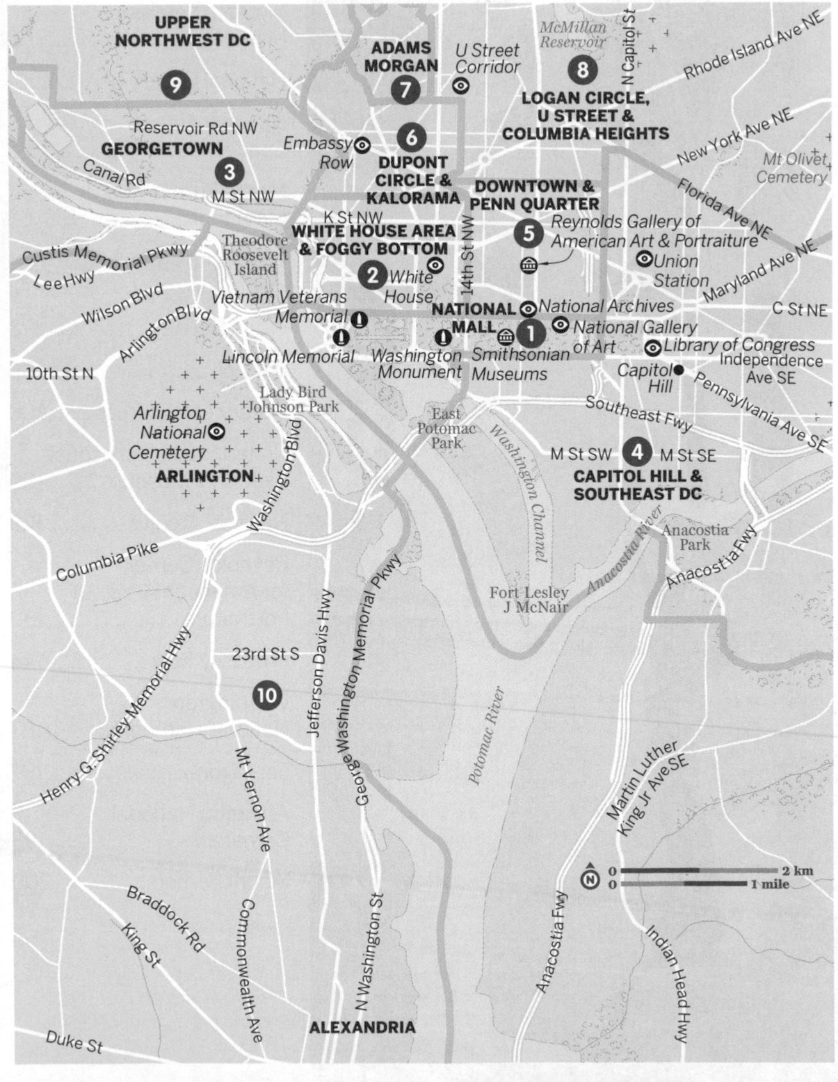

❶ National Mall p56

The Mall – aka 'America's front yard' – holds most of the Smithsonian museums and major monuments. The Lincoln Memorial, Washington Monument, Air and Space Museum, National Gallery of Art and much more crowd around a 2-mile-long strip of scrubby grass.

❷ White House Area & Foggy Bottom p76

The President lives at the center of the 'hood. The State Department, World Bank and other institutions hover nearby in Foggy Bottom. It's mostly a business district by day, and not terribly active by night, with the exception of the Kennedy Center for performing arts.

❸ Georgetown p92

Georgetown is DC's most aristocratic neighborhood, home to elite university students, ivory-tower academics and diplomats. Chi-chi brand-name shops, dark-wood pubs and upscale restaurants line the streets. Lovely parks and gardens color the edges.

❹ Capitol Hill & Southeast DC p104

The city's geographic and legislative heart surprises by being mostly a row-house-lined residential neighborhood. The vast area holds top sights such as the Capitol, Library of Congress and Holocaust Memorial Museum. The areas around Eastern Market and H St NE are locals' hubs, with good-time restaurants and nightlife.

❺ Downtown & Penn Quarter p127

Penn Quarter forms around Pennsylvania Ave as it runs between the White House and the Capitol. Downtown extends west beyond it. Major sights include the National Archives, Reynolds Center for American Art & Portraiture and Ford's Theatre. It's also DC's theater district and home to the basketball/hockey sports arena.

❻ Dupont Circle & Kalorama p142

Dupont offers flash new restaurants, hip bars, cafe society and cool bookstores. It's also the heart of the city's GLBT community. It used to be where turn-of-the-century millionaires lived. Today those mansions hold DC's greatest concentration of embassies. Kalorama sits in the northwest corner and ups the regal reserve.

❼ Adams Morgan p155

Adams Morgan has long been Washington's fun, nightlife-driven neighborhood. It's also a global village of sorts. The result today is a raucous mash-up centered on 18th St NW. Vintage boutiques, record shops and ethnic eats poke up between thumping bars and clubs.

❽ Logan Circle, U Street & Columbia Heights p164

This neighborhood covers a lot of ground. Logan Circle stars with hot-chef bars and bites amid stately old manors. Historic U St has been reborn as a jazzy arts and entertainment district. Columbia Heights booms with Latino immigrants and hipsters. Onward, Northeast DC is a stretch of prosperous residential blocks holding some great far-flung sights.

❾ Upper Northwest DC p185

The leafy lanes of Upper Northwest have long been the place for upper-income Washingtonians to settle their families. Sights scatter across the extensive area. The National Zoo and National Cathedral are foremost. Rock Creek Park and Russian-art-filled Hillwood Museum are less well known but equally worthwhile.

❿ Northern Virginia p195

Arlington has the solemn National Cemetery, the imposing Pentagon and ethnic enclaves for good eats. Colonial Alexandria is a posh collection of historic house museums, cobblestoned streets, outdoor cafes and a waterfront promenade. Nature areas and trails fringe both towns.

National Mall

Neighborhood Top Five

❶ Climb the steps of the **Lincoln Memorial** (p58), stare into Abe's stony eyes and read his Gettysburg Address chiseled in the wall. Then go stand where Martin Luther King Jr gave his 'I Have a Dream' speech and feel the sweep of history.

❷ Touch the moon and gawp at nuclear missiles at the **National Air and Space Museum** (p62).

❸ Reflect on the sea of names sprawled across the **Vietnam Veterans Memorial** (p60).

❹ Smell the roses, er, cherry blossoms around the **Tidal Basin** (p69) come springtime.

❺ Poke around the monumental trove of paintings and sculpture at the **National Gallery of Art** (p61).

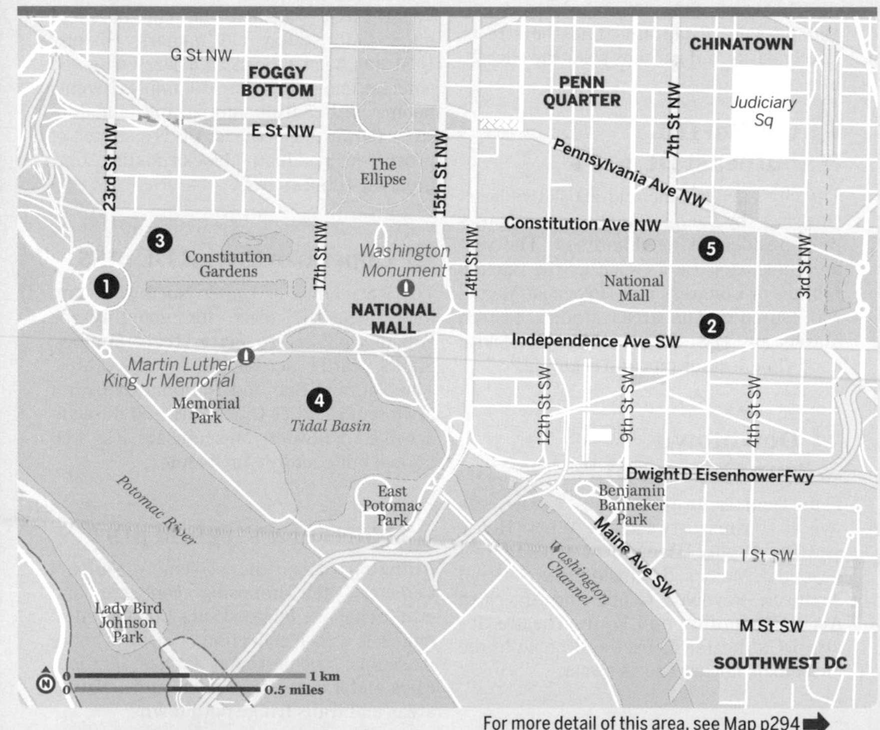

For more detail of this area, see Map p294

Explore the National Mall

A nation is many things: its people, its history, its politics and its amassed knowledge. Somehow, every item listed above is given architectural life on the National Mall, the center of iconography of the most iconic city in America. This is where the nation's ideals are expressed in stone, landscaping, educational institutions, monuments and memorials.

It's also, for you first-timers, a big old lawn. Really, that's the gist of it – a couple of miles of scrubby grass sandwiched between the Capitol and Lincoln Memorial, pinned down by the Washington Monument, flanked by hot-dog vendors and T-shirt stands, and containing therein the American experience. This communal space is where Americans come to protest, to rally, to watch presidents get inaugurated. It's also where locals come to jog, dog-walk and toss a Frisbee.

With all the monuments and museums to see (for free!), you could spend your entire trip here. It's easy to get lost in the National Gallery of Art or the Air and Space Museum for half a day. Whatever you decide to explore, be prepared to walk. The main row of sights, from the Smithsonian museums west to the Lincoln Memorial, is about 2 miles tip to tip. The DC Circulator bus route stops by many of the hot spots, but you'll still be hoofing it quite a bit. Eating and drinking options are thin on the ground beyond the museum cafes. And while it's beautiful at night, there's not much going on after hours.

Local Life

➡ **Early to Rise** Many locals say the best cherry-blossom viewing is from the Franklin Delano Roosevelt Memorial (p69) at sunrise.

➡ **Sunset Kiss** Looking for a romantic place to smooch your sweetie? Constitution Gardens (p70) at sunset is a well-known hot spot.

➡ **Nighttime Stroll** Don't overlook visiting the Mall at night. A walk along Constitution Ave past the dramatically lit monuments is atmospheric (and safe).

Getting There & Away

➡ **Metro** Smithsonian (Blue, Orange, Silver Lines) and L'Enfant Plaza (Blue, Orange, Silver, Green and Yellow Lines) for most sights; Foggy Bottom-GWU for the Lincoln and Vietnam Memorials – though they're about a mile walk from the station.

➡ **Bus** The new DC Circulator National Mall bus runs from Union Station around the Mall and Tidal Basin, with stops at main sights.

➡ **Bicycle** Several Capital Bikeshare stations fringe the Mall.

Lonely Planet's Top Tip

Aside from a couple of notable museum cafes and scattered snack vendors, it's a food desert on the Mall. It's wise to bring your own nibbles. One strategy: hit Eastern Market (p125) first to assemble a picnic for later in the day. It's a short hop east on the Metro's Blue, Orange and Silver Lines in the Capitol Hill neighborhood.

Best Gardens

➡ National Sculpture Garden (p67)

➡ United States Botanic Garden (p67)

➡ Hirshhorn Sculpture Garden (p67)

➡ Enid A Haupt Garden (p66)

For reviews, see p66. ➡

Best Museums

➡ National Air and Space Museum (p62)

➡ National Gallery of Art (p61)

➡ Freer-Sackler Museums of Asian Art (p66)

➡ National Museum of Natural History (p67)

For reviews, see p66. ➡

Best Monuments

➡ Vietnam Veterans Memorial (p60)

➡ Lincoln Memorial (p58)

➡ Washington Monument (p59)

➡ Martin Luther King Jr Memorial (p63)

For reviews, see p66. ➡

PAUL FRANKLIN / GETTY IMAGES ©

TOP SIGHT
LINCOLN MEMORIAL

In a city of icons, the inspiration for the 16th president stands out in the crowd. Maybe it's the classicism evoked by the Greek temple design, or the stony dignity of Lincoln's gaze. Whatever the lure, a visit here while looking out over the Reflecting Pool is a defining DC moment.

The Design

Plans for a monument to Abraham Lincoln began in 1867 – two years after his assassination – but construction didn't begin until 1914. Henry Bacon designed the memorial to resemble a Doric temple, with 36 columns to represent the 36 states in Lincoln's union. Carvers used 28 blocks of marble to fashion the seated figure. Lincoln's face and hands are particularly realistic, since they are based on castings done when he was president. The words of his Gettysburg Address and Second Inaugural speech flank the statue on the north and south walls, along with murals depicting his principles. Look for symbolic images of freedom, liberty and unity, among others. More info is available via a **DIY cell-phone tour** (☎202-747-3420).

DON'T MISS...

- Martin Luther King's 'Dream' speech marker
- Lincoln's expressive face and hands
- Gettysburg Address text
- Murals
- Visiting at nighttime

PRACTICALITIES

- Map p294
- www.nps.gov/linc
- 2 Lincoln Memorial Circle NW
- 24hr
- Circulator, M Foggy Bottom-GWU

Civil Rights Rallying Point

From the get-go, the Lincoln Memorial became a symbol of the Civil Rights movement. Most famously, Martin Luther King Jr gave his 'I Have a Dream' speech here in 1963. An engraving of King's words marks the spot where he stood. It's on the landing 18 steps from the top, and is usually where everyone is gathered, snapping photos of the awesome view out over the Reflecting Pool and Washington Monument. Visiting the memorial at nighttime is particularly atmospheric (and there's less crowd jostling).

TOP SIGHT
WASHINGTON MONUMENT

Rising up on the Mall like an exclamation point, the 555ft obelisk embodies the awe and respect the nation felt for George Washington, the USA's first president and founding father. The monument is DC's loftiest structure, and by federal law no local building can reach above it. A 70-second elevator ride whisks you to the observation deck for the city's best views.

Mismatched Marble

Construction began in 1848, but a lack of funds during the Civil War grounded the monument at 156ft. President Ulysses S Grant got the ball rolling again in 1876.

There was a problem, though. The original marble was drawn from a quarry in Maryland, but the source dried up during the construction delay. Contractors had to turn to Massachusetts for the rest of the rock. If you look closely, there is a visible delineation in color where the old and new marble meet about a third of the way up (the bottom is a bit lighter).

DON'T MISS...

- Change in color a third of the way up
- Inscribed stones inside
- Views from the top

PRACTICALITIES

- Map p294
- www.nps.gov/wamo
- 2 15th St NW
- 9am-5pm, to 10pm Jun-Aug
- Circulator, Smithsonian

Pyramid Topper

In December 1884 workers heaved a 3300lb marble capstone on the monument and topped it off with a 9in pyramid of cast aluminum. At the time, aluminum was rare and expensive. Before the shiny novelty went to Washington, the designers displayed the pyramid in the window of Tiffany's in New York City.

The monument was the culmination of some 36,000 stacked blocks of granite and marble, weighing 81,000 tons. The 'Father of his Country' had his due.

Observation Deck & Memorial Stones

Inside the monument, an elevator takes you to the sky-high observation deck that provides grand city vistas. There are also exhibits that explain how the Washington Monument was the world's tallest structure until the Eiffel Tower surpassed it. And how in August 2011, an earthquake rattled the monument causing structural damage. It took 33 months and $15 million to fix.

On the way back down, the elevator slows so you can glimpse some of the 195 memorial stones that decorate the shaft's interior. Various states, cities and patriotic societies purchased them as part of the monument's initial construction. There's even one from the Pope.

Queues & Tickets

Same-day tickets for a timed entrance are available at the **kiosk** (15th St, btwn Madison Dr NW & Jefferson Dr SW; from 8:30am) by the monument. During peak season it's a good idea to **reserve tickets in advance** (877-444-6777; www.recreation.gov) by phone or online ($1.50 fee per ticket, plus additional $3 if you order more than 10 days prior). And don't despair if you look online and see that tickets are sold out; there are still 1000 more available each day to be given out at the kiosk. Rangers advise getting there by 7:30am in peak season, and 9am in the off-season to snag day-of tickets.

TOP SIGHT
VIETNAM VETERANS MEMORIAL

At this powerful site, a black granite 'V' cuts into the Mall, just as the war it memorializes cut into the national psyche. The monument eschews mixing conflict with glory. Instead, it quietly records the names of service personnel killed or missing in action in Vietnam, honoring those who gave their lives and explaining, in stark architectural language, the true price paid in war.

The Design

Maya Lin, a 21-year-old Yale architecture student, designed the memorial following a nationwide competition in 1981. The 'V' is comprised of two walls of polished granite that meet in the center at a 10ft peak, then taper to a height of 8in. The mirror-like surface lets visitors see their own reflection among the names of the dead, bringing past and present together. A DIY cell-phone tour that goes into detail about the design is available by calling ☎202-595-0093.

Order of Names

The wall lists soldiers' names chronologically according to the date they died (and alphabetically within each day). The list starts at the monument's vertex on panel 1E on July 8, 1959. It moves day by day to the end of the eastern wall at panel 70E, then starts again at panel 70W at the western wall's end. It returns to the vertex on May 15, 1975, where the war's beginning and end meet in symbolic closure. Paper indices at each end of the wall let you look up individual names and get their panel location. There are 58,272 names; new ones are added sporadically due to clerical errors in record keeping. Rank is not provided on the wall, and privates share space with majors.

DON'T MISS...

- Mementos left at the wall
- Your reflection in the wall
- Three Soldiers monument
- Women in Vietnam Memorial
- Symbols beside the names

PRACTICALITIES

- Map p294
- www.nps.gov/vive
- 5 Henry Bacon Dr NW
- 24hr
- Circulator, Foggy Bottom-GWU

Mementos, Diamonds & Plus Signs

A diamond next to the name indicates 'killed, body recovered.' A plus sign indicates 'missing and unaccounted for.' There are approximately 1200 of the latter. If a soldier returns alive, a circle is inscribed around the plus sign. To date, no circles appear.

Many people leave mementos at the wall, such as photos of babies and hand-scrawled notes that bring tears to the most hardened hearts. Rangers collect the items daily; the National Park Service then catalogs and warehouses them.

Reaction & Nearby Sculptures

In 1984 opponents of Maya Lin's design insisted that a more traditional sculpture be added to the monument. The **Three Soldiers** depicts three servicemen – one white, one African American and one Latino – who seem to be gazing upon the nearby sea of names. The tree-ringed **Women in Vietnam Memorial**, showing female soldiers aiding a fallen combatant, is also nearby.

TOP SIGHT
NATIONAL GALLERY OF ART

Affiliated with but not a part of the Smithsonian, the National Gallery needs two buildings to house its staggering collection that spans the Middle Ages to the present. Being a generalist sort of spot, it doesn't quite excel in any one area (the Hirshhorn has better modern art, and the Reynolds Center keeps a better national retrospective), but it's still mighty impressive.

West Building

The original neoclassical building, known as the West Building, exhibits primarily European works from the Middle Ages to the early 20th century. You could spend days wandering through the trove in this wing alone. The National Gallery is the only art museum in the western hemisphere displaying a Leonardo da Vinci (*Ginevra di' Benci,* in Gallery 6). Rembrandt's 1659 jowly *Self-Portrait* stares out from nearby Gallery 48. Impressionist and post-impressionist fans should beeline to galleries 80 to 93, where all the big-name brushmen hang. There are entire rooms devoted to Cézanne works (like *Boy in a Red Waistcoat*), Van Gogh's vivid swirls (as in *Self-Portrait* and *Roses*) and Monet's fleeting light *(Rouen Cathedral).* Renoir's *Girl with a Watering Can* remains a crowd favorite, as does Picasso's *Family of Saltimbanques.*

Free audio tours are available inside the main entrance near the coat check.

DON'T MISS...

- Leonardo da Vinci's *Ginevra di' Benci*
- Alexander Calder mobile
- Impressionist galleries
- Twinkling-light walkway
- Free films and concerts

PRACTICALITIES

- Map p294
- ☎202-737-4215
- www.nga.gov
- Constitution Ave NW, btwn 3rd & 7th Sts
- 10am-5pm Mon-Sat, 11am-6pm Sun
- Circulator, Ⓜ Archives

East Building

Across 4th St NW, the angular East Building, designed by IM Pei, holds modern art. Alas, most of the galleries are closed into 2016 for renovations and expansion. But you can still pop in and see Alexander Calder's incredible mobile *Untitled* – the largest one he ever produced – as it swings over the atrium, as well as a scattering of sculptures by Max Ernst, Henry Moore and others that rise up on the ground level.

Cafe & Artsy Walkway

To get between the two buildings, jump on the trippy, twinkling, moving sidewalk that connects them underground. It's a work of art itself, titled *Multiverse,* by Leo Villareal. The Cascade Cafe buzzes with patrons at the walkway's west end.

The gallery overall is huge and could easily fill a day. If you're short on time, ask for the see-it-in-an-hour highlights brochure; each building has its own, available at the main entrances.

Concerts, Films & Kids' Programs

The National Gallery's documentary and avant-garde film program takes place several times a month in the East Building auditorium. During renovations, the free screenings happen at other museums around town. Check www.nga.gov/film. Free classical concerts fill the air on Sundays at 6:30pm in the West Building's West Garden Court. Free 'Family Guide' activity booklets and a kids' audio tour make visits here especially good for children. See www.nga.gov/kids for more.

FUSE / GETTY IMAGES ©

TOP SIGHT
NATIONAL AIR AND SPACE MUSEUM

The Air and Space Museum is one of the Smithsonian's biggest crowd-pullers. Families flock in for the mind-blowing array of rockets, jets and other contraptions – and all of it is as rousing for adults as kids. Name the historic aircraft or spacecraft – the Wright brothers' flyer, Lindbergh's *Spirit of St Louis*, Skylab – and it's here amid the two-floor spread of awesomeness.

The museum gets jam-packed, but you have to come anyway. C'mon – it's got real nuclear missiles! Walk in the Mall-side entrance and you'll see them, along with rockets, Chuck Yeager's sound-barrier-breaking Bell X-1 and Charles Lindbergh's famed transatlantic-crossing plane. You can also touch the moon (or at least a lunar rock that you're invited to lay fingers on). The USS *Enterprise* from *Star Trek* should be joining the scene by 2016.

That's all by the entrance. Move onward into the galleries and you'll see the 1903 Wright Flyer (aka the world's first airplane), Amelia Earhart's natty red Lockheed 5B Vega (she flew it solo across the Atlantic Ocean in 1932 – the first woman to do so) and a model of the Apollo Lunar Module that Neil Armstrong and Buzz Aldrin stepped out of as the first men on the moon.

An IMAX theater screens films throughout the day, while shows at the Albert Einstein Planetarium send viewers hurtling through space on tours of the universe.

The museum has so much cool stuff they had to build extra hangars for it at the Steven F Udvar-Hazy Center near Washington Dulles International Airport. Together the two sites comprise the world's largest collection of aviation and space artifacts.

DON'T MISS...

- Chuck Yeager's Bell X-1
- Lindbergh's *Spirit of St Louis*
- Apollo Lunar Module
- Wright brothers' original airplane
- Amelia Earhart's plane

PRACTICALITIES

- Map p294
- 202-633-1000
- www.airandspace.si.edu
- cnr 6th St & Independence Ave SW
- 10am-5:30pm, to 7:30pm mid-Mar–early Sep
- Circulator, L'Enfant Plaza

TOP SIGHT
MARTIN LUTHER KING JR MEMORIAL

The newest memorial on the Mall, and the first one to honor an African American, occupies a lovely space along the Tidal Basin. The monument conveys themes of democracy, justice and hope, given form in the striking centerpiece: a 30ft-tall likeness of Dr King emerging from a mountain of granite. But like the man who inspired it, the monument has faced controversy.

Sculptor Lei Yixin carved the piece. Besides Dr King's image, known as the Stone of Hope, there are two blocks behind him that represent the Mountain of Despair. A wall inscribed with King's quotes flanks the statues. King's statue, incidentally, is 11ft taller than those of Lincoln and Jefferson in their nearby memorials.

The MLK monument broke ground in 2006, then got mired in funding difficulties. It finally opened in late 2011. But there was a problem. Chiseled on the Stone of Hope's side was the quote, 'I was a drum major for justice, peace and righteousness.' It was paraphrased from a sermon King gave in Atlanta in 1968, where he said, 'Yes, if you want to say that I was a drum major, say that I was a drum major for justice. Say that I was a drum major for peace. I was a drum major for righteousness. And all of the other shallow things will not matter.' Many pointed out the 'if' and the 'you' changed the quote's meaning from the paraphrased version. Poet Maya Angelou said the way the monument read made King sound like 'an arrogant twit.'

So, after much debate, the park service fixed it. Workers sandblasted off the quote in 2013. The moral, which King would surely appreciate: you *can* change what's written in stone.

DON'T MISS...

- Stone of Hope
- Mountain of Despair
- View of Washington and Jefferson monuments
- Wall of quotes

PRACTICALITIES

- Map p294
- www.nps.gov/mlkm
- 1850 W Basin Dr SW
- 24hr
- Circulator, Smithsonian

National Mall

Folks often call the Mall 'America's Front Yard,' and that's a pretty good analogy. It is indeed a lawn, unfurling scrubby green grass from the Capitol west to the Lincoln Memorial. It's also America's great public space, where citizens come to protest their government, go for scenic runs and connect with the nation's most cherished ideals writ large in stone, landscaping, monuments and memorials.

You can sample quite a bit in a day, though it'll be a full one that requires roughly 4 miles of walking. Start at the **Vietnam Veterans Memorial** ❶, then head counterclockwise around the Mall, swooping in on the **Lincoln Memorial** ❷, **Martin Luther King Jr Memorial** ❸ and **Washington Monument** ❹. You can also pause for the cause of the Korean War and WWII, among other monuments that dot the Mall's western portion.

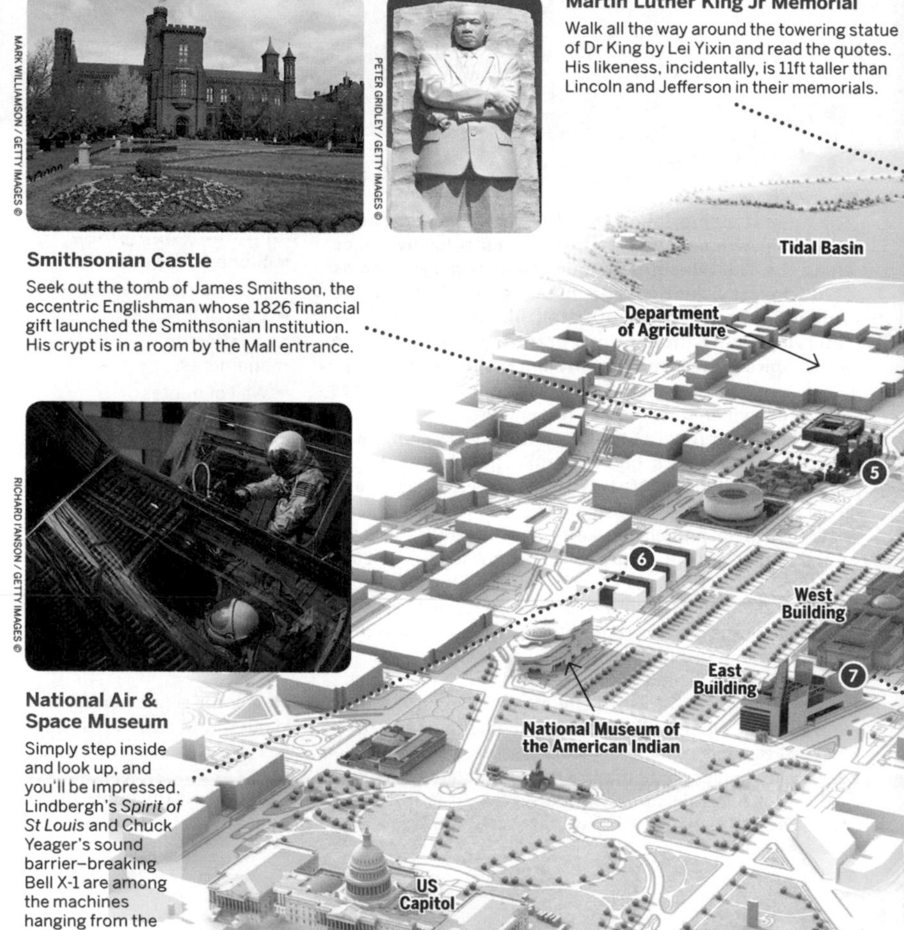

Martin Luther King Jr Memorial

Walk all the way around the towering statue of Dr King by Lei Yixin and read the quotes. His likeness, incidentally, is 11ft taller than Lincoln and Jefferson in their memorials.

Smithsonian Castle

Seek out the tomb of James Smithson, the eccentric Englishman whose 1826 financial gift launched the Smithsonian Institution. His crypt is in a room by the Mall entrance.

National Air & Space Museum

Simply step inside and look up, and you'll be impressed. Lindbergh's *Spirit of St Louis* and Chuck Yeager's sound barrier–breaking Bell X-1 are among the machines hanging from the ceiling.

Then it's onward to the museums, all fabulous and all free. Begin at the **Smithsonian Castle** ❺ to get your bearings – and to say thanks to the guy making all this awesomeness possible – and commence browsing through the **National Air & Space Museum** ❻, **National Gallery of Art & National Sculpture Garden** ❼ and **National Museum of Natural History** ❽.

TOP TIPS

Start early, especially in summer. You'll avoid the crowds, but more importantly you'll avoid the blazing heat. Try to finish with the monuments and be in the air-conditioned museums by 10:30am. Also, consider bringing snacks, since the only food available is from scattered cart vendors and museum cafes.

Lincoln Memorial

Commune with Abe in his chair, then head down the steps to the marker where Martin Luther King Jr gave his 'Dream' speech. The view of the Reflecting Pool and Washington Monument is one of DC's best.

STEVEN GREAVES /GETTY IMAGES ©

Korean War Veterans Memorial

National WWII Memorial

National Museum of American History

National Sculpture Garden

Vietnam Veterans Memorial

Check the symbol that's beside each name. A diamond indicates 'killed, body recovered.' A plus sign indicates 'missing and unaccounted for.' There are approximately 1200 of the latter.

Washington Monument

As you approach the obelisk, look a third of the way up. See how it's slightly lighter in color at the bottom? Builders had to use different marble after the first source dried up.

National Museum of Natural History

Wave to Henry, the elephant who guards the rotunda, then zip to the 2nd floor's Hope Diamond. The 45.52-carat bauble has cursed its owners, including Marie Antoinette, or so the story goes.

EDDIE BRADY / GETTY IMAGES ©

National Gallery of Art & National Sculpture Garden

Beeline to Gallery 6 (West Building) and ogle the Western Hemisphere's only Leonardo da Vinci painting. Outdoors, amble amid whimsical sculptures by Miró, Calder and Lichtenstein. Also check out IM Pei's design of the East Building.

SIGHTS

LINCOLN MEMORIAL MONUMENT

See p58.

WASHINGTON MONUMENT MONUMENT

See p59.

VIETNAM VETERANS MEMORIAL MONUMENT

See p60.

NATIONAL GALLERY OF ART MUSEUM

See p61.

NATIONAL AIR AND SPACE MUSEUM MUSEUM

See p62.

MARTIN LUTHER KING JR MEMORIAL MONUMENT

See p63.

SMITHSONIAN CASTLE NOTABLE BUILDING

Map p294 (202-633-1000; www.si.edu; 1000 Jefferson Dr SW; 8:30am-5:30pm; ; Circulator, Smithsonian) James Renwick designed this turreted, red-sandstone fairytale in 1855. Today the castle houses the **Smithsonian Visitor Center**, which makes a good first stop on the Mall. Inside you'll find history exhibits, multilingual touchscreen displays, a staffed information desk, free maps, a cafe – and the tomb of James Smithson, the institution's founder. His crypt lies inside a little room by the main entrance off the Mall.

FREER-SACKLER MUSEUMS OF ASIAN ART MUSEUM

Map p294 (www.asia.si.edu; cnr Independence Ave & 12th St SW; 10am-5:30pm; ; Circulator, Smithsonian) FREE This is a lovely spot in which to while away a Washington afternoon. Japanese silk scrolls, smiling Buddhas, rare Islamic manuscripts and Chinese jades spread through cool, quiet galleries. The Freer and Sackler are actually separate venues, connected by an underground tunnel. The Sackler focuses more on changing exhibits, while the Freer, rather incongruously, also houses works by American painter James Whistler. Don't miss the blue-and-gold, ceramics-crammed Peacock Room.

Like all Smithsonian institutions, the venues host free lectures, concerts and film screenings; the ones here typically have an Asian bent. The website has the schedule. Alas, the Freer will be closed for structural renovations from January 1, 2016 until summer of 2017. The Sackler will stay open throughout the period.

NATIONAL MUSEUM OF AFRICAN ART MUSEUM

Map p294 (www.nmafa.si.edu; 950 Independence Ave SW; 10am-5:30pm; ; Circulator, Smithsonian) FREE Enter the museum's ground-level pavilion through the Enid A Haupt Garden, then descend into the dim underground exhibit space. Devoted to ancient and modern sub-Saharan African art, the quiet galleries display wooden masks, beaded textiles, ceramics, fetish dolls and other examples of the region's visual traditions. Intentionally or not, there's a definite West African focus with lots of traditional art from Nigeria, Benin and Cameroon.

African dance troupes, theater companies and multimedia artists frequently stage shows here. An underground tunnel connects to the Sackler Gallery.

HIRSHHORN MUSEUM MUSEUM

Map p294 (www.hirshhorn.si.edu; cnr 7th St & Independence Ave SW; 10am-5:30pm; ; Circulator, L'Enfant Plaza) FREE The Smithsonian's cylindrical modern art museum stockpiles sculptures and canvases from modernism's early days to pop art to contemporary art. Special exhibits ring the 2nd floor. Rotating pieces from the permanent collection circle the 3rd floor, where there's also a swell sitting area with couches, floor-to-ceiling windows and a balcony offering Mall views.

Gallery spaces are infused with the right edge of cold showroom chic you expect in modern art museums. The permanent collection includes sculptures by Rodin, Brancusi, Calder and Moore, and canvases by Bacon, Miró, O'Keeffe, Warhol, Stella and Kiefer.

LOCAL KNOWLEDGE

ENID A HAUPT GARDEN

A few tourists find the green space hiding behind the Smithsonian Castle, but mostly it's workers escaping the office who hang out in the **Enid A Haupt Garden** (Map p294; www.gardens.si.edu; ; Circulator, Smithsonian). Shaded benches dot the grounds amid Asian moon gates and Moorish-style geometric flower beds. The peaceful retreat beckons just steps from the Mall, and as a bonus there is free wi-fi.

HIRSHHORN SCULPTURE GARDEN GARDENS

Map p294 (⏲7:30am-sunset; 🚌Circulator, Ⓜ L'Enfant Plaza) Outside and across Jefferson Dr from the Hirshhorn Museum, the sunken Sculpture Garden feels, on the right day, like a bouncy jaunt through a Lewis Carroll Wonderland all prettified up. Young lovers, lost tourists and serene locals wander by sculptures such as Rodin's *The Burghers of Calais*.

NATIONAL MUSEUM OF THE AMERICAN INDIAN MUSEUM

Map p294 (www.nmai.si.edu; cnr 4th St & Independence Ave SW; ⏲10am-5:30pm; 📶👪; 🚌Circulator, Ⓜ L'Enfant Plaza) FREE Ensconced in honey-colored, undulating limestone, this museum makes a striking architectural impression. Inside it offers cultural artifacts, costumes, video and audio recordings related to the indigenous people of the Americas. Exhibits are largely organized and presented by individual tribes, which provides an intimate, if sometimes disjointed, overall narrative. The 'Our Universes' gallery (on Level 4) about Native American beliefs and creation stories is intriguing.

The curving exterior has no sharp edges. The impression it gives is of nature flowing into the learning space, accentuated by an outside green area of wetlands and micro-biomes meant to simulate the ecosystem of the North American continent. The museum offers storytelling, percussion workshops and lots of other family programming. The ground-floor Mitsitam Native Foods Cafe (p71) is the best dining option on the Mall.

UNITED STATES BOTANIC GARDEN GARDENS

Map p294 (www.usbg.gov; 100 Maryland Ave SW; ⏲10am-5pm; 👪; 🚌Circulator, Ⓜ Federal Center SW) FREE The Botanic Garden is the Mall's overlooked gem. Built to resemble London's Crystal Palace, the iron-and-glass greenhouse provides a beautiful setting to roam by orchids, ferns and cacti. When you're done with those, seek out the *Amorphophallus titanum,* whose name translates to 'giant misshapen penis' and whose erratic blooms smell like rotting flesh. Mmm! Alas, it only blooms every three to five years and it's not on show during its hibernation.

A rose garden, butterfly garden and water garden fill the landscape just outside the building.

ℹ FREE WI-FI FOR FREE APPS

If you didn't already download the handy-dandy **National Mall app** (www.nps.gov/nama) and the **Smithsonian app** (www.si.edu/apps/smithsonian-mobile), and you want to save on data costs, swing into the Smithsonian Castle and use the free wi-fi to get them on your mobile device.

BARTHOLDI FOUNTAIN FOUNTAIN

Map p300 (cnr 1st St SW & Independence Ave SW) Behind the United States Botanic Garden, across Independence Ave, you'll find the grand Bartholdi Fountain. Frederic Auguste Bartholdi designed the 15-ton cast-iron squirter at the same time he was designing the Statue of Liberty. Benches and tables dot the flowery grounds. It's a sweet refuge where you can escape the Mall crowds.

NATIONAL SCULPTURE GARDEN GARDENS

Map p294 (cnr Constitution Ave NW & 7th St NW; ⏲10am-7pm Mon-Thu & Sat, 10am-9:30pm Fri, 11am-7pm Sun; 🚌Circulator, Ⓜ Archives) FREE The National Gallery of Art's 6-acre garden is studded with whimsical sculptures such as Roy Lichtenstein's *House,* a giant Claes Oldenburg typewriter eraser and Louise Bourgeois' leggy *Spider*. They are scattered around a fountain – a great place to dip your feet in summer. From November to March the fountain becomes a festive **ice rink** (adult/child $8/7, skate rental $3).

In summer, the garden hosts free evening jazz concerts on Fridays from 5pm to 8:30pm.

NATIONAL MUSEUM OF NATURAL HISTORY MUSEUM

Map p294 (www.mnh.si.edu; cnr 10th St & Constitution Ave NW; ⏲10am-5:30pm, to 7:30pm Jun-Aug; 👪; 🚌Circulator, Ⓜ Smithsonian) FREE Smithsonian museums don't get more popular than this one, so crowds are pretty much guaranteed. Wave to Henry, the elephant who guards the rotunda, then zip to the 2nd floor's Hope Diamond. The 45.52-carat bauble has cursed its owners, including Marie Antoinette, or so the story goes. The beloved Dinosaur Hall is under renovation until 2019, but the giant squid (1st floor, Ocean Hall) and tarantula feedings (2nd floor, Insect Zoo) fill in the thrills at this kid-packed venue.

Adults will find lots to love here too: Easter Island heads (lobby at the Constitution Ave entrance), enormous stuffed creatures in the Mammal Hall (1st floor) and creepy skeletons in the Bone Hall (2nd floor). In a somewhat political statement, which is uncommon for the Smithsonian, the museum has heavily promoted its Darwin and evolution exhibits as a counter to creationism proponents.

The Johnson IMAX Theater (per ticket $9) shows nature extravaganzas in 3D daily. Movies sell out so buy tickets as soon as you arrive, or online in advance. The Butterfly Pavilion has a separate admission fee ($6); it's free on Tuesdays.

NATIONAL MUSEUM OF AMERICAN HISTORY MUSEUM

Map p294 (www.americanhistory.si.edu; cnr 14th St & Constitution Ave NW; 10am-5:30pm, to 7:30pm Jun-Aug; ; Circulator, Smithsonian) FREE

The museum collects all kinds of artifacts of the American experience. The centerpiece is the flag that flew over Fort McHenry in Baltimore during the War of 1812 – the same flag that inspired Francis Scott Key to pen 'The Star-Spangled Banner'. Other highlights include Julia Child's kitchen (1st floor, Food exhibition), Dorothy's ruby slippers and a piece of Plymouth Rock (both on the 2nd floor, American Stories exhibition).

This is a better museum for children than adults; displays tend to be bright and interactive. It is one of the Smithsonian's most popular sights and typically quite crowded. The building continues to undergo significant renovations, so prime exhibits often disappear. Check the website for updates.

NATIONAL MUSEUM OF AFRICAN AMERICAN HISTORY AND CULTURE MUSEUM

Map p294 (www.nmaahc.si.edu; 1400 Constitution Ave NW; 10am-5:30pm; Circulator, Smith-

SHOPPING THE NATIONAL MALL

The Mall's museums all have shops where you'll unearth rare finds. Amazonian artwork, West African handicrafts and surreal space food are just a few things on offer.

National Gallery of Art (p61) It boasts several shops, including a huge one lining the underground corridor linking the East and West Buildings. You'll find framed and unframed reproductions of the museum's best-known works, greeting cards, jewelry, creative games and activities for kids, and loads of books.

National Museum of the American Indian (p67) The smaller 1st-floor shop sells pottery, artwork and jewelry made by tribes from across the Americas. The busier store upstairs has books, crafts and native-themed souvenirs (dream catchers, Mola purses, replica arrowheads).

National Museum of African Art (p66) This is a great gift-buying spot with African textiles, baskets, musical instruments and dolls. Be sure to check out the exquisite jewelry and wood-carved boxes.

National Air and Space Museum (p62) The three-floor emporium offers books, toys, kites, posters, model aircraft and such iconic DC souvenirs as freeze-dried astronaut ice cream. The shop even has child-size space suits, complete with official NASA patches.

National Museum of Natural History (p67) It has four different specialty shops, including a bottom-floor store devoted to toys, stuffed dinosaurs and East Asian–themed items (origami sets, silk purses, kimonos). Outside the Geology Hall, the gem store sells fine and costume jewelry, vases, bowls, candleholders and a variety of unpolished stones.

Freer-Sackler Museums of Asian Art (p66) The Sackler side features Asian art posters and limited-edition prints, exotic jewelry and world crafts. The Freer side stocks antique ceramics from Asia, plus unique prints, scarves, bags and Eastern music (though the Freer is closed for renovation until summer 2017).

National Museum of American History (p68) Replica souvenirs (brass binoculars, lanterns, wooden model ships) plus books and DVDs on all aspects of American culture and history fill the shelves.

sonian, Federal Triangle) FREE This most recent addition to the Smithsonian fold covers the diverse African American experience and how it helped shape the nation. The collection includes everything from Harriet Tubman's hymnal to Emmett Till's casket to Louis Armstrong's trumpet. The institution is constructing a brand-spankin' new building for the museum, to open in 2016. In the meantime, find exhibits from the collection on show at the next-door National Museum of American History (on the 2nd floor).

TIDAL BASIN — WATERFRONT

Map p294 (Circulator, Smithsonian) It's magnificent to stroll around this constructed inlet and watch the monument lights wink across the Potomac. The blooms here are loveliest during the Cherry Blossom Festival, the city's annual spring rejuvenation, when the basin bursts into a pink-and-white floral collage. The original Yoshino cherry trees were a gift from the city of Tokyo, and planted in 1912. Rent a paddleboat from the boathouse (p71) to get out on the water.

The Tidal Basin also serves a practical purpose: flushing the adjacent Washington Channel. At high tide, river waters fill the basin through gates under the Inlet Bridge. At low tide, gates under the Outlet Bridge open and water streams into the channel.

JEFFERSON MEMORIAL — MONUMENT

Map p294 (www.nps.gov/thje; 900 Ohio Dr SW; 24hr; Circulator, Smithsonian) FREE Set on the south bank of the Tidal Basin amid the cherry trees, this memorial honors the third US president, political philosopher, drafter of the Declaration of Independence and founder of the University of Virginia. Designed by John Russell Pope to resemble Jefferson's library at the university, the rounded monument was initially derided by critics as 'the Jefferson Muffin.' Inside is a 19ft bronze likeness, and excerpts from Jefferson's writings are etched into the walls.

Historians criticize some of the textual alterations (edited, allegedly, for space considerations). Regardless, there are wonderful views across the waterfront onto the Mall.

GEORGE MASON MEMORIAL — MONUMENT

Map p294 (www.nps.gov/gemm; cnr Ohio Dr & E Basin Dr SW; 24hr; Circulator, Smithsonian) FREE This little oasis of flowers and fountains honors the famed statesman and author of the Commonwealth of Virginia Declaration of Rights (a forerunner to the US Bill of Rights). A bronze sculpture of Mason sits (literally; his legs are crossed and the man looks eminently relaxed) under a pretty covered arcade, amid wise words against slavery and in support of human rights. Take a seat next to him and soak it all up.

FRANKLIN DELANO ROOSEVELT MEMORIAL — MONUMENT

Map p294 (www.nps.gov/frde; 400 W Basin Dr SW; 24hr; Circulator, Smithsonian) FREE The 7.5-acre memorial pays tribute to the longest-serving president in US history and the era he governed. Visitors are taken through four red-granite 'rooms' that narrate FDR's time in office, from the Depression to the New Deal to WWII. The story is told through statuary and inscriptions, punctuated with fountains and peaceful alcoves. It's especially pretty at night, when the marble shimmers in the glossy stillness of the Tidal Basin.

The irony is, FDR didn't want a grand memorial. Instead, he requested a modest stone slab (p132) by the Archives building. DC honored that request too.

NATIONAL WWII MEMORIAL — MONUMENT

Map p294 (www.nps.gov/wwii; 17th St; 24hr; Circulator, Smithsonian) FREE Dedicated in 2004, the WWII memorial honors the 400,000 Americans who died in the conflict, along with the 16 million US soldiers who served between 1941 and 1945. The plaza's dual arches symbolize victory in the Atlantic and Pacific theaters. The 56 surrounding pillars represent each US state and territory. Stirring quotes speckle the monument. You'll often see groups of veterans paying their respects here.

The Freedom Wall is studded with 4048 hand-sculpted gold stars, one for every 100 Americans who lost their lives in the war (the stars are replicas of those worn by mothers who lost their sons in the fighting). Bas-relief panels depict both combat and the mobilization of the home front. Beside the memorial to the south there is an **information kiosk** where you can look through the registry of war veterans.

DISTRICT OF COLUMBIA WAR MEMORIAL — MONUMENT

Map p294 (West Potomac Park, off Independence Ave; 24hr; Circulator, Foggy Bottom-GWU) FREE This small Greek-style temple commemorates local soldiers killed in WWI, making it the only local District memorial on the Mall. Twelve Doric 22ft-high marble columns support the circular structure; inside are the names of the 26,000 Washingtonians who served in the war and the 499 DC soldiers killed in action.

Various parties have tried to expand the site into a national WWI memorial. Congressional representatives have introduced bills to this effect, but to date nothing has been enacted.

KOREAN WAR VETERANS MEMORIAL — MONUMENT

Map p294 (www.nps.gov/kwvm; 10 Daniel French Dr SW; Circulator, Foggy Bottom-GWU) FREE Nineteen steel soldiers wander through clumps of juniper past a wall bearing images of the 'Forgotten War' that assemble, in the distance, into a panorama of the Korean mountains. It's best visited at night, when the sculpted patrol – representing all races and combat branches that served in the war – takes on a phantom cast. In winter, when snow folds over the infantry's field coats, the impact is especially powerful.

REFLECTING POOL — POOL

Map p294 (Circulator, Foggy Bottom-GWU) Henry Bacon, who designed the Lincoln Memorial, also conceived the iconic Reflecting Pool, modeling it after the canals at Versailles and Fontainebleau. The 0.3-mile-long pond holds 6.75 million gallons of water that circulate in from the nearby Tidal Basin. The site is all gussied up after a $34 million renovation completed in 2012.

CONSTITUTION GARDENS — GARDENS

Map p294 (24hr; Circulator, Foggy Bottom-GWU) FREE Constitution Gardens is a bit of a locals' secret. Quiet, shady and serene, it's a reminder of the size of the Mall – how can such isolation exist amid so many tourists? Here's the simple layout: a copse of trees set off by a small kidney-shaped pool, punctuated by a tiny island holding the **Signers' Memorial**, a plaza honoring those who signed the Declaration of Independence. If you're in need of a romantic getaway, the 'kiss me' vibes don't get much better than this spot at sunset.

The gardens are undergoing renovation to add a cafe, ice-skating facilities and more amenities, to be completed in late 2016.

C&O CANAL GATEHOUSE — HISTORIC BUILDING

Map p294 (near cnr Constitution Ave & 17th St NW) At the northeast corner of Constitution Gardens is an elegantly aged stone cottage, a remnant of the days when the Washington City Canal flowed through this area. The 1835 C&O Canal Gatehouse was the lock-keepers' house for the lock that transferred boats from the City Canal onto the C&O Canal, which begins in Georgetown.

EATING

The Mall has always been a bit of a food desert. The National Park Service operates a handful of kiosks that sell cold drinks, sandwiches and ice cream. Hot-dog cart vendors are scattered around. Meanwhile, most museums have overpriced restaurants with unremarkable menus. We've listed a few of the exceptions here.

CASCADE CAFE — CAFE $

Map p294 (National Gallery of Art, East Bldg; mains $7-14; 11am-3pm Mon-Sat, to 4pm Sun; Circulator, Archives) Located at the juncture of the National Gallery's two wings, the Cascade offers views of just that: a shimmering, IM Pei–designed artificial waterfall. The cafeteria-style eatery is divided

LOCAL KNOWLEDGE

CHOW BEYOND THE MALL

Granted, it's not particularly convenient, but for better food choices than the museums and Mall carts offer, hop on the Metro at the Smithsonian or Archives stations and make the quick trip to Eastern Market (p125).

Another option, especially from the Mall's north-side institutions, is to walk a quarter-mile or so along 12th St NW to the Ronald Reagan Building (p135). The food court inside has sandwiches, sushi, pizza and Chinese food among its stash.

You may find food trucks around the Mall, along Constitution Ave NW and Independence Ave SW. Check **Food Truck Fiesta** (www.foodtruckfiesta.com) for locations.

into different stations where you pick up a tray and choose among pizza, pasta, sandwiches, barbecue and salads. The adjoining espresso bar scoops 19 flavors of gelato. It's a lovely place for a quick bite, and a big family favorite given the sweet treats on offer.

PAVILION CAFE CAFE $

Map p294 (www.pavilioncafe.com; cnr Constitution Ave & 7th St NW; mains $9-12; ⏲10am-7pm Mon-Thu & Sat, 10am-9:30pm Fri, 11am-7pm Sun; Circulator, Archives) Set amid the rambling sylvan serenity of the National Sculpture Garden, this pizza and panini place bustles throughout the seasons. Eat in the glass-walled interior or at the umbrella-shaded outdoor tables. Even if you're not ravenous, the cafe makes a sweet pit stop for a French pastry and glass of wine or beer, a fine reward after all the Mall walking.

MITSITAM NATIVE FOODS CAFE NATIVE AMERICAN $$

Map p294 (www.mitsitamcafe.com; cnr 4th St & Independence Ave SW, National Museum of the American Indian; mains $10-18; ⏲11am-5pm; Circulator, L'Enfant Plaza) By far the most unique food on the Mall, the Mitsitam introduces visitors to the Native American cuisine of five different regions, including the northwest coast (such as cedar-planked wild salmon), Great Plains (buffalo chili) and northern woodlands (maple-brined turkey and wild rice). Menus rotate seasonally, and mixed among the tourists are scads of local office workers seeking a quality lunch.

ENTERTAINMENT

JAZZ IN THE GARDEN LIVE MUSIC

Map p294 (www.pavilioncafe.com/jazz.html; cnr Constitution Ave & 7th St NW; ⏲5-8:30pm Fri late May-early Sep; Circulator, Archives) FREE Lots of locals show up for these outdoor jazz, blues and world-music concerts at the National Sculpture Garden. Bring a blanket and picnic fare, and supplement with beverages from the Pavilion Cafe.

SCREEN ON THE GREEN CINEMA

Map p294 (www.friendsofscreenonthegreen.org; Mall btwn 7th & 12th Sts NW; ⏲8pm Mon mid-Jul–mid-Aug; Circulator, Smithsonian) FREE Classic movies such as *One Flew Over the Cuckoo's Nest* and *Willy Wonka and the Chocolate Factory* flicker on a large outdoor screen set up on the Mall. Bring a blanket, picnic fixin's and plenty of bug spray. Films start at sunset, usually around 8pm. Check the location before heading out, as it can vary due to construction on the Mall.

DISCOVERY THEATER THEATER

Map p294 (www.discoverytheater.org; 1100 Jefferson Dr SW; tickets $6-12; Circulator, Smithsonian) In the basement of the Ripley Center, Discovery stages delightful puppet shows and other productions for children.

SYLVAN THEATER THEATER

Map p294 (cnr 15th St & Independence Ave SW; Circulator, Smithsonian) This open-air theater, southeast of the Washington Monument, hosts a variety of performances. The summer-evening military band concerts (usually at 8pm) draw big crowds.

CYCLING THE MALL

Bicycles are welcome on the Mall, and two-wheeling is a great way to navigate the lengthy expanse. Capital Bikeshare (p270) has several stations around the area. Handy ones are by the Smithsonian Metro, Lincoln Memorial, Maryland and Independence Aves SW (near the National Air and Space Museum) and Jefferson and 14th Sts SW (near the Washington Monument). No companies rent bikes on the Mall proper, though Bike & Roll (p126) at L'Enfant Plaza isn't too far away.

SPORTS & ACTIVITIES

TIDAL BASIN BOATHOUSE BOATING

Map p294 (www.tidalbasinpaddleboats.com; 1501 Maine Ave SW; 2-/4-person boat rental $14/22; ⏲10am-6pm mid-Mar–Aug, Wed-Sun only Sep–mid-Oct, closed mid-Oct–mid-Mar; Circulator, Smithsonian) It rents paddleboats to take out on the Tidal Basin. Bring a camera. There are great views, of the Jefferson Memorial in particular, from the water.

CAROUSEL FUN RIDE

Map p294 (tickets $3.50; ⏲10am-6pm; Circulator, Smithsonian) A musical merry-go-round pleases kiddies on the Mall by the Smithsonian Castle.

The Smithsonian Institution

It's not a single place, as commonly thought. Rather, the Smithsonian Institution consists of 19 museums, the National Zoo and nine research facilities. Most are in DC, but others are further flung in the US and abroad. And to think it all started with a gift from an eccentric anti-monarchist Englishman...

Mr Smithson's Gift

The whole thing began with James Smithson, a British scientist who never set foot in the USA, let alone Washington, DC. He died in 1829 with a provision in his will to found 'at Washington, under the name of the Smithsonian Institution, an establishment for the increase and diffusion of knowledge.' Actually, that was the backup plan. The money first went to his nephew Henry, but Henry died a few years after Smithson, without heirs. So the 'institution' clause kicked in, and $508,318 arrived in Washington for the task.

The US government promptly ignored the amazing gift. 'Every whippersnapper vagabond...might think it proper to have his name distinguished in the same way,' grumbled Senator William Preston, while Senator John C Calhoun argued it was 'beneath American dignity to accept presents from anyone.' Anti-British sentiment informed some of this debate: the 1814 British torching of Washington remained fresh in many American minds. Finally, Congress accepted the money and began constructing the Smithsonian Institution in 1846.

Mysterious Motive

So who was Smithson? He was the illegitimate son of the Duke of Northumberland. A mineralogist by trade and shrewd investor by evidence (his donation was a fortune for its time), Smithson was well educated and wealthy by any measure. But his motivations for bequeathing so much money to the USA, as opposed to his native Britain, remain a mystery. Some say he was an anti-monarchist who took a particular shine to the American Republic. He may have just loved learning. To quote Smithson, 'Every man is a valuable member of society who by his observations, researches, and experiments procures knowledge for men.'

Smithson was 64 years old when he died in Genoa, Italy, and was buried

HIGHLIGHTS OF THE SMITHSONIAN

- ➡ Hope Diamond (National Museum of Natural History)
- ➡ Star-Spangled Banner flag (National Museum of American History)
- ➡ 1903 Wright brothers' flyer (National Air and Space Museum)
- ➡ Abraham Lincoln's top hat (National Museum of American History)
- ➡ Dorothy's ruby slippers (National Museum of American History)

1. Moon-landing display at the National Air and Space Museum (p62) **2.** Panda at the National Zoo (p188)

1

2

1

SMITHSONIAN'S DC ROSTER

- National Museum of Natural History (p67)
- National Air and Space Museum (p62)
- National Museum of American History (p68)
- National Zoo (p188)
- National Museum of the American Indian (p67)
- Steven F Udvar-Hazy Center (p200)
- Reynolds Center for American Art & Portraiture (two museums; p130)
- Smithsonian Castle (p66)
- Hirshhorn Museum and Sculpture Garden (p66)
- National Postal Museum (p111)
- Freer-Sackler Museums of Asian Art (two museums; p66)
- National Museum of African Art (p66)
- Anacostia Community Museum (p116)
- National Museum of African American History and Culture (opening 2016; p68)
- Renwick Gallery (reopening 2016; p82)
- Arts & Industries Building (closed)

there, until Alexander Graham Bell – in his role as Smithsonian regent – went to fetch the Englishman's remains and bring them to Washington in 1904. Today Smithson is entombed in the Smithsonian Castle on the Mall.

The Smithsonian Today

His gift morphed into a vast vault of treasures. The Smithsonian holds approximately 140 million artworks, scientific specimens, artifacts and other objects, of which only 1% are on display at any given time. The collection sprawls across 19 museums – 10 on the Mall, seven others around DC and two in New York City (the American Indian Museum Heye Center and Cooper Hewitt Design Museum). The Smithsonian also operates the National Zoo. There is no entry fee for any of the venues. They're all free, always.

The institution needs expensive upkeep, and it continues to expand. It has been suggested the museums start charging admission to help with costs, but the powers that be won't hear of it, arguing fees would hinder Smithson's original goal

MARK WILLIAMSON STOCK PHOTOGRAPHY / GETTY IMAGES ©

GREG DALE / GETTY IMAGES ©

1. The 1855 Smithsonian Castle (p66) now houses the Smithsonian Visitor Center
2. An interactive display at the National Museum of Natural History (p67)

to spread knowledge. So the quest for financing keeps on.

The Smithsonian is about 60% federally funded. In 2015 Congress appropriated $819.5 million to the institution. The rest comes from private sources such as corporations, foundations and individuals.

Research Centers

In addition to museums, the Smithsonian holds nine research centers under its umbrella, and they're scattered all over the place. They include the Archives of American Art (in DC and NYC), Astrophysical Observatory (Cambridge, MA), Conservation Biology Institute (Front Royal, VA), Environmental Research Center (Edgewater, MD), Marine Station (Fort Pierce, FL), Museum Conservation Institute (Suitland, MD), Smithsonian Archives (DC), Smithsonian Libraries (DC, NY, MA and Panama) and Tropical Research Institute (Panama). The Astrophysical Observatory, Environmental Research Center and Marine Station have public programs, and the Museum Conservation Institute offers artifact appraisals and instruction on antique restoration to the community. But for the most part the research centers are for scholarly endeavors.

Record Label

Yes, the institution even has its own record label. Smithsonian Folkways documents folk music, spoken word and sounds from around the world. It's an incredible enterprise that preserves everything from civil rights protesters' songs in Selma, AL, to 1940s Dixieland jazz, Comanche flute music and Norwegian lullabies. It also puts on the annual **Folklife Festival** (www.festival.si.edu), a 10-day music and cultural bash on the Mall in late June and early July.

Odds & Ends

Of the roughly 140 million specimens and artifacts, 127 million belong to the National Museum of Natural History. You can look up just about anything in the 9 million digital records available via the **Smithsonian Collections Search Center** (www.collections.si.edu/search).

White House Area & Foggy Bottom

Neighborhood Top Five

❶ It doesn't matter how many times you've seen it on TV: strolling through the **White House** (p78) thrills, from the ceremonial East Room to Thomas Jefferson's green dining room.

❷ Knock back a Scotch at the **Round Robin** (p89), reputed birthplace of the mint julep.

❸ Watch a free performance any night of the week at the **Kennedy Center** (p90).

❹ Browse exquisite rooms of fabrics and weavings at the new **Textile Museum** (p86).

❺ Play spot-the-politician while slurping oysters at the **Old Ebbitt Grill** (p87).

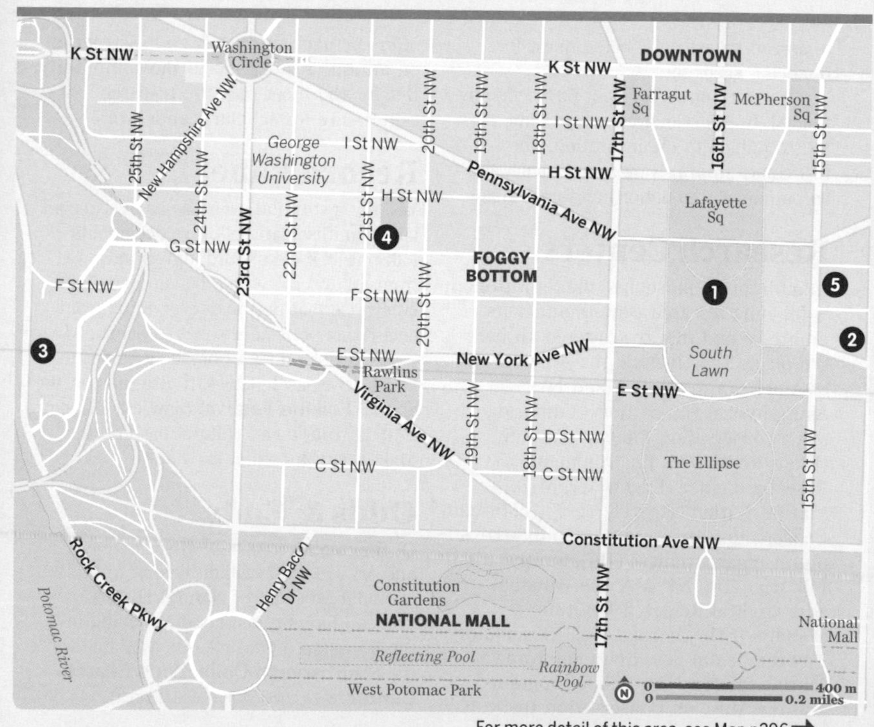

For more detail of this area, see Map p296

Explore White House Area & Foggy Bottom

When you play image association with the words 'Washington, DC,' the mental snapshot most people have of the city is the White House, a pale flame slipped into a grid of dark, manicured grounds. The president's pad does take your breath away the first time you see it, if only because you're standing in front of the *real thing*, the building you've seen a thousand times before in photos and on TV.

All in all, there's a sense of regal importance on these streets, blended with the bustle of a very alive nerve cluster of federal power. By day the area hums with the comings and goings of office workers, diplomats, lobbyists, tourists and bureaucrats. At night it dies a sudden death, like most urban business districts, aside from scattered fine dining restaurants and hotel bars mixing Manhattans.

West of the White House Area is Foggy Bottom, deriving its name from its low-lying geography, which serves as a catchment for Potomac mists. Foggy Bottom is synonymous with the State Department, World Bank, IMF and other hefty institutions. George Washington University infuses it with a bit of youthful energy.

With worthy art museums such as the Renwick Gallery, Textile Museum and Corcoran of Art (now part of the National Gallery), a slew of terrific architecture to browse – including that big white house – and the Kennedy Center for evening performances, plan on a full day here.

Local Life

➡**Cheap Eats** Follow local office workers to food trucks and lunch spots such as BreadLine for economical fare in this neighborhood of power-player dining.

➡**Romantic Drink** The terrace at the Kennedy Center unfurls fantastic views where sharp-dressed Washingtonians enjoy a romantic cocktail.

➡**Smell the Roses** Students and workers looking for a green respite grab a bench in rosebush-strewn University Yard.

Getting There & Away

➡**Metro** The Blue, Orange and Silver Lines run in tandem here. Get off at Federal Triangle or McPherson Sq for the White House; Farragut West for the Renwick and other museums; and Foggy Bottom-GWU for the university and Kennedy Center.

➡**Bus** A free shuttle runs every 15 minutes between the Foggy Bottom-GWU Metro station and the Kennedy Center.

Lonely Planet's Top Tip

Plan ahead! To visit the White House you need to make a tour request 21 days to six months in advance. For the best chance of success, do it three months beforehand. You also need to make advance arrangements to tour the Federal Reserve and the Department of the Interior – at least five days notice for the former, and two weeks for the latter.

Best Places to Eat

- Founding Farmers (p87)
- Old Ebbitt Grill (p87)
- Marcel's (p88)
- Bombay Club (p87)
- BreadLine (p87)

For reviews, see p87.➡

Best Places to Drink

- Round Robin (p89)
- Off the Record (p90)
- Le Bar (p90)
- Hamilton (p90)

For reviews, see p89.➡

Best Art Museums

- Renwick Gallery (p82)
- Textile Museum (p86)
- Corcoran Gallery of Art (p83)
- Art Museum of the Americas (p84)
- Daughters of the American Revolution (p84)

For reviews, see p82.➡

TOP SIGHT

WHITE HOUSE

The White House is a home as well as a symbol. It stuns visitors with its sense of pomp and circumstance, yet it also charms with little traces left behind by those who have lived here before, which includes every US president since John Adams. Icon of the American presidency? Yeah. But it's also someone's home.

The Building

George Washington picked the site for the White House in 1791. Pierre L'Enfant was the initial architect, but he was fired for insubordination. Washington held a national competition to find a new designer. Irish-born architect James Hoban won.

Hoban's idea was to make the building simple and conservative, so as not to seem royal, in keeping with the new country's principles. He modeled the neoclassical-style manor on Leinster House, a mid-18th-century duke's villa in Dublin that still stands and is now used by Ireland's Parliament.

The 'President's House' was built between 1792 and 1800. Legend has it that after the British burned the building in the War of 1812, the house was restored and painted white to cover the smoke marks, and people began to call it the White House. That's not true – it had been white almost from the get-go – but it makes a nice story. Hoban, incidentally, was hired to supervise the rebuilding. It was a big job, as all that remained were the exterior walls and interior brickwork.

DON'T MISS...

- View across South Lawn
- View across North Lawn
- FDR's fireside chat desk
- President Garfield's squirrel soup
- James Hoban's neoclassical design

PRACTICALITIES

- Map p296
- tours 202-456-7041
- www.whitehouse.gov
- tours 7:30-11:30am Tue-Thu, to 1:30pm Fri & Sat
- Federal Triangle, McPherson Sq, Metro Center

Presidential Rooms

The White House has 132 rooms and 35 bathrooms. This includes 412 doors, 147 windows, 28 fireplaces, eight staircases and three elevators (for those who are counting).

The Residence is in the middle, flanked by the East and West Wings. In general, the West Wing is the business side, and the East Wing is the social side. So the Situation Room – a 5000-sq-ft complex staffed 24/7 to monitor national and world intelligence information – is in the west. The Cabinet Room is there too, with its huge mahogany table around which the cabinet secretaries sit to discuss business with the president. The East Wing – where the public tours begin – holds the first lady's office, the social secretary's office, and the Graphics and Calligraphy Office (though you won't see any of these).

The Residence has three main levels: the Ground Floor, State Floor and Second Floor. The Ground and State floors have rooms used for official entertaining and ceremonial functions (many of which you see on the tour). The Second Floor holds the private living quarters of the president and family.

Tours

Tours are free, but they have to be arranged in advance. Americans must apply via one of their state's members of Congress, and non-Americans must apply through either the US consulate in their home country or their country's consulate in DC. Applications are taken from 21 days to six months in advance; three months ahead is the recommended sweet spot. Don't take it personally if you don't get accepted. Capacity is limited, and often official events take precedence over public tours. If you do get in, the self-guided walk-through takes about 30 minutes.

Visitor Center

The **visitor center** (www.nps.gov/whho; ⏰7:30am-4pm) FREE is your backup plan. It reopened in late 2014 after a $12.6 million renovation, and it's all spiffed up. Browse artifacts such as Roosevelt's desk for his fireside chats and Lincoln's cabinet chair. See the chocolate molds that White House pastry chefs use. Multimedia exhibits give a 360-degree view into the White House's rooms. It's obviously not the same as seeing the real deal first-hand, but the center does do its job very well, giving good history sprinkled with great anecdotes on presidential spouses, kids, pets and dinner preferences. Betcha didn't know President Garfield liked squirrel soup? The gift shop is excellent if you're looking for classy souvenirs.

PERSONAL TOUCHES

Presidents have customized the property over time. Franklin Roosevelt added a pool; Truman gutted the whole place (and simply discarded many of its historical features – today's rooms are replicas); Jacqueline Kennedy brought back antique furnishings and historic details; Nixon added a bowling alley; Carter installed solar roof panels, which Reagan then removed; Clinton added a jogging track; and George W Bush included a T-ball field.

Photography is forbidden inside the White House, so you'll have to snap pictures from outside. Cars aren't allowed to pass the building on Pennsylvania Ave, clearing the area for posing school groups and round-the-clock peace activists. You can get good photos across the North Lawn from here. Or move to E St NW and take pictures across the South Lawn. This is the view commonly used as the backdrop to TV news reports.

White House

The most striking thing about the White House is how much it feels like a house. A 55,000-sq-ft house, but still a real one where a family lives. If you're lucky enough to get inside on a public tour, you'll see several rooms in the main residence, each rich in presidential lore: this is where Thomas Jefferson ate; Abe Lincoln's coffin stood over there...

The walk-through is self-guided and starts at the visitor entrance by the White House's southeast gate. From there you pass by the **Library** ❶, Vermeil Room and China Room, all on the ground floor (they're roped off, so you don't actually go in). Next you go up a flight of stairs to the State Floor and continue on through the **East Room** ❷, Green Room, **Blue Room** ❸, Red Room and **State Dining Room** ❹. Unlike the floor below, you can enter these rooms. The Secret Service guys standing guard everywhere are ace at answering questions – really.

The White House's 2nd and 3rd floors, as well as the east and west wings, are off-limits. So you won't get to see two of the most famous rooms – the **Lincoln Bedroom** ❺ and the **Oval Office** ❻ – but you'll feel their aura.

You depart from the building's front (north) side. Before leaving the neighborhood, swing over to 15th St NW and stroll south to E St NW. Turn right and walk along the South Lawn, and you'll have a picture-perfect **view** ❼ of the house you just visited.

Oval Office
West Wing, Ground Floor
Suppose you were allowed into the west wing. You'd see the Oval Office, the president's official workspace. Each president has changed it to suit his taste, even designing his own carpet.

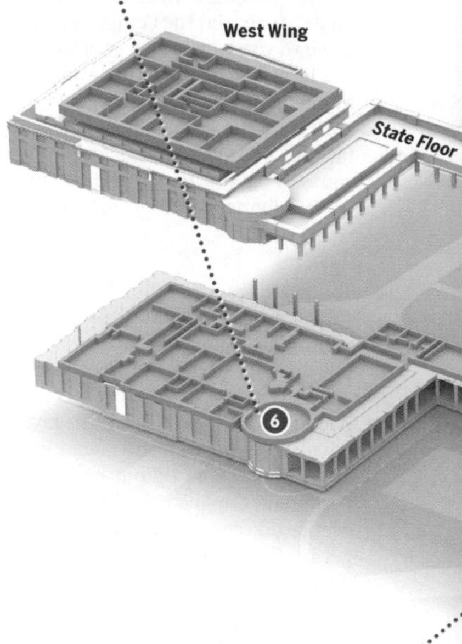

East Room
Residence, State Floor
Admire the White House's largest room, used for ceremonies and press conferences. Lincoln, Kennedy and five other presidents have lain in state here. Note how gilded eagles hold up the piano.

State Dining Room

Residence, State Floor

Imagine inviting over 130 of your closest kings, prime ministers and movie stars for a little poached lobster. The fireplace mantel's quote is from a letter John Adams wrote in 1800.

BARRY WINIKER / GETTY IMAGES ©

Blue Room

Residence, State Floor

Pretend the president is receiving you here, as he does other guests. Fifth prez James Monroe bought the gilded French Empire decor. Eighth prez Martin Van Buren painted the room blue.

Lincoln Bedroom

Residence, 2nd Floor

Keep watch for Lincoln's ghost, said to roam the White House from here. The room was formerly Abe's office, where he signed the Emancipation Proclamation. His Gettysburg Address draft sits on the desk.

5
4
Main Residence
3
2
Red Room
Green Room
East Wing
State Floor
Ground Floor
1
Diplomatic Reception Room
China Room
Vermeil Room
7

View from E St NW

Snap your keepsake pictures across the South Lawn (taking photographs inside the White House is forbidden). Recognize the view? It's commonly used as the backdrop to TV news reports.

STEPHEN BOITANO / GETTY IMAGES ©

Library

Residence, Ground Floor

Scan the shelves of history, fiction and biography, and check out that chandelier. It belonged to the family of James Fenimore Cooper (author of *Last of the Mohicans*, 1826).

SIGHTS

White House Area

WHITE HOUSE LANDMARK

See p78.

ELLIPSE PARK

Map p296 (Constitution Ave, btwn 15th & 17th Sts NW; Ⓜ Federal Triangle) The expansive, oval-shaped park on the White House's south side is known as the Ellipse. It's studded with a random collection of monuments, such as the **Zero Milestone** (the marker for highway distances all across the country) and the **Second Division Memorial**. It also hosts parades and public events such as the lighting of the national Christmas tree.

RENWICK GALLERY MUSEUM

Map p296 (www.americanart.si.edu/renwick; 1661 Pennsylvania Ave NW; 10am-5:30pm; ; Ⓜ Farragut West) FREE Part of the Smithsonian diaspora, the Renwick Gallery is set in a stately 1859 mansion and exhibits a superb collection of American crafts and decorative-art pieces. Alas, it's closed until early 2016 for infrastructure upgrades.

When it reopens, you'll see the 'crafts' here straddle a line between utilitarian and artistic expression, with a dash of whimsy thrown in. The playful pieces make it a wonderful place to introduce kids to art. Highlights include Larry Fuente's extravagantly kitsch *Game Fish* and Kim Schmahmann's *Bureau of Bureaucracy,* a hilariously accurate expression of the futility of dealing with official ineptitude realized in a cabinet plucked from MC Escher's nightmares.

BLAIR HOUSE HISTORIC BUILDING

Map p296 (1651 Pennsylvania Ave NW; closed to public; Ⓜ Farragut West) The 1824 Blair House has been the official presidential guesthouse since 1942, when Eleanor Roosevelt got sick of tripping over dignitaries in the White House. A plaque on the front fence commemorates the bodyguard killed here while protecting President Truman from a 1950 assassination attempt by pro-independence militants from Puerto Rico (Truman was living here while the White House was undergoing renovations).

The red-brick **building** (Map p296; 1653 Pennsylvania Ave NW; Ⓜ Farragut West) next door (now combined with Blair House) was built by Robert E Lee's cousin in 1859. This is where Lee declined command of the Union Army when the Civil War erupted.

LAFAYETTE SQUARE SQUARE

Map p296 (Pennsylvania Ave, btwn 15th & 17th Sts NW; Ⓜ Farragut West, McPherson Sq) The land north of 1600 Pennsylvania Ave was originally deeded as part of the White House grounds. However, in 1804 President Thomas Jefferson decided to divide the plot and give half back to the public in the form of a park, now known as Lafayette Sq. A statue of Andrew Jackson astride a horse holds court in the center, while the statues anchoring the four corners are all of foreign-born revolutionary leaders, a nice reminder that non-American freedom fighters helped ensure American independence.

In the southeast corner check out the likeness of the Marquis de Lafayette, a revolutionary war general by the age of 19. Although Lafayette was branded a traitor in his native France following the war, he was consistently lauded in the young America. In the northeast corner is a memorial to Tadeusz Kościusko, a Polish soldier and prominent engineer in Washington's army. The sculpture is one of the more in-your-face ones in town: Kosciusko towers over an angry imperial eagle killing a snake atop a globe, and an inscription at the base, taken from Scottish poet Thomas Campbell, reads: 'And Freedom shrieked as Kosciusko fell!'

ST JOHN'S CHURCH CHURCH

Map p296 (www.stjohns-dc.org; 1525 H St NW; 9am-3pm Mon-Sat, from 11am Tue; Ⓜ McPherson Sq) A small building, St John's isn't DC's most imposing church, but it is arguably its most important. That's because it's the 'Church of the Presidents' – every president since Madison has attended services here at least once, and pew 54 is reserved for the Big Guy (er, the president; not God). Abraham Lincoln's favorite pew is designated in the back. Services take place at 7:45am, 9am and 11am on Sunday, as well as weekdays at 12:10pm.

DECATUR HOUSE HISTORIC BUILDING

Map p296 (www.whha.org; 1610 H St NW; Ⓜ Farragut West) FREE Designed in 1818 by Benjamin Latrobe for the War of 1812 naval hero Stephen Decatur, the building holds the honor of being the first and last house on Lafayette Sq to be occupied as a private res-

PECULIAR PRESIDENTIAL PETS

Most people have probably heard of Bo and Sunny Obama, the Portuguese water dogs that are America's current first pets. Before them was Barney the terrier, preceded by Socks the cat, Buddy the Labrador and then...well, here are some suitably awesome pets you may never have known graced the presidential digs.

Billy the pygmy hippo Rubber-maker Harvey Firestone brought Billy all the way from Liberia for Calvin Coolidge in 1927, who, for the record, already owned a wallaby, a duiker (a kind of African antelope) and a raccoon. Billy ended up in the National Zoo when (contrary to his species name) he got too big for the White House.

The Adams alligators Let's say you're the Marquis de Lafayette and you want to get a present for John Quincy Adams, the kind of guy who likes to go swimming, naked, in the Potomac every morning. How about: two alligators! In the 1820s, Adams, skinny-dipping badass that he was, happily housed the two reptiles in the White House bathtub.

Pauline Wayne the cow William Taft let Pauline, a Holstein gift from a Wisconsin Senator, graze the front lawn of the White House from 1909 to 1913, during his term. The trade-off? Pauline provided milk for the first family during Taft's last three years in office.

Josiah the badger All of the above animals were thoughtful presents to sitting presidents. Josiah, on the other hand, was apparently a furry assassination attempt. In 1903, a girl in Kansas threw ornery Josiah directly at Theodore Roosevelt. Roosevelt, the kind of guy who hunted lions and charged fortified positions like San Juan hill on foot, ended up taking the little guy back to Washington.

idence. Architecturally, it's an interesting mash-up of austere Federal and wedding cake Victorian influences. Famous tenants include Martin Van Buren and Henry Clay. The White House Historical Association owns the site and offers occasional free tours. Check the website's 'public programs' link to see when.

K STREET — STREET

Map p296 (M Farragut North, McPherson Sq) K St is the center of the Washington lobbying industry. This is where high-powered lawyers, consultants and, of course, lobbyists ('K St' and 'lobbyist' have practically become synonymous since the 1990s) bark into their smartphones and enjoy expensive lunches. Come nightfall, the same power set comes back with hair considerably slicked and/or flattened to drink expensive cocktails while surrounded by the sort of people who swoon over everything we've just described.

MCPHERSON SQUARE — SQUARE

Map p296 (M McPherson Sq) The square is named for Civil War general James B McPherson who once commanded the Army of Tennessee, and a statue of him on his horse has dotted the center since 1876. Given its location near the White House, the square often hosts political protesters. Homeless people also cluster here.

CORCORAN GALLERY OF ART — MUSEUM

Map p296 (202-639-1704; www.corcoran.org; 500 17th St NW; M Farragut West) FREE DC's oldest art museum has always been terrific, but it had a tough time standing up to the free, federal competition around the block. In mid-2014 it gave up and let the National Gallery of Art take possession. The Corcoran's historic beaux-arts building will close for renovations into 2016 (at least). It will then reopen as a National Gallery annex showcasing modern and contemporary works from the merged collection.

The building will also have a 'legacy gallery' where old Corcoran favorites such as the gilded Salon Doré (part of an 18th-century Parisian mansion the Count d'Orsay had built for his princess bride) will be on view.

OCTAGON MUSEUM — MUSEUM

Map p296 (202-638-3221; www.theoctagon.org; 1799 New York Ave NW; 1-4pm Thu-Sat; M Farragut West) FREE The apex of the Federal style of architecture pioneered in the USA also happens to be the oldest museum in America dedicated to architecture and design. Designed by William Thornton (the Capitol's first architect) in 1800, the building is a symmetrically winged structure designed to fit an odd triangular lot. The inside is open for self-guided tours over creaky floors and into rooms with period furnishings.

President James Madison lived here after the British burned the White House during the War of 1812. The box that held the Treaty of Ghent (that ended the war) is on the 2nd floor. The American Institute of Architects operates the museum.

DAUGHTERS OF THE AMERICAN REVOLUTION MUSEUM

Map p296 (DAR; www.dar.org/museum; 1776 D St NW; ⌚8:30am-4pm Mon-Fri, 9am-5pm Sat; Ⓜ Farragut West) FREE The DAR's neoclassical behemoth, also known as Constitution Hall, is supposedly the largest complex of buildings in the world owned exclusively by women. They own the entire city block! Enter from D St to reach the museum, where you'll find a sweet spread of silver teapots, quilts, portrait paintings, crystal decanters and folk art.

Ask for the self-guided tour information to see more antiques in the 31 colonial revival 'Period Rooms' spread throughout the building. And FYI, if the group's name sounds familiar, it's because in 1939 the DAR barred African American contralto Marian Anderson from singing at its hall. Anderson then performed her famous civil rights concert on the Lincoln Memorial's steps. The DAR eventually changed its policies and mended fences with Anderson.

ORGANIZATION OF AMERICAN STATES GARDENS

Map p296 (OAS; www.oas.org; 201 18th St NW; ⌚10am-5pm Tue-Sun; Ⓜ Farragut West) FREE A forerunner to the UN, the OAS was founded in 1890 to promote cooperation among North and South American nations. Its main building at 17th St and Constitution Ave NW is a marble palazzo surrounded by the sculpture-studded **Aztec Gardens** (Map p296; Ⓜ Farragut West). In the small building behind it, the OAS operates the Art Museum of the Americas, which has a provocative collection.

ART MUSEUM OF THE AMERICAS MUSEUM

Map p296 (www.museum.oas.org; 201 18th St NW; ⌚10am-5pm Tue-Sun; Ⓜ Farragut West) The Organization of American States operates this mini art museum in a separate building on its property. It features changing exhibits of paintings and photography that span the 20th century and the western hemisphere. It's well worth popping in, though you'll likely be the only one there walking across the creaky floors to examine the surprisingly political works.

DEPARTMENT OF THE INTERIOR MUSEUM MUSEUM

Map p296 (☎202-208-4743; www.doi.gov/interiormuseum; 1849 C St NW; ⌚8:30am-4:30pm Mon-Fri; Ⓜ Farragut West) FREE Responsible for managing the nation's natural resources, the Department of the Interior operates this small, but excellent, museum to educate the public about its current goals and programs. It includes landscape art, Native American artifacts and some great historical photos of Native American life, as well as exhibits on wildlife and resource management. Bring photo ID to enter.

The building itself is striking and contains tremendous New Deal murals from the 1930s and 1940s, as well as 26 photographic murals by Ansel Adams, plus panels by Maynard Dixon and Allan Houser. You can see some of them on your own as you walk through the structure, but guided tours cover it all. The hour-long jaunts are at 2pm Tuesday and Thursday; call to make a reservation two weeks in advance (though staff can sometimes do it with less notice).

⊙ Foggy Bottom

GEORGE WASHINGTON UNIVERSITY UNIVERSITY

Map p296 (www.gwu.edu; 801 22nd St NW; Ⓜ Foggy Bottom-GWU) Known as 'G-dub' or 'GW,' the university has been a bedrock of Washington identity since its founding in 1821. Besides shaping much of the American political landscape, GW has shaped the capital itself, buying up townhouses on such a scale that it is now the city's second-biggest landowner after the federal government. Plenty of famous alumni have studied here: Edgar Hoover, Jacqueline Kennedy Onassis, Colin Powell, Brian Williams and Haddaway (you know, the guy who sang 'What Is Love?').

The school is spread over several blocks between F, 20th and 24th Sts and Pennsylvania Ave in Foggy Bottom. The best bit of the campus is **University Yard** (Map p296; Ⓜ Foggy Bottom-GWU), between G, H, 20th and 21st Sts, where Colonial-revival

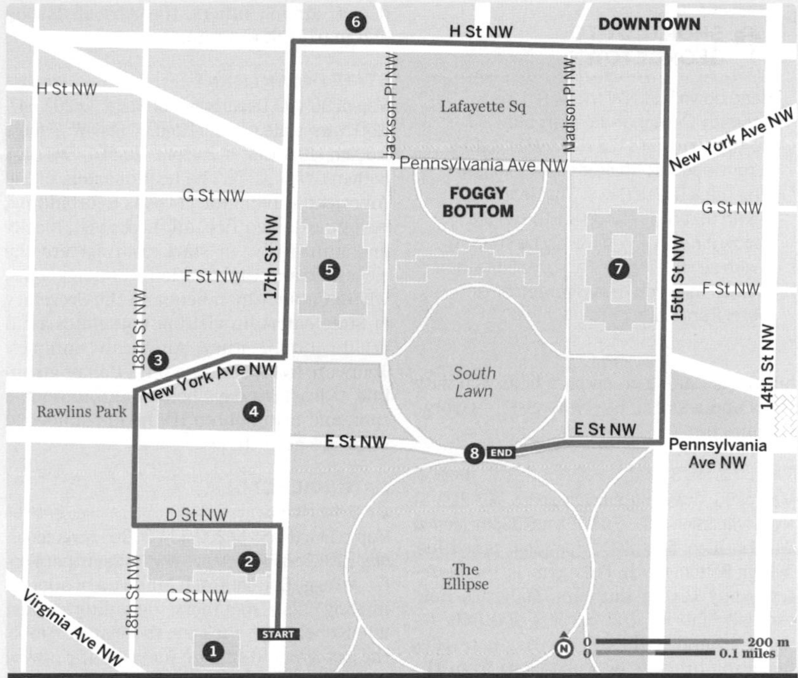

Neighborhood Walk
Architectural Accents

START ORGANIZATION OF AMERICAN STATES
END WHITE HOUSE SOUTH LAWN
LENGTH 2.25 MILES; 1½ HOURS

Powerful architecture rises throughout the neighborhood that is USA's seat of, well, power. Start at the 1 **Organization of American States** (p84), a marble palazzo offering pretty gardens and an impressive art museum. Stroll up to D St NW and check out the headquarters of the 2 **Daughters of the American Revolution** (p84). Also known as Constitution Hall, it's a great example of neoclassical architecture; go inside for a peek.

Onward to the 3 **Octagon Museum** (p83). The American Institute of Architects owns the 1801 Federal-style beauty, where President James Madison lived after the British burned Washington. The beaux-arts 4 **Corcoran Gallery of Art** (p83), now a branch of the National Gallery of Art, stands across the street.

At the corner of 17th St & Pennsylvania Ave, the 5 **Eisenhower Building** is done up with all the baroque flair of the late 19th-century, also known as the Gilded Age. The sloped mansard roof is European in origin, while its 900 columns are wonderfully ostentatious. Currently the building is used as an office wing of the executive branch.

Walk north on 17th St NW to H St NW and turn right. An office building by any other name, the designers of 6 **800 Connecticut Ave** knew lobbyists and politicos would be using it. As a result it prickles with terraces and corner offices that provide excellent lines of sight to the White House.

Head past Lafayette Sq to 15th St NW and turn south toward the 7 **Treasury Building**. It took a while to find a place to plop the building, and legend has it President Andrew Jackson, ticked off by foot-dragging, stood on the current spot and yelled, 'Build it here!' As a result, Pierre L'Enfant's planned clear line of sight between the White House and the Capitol was ruined.

Last stop: E St NW, for the quintessential view of the 8 **White House** (p78), strutting its stuff across the South Lawn.

SHORTCUT TO GEORGETOWN

Head down F St NW (between the Kennedy Center and Watergate Complex) toward the river. Veer right a bit and you'll see a crosswalk that goes over Rock Creek Pkwy. That leads to a path that runs alongside the water. Follow it north – you'll likely be sharing it with several joggers and cyclists – and in a half mile you're in Georgetown's Waterfront Park.

buildings flank a green park bedecked with roses and a statue of – who else? – George Washington.

TEXTILE MUSEUM MUSEUM

Map p296 (www.museum.gwu.edu; 701 21st St NW; admission $8; 11:30am-6:30pm Mon & Wed-Fri, 10am-5pm Sat, 1-5pm Sun, closed Tue; MFogg Bottom-GWU) This gem is the country's only textile museum. Galleries hold exquisite fabrics and carpets. Exhibits revolve around a theme, say Asian textiles depicting dragons or Kuba cloth from the Democratic Republic of Congo, and rotate a few times a year. Bonus: the museum shares space with George Washington University's Washingtonia trove of historic maps, drawings and ephemera.

The museum is old (founded in 1925) but the building is brand spankin' new (opened in early 2015). The collection also includes rare kimonos, pre-Columbian weaving, American quilts and Ottoman embroidery. (Find the flaw: traditional textile artists, from Islamic carpet makers to Appalachian quilters, weave intentional flaws into their work to avoid mimicking God's perfection.) Accompanying wall commentary explains how the textiles mirror the social, spiritual, economic and aesthetic values of the societies that made them.

ST MARY'S EPISCOPAL CHURCH CHURCH

Map p296 (728 23rd St NW; 9:30am-3pm Mon-Thu; MFoggy Bottom-GWU) Built in 1887, St Mary's was home to the first black Episcopal congregation in DC. James Renwick, designer of the Smithsonian Castle, created the beautiful red-brick building especially for the congregation. Above the altar are French-made painted-glass windows that depict, among others, the African bishop and martyr St Cyprian.

STATE DEPARTMENT BUILDING

Map p296 (US Department of State; 202-647-3241; www.state.gov; cnr 22nd & C Sts NW; tours 9:30am, 10:30am & 2:45pm Mon-Fri; MFoggy Bottom-GWU) FREE The headquarters of the American diplomatic corps is a forbidding, well-guarded edifice, all modernist, blocky and unfriendly. In stark contrast are the elegant grand diplomatic reception rooms, where Cabinet members and the Secretary of State entertain visiting potentates amid ornate 18th-century American antiques. Tours are by reservation only. Call or go online at least 90 days beforehand to book a spot, and bring photo ID; no kids under 12 years are admitted.

NATIONAL ACADEMY OF SCIENCES BUILDING

Map p296 (NAS; 202-334-2000; www.cpnas.org; 2101 Constitution Ave NW; 9am-5pm Mon-Fri; MFoggy Bottom-GWU) Made up of approximately 2250 members, including almost 200 Nobel Prize winners, these are the folks the government hits up for scientific advice (whether the government listens to them or not is, as you may have guessed, entirely up to the government). Inside the NAS hosts intriguing scientific and art exhibitions and symposiums. Bring photo ID to enter.

ALBERT EINSTEIN MEMORIAL SCULPTURE

Map p296 (Constitution Ave NW; MFoggy Bottom-GWU) The nicely landscaped grounds in front of the National Academy of Sciences feature DC's most huggable monument: the Albert Einstein statue. The larger-than-life, sandal-shod, chubby bronze reclines on a bench, while little kids crawl all over him and frolic on a 'star map,' which depicts the heavens that his theories reshaped for humanity.

FEDERAL RESERVE BUILDING

Map p296 (202-452-3778; www.federalreserve.gov; 20th St NW, btwn C St & Constitution Ave; tours by reservation Mon-Fri; MFarragut West) FREE 'The Fed,' which resembles a cross between a Greek temple and a Soviet-era bunker, is the Olympus of the Gods of the American Economy. Unfortunately, you won't see too much fiscal action on tours; these focus on the Fed's art collection, part of which is displayed in the atrium of the Eccles Building. The permanent collection is a survey of American art from the 1830s to the present. The group also presents rotating exhibitions of borrowed art on varied themes like currency design. Call to reserve at least five days in advance.

WATERGATE COMPLEX BUILDING

Map p296 (2650 Virginia Ave NW; MFoggy Bottom-GWU) The riverfront Watergate complex encompasses apartments, boutiques and the office towers that made 'Watergate' a byword for political scandal after it broke that President Nixon's 'plumbers' had bugged the headquarters of the 1972 Democratic National Committee here.

Monica Lewinsky, Ruth Bader Ginsburg and Condoleezza Rice are among the Washingtonians who have lived at Watergate. The interior of the complex is set to reopen as a top-end hotel by 2016.

EATING

As you might guess, this is high-end eating territory, the pinnacle of the power lunch and show-off dinner school of sartorial activity. With all that said, you usually get what you pay for – there's too much competition around for local chefs to rest lazily on their laurels.

BREADLINE SANDWICHES $

Map p296 (202-822-8900; www.breadline.com; 1751 Pennsylvania Ave NW; sandwiches $8-12; 7am-5:30pm Mon-Fri; MFarragut West) 'Food is ammunition – don't waste it!' commands a WWII-era poster on the wall of BreadLine, a polished bakery and sandwich shop. Come here for a good, cheap lunch alongside local office workers. It'll probably be crowded, and with reason. The fresh sandwiches – stacked with, say, Italian sausage or barbecue on ciabatta bread – are gorgeous, as are the sweet treats.

G STREET FOOD INTERNATIONAL $

Map p296 (202-842-8484; www.gstreetfood.com; 1030 15th St NW; mains $8-12; 7am-6pm Mon-Fri; ; MMcPherson Sq) G Street lives up to its tagline of 'globally inspired street food.' Breakfast might be a Hungarian omelet (with onion, red pepper and chives), lunch a Thai-spiced tuna salad sandwich. Plates of Turkish lamb kebabs and bowls of Japanese curry rice also hit the tables. The menu sprawls; gluten-free and vegetarian options abound.

★FOUNDING FARMERS MODERN AMERICAN $$

Map p296 (202-822-8783; www.wearefoundingfarmers.com; 1924 Pennsylvania Ave NW; mains $14-26; 11am-10pm Mon, to 11pm Tue-Thu, to midnight Fri, 9am-midnight Sat, 9am-10pm Sun; ; MFoggy Bottom-GWU, Farragut West) A frosty decor of pickled goods in jars adorns this buzzy dining space. The look is a combination of rustic-cool and modern art that reflects the nature of the food: locally sourced, New American fare. Buttermilk fried chicken and waffles and zesty pork and lentil stew are a few of the favorites that hit the wood tables. The restaurant is located in the IMF building.

OLD EBBITT GRILL AMERICAN $$

Map p296 (202-347-4800; www.ebbitt.com; 675 15th St NW; mains $12-22; 7:30am-1am Mon-Fri, from 8:30am Sat & Sun; MMetro Center) The Grill has occupied its prime, by the White House real estate since 1846. Political players (and lots of tourists) pack into the brass and wood interior, the sound of their conversation rumbling across a dining room where thick burgers, crab cakes and fish-and-chip type fare are rotated out almost as quickly as the clientele. Pop in for a drink and oysters during happy hour.

BOMBAY CLUB INDIAN $$

Map p296 (202-659-3727; www.bombayclubdc.com; 815 Connecticut Ave NW; mains $14-24; 11:30am-2:30pm & 5:30-10:30pm Mon-Fri, 5:30-11pm Sat, 11:30am-2:30pm & 5:30-9:30pm Sun; ; MFarragut West) No bad sitar music or heat-lamp-warmed buffets here; Bombay Club cooks eclectic, modern Indian fare. The duck kebab fires up the ginger-chili heat, while the fenugreek-laced lobster curry explodes with wild flavor. Sit inside where ceiling fans swirl lazily and piano tinklings fill the air, or outside on the breezy patio. Vegetarians have several options.

SICHUAN PAVILION CHINESE $$

Map p296 (202-466-7790; www.sichuan-pavilion.com; 1814 K St NW; mains $11-18; noon-10pm Mon-Fri, 11:30am-9:30pm Sat & Sun; MFarragut North, Farragut West) Many Chinese come to this unassuming restaurant to dine on fiery, oily classics of the old school. Piquant Sichuan (or Szechuan) cuisine is often blanded-up for Western customers around the world, but these guys keep it real for all their clientele, Asian or otherwise. The *ma-po tofu* (includes pork, fermented black beans and fiery peppercorns) is particularly stinky and sublime.

MARCEL'S FRENCH $$$

Map p296 (☎202-296-1166; www.marcelsdc.com; 2401 Pennsylvania Ave NW; 4-/5-/7-course menus $90/110/150; ⏰5-10pm Mon-Thu, to 11pm Fri & Sat, to 9:30pm Sun; Ⓜ Foggy Bottom-GWU) Marcel's keeps true to classic French cuisine while adding modern embellishments. Old school, fill-you-up-by-a-fire fare such as pork belly and turbot with peas is hearty and thick. But the sprucing on the side – quail egg and cornichons, or the miso that accompanies the Alaskan cod – is just understated enough to ratchet the experience to greatness.

A classy touch: Marcel's offers a complimentary limousine service to the Kennedy Center, so it's ideal for pre-theater dining.

BAYOU CAJUN $$$

Map p296 (☎202-223-6941; www.bayouonpenn.com; 2519 Pennsylvania Ave NW; mains $19-24; ⏰11am-10pm Sun & Tue-Thu, to 11pm Fri & Sat; Ⓜ Foggy Bottom-GWU) Here's your slice of New Orleans in DC. Is it the most phenomenal Cajun/Creole you'll ever have? No, but it's mighty fine. All the classics arrive at the jazzy red booths with heat and spice. Bite into oyster po'boy sandwiches, crawfish cheesecake (not a dessert!), seafood gumbo and sides of jalapeno grits. There's even a fried green tomato po'boy for vegetarians.

Wash it down with a mason jar of Hurricane. Then get your dance on at the live blues, jazz and R & B shows weekend nights at 10pm.

EQUINOX MODERN AMERICAN $$$

Map p296 (☎202-331-8118; www.equinoxrestaurant.com; 818 Connecticut Ave NW; mains $27-36; ⏰11:30am-2pm & 5:30-10pm Mon-Fri, 5:30-10:30pm Sat, to 9pm Sun; Ⓜ Farragut West) Equinox is as mom-and-pop as high-end White House–adjacent dining gets – Todd Gray and wife Ellen Kassoff are the respective chef and manager. The intimacy of the restaurant's executive staff extends to the menu, which has long eschewed pricey export ingredients in favor of meat, fish, fowl and fruit sourced from the Shenandoah Valley and Chesapeake Bay.

PRIME RIB STEAK $$$

Map p296 (☎202-466-8811; www.theprimerib.com; 2020 K St NW; mains $26-48; ⏰11:30am-3pm Mon-Fri, 5-10:30pm Mon-Sat; Ⓜ Foggy Bottom-GWU) There are lots of K St restaurants that serve up fusiony, modernist, wasabi-crusted-panko-seaweed-octopus-brioche kinda fare. Not the Prime Rib. Excuse a bit of stereotyping, but power, friends, is still best exemplified by sitting in a dark-wood dining room cutting deals over huge hunks of seared cow, then stepping outside for a cigar (damned smoking ban) and coming back in for a cognac.

The wait staff, clad in tuxedos, dress the part, and you'd better too – that means ties and jackets, men. Actually, you don't need the jacket at lunch, at which time the Rib delivers a $30 three-course set menu that is quite a good deal. The food lives up to the atmosphere; while this place may not be cutting edge, that doesn't mean it isn't good at what it does.

GEORGIA BROWN'S SOUTHERN $$$

Map p296 (☎202-393-4499; www.gbrowns.com; 950 15th St NW; mains $20-30; ⏰11:30am-10pm Mon-Thu, to 11pm Fri & Sat, 10am-10pm Sun; Ⓜ McPherson Sq) Georgia Brown's treats the humble ingredients of the American South (shrimp, okra, red rice, grits and sausage) with the respect great French chefs give their provincial dishes. The result is high-class cuisine from the Carolina Low country served in a warm, autumnal interior. The stalwart eatery was a favorite spot for the Clintons during Bill's presidency.

CAFE DU PARC FRENCH $$$

Map p296 (☎202-942-7000; www.cafeduparc.com; 1401 Pennsylvania Ave NW, Willard Intercontinental Hotel; mains $26-38; ⏰7am-10pm; Ⓜ Metro Center) Du Parc has been cooking traditional French fare in the swanky Willard Hotel for quite a while. So it knows how to bring out honest, strong flavors in its duck confit and red snapper-flecked bouillabaisse. Breakfast here is lovely – a nice blend of American and Continental dishes – and presents a good opportunity for politico spotting.

OVAL ROOM AMERICAN $$$

Map p296 (☎202-463-8700; www.ovalroom.com; 800 Connecticut Ave NW; mains $28-34; ⏰11:30am-2:30pm & 5:30-10pm Mon-Fri, 5:30-10:30pm Sat; Ⓜ Farragut West) The Oval serves standout food, generally of the American-hint-of-Mediterranean genre. The chef eschews heavy sauces in favor of allowing ingredients to hold their own intensity, such as foie gras with fig and vanilla, or

LOCAL KNOWLEDGE

FOOD TRUCKIN'

More than 150 food trucks roll in DC, and the White House neighborhood welcomes the mother lode. They congregate at Farragut Sq, Franklin Sq, the State Department and George Washington University on weekdays between 11:30am and 1:30pm. Follow the locals' lead, and stuff your face with a delicious meal for under $15 – maybe a lobster roll poached in butter or a bowl of Lao drunken noodles. **Food Truck Fiesta** (www.foodtruckfiesta.com) tracks the ever-evolving fleet via Twitter. Here are some favorites:

Lilypad on the Run (twitter.com/LilypadontheRun) Ethiopian meat and veggie combos that make you want to lick the styrofoam container.

Far East Taco Grille (twitter.com/fareasttg) Asian-flavored tacos using meats or tofu, corn or flour tortillas.

DC Pie Truck (twitter.com/ThePieTruckDC) The Dangerously Delicious piemakers swing out in a big red truck. Sweet and savory slices emerge from the window. Pies range from spinach with goat cheese to chocolate cream to coconut chess.

Red Hook Lobster Truck (twitter.com/LobsterTruckDC) Take your pick: mayo-based, Maine-style lobster rolls or butter-slathered Connecticut-style rolls.

bass laced with a delicate mix of fennel and toasted almonds. Condoleezza Rice agrees – this was her favorite restaurant in town when she was a Washingtonian.

CIRCLE BISTRO — MODERN AMERICAN $$$

Map p296 (☎202-293-5390; www.circlebistro.com; 1 Washington Circle NW; mains $19-27; ⊙7am-2:30pm & 5-10pm Mon-Sat, to 8pm Sun; ⓂFoggy Bottom-GWU) The Circle is an intimate neighborhood spot where locals often dine before seeing a show at the Kennedy Center. The changing menu uses hearty American ingredients, and while you may not be surprised by dishes such as scallops with wild mushrooms or braised lamb shanks, that doesn't mean you won't be delighted by them – the food is, simply, quite good.

KAZ SUSHI BISTRO — JAPANESE $$$

Map p296 (☎202-530-5500; www.kazsushibistro.com; 1915 I St NW; lunch specials $16, mains $22-36; ⊙11:30am-2pm Mon-Fri, 5:30-10pm Mon-Sat; ⓂFarragut West) Fusing East and West, chef Kaz Okochi presents his own invention, 'free-style Japanese cuisine.' The sushi on its own is fresh and flavorful and good enough. Many clever combinations, however, add a certain *je ne sais quoi* to the traditional tastes.

DC COAST — SEAFOOD $$$

Map p296 (☎202-216-5988; www.dccoast.com; 1401 K St NW; mains $22-32; ⊙11:30am-2:30pm Mon-Fri, 5:30-10:30pm Mon-Sat, to 9:30 Sun; ⓂMcPherson Sq) If Poseidon hired an art deco revivalist to redo his temple, the final result would probably end up looking something like DC Coast's interior. It's a beautiful space, more chaotic for the constant hum of lobbyist lunchers. Join the crowd indulging in pan-roasted trout and smoked lobster.

OCCIDENTAL GRILL — STEAK $$$

Map p296 (☎202-783-1475; www.occidentaldc.com; 1475 Pennsylvania Ave NW; mains $30-38; ⊙10am-11pm Mon-Sat, 11am-9pm Sun; ⓂMetro Center) This DC institution is practically wallpapered with mug shots of congressmen and other political celebs who have dined here throughout the years. Although the Occidental isn't the nerve center it once was, plenty of bigwigs still roll up their pinstripes to dive into hamburgers, chops, steaks and seafood.

DRINKING & NIGHTLIFE

College kids, doctors and journalists coexist in this neighborhood. For the most part the vibe is sort of white-yuppie-meets-college-scruffy at the local pub, although there are some genuine wheeler-dealer bars in the bigger hotels.

ROUND ROBIN — BAR

Map p296 (1401 Pennsylvania Ave NW, Willard InterContinental Hotel; ⊙noon-1am Mon-Sat,

KENNEDY CENTER FREEBIES

Don't have the dough for a big-ticket show? No worries. Each evening the Kennedy Center's **Millennium Stage** (www.kennedy-center.org/millennium; Kennedy Center; MFoggy Bottom-GWU) puts on a first-rate music or dance performance at 6pm in the Grand Foyer. The cost is absolutely nada. Check the website to see who's playing.

Guides also offer free, 45-minute **tours** (10am-5pm Mon-Fri, to 1pm Sat & Sun) of the Kennedy's chandelier- and art-filled complex. They depart every 10 minutes from the tour desk on Level A and take you into all the theaters and private lounges, as well as onto the viewtastic rooftop terrace.

to midnight Sun; MMetro Center) Dispensing drinks since 1850, the bar at the Willard hotel is one of DC's most storied watering holes. The small, circular space is done up in Gilded Age accents, all dark wood and velvet green walls, and while it's touristy, you'll still see officials here likely determining your latest tax hike over a mint julep or single-malt Scotch.

OFF THE RECORD BAR

Map p296 (800 16th St NW, Hay-Adams Hotel; 11:30am-midnight Sun-Thu, to 12:30am Fri & Sat; MMcPherson Sq) Intimate red booths, a hidden basement location in one of the city's most prestigious hotels, right across from the White House – no wonder DC's important people submerge to be seen and not heard (as the tagline goes) at Off the Record. Experienced bartenders swirl martinis and Manhattans for the suit-wearing crowd. Groovy framed political caricatures hang on the walls.

LE BAR BAR

Map p296 (806 15th St NW, Sofitel Lafayette Square; 11am-midnight; MMcPherson Sq) This is the kind of spot you should rightly enter in a trench coat in the midst of occupied Paris whilst delivering secret documents to a very attractive member of the Resistance. Seriously, that's the vibe: chandelier-like European glitz mixed with a bit of Washington power-player muscle. The outdoor patio is wonderful on spring and humid summer nights.

FROGGY BOTTOM PUB BAR

Map p296 (www.froggybottompub.com; 2021 K St NW; 11am-1am Mon-Thu, to 2am Fri & Sat; MFoggy Bottom-GWU) This popular GWU hangout attracts students with grub-and-pub deals, a frat-boy-esque atmosphere and the sort of shot specials that make you want to down a lot of hard alcohol very quickly. As you might have guessed, things can get messy in here, but in a good, all-American college kinda way.

POV LOUNGE

Map p296 (515 15th St NW, W Hotel Washington; 3pm-midnight Mon-Thu, to 2am Fri, to 2am Sat, 11am-midnight Sun; MMetro Center) It's all about the view at POV, which sits atop the W Hotel Washington. The sky terrace imparts terrific vistas, prime for sunset gazing. A chi-chi crowd congregates for the cocktails, which are fine but you do certainly do pay for them.

☆ ENTERTAINMENT

★KENNEDY CENTER PERFORMING ARTS

Map p296 (202-467-4600; www.kennedy-center.org; 2700 F St NW; MFoggy Bottom-GWU) Sprawled on 17 acres along the Potomac River, the magnificent Kennedy Center hosts a staggering array of performances – more than 2000 each year among its multiple venues including the Concert Hall (home to the National Symphony) and Opera House (home to the National Opera). A free shuttle bus runs to and from the Metro station every 15 minutes from 9:45am (noon on Sunday) to midnight.

Reduced-rate tickets are available for people aged 18 to 30 via the MyTix program; details are on the Kennedy website. Students can sometimes get half-price tickets for certain performances. Call or visit the box office. The center is undergoing an expansion into 2017, mostly adding rehearsal space and classrooms, but the public will benefit from the new gardens and outdoor video wall.

HAMILTON LIVE MUSIC

Map p296 (www.thehamiltondc.com; 600 14th St NW; MMetro Center) Upstairs it's a power-player restaurant, all mahogany paneling and pork chops and silver pots of coffee. There's also a long, convivial bar with 20 beers on tap (including several local ones). Downstairs it's a 500-person live music club that genre-jumps from funk to blues to alt-rock guitar pickers. Bands take the stage most nights of the week.

NATIONAL SYMPHONY ORCHESTRA PERFORMING ARTS

Map p296 (www.kennedy-center.org/nso; Kennedy Center; MFoggy Bottom-GWU) This is the affiliate orchestra of the Kennedy Center and one of the best chamber symphonies in the nation.

WASHINGTON NATIONAL OPERA PERFORMING ARTS

Map p296 (www.kennedy-center.org/wno; Kennedy Center; MFoggy Bottom-GWU) The Washington Opera is based at the Kennedy Center and puts on a varied showcase throughout the year. Placido Domingo helmed the company until 2011, when he stepped down after 15 years for Francesca Zambello.

WASHINGTON BALLET PERFORMING ARTS

Map p296 (www.washingtonballet.org; Kennedy Center; MFoggy Bottom-GWU) The Washington Ballet hasn't been known for many groundbreaking productions, although its reputation is beginning to change as it explores the work of younger choreographers. The troupe leaps at the Kennedy Center and THEARC in Southeast DC.

SHOPPING

★WHITE HOUSE HISTORICAL ASSOCIATION MUSEUM SHOP SOUVENIRS

Map p296 (shop.whitehousehistory.org; 1450 Pennsylvania Ave NW; ⌚7:30am-4pm; MFederal Triangle) Located inside the White House Visitor Center, this is the spot to get official White House-branded mementos, like the official Bo Obama Christmas ornament, or the official Blue Room necklace with glass beads, or the official Burning of the White House 1814 puzzle. The selection shocks and awes.

WHITE HOUSE GIFTS SOUVENIRS

Map p296 (www.whitehousegifts.com; 701 15th St NW; ⌚8am-9pm Mon-Sat, 9am-7pm Sun; MMetro Center) Not to be confused with the official White House gift shop (in the White House Visitor Center), this store sells, er, less official items. So while you can still find the official Christmas ornament among the stock, you'll also see caricature Obama bottle openers and the Political Inaction Figures paper doll set.

If you buy $10 worth of merchandise, you can take a cheesy photo sitting behind a replica of the president's desk.

INDIAN CRAFT SHOP ARTS & CRAFTS

Map p296 (www.indiancraftshop.com; 1849 C St NW, Dept of Interior; ⌚8:30am-4:30pm Mon-Fri; MFarragut West) Representing more than 45 tribal groups in the US, this compact shop sells gorgeous basketry, weavings, pottery, beadwork, sand paintings and fetish carvings made by Native Americans. The high-quality pieces don't come cheap. The shop hides inside the Department of the Interior; show photo ID to enter the building.

W CURTIS DRAPER TOBACCONIST TOBACCO

Map p296 (www.wcurtisdraper.com; 699 15th St NW; ⌚9:30am-6:30pm Mon-Fri, 10am-5pm Sat; MMetro Center) Follow your nose into W Curtis Draper, which has been selling cigars to politicos since 1887. Make your selection, then sit in one of the overstuffed leather chairs to puff with fellow enthusiasts young and old. Staff are friendly and helpful to stogie-smoking newbies.

AMERICAN INSTITUTE OF ARCHITECTS BOOKSTORE BOOKS

Map p296 (1735 New York Ave NW; ⌚9am-5pm Mon-Fri; MFarragut West) Architecture buffs are in good company in this small specialty shop, which stocks the latest architecture and design titles and periodicals. For the classic overview on the city's iconic buildings, pick up the AIA *Guide to the Architecture of Washington, DC*.

RENWICK GALLERY ARTS & CRAFTS

Map p296 (www.americanart.si.edu/renwick; 1661 Pennsylvania Ave NW; ⌚10am-5:30pm; MFarragut West) In one of DC's best museum shops, handmade textiles and hand-dyed silks are available, as is glasswork, woodwork and unique jewelry, much of it rather affordable. The excellent choice of books includes how-to manuals on jewelry- and fabric-making, ceramics, glassblowing and cabinetry, many appropriate for kids. The shop is closed along with the museum until 2016.

Georgetown

Neighborhood Top Five

❶ Swirl a cocktail in the same room where JFK proposed to Jackie at **Martin's Tavern** (p99).

❷ Meander the ponds, pools and terraced formal gardens of **Dumbarton Oaks** (p94).

❸ Escape the concrete jungle by walking or cycling a bit of the bucolic **C&O Canal Towpath** (p103).

❹ Sip an alfresco drink, ogle the yachts and watch rowing teams at **Georgetown Waterfront Park** (p94).

❺ Paddle past DC's stony monuments on a sunset tour with **Key Bridge Boathouse** (p103).

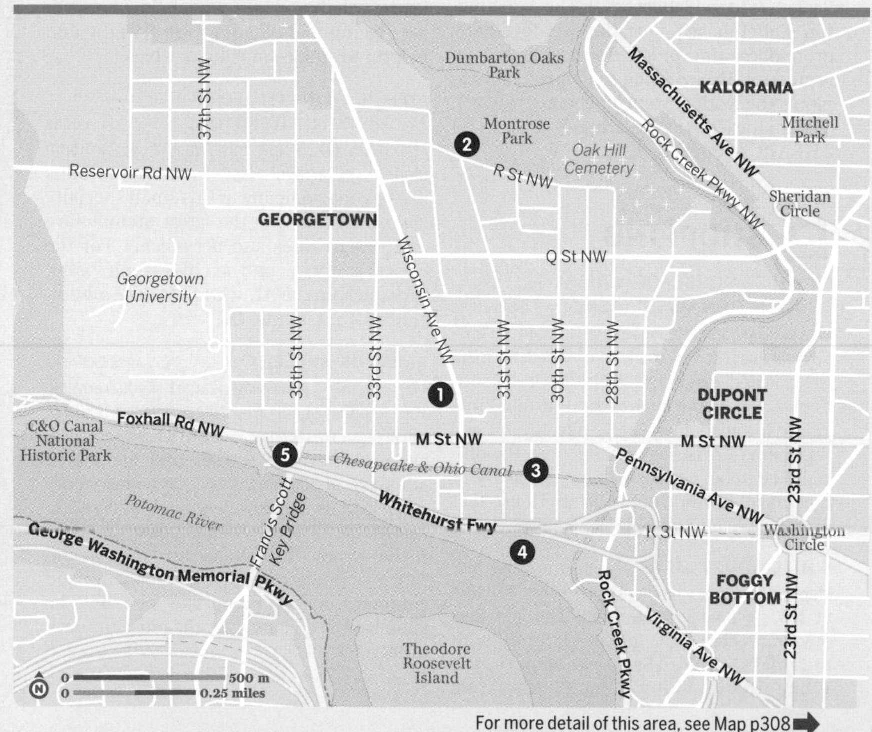

For more detail of this area, see Map p308

Explore Georgetown

Thousands of the bright and beautiful, from students to academics and diplomats, call this leafy, aristocratic neighborhood home. Georgetown is Washington's house on the hill. To be more accurate, it's a series of beautiful houses, reflecting the best of American Federal and Victorian architecture, interspersed with velvet green gardens, high-end shopping arcades, hushed restaurants and a preppie nightlife scene. Then there's the collegiate name behind the game: Georgetown University, the city's most prestigious school (sorry, GWU, but it's true).

This is an evocative place. In spring and summer, it's green and gorgeous, the trees waving over filigreed brick romance, laughing co-eds and well-off families. In fall and winter, Georgetown becomes dignified and reserved, her old-school atmosphere enhanced by the change of leaves or the flicker of gas lamps on snowy nights. There's a subtle but palpable sense of exclusivity in many haunts, and to keep the commoners out, Georgetown residents killed any Metro extensions into their neighborhood in 1980. The other hitch: Georgetown is expensive.

Still, it's hard not to fall for the allure of the capital's equivalent of the prettiest girl in school. Shopaholics have their chic boutiques lined up in a row along M St, hikers and cyclists have idyllic trails, and garden lovers have genteel landscapes to stroll through. Afterward, the cafes and pubs invite lingering into the night.

Local Life

➡ **Book Hill** A Paris-like row of art galleries, interior-design stores and antique shops slope down the 1600 block of Wisconsin Ave (between Q St and R St NW). The area is called Book Hill, and when Georgetowners need Chinese laquered chests or lavender linen-drawer liners for their home, it's their one-stop shop.

➡ **La Dolce Vita** Georgetown has the goods for DC sweet tooths: hulking pastries at Baked & Wired, creamy frosted Georgetown Cupcakes, flaky goodness at Pie Sisters and exotic gelato at Dolcezza.

➡ **Party at the Waterfront** On warm nights the outdoor cafes and boating action make Georgetown Waterfront Park the neighborhood hot spot.

Getting There & Away

➡ **Metro** The Foggy Bottom-GWU stop (Blue/Orange/Silver Lines) is a 0.75-mile walk from M St's edge.

➡ **Bus** The DC Circulator's Dupont–Georgetown–Rosslyn line runs from the Dupont Circle Metro station (south entrance), with stops along M St. The Union Station–Georgetown line runs via K St.

Lonely Planet's Top Tip

Georgetown is a terrific cycling spot. Two top trails are the C&O Canal Towpath, which is flat, wide, forested and scenic; and the Capital Crescent Trail, a paved path built on an old railroad bed that provides beautiful lookouts over the Potomac River. The neighborhood has several bike-rental shops that make it easy to get rolling.

Best Places to Eat

- Baked & Wired (p98)
- Chez Billy Sud (p99)
- Martin's Tavern (p99)
- Pie Sisters (p99)
- Fiola Mare (p100)

For reviews, see p98. ➡

Best Places to Drink

- Tombs (p101)
- Cafe Bonaparte (p101)
- J Paul's (p101)
- Kafe Leopold (p101)

For reviews, see p101. ➡

Best Parks & Gardens

- Dumbarton Oaks (p94)
- Georgetown Waterfront Park (p94)
- Tudor Place (p94)
- Oak Hill Cemetery (p98)
- Dumbarton Oaks Park (p94)

For reviews, see p94. ➡

SIGHTS

DUMBARTON OAKS — GARDENS, MUSEUM

Map p308 (www.doaks.org; 1703 32nd St NW; museum free, gardens adult/child $8/5; ⏲museum 11:30am-5:30pm Tue-Sun, gardens 2-6pm) The mansion's 10 acres of enchanting formal gardens are straight out of a storybook. In springtime, the blooms – including heaps of cherry blossoms – are stunning. The mansion itself is worth a walk through to see exquisite Byzantine and pre-Columbian art, as well as El Greco's *The Visitation* and a fascinating library of rare books.

In 1944, diplomatic meetings took place here that laid the groundwork for the UN. The trustees of Harvard University operate the house, so Harvard students, faculty and staff get in for free. From November to mid-March the gardens are free to all (and they close at 5pm). The garden entrance is at R and 31st Sts NW.

GEORGETOWN WATERFRONT PARK — PARK

Map p308 (Water St NW, btwn 30th St & Key Bridge; 👪) The park is a favorite with couples on first dates, families on an evening stroll and power players showing off their big yachts. Benches dot the way, where you can sit and watch the rowing teams out on the Potomac River. Alfresco restaurants cluster near the harbor at 31st St NW. They ring a terraced plaza filled with fountains (which become an ice rink in winter). The docks are also here for sightseeing boats that ply the Potomac to Alexandria, VA.

The park then curves along 10 riverside acres west to the Key Bridge. Kids splash in the fountains at Wisconsin Ave's foot. At 33rd St there's a labyrinth in the grass; walk the circles and see if you feel more connected to the universe.

GEORGETOWN UNIVERSITY — UNIVERSITY

Map p308 (www.georgetown.edu; cnr 37th & O Sts NW) Georgetown is one of the nation's top universities, with a student body that's equally hard-working and hard-partying. Founded in 1789, it was America's first Roman Catholic university. Notable Hoya (derived from the Latin *hoya saxa*, 'what rocks') alumni include Bill Clinton, as well many international royals and heads of state. Near the campus' east gate, medieval-looking **Healy Hall** impresses with its tall, Hogwarts-esque clock tower. Pretty **Dalghren Chapel** and its quiet courtyard hide behind it.

> **LOCAL KNOWLEDGE**
>
> **DUMBARTON OAKS PARK**
>
> Next door to Dumbarton Oaks garden, **Dumbarton Oaks Park** (Map p308; www.dopark.org; Lovers' Lane; ⏲sunrise-sunset) was once part of the estate but is now a public woodland beloved by joggers and dog walkers. Access it via Lovers' Lane (a paved path 200ft east of R and 31st Sts) and enter a world of forested trails, quaint stone bridges, mini waterfalls and deer-filled meadows.

EXORCIST STAIRS — FILM LOCATION

Map p308 (3600 Prospect St NW) The steep set of stairs dropping down to M St is a popular track for joggers, but more famously it's the spot where demonically possessed Father Karras tumbles to his death in the 1973 horror classic *The Exorcist*. Come on foggy nights, when the stone steps really are creepy.

TUDOR PLACE — MUSEUM

Map p308 (www.tudorplace.org; 1644 31st St NW; 1hr house tour adult/child $10/3, self-guided garden tour $3; ⏲10am-4pm Tue-Sat, from noon Sun, closed Jan) This 1816 neoclassical mansion was owned by Thomas Peter and Martha Custis Peter, the granddaughter of Martha Washington. Today the mansion functions as a small museum, and features furnishings and artwork from Mount Vernon, which give a nice insight into American decorative arts. The grand, 5-acre gardens bloom with roses, lilies, poplar trees and exotic palms.

DUMBARTON HOUSE — MUSEUM

Map p308 (www.dumbartonhouse.org; 2715 Q St NW; adult/child $5/free; ⏲11am-3pm Tue-Sun) Often confused with Dumbarton Oaks (the mansion and gardens), Dumbarton House is a modest Federal historic house, constructed by a wealthy family in 1798. Now it's run by the Colonial Dames of America, who are on hand to provide gently witty commentary. The focus isn't just the house – chockablock with antique china, silver, furnishings, gowns and books – but quaint Federal customs, like passing round the chamber pot after formal dinners so gentlemen could have a group pee.

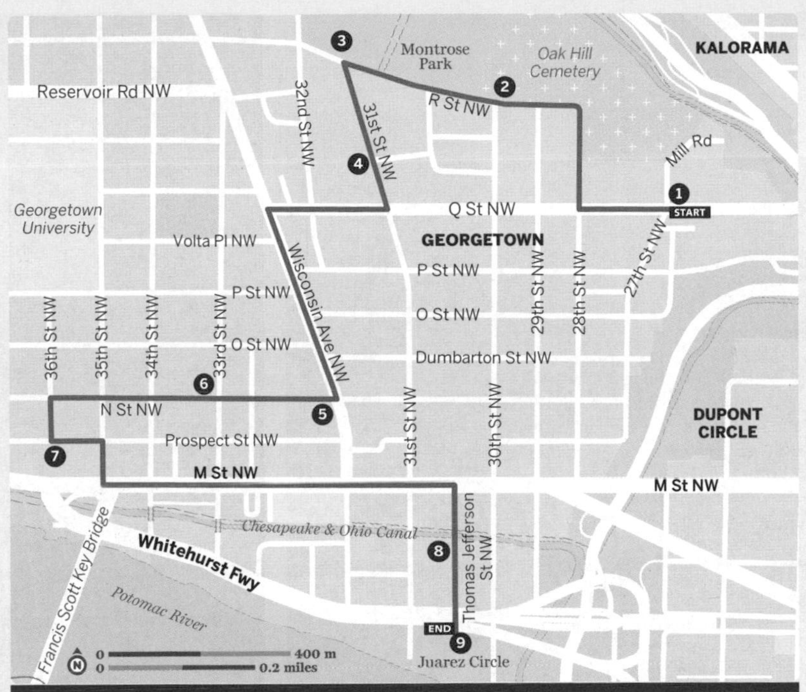

Neighborhood Walk
Genteel Georgetown

START MT ZION CEMETERY
END GEORGETOWN WATERFRONT PARK
LENGTH 3 MILES; THREE HOURS

If ever a neighborhood were prime for ambling, it's Georgetown, in all its leafy glory.

African American **1 Mt Zion Cemetery** (p98), near the intersection of 27th and Q Sts, dates from the early 1800s. The church was a stop on the Underground Railroad; escaping slaves hid in a vault in the cemetery.

2 Oak Hill Cemetery (p98) is a few blocks away. Stroll the obelisk-studded grounds and look for gravesites of prominent Washingtonians such as Edwin Stanton (Lincoln's war secretary). Up the road, **3 Dumbarton Oaks** (p94) offers exquisite Byzantine art inside and sprawling, fountain-dotted gardens outside.

George Washington's step-granddaughter Martha Custis Peter owned **4 Tudor Place** (p94), the neoclassical mansion at 1644 31st St NW. It has some of George's furnishings from Mount Vernon on show.

Head over to Wisconsin Ave NW, and stop in at **5 Martin's Tavern** (p99), where John F Kennedy proposed to Jackie. Walk west along N St NW and you'll pass several Federal-style townhouses in the 3300 block. JFK and Jackie lived at **6 3307 N St** between 1958 and 1961, when they left for the White House.

At the corner of 36th NW and Prospect Sts, stare down the **7 Exorcist Stairs** (p94). This is the spot where possessed Regan of *The Exorcist* sent victims to their screaming deaths. Joggers use them by day, but at night the stairs are legitimately creepy as hell.

Go down to M St NW, popping in to whatever tony boutiques and high-end chain stores your wallet permits. At Thomas Jefferson St turn right and sniff your way to **8 Baked & Wired** (p98) to replenish with a monster cupcake and cappuccino. From there you can stroll down to **9 Georgetown Waterfront Park** (p94) to watch the boats and other action along the Potomac River.

1

RICK GEHARTER / GETTY IMAGES ©

2

4

DAN HERRICK / GETTY IMAGES ©

1. Georgetown University (p94)
Founded in 1789, Georgetown was the USA's first Roman Catholic university.

2. Neighborhood streets
Georgetown's leafy streets, filled with handsome row houses, are evocative places to stroll.

3. Dumbarton Oaks (p94)
One of DC's finest mansions is set amid elegant gardens and formal courtyards.

4. Blues Alley (p101)
A former haunt of Dizzy Gillespie, this is still one of the city's best jazz and blues bars.

ALEXANDRE TOKOVININE / GETTY IMAGES ©

AFRICAN AMERICAN GEORGETOWN

Three sites recall the history of Georgetown's 19th-century free black community, who lived in an area known as Herring Hill. Founded in 1816, **Mt Zion United Methodist Church** (Map p308; www.mtzionumcdc.org; 1334 29th St NW) is DC's oldest black congregation. Its original site, on 27th St NW, was a stop on the Underground Railroad.

Nearby at **Mt Zion Cemetery** (Map p308; 27th & Q Sts NW) and the connected **Female Union Band Cemetery** (Map p308; 27th & Q Sts NW), the crumbling, overgrown headstones of many free black residents are scattered in a forlorn patch of trees. The church hid escaping slaves in a vault here. Look for the road leading into the graveyard just west of the building at 2531 Q St NW.

OAK HILL CEMETERY CEMETERY

Map p308 (www.oakhillcemeterydc.org; 3001 R St NW; ⌚9am-4:30pm Mon-Fri, 11am-4pm Sat, 1-4pm Sun) This 24-acre, obelisk-studded cemetery contains winding walks and 19th-century gravestones set into the hillsides of Rock Creek. It's a fantastic spot for a quiet walk, especially in spring, when it seems like every wildflower in existence blooms on the grounds. James Renwick designed the lovely gatehouse and charming gneiss (stone) chapel.

OLD STONE HOUSE HISTORIC SITE

Map p308 (www.nps.gov/olst; 3051 M St NW; ⌚noon-5pm Wed-Sun) FREE Built in 1765, the capital's oldest surviving building has been a tavern, brothel and boardinghouse (sometimes all at once). Today it's a small museum offering a peek into Revolutionary War–era life. The evocative little garden in back is worth a mosey.

It was almost demolished in the 1950s, but a persistent (albeit false) rumor that Pierre L'Enfant used it as a workshop while designing DC saved it for posterity.

EATING

★BAKED & WIRED BAKERY $

Map p308 (☎202-333-2500; www.bakedandwired.com; 1052 Thomas Jefferson St NW; baked goods $3-6; ⌚7am-8pm Mon-Thu, to 9pm Fri, 8am-9pm Sat, 9am-8pm Sun; wi-fi) Sniff out Baked & Wired, a cheery cafe that whips up beautifully made coffees, bacon cheddar buttermilk biscuits and enormous cupcakes. It's a fine spot to join students in both real and virtual chatter (free wi-fi, of course). When the weather permits, patrons take their treats outside to the adjacent grassy area by the C&O canal.

SIMPLY BANH MI VIETNAMESE $

Map p308 (www.simplybanhmidc.com; 1624 Wisconsin Ave NW; mains $6-9; ⌚11am-7pm Tue-Sun) There's nothing fancy about the small, below-street-level space, and the compact menu sticks to sandwiches and bubble tea. But the brother-sister owners know how to take a crusty baguette, stuff it with delicious lemongrass pork or other meat (or tofu!), and make your day. They're super attentive to quality and to customer needs (vegan, gluten free etc).

PATISSERIE POUPON CAFE $

Map p308 (www.patisseriepoupon.net; 1645 Wisconsin Ave NW; baked goods $3-5; ⌚8:30am-6pm Tue-Fri, 8am-5:30pm Sat, 8am-4pm Sun) The society ladies know where to replenish mid–shopping spree: Patisserie Poupon. Join them in nibbling almond croissants, macarons or a Niçoise salad at one of the little cafe's tables. Once the French-press coffee and *chocolat chaud* (hot chocolate) arrive, it's easy to linger.

GEORGETOWN CUPCAKE BAKERY $

Map p308 (www.georgetowncupcake.com; 3301 M St NW; cupcakes $3; ⌚10am-9pm Mon-Sat, to 8pm Sun) Here's what's going to happen: you'll be walking down M St and will see a gigantic line spilling out of a small shop: moms with kids, preppy students and ladies-who-lunch types. Shouts of 'They have salted caramel!', 'I'm getting the lava fudge!' will fill the air. You won't be able to resist and will fall in behind them.

Honestly, we don't think these are the best cupcakes in town. (That honor belongs to nearby Baked & Wired.) That said, the ladies do make a damn fine cake.

DOLCEZZA GELATERIA $

Map p308 (www.dolcezzagelato.com; 1560 Wisconsin Ave NW; gelato $5-8; ⌚noon-9pm Sun-Fri, to 10pm Fri & Sat; 📶) Dolcezza serves eclectic-flavored gelato from an ever-changing menu. Recent hits include lime cilantro, Mexican coffee and lemon ricotta cardamom. It may sound odd, but it's awesome. Other outposts scoop in Dupont Circle and Logan Circle.

CHING CHING CHA ASIAN $

Map p308 (www.chingchingcha.com; 1063 Wisconsin Ave NW; snacks $2-5, 3-course tea meal $14; ⏲11am-9pm) This airy, Zen-like teahouse feels a world away from the shopping mayhem of M St. Stop in for a pot of rare tea (they brew more than 70 varieties), and steamed dumplings, coconut tarts, or a three-course 'tea meal,' with little dishes along the lines of green squash and miso salmon.

SWEETGREEN HEALTH FOOD $

Map p308 (☎202-337-9338; www.sweetgreen.com; 3333 M St NW; mains $8-11; ⏲11am-10pm; 🖉) 🍃 Georgetown's teeny branch of the uber-healthy salad and frozen-yogurt chain was the first. Order your gigantic bowl of curry-yogurt-sauced roast chicken and greens (or other equally wholesome dish) at the counter, then take it to the waterfront park to consume.

QUICK PITA MIDDLE EASTERN $

Map p308 (☎202-338-7482; www.quick-pita.com; 1210 Potomac St NW; sandwiches $5-7; ⏲11am-2am Sun-Thu, to 3am Fri & Sat) A million late-night joints sell falafel to hard-drinking students. We love this one. Why? The yogurt's a little saltier, the stools are more stable so we don't fall on our faces, the shawarma (a meat-in-pita sandwich) is a little greasier and the counter guys curse at each other in Arabic with just a little more vehemence. It's cozy like that.

★CHEZ BILLY SUD FRENCH $$

Map p308 (☎202-965-2606; www.chezbillysud.com; 1039 31st St NW; mains $17-29; ⏲11:30am-2pm Tue-Fri, 11am-2pm Sat & Sun, 5-10pm Tue-Thu & Sun, 5-11pm Fri & Sat; 🖉) An endearing little bistro tucked away on a residential block, Billy's mint-green walls, gilt mirrors and wee marble bar exude laid-back elegance. Mustachioed servers bring baskets of warm bread to the white linen–clothed tables, along with crackling pork and pistachio sausage, golden trout, tuna niçoise salad and plump cream puffs.

LOCAL KNOWLEDGE

PIE SISTERS

The neighbors can't help but stop in to see what the **Pie Sisters** (Map p308; ☎202-338-7437; www.piesisters.com; 3423 M St NW; slices $5; ⏲11am-7pm Tue, Wed & Sun, to 9pm Thu-Sat) have cooling on the rack. Chocolate cream and jumbleberry tempt among the sweet wares, while chicken pot pie and pork barbecue pie waft savory goodness. The sweet ones come in bite-size and cupcake-size versions, but go for a full slice for best results. A smattering of tables let you fork in immediately.

Staff members are attentive to vegetarians and diners with food allergies. If the name sounds familiar, it's because Chez Billy Sud has a sibling restaurant in Petworth.

MARTIN'S TAVERN AMERICAN $$

Map p308 (☎202-333-7370; www.martins-tavern.com; 1264 Wisconsin Ave NW; mains $17-32; ⏲11am-1:30am Mon-Thu, to 2:30am Fri, 9am-2:30am Sat, 8am-1:30am Sun) John F Kennedy proposed to Jackie in booth three at Georgetown's oldest saloon, and if you're thinking of popping the question there today, the attentive waitstaff keep the champagne chilled for that very reason. With an old-English country scene, including the requisite fox-and-hound hunting prints on the wall, this DC institution serves unfussy classics like thick burgers, crab cakes and icy-cold beers.

PIZZERIA PARADISO PIZZA $$

Map p308 (☎202-337-1245; www.eatyourpizza.com; 3282 M St NW; mains $13-20; ⏲11:30am-10pm Mon & Tue, to 11pm Wed & Thu, to midnight Fri & Sat, noon-10pm Sun) Casual Paradiso serves wood-oven Neapolitan-style pizzas with scrumptious toppings to crowds of hungry patrons. The pizza crust is perfect: light, crisp and a little flaky. There's great people-watching from the big plate-glass windows and popular happy hours. A fine beer and ale selection heightens the appeal.

UNUM MODERN AMERICAN $$

Map p308 (☎202-621-6959; www.unumdc.com; 2917 M St NW; mains $19-28; ⏲5:30-10pm Sun-Thu, to 11pm Fri & Sat) Unum hops on the upscale-casual, modern-American-fare bandwagon with its shareable plates and

NEIGHBORHOOD RESOURCE

The **Georgetown Business Improvement District** (www.georgetowndc.com) has maps, transport and parking info, and a directory of bars, restaurants and shops on its website.

mains (most of which are available by the half-order) such as Indian-spiced lamb shank and kale-pesto-sauced goat cheese ravioli. Sides of cashew-raisin Brussels sprouts and lots of California wines go alongside. The intimate room, glimmering in warm golds and light wood, will please romantics.

KOTOBUKI JAPANESE **$$**

(202-281-6679; www.kotobukiusa.com; 4822 MacArthur Blvd NW; mains $17-27; noon-2:30pm Mon-Sat, 5-9:30pm Mon-Thu & Sun, to 10:30pm Fri & Sat) Kotobuki is one of the better spots for sushi, thanks to its excellent platters (at around $15 for a lunch and $25 for a dinner platter), its tucked-away location, which adds a feeling of discovery, and its oh-so-Japanese interior, all stripped-down aesthetic overlaid by running cursive kanji script on the walls. It's located upstairs above a more expensive sushi joint.

LA CHAUMIÈRE FRENCH **$$**

Map p308 (202-338-1784; www.lachaumieredc.com; 2813 M St NW; mains $19-29; 11:30am-2:30pm Mon-Fri, 5:30-10:30pm Mon-Sat) There are artists and there are craftspeople, and La Chaumière's kitchen seems to fall into the second category. This isn't a bad thing; there's no fooling around with funny envelope-pushing here, just very good, classic French food prepared in an intimate dining room that screams 'expensive date'.

This is hearty, stick-to-your-ribs stuff straight from the terroir – duck breast, saddle of rabbit, calf brains – things that are long- and slow-braised with love. The central stone fireplace adds to the warmth.

FIOLA MARE SEAFOOD **$$$**

Map p308 (202-628-0065; www.fiolamaredc.com; 3050 K St NW; mains $26-45; 11:30am-2:30pm Tue-Sun, 5:30-10:30pm Mon-Thu, to 11pm Fri, 5-11pm Sat, to 9pm Sun) Fiola Mare delivers the chi-chi Georgetown experience. It flies in fresh fish and crustaceans from Maine, and even Tasmania, Australia, daily. The yacht-bobbling river view rocks. The see-and-be-seen multitudes are here. It's DC at its luxe best. Try it at lunchtime on a weekday, when $22 gets you an Italian-style seafood main and a drink in the bar area. Make reservations.

1789 AMERICAN **$$$**

Map p308 (202-965-1789; www.1789restaurant.com; 1226 36th St NW; mains $28-48; 6-10pm Mon-Thu, to 11pm Fri, 5:30-11pm Sat, to 10pm Sun) This place was one of the first high-end purveyors of 'rustic New American' fare, so if you're going to try local ingredients sexed up with provincial flair (think Shenandoah Valley beef with wild-mushroom bread pudding), this is the spot to indulge. Political bigwigs flock to the cozy, colonial room. While there's no longer a jacket requirement, most folks still look sharp.

BLACKSALT SEAFOOD **$$$**

(202-342-9101; www.blacksaltrestaurant.com; 4883 MacArthur Blvd NW; mains $30-38; 11:30am-2:30pm, 11am-2pm Sun, 5:30-9:30pm Mon-Thu, to 11pm Fri & Sat, to 9pm Sun) There are many who claim BlackSalt serves the best seafood in the city. The chef always seems to find new flavors, delving into whatever culinary pleasure one can ratchet out of a sole, skate or soft-shell crab. Smoky, buttery, minty – the shifting, innovative menu is typically spot on. Five-/seven-course tasting menus ($80/98) are also available.

If you can't get enough, BlackSalt doubles as a fish market, overflowing with fresh, organic sea creatures for cooking at home.

MAKOTO JAPANESE **$$$**

(202-298-6866; www.makotorestaurantdc.com; 4844 MacArthur Blvd NW; 8-course set menu $95; noon-2pm Tue-Fri, 6:30-8:30pm Tue-Fri, 5-9:30 Sat, 6:30-8pm Sun) When the sushi craving strikes we often opt for Makoto, simply because it's so classically...*Japanese.* The napkins look like origami. The wasabi is freshly grated. You leave your shoes at the door. And the food, needless to say, is excellent. There's no mucking about: this is old-school stuff prepared with the height of focus and technique.

Reservations are a good idea, since the restaurant is tiny. Note there's a business-casual dress code (no athletic gear allowed).

CAFE MILANO
ITALIAN $$$

Map p308 (☎202-333-6183; www.cafemilano.com; 3251 Prospect St NW; mains $25-45; ⊙11:30am-11pm Sun-Tue, to midnight Wed-Sat) Milano has been reeling in the political glitterati and besotted Georgetown couples for years with its executions of northern Italian favorites. Be prepared to pay for the European-chic ambience and celebrity-spotting. The pastas get the biggest praise, especially the ones prepared tableside.

DRINKING & NIGHTLIFE

Several British-style pubs with heavy wood and dark nooks line up on M St. Drinks can be amazingly expensive in this cashed-up 'hood.

TOMBS
PUB

Map p308 (www.tombs.com; 1226 36th St NW; ⊙11:30am-1:30am Mon-Thu, to 2:30am Fri & Sat, 9:30am-1:30am Sun) Every college of a certain pedigree has 'that' bar – the one where faculty and students alike sip pints under athletic regalia of the old school. The Tombs is Georgetown's contribution to the genre. If it looks familiar, think back to the '80s: the subterranean pub was one of the settings for the film *St Elmo's Fire*.

CAFE BONAPARTE
CAFE

Map p308 (www.cafebonaparte.com; 1522 Wisconsin Ave NW; ⊙10am-11pm Mon-Thu, to midnight Fri & Sat, 9am-10pm Sun) This jewel-box cafe feels as though it's been plucked straight from the streets of Paris. Come to sip a *cafe au lait* or a glass of sparkling wine. Hopefully you're not in a hurry, because service can be slow. *Frites*, crepes and chocolate tortes emerge from the kitchen for those in need of a nosh.

J PAUL'S
PUB

Map p308 (☎202-333-3450; 3218 M St NW; ⊙11:30am-2am Mon-Fri, from 10:30am Sat & Sun) Politicians, lobbyists, students and other locals belly up at J Paul's to knock beers back and enjoy great burgers, steaks, ribs and seared salmon. Join the group at the long mahogany shotgun bar, especially during happy hour, when there are deals on oysters and other menu items.

KAFE LEOPOLD
CAFE

Map p308 (www.kafeleopolds.com; Cady's Alley, 3315 M St; ⊙8am-10pm Sun-Tue, to 11pm Wed, to midnight Thu-Sat) Leopold serves full meals, but it shines most as a European-vibed spot for coffee and German and Austrian wines. Sip at one of the umbrella-shaded tables that spill out into the courtyard. Banana rum macarons, five-layer hazelnut cake and chocolatey Sacher torte entice from the glass case. Service can be lackluster, though it doesn't seem to deter the crowds.

The cafe hides along the cobblestones of Cady's Alley.

MR SMITH'S
BAR

Map p308 (www.mrsmiths.com; 3205 K St NW; ⊙11:30am-2am Sun-Thu, to 3am Fri & Sat) This is as divey as they come in Georgetown – sawdust and dusky interior concealing patrons that only get more rowdy and roaring with the night. That said, Mr Smith's is as popular with Georgetown Jonathan as with Average Joe, which makes for an intriguing and generally affable atmosphere. Wednesday through Saturday a sing-a-long piano player gets the crowd crooning.

SEQUOIA
BAR

Map p308 (www.sequoiadc.com; Waterfront Harbour, 3000 K St NW; ⊙11:30am-9pm Mon-Thu, to 10pm Fri & Sat, 10am-9pm Sun) On a steamy summer night, Sequoia's patio is the place to be. Plop down on a plastic chair on the cascading terrace overlooking the Potomac. Or fight your way through the throng at the bar, grab an overpriced beer, then start flirting with the hottie of your choice.

The bar attracts all types – from pretty gays to trustafarian college kids to 30-something lawyers – and has a reputation as a pick-up spot.

ENTERTAINMENT

BLUES ALLEY
JAZZ

Map p308 (www.bluesalley.com; 1073 Wisconsin Ave NW; admission from $20; ⊙shows 8pm & 10pm) Greats such as Dizzy Gillespie and Sarah Vaughan played this venerable club back in the day. The talent remains just as sterling now, and the setting just as sophisticated. Reserve a ticket in advance if a big name is making music. Enter through the alley just off M St, south of Wisconsin Ave.

SHOPPING

M St and Wisconsin Ave are the main thoroughfares, packed with Urban Outfitters, Juicy Couture, Apple and a slew of other tony brand stores. Stroll down the side streets to find the more imaginative shops.

★OLD PRINT GALLERY — MAPS

Map p308 (www.oldprintgallery.com; 1220 31st St NW; ⏲10am-5:30pm Tue-Sat) The small store sells a fantastic array of vintage maps and prints. Looking for a chart of Kentucky c 1794, or maybe Hindustan (India) in 1855? What about an 1844 hand-colored Audubon lithograph of a cayenne tern? The globe-spanning trove is a great place to browse and hold a bit of history in your hands.

APPALACHIAN SPRING — ARTS, CRAFTS

Map p308 (www.appalachianspring.com; 1415 Wisconsin Ave NW; ⏲10am-6pm Mon-Sat, from noon Sun) Touting its motto, 'fine American craft', Appalachian Spring features handmade pottery, woodcarvings, quilts and jewelry. The carved wooden boxes and hand-blown glass bowls make handsome gifts.

OLIVER DUNN, MOSS & CO AND CATHARINE ROBERTS — ANTIQUES

Map p308 (1657 Wisconsin Ave NW; ⏲11am-5pm Tue-Sat, noon-4pm Sun) The lengthy name comes from three businesses under one roof. Located in a cute row house in the thick of Book Hill (Georgetown's antique-laden block of shops), this spot spreads posh linens, Scandinavian textiles, French signs and concrete garden ornaments through six rooms and into the back yard.

TUGOOH TOYS — CHILDREN

Map p308 (www.tugoohtoys.com; 1355 Wisconsin Ave NW; ⏲10am-7pm Mon-Thu, to 8pm Fri & Sat, 11am-6pm Sun) If you've ever been nostalgic for the great wooden toys of childhood, this hip wonderland has the goods with clever modern touches. Lots of ecofriendly playthings (ie cuddly animals made with high-quality organic cotton) and educational games stack the shelves, too.

CADY'S ALLEY — HOMEWARES

Map p308 (www.cadysalley.com; ⏲hours vary) Not a store per se, Cady's Alley is a small cobblestone lane lined with uber-cool (and often expensive) clothing and interior-design boutiques selling everything from little black dresses to concept furniture. It runs parallel to M St NW, between 33rd and 34th Sts NW; you can enter off M St.

RELISH — CLOTHING

Map p308 (www.relishdc.com; 3312 Cady's Alley NW; ⏲10am-6pm Mon-Sat) Set on Cady's Alley, Relish sells high-end fashion for the ladies. The two-level store boasts top-name labels and indie designers alike, including pieces by Marni, Jil Sander and Nicole Farhi. Shoes, bags and accessories all make nice eye candy.

SHOPS AT GEORGETOWN PARK — MALL

Map p308 (3222 M St NW; ⏲10am-8pm Mon-Sat, noon-6pm Sun) Set in a 19th-century cast-iron building that once sheltered horse-drawn omnibuses, this mall (with skylights and hanging plants) has become a hub for trendy, bargain-friendly chain stores. Inside you'll find retailers such as H&M, Forever 21, Anthropologie and DSW shoes. The food court is meager but in the process of getting an upgrade.

APPLE STORE — ELECTRONICS

Map p308 (www.apple.com; 1229 Wisconsin Ave NW; ⏲10am-9pm Mon-Sat, 11am-7pm Sun) iPads, iPhones and 'i' everything else for Mac enthusiasts are splayed across the bright, airy space. Plenty of clued-up staff are on hand to answer product questions, and there's free internet access on machines throughout the store.

LUSH — BEAUTY

Map p308 (www.twitter.com/lushgeorgetown; 3066 M St NW; ⏲10am-9pm Mon-Sat, 11am-6pm Sun) A cleaner world awaits inside sweet-smelling Lush. The international chain of handmade, all-natural soaps brings high art to the common bath experience. Top selections include honey- and toffee-scented lump soap, rosebud-filled bath bombs and bergamot-and-lemon bubble bars (for the bubble-bath experience).

PATAGONIA — OUTDOOR EQUIPMENT

Map p308 (www.patagonia.com; 1048 Wisconsin Ave NW; ⏲11am-7pm Mon-Fri, 10am-7pm Sat, 11am-5pm Sun) Staffed with knowledgeable sales clerks and stocked with everything you need for a trip to the great outdoors, this tri-level shop has a giant collection of Patagonia's trusted gear, including trendy garb for women and men along with camping supplies, down jackets and hiking shoes and shorts.

SPORTS & ACTIVITIES

C&O CANAL TOWPATH — WALKING, CYCLING

Map p308 (www.nps.gov/choh; 1057 Thomas Jefferson St NW) The shaded hiking-cycling path – part of a larger national historic park – runs alongside a waterway constructed in the mid-1800s to transport goods to West Virginia. Step on at Jefferson St for a lovely green escape from the crowd.

In its entirety, the gravel path runs for 185 miles from Georgetown to Cumberland, MD. Lots of cyclists do the 14-mile ride from Georgetown to Great Falls, MD. The tree-lined route goes over atmospheric wooden bridges and past water wheels and old lock houses. It's mostly flat, punctuated by occasional small hills. The park's website and **Bike Washington** (www.bikewashington.org/canal) have trail maps.

CAPITAL CRESCENT TRAIL — CYCLING

Map p308 (www.cctrail.org; Water St) Stretching between Georgetown and Bethesda, MD, the constantly evolving Capital Crescent Trail is a fabulous (and very popular) jogging and cycling route. Built on an abandoned railroad bed, the 11-mile trail is paved and is a great leisurely day trip. It has beautiful lookouts over the Potomac River, and winds through woodsy areas and upscale neighborhoods.

In Georgetown, the trail begins under the Key Bridge on Water St (which is what K St becomes as it moves west along the waterfront); the trailhead is clearly marked. In Bethesda, it starts at the Wisconsin Ave Tunnel, on Wisconsin Ave just south of Old Georgetown Rd (it's clearly marked here, too, and accessible from Bethesda Metro station).

The trail also links up with the C&O Canal Towpath and trails through Rock Creek Park.

BIG WHEEL BIKES — BICYCLE RENTAL

Map p308 (www.bigwheelbikes.com; 1034 33rd St NW; per 3hr/day $21/35; ⏲11am-7pm Tue-Fri, 10am-6pm Sat & Sun) Big Wheel has a wide variety of two-wheelers to rent, and you can spin onto the C&O Canal Towpath practically from the front door. Staff members also provide the lowdown on the nearby Capital Crescent Trail and Mount Vernon Trail. There's a three-hour minimum with rentals.

KEY BRIDGE BOATHOUSE — KAYAKING

Map p308 (www.boatingindc.com; 3500 Water St NW; ⏲hours vary Mar-Oct) Located beneath the Key Bridge, the boathouse rents canoes, kayaks and stand-up paddleboards (prices start at $15 per hour). It also offers guided, 90-minute kayak trips ($45 per person) in summer that glide past the Lincoln Memorial as the sun sets. If you have a bike, the boathouse is a mere few steps from the Capital Crescent Trail.

THOMPSON BOAT CENTER — KAYAKING, BICYCLE

Map p308 (www.thompsonboatcenter.com; 2900 Virginia Ave NW; bicycle/watercraft per hr from $10/15; ⏲8am-5pm Mar-Oct) At the Georgetown waterfront's eastern edge, Thompson Boat Center rents canoes and kayaks and offers rowing classes. This is also a convenient place to rent bicycles.

THE TOWPATH: FUELED BY MULE

When work began on the C&O in 1828, the canal was considered an engineering marvel. Unfortunately, by the time it was completed in 1850, the waterway was already obsolete, rendered out of date by the railroad. Nonetheless, the C&O remained in operation for 74 years until a series of floods closed it in 1924.

Mules typically were the 'engines' of the canal boats, pulling them along the water from the roadside. The 1000lb creatures were sturdier and cheaper than horses. Some mules worked on the C&O for more than 20 years.

After the canal closed, it almost became a highway but for the efforts of Supreme Court judge William Douglas, one of the court's most committed civil libertarians and environmentalists. He felt the towpath should be set aside for future generations, and to prove his point he organized a creative publicity stunt. In March 1954, Douglas led an eight-day hike from Cumberland to DC; of the 58 people who set out, only nine (including Douglas) made it to Georgetown. The ploy worked: press coverage of the hike was positive, as was the public reaction, and the towpath became a national park.

Capitol Hill & Southeast DC

CAPITOL HILL | SOUTHEAST DC | SOUTHWEST DC

Neighborhood Top Five

1. Count the statues, ogle the frescoes, eat the bean soup and visit the chambers of the guys and gals who run the country under the big white dome of the **Capitol** (p106).

2. Be wowed by the sheer volume of, well, volumes at the **Library of Congress** (p108).

3. Immerse yourself in the good and bad sides of human nature at the haunting **United States Holocaust Memorial Museum** (p109).

4. Listen in on case arguments at the **Supreme Court** (p110).

5. Catch a baseball game and see the famous racing presidents at **Nationals Park** (p125).

For more detail of this area, see Map p300

Explore Capitol Hill & Southeast DC

First-time visitors will be forgiven for assuming Capitol Hill, the city's geographic and legislative heart, is all about power-broking and wheeling-dealing. Truth is, it's pretty much a traditional neighborhood, where people live in brownstone row houses clumped into a community that revolves around Eastern Market. The feel of the area is more cozy borough than clandestine backroom.

But there's no denying that the big domed building grabs all the attention. The Capitol, appropriately, sits atop Capitol Hill (what Pierre L'Enfant called 'a pedestal waiting for a monument') across a plaza from the almost-as-regal Supreme Court and Library of Congress. They're all DC highlights, and touring them requires the better part of a day. The Holocaust Memorial Museum and money-churning Bureau of Engraving and Printing are other must-sees. They're in Southwest DC, a little sliver of spillover from the Mall. Beyond, in farther flung Southeast, the Nationals' stadium has sparked development of a mod riverside park and brewery. Frederick Douglass' historic home lies across the water in hardscrabble Anacostia.

The neighborhood is quite large, so plan on some serious Metro-ing to get between sights. And count on lingering into the night. The eating and entertainment options rock, especially along H St NE and around Eastern Market.

Local Life

➡ **Hangout** Eastern Market (p125) is the true heart of Capitol Hill: a neighborhood hangout, covered bazaar and all-round great place to soak up local flavor.

➡ **Bard's B-day** On April 23 – Shakespeare's birthday – the Folger Shakespeare Library (p110) throws a party with jugglers, jesters, cake and sonnet contests. It's a big DC to-do for families.

➡ **Secret Cafe** Join Library of Congress workers in the Madison Building's covert 6th-floor cafeteria. It's open to the public, and the floor-to-ceiling windows provide eye-popping vistas over DC's river-sliced landscape.

Getting There & Away

➡ **Metro** Union Station (Red Line), Capitol South (Blue, Orange and Silver), Eastern Market (Blue, Orange and Silver) and Navy Yard (Green) are the main stations.

➡ **Bus** To reach H St from Union Station, catch the X2 bus on the corner of N Capitol and H Sts NE.

➡ **Streetcar** DC's new line will cover H St when completed; check route info at www.dcstreetcar.com.

Lonely Planet's Top Tip

During the March to May peak season, it pays to plan ahead for certain sights, given the crowds and potential sell-out of tickets. The Capitol lets you reserve tours online for free. The Holocaust Memorial Museum lets you reserve tickets for a $1 fee. The Bureau of Engraving and Printing does not take advance bookings, so show up around 8am to get a ticket. For the Marines' drill parade, book online starting March 1.

Best Places to Eat

➡ Rose's Luxury (p122)
➡ Toki Underground (p118)
➡ Atlas Room (p120)
➡ Seventh Hill Pizza (p120)

For reviews, see p117.➡

Best Places to Drink

➡ Little Miss Whiskey's Golden Dollar (p122)
➡ Bluejacket Brewery (p122)
➡ H Street Country Club (p122)
➡ Granville Moore's (p123)

For reviews, see p122.➡

Best Underrated Museums

➡ Folger Shakespeare Library (p110)
➡ Frederick Douglass National Historic Site (p112)

For reviews, see p110.➡

ALLAN BAXTER / GETTY IMAGES ©

TOP SIGHT
CAPITOL

The political center of the US government and geographic heart of the District, the Capitol sits atop a high hill overlooking the National Mall and the wide avenues flaring out to the city beyond. The towering 288ft cast-iron dome, ornate fountains and marble Roman pillars set on sweeping lawns scream: 'This is DC.'

Background & History

Since 1800, the Capitol is where the legislative branch of the US government – ie Congress – has met. The lower House of Representatives (435 members) and upper Senate (100 members) meet respectively in the south and north wings of the building.

Pierre L'Enfant chose the site for the Capitol in his original 1791 city plans; construction began in 1793. George Washington laid the cornerstone, anointing it with wine and oil in Masonic style. In 1814, midway through construction, the British marched into DC and burnt the Capitol (and much of the city) to the ground. The destruction tempted people to abandon Washington altogether, but the government finally rebuilt both city and structure. In 1855 the iron dome (weighing nine million pounds) was designed, replacing a smaller one; the House and Senate wings were added in 1857. The final touch, the 19ft *Statue of Freedom* sculpture, was placed atop the dome in 1863.

DON'T MISS...

- Constantino Brumidi frieze around rotunda
- *Freedom* sculpture atop dome
- Hall of Statues
- Grotto
- Military bands playing on Capitol steps

PRACTICALITIES

- Map p300
- www.visitthecapitol.gov
- First St NE & E Capitol St
- ⏲8:30am-4:30pm Mon-Sat
- Ⓜ Capitol South

Visiting the Building

The **Capitol Visitor Center** (Map p300; www.visitthecapitol.gov; 1st St NE & E Capitol St; ⏲8:30am-4:30pm Mon-Sat) sits below the East Plaza and is where all visits begin. Tours are free, but you need a ticket. Get one at the information desk, or reserve online in advance (there's no fee). It's a good idea to make reservations between March and August.

The hour-long jaunt starts with a cheesy film where you'll hear a lot about 'E Pluribus Unum' (Out of Many, One) and how the US government works. Then staff members lead you to the good stuff.

Inside the halls and ornate chambers you really get a feel for the power-playing side of DC. The centerpiece of the Capitol is the magnificent Rotunda (the area under the dome). It's 96ft in diameter and 180ft high. A Constantino Brumidi frieze around the rim replays more than 400 years of American history. Look up into the eye of the dome for the *Apotheosis of Washington*, an allegorical fresco by Brumidi. Alas, the dome is getting a facelift until early 2017, so parts of it are obscured.

The Capitol also contains sculptures of two famous residents per state. Many of these are found in the Hall of Statues. You might recognize likenesses of George Washington (Virginia) and Ronald Reagan (California), less so Uriah Milton Rose (Arkansas). After the tour, swing by the Exhibition Hall and check out the plaster model for the *Statue of Freedom* that crowns the dome.

Note you cannot bring food or drinks inside the building. Security staff will make you get rid of them before entering.

Capitol Grounds

The Capitol's sweeping lawns owe their charm to famed landscape architect Frederick Law Olmsted, who also designed New York City's Central Park. During the Civil War, soldiers camped in Capitol halls and stomped around its lawns. In 1874, spring cleaning was in order: Olmsted added lush greenery and majestic terraces, creating an elegant landscape that gave rise to over 4000 trees from all 50 states and many countries. Northwest of the Capitol is the charming 1879 **grotto** (Map p300), a red-brick hexagon with black-iron gates and an interior well. Its official name is the Summer House, so called because this is where women back in the day came to stay cool in their big hoop dresses during the warmer months.

At the base of Capitol Hill, the **Capitol Reflecting Pool** (Map p294) echoes the larger Reflecting Pool by the Lincoln Memorial at the Mall's western end. The Capitol pool actually caps the I-39 freeway, which dips under the Mall here. The ornate **Ulysses S Grant Memorial** (Map p294) dominates the pool's eastern side, showing the general in horseback action.

VISITING THE HOUSE & SENATE FLOORS

To watch Congress in session, you need a separate visitor pass. US citizens must get one from their representative or senator; foreign visitors should take their passports to the House and Senate Appointment Desks on the upper level. Congressional committee hearings are actually more interesting (and substantive) if you care about what's being debated; check for a schedule, locations and to see if they're open to the public (they often are) at www.house.gov and www.senate.gov. Prepare to go through rigid security; you'll have to store most of your belongings before entering the chambers.

The Army, Navy, Marine Corps and Air Force bands take turns performing on the steps of the Capitol on weekdays (except Thursday) June through August. Look for them at 8pm on the West Front.

LESTER LEFKOWITZ / GETTY IMAGES ©

TOP SIGHT
LIBRARY OF CONGRESS

The world's largest library – with 29 million books and counting – awes in both scope and design. Its mission: to further the progress of knowledge and creativity. Not a small undertaking! Films, photographs and manuscripts join all those books. A browse through turns up everything from Thomas Jefferson's dusty tomes to 500-year-old maps to free concerts.

The library spreads through three buildings. The centerpiece is the 1897 Jefferson Building, where you can wander around the spectacular Great Hall, done up in stained glass, marble and mosaics of mythical characters. Multimedia kiosks provide the minutest details of it all.

Pick up a map at the entrance, which will take you to sweet spots such as the Gutenberg Bible (c 1455) on the 1st floor. The 2nd floor holds Thomas Jefferson's round library (well, a reconstruction, though several of the books are really his), the Waldseemuller World Map from 1507 (the first to show America) and the overlook into the Main Reading Room (famed setting for the film *All the President's Men*). Guides lead free 45-minute tours from the ground floor at 10:30am, 11:30am, 12:30pm, 1:30pm, 2:30pm and 3:30pm that take it all in.

A groovy underground tunnel runs from the Jefferson Building to the **Madison Building** (Map p300; 1st St SE, btwn Independence Ave & C St SE), where the Madison Cafe (open 8:30am to 3:30pm weekdays) hides on the 6th floor and offers killer views of the city. Room 140 is where staff members issue library cards to anyone who wants to do research. The **Adams Building** (Map p300; 2nd St SE) is also connected by underground tunnel (as is the Capitol Visitor Center). Free concerts, lectures, films and other events take place throughout the complex daily; check www.loc.gov/loc/events.

DON'T MISS...

- Great Hall
- 1507 Waldseemuller World Map
- Main Reading Room overlook
- Thomas Jefferson's library
- Gutenberg Bible

PRACTICALITIES

- Map p300
- www.loc.gov
- 1st St SE
- 8:30am-4:30pm Mon-Sat
- M Capitol South

TOP SIGHT
UNITED STATES HOLOCAUST MEMORIAL MUSEUM

For a deep understanding of the Holocaust, this harrowing museum is a must-see. It gives visitors the identity card of a single Holocaust victim, whose story gets revealed as you take a winding route into a past marked by ghettos, rail cars and death camps. It also shows the flip side of human nature, documenting the risks many citizens took to help the persecuted.

Design

James Ingo Freed designed the extraordinary building in 1993, and its stark facade and steel-and-glass interior echo the death camps themselves. Look up at the skylight in the Hall of Witness when you enter the building. Many survivors say this reminds them of the sky above the camps. For them it was symbolic, the only thing the Nazis couldn't control.

Permanent Exhibit

The permanent exhibit presents the Holocaust's history chronologically from 1933 to 1945. Galleries span three floors and use more than 900 artifacts, 70 video monitors, historic film footage and eyewitness testimonies.

Start on the 4th floor, which is titled 'Nazi Assault' and covers the period between 1933 and 1939. Watch propaganda videos of Hitler, Goebbels and others, and learn how the Nazis used modern techniques such as video to craft their message to sway citizens.

The 3rd floor is 'The Final Solution,' covering the period between 1940 and 1945. Here you'll see a rail car used to transport people to the camps, a wooden bunk bed from Auschwitz and a harrowing scale model of Crematorium II at Auschwitz. There's also a listening room where you can hear recordings of people speaking about their experiences in the camps.

The 2nd floor is the 'Last Chapter,' where old film footage shows the camps' liberation, and videos flicker across screens illuminating individual survivors telling their stories. From here you come out into the candlelit Hall of Remembrance, a sanctuary for quiet reflection. The Wexner Center is likewise on this floor, featuring exhibits on other genocides around the world. The museum is a major advocate against, and information clearing house on, ongoing genocides such as in Darfur. Here's something you'll learn: the word genocide didn't exist until 1944. That's when Raphael Lemkin, a Jewish refugee from Poland, coined it to describe what was happening in German-occupied Europe.

If you have young children, a gentler kids' installation – 'Remember the Children: Daniel's Story' – is on the 1st floor.

Entry Tickets

Same-day passes to view the permanent exhibit are required March through August, available at the desk on the 1st floor. The passes allow entrance at a designated time. Arrive early because they do run out. Better yet, reserve tickets in advance via the museum's website for a $1 surcharge.

DON'T MISS...

- Hall of Remembrance
- Skylight in the Hall of Witness
- Propaganda videos
- Survivor testimonies
- Wexner Center

PRACTICALITIES

- Map p300
- ☎202-488-0400
- www.ushmm.org
- 100 Raoul Wallenberg Pl SW
- ⌚10am-5:20pm, to 6:20pm Mon-Fri Apr & May
- Ⓜ Smithsonian

THE SUPREME COURT'S CONTROVERSIAL ARCHITECTURE

The issue of separating church and state is one of the main battlefronts in US culture wars, and Supreme Court architecture has often been in the middle of the cross fire.

The sculpture *Justice the Guardian of Liberty*, on the east (ie back) pediment of the court's exterior, displays Moses bearing two tablets. In addition, an interior frieze in the main courtroom also depicts Moses, again with tablets in hand. This is proof, according to some, that the Ten Commandments should be displayed in American courthouses and schools, a traditional aim of the anti–separation of church and state movement.

The problem is, these claims take Moses out of artistic context. In the exterior sculpture he is presented with Solon of Athens and Confucius; the figures are meant to represent great lawgivers of 'the East' and Moses' tablets are deliberately left blank. In the interior frieze, Moses' tablets are numbered, Roman style, I to X, but Adolph Weinman, who designed the frieze, told the court (his letter is kept in court archives) that the numbers represent the Bill of Rights, not the Ten Commandments.

Moses is also represented with 17 other lawgivers in a frieze that runs along the north and south walls of the main courtroom. Included among these lawgivers are Hammurabi, Napoleon and the Prophet Muhammad. The Council on American Islamic Relations has asked for the Muhammad depiction to be removed, as Islamic law forbids depictions of the prophet, but that request was turned down by Justice William Rehnquist, who argued the depiction is a respectful one meant to honor Muhammad's jurisprudence.

SIGHTS

Capitol Hill

CAPITOL LANDMARK

See p106.

LIBRARY OF CONGRESS LIBRARY

See p108.

SUPREME COURT LANDMARK

Map p300 (202-479-3030; www.supremecourt.gov; 1 1st St NE; h9am-4:30pm Mon-Fri; mCapitol South) F The highest court in the USA sits in a pseudo-Greek temple that you enter through 13,000lb bronze doors. Arrive early to watch arguments (periodic Monday through Wednesday October to April). You can visit the permanent exhibits and the building's five-story, marble-and-bronze, spiral staircase year-round. On days when court is not in session you also can hear lectures (every hour on the half-hour) in the courtroom.

To attend arguments, lines form out front by the court steps from 8am. There are usually two queues: one for people who wish to sit through the entire argument, and another for people who want to observe the court in session for 10 to 15 minutes. Bring quarters for lockers; you're not allowed to take anything into the courtroom.

When the building was erected in 1935, some justices felt it was too large and didn't properly reflect the subdued influence of the nine justices within. The neoclassical design was meant to evoke a Greek temple. The seated figures in front of the building represent the female Contemplation of Justice and the male Guardian of Law; panels on the front doors depict the history of jurisprudence. The interior grand corridor and Great Hall are no less impressive. Downstairs is an exhibit on the history of the court. Friezes within the courtroom also depict legal history and heroes, which has caused no little debate among Americans. The separation of church and state gets muddled even here.

FOLGER SHAKESPEARE LIBRARY LIBRARY

Map p300 (www.folger.edu; 201 E Capitol St SE; 10am-5pm Mon-Sat, noon-5pm Sun; ; Capitol South) FREE Bard-o-philes will be all of a passion here, as the library holds the largest collection of old Billy's works in the world. Stroll through the Great Hall to see Elizabethan artifacts, paintings, etchings and manuscripts. The highlight is a rare First Folio that you can leaf through digitally. The evocative theater on-site stages Shakespearean plays.

Most of the items are housed in the library's reading rooms, closed to all but scholars, except on Shakespeare's birthday

(April 23) and during Saturday tours (noon to 1pm; book online in advance). Docents also give hour-long tours (11am and 3pm Monday through Friday, 11am and 1pm Saturday, 1pm Sunday) of the building and exhibitions; no reservations are required for those. An Elizabethan garden, full of flowers and herbs cultivated during Shakespeare's time, blooms on the building's eastern end.

The Folger building itself is notable for being the most prominent example of the modernist-classical hybrid movement that swept Washington, DC, during the Great Depression. Jokingly referred to as 'Stark Deco,' it tends to inspire strong feelings: lovers say it elegantly pays homage to Greek classicism and 20th-century modernism, while haters say it ruins both styles.

NATIONAL PUBLIC RADIO BUILDING

(www.npr.org/about-npr/177066727/visit-npr; 1111 N Capitol St NE; ⌚tours 11am Mon-Fri; MNoMa) FREE Fans of *Morning Edition* and *All Things Considered* can see where the magic happens at National Public Radio's eco-friendly headquarters. Hour-long tours peek into the newsroom and a high-tech production studio. The guides – usually former employees – entertain with insider stories. Reservations required. The on-site shop sells gifts such as the Nina Totin' bag (named for longtime reporter Nina Totenberg).

SEWALL-BELMONT HOUSE MUSEUM

Map p300 (☎202-546-1210; www.sewallbelmont.org; 144 Constitution Ave NE; admission $8; ⌚tours 11am, 1pm & 3pm Thu-Sat; MUnion Station, Capitol South) The District lacks a specific monument and museum to the women's rights movement, but it does have this historic house – headquarters of the National Woman's Party since 1929, and 43-year residence of the party's legendary founder, suffragette Alice Paul. Paul spearheaded efforts to gain the vote for women (enshrined in the 19th Amendment) and wrote the Equal Rights Amendment. Docents show off historical exhibits, portraits, sculpture and a library that celebrates feminist heroes. Book online a day or so in advance.

The entrance is on 2nd St, next to the Hart Senate Office Building.

UNION STATION LANDMARK

Map p300 (www.unionstationdc.com; 50 Massachusetts Ave NE; MUnion Station) DC's main rail and bus hub, a 1907 beaux-arts beauty designed by Daniel Burnham, is an eye popper. The Grand Concourse is patterned after the Roman Baths of Diocletian and is awash in marble and gold filigree. Check out the legionnaire statues atop the arches that span the entrances and exits. Although shields are strategically placed across their waists, the guys' man-bits are supposed to be anatomically correct, but rumor holds that only one was built that way.

Besides being an architectural gem, Union Station also has an arcade of shops and fast-food restaurants. A big structural renovation is ongoing; expect lots of scaffolding in the interim.

NATIONAL POSTAL MUSEUM MUSEUM

Map p300 (www.postalmuseum.si.edu; 2 Massachusetts Ave NE; ⌚10am-5:30pm; 👪; MUnion Station) FREE The Smithsonian-run Postal Museum is way cooler than you might think. Level 1 has exhibits on postal history from the Pony Express to modern times, where you'll see antique mail planes and touching old letters from soldiers and pioneers. Level 2 holds the world's largest stamp collection. Join the stamp geeks pulling out drawers and snapping photos of the world's rarest stamps (the Ben Franklin Z Grill!), or start your own collection choosing among thousands of free international stamps (Guyana, Congo, Cambodia...).

The museum is kid-friendly and hosts story times and card-making workshops. It

STREET ADDRESSES

In Capitol Hill, different streets in close proximity can have the same letter, depending on whether they are north or south of E Capitol St (ie A St NE is just two blocks north of A St SE). Pay attention to the directional (NE or SE) to avoid confusion.

LOCAL KNOWLEDGE

LIBRARY OF CONGRESS FREEBIES

The Library of Congress offers free lectures, concerts and other events throughout its multi-building complex each day. Appearances by famous actors, Nobel laureates and world musicians pepper the schedule. Check www.loc.gov/loc/events.

also has a stamp shop where you can browse the catalog of oddball US Postal Service stamps and have the 'philatelic clerk' (excellent job title) fetch your selection. Many of the stamps are hot off the press and aren't available elsewhere.

TAFT MEMORIAL CARILLON MONUMENT

Map p300 (Constitution Ave NW, btwn New Jersey Ave & 1st St NW) What is that chiming you hear every quarter-hour? It's the 27 bells of the Taft Memorial Carillon, built to honor Senator Robert A Taft from Ohio in 1959. The tower is part of the Capitol grounds.

NATIONAL JAPANESE AMERICAN MEMORIAL MONUMENT

Map p300 (www.njamf.com; btwn Louisiana Ave, New Jersey Ave & D St NW; 24hr; M Union Station) Tucked back from the road and providing a peaceful sanctuary, the memorial centers on a statue of two cranes bound with barbed wire. During WWII, thousands of West Coast Japanese American citizens were held in internment camps as suspected 'enemy aliens.' Even as this discrimination occurred under government mandate, hundreds of their relatives enrolled in the all–Japanese American 442nd Infantry Regiment, which went on to become the war's most decorated American combat unit. The memorial honors both the soldiers and interred civilians.

LINCOLN PARK PARK

Map p300 (E Capitol St, btwn 11th & 13th Sts NE; M Eastern Market) Lincoln Park is the lively center of Capitol Hill's east end. Joggers and stroller-pushing families zip past the **Emancipation Memorial** (Map p300; Lincoln Park; M Eastern Market), a statue of a chained slave kneeling at Lincoln's feet. Freed black slaves raised the funds to erect it in 1876, but the slave's supplicant position makes it DC's most bizarrely uncomfortable monument. Across the park, the **Mary McLeod Bethune Memorial** (Map p300; Lincoln Park) is DC's first statue of a black woman. Bethune was an educator and founder of the National Council of Negro Women.

Southeast DC

MARINE BARRACKS BUILDING

Map p300 (www.barracks.marines.mil; cnr 8th & I Sts SE; parade 8:45pm Fri May-Aug; M Eastern Market) FREE The 'Eighth and Eye Marines' are on largely ceremonial duty at the nation's oldest Marine Corps post. Most famously, this is the home barracks of the Marine Corps Band, once headed by John Philip Sousa, king of the military march, who was born nearby at 636 G St SE. On Friday evenings in summer the 1¼-hour ceremonial drill parade featuring the band, drum and bugle corps and silent drill team is a must-see. Make reservations online weeks in advance; tickets become available March 1.

You can also show up for general admission at 8pm when they distribute any unclaimed tickets. In addition, the band performs on summer Tuesdays at 7pm at the Marine Corps War Memorial by Arlington National Cemetery; no reservations are required for that one.

YARDS PARK PARK

Map p300 (www.yardspark.org; 355 Water St SE; 7am-2hr past sunset; M Navy Yard) The riverside green space is just down the road from the Nationals' stadium. There are shaded tables by the water, a wooden boardwalk, fountains and a funky modernist bridge that looks like a giant, open-faced plastic straw. Look left and you'll see ships docked at the Navy Yard. Several new restaurants and an excellent brewery at the park's edge ensure you won't hunger or thirst.

FREDERICK DOUGLASS NATIONAL HISTORIC SITE HISTORIC SITE

(877-444-6777; www.nps.gov/frdo; 1411 W St SE; 9am-5pm Apr-Oct, to 4:30pm Nov-Mar; M Anacostia to B2 bus) FREE Escaped slave, abolitionist, author and statesman Frederick Douglass occupied this beautifully sited hilltop house from 1878 until his death in 1895. Original furnishings, books, photographs and other personal belongings paint a compelling portrait of both the private and public life of this great man. Keep an eye out for his wire-rim eyeglasses on his roll-top desk. Visits into the home – aka Cedar Hill – are by guided tour only.

Tour times are 9am, 12:15pm, 1:15pm, 3pm and 3:30pm (plus 4pm from April to October). It's best to reserve a ticket online (for a $1.50 fee) at least a day in advance, though unreserved tickets are available at the site's visitor center on a first-come basis.

The B2 bus runs from the Metro station to a stop right in front of Cedar Hill. However, you can't catch the return bus from

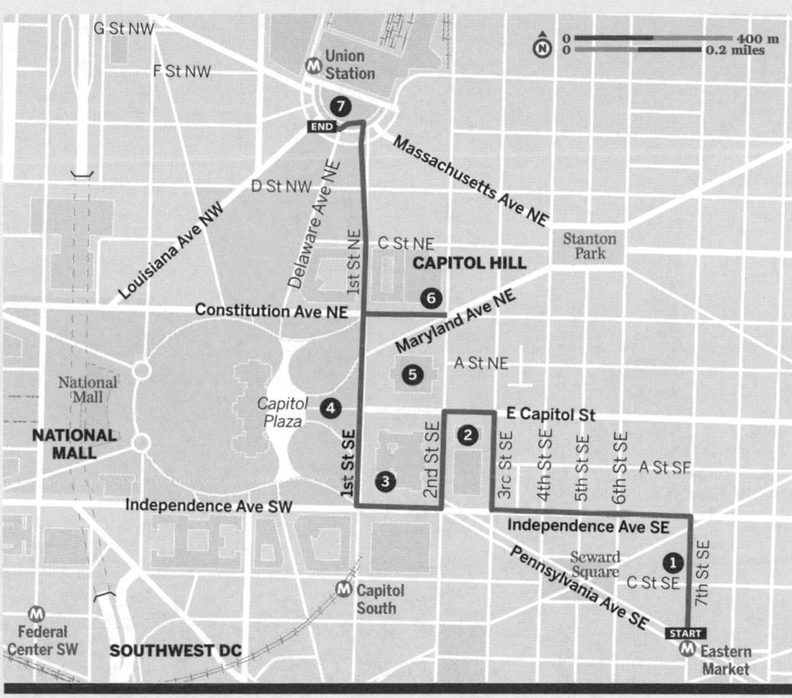

Neighborhood Walk
Cap Hill Crawl

START EASTERN MARKET METRO
END UNION STATION
LENGTH 2 MILES; THREE TO FOUR HOURS

Start by fueling up at **1 Eastern Market** (p125; about 20m north of Eastern Market Metro). This is the heart of Capitol Hill: a neighborhood hangout, covered bazaar and just great place to soak up local flavor.

Walk west on Independence Ave SE toward the Capitol Dome, which is hard to miss. At 3rd St SE, detour a couple of blocks north to the **2 Folger Shakespeare Library** (p110). The building, jokingly referred to as 'Stark Deco,' holds the world's largest collection of Shakespeare's works, along with cool exhibits. Get ready for a literary comparison, because our next stop is the **3 Library of Congress** (p108). Pop in for a guided tour of a building that's almost as impressive as its mission: to gather all the knowledge in the world under one roof.

Now go underground into the **4 Capitol Visitor Center** (p106). You can easily spend two or more hours here learning about the seat of the legislative branch of government (ie Congress). Across the street the government's judiciary branch – the **5 Supreme Court** (p110) – rises up in Greek temple-esque splendor. If you happen to stumble upon the day of an interesting case, you may find that your tour has come to an abrupt, albeit serendipitous end – watching verbal arguments conducted in front of the nine justices is an opportunity that shouldn't be passed up.

Make another little detour to **6 Sewell-Belmont House** (p111), home base of the National Woman's Party since 1929, and 43-year residence of the party's legendary founder, suffragette Alice Paul. US women: she's why you can vote.

Return to 1st St NE and head north until you get to **7 Union Station** (p111). This is one of the masterpieces of the early-20th-century beaux-arts movement, patterned after the Roman Baths of Diocletian. We like to think even an emperor would be awed by the sights just traversed.

1

3

STEPHEN J BOITANO/GETTY IMAGES ©

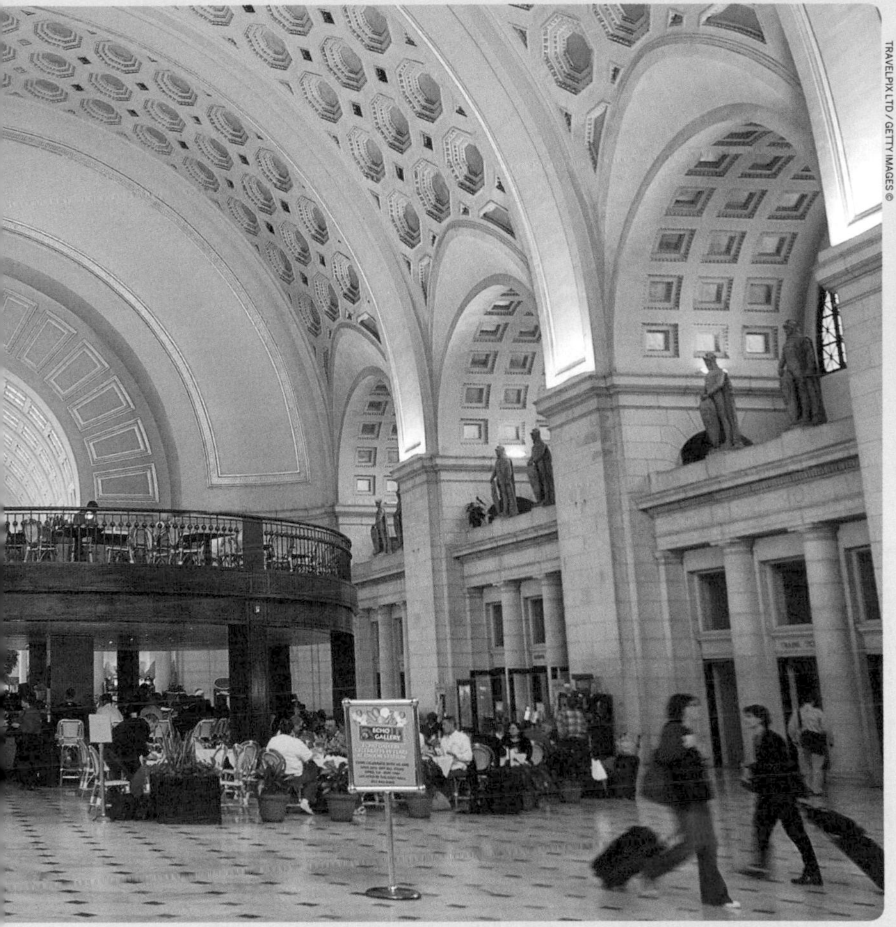

TRAVELPIX LTD / GETTY IMAGES ©

1. Union Station (p111)
Union Station is one of the best examples of the US beaux-arts movement.

2. Supreme Court (p110)
Built in 1935, the Supreme Court's grand, neoclassical design was meant to evoke a Greek temple.

3. Eastern Market (p125)
Going strong since 1873, the market is a local favorite for food and crafts.

FLYSNOW / GETTY IMAGES ©

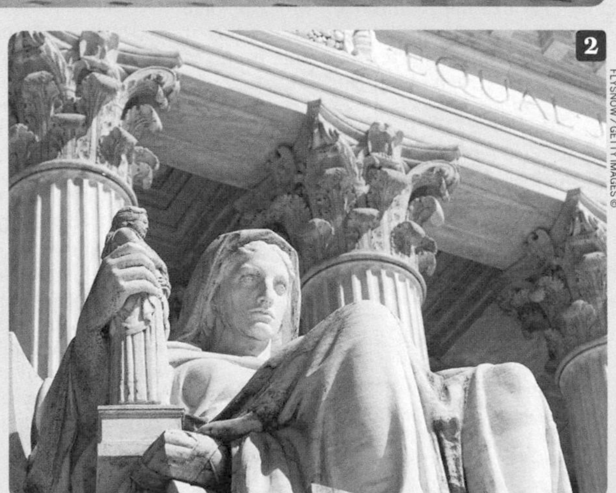

the house. Instead, walk three blocks north to Good Hope Rd and get the B2 bus to the Metro there.

ANACOSTIA MUSEUM MUSEUM

(☎202-633-4820; www.anacostia.si.edu; 1901 Fort Pl SE; ⏰10am-5pm; Ⓜ Anacostia to bus W2, W3) FREE This Smithsonian museum has good rotating exhibitions on the African American experience in the USA. They typically focus on art (quilts of a certain region; landscape paintings by an overlooked artist) or history (the first black baseball teams in the area; a slave family's story). The museum also serves as a community hall for the surrounding neighborhood of Anacostia. Call ahead, as it often closes between installations.

It's easiest to get here by car or taxi. From the Metro station, take the 'Local' exit to Howard Rd and transfer to the W2 or W3 bus. The W2 runs during rush hours, the W3 every 30 minutes.

THEARC ARTS CENTER

(www.thearcdc.org; 1901 Mississippi Ave SE; Ⓜ Southern Ave) The Town Hall Education, Arts and Recreation Campus (THEARC) has been a cornerstone for community redevelopment in River East/Far Southeast. A multipurpose community center, arts education campus and performance space, the building was the first one of its kind in what was then a neglected area of town. If you want a sense of the pulse of contemporary African American DC, catch a show or see one of the center's frequent special exhibitions.

Thearc's impact has really brought some of the surrounding blocks back to life. It is about three-quarters of a mile from the closest Metro; it's best to drive here.

11TH STREET BRIDGE PARK PARK

Map p300 (www.bridgepark.org; 11th St SE & riverfront; Ⓜ Navy Yard) FREE It won't come to fruition until 2018 or so, but keep an eye on the space at 11th St SE and the Anacostia River. The city is converting the piers from an old bridge into a mod park that will span the water, linking touristy DC to the neglected Anacostia neighborhood. Play spaces, public art, urban agriculture and kayak and canoe launches will all be part of the $45-million project.

LOCAL KNOWLEDGE

HAINS POINT

The southern tip of East Potomac Park that juts out into the river is called Hains Point. Lots of folks come here to picnic, and the spot provides great views of the planes taking off from nearby Reagan National Airport.

Southwest DC

Washington's smallest quadrant consists of Smithsonian spillover from the Mall, the federal center (which includes several executive-branch department buildings) and the two residential neighborhoods of Bellevue and Southwest Waterfront (which is undergoing extensive redevelopment).

UNITED STATES HOLOCAUST MEMORIAL MUSEUM MUSEUM

See p109.

BUREAU OF ENGRAVING & PRINTING LANDMARK

Map p294 (www.moneyfactory.gov; cnr 14th & C Sts SW; ⏰9-10:45am, 12:30-3:45pm & 5-6pm Mon-Fri Mar-Aug, reduced hours Sep-Feb; Ⓜ Smithsonian) FREE Cha-ching! The nation's paper currency is designed and printed here. Guides lead 40-minute tours during which you peer down onto the work floor where millions of dollars roll off the presses and get cut (by guillotine!). In peak season (March to August), timed entry tickets are required. Get in line early at the **ticket kiosk** (Map p294; Raoul Wallenberg Pl, aka 15th St). It opens at 8am.

During non-peak season (September through February), no tickets are required and you can come in through the main entrance at 14th and C Sts; tours take place every 15 minutes from 9am to 10:45am and from 12:30pm to 2pm.

EAST POTOMAC PARK PARK

Map p300 (Ohio Dr SW; Ⓜ Smithsonian) Although only a stone's throw from the National Mall, as far as tourists go, East Potomac Park may as well be in Siberia. The pleasant, green, cherry-blossom-lined expanse is a lovely spot for walking, fishing and general gamboling. A 5-mile paved trail, great for biking or in-line skating, runs around the park's circumference, paralleling Ohio Dr. The East Potomac Park golf course lies at the center.

LOCAL KNOWLEDGE

CONGRESSIONAL CEMETERY: WHERE THE DEAD MEET THE DOGS

It is jarring the first time you see a dachshund lower its haunches and poo right next to a tombstone. Some people say it's disrespectful. Others say the dogs saved Washington, DC's **Congressional Cemetery** (Map p300; www.congressionalcemetery.org; 1801 E St SE; ⏲sunrise-sunset; Ⓜ Stadium Armory).

Founded in 1807, the burial ground had become a forlorn place of crack deals and toppled monuments by the 1990s. But then a group of locals had an idea: turn the graveyard into a members-only dog park, and use the fees to restore the site.

It's now a lovely spot to ramble, and the cemetery has done a fab job documenting the dead. Pick up maps at the entrance (at 18th and E Sts) to find famed civil rights heroes, global explorers, beer brewers, War of 1812 officers, and loads of other people you should know. Favorite spirits to seek out:

➡ Mathew Brady: The Civil War photographer is known as the father of photojournalism. He took the picture of Lincoln that's now on the $5 bill.

➡ Belva Lockwood: She ran for US president in 1884 as the Equal Rights Party's candidate. Yes, she was aware women didn't have voting rights at the time. She still got 4000 votes.

➡ J Edgar Hoover: The infamous FBI director has a grave that's surrounded by a fence and faces DC's jail.

Just watch out for loping black labs, stick-chasing Yorkies and other members of the K9 Corps patrolling the stony rows. Incidentally, it's a year-long waiting list to join the pack.

The park sits on a finger of land that extends southward from the Tidal Basin into the Potomac River. On foot, you can access it by following trails that lead from the Thomas Jefferson Memorial under the bridges. If you drive out this way, you can park on the shoulder of Ohio Dr.

WOMEN'S TITANIC MEMORIAL — MEMORIAL

Map p300 (waterfront & P St SW; Ⓜ Waterfront) Set in Waterside Park, the red-granite memorial honors the men who sacrificed their lives to save the women and children aboard the sinking ship. The statue's outstretched arms look a lot like Kate Winslet's pose in the 1997 film *Titanic,* but the sculptor carved it in 1931.

FORT LESLEY J MCNAIR — BUILDING

Map p300 (P St & 3rd Ave SW; Ⓜ Waterfront) The army post at Fort McNair was established in 1791. The British burned it in 1814. The Lincoln-assassination conspirators were hanged here in 1865. McNair now houses the National Defense University and National War College (closed to the public).

LAW HOUSE — LANDMARK

Map p300 (1252 6th St SW; Ⓜ Waterfront) This 1784 Federalist mansion was the home of Thomas Law and Eliza Parke Custis, oldest granddaughter of Martha Washington. It's now part of a housing co-op.

BENJAMIN BANNEKER PARK — PARK

Map p300 (cnr 10th & G Sts SW; Ⓜ L'Enfant Plaza) This park honors Benjamin Banneker, a free black, self-taught astronomer, mathematician and one of the original surveyors of the 10-sq-mile plot that would define the District. A grassy little circle near the waterfront, the park is swiped by a tangle of highways, about a half-mile from the Metro.

AMERICAN VETERANS DISABLED FOR LIFE MEMORIAL — MEMORIAL

Map p300 (www.avdlm.org; 150 Washington Ave SW; Ⓜ Federal Center SW) Oddly situated in a triangular plaza between drab federal buildings and busy roadways, this subtle memorial opened in late 2014. It's dedicated to the more than four million US soldiers who have returned home with life-changing disabilities. It features a still, star-shaped fountain, glass-etched walls and benches for contemplation.

EATING

Capitol Hill has long been an outpost for the DC burger bar, the sort of unpretentious spot where you roll up your sleeves, slather on some ketchup and – 'Sorry, yes, Senator? I'll be back on the Hill right away! Damn, there goes my lunch.' Hip, upscale spots also have arrived in the neighborhood, especially along Pennsylvania Ave, Barracks Row (8th St SE, near the Marine Barracks) and around the Navy Yard (near the baseball park). H St NE, east of Union Station, has also seen action. The formerly beat-up section of town is being transformed by a glut of fun, offbeat restaurants and bars clustered between 10th and 14th Sts NE.

Capitol Hill

★**TOKI UNDERGROUND** ASIAN $

Map p300 (☎202-388-3086; www.tokiunderground.com; 1234 H St NE; mains $10-12; ⏰11:30am-2:30pm & 5-10pm Mon-Thu, to midnight Fri & Sat; 🚌X2 from Union Station) Spicy ramen noodles and dumplings sum up wee Toki's menu. Steaming pots obscure the busy chefs, while diners slurp and sigh contentedly. The eatery doesn't take reservations and there's typically a wait. Take the opportunity to explore surrounding bars; Toki will text when your table is ready. The restaurant isn't signposted; look for the Pug bar, and Toki is above it.

DANGEROUSLY DELICIOUS PIES AMERICAN $

Map p300 (www.dangerouspiesdc.com; 1339 H St NE; slices $6.50-7.50; ⏰11am-midnight Mon-Thu, to 3:30am Fri, 9am-3:30am Sat, 9am-10pm Sun; 📝; 🚌X2 from Union Station) The eponymous wares come in both sweet and savory varieties, which means you can – without shame – make a meal of pie. Pull up a retro chair in the cozy, pine-green-walled room and scan the chalkboard for options such as vegan vegetable pie, pork barbecue pie and the mega-rich, cookie-infused Baltimore Bomb. Bonus: they serve alcohol to go with the flaky goodness.

GOOD STUFF EATERY BURGERS $

Map p300 (www.goodstuffeatery.com; 303 Pennsylvania Ave SE; burgers $7-9; ⏰11:30am-11pm Mon-Sat; 👪; Ⓜ Capitol South, Eastern Market) 🍃 Spike Mendelsohn (of *Top Chef* TV fame) is the cook behind Good Stuff, a

Local Life

A Local's Day on Capitol Hill

Pretend you're a resident of one of the brownstone homes along the red-brick sidewalks and shop for seafood at Eastern Market or browse the Flea Market's curios. Have breakfast anytime in a dive bar, then stop by the rambling, double-stacked bookshop. Knock back a beer across from the Marine Barracks and wave to neighbors at the riverside park.

1 The Dive Bar: Tune Inn

Tune Inn (Map p300; 331 Pennsylvania Ave SE; mains $7-14; ⏰8am-2am Sun-Fri, to 3am Sat; Ⓜ Capitol South, Eastern Market) has been around for decades and is where the neighborhood's older residents come to down Budweisers. The mounted deer heads and antler chandelier set the mood, as greasy-spoon grub and all-day breakfasts get gobbled in the vinyl-backed booths.

2 Capitol Hill Books

Rambling Capitol Hill Books (p124) has so many used tomes they're stacked two deep on the shelves. They're even stacked in the bathroom. Floors creak and classical music plays as neighborhood bibliophiles sift through the whopping selection.

3 Eastern Market

Eastern Market (p125) is the true heart of Capitol Hill. The covered arcade holds bakery, dairy, butcher, blue-crab-and-shrimp company, and produce vendors. It's not that large...until the weekend, when artisans and farmers join the fun and the market spills onto the street.

4 Flea Market Finds

On weekends the Flea Market (p125) sets up across from Eastern Market in the Hines schoolyard, doubling the browsing acreage. Vendors sell cool art, antiques, furniture, maps, prints, global wares, clothing and curios. Sunday is the busier day, with more stalls.

5 Street Art at the Fridge

First you have to find the **Fridge** (Map p300; www.thefridgedc.com; 516½ 8th St

Inside the Eastern Market (p125)

SE, rear alley; ⌚noon-8pm Wed-Sat, to 5pm Sun; Ⓜ Eastern Market), a friendly gallery specializing in street art. Follow the murals and graffiti into the alley beside the oyster shop. The space hosts music and theater performances, too.

6 Beer at Lola's Barracks

Lola's Barracks Bar & Grill (Map p300; www.lolasbarracksbarandgrill.com; 711 8th St SE; ⌚5pm-2am Mon & Tue, 11am-2am Wed-Thu & Sun, to 3am Fri & Sat; Ⓜ Eastern Market) sits across the street from the Marine Barracks, hence the name. Cap Hill professionals drink wine and craft beer in the snug, low-lit main room. Check out the old neighborhood photos hanging on the walls.

7 Dinner at Rose's Luxury

Locals line up for shabby-chic Rose's Luxury (p121), which offers a small, changing menu of 10 or so plates a day. The pork sausage, habanero and lychee salad is the salty-sweet dish on everyone's lips.

8 River Views at Yards Park

Lovely Yards Park (p112) is a sculpted public space with a wooden boardwalk, excellent river views, a funky modernist bridge and a mini tidal pool that is popular with neighborhood families on summer evenings.

popular burgers-shakes-and-fries spot. You can top off fries at the 'dipping bar' of various sauces, and the toasted-marshmallow milkshake comes with an honest-to-god toasted marshmallow. The ambience is that of a fast-food joint, and seats are at a premium weekend nights, when Cap Hill youth descend on the place.

JIMMY T'S DINER **$**

Map p300 (501 E Capitol St SE; mains $6-10; ⌚6:30am-3pm Tue-Fri, from 8am Sat & Sun; 🚼; Ⓜ Eastern Market) Jimmy's is a neighborhood joint of the old school, where folks come in with their dogs, cram in to read the *Post,* have a burger or a coffee or an omelet (breakfast all day, by the way), and basically be themselves. If you're hungover on Sunday and in Cap Hill, come here for a greasy cure. Cash only.

BOLD BITE AMERICAN **$**

Map p300 (www.boldbite.net; 50 Massachusetts Ave NE, lower level; mains $5-7; ⌚10am-9pm Mon-Sat, noon-6pm Sun; Ⓜ Union Station) Located in Union Station's lower-level food court, Bold Bite is a purveyor of local specialty the half-smoke (basically a bigger, smokier hot dog). You can get it classic style with onions, mustard and chili, but Bold Bite also riffs on the genre with a Mexican style (topped by guacamole and cheese) and Asian style (slaw and hot sauce).

PITANGO GELATO GELATERIA **$**

Map p300 (www.pitangogelato.com; 660 Pennsylvania Ave SE; gelato $4-6; ⌚11:30am-9pm Mon-Thu, to 10:30pm Fri, 10am-10:30pm Sat, to 10pm Sun, closed Mon in winter; Ⓜ Eastern Market) The DC mini-chain scoops terrific all-natural gelato, but the sorbet is the standout. Fruity flavors made from Haitian mangoes, white grapefruits and Bosc pears from a nearby farm explode on the tongue. Staff are sweet (pun!) about letting you try lots of samples.

TAYLOR GOURMET DELI **$**

Map p300 (www.taylorgourmet.com; 1116 H St NE; sandwiches $8-12; ⌚11am-9pm Sun-Thu, to 3:30am Fri & Sat; 🚌 H St shuttle) When you just need a good sandwich, Taylor has got you covered. For about $11 you can walk out of here with a foot of excellent anything between two pieces of bread, dressed with nicely shredded lettuce and brilliant oil and vinegar. We race here for the Race Street – turkey, prosciutto, pesto and mozzarella. Several other branches dot the DC area.

ATLAS ROOM AMERICAN **$$**

Map p300 (☎202-388-4020; www.theatlasroom.com; 1015 H St NE; mains $21-25; ⌚5:30-9:30pm Tue-Thu, to 10pm Fri & Sat, 5-9pm Sun; 🚌 X2 from Union Station) Set in a snug, candle-shimmering room, Atlas is a neighborhood favorite on edgy H St. The bistro takes cues from classical French and Italian gastronomy but blends them in approachable American ways using seasonal ingredients. In summer you might enjoy crab fritters, while in winter a braised daube of beef will melt your tongue (in a good way!).

MONTMARTRE FRENCH **$$**

Map p300 (☎202-544-1244; www.montmartredc.com; 327 7th St SE; mains $19-27; ⌚11:30am-2:30pm & 5:30-10pm Tue-Fri, 10:30am-3pm & 5:30-10:30pm Sat, 10:30am-3pm & 5:30-9pm Sun; Ⓜ Eastern Market) Montmartre is the place French expats take their friends to give them a taste of home. Great wines, very fine steak, silky homemade pâté and delightful desserts emerge from clanging pans in the kitchen. The cozy space is cluttered in a *maman*'s-dining-room kinda way, and the overall vibe is much more neighborhood spot than highbrow restaurant.

SEVENTH HILL PIZZA PIZZA **$$**

Map p300 (www.montmartredc.com/seventhhill; 327 7th St SE; pizzas $11-17; ⌚11:30am-2:30pm & 5-10pm Tue-Fri, 11:30am-10pm Sat, noon-9pm Sun; Ⓜ Eastern Market) It's just blistered, thin-crust pizza, but it's soooo addictive. Each pie is named for a local street or park, like the 'Potomac Ave,' topped with Felino salami and arugula, or the 'Maryland Ave' with egg, pesto and pecorino. Seventh Hill is the sibling of genial Montmartre next door, and some of the French wines find their way over to accompany the pizzas.

ETHIOPIC ETHIOPIAN **$$**

Map p300 (☎202-675-2066; www.ethiopicrestaurant.com; 401 H St NE; mains $12-18; ⌚5-10pm Tue-Thu, from noon Fri-Sun; 🌿; Ⓜ Union Station) In a city with no shortage of Ethiopian joints, Ethiopic stands above the rest. Top marks go to the various *wats* (stews) and the signature *tibs* (sauteed meat and veg), derived from tender lamb that has sat in a bath of herbs and hot spices. Vegans get lots of love here.

TED'S BULLETIN AMERICAN **$$**

Map p300 (☎202-544-8337; www.tedsbulletincapitolhill.com; 505 8th St SE; mains $10-19;

⌚7am-10pm Sun-Thu, to 11pm Fri & Sat; 👪; Ⓜ Eastern Market) Plop into a booth in the art-deco-meets-diner ambience, and loosen the belt. Beer biscuits and sausage gravy for breakfast, meatloaf with ketchup glaze for dinner and other hipster spins on comfort foods hit the table. You've got to admire a place that lets you substitute pop tarts for toast. Breakfast is available all day.

There's another Ted's on 14th St NW in Logan Circle.

MARKET LUNCH — AMERICAN $$

Map p300 (www.easternmarket-dc.org; 225 7th St SE; mains $9-17; ⌚7:30am-2:30pm Tue-Fri, 8am-3pm Sat, 11am-3pm Sun; Ⓜ Eastern Market) The popular food stall sits smack in the middle of Eastern Market. The ingredients are local and fresh, plucked from surrounding vendors. The oyster sandwich and lemonade lead the pack of favorite DC weekend lunches. Eat at the long communal table or outside at the picnic tables. Cash only. The stall also serves burgers and breakfast dishes like blueberry buckwheat pancakes.

POUND — CAFE $$

Map p300 (www.poundcoffee.com; 621 Pennsylvania Ave SE; sandwiches $6-9, mains $14-19; ⌚7am-4pm Mon, to 10pm Tue-Thu, to 11pm Fri, 7:30am-11pm Sat, 8am-10pm Sun; 📶; Ⓜ Eastern Market) Pound serves high-quality coffees amid an elegant rustic interior (exposed brick and timber, original plaster ceilings, wooden floors and nicely lit artwork). Breakfast quesadillas, panini and daily lunch specials are tops – as is the Nutella latte. In the evening, Pound turns into a wine-slinging bistro offering wholesome American fare such as shrimp tacos and goat-cheese burgers.

SONOMA RESTAURANT & WINE BAR — AMERICAN $$

Map p300 (☎202-544-8088; www.sonomadc.com; 223 Pennsylvania Ave SE; small plates $8-12, mains $15-28; ⌚11:30am-10pm Mon-Thu, to 11pm Fri, 5-11pm Sat, 11am-9pm Sun; Ⓜ Capitol South) The decor is sleek-chic but warm, like a fireplace den decorated by a Scandinavian couture designer's grandmother. The food is fantastic, a nice sampling of mid-Atlantic delicacies, such as Virginia fried oysters with cabbage and bacon jam. If you're an oenophile the extensive grape menu won't disappoint. You can rely on the staff to pick good pairings.

Note Sonoma closes between lunch and dinner (between 2:30 and 4:30).

LA PLAZA — LATIN AMERICAN $$

Map p300 (☎202-546-9512; www.laplazadc.com; 629 Pennsylvania Ave SE; mains $11-20; ⌚11:30am-11pm Mon-Thu, to midnight Fri, 11am-midnight Sat, to 10:30pm Sun; Ⓜ Eastern Market) The two prime times to visit La Plaza are at lunch, when it's occupied by Hill types seeking cheap Tex-Mex and Salvadorian fare, and at night, when they serve margaritas that will *kick your ass*. The staff are crazy friendly; if you chat with them enough, the tequila starts pouring so quick you don't even know when you shtart shlurrin' yer speesh…uh oh.

ARMAND'S PIZZERIA — PIZZA $$

Map p300 (www.armandspizza.com; 226 Massachusetts Ave NE; pizzas $12-18; ⌚11:30am-9:30pm Mon-Thu, to 10pm Fri & Sat, 4-9:30pm Sun; Ⓜ Union Station) The best pizza on the Hill is served Chicago style (deep crust) and pleasantly greasy. It's almost next door to the right-wing Heritage Foundation, so depending on your politics, you can share some pie with the neighboring conservatives or throw it at them.

★ ROSE'S LUXURY — MODERN AMERICAN $$$

Map p300 (☎202-580-8889; www.rosesluxury.com; 717 8th St SE; small plates $12-14,

LOCAL KNOWLEDGE

PRETZEL BAKERY

Here's how **Pretzel Bakery** (Map p300; www.thepretzelbakery.com; 340 15th St NE; items $2-3; ⌚8am-5pm Tue-Fri, from 9am Sat & Sun; Ⓜ Potomac Ave) works: a dude sells soft pretzels warm from the oven out of a house in the middle of a residential neighborhood across from a baseball field. Yes, it's a mouthful, but what a mouthful. Walk up to the window and order, then enjoy at the scattering of umbrella-shaded benches on the patio. The proprietor cooks fresh dough every 30 minutes, and offers mustards and dips to enhance the experience. He also serves a great breakfast sandwich with cheddar cheese, bacon and eggs (on a pretzel bun, of course). He sells out, so check Facebook or Twitter before you go to make sure he's still stocked.

family-style plates $28-33; ⌚5:30-10pm Mon-Thu, to 11pm Fri & Sat; Ⓜ Eastern Market) Rose's is DC's most buzzed-about eatery – and that was before *Bon Appetit* named it the nation's best new restaurant in 2014. Crowds fork into worldly Southern comfort food as twinkling lights glow overhead and candles flicker around the industrial, half-finished room. Rose's doesn't take reservations, but ordering your meal at the upstairs bar can save time (and the cocktails are delicious).

The pork sausage, habanero and lychee salad wows, as does the staff, which has an uncanny knack for treating everyone right. Rose's lives up to its hype.

BEUCHERT'S SALOON MODERN AMERICAN **$$$**
Map p300 (☎202-733-1384; www.beuchertssaloon.com; 623 Pennsylvania Ave SE; sandwiches $15-16, mains $26-29; ⌚5:30-11pm Mon-Thu, to midnight Fri & Sat, to 10pm Sun, 11am-2:30pm Sat & Sun; Ⓜ Eastern Market) Beuchert's has an old-timey, hipster vibe with antique wallpaper and sweet cocktails. It takes the locally sourced concept seriously, and everyone who works at the restaurant also has to work on the owner's farm in Maryland, where the chicken, eggs and vegetables come from. The playful dishes span cardamom-braised cabbage to horseradish egg custard to pork and sweet-potato dumplings. It's all lovely.

MONOCLE AMERICAN **$$$**
Map p300 (☎202-546-4488; www.themonocle.com; 107 D St NE; mains $19-34; ⌚11am-midnight Mon-Fri; Ⓜ Union Station) The Monocle's food – very American, surf-and-turf-type stuff – is generally good, occasionally great, sometimes disappointing. But people don't come here to eat so much as to celebrity spot, and seeing as this good ol' boys' club is just behind the Capitol, your chances of seeing Senator Smith aren't bad.

The dark bar and the walls help drive home the fact that it is a politicians' place first and foremost; note the quotes ('If you want a friend in Washington, get a dog').

Southwest DC

MAINE AVENUE FISH MARKET SEAFOOD **$**
Map p300 (1100 Maine Ave SW; mains $7-13; ⌚8am-9pm; Ⓜ L'Enfant Plaza) The pungent, open-air Maine Avenue Fish Market is a local landmark. No-nonsense vendors sell fish, crabs, oysters and other seafood so fresh it's almost still flopping. They'll kill, strip, shell, gut, fry or broil your desire, which you can take to the waterfront benches and eat blissfully (mind the seagulls!).

The surrounding area is being heavily redeveloped, but supposedly the market will remain as is.

DRINKING & NIGHTLIFE

The boozing atmosphere on Capitol Hill, still very much a residential neighborhood, is one of cozy pubs where policy talk gives way to Redskins predictions in the NFL. H St NE, otherwise known as the Atlas District, is a funky contrast to the Hill's red-brick conviviality.

★LITTLE MISS WHISKEY'S GOLDEN DOLLAR BAR
Map p300 (www.littlemisswhiskeys.com; 1104 H St NE; ⌚5pm-2am; 🚌X2 from Union Station) If Alice had returned from Wonderland so traumatized by her near beheading that she needed a stiff drink, we imagine she'd pop down to Little Miss Whiskey's. She'd love the whimsical-meets-dark-nightmares decor. And she'd probably have fun with the club kids partying on the upstairs dance floor on weekends. She'd also adore the weirdly fantastic back patio.

The excellent beer and whiskey menu and savvy staff make this feel like a bartender's bar. Cash only.

★BLUEJACKET BREWERY BREWERY
Map p300 (☎202-524-4862; www.bluejacketdc.com; 300 Tingey St SE; ⌚11am-1am Sun-Thu, to 2am Fri & Sat; Ⓜ Navy Yard) Beer lovers' heads will explode in Bluejacket. Pull up a stool at the mod-industrial bar, gaze at the silvery tanks bubbling up the ambitious brews, then make the hard decision about which of the 25 tap beers you want to try. A dry-hopped kolsch? Sweet-spiced stout? A cask-aged farmhouse ale? Four-ounce tasting pours help with decision-making.

H STREET COUNTRY CLUB BAR
Map p300 (www.thehstreetcountryclub.com; 1335 H St NE; ⌚5pm-1am Mon-Thu, 4pm-3am Fri, 11am-3am Sat, 11am-1am Sun; 🚌X2 from Union Station) The Country Club is two levels of great. The bottom floor is packed with pool

H STREET CORRIDOR

H St NE rolls out several blocks of awesomeness east of Union Station. Pie cafes, noodle shops, German beer gardens and more stack up one after the other between 10th and 14th Sts.

The road was once one of Washington's major shopping strips. That was before the race riots of 1968, which sadly gutted the area. It has come back over the past five years or so, thanks to a profusion of creative businesses. The Atlas Performing Arts Center was one of the leaders of the charge, which is why the area is sometimes referred to as the Atlas District.

H St rocks hardest at night. By day it's a bit deserted and edgy. The District's long-awaited streetcars should energize the scene. They clang from Union Station past all the H St hot spots. Check www.dcstreetcar.com for route info.

Otherwise, the corridor is about a 25-minute, desolate walk from Union Station. You can always catch a cab (about $8) from there, or take the X2 bus (catch it on the corner of N Capitol and H Sts NE).

tables, skeeball and shuffleboard, while the top contains its own minigolf course ($7 to play) done up to resemble a tour of the city on a small scale. You putt-putt past a trio of Lego lobbyists, through Beltway traffic snarls and past a King Kong–clad Washington monument.

The whole vibe of the place just facilitates a relaxed atmosphere where it's very easy to strike up conversations with locals – if you're shy and new to town, we'd highly recommend joining the Country Club.

GRANVILLE MOORE'S PUB

Map p300 (www.granvillemoores.com; 1238 H St NE; 5pm-midnight Mon-Thu, to 3am Fri, 11am-3am Sat, 11am-midnight Sun; X2 from Union Station) Besides being one of DC's best places to grab *frites* and a steak sandwich, Granville Moore's has an extensive Belgian beer menu that should satisfy any fan of low-country boozing. With its raw, wooden fixtures and walls that look as if they were made from daub and mud, the interior resembles a medieval barracks. The fireside setting is ideal on a winter's eve.

SIDAMO COFFEE & TEA CAFE

Map p300 (www.sidamocoffeeandtea.com; 417 H St NE; 7am-7pm Mon-Fri, 8am-6pm Sat, to 5pm Sun; ; Union Station) Owned by an Ethiopian family, Sidamo offers excellent, organic African coffee, tasty and strong as hell. There's friendly staff and that just-right bohemian atmosphere. You can use the wi-fi and smell the beans roasting and write books while blustery days go by. On Sunday at 2pm, the family puts on a free Ethiopian coffee ceremony; all customers are invited to participate.

ARGONAUT BAR

Map p300 (www.argonautdc.com; 1433 H St NE; 5pm-2am Mon-Wed, from 10am Thu-Sun; X2 from Union Station) The 'Naut looks and feels like a corner spot where folks repair for a beer after work, and in truth, people still do so here. The 12 draught lines flow with local brews. Many are half-price during happy hour (from 5pm to 7pm), and you can order a four-beer sampler to get acquainted with the options.

Take your drinks out to the dog-friendly patio, play a little cornhole (beanbag toss), and if hunger strikes, try the fish tacos or sweet-potato fries. Children are welcome and get their own menu. Hipster enough to be different, but not so much that locals have fled the premises, the Argonaut is a great date spot for someone who's a little off-kilter.

PEREGRINE ESPRESSO COFFEE

Map p300 (www.peregrineespresso.com; 660 Pennsylvania Ave SE; 7am-9pm Mon-Sat, 8am-8pm Sun; ; Eastern Market) The local mini-chain wins lots of 'best coffee' awards, and locals agree it's the real caffeinated deal. Join the laptop pack and sip your foam art in the sleek interior or on the outdoor patio.

STAR & SHAMROCK PUB

Map p300 (www.starandshamrock.com; 1341 H St NE; 11am-2am Sun-Thu, to 3am Fri & Sat; X2 from Union Station) It's not every day you come across an Irish pub–Jewish deli fusion. So fork right in to fried matzo balls with 'au Jew' dipping sauce, meaty bagel sandwiches and latkes (though the latter will not be as good as your bubbe's) while sipping Guinness or Harp. Of course, Manischewitz sangria and Hebrew Genesis ale are also part of the shtick.

PHASE 1 — LESBIAN

Map p300 (www.phase1dc.com; 525 8th St SE; 7:30pm-2am Thu, to 3am Fri & Sat, to 2am Sun; Eastern Market) 'The Phase' claims to be the oldest lesbian bar in the country; it's certainly the best lesbian dive in DC, not that there's much competition for the crown. It's great, friendly fun by any measure, chockablock with jelly wrestling, free pizza nights and an unpretentious but raucous enough atmosphere for ladies on the prowl.

Come early to mingle in peace and quiet, or late to shake your booty on the packed dance floor.

KELLY'S IRISH TIMES — IRISH PUB

Map p300 (www.kellysirishtimesdc.com; 14 F St NW; 11am-2am Sun-Thu, to 3am Fri & Sat; Union Station) Kelly's implores: 'Give me your tired, your hungry, your befuddled masses,' and the masses respond. Fans of the on-tap Guinness and the Thursday-to-Saturday live music tend to be younger than the patrons next door at the Dubliner pub – mostly students and Congressional staffers. The layout is like every Irish pub you've ever been in, but it's an exemplar of the genre.

UGLY MUG — SPORTS BAR

Map p300 (www.uglymugdc.com; 723 8th St SE; 11am-2am Sun-Thu, to 3am Fri & Sat; ; Eastern Market) The Mug is typical of the dives in this part of town: kinda scuzzy, but self-consciously so, attracting an interesting mix of preppie Hill types, Marines from the nearby barracks and 20-something locals. The predominating crowd is usually pretty loud and raucous, making this the 8th St SE option for those wanting a bit more of a frat-party ambience.

☆ ENTERTAINMENT

★ROCK & ROLL HOTEL — LIVE MUSIC

Map p300 (www.rockandrollhoteldc.com; 1353 H St NE; X2 from Union Station) The R&R Hotel is a great, grotty spot to catch rockin' live sets from the likes of Thurston Moore, Mudhoney and the Dead Kennedys. Don't let the name fool you; this hotel hosts all kinds of music genres from Afrofunk to the city's freshest hip-hop acts, with indie, punk and metal, too.

ARENA STAGE — THEATER

Map p300 (www.arenastage.org; 1101 6th St SW; tickets from $35; Waterfront-SEU) The mod, glassy Arena Stage is the second-largest performing-arts complex in Washington after the Kennedy Center. The three theaters inside (including a theater-in-the-round) are top venues for traditional and experimental works, especially American classics, premieres of new plays and contemporary stories. Arena Stage was the city's first racially integrated theater and has continued its progressive tradition through performances addressing African American history.

FOLGER THEATRE — THEATER

Map p300 (www.folger.edu/theatre; 210 E Capitol St SE; tickets from $30; Capitol South) The 250-seat, Renaissance-style theater attached to the Folger Shakespeare Library stages classic and modern interpretations of the bard's plays, as well as new works inspired by Shakespeare. Literary readings (including the PEN/Faulkner series) and great programs for children are also all part of the venue's repertoire.

With its three-tiered wooden balconies, half-timbered facade and sky canopy, the theater evokes an inn courtyard, where troupes often staged plays in Shakespeare's day.

ATLAS PERFORMING ARTS CENTER — THEATER

Map p300 (www.atlasarts.org; 1333 H St NE; tickets $5-25; X2 from Union Station) The art-deco Atlas theater is the backbone of the H St NE revival. All kinds of indie goodness gets performed here, from operettas to innovative new plays, ethnic dance shows and chamber music.

SHOPPING

★CAPITOL HILL BOOKS — BOOKS

Map p300 (www.capitolhillbooks-dc.com; 657 C St SE; 11:30am-6pm Mon-Fri, from 9am Sat & Sun; Eastern Market) A trove of secondhand awesomeness, this shop has so many books staff has to double-stack them on the shelves. Superb notes by the cantankerous

LOCAL KNOWLEDGE

EASTERN MARKET

One of the icons of Capitol Hill, **Eastern Market** (Map p300; www.easternmarket-dc.org; 225 7th St SE; ⌚7am-7pm Tue-Fri, to 6pm Sat, 9am-5pm Sun; Ⓜ Eastern Market) sprawls with delectable chow and good cheer, especially on the weekends. Built in 1873, it is the last of the 19th-century covered bazaars that once supplied DC's food. The South Hall has bakery, dairy, fishmonger, butcher, flower vendors, and fruit and vegetable sellers. The Market Lunch stall sells prepared foods and is a crowd favorite for its oyster sandwiches and blueberry buckwheat pancakes.

Come the weekend, the market doubles in size. Artisans and farmers bring their wares and set up outside. Besides fresh apples, peppers, eggplants and other produce, you can pick up handmade soaps, colorful pottery, painted ceramics and unusual jewelry.

But wait, there's more. The **Flea Market** (Map p300; www.easternmarket.net; 7th & C Sts SE; ⌚10am-5pm Sat & Sun; Ⓜ Eastern Market) also gets its groove on. It pops up across the street in the Hines schoolyard, where vendors sell all kinds of cool antiques, wood-block art, global wares, clothing and restored furniture. Sunday is the busier day, with more stalls.

clerks help guide your selection. For instance, there's the 'Wacko Stacko' offering pages by Sarah Palin, Newt Gingrich and Mike Huckabee. The section on US presidents is huge (Chester Arthur books! An entire shelf of Truman books!).

Bookworms will find vintage cookbooks and mystery novels in abundance. Be sure to check the table outside for any freebies on offer. Sometimes items besides books appear, such as old TVs.

HILL'S KITCHEN — HOMEWARES

Map p300 (www.hillskitchen.com; 713 D St SE; ⌚10am-6pm Tue-Sat, to 5pm Sun; Ⓜ Eastern Market) A great variety of spices, cookbooks, whisks, cast-iron pans and other colorful kitchenwares stuff this 1884 townhouse near Eastern Market. Behold the cookie cutters that come in the shape of every US state. The proprietor is super welcoming to cooks both pro and novice. The shop holds pie-making, knife-skills and other classes (around $50) most weeks.

HUNTED HOUSE — HOMEWARES

Map p300 (☎202-549-7493; www.huntedhousedc.com; 510 H St NE; ⌚1-7pm Thu, noon-6pm Fri-Sun; Ⓜ Union Station) Every piece of vintage furniture cramming this walk-up abode is a gem of the deco or modernist design movement. It's laid out to resemble a functioning apartment. Be sure to admire the Jetsonsesque TV in the sitting room, which is, sadly, never for sale. The shop is also open Tuesday by appointment.

WOVEN HISTORY — ARTS, CRAFTS

Map p300 (www.wovenhistory.com; 315 7th St SE; ⌚10am-6pm Tue-Sun; Ⓜ Eastern Market) It's as if a Silk Road caravan got lost and pitched up near the Eastern Market. The lovely emporium is stuffed with crafts, carpets and tapestries from across Central Asia, Tibet and Mongolia. Unlike a lot of stores of this genre, Woven History feels more like an authentic tented bazaar than a hippie hangout.

HOMEBODY — HOMEWARES

Map p300 (www.homebodydc.com; 715 8th St SE; ⌚11am-7pm Tue-Sat, noon-6pm Sun; Ⓜ Eastern Market) A good stop on your way to or from Eastern Market is the fun and colorful Homebody. Here you'll encounter a range of eye-catching gift ideas, including painted candelabras, decorative wall clocks, painted drinking glasses, graphic dinner plates and windup robot insects.

SPORTS & ACTIVITIES

★WASHINGTON NATIONALS — BASEBALL

Map p300 (www.nationals.com; 1500 S Capitol St SE; 📶; Ⓜ Navy Yard) The major-league Nats play baseball at **Nationals Park** (Map p300) beside the Anacostia River. Don't miss the mid-fourth-inning 'Racing Presidents' – an odd foot race between giant-headed caricatures of George Washington,

CYCLING EAST POTOMAC PARK

East Potomac Park makes a fine cycling destination. Ohio Dr starts at the Tidal Basin and circumnavigates the peninsula that contains the park. A wide, paved sidewalk runs parallel for cyclists who are not at ease sharing the road with cars. The 5-mile loop runs along the Washington Channel on one side and the Potomac River on the other. It's easy, breezy and pleasing.

Abraham Lincoln, Thomas Jefferson, Teddy Roosevelt and William Taft. The stadium itself is spiffy, and hip eateries and mod Yards Park have cropped up around it as the area gentrifies.

Catch a game if you can. The Nats act as a strong social glue among DC's transients and natives. And tickets are cheap, starting at around $15.

WASHINGTON REDSKINS FOOTBALL

(☎301-276-6800; www.redskins.com; 1600 Fedex Way, Landover, MD; Ⓜ Morgan Blvd) Washington's NFL team, the Redskins, play September through January at FedEx Field. The team has experienced a lot of controversy recently, and not only because of its woeful play. Many groups have criticized the Redskins' name and logo as insulting to Native Americans. The US Patent and Trademark Office agreed, and revoked the team's trademark.

Tickets used to be difficult to get, but by the end of the 2014 season, some fans were selling their seats online for as little as $4. FedEx Field is about 10 miles east of the Capitol. The Morgan Blvd Metro station is closest, a 1-mile walk along a sidewalk.

PRESIDENTIAL PHOTO OP

There's no better keepsake photo than one where you're surrounded by the Washington Nationals' Racing Presidents while at the ballpark. After George, Abe, Tom, Teddy and Bill race in the middle of the fourth inning, they hang out behind Section 131 until the end of the fifth inning to take pictures with fans. Just do it.

DC UNITED SOCCER

(www.dcunited.com; 2400 E Capitol St; Ⓜ Stadium-Armory) Multiple-time Major League Soccer champions DC United play March through October at RFK Stadium. Tickets start at around $20. The team is building a new arena in Southwest DC by Fort McNair, to be completed in late 2017.

BIKE & ROLL – UNION STATION BICYCLE RENTAL

Map p300 (☎202-962-0206; www.bikeandrolldc.com; 50 Massachusetts Ave NE; bikes per 2hr/day from $16/40; ⏲9am-7pm summer, 10am-4pm winter; Ⓜ Union Station) Rent a bike to explore the city; the rental price includes a lock and safety equipment. The shop is on the western side of Union Station, between it and the National Postal Museum. Bike & Roll has a couple of outposts around town, but this is the one that's open year-round.

BIKE & ROLL – L'ENFANT PLAZA BICYCLE TOUR

Map p300 (www.bikeandrolldc.com; 955 L'Enfant Plaza SW; tours adult/child $40/30; ⏲mid-Mar–early Dec; Ⓜ L'Enfant Plaza) This branch of the bike-rental company (per two hours from $16) is the one closest to the Mall. In additional to bike rental, it also provides tours. Three-hour jaunts wheel by the main sights of Capitol Hill and the National Mall. The evening rides to the monuments are particularly good.

EAST POTOMAC PARK GOLF COURSE GOLF

Map p300 (www.eastpotomacgolf.com; Ohio Dr SW; 18 holes weekday/weekend $28/32, 9 holes from $10/13; ⏲sunrise-sunset; Ⓜ Smithsonian) It's a bit scrubby, with three courses (red, blue and white). There's also a year-round driving range and summer mini golf.

LANGSTON GOLF COURSE GOLF

(www.langstongolfcourse.com; 2600 Benning Rd NE; 18 holes weekday/weekend $25/31, 9 holes $18/22; ⏲sunrise-sunset; 🚌X1, X2 or X3 from Union Station) The fairways are flat, with lots of trees on the back nine.

Downtown & Penn Quarter

PENN QUARTER | JUDICIARY SQUARE | CHINATOWN | CONVENTION CENTER

Neighborhood Top Five

❶ Gawp at the Declaration of Independence, Constitution and Bill of Rights – the real, live, yellowing, spidery-handwriting-scrawled documents themselves – at the **National Archives** (p129).

❷ Browse the world's largest collection of US art at the **Reynolds Center for American Art & Portraiture** (p130).

❸ See the very seat where Abraham Lincoln was assassinated at **Ford's Theatre** (p131).

❹ Read the day's newspapers from around the globe and learn about the journalist lifestyle at the **Newseum** (p131).

❺ Behold the palatial room that has held 17 inaugural balls at the **National Building Museum** (p133).

For more detail of this area, see Map p302

Lonely Planet's Top Tip

Many restaurants in the neighborhood offer pre-theater menus. This generally means a three-course meal for around $35, offered before 6:30pm. Our favorite is Bistro D'Oc ($25, including a glass of wine). Rasika, Brasserie Beck, Jaleo and Central Michel Richard are among the others that offer pre-theater deals.

Best Places to Eat

- Central Michel Richard (p136)
- Red Apron Butchery (p134)
- Minibar (p136)
- Hill Country Barbecue (p135)
- Zaytinya (p135)

For reviews, see p134.

Best Places to Drink

- RFD Washington (p138)
- City Tap House (p138)
- Poste Lounge (p138)
- Rocket Bar (p138)
- Green Lantern (p138)

For reviews, see p138.

Best Theaters

- Shakespeare Theatre Company (p138)
- Capitol Steps (p138)
- National Theatre (p138)
- Woolly Mammoth Theatre Company (p138)
- E Street Cinema (p139)

For reviews, see p131.

Explore Downtown & Penn Quarter

Washington's downtown is less conventional city center and more of a gussied-up transition space between the National Mall and Washington's residential communities. The neighborhood both emerges from and is attached to Penn Quarter, a corridor formed by the line Pennsylvania Ave creates between the White House and the Capitol. There are the usual chain stores and bright lights, but the area revolves around the enormous, gaudy Verizon Center, home of DC's professional basketball and hockey teams, and some of the city's best museums.

We're talking about the National Archives, where the Declaration of Independence lies enshrined for viewing; the Reynolds Center for American Art, filled with famed portraits and a who's who of big-name artists' works; Ford's Theatre, where John Wilkes Booth shot Abraham Lincoln; and the Newseum, a whiz-bang, multi-story collection of artifacts and current-events exhibits. The elegant National Building Museum, cheeky International Spy Museum and creepy Crime Museum are also on tap. You'll need a few days to do them all justice.

Downtown is also the theater district. The Capitol Steps do their political shtick. Shakespeare Theatre puts on well-regarded productions of the bard's plays (including a free summer series). And Woolly Mammoth Theatre Company stages contemporary and experimental works.

In case you hadn't figured it out, the neighborhood bustles day and night. Trendy restaurants and bars cater to conventioneers (the Convention Center is in the 'hood), theatergoers and sports fans. While this good life tends to come with a not-so-lovely price tag, there are a few cheap surprises to be discovered here as well.

Local Life

- **Start the day right** Office workers cluster here on their way to work, because Red Apron Butchery (p134) makes a killer breakfast sandwich.
- **Oasis** Locals seeking peace and quiet from downtown's hullabaloo head to the Reynolds Center for American Art (p130) and its 1st-floor interior courtyard of trees, peaceful fountains and free wi-fi.
- **Evening movie** E Street Cinema (p139) is a quirky theater screening quirky movies for neighborhood types.

Getting There & Away

- **Metro** All five Metro lines cross downtown, so there are several stations here. The main ones are Metro Center (where the Red, Blue, Orange and Silver Lines hub), and Gallery Pl (where the Green, Yellow and Red Lines merge).

TOP SIGHT
NATIONAL ARCHIVES

It's hard not to feel a little in awe of the big three documents in the National Archives: the Declaration of Independence, the Constitution and the Bill of Rights. Seeing them in person is one of those DC experiences that gets even hard-bitten locals to whisper 'Wow.'

The star documents are laid out in chronological order from left to right in the dimly lit rotunda. Don't expect to linger over any of them – guards make you keep moving. First up is the Declaration (1776). Next is the Constitution (1787). Editors in the group can try to spot the spelling error (hint: look at the list of signatories, at the word that starts with 'p' and ends with 'sylvania'). The Bill of Rights (1789) unfurls in the next display case.

After the rotunda, head through the hall to the Public Vaults. Browse George Washington's handwritten letters and Abraham Lincoln's wartime telegrams. There's a nifty piece of paperwork from Charles 'Pa' Ingalls (of *Little House on the Prairie* fame) showing his grant application for 154 acres in the Dakota Territory. You can also watch vintage D-Day reels.

Go down a floor to the Rubenstein Gallery, and a 1297 version of the Magna Carta is on view. The Constitution's Fifth Amendment is a direct descendant of this document. The excellent Archives Shop and the building's entrance/exit are also here.

In spring and summer, reserve tickets in advance on the website for $1.50 each. This lets you go through the fast-track entrance on Constitution Ave (to the right of the steps) versus the general entrance (to the left of the steps), where queues can be lengthy.

DON'T MISS...

- Declaration of Independence
- Constitution
- Bill of Rights
- Magna Carta
- Pa Ingalls' land grant

PRACTICALITIES

- Map p302
- 866-272-6272
- www.archives.gov/museum
- 700 Pennsylvania Ave NW
- 10am-5:30pm Sep–mid-Mar, to 7pm mid-Mar–Aug
- M Archives

ROSAIRENEBETANCOURT 1 / ALAMY ©

TOP SIGHT
REYNOLDS CENTER FOR AMERICAN ART & PORTRAITURE

If you only visit one art museum in DC, make it the Reynolds Center, which combines the National Portrait Gallery and the American Art Museum. There is, simply put, no better collection of American art in the world than at these two Smithsonian museums.

The American Experience gallery (1st floor) hangs blockbusters such as Georgia O'Keeffe's flowery pink *Manhattan* and Edward Hopper's trapped woman in *Cape Cod Morning*. The nearby folk-art gallery holds a vivid collection, especially by African American artists. Look for James Hampton's exquisite, foil-made throne.

The America's Presidents gallery (2nd floor) gives historic due to 43 heads of state. Gilbert Stuart's rosy-cheeked *George Washington* is the most beloved. The 'cracked plate' photo of Abraham Lincoln is also here. Then seek out Benjamin Franklin. You'll recognize the image, as it's the same one that now graces the $100 bill. Ben's portrait enriches the American Origins gallery (1st floor).

The 3rd floor has Andy Warhol's pop-art version of Marilyn Monroe and groovy paintings by Roy Lichtenstein, Franz Kline and more modern blue-chip artists. The Luce Center, the museum's open storage area, spills across the 3rd and 4th floors. Wander around the trove and ogle cases of paintings. Open drawers filled with portrait miniatures, antique medals and vintage jewelry. Peruse shelves stacked with sculptures, ceramics and other gorgeous *objets d'art*. The center has its own information desk that provides free audio tours.

The museum's other bit of awesomeness is the 1st-floor inner courtyard dotted with olive trees, peaceful fountains and a cafe.

DON'T MISS...

- Luce Center
- Gilbert Stuart's *George Washington*
- Joseph Siffred Duplessis' *Benjamin Franklin*
- Edward Hopper's *Cape Cod Morning*
- Georgia O'Keeffe's *Manhattan*

PRACTICALITIES

- Map p302
- ☎202-633-1000
- www.americanart.si.edu
- cnr 8th & F Sts NW
- ⌚11:30am-7pm
- Ⓜ Gallery Pl

SIGHTS

Penn Quarter

NATIONAL ARCHIVES LANDMARK

See p129.

REYNOLDS CENTER FOR AMERICAN ART & PORTRAITURE MUSEUM

See p130.

NEWSEUM MUSEUM

Map p302 (www.newseum.org; 555 Pennsylvania Ave NW; adult/child $23/14; 9am-5pm; ; Archives, Judiciary Sq) This six-story, highly interactive news museum is worth the admission price. You can delve into the major events of recent years (the fall of the Berlin Wall, September 11, Hurricane Katrina), and spend hours watching moving film footage and perusing Pulitzer Prize–winning photographs. The concourse level displays FBI artifacts from prominent news stories, such as the Unabomber's cabin and John Dillinger's death mask.

Level 2 has video stations where kids read news stories from a teleprompter and 'report' the news in front of a DC backdrop. Level 3 holds a memorial to journalists killed in pursuit of the truth. Level 4 has twisted wreckage from the September 11, 2001 attacks and haunting final images from Bill Biggart's camera (Biggart was the only journalist to be killed that day). Level 6 offers a terrace with awesome views of Pennsylvania Ave up to the Capitol. Tickets are usable for two consecutive days, so you don't have to view everything at once.

FORD'S THEATRE HISTORIC SITE

Map p302 (202-426-6924; www.fords.org; 511 10th St NW; 9am-4:30pm; Metro Center) FREE On April 14, 1865, John Wilkes Booth assassinated Abraham Lincoln in his box seat here. Timed-entry tickets let you see the flag-draped site. They also provide entry to the basement museum (displaying Booth's .44-caliber pistol, his muddy boot etc) and to Petersen House (across the street), where Lincoln died. Arrive early because tickets do run out. Reserve online ($6.25 fee) to ensure admittance.

The play the president and Mrs Lincoln watched was *Our American Cousin*. Booth knew the farce and knew at what line the audience would laugh most. He shot Lincoln at that moment to muffle the sound. Park Service rangers tell the full story.

The theater still holds performances, and sometimes the venue is closed to the public. It's always smart to check the schedule before heading out. Ford's posts it online, or you can call the box office to make sure the site is open.

NEWS SOURCE

Want to know what's happening back home? Stroll over to the Newseum, where the front pages of newspapers from around the world – as well as from every US state – are displayed daily by the entrance.

PETERSEN HOUSE HISTORIC SITE

Map p302 (www.nps.gov/foth; 516 10th St NW; 9am-4:30pm; Metro Center) FREE After being shot at Ford's Theatre, the unconscious president was carried across the street to Petersen House, where he died the next day. Its tiny, unassuming rooms create a moving personal portrait of the president's death. Entrance to the home is in conjunction with the Ford's Theatre tour, so obtain tickets at the box office there.

FORD'S THEATRE CENTER MUSEUM

Map p302 (www.fords.org; 514 10th St NW; 9am-5pm; Metro Center) FREE More exhibits for Lincoln-o-philes. Displays on the 3rd and 4th floors show the assassination's aftermath and how Lincoln's legacy lives on in current politics and pop culture. The center is operated in conjunction with the Ford's Theatre historic site. You'll need a ticket for entry; get it across the street at the theater box office.

The 1st floor holds a Lincoln-stuffed gift shop, as well as a 34ft tower of Lincoln books (they're actually an aluminum sculpture) that rise up in the middle of the space – a testament to how much has been written about the 16th president.

INTERNATIONAL SPY MUSEUM MUSEUM

Map p302 (202-393-7798; www.spymuseum.org; 800 F St NW; adult/child $22/15; 9am-7pm May-Aug, 10am-6pm Sep-Apr; ; Gallery Pl) One of DC's most popular museums is flashy, over the top, and probably guilty of overtly glamming up a life of intelligence gathering. But who cares? You basically want to see Q's lab, and that's what the

Spy Museum feels like. Check out James Bond's tricked-out Aston Martin, the KGB's lipstick-concealed pistol and more. Kids go crazy for this spot, but be warned: lines form long and early. Ease the wait somewhat by reserving online (there's a $2 surcharge per ticket).

There are all kinds of artifacts and interactive displays, and guests are invited to play the role of a secret agent by adopting a cover at the start of their visit. You can try to identify disguises, listen to bugs and spot hidden cameras throughout the museum. A lot of the exhibits are historical in nature, focusing on the Cold War in particular (a re-creation of the tunnel under the Berlin Wall is an eerie winner). The museum also offers several tours, such as 'Spy in the City' ($15), a sort of GPS-driven scavenger hunt across DC. Alas, the museum is planning to move elsewhere in DC sometime before mid-2017.

CRIME MUSEUM MUSEUM

Map p302 (202-393-1099; www.crimemuseum.org; 575 7th St NW; adult/child $22/15; 10am-7pm; Gallery Pl) If you're a fan of forensics and crime-investigation TV shows, or if you enjoy gruesome torture devices and artifacts, the Crime Museum entertains. Spend a few hours wandering through and ogling things such as the bloodstained floorboards from Jesse James' hideout, Al Capone's rosary and serial killer John Wayne Gacy's clown costume. The heretic fork and neck violin (a shackle that locks two quarrelers face-to-face) show how past crimes were punished. Buy tickets online to save a few dollars.

The museum is very interactive, with exhibits that teach how to crack a safe and what it's like to be in a prison cell. Older kids love it. The museum also sells add-on experiences such as forensics workshops.

NATIONAL MUSEUM OF WOMEN IN THE ARTS MUSEUM

Map p302 (www.nmwa.org; 1250 New York Ave NW; adult/child $10/free; 10am-5pm Mon-Sat, from noon Sun; Metro Center) The only US museum exclusively devoted to women's artwork fills this Renaissance Revival mansion. Its collection – 2600 works by almost 700 female artists from 28 countries – moves from Renaissance artists such as Lavinia Fontana to 20th-century works by Frida Kahlo, Georgia O'Keeffe and Helen Frankenthaler. Placards give feminist interpretations of various art movements. It's free the first Sunday of each month.

The building's chandeliered interior is gorgeous. Head up the sweeping staircase to the 3rd floor, which is where most of the collection resides. Free chamber-music concerts take place on occasional Wednesdays.

NAVY MEMORIAL & NAVAL HERITAGE CENTER MONUMENT

Map p302 (www.navymemorial.org; 701 Pennsylvania Ave NW; memorial 24hr, center 9:30am-5pm; Archives) FREE The hunched figure of the *Lone Sailor*, warding off the wind with his flipped-up pea coat, is an oft-overlooked memorial in the city. The sailor waits quietly by his duffel in a circular plaza bordered by masts sporting semaphore flags; the space evokes the vastness and the ubiquity of the sea. The Naval Heritage Center, on the same grounds, displays artifacts and a couple of ship models.

MARTIN LUTHER KING JR MEMORIAL LIBRARY LIBRARY

Map p302 (www.dclibrary.org/mlk; 901 G St NW; 9:30am-9pm Mon-Thu, to 5:30pm Fri & Sat, 1-5pm Sun; ; Metro Center, Gallery Pl) FREE Designed by famed modern architect Ludwig Mies van der Rohe, this low-slung, sleek central branch of the DC public library system is as warm and fuzzy as a goodnight story on the inside, especially the colorful mural portraying the Civil Rights movement. This is an important community and cultural center, sponsoring readings, concerts, films and children's activities.

FLASHPOINT GALLERY GALLERY

Map p302 (315 1310; www.culturaldc.org; 916 G St NW; noon-6pm Wed-Sat; Metro Center, Gallery Pl) FREE The nonprofit gallery shows experimental contemporary art by both local and international artists working in a variety of media. It's usually cool, thought-provoking stuff. The building also holds a 60-seat theater used as a laboratory for emerging works.

FDR MEMORIAL STONE MEMORIAL

Map p302 (cnr 9th St & Pennsylvania Ave NW; Archives) President Franklin Delano Roosevelt didn't want a grand memorial like the one that's now on the Mall. He reportedly said, 'If any memorial is erected to me, I should like it to consist of a block about the size of this desk and placed in front of the Archives Building. I want it plain, without any ornamentation, with the simple carving

"In Memory Of".' This request was honored in 1965, with a small stone slab.

Judiciary Square

NATIONAL BUILDING MUSEUM MUSEUM

Map p302 (www.nbm.org; 401 F St NW; adult/child $8/5; ⌚10am-5pm Mon-Sat, from 11am Sun; 👪; Ⓜ Judiciary Sq) Devoted to architecture and urban design, the museum is appropriately housed in a magnificent 1887 edifice modeled after the Renaissance-era Palazzo Farnese in Rome. Four stories of ornamented balconies flank the dramatic 316ft-wide atrium and the Corinthian columns rise 75ft high. There's no charge to view the public areas; the admission fee is for the exhibits, which will please architecture buffs.

The space has hosted 17 inaugural balls, from Grover Cleveland's in 1885 to Barack Obama's in 2013. Step inside to see the inventive system of windows and archways that keep the Great Hall constantly glimmering in natural light. For more information, pick up a self-guided-tour brochure at the information desk, or join a free 45-minute docent-led tour (11:30pm, 12:30pm and 1:30pm). There's also a cafe and a bookstore inside.

The museum's Building Zone for kids is a local secret, where two- to six-year-olds stack block towers, drive toy bulldozers and otherwise construct in the hands-on play area.

NATIONAL LAW ENFORCEMENT OFFICERS MEMORIAL MONUMENT

Map p302 (www.nleomf.com; E St NW, btwn 4th & 5th Sts NW; ⌚24hr; Ⓜ Judiciary Sq) The memorial on Judiciary Sq commemorates US police officers killed on duty since 1794. In the style of the Vietnam Veterans Memorial, names of the dead are carved on two marble walls curving around a plaza; new names are added during a moving candlelight vigil each year in May. Peeking over the walls, bronze lion statues protect their sleeping cubs (presumably as law enforcement officers protect us).

The group has broken ground on the **National Law Enforcement Museum**, which will open across from the memorial sometime in 2016 or after.

NATIONAL LAW ENFORCEMENT MEMORIAL VISITORS CENTER MUSEUM

Map p302 (400 7th St NW; ⌚9am-5pm Mon-Fri, from 10am Sat, from noon Sun; Ⓜ Archives) FREE Located a few blocks from the National Law Enforcement Officers Memorial, the visitor center houses a small shop and a couple of exhibits about the memorial's history and the men and women it honors.

LOCAL KNOWLEDGE

THE FBI

If you're just dying to make your eyes bleed, take a gander at the headquarters of the **Federal Bureau of Investigation** (FBI; Map p302; 10th St & Pennsylvania Ave NW; Ⓜ Archives). This concrete, brutalist affront to all that is good and holy should be seen, if only to say you have laid eyes on – and we're not kidding – the single ugliest building in the entire District. Better do it soon, though. Plans are in the works to move the FBI headquarters to either Maryland or Virginia and knock down DC's most hated building. No firm date on its demise has been given.

Chinatown & Convention Center

CHINATOWN AREA

Map p302 (7th & H Sts NW; Ⓜ Gallery Pl) DC's dinky Chinatown is anchored on 7th and H Sts NW. It was once a major Asian entrepôt, but today most Asians in the Washington area live in the Maryland/Virginia suburbs. That said, Chinatown is still an intriguing browse. Enter through **Friendship Arch** (Map p302), the largest single-span arch in the world. This used to be an infamous boozer strip, now scrubbed and shiny thanks to the nearby Verizon Center.

SURRATT HOUSE SITE (WOK & ROLL) BUILDING

Map p302 (604 H St NW; Ⓜ Gallery Pl) At this inauspicious address, now the restaurant Wok & Roll, Lincoln's assassins met and plotted their scheme in 1865. The home's owner, Confederate sympathizer Mary Surratt, ran it as a boarding house. She was eventually hanged at Fort McNair for her role in the murder – the first white woman executed by the US federal government.

TO PAY OR NOT TO PAY

One of the best things about DC is the abundance of top-notch museums you can visit for free. So why go to a museum with a hefty admission price like the Newseum, International Spy Museum or Crime Museum? Good question. These attractions are flashier and more interactive than most of their gratis peers. They hold one-of-a-kind collections. And they tend to manage crowds better via online ticket sales. But jeez, given all the excellent free competition…

Our advice: if you're only going to visit one museum with a fee, make it the Newseum. It's the most educational of the bunch, and your ticket is good for two days. The International Spy Museum and Crime Museum are somewhat similar in their approach and exhibits, so if you must choose between the two, decide whether espionage or forensics appeals most.

TOUCHSTONE GALLERY GALLERY

Map p302 (www.touchstonegallery.com; 901 New York Ave NW; ⌚11am-6pm Wed-Fri, noon-5pm Sat & Sun; Ⓜ Metro Center) Touchstone Gallery exhibits contemporary pieces created by its 45 member artists. Works cover multiple media, including sculpture, painting and the occasional esoteric installation. The bright, welcoming space always has something eye-popping going on.

HISTORICAL SOCIETY OF WASHINGTON, DC MUSEUM

Map p302 (www.historydc.org; 801 K St NW; ⌚10am-4pm Tue-Fri; Ⓜ Mt Vernon Sq) FREE Located in the Carnegie Library building at Mount Vernon Sq, the Historical Society has an extensive collection of books, photographs, maps and other archives. The bit that's open to the public is on the 2nd floor in the Small-Alper Gallery. It's a quick-see, but intriguing, exhibit that traces DC development over the years through artworks and photos.

EATING

Restaurants are thick on the ground along 7th and 8th Sts NW as well as H St NW in Chinatown.

Penn Quarter

★**RED APRON BUTCHERY** DELI $

Map p302 (☎202-524-5244; www.redapron-butchery.com; 709 D St NW; mains $5-10; ⌚7:30am-8pm Mon-Fri, 9am-8pm Sat, 9am-5pm Sun; Ⓜ Archives) Red Apron makes a helluva breakfast sandwich. Plop into one of the comfy booths and wrap your lips around the ricotta, honey and pine-nut 'aristocrat' or the egg and chorizo 'buenos dias.' They're all heaped onto tigelle rolls, a sort of Italian flatbread. But you have to order before 10:30am (2:30pm on weekends).

The surrounding foodie market sells everything from nut butters to duck fat.

DAIKAYA JAPANESE $

Map p302 (☎202-589-1600; www.daikaya.com; 705 6th St NW; mains $12-14; ⌚11:30am-10pm Sun & Mon, to 11pm Tue-Thu, to midnight Fri & Sat; Ⓜ Gallery Pl) Daikaya offers two options. Downstairs it's a casual ramen-noodle shop, where locals swarm in and slurp with friends in the slick wooden booths. Upstairs it's a sake-pouring Japanese *izakaya* (tavern), with rice-bowl lunches and fishy small plates for dinner. Note the upstairs closes between lunch and dinner (ie between 2pm and 5pm).

MERZI INDIAN $

Map p302 (☎202-656-3794; www.merzi.com; 415 7th St NW; mains $7-9; ⌚11am-10pm Mon-Sat, to 9pm Sun; 🖉; Ⓜ Archives, Gallery Pl) For cheap Indian food – especially cheap Indian vegetarian – in downtown DC, this is where to be. Merzi's setup is simple: choose a base (roti, rice, salad, etc), a protein (chicken, lamb, veg, etc), then add sauces, chutney and such. Your wallet will barely feel lighter for the visit.

ASTRO DOUGHNUTS & FRIED CHICKEN AMERICAN $

Map p302 (www.astrodoughnuts.com; 1308 G St NW; doughnuts $2.50-3, chicken $6-8; ⌚7:30am-5:30pm Mon-Fri, 9am-3pm Sat & Sun; Ⓜ Metro Center) Eleven doughnut flavors and fried bird – what more do you need? The chicken is the winner here, cooked crisp with buttermilk or hot Sriracha sauce, though the creme brûlée doughnut also awes as you crunch into the sugar crust and strike the creamy center. The chicken becomes available at 11:30am (11am weekends).

A couple of outdoor tables flank the door, but wee Astro is mostly for takeaway.

SHAKE SHACK BURGERS $

Map p302 (www.shakeshack.com; 800 F St NW; mains $5-10; ⌚11am-11pm Sun-Thu, to midnight Fri & Sat; 👪; Ⓜ Gallery Pl) The NYC chain has come to DC. The self-proclaimed 'modern roadside burger stand' is beloved for its well-griddled patties under a sweet-and-tangy Shake Sauce, crinkle-cut fries and milkshakes made with creamy custard. Are the shakes really the nation's best? The endless crowd of happy slurpers provides the answer.

This branch is typically mobbed with families, thanks to its location next to the Spy Museum.

TEAISM ASIAN $

Map p302 (www.teaism.com; 400 8th St NW; mains $9-12; ⌚7:30am-10pm Mon-Fri, 9:30am-9pm Sat & Sun; Ⓜ Archives) This teahouse is unique in the area for its affordable lunch options – hot noodle dishes and fresh bento boxes – and its relaxing atmosphere. It's a grand spot for a bite after a day of Mall sightseeing. The salty oat cookies are a local favorite. Teaism has locations in Dupont Circle and near the White House as well.

RASIKA INDIAN $$

Map p302 (☎202-637-1222; www.rasikarestaurant.com; 633 D St NW; mains $14-28; ⌚11:30am-2:30pm Mon-Fri, 5:30-10:30pm Mon-Thu, 5-11pm Fri & Sat; 🍷; Ⓜ Archives) Rasika is as cutting edge as Indian food gets. The room resembles a Jaipur palace decorated by a flock of modernist art-gallery curators. Narangi duck is juicy, almost unctuous, and pleasantly nutty thanks to the addition of cashews; the deceptively simple *dal* (lentils) have the right kiss of sharp fenugreek. Vegans and vegetarians will feel a lot of love here.

HILL COUNTRY BARBECUE BARBECUE $$

Map p302 (☎202-556-2050; www.hillcountrywdc.com; 410 7th St NW; mains $13-22; ⌚11:30am-10pm Sun-Thu, to 11pm Fri & Sat; Ⓜ Archives) Hill Country is an anomaly for DC – a Texas-themed, cowboy-hat-filled joint that doesn't feel corny; a barbecue spot that serves excellent smoked meat; and a live-music venue that hosts great honky-tonk shows. From May through August, it operates a popular alfresco outpost on the National Building Museum's lawn. Grab a hay-bale seat and join the fun 4pm to 9pm Thursday to Saturday.

ZAYTINYA MEDITERRANEAN $$

Map p302 (☎202-638-0800; www.zaytinya.com; 701 9th St NW; mezze $8-13; ⌚11:30am-11:30pm Tue-Sat, to 10pm Sun & Mon; 🍷; Ⓜ Gallery Pl) One of the culinary crown jewels of chef José Andrés, ever-popular Zaytinya serves superb Greek, Turkish and Lebanese mezze (small plates) in a long, noisy dining room with soaring ceilings and all-glass walls. It's a favorite after-work meet-up spot.

CAFE MOZART GERMAN $$

Map p302 (☎202-347-5732; www.cafemozartdc.com; 1331 H St NW; mains $15-26; ⌚7am-10pm Mon-Fri, 9am-10pm Sat, 11am-10pm Sun; Ⓜ Metro Center) This German grocery store–deli-bakery has a cute restaurant hiding out the back that serves great sauerkraut, spaetzle and schnitzel. Best of all, it hosts accordion concerts on Tuesday, Wednesday and Sunday, and classical piano concerts on Saturday; they all start at 6pm. If nothing else, stop in the front to pick up some European chocolates or pastries.

JALEO SPANISH $$

Map p302 (☎202-628-7949; www.jaleo.com; 480 7th St NW; tapas $8-15; ⌚11:30am-10pm Mon, to 11pm Tue-Thu, to midnight Fri & Sat, 11am-10pm Sun; Ⓜ Archives) The whole tapas thing has

LOCAL KNOWLEDGE

CHEAP EATS

For a quick bite, Downtown offers a couple of food courts popular with office workers. One is inside the **Ronald Reagan Building** (Map p302; 1300 Pennsylvania Ave NW; ⌚10:30am-7pm Mon-Fri, 11am-6pm Sat; Ⓜ Federal Triangle), which has sandwiches, sushi, pizza and Chinese food among its stash. Since it's inside a federal building, you have to go through security to enter. The other is the **Shops at National Place** (Map p302; 529 W 14th St NW; ⌚7am-8pm Mon-Fri, 11am-5pm Sat; Ⓜ Metro Center), inside the National Press Club Building, where Five Guys wafts its burgery goodness.

been done to death, but Jaleo helped start the trend in DC and it still serves some of the best Spanish cuisine in town. The interior is an Iberian pastiche of explosive color and vintage mural-dom. Garlicky shrimps, beet salad with pistachios and housemade pork sausage with white beans are favorites in the lineup.

BISTRO D'OC FRENCH $$

Map p302 (202-393-5444; www.bistrodoc.com; 518 10th St NW; mains $20-28; 11:30am-2:30pm & 5:30-10:30pm Mon-Sat, 11:30am-8:30pm Sun; Metro Center) D'Oc is widely acknowledged as Washington's best place to impress with old-school French cuisine. It's supremely cozy, more Languedoc basement than lobbyist banter-bar. Think rich cassoulet and heavenly cheese plates, then stop thinking and order them.

★CENTRAL MICHEL RICHARD MODERN AMERICAN $$$

Map p302 (202-626-0015; www.centralmichelrichard.com; 1001 Pennsylvania Ave NW; mains $19-34; 11:30am-2:30pm Mon-Fri, 5-10:30pm Mon-Thu, 5-11pm Fri & Sat; Federal Triangle) Michel Richard is known for his high-end eating establishments in the District, but Central stands out as a special dining experience. It's aimed at hitting a comfort-food sweet spot. You're dining in a four-star bistro where the food is old-school favorites with a twist: lobster burgers, a sinfully complex meatloaf and fried chicken that redefines what fried chicken can be.

MINIBAR AMERICAN $$$

Map p302 (202-393-0812; www.minibarbyjoseandres.com; 855 E St NW; tasting menu $250; 6pm & 8:30pm Tue-Sat; Archives) Whimsical Minibar is foodie nirvana, where the lucky 12 (just 12 seats, folks) get wowed by animal bits spun into cotton candy and cocktails frothed into clouds. The tasting menu, entirely determined by chef Jose Andres, is often delicious and never dull. There's a sense of madcap experimentation among the 25 to 30 courses, as you'd expect from a molecular gastronomist like Andres.

Reservations are tough to get. Mark these dates on your calendar: March 1, June 1, September 1 and December 1. That's when you can reserve online for the three-month season ahead (in other words, on March 1 you can make reservations for April, May and June; on June 1 you can reserve for July, August and September, etc).

BIBIANA ITALIAN $$$

Map p302 (202-216-9550; www.bibianadc.com; 1100 New York Ave NW; mains $20-32; 11:30am-2:30pm Mon-Fri, 5:30-10:30pm Mon-Wed, to 11pm Thu-Sat; ; Metro Center) Owned by Ashok Bajaj of Rasika, Bibiana pushes contemporary Italian just as its sister establishment does with Indian cuisine. Chiluluy-esque chandeliers and light fixtures hang over an ultramodern dining room, where diners enjoy tortellini with guinea fowl and foie gras, or poached halibut over green-tomato polenta. A meat-free tasting menu is a standout in DC's vegetarian repertoire.

PROOF AMERICAN $$$

Map p302 (202-737-7663; www.proofdc.com; 775 G St NW; small plates $10-15, mains $25-35; 11:30am-2pm Tue-Fri, 5:30-10pm Mon-Thu, to 11pm Fri & Sat, to 9:30pm Sun; Gallery Pl) Everything at this wine bar–small plates restaurant is excellent, but if you want to keep costs down and still eat well, opt for the excellent cheese and charcuterie dishes, which are the best complements to the epic wine menu. If you're in a group, try to mix and match off sexy small plates such as cozy flatbread under creamy ricotta.

POSTE FRENCH $$$

Map p302 (202-783-6060; www.postebrasserie.com; Hotel Monaco, 555 8th St NW; mains $25-34; 7am-10pm Mon-Fri, 8am-10:30pm Sat, 8am-9pm Sun; Gallery Pl) Named for its previous incarnation as the mail-sorting room for the city post office, Poste does the nouveau-brasserie thing with style. Fork into top-notch *steak-frites*, crispy duck, and wine-and-herb-sauced sea bass, among other dishes. The outdoor courtyard is one of the best alfresco dining spaces in the city.

Poste gets green points by using vegetables and herbs from its organic garden, composting its food waste and offering a list of organic and local Virginia wines. Note the kitchen shuts down between 2:30pm and 5pm.

Chinatown & Convention Center

DANGEROUSLY DELICIOUS PIES AMERICAN $

Map p302 (www.dangerouspiesdc.com; 675 I St NW; slices $6.50-7.50; 10am-4pm Mon-Fri; Gallery Pl) This is a small outpost of the Dangerously Delicious shop on H St NE. The pies come in sweet and savory styles.

The latter – the beer brat pie, tofu curry pie, chicken pot pie – tend to get wiped off the chalkboard menu first, as this location does a big lunchtime business. It's kitschy-cute inside, though there isn't much seating.

NANDO'S PERI-PERI FAST FOOD **$**

Map p302 (www.nandosperiperi.com; 819 7th St NW; mains $9-14; ⏲11am-10pm Sun-Thu, to 11pm Fri & Sat; ; Ⓜ Gallery Pl) South African chain Nando's is about hot-spiced, flame-grilled chicken. Peri-peri, for the uninitiated, is a vinegary, chili-laden sauce in which they marinate the meat. Choose the spice level you want (it ranges from tongue-scorching to plain), order at the counter (including beer and wine), and staff brings the meal to your table. It's akin to fast food, but a winning step up.

Check out the walls: they hang original artworks by South African artists.

PING PONG ASIAN **$**

Map p302 (☎202-506-3740; www.pingpong-dimsum.us; 900 7th St NW; dim sum $7-15; ⏲11:30am-11pm Mon-Thu, to midnight Fri & Sat, 11am-10pm Sun; Ⓜ Gallery Pl) At Ping Pong, you can enjoy delectable dim sum any time. In fact, the stylish and open dining room gathers the liveliest crowds at night. The pan-Asian menu features delicate steamed dumplings, honey-roasted pork buns, seafood clay pots and other hits, plus tasty libations such as plum wine and elderflower *saketini* (sake-based cocktail).

MATCHBOX PIZZA PIZZA **$$**

Map p302 (☎202-289-4441; www.matchbox chinatown.com; 713 H St NW; pizzas $13-15; ⏲11am-10:30pm Mon-Thu, to 11:30pm Fri, 10am-11:30pm Sat, to 10:30pm Sun; ; Ⓜ Gallery Pl) The pizza here has a devout following of gastronomes and the restaurant's warm, exposed-brick interior typically is packed. What's so good about it? Fresh ingredients, a thin, blistered crust baked by angels, and more fresh ingredients. Oh, and the beer list rocks, with Belgian ales and hopped-up craft brews flowing from the taps. Reserve ahead to avoid a wait.

BUSBOYS & POETS CAFE **$$**

Map p302 (www.busboysandpoets.com; 1025 5th St NW; mains $11-21; ⏲8am-midnight Mon-Thu, to 1am Fri, 9am-1am Sat, to midnight Sun; ; Ⓜ Gallery Pl) Busboys & Poets is a local mini-chain of cool cafes. Each has a multiracial, opinionated, creative vibe along with well-priced sandwiches, Southern dishes, coffee, beer and other cafe fare. Open-mikes, literary readings and discussions take place several nights a week.

FULL KEE CHINESE **$$**

Map p302 (www.fullkeedc.com; 509 H St NW; mains $10-20; ⏲11am-2am; Ⓜ Gallery Pl) Although you may find more atmosphere on the moon, you won't find a better Chinese dive in the city limits. Fill yourself for next to nothing with a simple noodle dish or stir-fry, but make sure you leave some room for the duck, which is divine. Try it with some mambo sauce (DC's almost citrusy version of sweet and sour). Cash only.

BRASSERIE BECK BELGIAN **$$$**

Map p302 (☎202-408-1717; www.brasseriebeck.com; 1101 K St NW; mains $20-32; ⏲11:30am-10pm Sun-Thu, to 11:30pm Fri & Sat; Ⓜ Metro Center) The chef cooks the foods of his family's homeland at boisterous Beck. It's a meaty affair, with beef braised in dark beer, duck lasagna and pots of mussels alongside crisp *frites*. Peek in the glass-walled kitchen to see the magic happen. The beer list – a fat book of unusual brews meant to pair with the dishes – rocks hard.

Big props to the chocolate desserts, as well.

ACADIANA CAJUN, CREOLE **$$$**

Map p302 (☎202-408-8848; www.acadianarestaurant.com; 901 New York Ave NW; mains $25-35; ⏲11:30am-2:30pm Mon-Fri, 5:30-10:30pm Mon-Sat, 11am-9pm Sun; Ⓜ Metro Center) This is rich, regional Louisiana cookin', so come prepared for duck glazed in pepper jelly, sweet watermelon salad set off by spicy pecans, and veal dunked in mushroom gravy set atop a hot bed of jalapeno grits. The interior is a bit sterile – not nearly colorful enough for a Louisiana restaurant – but the food more than makes up for it.

DRINKING & NIGHTLIFE

RFD WASHINGTON BAR

Map p302 (www.lovethebeer.com; 810 7th St NW; ⏲11am-2am; Ⓜ Gallery Pl) Compared with other bars that have a wildly extensive beer menu, RFD has a slick, corporate feel, but the service is fast, it's rarely out of any one brand and the actual drinking space is huge. More than 300 brews are available, including many locally made elixirs (try DC Brau). RFD gets busy when the nearby Verizon Center hosts an event.

CITY TAP HOUSE PUB

Map p302 (www.citytaphousedc.com; 901 9th St NW; ⌚11:30am-midnight Sun-Wed, to 1:30am Thu, to 2:30am Fri & Sat; MGallery Pl) What's not to like about a wood-paneled, lodgelike gastropub with craft beers flowing from 40 taps? The vintage photos of folks boozing set the good-time mood. Settle in and make your own four-beer flight (4.5oz each) for $15. The brick-oven pizzas, Korean-short-rib tacos and other upscale bar food help soak it up.

POSTE LOUNGE LOUNGE

Map p302 (www.postebrasserie.com; Hotel Monaco, 555 8th St NW; ⌚5-10pm; MGallery Pl) At the back of the Hotel Monaco, Poste is a fantastic spot for a strong cocktail and some eye candy. Sip in the glass atrium or at the outdoor courtyard, an enormous, friendly space that's especially lovely on summer nights. In winter on Thursday, Friday and Saturday, heat lamps warm the area, and you can snuggle under the blankets draped over the couches.

ROCKET BAR BAR

Map p302 (www.rocketbardc.com; 714 7th St NW; ⌚4pm-1:30am Sun-Thu, to 2:30am Fri & Sat; MGallery Pl) Rocket Bar is an almost inexplicably popular pool hall, although there's lots more going on than some stick – shuffle board, Golden Tee, all the oldies. If you're looking for a place to check out the local talent without all the pomp, circumstance and dressing up that comes with a night of clubbing, this might be your spot.

GREEN LANTERN GAY

Map p302 (www.greenlanterndc.com; 1335 Green Ct NW; ⌚4pm-2am Sun-Thu, to 3am Fri & Sat; MMcPherson Sq) The Green Lantern is a bar downstairs, while the 2nd floor is more frisky and clubby. It attracts a slightly older crowd, and there are all kinds of daily promotions – free beer for shirtless men Thursday (10pm to 11pm), Monday karaoke etc. All in all there's a hairier, bear-ier crowd here than at many other DC gay bars.

ENTERTAINMENT

SHAKESPEARE THEATRE COMPANY THEATER

Map p302 (☎202-547-1122; www.shakespearetheatre.org; 450 7th St NW; MArchives) The nation's foremost Shakespeare company presents masterful works by the bard, as well as plays by George Bernard Shaw, Oscar Wilde, Ibsen, Eugene O'Neill and other greats. The season spans about a half-dozen productions annually, plus a free summer Shakespeare series on-site for two weeks in late August.

CAPITOL STEPS COMEDY

Map p302 (www.capsteps.com; Ronald Reagan Bldg, 1300 Pennsylvania Ave NW; tickets $40.50; ⌚shows 7:30pm Fri & Sat; MFederal Triangle) This singing troupe claims to be the only group in America that tries to be funnier than Congress. It's composed of current and former congressional staffers, so they know their political stuff, although sometimes it can be overtly corny. The satirical, bipartisan jokes poke fun at both sides of the spectrum.

NATIONAL THEATRE THEATER

Map p302 (☎202-628-6161; www.thenationaldc.org; 1321 Pennsylvania Ave NW; MMetro Center) Washington's oldest continuously operating theater shows flashy Broadway musicals and big-name productions. A lottery for $25 tickets (cash only) takes place two hours prior to every show; submit your name at the box office. Saturday mornings feature free performances for children at 9:30am and 11am. Grown-ups get their free show (a classic-movie screening) Monday evenings from September through May.

WOOLLY MAMMOTH THEATRE COMPANY THEATER

Map p302 (☎202-393-3939; www.woollymammoth.net; 641 D St NW; MArchives) Woolly Mammoth is the edgiest of DC's experimental groups. Assuming the show is not a sell-out, $15 'stampede' seats are available at the box office two hours before performances.

E STREET CINEMA CINEMA

Map p302 (www.landmarktheatres.com; 555 11th St NW; MMetro Center) The eight screens flicker with first-run independent and foreign films, documentaries and classic revivals. Crab-cake bites, chicken satay, wine and craft beer stock the beyond-the-norm concession stand. This is a great neighborhood spot to see a movie.

FORD'S THEATRE THEATER

Map p302 (www.fordstheatre.org; 511 10th St NW; Ⓜ Metro Center) The historical theater – where John Wilkes Booth killed Abraham Lincoln – stages works related to Lincoln's life and times (including world premieres and musicals), as well as American classics.

WARNER THEATRE THEATER

Map p302 (www.warnertheatredc.com; 513 13th St NW; Ⓜ Federal Triangle) The beautifully restored 1924 art-deco theater was originally built for vaudeville and silent films, but it now stages headliner concerts, comedians and national runs of Broadway musicals.

SHOPPING

★**NATIONAL ARCHIVES SHOP** SOUVENIRS

Map p302 (www.myarchivesstore.org; 700 Pennsylvania Ave NW; ⏲10am-5:30pm Sep–mid-Mar, to 7pm mid-Mar–Aug; Ⓜ Archives) Whether you're looking for a Thomas Jefferson biography, a Declaration of Independence–inscribed ruler, a John Adams stuffed toy or an Elvis-meets-Nixon magnet, the Archives Shop has a huge array of fun, historical goods.

INTERNATIONAL SPY MUSEUM SHOP SOUVENIRS

Map p302 (www.spymuseumstore.org; 800 F St NW; ⏲10am-6pm; Ⓜ Gallery Pl) Let's face it: every so often everyone needs a pair of reverse-mirrored sunglasses. Now you know where to get them, and piles of other nifty spy gadgets. James Bond–type gear that might come in handy includes concealed listening devices, disguise kits, micro cameras and recorder pens.

NATIONAL BUILDING MUSEUM SHOP ARTS

Map p302 (www.nbm.org; 401 F St NW; ⏲10am-5pm Mon-Sat, from 11am Sun; Ⓜ Judiciary Sq) The museum shop is an amateur architect's dream, with small pieces of furniture, paper models of famed buildings, groovy stationery and a collection of books on American and international architecture. There's also a big selection of build-it-yourself educational toys for kids.

NATIONAL MUSEUM OF WOMEN IN THE ARTS SHOP ARTS

Map p302 (www.nmwa.org; 1250 New York Ave NW; ⏲10am-5pm Mon-Sat, from noon Sun; Ⓜ Metro Center) This small room left of the museum entrance holds unique books, prints, posters, jewelry and handicrafts – all created by women.

COUP DE FOUDRE CLOTHING

Map p302 (www.coupdefoudrelingerie.com; cnr 11th & E Sts NW; ⏲11am-6pm Mon-Sat; Ⓜ Metro Center) Local men dream of the day their girlfriends take them here and say, 'What should I get, honey?' Women also love Coup; the lingerie makes Victoria's Secret look gauche, and the mom-and-daughter owners have a passion for prettying up your bottom drawer.

TEAISM SHOP FOOD & DRINK

Map p302 (www.teaism.com; 400 8th St NW; ⏲10am-6pm Mon-Sat, from 11am Sun; Ⓜ Archives) Next to the inviting cafe of the same name, Teaism sells dozens of loose-leaf teas, from smoky Lapsang Souchong to organic jasmine and rich green teas – all concealed in artful boxes behind the counter. You can also buy teapots, mugs, strainers and ornate display boxes (covered with handmade paper).

SPORTS & ACTIVITIES

WASHINGTON WIZARDS BASKETBALL

Map p302 (www.nba.com/wizards; 601 F St NW; Ⓜ Gallery Pl) Washington's winning pro basketball team plays at the Verizon Center from October through April. The lowest-price tickets are around $30 for the nosebleed section, and the cost goes way up from there.

WASHINGTON CAPITALS HOCKEY

Map p302 (http://capitals.nhl.com; 601 F St NW; Ⓜ Gallery Pl) Washington's rough-and-tumble pro hockey team skates at the Verizon Center from October through April. Tickets start from around $40.

WASHINGTON MYSTICS BASKETBALL

Map p302 (www.wnba.com/mystics; 601 F St NW; Ⓜ Gallery Pl) DC's women's NBA team plays at the Verizon Center from May to September.

National Cherry Blossom Festival

It's a rite of spring: each year in late March or early April, DC's 3700-plus cherry trees burst into a shimmering sea of pale-pink blossoms. The festival celebrates the occasion, with 1.5 million people descending on the Tidal Basin to revel in the fairy-tale sight and intoxicating scent.

Japan's Gift to DC

In 1912, the mayor of Tokyo gave 3000 cherry trees to Washington, DC, as a gift of friendship between Japan and the USA. It was actually his second gift: the first group of trees arrived two years prior, but insects and disease infested them and they had to be destroyed.

The 1912 batch fared better. First Lady Helen Herron Taft and Viscountess Chinda, wife of the Japanese ambassador, planted the first two trees in West Potomac Park on March 27. Workers placed the rest elsewhere around the Tidal Basin. Since then, the number of trees has expanded to approximately 3750. A crew of dedicated National Park Service arborists tends them.

Festival Dates & Activities

The festival kicks off on March 20 and runs for three weeks or so. Events take place all over town. The highlight is the Cherry Blossom Parade, which occurs the last Saturday of the fest and brings elaborate floats, marching bands and celebrity entertainers for a procession along Constitution Ave. Immediately afterward the Sakura Matsuri Japanese Street Festival lets loose downtown. The Kite Festival swoops and soars by the Washington Monument on a late-March

SEAN PAVONE / GETTY IMAGES ©

LISSANDRA MELO / SHUTTERSTOCK ©

1. Spring blossoms in one of the city's gardens
2. A float in the annual Cherry Blossom Parade
3. Martin Luther King Jr Memorial (p63) in spring

OFHAN CAM / SHUTTERSTOCK ©

Saturday, while the Southwest Waterfront Fireworks illuminate the night sky the following weekend. Most events are kid-friendly and free. Photography workshops; boat, bike and walking tours; garden-design seminars; and theater and musical performances are also on offer.

Viewing Tips

Everyone wants to visit during the 'peak bloom' date, when 70% of the blossoms are open. The average peak bloom in recent years has been March 31. Warm weather makes it happen earlier (March 15, 1990, is the record), cold weather makes it happen later (April 18, 1958, wins the prize). The festival website (www.nationalcherryblossomfestival.org) tracks the predicted date via its Bloom Watch.

If you miss the Tidal Basin explosion, all is not lost. Smaller groves of cherry trees pop up at the National Arboretum and Dumbarton Oaks, and they usually peak a bit later.

TOP CHERRY-BLOSSOM EXPERIENCES

- Snapping photos of the shimmering scene from the Jefferson Memorial or Martin Luther King Jr Memorial.
- Seeing the trees from the water. Do it DIY style with a Tidal Basin Boathouse paddleboat or on a guided kayak tour with Key Bridge Boathouse.
- Joining the Kite Festival by the Washington Monument.
- Wearing pink and readying the confetti for the Cherry Blossom Parade.

Dupont Circle & Kalorama

Neighborhood Top Five

❶ Travel to India, Kenya, Laos, Luxembourg, Malawi, Morocco and Zambia during an hour's walk (literally – embassy grounds are technically another nation's territory) along **Embassy Row** (p144).

❷ Stand face to face with Renoirs and Gauguins in the intimate setting of the **Phillips Collection** (p145).

❸ Browse the stacks, sip cocktails and stuff your face at **Kramerbooks** (p153).

❹ Expand your mind at **Studio Gallery** (p145) or other neighborhood showplaces.

❺ Experience the genteel Washingtonian lifestyle, both past and present, at **Woodrow Wilson House** (p145).

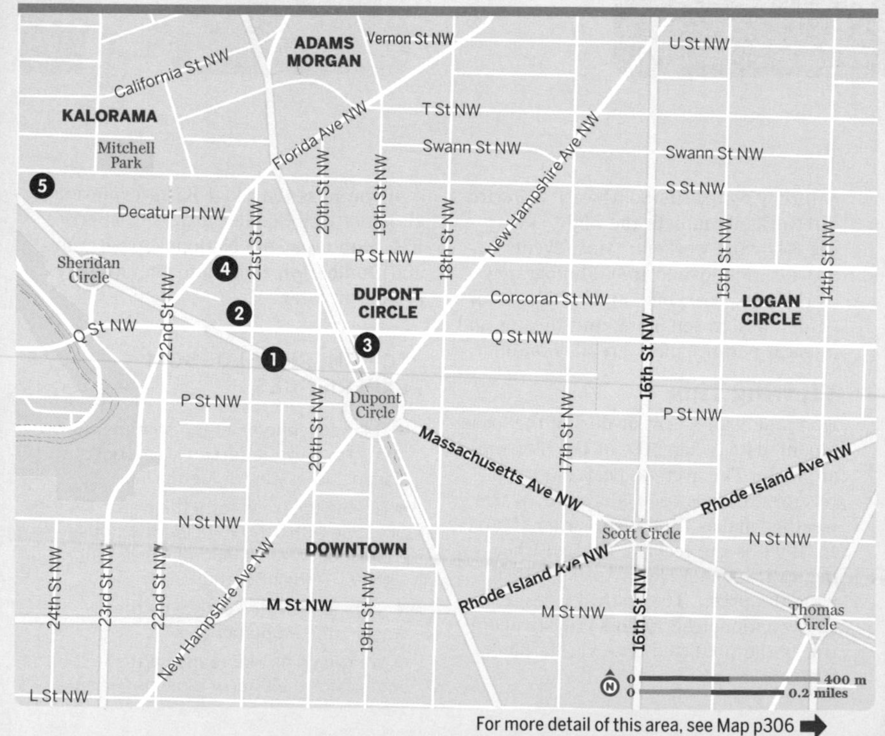

For more detail of this area, see Map p306

Explore Dupont Circle & Kalorama

A well-heeled splice of gay community and DC diplomatic scene, Dupont Circle – or, much more commonly, Dupont – is city life at its best. Here you'll find flash new restaurants, hip bars, cafe society and nifty bookstores. The neighborhood has Washington's highest concentration of embassies, many set in captivating historic mansions along Massachusetts Ave NW (aka Embassy Row). Dupont is also the out-and-about heart of DC's gay and lesbian community. This combination gay and international pulse tends to beat out the social rhythm for young professionals of all stripes and persuasions.

Kalorama adjoins Dupont to the northwest. Greek for 'beautiful view,' it was named for an estate built by Jefferson confidant Joel Barlow that dominated this hilly area in the 19th century. These days it's a sort of Dupont with an extra helping of regal reserve and mansions.

The neighborhood is easy to explore, since almost everything radiates from the literal Dupont Circle, the traffic rotunda. Spend the morning getting cultured in under-the-radar museums. An embassy stroll coupled with artsy shopping is a fine way to spend the afternoon. Have dinner in one of the international eateries, then get ready for a big night out. Romantic cocktails, crazy dance parties, retro board games and 24-hour bookstores await.

Local Life

➡ **Midnight bite** Afterwords Cafe (p148) hops late-night on weekends, when it slings chow – and tomes at attached store Kramerbooks – 24/7. Brunch is equally jam-packed.

➡ **Lunchtime journey** During the spring and fall, the National Geographic Society Museum (p146) shows a free documentary on Tuesdays at noon. Join locals on their lunch break to explore distant lands.

➡ **Happy hours** Lots of bars and clubs mean lots of happy hours. Dupont is a great spot for post-work tipples that won't flatten your wallet.

Getting There & Away

➡ **Metro** Access most points from Dupont Circle (Red Line). Use the Q St exit for destinations north of P St, and the 19th St exit for destinations south. Farragut North (Red Line) is closer to M St.

➡ **Bus** To catch the DC Circulator's Dupont–Georgetown–Rosslyn bus, depart Dupont Circle Metro station from the south exit; the bus stop is at 19th and N Sts.

Lonely Planet's Top Tip

If you really want to take advantage of the embassy scene, check out the **International Club** (www.internationalclubdc.com). It organizes concerts, dinners and cultural events – many held at embassies – for 'internationally minded' locals to socialize. Anyone can join and be off to dinners at the Ukrainian Embassy, concerts at the Austrian Embassy and more.

Best Places to Eat

➡ Little Serow (p148)
➡ Bistrot du Coin (p148)
➡ Duke's Grocery (p148)
➡ Komi (p148)
➡ Bub & Pop's (p147)

For reviews, see p147. ➡

Best Places to Drink

➡ Tabard Inn Bar (p151)
➡ Firefly Bar (p151)
➡ Bar Charley (p151)
➡ Filter (p152)
➡ Russia House (p150)

For reviews, see p151. ➡

Best Museums

➡ Phillips Collection (p145)
➡ National Geographic Society Museum (p146)
➡ Woodrow Wilson House (p145)
➡ Society of the Cincinnati (p145)
➡ Laogai Museum (p145)

For reviews, see p145. ➡

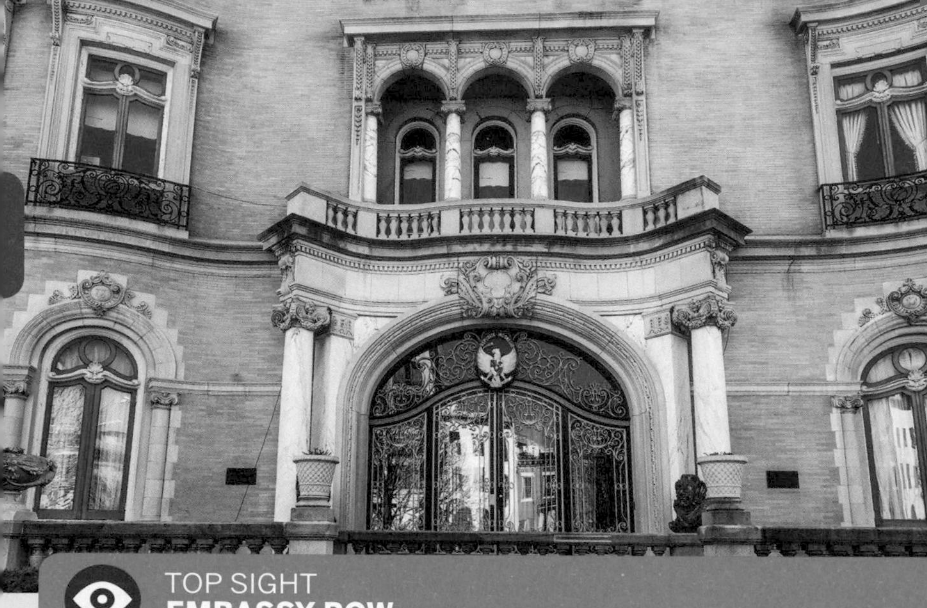

BILL PERRY / SHUTTERSTOCK ©

TOP SIGHT
EMBASSY ROW

How quickly can you leave the country? It takes about five minutes; just stroll north along Massachusetts Ave from Dupont Circle and you pass more than 40 embassies housed in mansions that range from elegant to imposing to discreet. Technically, they're on foreign soil, as embassy grounds are the embassy nation's territory.

Embassies sprinkle the District, but Dupont has the most. Massachusetts Ave was once Millionaire's Row, and the mansions of the old elite are still thick on the ground. Most embassies were residences built by industrialists and financiers at the turn of the 20th century. The Great Depression caused many to lose their manors, which then stood gracefully decaying until WWII's end. As nations came to Washington to set up shop, the old homes were uniquely fit to be embassies.

The **Indonesian Embassy** (Map p306; 2020 Massachusetts Ave NW) is an impressive example. Gold-mining magnate Thomas Walsh commissioned the home in 1903, when it was said to be the costliest house in the city (not surprising, considering the gold-flecked marble pillars). The **Luxembourg Embassy** (Map p306; 2200 Massachusetts Ave NW) is another show-stopper. Congressman Alexander Stewart built the home in 1909 in the grand court style of Louis XIV. In 1941 the Grand Duchess of Luxembourg bought it and lived here in exile during WWII. Edward Everett, inventor of the grooved bottle cap, built the structure that is now the **Turkish Ambassador's Residence** (Map p306; cnr Sheridan Circle & 23rd St). George Oakley Totten designed the building, which has some Ottoman influences. Totten was the official architect of Ottoman sultan Abdul Hamid II. At the nearby **Croatian Embassy** (Map p306; 2343 Massachusetts Ave NW) an impressive sculpture marks the spot: a life-size, cross-legged St Jerome dreaming over his book, by sculptor Ivan Meštrović.

DON'T MISS...

- Indonesian Embassy
- Luxembourg Embassy
- Turkish Ambassador's Residence
- Croatian Embassy

PRACTICALITIES

- Map p306
- www.embassy.org
- Massachusetts Ave NW btwn Observatory & Dupont Circles NW
- Ⓜ Dupont Circle

SIGHTS

EMBASSY ROW ARCHITECTURE

See p144.

PHILLIPS COLLECTION MUSEUM

Map p306 (www.phillipscollection.org; 1600 21st St NW; Sat & Sun $10, Tue-Fri free, ticketed exhibitions per day $12; ⊙10am-5pm Tue, Wed, Fri & Sat, to 8:30pm Thu, 11am-6pm Sun, chamber-music series 4pm Sun Oct-May; Ⓜ Dupont Circle) The first modern-art museum in the country (opened in 1921) houses a small but exquisite collection of European and American works. Renoir's *Luncheon of the Boating Party* is a highlight, along with pieces by Gauguin, Van Gogh, Matisse, Picasso and many other greats. The intimate rooms, set in a restored mansion, put you unusually close to the artworks. The permanent collection is free on weekdays.

The Rothko Room, which hangs four of the abstract expressionist's pieces, is worth a peek, although sometimes it's part of the museum's ticketed exhibits (in which case extra admission fees apply). The Phillips' Sunday chamber-music series has been making sweet sounds since 1941.

WOODROW WILSON HOUSE MUSEUM

Map p306 (www.woodrowwilsonhouse.org; 2340 S St NW; adult/child $10/free; ⊙10am-4pm Tue-Sun; Ⓜ Dupont Circle) This Georgian-revival mansion offers guided hour-long tours focusing on the 28th president's life and legacy. Genteel docents discuss highlights of Wilson's career (WWI, the League of Nations) and home, which has been restored to the period of his residence (1921–24). The tour features European bronzes, a stairwell conservatory, exquisite china and Mrs W's flapper dresses, all of which offer a glamorous portrait of Roaring '20s DC society.

The docents' entertaining stories spread beyond the Wilson house: they can point out the rich eccentrics and ambassadors who live nearby and give you directions to the Clintons' Georgian Colonial pad about a mile up the road.

STUDIO GALLERY GALLERY

Map p306 (www.studiogallerydc.com; 2108 R St NW; ⊙1-7pm Wed-Fri, to 6pm Sat; Ⓜ Dupont Circle) Studio Gallery shows contemporary works by 35 emerging DC-area artists. Paintings, sculpture, mixed media and video are represented. The relatively small space spans the main floor and basement, with exhibits that always feel fresh. Openings are held on the first Friday of the month.

> **LOCAL KNOWLEDGE**
>
> **THE SPANISH STEPS**
>
> You're walking up 22nd St to S St NW, and suddenly an enchanting staircase appears. The **Spanish Steps** (Map p306), as they're known, were modeled on those in Rome's Piazza di Spagna. Why are they here? The rise up to S St was deemed too steep, so city planners built the steps to bridge the gap. Climb up for an atmospheric view of Embassy Row.

SOCIETY OF THE CINCINNATI MUSEUM

Map p306 (www.societyofthecincinnati.org; 2118 Massachusetts Ave NW; ⊙1-4pm Tue-Sat; Ⓜ Dupont Circle) FREE The Society of the Cincinnati is a private patriotic group that educates the public about the Revolutionary War. Who knew? What's key here is the chance to go inside the Renaissance Revival mansion (aka Anderson House) where it has its headquarters and check out the opulent interior. The gilded ballrooms, chandeliers, tapestries, sweeping staircases and marble pillars drop the jaw.

You can poke around a little bit on your own, but allow an hour for a docent-guided tour to see the majority of the rooms.

LAOGAI MUSEUM MUSEUM

Map p306 (☎202-730-9308; www.laogaimuseum.org; 1734 20th St NW; ⊙10am-6pm; Ⓜ Dupont Circle) FREE The small Laogai Museum sits on a peaceful Dupont residential street, so it's jarring to enter and confront the roomful of harrowing exhibits about Chinese labor camps. Red and white placards fill the walls telling the stories of people – mostly political dissidents – sentenced to the camps and the harsh treatment they face. Artifacts such as prisoners' tattered clothing and everyday products made in the camps (black tea, toys, plastic bags) add to the haunting effect.

Exhibit space is also given to Soviet gulags, Nazi concentration camps and the Khmer Rouge's forced-labor camps in Cambodia.

HEURICH HOUSE MUSEUM

Map p306 (www.heurichhouse.org; 1307 New Hampshire Ave NW; tours $5; ⊙11:30am & 1pm Thu & Fri, 11:30am, 1pm & 2:30pm Sat; Ⓜ Dupont

LOCAL KNOWLEDGE

ANOTHER EMBASSY ROW

While Massachusetts Ave has the most embassies, New Hampshire Ave also has its share: 12 embassies, to be exact, in a four-block stretch heading northeast from Dupont Circle. Saunter along and wave to the good folks of Mozambique, Argentina, Belarus and Eritrea, among others.

Circle) Welcome to 'the castle that beer built.' John Granville Myers designed the 31-room mansion for German-born brewer Christian Heurich, a man who loved beer with a passion. One quote along the walls states: '*Raum ist in der kleinsten Kammer fur den grossten Katzenjammer*' ('There is room in the smallest chamber for the biggest hangover'). Entry is by guided tour only, though DIY explorations of the gardens (11am to 3pm April to October) are permitted.

MANSION ON O STREET BUILDING

Map p306 (www.omansion.com; 2020 O St NW; tours $10; ⏲11am-8pm Mon, to 4pm Tue-Sat, 1:30-4pm Sun; Ⓜ Dupont Circle) This 100-room 1892 mansion is part inn, part gallery performance space and part private club. In this latter incarnation, it has hosted Hollywood celebrities and Chelsea Clinton's sweet-16 party. The decor is like a wedding at Castle Dracula: swags of velvet drapery, ornate chandeliers, candelabras and concealed doorways. And it's all for sale! The mansion serves food and drinks, but we recommend sticking to the bizarro self-guided tour. Register online for a time slot at least 24 hours in advance.

FOUNDRY GALLERY GALLERY

Map p306 (www.foundrygallery.org; 1314 18th St NW; ⏲noon-6pm Wed-Sun; Ⓜ Dupont Circle) A nonprofit member-run organization, this gallery features a diverse range of super-contemporary art, including paintings, sculptures and drawings, made in the last decade, all created by local artists. Openings are held on various Fridays.

CATHEDRAL OF ST MATTHEW THE APOSTLE CHURCH

Map p306 (www.stmatthewscathedral.org; 1725 Rhode Island Ave NW; ⏲6:30am-6:30pm Sun-Fri, from 7:30am Sat; Ⓜ Dupont Circle) The sturdy redbrick exterior doesn't hint at the marvelous mosaics and gilding within this 1893 Catholic cathedral, where JFK was laid in state and his funeral mass was held. Its vast central dome, altars and chapels depict biblical saints and eminent New World personages – from Simón Bolívar to Elizabeth Ann Seton – in stained glass, murals and scintillating Italianate mosaics; almost no surface is left undecorated. Pick up a self-guided-tour brochure by the entrance (beneath the guest register).

Evening is the best time to visit, when flickering candles illuminate the sanctuary, but you can attend mass on Sunday morning or slip in almost any time to look around.

NATIONAL GEOGRAPHIC SOCIETY MUSEUM MUSEUM

Map p306 (☎202-857-7700; www.ngmuseum.org; 1145 17th St NW; adult/child $11/7; ⏲10am-6pm; Ⓜ Farragut North) The museum at National Geographic Society headquarters can't compete with the Smithsonian's more extensive offerings, but it can be worth a stop, depending on what's showing. Exhibits are drawn from the society's well-documented expeditions to the far corners of the Earth, and they change every three months or so. In spring and fall, the on-site theater shows free documentary films on Tuesdays at noon.

The society also hosts concerts and lectures by famed researchers and explorers; most programs have a fee.

CHARLES SUMNER SCHOOL & ARCHIVES MUSEUM

Map p306 (1201 17th St NW; ⏲10am-5pm Mon-Fri; Ⓜ Farragut North) FREE The stately, dignified Sumner building is a great example of solidly beautiful red-brick 19th-century urban design, but it is an even better testament to civil rights and education. Back in 1877, this was where the first high-school class of African Americans was graduated out of the school system. Today you can find the DC Public School archives here, as well as a museum that displays local public school memorabilia along with exhibits on statesman and orator Frederick Douglass.

METROPOLITAN AME CHURCH CHURCH

Map p306 (Metropolitan African Methodist Episcopal Church; www.metropolitanamec.org; 1518 M St NW; ⏲10am-6pm Mon-Sat; Ⓜ McPherson

Sq) Built and paid for in 1886 by former slaves (quite a feat considering its impressive size), the Metropolitan AME Church occupies an imposing redbrick Gothic structure and is one of the city's most striking churches. Frederick Douglass often preached here, and his state funeral was held here in February 1895. On the day of his burial, black schools closed, crowds packed the exterior to pay respect and flags flew at half-mast.

SCOTTISH RITE TEMPLE BUILDING

Map p306 (www.scottishrite.org; 1733 16th St NW; ⏲10am-4pm Mon-Thu Sep-May, from 9am Jun-Aug; Ⓜ Dupont Circle) FREE The regional headquarters of the Scottish Rite Freemasons, also known as the House of the Temple, is one of the most eye-catching buildings in the District. That's because it looks as if a magic temple lifted out of a comic book, all the more incredible for basically sitting amid a tangle of residential row houses. It's as if someone plopped the Parthenon in the middle of Shady Acres suburbia.

There's a lot of heavy Masonic symbolism and ritual associated with the building. Thirty-three columns surround the building, representing the 33rd Degree, an honorary distinction conferred on outstanding Masons. Two sphinxes, Wisdom and Power, guard the entrance, and past the gates of bronze that front the building (really), the grand atrium looks like a collision zone between the Egyptian and Greek antiquities departments of a major museum. Note the pharaonic statues and chairs modeled to resemble thrones from the Temple of Dionysus. Guides provide tours of all this fascinating minutiae.

EATING

Classy nouveau cuisine and upscale ethnic eateries cater to the flocks of diplomats and businesspeople, while casual cafes cater to the more bohemian.

BUB & POP'S SANDWICHES $

Map p306 (www.bubandpops.com; 1815 M St NW; sandwiches $7-13; ⏲11am-7pm Mon-Fri, noon-7pm Sat; Ⓜ Dupont Circle) A chef tired of the fine-dining rat race opened this gourmet sandwich shop with his parents. Ingredients are made from scratch in house – the meatballs, pickles, mayonnaise, roasted pork. Congenial mom Arlene rules the counter and can answer questions about any of it. The sandwiches are enormous, best consumed hot off the press in the bright aqua and red room.

DOLCEZZA GELATERIA $

Map p306 (www.dolcezzagelato.com; 1704 Connecticut Ave NW; gelato $5-8; ⏲7am-10pm Mon-Thu, to 11pm Fri, 8am-11pm Sat, to 10pm Sun; 📶; Ⓜ Dupont Circle) The local mini-chain Dolcezza whips up the District's best gelato. Some flavors are unusual, such as sweet-potato pecan and Thai coconut milk, and change with the seasons. Traditionalists can always get their licks with chocolate, salted caramel and peppermint. Good coffee, vintage-chic decor and free wi-fi add to the pleasure.

SWEETGREEN HEALTH FOOD $

Map p306 (www.sweetgreen.com; 1512 Connecticut Ave NW; mains $8-11; ⏲11am-10pm; 🖉; Ⓜ Dupont Circle) Dupont Circle's branch of the healthful salad purveyor often has a line out the door. Order your huge bowl of

CAPITALLY KOSHER

Two of Washington's most prominent Judaica sights can be found amid the brown-red bricks of Dupont Circle. The **Washington DC Jewish Community Center** (Map p306; www.washingtondcjcc.org; 1529 16th St NW; Ⓜ Dupont Circle) hosts plenty of arts activities, interfaith dialogues, community action programs and the like. The community center's sleek, boxlike headquarters is a treat in itself, resembling the exterior of a modern art museum.

The **National Museum of American Jewish Military History** (Map p306; www.nmajmh.org; 1811 R St NW; ⏲9am-5pm Mon-Fri; Ⓜ Dupont Circle) FREE offers a small but fascinating peek into the wartime exploits of American Jews. Displays on Jewish Medal of Honor recipients and the history of death-camp liberation – among others – are brought to life with touch screens, large-scale videos, listening stations and other multimedia experiences.

roast chicken and kale or spicy shrimp and arugula at the counter, then take it to the communal tables to consume with the rest of the young and fit.

WELL-DRESSED BURRITO TEX-MEX $

Map p306 (www.thewelldressedburrito.com; 1220 19th St NW; mains $6-10; ⏲11:45am-2:15pm Mon-Fri; Ⓜ Dupont Circle) The Well-Dressed Burrito deals in...well, do we need to spell it out? These burritos are big, fat and the perfect antidote to last night's alcohol overindulgence. Enter through the alley between M and N Sts.

★BISTROT DU COIN FRENCH $$

Map p306 (☎202-234-6969; www.bistrotducoin.com; 1738 Connecticut Ave NW; mains $14-24; ⏲11:30am-11pm Sun-Wed, to 1am Thu-Sat; Ⓜ Dupont Circle) The lively and much-loved Bistrot du Coin is a neighborhood favorite for roll-up-your sleeves, working-class French fare. The kitchen sends out consistently good onion soup, classic *steak-frites* (grilled steak and French fries), cassoulet, open-face sandwiches and nine varieties of its famous *moules* (mussels). Regional wines from around the motherland accompany the food by the glass, carafe and bottle.

The clientele is a fun mix of Dupont locals and nostalgic Europeans, and the atmosphere feels plucked out of Orwell's *Down and Out* descriptions of Paris. Make reservations.

DUKE'S GROCERY CAFE $$

Map p306 (☎202-733-5623; www.dukesgrocery.com; 1513 17th St NW; mains $11-16; ⏲5:30-10pm Mon, 8am-10pm Tue & Wed, to 1am Thu & Fri, 11am-1am Sat, to 10pm Sun; 📶✍; Ⓜ Dupont Circle) 'The taste of East London in East Dupont' is the Duke's tagline, and that means black pudding and baked beans in the morning, spiced-lentil rotis in the afternoon and Brick Lane salt-beef sandwiches late at night. Couples on low-maintenance dates and groups of chitchatty friends angle for tables by the bay windows to people watch. The genial vibe invites all-day lingering.

Menu items change, but there's always a curry of the day, a few vegetarian items and killer cocktails.

AFTERWORDS CAFE AMERICAN $$

Map p306 (☎202-387-3825; www.kramers.com; 1517 Connecticut Ave; mains $15-21; ⏲7:30am-1am Sun-Thu, 24hr Fri & Sat; Ⓜ Dupont Circle) Attached to Kramerbooks, this buzzing spot is not your average bookstore cafe. The packed indoor tables, wee bar and outdoor patio overflow with good cheer. The menu features tasty bistro fare and an ample beer selection, making it a prime spot for happy hour, for brunch and at all hours on weekends (open 24 hours, baby!).

Browsing the stacks before stuffing the gut is many locals' favorite way to spend a Washington weekend.

ZORBA'S CAFE GREEK $$

Map p306 (☎202-387-8555; www.zorbascafe.com; 1612 20th St NW; mains $13-16; ⏲11am-11:30pm Mon-Sat, to 10:30pm Sun; 👪; Ⓜ Dupont Circle) Generous portions of moussaka and souvlaki, as well as pitchers of Rolling Rock beer, make family-run Zorba's Cafe one of DC's best bargain haunts. On warm days the outdoor patio is packed with locals. With the bouzouki music playing in the background, you can almost imagine you're in the Greek islands.

★LITTLE SEROW THAI $$$

Map p306 (www.littleserow.com; 1511 17th St NW; fixed menu per person $45; ⏲5:30-10pm Tue-Thu, to 10:30pm Fri & Sat; Ⓜ Dupont Circle) Little Serow has no phone, no reservations and no sign on the door. It only seats groups of four or fewer (larger parties will be separated), but despite all this, people line up around the block. And what for? Superlative Northern Thai cuisine. The single-option menu – which consists of six or so hot-spiced courses – changes by the week.

You might get chicken livers and long peppers, or shrimp paste, eggplant and chilies. Every dish comes with mountains of fresh herbs.

KOMI FUSION $$$

Map p306 (☎202-332-9200; www.komirestaurant.com; 1509 17th St NW; set menu $135; ⏲5-9:30pm Tue-Thu, to 10pm Fri & Sat; Ⓜ Dupont Circle) There is an admirable simplicity to Komi's changing menu, which is rooted in Greece and influenced by everything – primarily genius. Suckling pig for two; scallops and truffles; a roasted baby goat. Komi's fairytale of a dining space doesn't take groups larger than four, and you need to reserve way in advance – like, now.

It's one of Washington's most knockout dining experiences, with the incredible attention and measured pacing that the staff provides adding to the effect.

OBELISK

ITALIAN **$$$**

Map p306 (☎202-872-1180; http://www.obeliskdc.com; 2029 P St NW; 5-course menu $75-85; ⏰6-10pm Tue-Sat; Ⓜ Dupont Circle) Obelisk pushes the boundaries of what can be done in an Italian *cucina*. The small and narrow dining room feels almost like eating at someone's kitchen table. The set-course Italian feasts are lovingly prepared with first-rate ingredients; the antipasti in particular is a revelation. The menu changes daily but doesn't give you much selection (picky eaters should call ahead). Make reservations.

SUSHI TARO

JAPANESE **$$$**

Map p306 (☎202-462-8999; www.sushitaro.com; 1503 17th St NW; tasting menu from $80; ⏰11:30am-2pm Mon-Fri, 5:30-10pm Mon-Sat; Ⓜ Dupont Circle) Many locals say this contemporary Japanese place serves the best sushi in town. The kitchen obsesses over preparing the finest, freshest fish possible, arranged with beautiful sides and garnishes. The tastes have almost mathematical layers of complexity, yet the intricacy is arrived at from the simple combination of a few fresh ingredients.

For instance, a quivering bit of fatty tuna comes with a side of wasabi freshly grated from one long stem of Japanese horseradish into slivers of nose-tingling happiness.

TABARD INN RESTAURANT

AMERICAN **$$$**

Map p306 (☎202-331-8528; www.tabardinn.com/restaurant; 1739 N St NW; mains $24-34; ⏰7-10am, 11:30am-2:30pm & 5:30-9:30pm Mon-Fri, 7-9am, 10:30am-2:30pm & 5:30-9:30pm Sat & Sun; Ⓜ Dupont Circle) Dinners are seasonal twists on classic fare – scallops with parsnip puree, veal with sugar snap peas – but it's the deceptively normal weekend brunch menu that stands out. The poached eggs, chocolate waffles and oysters (which are caught specifically for the inn) are sublime. Grab a table in the cozy, English manor–like interior or the splendid, ivy-walled garden courtyard. Reservations recommended.

BLUE DUCK TAVERN

AMERICAN **$$$**

Map p306 (☎202-419-6755; www.blueducktavern.com; 1201 24th St NW; mains $20-36; ⏰6:30am-2:30pm & 5:30-10:30pm Sun-Thu, to 11:30pm Fri & Sat; ✍; Ⓜ Dupont Circle) The Blue Duck creates a rustic kitchen ambience in the midst of an uber-urbanized concrete corridor of M St. The menu draws from farms across the country, mixing mains such as venison tartare and suckling pig sourced from Pennsylvania, crab cakes from nearby Chesapeake Bay and grits from South Carolina.

The interior mashes up modernist clean lines and high ceilings with countrified quilts and wooden tables and chairs. The restaurant is located inside the Park Hyatt hotel.

> **LOCAL KNOWLEDGE**
>
> **FARMERS MARKET**
>
> The **Dupont Circle Market** (Map p306; www.freshfarmmarkets.org; 1560 20th St NW; ⏰9am-2pm Sun Apr-Dec, 10am-1pm Jan-Mar; Ⓜ Dupont Circle) teems with locals on Sunday morning. It's part of the Fresh Farm Market program, one of the leaders of the Chesapeake Bay region local-food movement. Browse stalls selling rosemary-salt bread, goat Brie, bluefish empanadas and fruits and veggies galore.

HANK'S OYSTER BAR

SEAFOOD **$$$**

Map p306 (☎202-462 4265; www.hanksoysterbar.com; 1624 Q St NW; mains $20-30; ⏰11:30am-3pm & 5:30-10pm Sun-Tue, to 11pm Wed-Sat; Ⓜ Dupont Circle) DC has several oyster bars, but mini-chain Hank's is our favorite, mixing power-player muscle with good-old-boy ambience. As you'd expect, the oyster menu is extensive and excellent; there are always at least four varieties on hand. Quarters are cramped, and you often have to wait for a table – nothing a sake oyster bomb won't fix.

NORA

MODERN AMERICAN **$$$**

Map p306 (☎202-462-5143; www.noras.com; 2132 Florida Ave NW; mains $30-40; ⏰5:30-10pm Mon-Thu, from 5pm Fri & Sat; Ⓜ Dupont Circle) Opened in 1979, this was by many accounts the first organic restaurant in the country. Chef Nora was a pioneer of New American–style cooking, and she still crushes it. Alaskan halibut arrives on a bed of corn succotash, while Amish chicken livers soak deliciously in their own *jus*. All this happens in a quaint carriage house on one of Dupont's loveliest corners.

VIDALIA

SOUTHERN **$$$**

Map p306 (☎202-659-1990; www.vidaliadc.com; 1990 M St NW; mains $30-36; ⏰11:30am-2:30pm

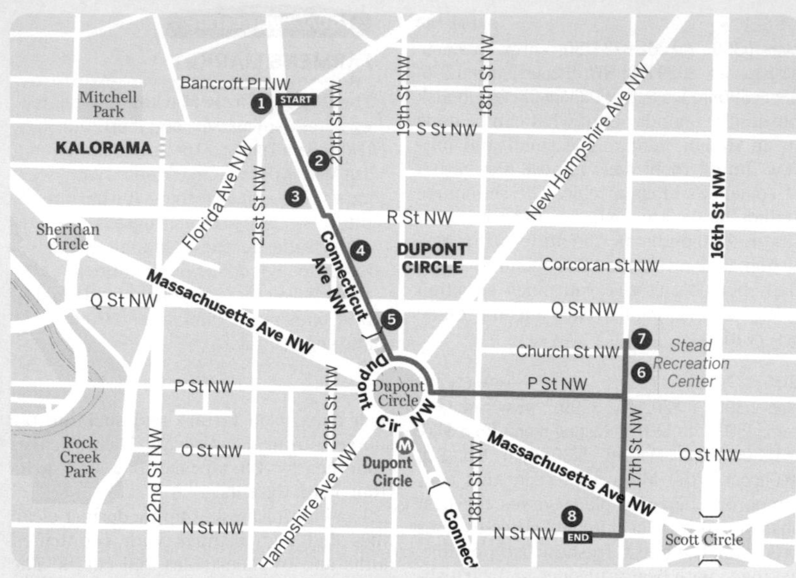

Local Life
A Night Out in Dupont Circle

Dupont gets busy once the sun goes down. Young professionals of all stripes and persuasions gather with friends to drink, dine and sing karaoke. They play board games, knock back vodka shots, indulge in late-night gelato and curries, and flirt with each other in the 24-hour bookshop on weekends.

1 Caviar at Russia House

Russophiles flock to faded but elegant **Russia House** (Map p306; www.russiahouselounge.com; 1800 Connecticut Ave NW; ⏲5pm-midnight Sun-Thu, to 2:30am Fri & Sat; Ⓜ Dupont Circle), with its brassy chandeliers, candlelit chambers and stupefying vodka selection. It's a great spot for conversation and caviar.

2 Board Room's Game Stash

Grab a beer, settle in at a table and crush your opponent at Hungry Hungry Hippos. Or summon spirits with a ouija board. **Board Room** (Map p306; www.boardroomdc.com; 1737 Connecticut Ave NW; ⏲4pm-2am Mon-Thu, to 3am Fri, noon-3am Sat, to 2am Sun; Ⓜ Dupont Circle) lets you flash back to childhood via stacks of board games.

3 Gelato at Dolcezza

Dolcezza (p147) scoops a dozen or so creamy flavors of gelato. They're not your everyday spoonful, with varieties such as lemon ricotta cardamom and strawberry tarragon. Don't be timid – they're divine. But they're not the only reason so many people are hanging out here. The pour-over coffee and espresso drinks provide the perfect zap for the night ahead.

4 Worldly Photos

At **Claude Taylor Photography** (Map p306; www.travelphotography.net; 1627 Connecticut Ave NW; ⏲10am-9pm Mon-Sat, to 8pm Sun; Ⓜ Dupont Circle), the local lensman sells his glossy travel shots featuring people and landscapes from around the world. The prints come in all shapes and sizes, starting at around $35.

5 Twenty-Four-Hour Books

Open round the clock on weekends, Kramerbooks (p153) – along with its attached Afterwords cafe and bar – is as much a spot for schmoozing as for shopping. Grab a meal, have a pint and flirt with

JASON COLSTON / GETTY IMAGES ©

Kramerbooks (p153), Dupont Circle

comely strangers (the store is a fabled pick-up spot for straights and gays).

6 Curry at Duke's Grocery

Duke's Grocery (p148) takes its cue from East London's corner cafes. Runny eggs and toast for breakfast, lamb *kofta* (meatballs) for dinner – a chalkboard lists the changing menu. The convivial tables spread over two floors amid mismatched armchairs and old photos.

7 Karaoke at JR's

Gay hangout JR's (p152) is usually packed. While it's mostly guys under age 40 in natty-casual attire who are chatting over their beers, the dark-wood and stained-glass bar is welcoming to all. Show-tunes karaoke is great fun on Monday nights.

8 Tabard Inn Cocktails

The **Tabard Inn Bar** (Map p306; www.tabardinn.com; 1739 N St NW; ⌚11:30am-1:30am Mon-Fri, from 10:30am Sat & Sun; Ⓜ Dupont Circle) is in a hotel, but plenty of locals come to swirl an old-fashioned or gin and tonic in the wood-beamed, lodge-like lounge. On warm nights, maneuver for an outdoor table on the ivy-clad patio.

Mon-Fri, 5:30-9:30pm Mon-Sun; Ⓜ Dupont Circle) Subterranean Vidalia blends Southern roots with French influences. The menu changes regularly, but it always revolves around unique, approachable flavors, say sweetbreads and waffles under bacon fondue. The signature side is a slow-cooked version of the titular onion with toasted hazelnuts and ham. And just try to keep your paws off the housemade breads that come pre-meal.

DRINKING & NIGHTLIFE

DC's gay and lesbian nightlife mecca, this neighborhood is packed with bars ranging from raunchy to ritzy. Regardless of your sexual orientation, there's something to keep you drinking around the circle. Chill coffeehouses, super-sleek lounges and ramshackle joints known for cheap happy hours abound.

FIREFLY BAR BAR

Map p306 (www.firefly-dc.com; 1310 New Hampshire Ave NW; ⌚4-11pm; Ⓜ Dupont Circle) Firefly is a restaurant first – the Hotel Madera's restaurant, to be precise – but we're not listing it for those merits. We can say it's one of the coolest bars in Dupont, decked out with its surreal, magically happy 'firefly trees,' all candlelit and reminiscent of childhood summer evenings, and romantic as hell to boot. The cocktail menu is a glorious thing.

Knock back a bourbon cream soda and see if the world doesn't just glow a little more…wait, that's the firefly trees.

BAR CHARLEY BAR

Map p306 (www.barcharley.com; 1825 18th St NW; ⌚5pm-12:30am Mon-Thu, 4pm-1:30am Fri, 10am-1:30am Sat, to 12:30am Sun; Ⓜ Dupont Circle) Bar Charley draws a mixed crowd from the neighborhood – young, old, gay and straight. They come for groovy cocktails sloshing in vintage glassware and ceramic tiki mugs, served at very reasonable prices by DC standards. Try the gin and gingery Suffering Bastard. The beer list isn't huge, but it is thoughtfully chosen with some wild ales. Around 60 wines are available, too.

If you're hungry, Charley concocts globe-trotting small plates (poutine, curried mussels). The drinks are the prize here, though.

FILTER CAFE

Map p306 (www.filtercoffeehouse.com; 1726 20th St NW; ⌚7am-7pm Mon-Fri, 8am-7pm Sat & Sun; 📶; Ⓜ Dupont Circle) Set on a quiet street, Filter is a jewel-box-sized cafe with a tiny front patio, a hipsterish laptop-toting crowd and, most importantly, great coffee. Those who seek caffeinated perfection can get a decent flat white here.

BIER BARON BAR

Map p306 (www.bierbarondc.com; 1523 22nd St NW; ⌚4pm-midnight Mon-Thu, to 2am Fri, 3pm-2am Sat, to midnight Sun; Ⓜ Dupont Circle) Enter the Bier Baron's underground lair and prepare your liver for an onslaught of brews. The dark, dingy, pubby bar taps 50 different beers – emphasis on local and unusual craft suds – and offers 500 more bottled beers from around the world. Aim for a corner seat, order a sampler and settle in for an impressive taste tour.

18TH STREET LOUNGE CLUB

Map p306 (www.eighteenthstreetlounge.com; 1212 18th St NW; ⌚5:30pm-2am Tue-Fri, 9:30pm-3am Sat, 9pm-2am Sun; Ⓜ Dupont Circle) Chandeliers, velvet sofas, antique wallpaper and a ridiculously good-looking, dance-loving crowd adorn this multifloored mansion. The DJs – spinning funk, soul and Brazilian beats – are phenomenal, which is not surprising given Eric Hilton (of Thievery Corporation) is co-owner. The lack of a sign on the door proclaims the club's exclusivity. No denim or sneakers. Covers range from $10 to $20.

SCIENCE CLUB LOUNGE

Map p296 (www.scienceclubdc.com; 1136 19th St NW; ⌚5pm-2am Mon-Sat; Ⓜ Dupont Circle) In a warren of rooms scattered about a townhouse, the Science Club attracts a varied crowd of interns, transplants and young geeky types. They bond over wine, vegetarian snacks and nightly DJ music.

JR'S GAY

Map p306 (www.jrsbar-dc.com; 1519 17th St NW; ⌚4pm-2am Mon-Thu, 4pm-3am Fri, 1pm-3am Sat, 1pm-2am Sun; Ⓜ Dupont Circle) Button-down shirts are de rigueur at this popular gay hangout frequented by the 20- and 30-something, work-hard-and-play-hard set. Some DC residents claim that the crowd at JR's epitomizes the conservative nature of the capital's gay scene, but even if you love to hate it, as many do, JR's knows how to rock a happy hour and is teeming more often than not.

COBALT GAY

Map p306 (www.cobaltdc.com; 1639 R St NW; ⌚5pm-2am; Ⓜ Dupont Circle) Featuring lots of hair product and faux-tanned gym bodies, Cobalt tends to gather a well-dressed late-20s to 30-something crowd who come for fun (but loud!) dance parties throughout the week. The time-hallowed dance club is on the 3rd floor; the venue also has a restaurant on the 1st floor and a lounge on floor two.

There's no cover charge early in the week; it ranges from $3 to $10 Thursday through Saturday.

LAURIOL PLAZA BAR

Map p306 (www.lauriolplaza.com; 1835 18th St NW; ⌚11:30am-11pm Sun-Thu, to midnight Fri & Sat; Ⓜ Dupont Circle) Lauriol doubles as a decent Mexican restaurant by day; by night, it's extremely popular with the young and frolicsome. Most folks go for multicolored margaritas – y'know, the ones that don't taste like they've got any booze in them, and you really shouldn't have ordered another three but whatever, man, there's nothing in these...(30 minutes later)...Wooh! I love you, bro!

LARRY'S LOUNGE BAR

Map p306 (1836 18th St NW; ⌚4pm-1am; Ⓜ Dupont Circle) An agreeably worn neighborhood joint, Larry's is known for its generous pours, dog-friendly patio and big windows prime for people watching. It's a gay bar, but plenty of straight patrons settle in to take advantage of its virtues. Prepare for a chat with a cast of characters.

CAFE CITRON CLUB

Map p306 (www.cafecitrondc.com; 1343 Connecticut Ave NW; ⌚4-11pm Mon, to 2am Tue-Fri, to 3am Sat; Ⓜ Dupont Circle) Cafe Citron is one of DC's most popular Latin-music clubs (in fairness, it plays everything, but the focus is salsa, samba et al). Girls dance; guys watch; the hours tick on. Late night it morphs to an all-dance crowd shaking it to mega-loud music. Nights out here can be fun, if only to observe the above unfolding epic pick-up scene.

BIG HUNT BAR

Map p306 (www.thebighunt.net; 1345 Connecticut Ave NW; ⌚4pm-2am Mon-Fri, from 5pm Sat & Sun; Ⓜ Dupont Circle) If you just said the name of this bar and smiled a little inner smile (or turned red), well, that's kinda the point. The irreverence is carried on inside via two floors of general tomfoolery, plus one of the city's better rooftop patios and some pool tables. For a dive bar, Big Hunt has several surprisingly fine small-batch beers on tap.

BUFFALO BILLIARDS BAR

Map p306 (www.buffalobilliards.com; 1330 19th St NW; ⏲4pm-2am Mon-Fri, from noon Sat & Sun; 📶; Ⓜ Dupont Circle) The 15 pool tables pull college kids and yuppies into this bright, below-street-level cave. There's usually a wait for a table, so play a little foosball, ping pong or skeeball before taking up some stick. A couple of good craft beers hide among taps.

LUCKY BAR BAR

Map p306 (www.luckybardc.com; 1221 Connecticut Ave NW; ⏲3pm-2am Mon-Fri, from noon Sat & Sun; Ⓜ Dupont Circle) Lucky's interior is nothing special – your standard double-decker dark wood and cozy chairs. It's the crowd that sets it apart: an amalgamation of capital subcultures ranging from politicos, Dupont gay couples, club kids needing a break from thumpa-thumpa and the occasional tourist, everyone enjoying themselves amid a happy booze-fueled drone. Lots of sports, including international soccer, flicker on the 22 big screens.

SIGN OF THE WHALE BAR

Map p306 (www.signofthewhaledc.com; 1825 M St NW; ⏲11:30am-2am; Ⓜ Dupont Circle) The Sign (which is next to strip club Camelot) attracts a raucous university crowd, plus a fair few lawyers, on weekends. That's when servers in skimpy clothes make the rounds with shots on trays. On other days of the week it comes off as a divey pub with low-level buzz.

☆ ENTERTAINMENT

DC IMPROV COMEDY

Map p306 (www.dcimprov.com; 1140 Connecticut Ave NW; tickets from $15; ⏲closed Mon; Ⓜ Farragut North) DC Improv is comedy in the more traditional sense, featuring stand-up by comics from Comedy Central, Saturday Night Live and HBO, among others. It also offers workshops for those who would like to hone their laugh-getting skills.

LOCAL KNOWLEDGE

PHILLIPS COLLECTION CONCERTS

If you like chamber music, don't forget about the Sunday concerts at the **Phillips Collection** (Map p306; www.phillipscollection.org; 1600 21st St NW; tickets $20; ⏲4pm Sun Oct-May; Ⓜ Dupont Circle). They have been a local tradition since 1941.

THEATER J THEATER

Map p306 (www.washingtondcjcc.org/center-for-arts/theater-j; 1529 16th St NW; Ⓜ Dupont Circle) Well-respected Theater J addresses the urban American Jewish experience through its plays.

SHOPPING

The shopping action in Dupont Circle centers on Connecticut Ave north and south of the roundabout.

KRAMERBOOKS BOOKS

Map p306 (www.kramers.com; 1517 Connecticut Ave NW; ⏲7:30am-1am Sun-Thu, 24hr Fri & Sat; Ⓜ Dupont Circle) This flagship independent – which leapt into First Amendment history when it refused to release Monica Lewinsky's book-buying list to Ken Starr's snoops – features first-rate literature, travel and politics sections. The bookstore attaches to the fun-loving Afterwords Cafe, which brings in a frisky crowd that flirts over drinks and pages into the wee hours.

SECOND STORY BOOKS BOOKS, MUSIC

Map p306 (www.secondstorybooks.com; 2000 P St NW; ⏲10am-10pm; Ⓜ Dupont Circle) Packed with dusty secondhand tomes, atmospheric Second Story also sells used CDs (mostly jazz and classical), antiquarian books and old sheet music. The prices are decent and the choices are broad (particularly in history and Americana). Be sure to browse the sidewalk bins, which have books from 50¢ to $2.

TABLETOP HOMEWARES

Map p306 (www.tabletopdc.com; 1608 20th St NW; ⏲noon-8pm Mon-Sat, 10am-6pm Sun; Ⓜ Dupont Circle) Also known as the best little design store in Dupont, Tabletop is evidence that DC is a lot more stylish than some give it credit for. The whimsical candles, postmodern wine carafes and vintage table linens are sure to impress your artsy and creative friends.

RED ONION RECORDS MUSIC

Map p306 (www.redonionrecords.com; 1901 18th St NW; ⊙noon-7pm Mon-Sat, to 5pm Sun; Ⓜ Dupont Circle) Small, indie Red Onion deals in vintage vinyl. It stocks a good selection of disco, funk, jazz and classic rock. The owner will do trades if you bring in your old records. The bin of $1 bargain buys is worth a flick-through.

PROPER TOPPER ACCESSORIES

Map p306 (www.propertopper.com; 1350 Connecticut Ave NW; ⊙10am-8pm Mon-Fri, to 7pm Sat, noon-6pm Sun; Ⓜ Dupont Circle) Fedoras, panama hats, short- and wide-brimmed straw hats – they're all for sale at the Proper Topper, along with children's books, wallets, jewelry, scarves and a few snazzy black dresses.

BEADAZZLED JEWELRY

Map p306 (☎202-265-2323; www.beadazzled.net; 1507 Connecticut Ave NW; ⊙10am-8pm Mon-Sat, 11am-6pm Sun; Ⓜ Dupont Circle) Crafty types and jewelry lovers should not miss this specialty shop, which carries all things small and stringable. The selection from around the world ranges from 5¢ clay doohickeys to expensive pearls. Helpful staff will tell you how to put them together, and classes are offered on weekends (call to register).

PHILLIPS COLLECTION ARTS

Map p306 (www.phillipscollection.org; 1600 21st St NW; ⊙10am-5pm Tue-Sat, to 8:30pm Thu, noon-7pm Sun; Ⓜ Dupont Circle) The museum shop has a good collection of posters, pop and scholarly art books, and knickknacks imprinted with famous paintings, such as umbrellas sporting Renoir's *Luncheon of the Boating Party* and Monet water-lily mugs.

SECONDI CLOTHING

Map p306 (☎667 1122; www.secondi.com; 1702 Connecticut Ave NW; ⊙11am-6pm Mon & Tue, to 7pm Wed-Fri, to 6pm Sat, 1-5pm Sun; Ⓜ Dupont Circle) Up a narrow row of stairs, Secondi is filled with top labels for women such as Marc Jacobs jackets and slightly preloved Manolo Blahnik shoes. It's not the cheapest shop in the city (it's a consignment versus thrift shop), but it has a good collection of big-name designers.

BETSY FISHER CLOTHING

Map p306 (www.betsyfisher.com; 1224 Connecticut Ave NW; ⊙10am-7pm Mon-Fri, to 6pm Sat, 1-5pm Sun; Ⓜ Dupont Circle) The sales team at this classy women's boutique makes you feel like a queen while trying on fantastic pieces by designers such as Diane von Furstenberg and Nicole Miller. The styles run the gamut from funky and fashion forward to elegant, but they're a touch on the conservative side.

Adams Morgan

Neighborhood Top Five

❶ Explore **18th St NW**, where Africans, Latin Americans and hard drinkers collide in a row of restaurants, music clubs, dive bars, vintage boutiques, and indie book and record shops.

❷ Make a bleary-eyed stumble into the **Diner** (p157) to quell late-night munchies.

❸ Soak up the previous night's debauchery with a drag-queen brunch at **Perrys** (p160).

❹ Catch a band at **Madam's Organ** (p162) and snap a photo under the bawdy mural.

❺ Indulge in a squirt bottle of booze at **Dan's Cafe** (p161), DC's premier dive bar.

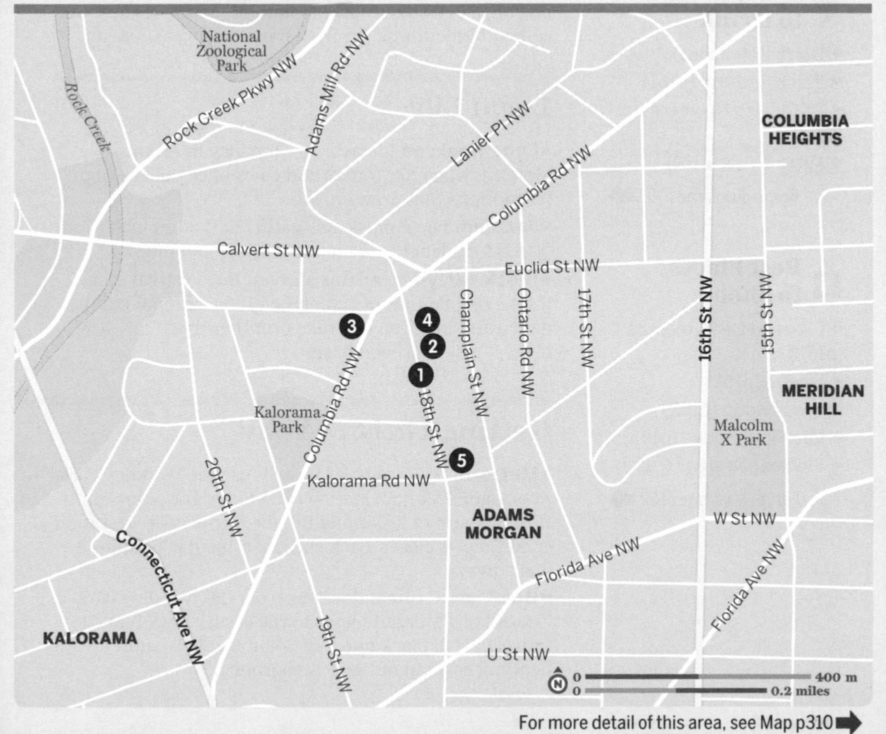

For more detail of this area, see Map p310

Lonely Planet's Top Tip

Hit the roof. Several bars and restaurants in the 'hood have rooftop decks where you can eat, drink and survey the scene playing out below. Madam's Organ and Perrys offer swell vistas. If heights aren't your thing, settle in at ground level for al fresco drinks on the patios at Tryst or Mintwood Place.

Best Places to Eat

- Donburi (p157)
- Mintwood Place (p160)
- Diner (p157)
- Perrys (p160)
- BUL (p160)

For reviews, see p157.

Best Places to Drink

- Dan's Cafe (p161)
- Black Squirrel (p161)
- Dr Clock's Nowhere Bar (p161)
- Millie & Al's (p161)

For reviews, see p161.

Best Places to Shop

- Crooked Beat Records (p162)
- Meeps (p162)
- Brass Knob (p162)
- Idle Time Books (p162)
- Skynear Designs (p163)

For reviews, see p162.

Explore Adams Morgan

Adams Morgan has long been Washington's fun, nightlife-driven neighborhood. It's also a global village of sorts, from an earlier time when rents were cheap and immigrants set up shop. The result is a raucous mashup centered on 18th St NW. Walk the half-mile stretch between Columbia Rd and Florida Ave and you'll sniff shish kebabs, Ethiopian lamb stew, jerk chicken and vegetable biryani mingling in the air. Vintage boutiques, arty homewares stores and record shops poke up between the ethnic eats, and make for good browsing by day.

But nighttime is when AdMo (as it's called in local text message–ese) really lets loose. Whether you love it or hate it – and everyone in DC seems to experience both emotions at some point – 18th St becomes one of the great bar crawls in town. It's a youthful crowd: bored kids from the 'burbs, Hill interns, fraternity guys and sorority gals, multiracial young professionals and even a fair number of party people from the rough side of town. All throw aside their differences for a while to shake a tail feather and scream in your face. If you're looking for a quiet night out, this is *not* your place.

There are no real sights here, unless it's the foot-and-a-half-long, 1000-calorie pizza slices that everyone chows on late at night. That said, Adams Morgan has recently shed a few of its get-hammered venues and welcomed high-aiming foodie restaurants in their stead.

Local Life

Long weekend It starts on Thursday in Adams Morgan, when many bars and clubs offer 'college night' promotions that draw crowds.

Jazz jam Local musicians gather at Columbia Station (p162) for a lengthy open jam session on Sunday.

Block party The Adams Morgan Day Festival rocks the second Sunday of September. International bands, dance and food vendors take over the streets for DC's biggest neighborhood bash.

Getting There & Away

Metro To reach most of 18th St, use the Woodley Park-Zoo/Adams Morgan station (Red Line). For points on 18th St south of Kalorama Rd, the Dupont Circle station (Red Line) is closer. Each station is about a 15-minute walk away.

Bus The DC Circulator runs from the Woodley Park-Zoo/Adams Morgan Metro to the corner of 18th and Calvert Sts (a block north of Columbia Rd), before heading east out of the neighborhood.

SIGHTS

DISTRICT OF COLUMBIA ARTS CENTER

ARTS CENTER

Map p310 (DCAC; www.dcartscenter.org; 2438 18th St NW; 2-7pm Tue-Sun; M Woodley Park-Zoo/Adams Morgan) FREE The grassroots DCAC offers emerging artists a space to showcase their work. The 800-sq-ft gallery features rotating visual-arts exhibits, while plays, improv, avant-garde musicals and other theatrical productions take place in the 50-seat theater. The gallery is free and worth popping into to see what's showing.

LOCAL KNOWLEDGE

HIDDEN ART GALLERY

Tucked away in a basement beneath Napoleon Bistro, **Hierarchy** (Map p310; www.hierarchydc.com; 1847 Columbia Rd NW; noon-5pm Sat & Sun; M Woodley Park-Zoo/Adams Morgan) FREE hosts cool pop-up art exhibitions. The contemporary shows change every month or so, and the space transforms along with them, so it'll look different each time you visit. The gallery sometimes opens at night for special events including a bar and DJ. Check the Twitter feed (@HierarchyDC) for updates.

EATING

★DONBURI

JAPANESE $

Map p310 (202-629-1047; www.facebook.com/donburidc; 2438 18th St NW; mains $9-12; 11am-10pm; M Woodley Park-Zoo/Adams Morgan) Hole-in-the-wall Donburi has 15 seats at a wooden counter where you get a front-row view of the slicing, dicing chefs. *Donburi* means 'bowl' in Japanese, and that's what arrives steaming hot and filled with, say, panko-coated shrimp atop rice and blended with the house's sweet-and-savory sauce. It's a simple, authentic meal. There's often a line, but it moves quickly. No reservations. It's located in the same building as the DC Arts Center.

TRYST

CAFE $

Map p310 (www.trystdc.com; 2459 18th St NW; breakfast & sandwiches $6-10; 6:30am-midnight Mon-Thu, to 3am Fri & Sat, 7am-midnight Sun; ; M Woodley Park-Zoo/Adams Morgan) The couches, armchairs and bookshelves, and the light flooding through streetside windows, lure patrons so faithful they probably should pay rent at Tryst. They crowd in for the coffee, stellar omelet and waffle breakfasts, and creative sandwiches. Come nightfall, baristas become bartenders, and the cafe hosts jazzy live music several nights a week.

Tryst turns off the wi-fi on weekends.

DINER

AMERICAN $

Map p310 (www.dinerdc.com; 2453 18th St NW; mains $9-17; 24hr; ; M Woodley Park-Zoo/Adams Morgan) The Diner serves hearty comfort food, any time of the day or night. It's ideal for wee-hour breakfast scarf-downs, weekend bloody-Mary brunches (if you don't mind crowds) or any time you want unfussy, well-prepared American fare. Omelets, fat pancakes, mac and cheese, grilled Portobello sandwiches and burgers hit the tables with aplomb. It's a good spot for kids, too.

AMSTERDAM FALAFELSHOP

MIDDLE EASTERN $

Map p310 (www.falafelshop.com; 2425 18th St NW; items $6-7; 11am-midnight Sun-Mon, to 2:30am Tue-Thu, to 4am Fri & Sat; ; M Woodley Park-Zoo/Adams Morgan) Cheap and cheerful, fast and delicious, the Falafelshop rocks the world of vegetarians and those questing for late-night munchies. Bowl up to the counter, order your falafel sandwich, then take it to the topping bar and pile on pickles, tabbouleh, olives and 20 other items. Take away, or dribble away at the scattering of stools and tables.

French fries are the only other dish on the menu, and they head to the topping bar too, best slathered with a mayo and peanut sauce combination.

PLEASANT POPS

CAFE $

Map p310 (202-558 5224; www.pleasantpops.com; 1781 Florida Ave NW; mains $3-6; 7:30am-7pm Mon, 7:30am-9pm Tue-Fri, 8:30am-9pm Sat, 8:30am-8pm Sun; ; M Dupont Circle) The cafe is definitely pleasant, with big windows that let in plenty of natural light. The 'pops' are popsicles, or Mexican *paletas* to be exact, in flavors such as peach hibiscus, Mexican sweet cream and cinnamon. The good-vibe little eatery also brews zippy coffee and prepares hit-the-spot vegetarian soups and sandwiches.

STEPHEN BOITANO / GETTY IMAGES ©

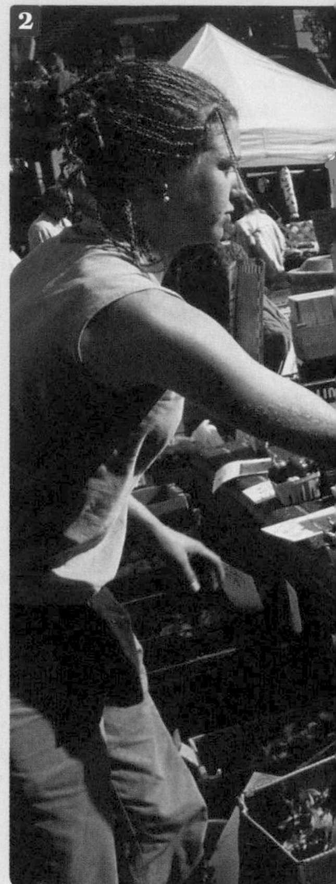

RICK GEHARTER / GETTY IMAGES ©

1. Madam's Organ (p162)
Patrons gather on the balcony of this famously quirky bar.

2. Adams Morgan Farmers Market (p160)
Shoppers abound at this Saturday-morning fresh-produce market.

3. Rumba Cafe (p160)
Minty mojitos and mouthwatering South American cuisine are on offer at Rumba.

4. Tryst (p157)
A popular coffee-and-breakfast joint by day and a bar after dark.

STEPHEN J BOITANO / GETTY IMAGES ©

CAKEROOM BAKERY $

Map p310 (☎202-450-4462; www.facebook.com/cakeroombakery; 2006 18th St NW; baked goods $2-5; ⊙9am-9pm Mon-Thu, to 10pm Fri, 10am-10pm Sat, to 9pm Sun; 📶; MDupont Circle) Ogle the glass cases bursting with creamy-frosted cakes and pies. The banoffee pie (a sublime banana-toffee mix) and date cupcake are the sweets to beat. Fadi, the baker, is from Jordan, and he invites guests to linger on the comfy couches and armchairs upstairs in the old-timey shop.

JULIA'S EMPANADAS LATIN AMERICAN $

Map p310 (www.juliasempanadas.com; 2452 18th St NW; empanadas from $4; ⊙11am-2am; MWoodley Park-Zoo/Adams Morgan) A frequent winner in DC's 'best late-night eats' polls, Julia's stuffs its dough bombs with chorizo, Jamaican beef and curry, spinach and more. Flavors peak if you've been drinking. The little chain has a handful of takeaway shops around town. Cash only.

MINTWOOD PLACE MODERN AMERICAN $$

Map p310 (☎202-234-6732; www.mintwood-place.com; 1813 Columbia Rd NW; mains $17-27; ⊙5:30-10pm Tue-Thu, to 10:30pm Fri & Sat, to 9pm Sun, 10:30am-2:30pm Sat & Sun; MWoodley Park-Zoo/Adams Morgan) In a neighborhood known for jumbo pizza slices and Jell-o shots, Mintwood Place is a romantic anomaly. Take a seat in a brown-leather booth or at a reclaimed-wood table under twinkling lights. Then sniff the French-American-fused dishes that emerge from the wood-burning oven. The cassoulet made with five types of meat, chicken-liver tartine and escargot hush puppies show how it's done.

PERRYS ASIAN $$

Map p310 (☎202-234-6218; www.perrysadamsmorgan.com; 1811 Columbia Rd NW; mains $14-25; ⊙5:30-10:30pm Mon-Thu, to 11:30pm Fri, 11am-3pm & 5:30-11:30pm Sat, 10am-3pm & 5:30-10:30pm Sun; MWoodley Park-Zoo/Adams Morgan) You can munch sushi at Perrys, but it's the creative fusion fare that really deserves your tongue's attention. Eat in the attractive lounge or under the stars on the rooftop. Sunday brings something entirely different: drag-queen brunch. The mega-popular campy show plus buffet is a scene to behold. Get in line by 9:30am; the rest of the week Perrys takes reservations.

LOCAL KNOWLEDGE

FARMERS MARKET

On Saturday morning the **Adams Morgan Farmers Market** (Map p310; bank plaza, cnr Columbia Rd NW & 18th St NW; ⊙8am-1pm Sat May-Nov; MWoodley Park-Zoo/Adams Morgan) pops up for a few brief hours. Join locals filling their reusable bags with produce, eggs, cheese, honey and cider from nearby small farms.

BUL KOREAN $$

Map p310 (☎202-733-3921; www.buldc.com; 2431 18th St NW; mains $10-20; ⊙5:30-10:30pm Tue-Sun; MWoodley Park-Zoo/Adams Morgan) BUL is DC's first *pojangmacha* ('covered wagon'), or Korean street-food eatery. Trendy locals love it, gobbling up grilled skewers of meat and vegetables, seafood pancakes, and a fishcakey 'hangover soup.' The pork belly fried rice comes with roasted kimchi made by the chefs' mothers.

For drinks, BUL pours seasonal flavors from a local kombucha brewery, as well as Asian spirits and beers.

CASHION'S EAT PLACE AMERICAN $$$

Map p310 (☎202-797-1819; www.cashionseat-place.com; 1819 Columbia Rd NW; mains $22-29; ⊙5:30-10pm Tue, to 11pm Wed-Fri, 10:30am-2:30pm & 5:30-11pm Sat & Sun; MWoodley Park-Zoo/Adams Morgan) With an original menu and inviting decor, this little bistro is lauded as one of the city's best. The mismatched furniture and flower boxes create an unpretentious setting to enjoy rich dishes such as scallion-cream-sauced crab and bison rib-eye with wild mushroom bordelaise sauce. The bar serves fancy small plates, such as pork-cheek quesadillas, until 1am on Friday and Saturday.

RUMBA CAFE LATIN AMERICAN $$$

Map p310 (☎202-588-5501; www.rumbacafe.com; 2443 18th St NW; tapas $9-16, mains $23-32; ⊙4:30pm-midnight Mon-Thu, 11am-midnight Fri-Sun; MWoodley Park-Zoo/Adams Morgan) Sit outside on the sidewalk and watch the passing parade while sipping some of the mintiest mojitos in the city and munching on mouthwatering morsels from South America. The tiny, eclectic restaurant's menu is mainly Brazilian, although it pops around the rest of the continent. We love the empanadas. After dinner Rumba hosts live Latin bands in its shabby-chic, red-and-mirror-clad interior.

DRINKING & NIGHTLIFE

★DAN'S CAFE — BAR

Map p310 (2315 18th St NW; ⏲7pm-2am Tue-Thu, to 3am Fri & Sat; Ⓜ Woodley Park-Zoo/Adams Morgan) This is one of DC's great dive bars. The interior looks sort of like an evil Elks Club, all unironically old-school 'art,' cheap paneling and dim lights barely illuminating the unapologetic slumminess. It's famed for its whopping, mix-it-yourself drinks, where you get a ketchup-type squirt bottle of booze, a can of soda and bucket of ice for barely $20. Cash only.

Dan's isn't marked, as the sign fell by the wayside a while ago, so keep an eye on the surrounding street addresses.

BLACK SQUIRREL — BAR

Map p310 (www.blacksquirreldc.com; 2427 18th St NW; ⏲5pm-1am Mon-Fri, from 11am Sat & Sun; Ⓜ Woodley Park-Zoo/Adams Morgan) Sometimes in Adams Morgan all you want is a good friggin' beer – no suds in plastic cups, no Jaeger shots – just a succulent microbrew. The warm, exposed-brick Squirrel stocks more than 100 unusual ales, from Mexican-spiced elixirs to abbey-style triple brews. Hungry? Pair them with the gastropub grub, such as the Gruyere-smothered, house-ground burgers.

DR CLOCK'S NOWHERE BAR — BAR

Map p310 (2nd fl, 2226 18th St NW; ⏲6pm-2am; Ⓜ Woodley Park-Zoo/Adams Morgan) The young and frisky seek out Dr Clock's for the offbeat Star Wars meets Soviet-style decor, the cheap local beers and absinthe cocktails, and the solid DJs spinning weird techno and house music on Thursday, Friday and Saturday nights (no cover charge).

The bar hides above the Rendezvouz Lounge.

MILLIE & AL'S — BAR

Map p310 (www.millienals.com; 2440 18th St NW; ⏲4pm-2am Sun-Thu, to 3am Fri & Sat; Ⓜ Woodley Park-Zoo/Adams Morgan) This comfortably worn dive is a neighborhood mainstay, famous for its $2 drafts, Jell-o shots and hit-the-spot pizza (best consumed in that order). M&A has always been, and probably will always be, a yuppie bar with a frat-house flavor – the kind of place where you can expect to be hit on and have beer spilled on you in the same night.

LOCAL KNOWLEDGE

MIDNIGHT BITES & BRUNCH

Adams Morgan is famed for its late-night eateries. Lots of people come here post-party on weekend nights to soak up the booze. Huge slices of pizza are a traditional snack: they're sold everywhere around the neighborhood and are uniformly greasy and delicious after several libations.

Other places to stuff your face in the wee hours:

- ➡ Diner (p157)
- ➡ Amsterdam Falafelshop (p157)
- ➡ Julia's Empanadas (p160)

Brunch is another favorite meal in the 'hood. It's usually decadent at:

- ➡ Perrys (p160)
- ➡ Cashion's Eat Place (p160)
- ➡ Diner (p157)

BOSSA — LOUNGE

Map p310 (☎202-650-9351; www.bossadc.com; 2463 18th St NW; ⏲5:30pm-2am Tue-Sun; Ⓜ Woodley Park-Zoo/Adams Morgan) Dark, intimate, close and sexy – that's the scene at Bossa. The soundtrack, if you couldn't guess: jazz, flamenco and bossa nova played in the candlelit lounge. It's a relatively chilled-out spot to drink mojitos and caipirinhas early on, and then it gets its groove on, so bring your dancing feet and prepare to samba (or salsa, or bachata…).

Often there's a cover charge, but it's rarely more than $5.

BLAGUARD — IRISH PUB

Map p310 (www.blaguarddc.com; 2003 18th St NW; ⏲5pm-2am Mon & Tue, 12:30pm-2am Wed-Sun; Ⓜ Dupont Circle) The Blaguard is a great bar in which to finish an Adams Morgan night. After you've had too much time dancing and screaming into someone's ear, you want a place that'll keep the party going but is a few notches lower on the crazy scale than a club. This youthful, slightly grungy, neighborhood spot delivers.

HABANA VILLAGE — CLUB

Map p310 (www.habanavillage.com; 1834 Columbia Rd NW; ⏲6-10:30pm Mon, to midnight Wed, to 1am Thu, to 3am Fri & Sat; Ⓜ Woodley Park-Zoo/Adams Morgan) Squeezed into an old townhouse with a cosmopolitan bar and romantic back room, the Village is as close as DC gets to Cuba. That's not particularly close, but you do get good, stiff mojitos here, and the music – salsa, meringue, mambo and bossa nova – packs the dance floor fairly often. Instructors give salsa lessons ($10) each evening at 7:30pm.

☆ ENTERTAINMENT

MADAM'S ORGAN
LIVE MUSIC

Map p310 (www.madamsorgan.com; 2461 18th St NW; admission $5-10; ⏲5pm-2am Sun-Thu, to 3am Fri & Sat; Ⓜ Woodley Park-Zoo/Adams Morgan) *Playboy* magazine once named Madam's Organ one of its favorite bars in America. The ramshackle place has been around forever, and its nightly blues, rock and bluegrass shows can be downright riot-inducing. There's a raunchy bar-dancing scene and funky decor with stuffed animals and bizarre paintings on the 1st floor. The rooftop deck is more mellow. The big-boobed mural outside is a classic.

BUKOM CAFE
LIVE MUSIC

Map p310 (www.bukomcafe.com; 2442 18th St NW; ⏲4:30pm-2am; Ⓜ Woodley Park-Zoo/Adams Morgan) Killer reggae and highlife bands take the stage nightly at Bukom. Be prepared for sore but happy hips as you join the mix of West African immigrants and ex–Peace Corps types who've earned their dancing chops on the continent. The music starts at 10pm (earlier weekdays); there's no cover.

Come early and sample the chicken *yassa* (spicy marinated dish with onions and poultry or fish) and other West African fare.

COLUMBIA STATION
LIVE MUSIC

Map p310 (www.columbiastationdc.com; 2325 18th St NW; ⏲4pm-2am Tue-Sun; Ⓜ Woodley Park-Zoo/Adams Morgan) FREE Columbia Station is an intimate spot to listen to nightly jazz and blues, and if you're on a budget it's especially appealing – it doesn't have a cover charge. It's a good date spot (well, assuming your date likes jazz), with lots of low light and, natch, romantic music.

Sunday's jam session, which starts at 4:30pm and goes all evening, brings out a sweet group of regulars.

 SHOPPING

Funky boutiques, antique shops and stores selling ethnic knickknacks are the strong suits here.

CROOKED BEAT RECORDS
MUSIC

Map p310 (www.crookedbeat.com; 2116 18th St NW; ⏲1:30-8pm Mon, noon-9pm Tue-Sat, to 7pm Sun; Ⓜ Dupont Circle) Go underground to enter this all-vinyl shop, the sort of place that in the '90s could have been its own movie about a bunch of aimless 20-somethings finding love amid stacks of indie, hip-hop and soul...you get the idea. The folks behind the counter are eminently down to earth, and if they don't have a certain record, they'll find you somewhere that does.

MEEPS
VINTAGE

Map p310 (www.meepsdc.com; 2104 18th St NW; ⏲noon-7pm Mon-Thu, to 8pm Fri & Sat, to 6pm Sun; Ⓜ Dupont Circle) There's this girl you know: extremely stylish and never seems to have a brand name on her body. Now, picture her wardrobe. Mod dresses, cowboy shirts, suede jackets, beaded purses, leather boots, Jackie O sunglasses and denim jumpsuits: there's Meeps mapped out for you. The store also carries a selection of clever, locally designed T-shirts.

BRASS KNOB
ANTIQUES

Map p310 (www.thebrassknob.com; 2311 18th St NW; ⏲10:30am-6pm Mon-Sat, noon-5pm Sun; Ⓜ Woodley Park-Zoo/Adams Morgan) This unique two-floor shop sells 'rescues' from old buildings: fixtures, lamps, tiles, mantelpieces and mirrors. The store's raison d'être, though, is the doorknob – brass, wooden, glass, elaborate, polished and antique. If you need to accent your crib like the interior of the best old DC row houses, look no further. Staff can help you find whatever you need.

IDLE TIME BOOKS
BOOKS

Map p310 (www.idletimebooks.com; 2467 18th St NW; ⏲11am-10pm; Ⓜ Woodley Park-Zoo/Adams Morgan) Three creaky floors are stuffed with secondhand literature and nonfiction, including one of the best secondhand political and history collections in the city. Its sci-fi, sports and humor sections are top-notch, and there's a good newsstand in its front window.

SKYNEAR DESIGNS
HOMEWARES

Map p310 (www.skyneardesigns.com; 2122 18th Ave NW; ⏲11am-7pm Mon-Sat, from noon Sun; Ⓜ Dupont Circle) How much hip can fit over four floors of fab, and what is hip anyway? Gorilla-shaped pillows? Uber-mod seatbelt chairs and other artisan furniture? Bronze candelabras and kitschy coffee tables? How about Japanese-style removable room partitions? It's all for sale in Skynear.

TORO MATA
HANDICRAFTS

Map p310 (www.toromata.com; 2410 18th St NW; ⏲noon-8pm Tue-Fri, 10am-8pm Sat, noon-6pm Sun; Ⓜ Woodley Park-Zoo/Adams Morgan) Inside the handsomely laid-out store you'll find a well-curated selection of Peruvian objects, including fluffy Alpaca rugs and cuddly stuffed animals, hand-carved chess sets and folk-art tableaus, colorful tapestries and woven hats and sweaters. The friendly owners have a wealth of knowledge on Peru.

SMASH!
MUSIC

Map p310 (www.smashrecords.com; 2314 18th St NW; ⏲noon-9pm Mon-Thu, to 9:30pm Fri & Sat, to 7pm Sun; Ⓜ Woodley Park-Zoo/Adams Morgan) There's a punk-rock vibe to this small upstairs shop. In addition to a solid selection of vinyl (covering mostly classic and indie rock and soul), Smash! sells used and new CDs, punky T-shirts, Doc Martens and secondhand clothing.

COMMONWEALTH
CLOTHING

Map p310 (www.commonwealth-ftgg.com; 1781 Florida Ave NW; ⏲noon-8pm Mon-Sat, to 5pm Sun; Ⓜ Dupont Circle) With a purely hip-hop aesthetic, this shop sells one-of-a-kind sneakers and graphic T-shirts. You can add to the wardrobe at a couple of other street-fashion shops in the same building.

B&K NEWSSTAND
GIFTS

Map p310 (2414 18th St NW; ⏲9am-9pm; Ⓜ Woodley Park-Zoo/Adams Morgan) No one asks for the *New York Times,* because B&K is really a pipe shop, one of the most famed among the city's stoner set. All of the glassware is, of course, to be used for tobacco smoking. Beyond all of the cigars, pipes and bongs is an almost clichéd array of Bob Marley paraphernalia along with other Amsterdam-esque accoutrements.

FLEET FEET
SHOES

Map p310 (www.fleetfeetdc.com; 1841 Columbia Rd NW; ⏲10am-8pm Mon-Fri, to 7pm Sat, noon-4pm Sun; Ⓜ Woodley Park-Zoo/Adams Morgan) Shoes for every sporting activity are on sale at this outlet of the national chain, and the personalized service ensures your feet get what they need. The store hosts free runs at 9am Sunday; they're typically 5 miles and often swing through nearby Rock Creek Park. Women-only runs take place Wednesday at 6pm.

Logan Circle, U Street & Columbia Heights

LOGAN CIRCLE | SHAW | COLUMBIA HEIGHTS | MT PLEASANT | NORTHEAST DC

Neighborhood Top Five

1. Wander along U St and take in its jazzy history, troubled descent and vibrant rebirth as an arts and entertainment district, then contemplate it over a meal at **Ben's Chili Bowl** (p173).

2. Walk through wooded groves at the **United States National Arboretum** (p167).

3. Feel the neighborhood vibe at cheery beery **Right Proper Brewing Co** (p177).

4. Discuss politics, sip free-trade coffee or spout verse at **Busboys & Poets** (p175).

5. Gawk at Lincoln's assassination bullet and more macabre exhibits at the **National Museum of Health and Medicine** (p170).

For more detail of this area, see Map p312

Explore Logan Circle, U Street & Columbia Heights

These neighborhoods have changed more in recent years than almost anywhere else in DC. The U St Corridor – DC's richest nightlife zone – has quite a history. It was once the 'Black Broadway' where Duke Ellington and Ella Fitzgerald hit their notes in the early 1900s. It was the smoldering epicenter of the 1968 race riots. There was a troubled descent, and then a vibrant rebirth in recent years. A stroll here is a must and rewards with mural-splashed alleys, red-hot music clubs and antique-crammed shops.

U St becomes part of the larger Shaw district, which is DC's current 'it' 'hood. But it's not annoyingly trendy. Instead, the breweries, bars and cafes that seem to pop up weekly are true local places, where neighbors come to sip among neighbors (and students among students, as Howard University is here). Logan Circle is next door and also booming. Walk down 14th St NW and hot-chef wine bars, beer bars, tapas bars and oyster bars flash by. The side streets hold stately old manors that give the area its class.

To the north, Columbia Heights has a reputation as an enclave for Latino immigrants and hipsters. There are no real sights, but the cheap ethnic food and unassuming punk dive bars can occupy many an evening.

Northeast DC is a vast stretch of leafy residential blocks holding several far-flung sights (and breweries). Nature lovers have a couple of groovy, free landscapes to explore, as long as you have a car or don't mind lengthy public-transportation trips.

Local Life

➡**Be at Ben's** The Chili Bowl (p173) is no secret, and you'll probably find a bus load of tourists inside. But it remains a real neighborhood spot, with locals downing half-smokes and gossiping over sweet iced tea.

➡**Bang on the Drum All Day** When the weather warms, a multicultural group gathers in Meridian Hill Park (p167) for a drum circle on Sunday afternoons.

➡**Get Funky** The neighborhood revs up the first Saturday in May with the Funk Parade, a musical street fair that celebrates the spirit of U St.

Getting There & Away

➡**Metro** The Green and Yellow Lines run in tandem to most sites. Useful stops are U St, Shaw-Howard U and Columbia Heights. Religious sites cluster near Brookland-CUA (Red Line). For Logan Circle points south of P St use McPherson Sq (Blue, Orange, Silver Line); for points north, use the U St Metro station.

Lonely Planet's Top Tip

Loosen the belt. These areas have fantastic eating and drinking options. Pick a street and meander until you find a favorite. There's 14th St in Logan Circle (trendy), 11th St in Columbia Heights (neighborly), 7th St by the Shaw Metro station (eclectic) and U St in the heart of it all (budget fare and soul food).

Best Places to Eat

➡ Ben's Chili Bowl (p173)
➡ Compass Rose (p174)
➡ Le Diplomate (p173)
➡ Estadio (p171)
➡ Bistro Bohem (p175)

For reviews, see p171.

Best Places to Drink

➡ Right Proper Brewing Co (p177)
➡ Room 11 (p181)
➡ Churchkey (p176)
➡ Bardo Brewpub (p177)
➡ A&D Bar (p177)

For reviews, see p176.

Best Places for Music

➡ Black Cat (p181)
➡ 9:30 Club (p182)
➡ Bohemian Caverns (p182)
➡ U Street Music Hall (p180)
➡ Velvet Lounge (p183)

For reviews, see p181. 

SIGHTS

Logan Circle

BETHUNE COUNCIL HOUSE — HISTORIC SITE

Map p312 (www.nps.gov/mamc; 1318 Vermont Ave NW; ⌚9am-4pm; Ⓜ McPherson Sq) FREE Mary McLeod Bethune served as President Franklin Roosevelt's special advisor on minority affairs. She rose through the political ranks to become the first African American woman to head a federal office. Her Vermont Ave home, where she lived for seven years, has been transformed into an archive, research center and small museum administered by the National Park Service. Rangers lead tours and show videotapes about Bethune's life, and exhibits, lectures and workshops on black history are held here as well.

The house was the first headquarters of the National Council of Negro Women.

U Street & Shaw

AFRICAN AMERICAN CIVIL WAR MEMORIAL — MONUMENT

Map p312 (www.afroamcivilwar.org; cnr U St & Vermont Ave NW; Ⓜ U St) Standing at the center of a granite plaza, this bronze memorial depicting rifle-bearing troops is DC's first major art piece by black sculptor Ed Hamilton. The statue is surrounded on three sides by the Wall of Honor, listing the names of 209,145 black troops who fought in the Union Army, as well as the 7000 white soldiers who served alongside them. You can use the directory to locate individual names within each of the regiments.

To get there, depart the Metro station via the 10th St exit (follow the 'memorial' signs as you leave the train).

AFRICAN AMERICAN CIVIL WAR MUSEUM — MUSEUM

Map p312 (☎202-667-2667; www.afroamcivilwar.org; 1925 Vermont Ave NW; ⌚10am-6:30pm Tue-Fri, to 4pm Sat, noon-4pm Sun; Ⓜ U St) FREE Set in an old schoolhouse behind the African American Civil War Memorial, the museum makes the point that for some, the Civil War was about secession versus union, but for others, it was a matter of breaking human bondage. The permanent exhibit uses photographs, videos and artifacts like slave shackles and a slave bill of sale to follow African American history from the Civil War through the Civil Rights movement. Visitors can search for ancestors in databases of black troops, regiments and battles.

HOWARD UNIVERSITY — UNIVERSITY

Map p312 (www.howard.edu; 2400 6th St NW; Ⓜ Shaw-Howard U) Founded in 1867, Howard remains the nation's most prestigious traditionally African American institute of higher education. Distinguished alumni include the late Supreme Court Justice Thurgood Marshall (who enrolled after he was turned away from the University of Maryland's then all-white law school), Ralph Bunche, Nobel laureate Toni Morrison and former New York City mayor David Dinkins. Today Howard enrolls around 10,000 students in 18 schools. The Shaw neighborhood is as defined by Howard University as Georgetown is by her titular school.

MURAL MANIA

Keep an eye out for all the murals splashed across the neighborhood's walls, especially around U St. Cool ones include the following:

➡ *Marvin Gaye,* on S St NW between 7th and 8th Sts, by artist Aniekan Udofia. The soul singer – and DC native son – is shown crooning into a microphone.

➡ *Silent George,* at 1502 U St NW, also by Aniekan Udofia. The image of George Washington with a gag over his mouth symbolizes DC's lack of representation in Congress.

➡ *The Alchemy of Ben Ali,* in the alley by Ben's Next Door at 1211 U St, by Eric B Ricks. It pays colorful homage to the founder of Ben's Chili Bowl. More murals cover the wall between Ben's and the Lincoln Theatre.

➡ *Duke Ellington,* by G Byron Peck. This mural used to stare out from the True Reformer Building at 1200 U St, but it was removed for repairs. It's supposed to return any day now...

Staff and students give free campus **tours** (www.howard.edu/explore). You must reserve in advance.

HOWARD UNIVERSITY GALLERY OF ART GALLERY

Map p312 (2455 6th St NW, Childers Hall; ⌚10am-5pm Mon-Fri, 1-4pm Sun; Ⓜ Shaw-Howard U) FREE The uni's Gallery of Art holds an impressive collection of work, largely dominated by African and African American artists.

MOORLAND-SPINGARN RESEARCH CENTER LIBRARY

Map p312 (202-806-7480; library.howard.edu/msrc; 500 Howard Pl NW; ⌚9:30am-4:30pm Mon-Fri; Ⓜ Shaw-Howard U) The Moorland-Spingarn Research Center boasts the nation's largest collection of African American literature. Tours are by appoinment only. The center sits inside thc **Founders' Library**, a handsome Georgian building with a gold spire and giant clock that is the campus' architectural centerpiece.

PROJECT 4 GALLERY

Map p312 (www.project4gallery.com; 1353 U St NW, 3rd fl; ⌚noon-6pm Wed-Sat; Ⓜ U St) Extremely hip (and quite small) Project 4 showcases some of the best of the contemporary and pop-art scene.

Columbia Heights & Mt Pleasant

MERIDIAN HILL PARK PARK

Map p312 (www.nps.gov/mehi; btwn 15th, 16th, Euclid & W Sts NW; ⌚5am-midnight May-Oct, to 9pm Nov-Apr; Ⓜ Columbia Heights) This is an incredible bit of urban green space. The grounds are terraced like a hanging garden replete with waterfalls, sandstone terraces and assorted embellishments that feel almost Tuscan. The prettiest bits reside in the park's south end, including – wait for it – DC's only memorial to James Buchanan (the USA's 15th president). Many locals still call this Malcolm X Park from its days of hosting political rallies. The Sunday drum circle (from 3pm to 9pm) has been going on for 50 years.

MUSEUM OF UNNATURAL HISTORY MUSEUM

Map p312 (202-525-1074; www.826dc.org; 3233 14th St NW; ⌚noon-6pm; Ⓜ Columbia Heights) FREE Step inside and be amazed at exhibits that feature an 'owlephant' (owl with an elephant trunk), Dr Luis Amarillo Urrea's forgotten trunk (from Papua New Guinea) and unicorn tears (putting 'the sparkle in sadness'). The tongue-in-cheek funhouse fronts 826DC, a nonprofit afterschool writing and tutoring program for kids. Be sure to check the shelf of used books for sale (all $2 or less).

LOCAL KNOWLEDGE

NAME GAME: MALCOLM X OR MERIDIAN HILL?

Officially, the park's name is Meridian Hill, because it's located on the exact longitude of DC's original milestone marker. Locals started calling it Malcolm X Park in 1970, after activist Angela Davis gave a speech there and rechristened it. Leaders then introduced a bill in Congress to change the moniker, but it was shot down because the park contains a memorial to President James Buchanan (the nation's 15th commander in chief). Thus the grounds' name cannot represent another person, according to the National Park Service, which operates the site. Locals pay the rule no mind, and everyone still calls it Malcolm X. Peculiar statues of Dante and Joan of Arc also dot the grounds.

Northeast DC

UNITED STATES NATIONAL ARBORETUM GARDENS

(202-245-2726; www.usna.usda.gov; cnr 24th & R Sts NE; ⌚8am-5pm Fri-Mon; Ⓜ Stadium-Armory to bus B2) FREE The greatest green space in Washington unfurls almost 450 acres of meadowland, sylvan theaters and a pastoral setting that feels somewhere between bucolic Americana countryside and a classical Greek ruralscape. Highlights include the Bonsai & Penjing Museum (exquisitely sculpted mini trees), the National Herb Garden (lots of hot peppers) and the otherworldly Capitol Columns Garden (studded with Corinthian pillars that were once part of the Capitol building). All are near the R St entrance.

A short distance onward, the National Grove of State Trees rises up. It sprouts

VISITORS CENTER & DIY TOURS

The **Greater U Street Visitors Center** (Map p312; 1211 U St; ⌚10am-8pm; ⓂU St) sits on the floor above Ben's Next Door. It's a partnership between the restaurant and **Cultural Tourism DC** (www.culturaltourismdc.org), with photos and simple exhibits on U St's history, info on local businesses and, of course, Ben's Chili Bowl souvenirs. Pick up the free booklet *City Within a City: Greater U Street Heritage Trail* or download it from the website. It's also available as an excellent **free audio tour** (http://dc.toursphere.com).

everything from New York's sugar maple to California's giant sequoia. Stop at the Administration Building for a map and self-guided tour information. Prepare to do a lot of walking. A **tram** (adult/chld $4/2) runs on weekends from mid-April to mid-October.

To reach the aboretum, take the Metro to bus B2. Get off on Bladensburg Rd at Rand St, which puts you a few blocks from the R St entrance. (There's another entrance on New York Ave NE, but R St is more convenient.)

KENILWORTH AQUATIC GARDENS GARDENS

(☎202-426-6905; www.nps.gov/keaq; 1550 Anacostia Ave NE; ⌚8am-4pm; ⓂDeanwood) FREE DC was built on a marsh, a beautiful, brackish, low-lying ripple of saw grass and steel-blue water, wind-coaxed and tide-touched by the inflow of the Potomac from Chesapeake Bay. You'd never know all that now, of course, unless you come to the USA's only national park devoted to water plants. See the natural wetlands the District sprang from; look out for beaver dams, clouds of birds and the more traditional manicured grounds, quilted in water lilies and lotus.

The aquatic gardens were begun as the hobby of a Civil War veteran and operated for 56 years as a commercial water garden, until the federal government purchased them in 1938. The park is about a mile walk from the Metro. Depart the station from the lower Polk St exit and take the pedestrian overpass across Kenilworth Ave. Go left on Douglas St, then go right on Anacostia Ave and enter any gate on your left.

BASILICA OF THE NATIONAL SHRINE OF THE IMMACULATE CONCEPTION CHURCH

(www.nationalshrine.com; 400 Michigan Ave NE; ⌚7am-7pm Apr-Oct, to 6pm Nov-Mar; ⓂBrookland-CUA) The largest Catholic house of worship in North America can host 6000 worshippers. It is an enormous, impressive, but somehow unimposing edifice, more Byzantine than Vatican in its aesthetic. Outlaid with some 75,000 sq ft of mosaic work and a crypt modeled after early Christian catacombs, the (literal) crowning glory is a dome that could have been lifted off the Hagia Sophia in Istanbul.

The Marian shrine sports an eclectic mix of Romanesque and Byzantine motifs, all anchored by a 329ft minaret-shaped campanile. Downstairs, the original Eastern-style crypt church has low, mosaic-covered vaulted ceilings lit by votives and chandeliers. Upstairs, the main sanctuary is lined with elaborate saints' chapels, lit by rose windows and fronted by a dazzling mosaic of a stern Christ. Hour-long guided tours cover all of it; they leave on the hour between 9am and 3pm (except no tour at noon) from the downstairs information desk.

The church is about a half-mile from the Metro. Exit the station and head west across Catholic University's campus.

SAINT JOHN PAUL II NATIONAL SHRINE MUSEUM

(www.jp2shrine.org; 3900 Harewood Rd NE; ⌚10am-5pm Mon-Sat, noon-5pm Sun; ⓂBrookland-CUA) FREE An adjunct for many devotees who visit the Basilica of the National Shrine of the Immaculate Conception, this modernist-style structure is an unexpected setting for a shrine to Karol Wojtyla, the Polish lad who went on to became Pope John Paul II and eventually a saint. Exhibits feature photos, videos and papal relics (like a vial of his blood).

The Knights of Columbus operate the site, which is undergoing renovations, including the addition of a 500-seat devotional chapel. It's about a quarter-mile north of the basilica on Harewood Rd.

FRANCISCAN MONASTERY MONASTERY

(www.myfranciscan.org; 1400 Quincy St NE; ⌚9am-5pm Mon-Fri, 9am-6pm Sat, 8am-5pm Sun; ⓂBrookland-CUA) FREE Also known as Mt St Sepulchre, the monastery offers serene grounds shimmering with 42 acres of tulips, dogwoods, cherry trees, roses – and some peculiar recreations of venerated

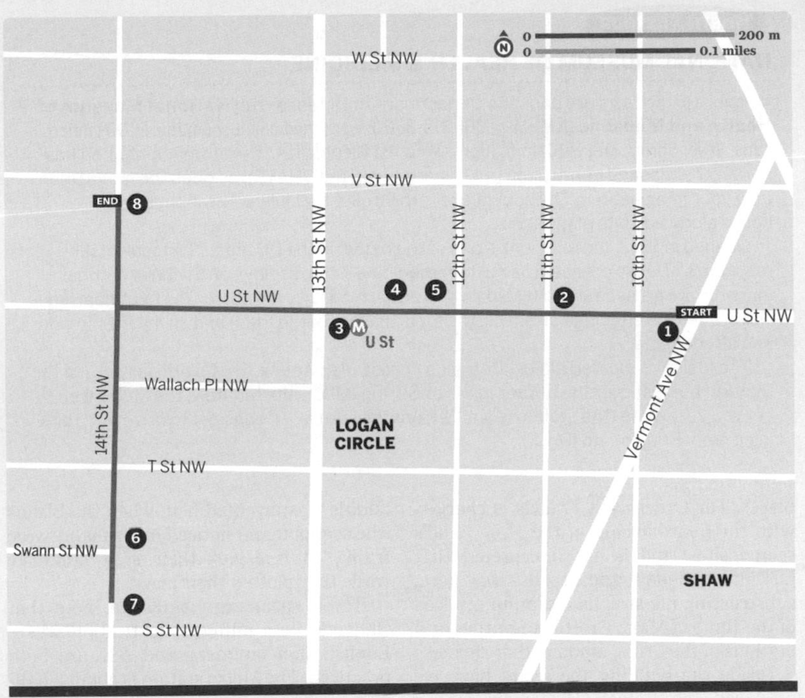

Neighborhood Walk U Street Stroll

START AFRICAN AMERICAN CIVIL WAR MEMORIAL
END BUSBOYS & POETS
LENGTH 1 MILE; 1½ HOURS

Wander and learn about the U St Corridor's rich African American heritage and renewal.

Exit the U St Metro station at the 10th St exit and saunter around the **1 African American Civil War Memorial** (p166) plaza. Why is this sculpture here? Because the Metro stop, which opened in 1991, was one of the first heralds of new development in the formerly downtrodden area. The memorial reminds black residents that the rebuilding of their community has been accomplished before, by ancestors who fought for their people's freedom.

Now walk west along U St – the numbered cross streets should be going up. At the corner of U and 11th Sts, the legendary jazz club **2 Bohemian Caverns** (p182) hosted names like Miles, Coltrane and Ellington. Duke Ellington grew up in this neighborhood and played his first public gig in a ballroom at the landmark **3 True Reformer Building** (1200 U St).

Cross the street and pop into **4 Ben's Chili Bowl** (p173), an iconic restaurant and one of the few businesses to survive since the 1950s. Grab a counter stool and chow down a chili half-smoke.

Next door, the **5 Lincoln Theatre** (p183) is the heart of what was once termed 'Black Broadway' – Billie Holiday, Ella Fitzgerald, Louis Armstrong and Cab Calloway all graced the stage. The '68 riots shut it down until the '90s.

Shops and clubs dot 14th St. Turn left, and after passing T St you'll run into the **6 Black Cat** (p181). The Foo Fighters' Dave Grohl helped start the club, and it hosts ripping rock sets most nights. Nearby **7 Home Rule** (p184) sells bright homewares. Artists made the counter mosaic with smashed glass from the 1968 riots.

Now head north to **8 Busboys & Poets** (p175), a cafe and bookstore that hosts readings and performances. It remains one of the artistic linchpins of the U St revival.

WORTH A DETOUR

NATIONAL MUSEUM OF HEALTH & MEDICINE

Macabre exhibits galore pack the Department of Defense–run **National Museum of Health and Medicine** (NMHM; ☎301-319-3300; www.medicalmuseum.mil; 2500 Linden Lane, Silver Spring, MD; ⌚10am-5:30pm; Ⓜ Forest Glen) FREE. The stomach-shaped hairball leaves a lasting impression (a 12-year-old girl ate THAT?), as does the megacolon (use your imagination). The showpiece is the bullet that killed Abraham Lincoln, encased alongside bits of his skull.

Opened in 1862, the museum is one of the oldest in the DC area. The focus of the museum's eclectic collection is military medicine – the displays on Civil War combat 'nursing' are gruesome and fascinating in equal measure. It's not for the faint-hearted – visitors see the effects of diseases, the tools used to battle them and all the messy side and after effects.

The facility is located at Fort Detrick's Forest Glen Annex. That's officially out of the District, but just over the border in Silver Spring, MD. Unfortunately, the Metro won't get you very close (the station is a mile from the site), so it's easiest to drive out. Parking is free. Bring photo ID.

places. The Order of St Francis is charged with the guardianship of the Holy Land's sacred sites, and it has interpreted that task in a unique – and broad – way here, constructing life-size, fake-granite replicas of the Tomb of Mary, Grotto at Lourdes and Stations of the Cross, among other shrines.

Inside the building the friars have reproduced the Roman Catacombs under the sanctuary floor. The dark, narrow passages wind past some fake tombs and the very real remains of Sts Innocent and Benignus; claustrophobes need not apply. You can walk around the church and grounds on your own, but the catacombs are accessible only on a guided tour (free; departs at 10am, 11am, 1pm, 2pm and 3pm Monday through Saturday, and afternoons only on Sunday). The whole place is creepy and fascinating, like a holy Disneyland.

Reach it from the Metro station by exiting toward the bus depot, then heading to Newton St NE; walk east until Newton meets 12th St NE, then go north (left) to Quincy St. It's about a mile overall, through a mostly residential neighborhood.

GALLAUDET UNIVERSITY — UNIVERSITY

(www.gallaudet.edu; 800 Florida Ave NE; Ⓜ NoMa) The first university for deaf and hard-of-hearing students in the world occupies a lovely manicured campus of bucolic green and Gothic accents north of Capitol Hill. Notable buildings include **College Hall**, an antique vision in brownstone, and **Chapel Hall**, a gorgeous Gothic structure that screams academia. The American football huddle was invented here when the Bisons (the school team) noticed other teams were trying to interpret their sign language while they plotted their plays.

If you speak sign language, note that Gallaudet is a bilingual institution where English sign language and ASL are both practiced. The Metro station is about a half-mile west.

FORT STEVENS PARK — HISTORIC SITE

(www.nps.gov/cwdw; cnr 13th & Quackenbos Sts NW; ⌚sunrise-sunset; 🚌70, 79 from Gallery Pl) FREE In a raid on July 11, 1864, Confederate General Jubal Early attacked Fort Stevens, the northernmost of the defensive ramparts ringing DC. A small but fierce battle raged for two days – the only time the Civil War touched District soil – until Early's men withdrew across the Potomac. The fort has been partially restored.

Abraham Lincoln himself was drawn into the shooting: the president, observing the battle from Fort Stevens' parapet, popped his head up so many times that Oliver Wendell Holmes, Jr, then a Union captain, yelled 'Get down, you damn fool, before you get shot!'

BATTLEGROUND NATIONAL CEMETERY — CEMETERY

(6625 Georgia Ave NW; ⌚sunrise-sunset; 🚌70, 79 from Gallery Pl) The 41 Union men who died defending Fort Stevens are buried at tiny Battleground National Cemetery, a half-mile north of the old fortifcation.

EATING

Logan Circle

ESTADIO

SPANISH $$

Map p312 (202-319-1404; www.estadio-dc.com; 1520 14th St NW; tapas $5-15; 5-10pm Mon-Thu, to 11pm Fri & Sat, to 9pm Sun, 11:30am-2pm Fri-Sun; U St) Estadio buzzes with a low-lit, date-night vibe. The tapas menu (which is the focus) is as deep as an ocean trench. There are three variations of Iberico ham and a delicious foie gras, scrambled egg and truffle open-faced sandwich. Wash it down with some traditional *calimocho* (red wine and Coke). No reservations after 6pm, which usually means a wait at the bar.

PIG

AMERICAN $$

Map p312 (202-290-2821; www.thepigdc.com; 1320 14th St NW; mains $12-21; 4-10:30pm Mon-Thu, 11:30am-11:30pm Fri, from 10:30am Sat & Sun; McPherson Sq) The Pig lives up to its name, offering plenty of porcine-inspired treats, from crispy shank to a decadent cutlet-and-Gruyère sandwich that will leave you lost for words. There's non-porky goodness as well, including some wonderful cornmeal-dusted oysters and a surprisingly vegetarian-friendly chickpea hash (that said, this isn't the best spot for herbivores). Great brunch value.

VERANDA ON P

MEDITERRANEAN $$

Map p312 (202-234-6870; www.verandaonp.com; 1100 P St NW; mains $12-21; 5pm-12:30am Mon-Thu, 5pm-1:30am Fri, 10:30am-1:30am Sat, 10:30am-midnight Sun; Mt Vernon Sq) Lots of locals stroll over for the stuffed grape leaves, lamb shanks and other good-value Mediterranean fare at Veranda on P. The interior of the homey little nook brings to mind an Ionian island, but most folks prefer the outdoor eponymous veranda, which sits amid the handsome red-brick townhouses of Logan Circle. Tuesdays bring crowds for half-price bottles of wine.

ETTO

ITALIAN $$

Map p312 (www.ettodc.com; 1541 14th St NW; mains $12-23; 5-10pm Mon-Thu, 5-11pm Fri, noon-11pm Sat, noon-10pm Sun; U St) The sun-splashed, tiled cafe is known for its thin-crust pizzas, salamis, anchovies and cheeses – all of which go smashingly with a nice glass of wine. The chefs are serious about quality: they grind their own flour and cure their own meats. It's worth swinging by Etto if queues at other 14th St eateries overwhelm.

BIRCH & BARLEY

AMERICAN $$

Map p312 (202-567-2576; www.birchandbarley.com; 1337 14th St NW; mains $16-29; 5:30-10pm Tue-Thu, 5:30-11pm Fri & Sat, 11am-8pm Sun; McPherson Sq) The menu of modern comfort foods focuses on housemade pastas, flatbreads and the crowd-favorite brat burger, all of which pairs with the enormous beer list. Sunday's 'boozy brunch' (prix fixe $30) pulls crowds for the doughnut appetizer (mmm, toffee-bacon), main, bottomless cups of coffee and two mind-altering cocktails. Good gluten-free options are available.

If it's crowded, try heading to the upstairs bar Churchkey (p176), which serves pretty much the same menu.

PEARL DIVE OYSTER PALACE

SEAFOOD $$

Map p312 (www.pearldivedc.com; 1612 14th St NW; mains $19-26; 5-10pm Mon, 5-11pm Tue-Thu, 11am-11pm Fri-Sun; U St) Flashy Pearl Dive serves exceptional, sustainable oysters from both coasts, along with braised duck and oyster gumbo, crab cakes and insanely rich peanut butter chocolate pie. Fresh air from the big front windows wafts through

WHAT'S A HALF-SMOKE?

DC's claim to native culinary fame is the half-smoke, a bigger, coarser, spicier and better version of the hot dog. There's little agreement on where the name comes from – half beef/half pork? (But some are all beef!) Because the sausage is usually split down the middle? Because they can be grilled or steamed? Who knows? But there is general consensus as to what goes on a half-smoke. New Yorkers like their mustard and relish, Chicagoans dress their dogs with a freakin' garden, and in DC? Chili and chopped onions, baby. Ben's Chili Bowl (p173) is the half-smoke standard bearer. Bold Bite (p120) at Union Station grills a fine one, while Churchkey (p176) serves an avant-garde version.

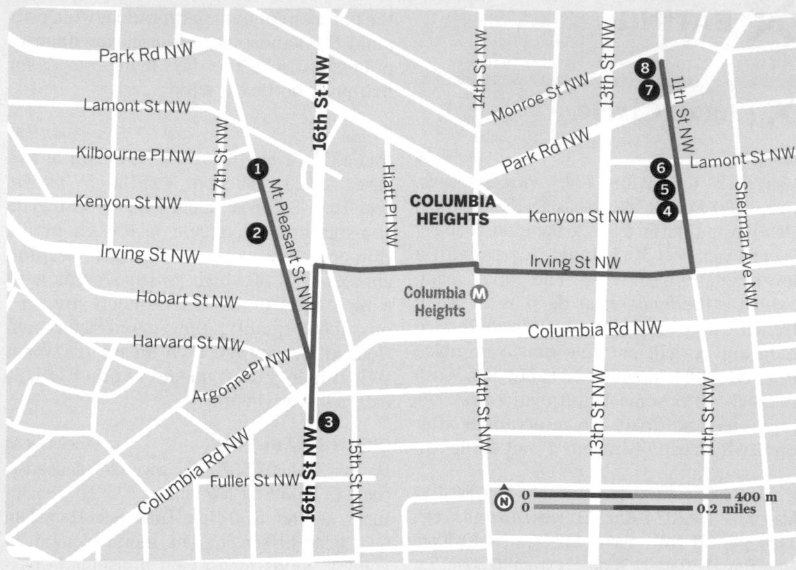

Local Life
Mixing it up in Columbia Heights

Columbia Heights booms with Latino immigrants and hipsters. A few decades ago the neighborhood was a tumbledown mess. Then the Metro station was built, followed by a slew of big-box retailers. And then – this is why you're here – it morphed into a cool-cat mix of ethnic eateries and unassuming corner taverns chock-full of local color.

❶ Mt Pleasant Street

Mt Pleasant St (Map p312; Ⓜ Columbia Heights) is the *corazón* (heart) of DC's Latino, largely Salvadoran community. Many businesses advertise money-transfer services to San Salvador or surrounds, or sell snacks from the homeland, or both.

❷ Pupuseria San Miguel

Pupuseria San Miguel (Map p312; ☎202-387-5140; 3110 Mt Pleasant Ave NW; pupusas $2; ⏰9am-10pm; Ⓜ Columbia Heights) is below street level and easy to miss.The humble little restaurant fries up delicious cheap *pupusas* (stuffed cornmeal pockets). They're a Salvadoran specialty and San Miguel's are renowned neighborhood-wide. Cash only.

❸ Mexican Cultural Institute

The **Mexican Cultural Institute** (Map p312; www.instituteofmexicodc.org; 2829 16th St NW; ⏰10am-6pm Mon-Fri, noon-4pm Sat; Ⓜ Columbia Heights) FREE looks imposing, but don't be deterred. The gilded beaux-arts mansion is open to the public and hosts excellent art and cultural exhibitions. Ring the doorbell for entry.

❹ Wonderland Ballroom

Divey **Wonderland Ballroom** (Map p312; www.thewonderlandballroom.com; 1101 Kenyon St NW; ⏰5pm-2am Mon-Thu, 4pm-3am Fri, 11am-3pm Sat, 10am-2am Sun; Ⓜ Columbia Heights) flaunts a spacious patio with outsized wooden benches that are just right on warm evenings. The upstairs dance floor sees a mix of DJs and bands, and gets packed on weekends.

❺ BloomBars

You never know what you'll find going on at **BloomBars** (Map p312; www.bloombars.com; 3222 11th St NW; by donation; ⏰hours vary; Ⓜ Columbia Heights), a cool community arts center. By day children's story times and music classes take place. By night gallery shows and world music take over.

Maple, Columbia Heights

6 Room 11
While Room 11 (p181) is known as an evening wine pourer, the cute-as-a-button cafe is open all day serving locally roasted coffee, egg and biscuit sandwiches and eclectic soups. The on-site bakery means the blackberry lime scones, honey goat's cheese cheesecake and chocolate pistachio biscotti are fresh as can be.

7 Meridian Pint
Staffed by neighborhood locals, **Meridian Pint** (Map p312; www.meridianpint.com; 3400 11th St NW; ⏲5pm-2am Mon-Thu, 5pm-3am Fri, 10am-3am Sat, 10am-2am Sun; Ⓜ Columbia Heights) is the quintessential corner tavern for Columbia Heights. Sports flicker on TV, folks play pool and shuffleboard, and American craft beers flow.

8 Maple
At **Maple** (Map p312; ☎202-588-7442; www.dc-maple.com; 3418 11th St NW; mains $14-22; ⏲5:30pm-midnight Mon-Thu, 5pm-1am Fri & Sat, 11am-11pm Sun; Ⓜ Columbia Heights), hot young residents eat pasta on a reclaimed wood bar. Housemade *limoncello*, Italian craft beers and unusual wine varietals move across the lengthy slab of maple wood.

the open industrial space, done up in a nautical, weathered-wood motif. No reservations; you'll need to take a number (like at a deli).

You can wait at the upstairs bar, Black Jack, where fedora-wearing bartenders will swirl you a glamorous cocktail.

★LE DIPLOMATE FRENCH $$$
Map p312 (☎202-332-3333; www.lediplomatedc.com; 1601 14th St NW; mains $22-31; ⏲5-10pm Mon & Tue, 5-11pm Wed & Thu, 5pm-midnight Fri, 9:30am-midnight Sat, 9:30am-10pm Sun; Ⓜ U St) This charming French bistro is a relative newcomer, but it has skyrocketed to one of the hottest tables in town. DC celebrities galore cozy up in the leather banquettes and at the sidewalk tables. They come for an authentic slice of Paris, from the coq au vin (wine-braised chicken) and aromatic baguettes to the vintage curios and nudie photos decorating the bathrooms. Make reservations.

U Street & Shaw

★BEN'S CHILI BOWL AMERICAN $
Map p312 (www.benschilibowl.com; 1213 U St; mains $5-10; ⏲6am-2am Mon-Thu, 6am-4am Fri, 7am-4am Sat, 11am-midnight Sun; Ⓜ U St) Ben's is a DC institution. The main stock in trade is half-smokes, DC's meatier, smokier version of the hot dog, usually slathered in mustard, onions and the namesake chili. For nearly 60 years presidents, rock stars and Supreme Court justices have come in to indulge in the humble diner, but despite the hype, Ben's remains a true neighborhood establishment. Cash only.

To place your order, join the locals clustered at the counter and gabbing over sweet ice tea. Ben and Virginia Ali opened the Chili Bowl in 1958. It's one of the only businesses on U St to have survived the 1968 riots and the disruption that accompanied construction of the U St Metro stop. Ben died in 2009. His sons now run the business, which includes outlets on H St NE and at Ronald Reagan Washington National Airport.

&PIZZA PIZZA $
Map p312 (☎202-733-1286; www.andpizza.com; 1250 U St NW; mains $8-12; ⏲11am-11pm Sun-Wed, to 2am Thu, to 3:30am Fri & Sat; 📶✍; Ⓜ U St) &pizza outlets are popping up all over DC, and no wonder: this is high-quality fast food. Create your own individual-sized pie

LOCAL KNOWLEDGE

UNION MARKET

The cool crowd hobnobs at **Union Market** (www.unionmarketdc.com; 1309 5th St NE; ⌚11am-8pm Tue-Sun; ⓂNoMa), where foodie entrepreneurs sell their banana-ginger chocolates, herbed goat's cheeses and oysters straight from Chesapeake Bay. Pop-up restaurants use the space to try out concepts for everything from Taiwanese ramen to Indian dosas. Craft beers and coffee drinks help wash it all down. Tables dot the sunlit warehouse, and many locals make an afternoon of it here, browsing, nibbling and reading. The market is about a half-mile walk from the NoMa Metro station, in the midst of several other food supply warehouses.

(big enough for two meals) using house-made mozzarella, vegan mozzarella, red chickpea puree, truffle sauce and a host of other ingredients. Or choose a signature pizza like the Farmer's Daughter with spicy tomato, Italian sausage and an egg cracked on top.

Wine, craft beer and the eatery's own wild sodas (pear and fig, anise root beer) accompany the goodness. Order at the counter and take to the scattering of communal seats. The place booms late night.

AMERICAN ICE COMPANY — BARBECUE $

Map p312 (☎202-758-3562; www.amicodc.com; 917 V St NW; mains $10-14; ⌚5pm-2am Mon-Thu, to 3am Fri, 1pm-3am Sat, 1pm-2am Sun; ⓂU St) The usual U St/Columbia Heights crew of hipsters, policy wonks and policy wonks who kind of look like hipsters packs the cluttered interior and much nicer outdoor patio of this casual eatery, which focuses on barbecue and canned beer, pretty much in that order. Try the gooey pork and cheese sandwich or the delicious pork nachos (yes, pork nachos).

ZENEBECH — ETHIOPIAN $

Map p312 (☎202-667-4700; www.zenebechdc.com; 608 T St NW; mains $10-12; ⌚9am-11pm, 🌶; ⓂShaw-Howard U) The area around 9th and U Sts is known as Little Ethiopia for its slew of shops and restaurants. Hole-in-the-wall Zenebech is a bit off the path, but it prepares terrific *injera* (spongy bread) and hot spiced *wats* (stews).

SATELLITE ROOM — DINER $

Map p312 (www.satellitedc.com; 2047 9th St NW; mains $9-13; ⌚5pm-2am Sun-Thu, to 3am Fri & Sat; ⓂU St) This diner located next to the 9:30 Club is a prime place to go before or after a show. The cheeky burgers are named after musicians, like the Dave Grohl, a goat's cheese and arugula-topped patty. A swell tater tot selection and booze-spiked milkshakes complement the main course.

FLORIDA AVENUE GRILL — SOUTHERN $

Map p312 (☎202-265-1586; www.floridaavenuegrill.com; 1100 Florida Ave NW; mains $10-16; ⌚8am-9pm Tue-Sat, to 4:30pm Sun; ⓂU St) The Grill is one of DC's quintessential diners. Be they president, Harlem Globetrotter or college student, they've all come here for more than 70 years to eat turkey legs, catfish and meatloaf served with sides of sweet tea and more character than Shakespeare's collected works.

CHIX — LATIN AMERICAN $

Map p312 (☎202-234-2449; www.chixdc.com; 2019 11th St NW; mains $8-10; ⌚11:30am-10pm Mon-Fri, from noon Sat & Sun; 📶🌶; ⓂU St) 🍃 The DC area takes its Peruvian chicken seriously. If you haven't had the stuff, it's slow-roasted, rotisserie style, and it's sooo good: succulent, juicy, the savory skin complementing the comforting pillows of meat. Plus, Chix is ecofriendly: the decor was built with sustainable materials and the cups are made out of fast-degrading corn.

Vegetarian dishes – mostly sides such as black beans and lentil soup – are available, too.

★COMPASS ROSE — INTERNATIONAL $$

Map p312 (☎202-506-4765; www.compassrosedc.com; 1346 T St NW; small plates $10-15; ⌚5pm-2am Sun-Thu, to 3am Fri & Sat; ⓂU St) Compass Rose feels like a secret garden, set in a discreet townhouse a whisker from 14th St's buzz. The exposed brick walls, rustic wood decor and sky-blue ceiling give it a casually romantic air. The menu is a mash-up of global comfort foods, so dinner might entail, say, a Chilean *lomito* (pork sandwich), Lebanese *kefta* (ground lamb and spices) and Georgian *khachapuri* (buttery, cheese-filled bread).

They're unique flavors for DC, but Rose manages to steer clear of trendiness. No reservations, though waiting at the bar sipping offbeat wines and cocktails from around the world makes time pass quickly.

BISTRO BOHEM
EASTERN EUROPEAN $$

Map p312 (202-735-5895; www.bistrobohem.com; 600 Florida Ave NW; mains $12-21; 5-11pm Mon-Thu, 5pm-2am Fri, 10am-2am Sat, 10am-11pm Sun; ; Shaw-Howard U) Cozy Bistro Bohem is a community favorite for its rib-sticking Czech schnitzels, goulash and pilsners, served with a side of local art on the walls and occasional live jazz. By day the action shifts to adjoining Kafe Bohem, which opens at 7am (8am weekends) for espresso, pastries and fat sandwiches. The warm, bohemian environs make you swear you're in Prague.

BUSBOYS & POETS
CAFE $$

Map p312 (202-387-7638; www.busboysandpoets.com; 2021 14th St NW; mains $11-21; 8am-midnight Mon-Thu, 8am-2am Fri, from 9am Sat & Sun; ; U St) Busboys & Poets (named for a Langston Hughes poem) is one of U St's linchpins. Locals gather for coffee, wi-fi and a progressive vibe (and attached bookstore) that make San Francisco feel conservative. The hearty menu spans sandwiches, pizzas and Southern fare like shrimp and grits. Tuesday night's open-mike poetry reading ($5 admission, from 9pm to 11pm) draws big crowds.

The cafe's slate of events also includes story slams, film screenings and discussion series. B&P has grown to include five locations in the DC region, but this one is the flagship.

TICO
LATIN AMERICAN $$

Map p312 (202-319-1400; www.ticodc.com; 1926 14th St NW; small plates $9-14; 4pm-midnight Sun-Thu, from 10am Fri & Sat; ; U St) Loud, fun and clattering, Tico draws a young and artsy crowd for its nouveau tacos, small plates and 140 tequilas. Top honors go to the scallop ceviche with crispy rice, the Manchego cheese fritters and hibiscus margaritas. Vegetarians get some love from the edamame tacos, roasted cauliflower and other dishes.

The bright-hued, mural-splashed eatery is mega popular, so make reservations.

BEN'S NEXT DOOR
AMERICAN $$

Map p312 (202-667-0909; www.bensnextdoor.com; 1211 U St; mains $12-20; 11am-midnight Mon-Thu, to 2am Fri & Sat, to 11pm Sun; U St) Ben's Next Door is, yes, next door to Ben's Chili Bowl. It offers upscale Southern fare (she crab soup, fried chicken, ribs), along with local beer and cocktails, in a warm, wood-floored room. That said, you can also get half-smokes and the rest of the Chili Bowl items over here (though we prefer to scarf them while sitting at the counter in their original environment).

EATONVILLE
SOUTHERN $$

Map p312 (202-332-9672; www.eatonville-restaurant.com; 2121 14th St NW; mains $12-21; 11am-10pm Mon-Thu, 11am-midnight Fri, 9am-midnight Sat, 9am-10pm Sun; U St) Novelist Zora Neal Hurston is the unconventional theme at Eatonville. The atmosphere is superb, a sort of bayou dripped through impressionist-style murals of the South, then resurrected upon a modernist, cavernous dining hall that looks like nothing less than a cathedral to black intelligentsia. And the food? Very fine. Catfish come correct with cheese grits, and the honey-cornbread muffins…revelatory. Wash it all down with a lavender lemonade.

OOHH'S & AAHH'S
SOUTHERN $$

Map p312 (202-667-7142; www.oohhsnaahhs.com; 1005 U St NW; mains $14-22; noon-10pm Mon-Thu, to 4am Fri & Sat, to 7pm Sun; U St) Un-notch the belt: the cornbread, collard greens, meatloaf and other soul-food dishes at this bare-bones joint come in enormous portions. Not that hungry? Stop in for a piece of hummingbird (banana-pineapple) cake. Sit at the counter and immerse yourself in the before-U-St-became-gentrified crowd. It's a great slice of local life. A more spacious dining room hides upstairs.

Columbia Heights & Mt Pleasant

STICKY FINGERS
VEGAN $

Map p312 (202-299-9700; www.stickyfingers-bakery.com; 1370 Park Rd NW; mains $6-10; 8am-8pm Mon-Thu, 8am-9pm Fri, 9am-9pm Sat, 9am-8pm Sun; ; Columbia Heights) The tempeh bacon, gluten-free pancakes and tofu scramble are but foreplay to the peanut butter fudge and raspberry cream cupcakes. Sticky Fingers is primarily a bakery, with a wee dining area attached. Order at the counter, then salivate over your purchases at the close-quartered retro tables where fellow vegans tap away on their Macbooks.

EL CHUCHO MEXICAN $

Map p312 (☎202-290-3313; 3313 11th St NW; tacos $6-12; ⊙4pm-2am Mon-Fri, 11:30pm-3am Sat, 11:30am-midnight Sun; Ⓜ Columbia Heights) There's a Day of the Dead–inspired interior, margaritas on tap, excellent *elote* (corn) smothered in white cheese and spices, and fresh guacamole. The tiny tacos leave us wanting more. It's home to lots of cool tattooed staff members, and the customers who love them.

PHO 14 VIETNAMESE $

Map p312 (☎202-986-2326; www.dcpho14.com; 1436 Park Rd NW; mains $9-16; ⊙11am-9:30pm Sun-Wed, to 10pm Thu-Sat; ✎; Ⓜ Columbia Heights) Smart, solid Pho 14 ladles out steaming bowls of the namesake noodle soup, as well as stir-fry dishes and *banh mi* sandwiches (baguettes filled with meat and/or spicy veggies) to brisk lunchtime and dinner crowds.

RED ROCKS PIZZERIA PIZZA $

Map p312 (☎202-506-1402; www.redrocksdc.com; 1063 Park Rd NW; pizzas $9-17; ⊙4-11pm Mon, 11am-11pm Tue-Thu & Sun, 11am-1am Fri & Sat; Ⓜ Columbia Heights) Red Rocks has been voted best pizza in the city in a glut of DC publications. That's testament to the unswerving excellence of its irregularly shaped, brick-fired pizzas. You're not gonna be shocked by any of the ingredients, except when it comes to their quality, which is impeccable: fresh basil, and flour, tomatoes and cheese all imported from Italy.

KANGAROO BOXING CLUB AMERICAN $$

Map p312 (KBC; ☎202-505-4522; www.kangaroodc.com; 3410 11th St NW; mains $13-18; ⊙5-11pm Mon-Thu, 5pm-1:30am Fri, 10am-1:30am Sat, 10am-10pm Sun; Ⓜ Columbia Heights) The gastropub concept – but a hip, laid-back, Brooklyn-esque gastropub – is all the rage among DC's hip young things and the restaurateurs who cater to them. Enter the KBC: it has a quirky theme (vintage boxing), a delicious menu (burgers, barbecue, sweet spoon bread and loaded mac 'n' cheese and the like) and a deep beer menu.

HEIGHTS AMERICAN $$

Map p312 (☎202-797-7227; www.theheightsdc.com; 3115 14th St NW; mains $16-22; ⊙11:30am-10:30pm Mon-Thu, 11:30am-11:30pm Fri, 9am-11:30pm Sat, 9am-10:30pm Sun; Ⓜ Columbia Heights) Heights' food is excellent Americana stuff – the fried chicken and mashed potatoes is wonderful – but whatever you do, come on a weekend and order off the greatest Bloody Mary menu on Earth. Select from 10 different types of vodka, or tequila, or gin, then add from options including clam juice, Old Bay seasoning, lump crabmeat, bacon – well, we could go on.

DRINKING & NIGHTLIFE

The U St Corridor has evolved into one long strip of bars, plus a fair few jazz spots and concert halls. Further north, Columbia Heights and beyond has become trendy among nighthawks.

Logan Circle

CHURCHKEY BAR

Map p312 (www.churchkeydc.com; 1337 14th St NW; ⊙4pm-1am Mon-Thu, 4pm-2am Fri, noon-2am Sat, noon-1am Sun; Ⓜ McPherson Sq) Coppery, mod-industrial Churchkey glows with hipness. Fifty beers flow from the taps, including five brain-walloping, cask-aged ales. If none of those please you, another 500 types of brew are available by bottle (including gluten-free suds). Churchkey is the upstairs counterpart to Birch & Barley (p171), a popular nouveau comfort-food restaurant, and you can order much of its menu at the bar.

CORK WINE BAR WINE BAR

Map p312 (www.corkdc.com; 1720 14th St NW; ⊙5pm-midnight Tue & Wed, 5pm-1am Thu-Sat, 11am-3pm & 5-10pm Sun; Ⓜ U St) This dark 'n' cozy wine bar manages to come off as foodie magnet and friendly neighborhood hangout all at once, which is a feat. Around 50 smart wines are available by the glass and 160 types by the bottle. Accompanying nibbles include cheese and charcuterie platters, as well as small plates like chicken livers on marmalade-dolloped rosemary bruschetta.

NUMBER NINE GAY

Map p306 (www.numberninedc.com; 1435 P St NW; ⊙5pm-2am Mon-Sat, from 3pm Sun; Ⓜ Dupont Circle) Number Nine looks like it should be a total den of obnoxiousness, what with its super-sleek spaceship-style furniture and Euro I'm-too-cool-for-school vibe, but then you go inside and it's a totally friendly, even laid-back gay bar. This is a great bar for gay meet-and-greet early in the evening, although things definitely get a bit more cruise-y as the night wears on.

U Street & Shaw

★RIGHT PROPER BREWING CO BREWERY

Map p312 (www.rightproperbrewery.com; 624 T St NW; ⏲5-11pm Tue-Thu, to midnight Fri & Sat, to 10pm Sun; Ⓜ Shaw-Howard U) As if the artwork – a chalked mural of the National Zoo's giant pandas with laser eyes destroying downtown DC – wasn't enough, Right Proper Brewing Co makes sublime ales in a building where Duke Ellington used to play pool. It's the Shaw district's neighborhood clubhouse, a big, sunny space filled with folks gabbing at reclaimed wood tables.

A&D BAR BAR

Map p312 (www.andbardc.com; 1314 9th St NW; ⏲5pm-1am Mon-Thu, to 2am Fri & Sat; Ⓜ Mt Vernon Sq) Neighborhood hipsters rally under the pressed tin ceiling and dangling vintage lights at this comfy tavern. A&D takes cocktails seriously, shaking and stirring housemade ingredients and local spirits, and there's a small but solid beer list. Trendy pub snacks help soak up the booze, or carry out from Sundevich, the bar's sibling shop of global sandwiches located next door (in the alley).

THE COFFEE BAR COFFEE

Map p312 (www.thecoffeebardc.com; 1201 S St NW; ⏲7am-6pm Mon-Fri, 8am-7pm Sat & Sun; 📶; Ⓜ U St) Many locals point to the Coffee Bar as their favorite spot to hang out all day reading and laptop typing. Located on a quiet residential corner, with tables spilling onto the sidewalk, it feels like the lived-in neighborhood cafe you've been coming to forever. Huge windows, retro couches, hipster baristas and truly delicious coffee stoke the love.

MARVIN BAR

Map p312 (www.marvindc.com; 2007 14th St NW; ⏲5:30pm-2am Mon-Sat, from 11am Sun; Ⓜ U St) Cool-cat Marvin has a low-lit lounge with vaulted ceilings where DJs spin soul and rare grooves to a mixed 14th St crowd. Upstairs, the splendid roof deck packs 'em in on summer nights and in winter, when folks huddle under roaring heat lamps sipping cocktails and Belgian beers. The bar is named for native son Marvin Gaye.

The theme pays homage to when Marvin Gaye lived in Belgium.

WORTH A DETOUR

LOCAL BREWERIES

Breweries have been bubbling up throughout Northeast DC. The following are far-flung but oh-so-worth the trip. Most visitors drive or rideshare, as the beer makers aren't easy to reach by public transportation.

DC Brau (www.dcbrau.com; 3178b Bladensburg Rd; ⏲4-9pm Thu & Fri, noon-5pm Sat, noon-4pm Sun) It was the first craft brewer in town, launching in 2011 with bodacious beers like Thyme After Thyme and seasonal specialties like the pumpkin porter Fermentation Without Representation. They're widely available around DC. The brewery has a taproom and offers free tours on most Saturdays at 2pm, 3pm and 4pm. It's north of the National Arboretum near the Maryland border.

Atlas Brew Works (www.atlasbrewworks.com; 2052 West Virginia Ave NE, Suite 102; ⏲5-8pm Fri, 1-8pm Sat & Sun) Atlas' tap room doesn't have tables and chairs, or loads of drink options. So why do beer geeks make the trek? Because the four rotating brews on offer are hopped-up, delicious and cheap. Patrons stand and guzzle at the bar, discussing the merits of 2-row malt versus midnight wheat with staff. Free tours of the brewery take place every Saturday on even-numbered hours.

Bardo Brewpub (www.bardodc.com; 1216 Bladensburg Rd NE; ⏲6pm-midnight Tue-Fri, 1pm-2am Sat, 1pm-midnight Sun; 🚌B2) Part beer garden with picnic tables, part brewery, part dog park, part corn hole sportsplex, part backyard of your crazy uncle who collects junk, Bardo is, um, eclectic. It rarely feels crowded (because it's huge), and almost always is relaxed with young, Frisbee-throwing types knocking back the 20 beers on tap. The suds tend toward ass-kicking stouts and India pale ales.

1

2

KRISTA ROSSOW / ALAMY ©

1. Bohemian Caverns (p182), mural by Alonso Tamayo
2. Diners upstairs at Meridian Pint (p173)
3. H Street Country Club (p122) has its own minigolf course

Five Neighborhoods for a Night Out

After a day of museums and monuments, it's time to let loose. Bohemian jazz clubs? Wee-hour half-smokes? Dive bars for nighthawks? DC has several buzzy neighborhoods to make it happen.

Logan Circle

North of downtown in trendy Logan Circle, 14th St NW bursts with wine bars, beer bars, tapas bars and oyster bars. Churchkey (p176) glows with the requisite hipness. DC's political glitterati cozy up nearby at Le Diplomate (p173).

U Street NW

Just north of Logan Circle, U St is DC's richest nightlife zone. Seasoned jazz players bop at historic Bohemian Caverns (p183), while DJ-savvy groovesters hit the dance floor at U Street Music Hall (p180). Late-night half-smokes await at Ben's Chili Bowl (p173).

H Street NE

Pie cafes, noodle shops and beer gardens roll out east of Union Station. Little Miss Whiskey's Golden Dollar (p122) sets the frisky standard with hallucinogenic decor and boogaloo-spinning DJs. H Street Country Club (p123) pours beer alongside a DC-themed minigolf course.

Barracks Row

In Capitol Hill along 8th St SE, locals line up for shabby-chic Rose's Luxury (p122). They also sip at convivial Lola's Barracks Bar & Grill (p119) and see what's on at The Fridge (p118) street art gallery.

Columbia Heights

The main vein is 11th St NW. In good weather the patio at Wonderland Ballroom (p172) fills with neighborhoodies hoisting brews. It's the same scene at wine-pouring Room 11 (p181) and beer-and-pool bar Meridian Pint (p173).

U STREET MUSIC HALL CLUB

Map p312 (www.ustreetmusichall.com; 1115 U St NW; ⊙hours vary; Ⓜ U St) FREE This is the spot to get your groove on sans the VIP/bottle service crowd. Two local DJs own and operate the basement club. It looks like a no-frills rock bar, but it has a pro sound system, cork-cushioned dance floor and other accoutrements of a serious dance club. Alternative bands also thrash a couple of nights per week to keep it fresh.

Shows start between 7pm and 10pm. Tickets cost $10 to $20.

MOCKINGBIRD HILL CAFE

Map p312 (www.drinkmoresherry.com; 1843 7th St NW; ⊙5-11:30pm Mon, 5pm-12:30am Tue-Thu, 5pm-1:30am Fri, 10am-1:30am Sat, 10am-11:30pm Sun; Ⓜ Shaw-Howard U) It's an expensive coffee bar by day (topping out at $30 for a cuppa, using some of the world's rarest beans). By night the focus is on sherry and the hams it goes so well with. If you're unfamiliar with Spanish fortified wine, tasting flights are available. It's niche, but the cozy-mod, Andalusian-tapas-bar aura wins you over in the end.

The owner also owns the next-door bourbon bar and oyster bar. They're among several stylish eateries and cafes that have sprung up along 7th St by the Shaw Metro station.

BRIXTON BAR

Map p312 (☎202-560-5045; www.brixtondc.com; 901 U St NW; ⊙5pm-2am Mon-Fri, to 3am Sat, from 11am Sun; Ⓜ Shaw-Howard U) As the name implies, this is a slice of England in DC, although it's not corny Olde England. Rather, it's hip young tight jeans and ethnic scarves and stiff drinks and London slang and East End pop art on the walls. It has a decent pub-grubby menu if such is your fancy, and a rooftop patio with great views over U St.

DACHA BEER GARDEN BEER GARDEN

Map p312 (www.dachadc.com; 1600 7th St NW; ⊙4-10:30pm Mon-Thu, 4pm-midnight Fri, noon-midnight Sat, noon-10:30pm Sun; Ⓜ Shaw-Howard U) Happiness reigns in Dacha's free-wheeling beer garden. Kids and dogs bound around the picnic tables, while adults hoist glass boots filled with German brews. When the weather gets nippy, staff bring heaters and blankets and stoke the fire pit. And it all takes place under the sultry gaze of Elizabeth Taylor (or a mural of her, which sprawls across the back wall).

It can get packed with a bro-hugging crowd as the evening progresses, but in general everyone remains good spirited and willing to share a table.

FLASH CLUB

Map p312 (www.flashdc.com; 645 Florida Ave NW; ⊙6pm-midnight Wed & Thu, to 3am Fri & Sat; Ⓜ Shaw-Howard U) A diverse group packs into Flash. The 1st floor is a bar, while upstairs is a pocket-sized club (you pass through a photo booth into a hidden room to reach it). Deep house, techno and dubstep DJs from the East Coast and Europe spin. Tickets usually cost $10 to $15.

SALOON BAR

Map p312 (1205 U St NW; ⊙5pm-2am Tue-Sat; Ⓜ U St) The Saloon doesn't allow patrons to pack in like sardines, with posted rules against standing between tables. That's great, because the added elbow room better allows you to enjoy a brew ordered off one of the most extensive beer menus in town (Belgian ales are the tour de force). The bar usually closes in August, when the owners go build schools in developing countries.

DICKSON WINE BAR WINE BAR

Map p312 (www.dicksonwinebar.com; 903 U St NW; ⊙6pm Sun-Wed, to 2am Thu-Sat; Ⓜ Shaw-Howard U) Cozy and candlelit, with walls covered in wine bottles, Dickson pours romantic, first-date ambience throughout a three-story row house. The entrance is not marked by name; look for 'Dickson Building 903' above the door. It's a cool spot to swing into before a show at a nearby club.

NELLIE'S GAY

Map p312 (www.nelliessportsbar.com; 900 U St NW; ⊙5pm-1am Mon-Thu, from 3pm Fri, from 11am Sat & Sun; Ⓜ Shaw-Howard U) The atmosphere is low-key, and Nellie's is a good place to hunker down among a friendly crowd for toothsome bar bites (including Venezuelan corn muffins), event nights (including karaoke Tuesdays) or early drink specials. Twelve plasma screens show sporting events; there's also a roof deck and board games on hand.

BAR PILAR BAR

Map p312 (www.barpilar.com; 1833 14th St NW; ⊙5pm-1:30am Sun-Thu, to 2:30am Fri & Sat; Ⓜ U St) Friendly neighborhood favorite Bar Pilar serves excellent cocktails and seasonal organic tapas dishes in a snug, nicely designed space. The mustard-colored walls and curious collections (hats, Hemingway regalia) give it an old-fashioned feel. There's a 2nd-floor dining room, but it's best to stay downstairs to drink and nibble.

TOWN DANCEBOUTIQUE GAY

Map p312 (www.towndc.com; 2009 8th St NW; ⏲6pm-4am Fri, 7pm-4am Sat; Ⓜ Shaw-Howard U) With a great sound system and fine DJs, Town is the go-to spot for dancing, with two floors, various rooms (including an outdoor smoking area) and hilarious drag shows on weekends. The cover charge is usually $5 to $12.

Columbia Heights & Mt Pleasant

★ROOM 11 CAFE

Map p312 (www.room11dc.com; 3234 11th St NW; ⏲8am-1am Sun-Thu, to 2am Fri & Sat; Ⓜ Columbia Heights) Room 11 isn't much bigger than an ambitious living room, and as such it can get pretty jammed. On the plus side, everyone is friendly, the intimacy is warmly inviting on chilly winter nights and there's a spacious outdoor area for when it gets too hot inside. The low-key crowd sips excellent wines hand-selected by the management and whiz-bang cocktails.

There's beer, too, of course. For dinner Room 11 cooks up a smallish, evolving menu of comfort foods. By day the space is a breezy coffee shop wafting quiches, sandwiches and baked-on-site chocolate bourbon pies and cookies.

RED DERBY BAR

(www.redderby.com; 3718 14th St NW; ⏲5pm-2am Mon-Fri, from 11am Sat & Sun; Ⓜ Columbia Heights) Welcome to a hipster-punk lounge where the 'tenders know the names, the sweet-potato fries soak up the beer ordered off an impressively long list and – why yes, that is *The Princess Bride* – cult movies play on a projector screen. The rooftop deck and board games add to the festivities. Note it's cash only, and the brews come in cans only.

The lighting is blood red and sexy; you can't help but look good under it. The bar is about a half-mile walk from the Metro north on 14th St. There's no sign, so look for the address and a painted symbol of a red hat.

RAVEN BAR

Map p312 (3125 Mt Pleasant St NW; ⏲4pm-1am Mon, from 2:30pm Tue-Sat, from 1pm Sun; Ⓜ Columbia Heights) The best jukebox in Washington, a dark interior crammed with locals and lovers, that neon lighting that casts you under a glow Edward Hopper should rightly paint and a tough but friendly bar staff are the ingredients in this shot, which, when slammed, hits you as DC's best dive by a mile.

☆ ENTERTAINMENT

☆ Logan Circle, U Street & Shaw

HOWARD THEATRE THEATER

Map p312 (www.thehowardtheatre.com; 620 T St NW; Ⓜ Shaw-Howard U) Built in 1910, Howard Theatre was the top address when U St was known as 'Black Broadway.' Duke Ellington, Ella Fitzgerald and other famed names lit the marquee. Now big-name comedians, blues and jazz acts fill the house, as does the Sunday gospel brunch. There's a photo op out front with the steel-and-granite statue of Ellington pounding the keys of a swirling treble clef.

The Howard was the first major theater to feature black entertainers performing for a predominantly black clientele. It shuttered in 1980 when the neighborhood declined, then reopened in 2012 after a $29 million renovation. The interior sparkles, from the the black walnut paneling to the oak floors and huge portraits of Duke and his jazzy friends.

★BLACK CAT LIVE MUSIC

Map p312 (www.blackcatdc.com; 1811 14th St NW; Ⓜ U St) A pillar of DC's rock and indie scene since the 1990s, the battered Black Cat has hosted all the greats of years past (White Stripes, the Strokes, Arcade Fire among others). If you don't want to pony up for $20-a-ticket bands on the upstairs main stage (or the smaller Backstage below), head to the Red Room for jukebox, pool and strong cocktails.

9:30 CLUB LIVE MUSIC

Map p312 (www.930.com; 815 V St NW; admission from $10; Ⓜ U St) The 9:30, which can pack

WORTH A DETOUR

PETWORTH

It wasn't long before Columbia Heights' gentrification spilled over to Petworth, the next stop north on the Metro. Originally a working-class community, younger, progressive types have moved in, bringing a hodgepodge of indie shops and funky bars with them. Georgia Ave is the main vein. Upshur St is also abuzz. Plus an uncommon historic site rises in the 'hood. Here are some favorite spots:

President Lincoln's Cottage (202-829-0436; www.lincolncottage.org; 140 Rock Creek Church Rd NW; adult/child $15/5; 10am-3pm Mon-Sat, 11am-3pm Sun; M Georgia Ave-Petworth) History buffs can make the trek to President Lincoln's summer house tucked away on the grounds of the old Soldiers' Retirement Home. Abe came here to beat the heat and jot notes for the Emancipation Proclamation in leafy seclusion. Ghosts float on the veranda's breeze. Tours of the empty home tell the tale. Reserve tickets in advance. The site is about a mile from the Metro station.

Hitching Post (202-726-1511; www.hitchingpostdc.com; 200 Upshur St NW; mains $15-24; 11:30am-11pm; M Georgia Ave-Petworth) Across the street from President Lincoln's Cottage, this neighborly diner looks like a house from the outside. Inside red-vinyl-backed booths and a bar fill the intimate room. Waitstaff call customers by name and bring them plates heaped with fried chicken, the house specialty. Grilled pork chops and catfish also hit the tables.

W Domku (202-722-7475; www.domkucafe.com; 821 Upshur St NW; mains $16-22; 5-11pm Tue-Thu, 5pm-midnight Fri, 10am-midnight Sat, 10am-10:30pm Sun; M Georgia Ave-Petworth) W Domku spreads a broad mix of Polish, Russian and Scandinavian fare – from goulash, fish stew and gravlax to house-infused aquavit. Retro furnishings (one fan referred to it as 'Ikea on good drugs') and an easy-going vibe add to its appeal. It's about a half-mile north of the Metro station.

Qualia Coffee (www.qualiacoffee.com; 3917 Georgia Ave NW; 7am-7pm Mon-Fri, 8am-6pm Sat & Sun; wi-fi; M Georgia Ave-Petworth) Follow your nose a couple of blocks north of the Metro to this hardcore coffee shop. Staff roast beans from around the world and offer free tasting sessions on the second and fourth Sunday of each month at 2pm. There's not a lot of seating indoors, but tables and chairs spill into the groovy backyard, too.

Looking Glass Lounge (www.thelookingglasslounge.com; 3634 Georgia Ave NW; 5pm-2am Sun-Thu, to 3am Fri & Sat; M Georgia Ave-Petworth) An old guy in a broad-brimmed cap clutches a highball of Jameson, while drinking next to him is a crowd of 20-somethings who respect his presence, even as they crank the music under dark chandelier-ish lighting and commiserate in the beer garden out back. Looking Glass is Petworth's neighborhood bar, a welcome-one, welcome-all dive with a great jukebox and first-rate pub grub. It's a block south of the Metro station.

DC Reynolds (202-506-7178; 3628 Georgia Ave NW; 11am-2am, to 3am Fri & Sat; M Georgia Ave-Petworth) A few doors away from Looking Glass Lounge, DC Reynolds is a comfy, dart-board-and-trivia-night pub. The main draw is the enormous outdoor patio that's perfect for a cool beer and a pickle back (whiskey followed by pickle juice). The free jukebox and deep happy-hour specials enhance its merits.

1200 people into a surprisingly compact venue, is the granddaddy of the live-music scene in DC. Pretty much every big name that comes through town ends up on this stage, and a concert here is the first-gig memory of many a DC-area teenager. Headliners usually take the stage between 10:30pm and 11:30pm.

BOHEMIAN CAVERNS — JAZZ

Map p312 (www.bohemiancaverns.com; 2001 11th St NW; admission $7-22; 7pm-midnight Mon-Thu, 7:30pm-2am Fri & Sat, 6pm-midnight Sun; M U St) Back in the day, Bohemian Caverns hosted the likes of Miles Davis, John Coltrane and Duke Ellington. Today the timeless jazz club stages a mix of youthful renegades and soulful legends. Monday night's swingin' house band draws an all-ages crowd.

STUDIO THEATRE THEATER

Map p312 (www.studiotheatre.org; 1501 14th St NW; Ⓜ Dupont Circle) The contemporary four-theater complex has been staging Pulitzer Prize–winning and premiere plays for more than 35 years. It cultivates a lot of local actors.

VELVET LOUNGE LIVE MUSIC

Map p312 (www.velvetloungedc.com; 915 U St NW; admission from $8; Ⓜ Shaw-Howard U) Velvet is tiny, red and awesome. It's a hole-in-the-wall, almost literally given its diminutive size, but that doesn't stop a steady stream of great rock and hip-hop artists from taking the stage upstairs. Top DJs spin house, funk and R & B in the downstairs bar.

DC9 LIVE MUSIC

Map p312 (www.dcnine.com; 1940 9th St NW; admission $10-15; ⌚from 5pm; Ⓜ Shaw-Howard U) DC9 is as intimate as DC's live-music venues get, and about as divey as well. Not that we're complaining; there's always a good edge on in this spot. Up-and-coming local bands, with an emphasis on indie rockers, play most nights of the week; when the live music finishes (often around 11pm) DJs keep the place going until about 3am.

On the 2nd floor, zodiac murals and diner booths set the mellow mood; downstairs you'll find a narrow shotgun bar that's often packed wall to wall. There's also a rooftop where folks gather to chill and drink.

SOURCE THEATRE THEATER

Map p312 (www.culturaldc.org; 1835 14th St NW; Ⓜ U St) Source hosts mostly new works across an array of disciplines. You might see improv, Spanish-language opera or a dreamy interpretation of Strindberg in the 150-seat theater. The popular Source Festival in June puts on a slew of 10-minute plays.

LINCOLN THEATRE THEATER

Map p312 (www.thelincolndc.com; 1215 U St NW; Ⓜ U St) Duke Ellington, Louis Armstrong and Billie Holiday are among the many African American luminaries who performed at this 1922 ballroom. The District renovated the venue in the 1990s to host music and theater. It's classy, but it kind of limps along with sporadic performances.

LOCAL KNOWLEDGE

NEIGHBORHOOD NEWS

Known as the 'king of local blogs,' **PoPville** (www.popville.com) posts information about restaurants, bars and shops that are opening, as well as political goings-on in DC's neighborhoods. It covers the whole city, but it has an emphasis on U St, Shaw and Petworth (the blog started with the title 'Prince of Petworth' and then expanded). It's a great source for the local lowdown.

☆ Columbia Heights & Northeast DC

DANCE PLACE DANCE

(www.danceplace.org; 3225 8th St NE; Ⓜ Brookland-CUA) The only truly cutting-edge dance space in the capital is tucked away in Northeast DC. It's run by five resident modern-dance companies offering a year-round calendar of new work, which includes festivals featuring African dance, tap dancing, step dancing and other genres. It also hosts the work of top-notch national companies. The theater is a few blocks south of the Metro station.

GALA HISPANIC THEATRE THEATER

Map p312 (☎202-234-7174; www.galatheatre.org; 3333 14th St NW; Ⓜ Columbia Heights) The Gala maintains a 40-year tradition of staging Spanish and Latin American plays.

SHOPPING

Upscale boutiques, quirky design and furniture shops, galleries and vintage stores are rife along U St and 14th St as it makes its way south into Logan Circle. In Columbia Heights, Target, Staples, Giant Foods and other big-box retailers throng the area around the Metro station.

★MISS PIXIE'S ANTIQUES

Map p312 (www.misspixies.com; 1626 14th St NW; ⌚11am-7pm; Ⓜ U St) One of the best places to browse in the neighborhood, Miss Pixie's is piled high with relics from the past, from stuffed leather armchairs to 1960s lawn ornaments. You'll find dishes, ashtrays, rocking chairs, farm tables, black-and-white photos and plenty of other vintage curiosities. New items arrive on Wednesday nights and hit the shelves by Thursday morning.

HOME RULE HOMEWARES

Map p312 (www.homerule.com; 1807 14th St NW; ⌚11am-7pm Mon-Sat, noon-5:30pm Sun; Ⓜ U St) Tired of Pottery Barn homogeneity around your house? Check out Home Rule's amusingly original stock: frog-shaped toothbrush holders, brightly colored martini glasses, animal-shaped salt-and-pepper sets, and rugs and linens, too. The mosaic decorating the front counter symbolizes the U St district's revitalization – it's made with smashed glass from the 1968 riots.

GOOD WOOD ANTIQUES

Map p312 (www.goodwooddc.com; 1428 U St NW; ⌚noon-7pm Mon-Sat, to 5pm Sun; Ⓜ U St) Even if you're not in the market for a mid-century armoire, Good Wood is well worth a visit. The warm, atmospheric store has a cool selection of antiques, including handcrafted chairs and tables, elegant lamps and wall hangings, plus other decorative items.

TREASURY VINTAGE

Map p312 (www.shoptreasury.com; 1843 14th St NW; ⌚noon-7pm Mon-Wed, noon-8pm Thu & Fri, 11am-7pm Sat, 11am-6pm Sun; Ⓜ U St) Looking for a flapper dress? An ostrich-skin satchel? A 1970s tweed vest and skirt set? Wooden clog sandals? Climb the stairs to this small shop and behold the vintage trove. Items don't come cheap, but they will be one-of-a-kind conversation starters.

REDEEM CLOTHING

Map p312 (www.redeemus.com; 1810 14th St NW; ⌚noon-8pm Mon-Sat, to 6pm Sun; Ⓜ U St) 'It's never too late to change,' is the motto of this enticing little clothier on 14th St. Redeem carries indie labels and a small selection of local designers, and targets urban and hip but cashed-up customers. Look for Earnest Sewn denim, Colcci ankle boots, Corpus sweaters and other unique labels.

BIG PLANET COMICS BOOKS

Map p312 (www.bigplanetcomics.com; 1520 U St NW; ⌚11am-7pm Mon, Tue, Thu & Fri, to 8pm Wed, to 6pm Sat, noon-5pm Sun; Ⓜ U St) Not just for comic-book-loving geeks, Big Planet appeals to a surprisingly diverse audience, with an excellent collection of limited editions and graphic novels, plus posters, T-shirts, manga material and collectible stuff.

CARAMEL CLOTHING

Map p312 (www.caramelfashion.com; 1603 U St NW; ⌚noon-7pm Sat, to 6pm Sun; Ⓜ U St) This dapper little boutique sells a well-edited selection of men's and women's clothing and accessories that aim for a stylish effortlessness. Look for comely I-Shandi dresses, eye-catching Leather Island belts and incredibly soft denim apparel. The artwork on the walls is also for sale – all created by local artists.

SPORTS & ACTIVITIES

ROCK CREEK PARK GOLF COURSE GOLF

(☎202-882-7332; www.golfdc.com; 6100 16th St NW; 18 holes weekday/weekend $20/25; ⌚sunrise-sunset; 🚌S1, S2, S4) The hilly and narrow fairways have large elevation changes. Dense woods on either side replace water hazards.

Upper Northwest DC

Neighborhood Top Five

❶ Seek out the sacred and profane in the architectural treasures of **Washington National Cathedral** (p187). A Darth Vader gargoyle, a moon rock and a secret garden are but a fraction of the esoteric offerings.

❷ Wave to the giant pandas and swinging orangutans at the **National Zoo** (p188).

❸ Hike, bike or saddle up a horse in **Rock Creek Park** (p188).

❹ Gaze at the exquisite collections from Russian royals at the **Hillwood Museum & Gardens** (p189).

❺ Browse books by big-name authors, then meet them in person at **Politics & Prose Bookstore** (p192).

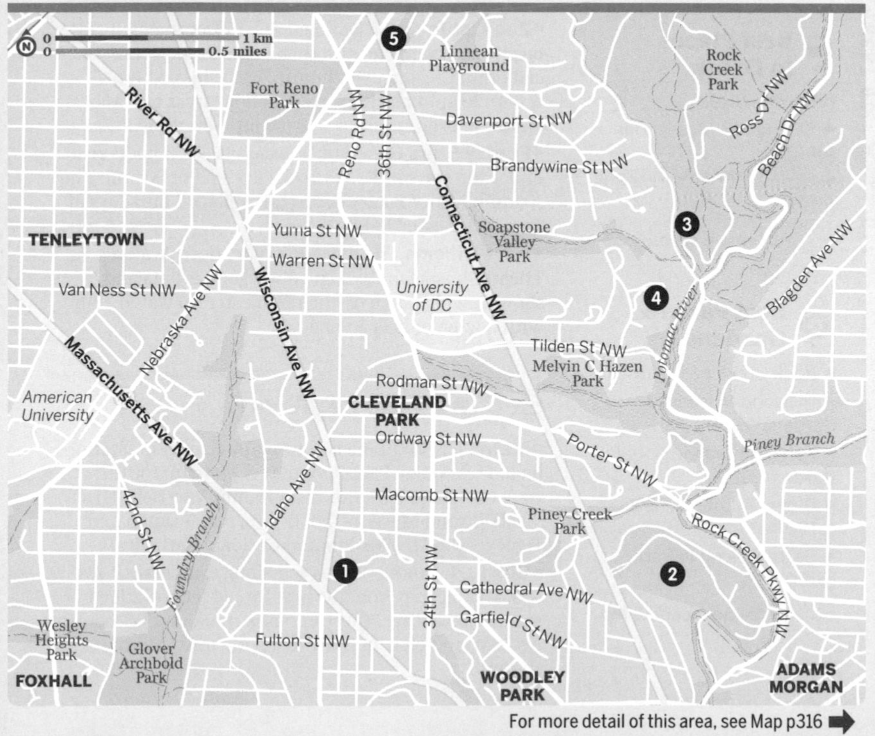

For more detail of this area, see Map p316 ➡

Lonely Planet's Top Tip

Remember your geography. The Upper Northwest may seem far from the action, but it's right next door to Georgetown (to the southwest), Dupont (to the southeast) and Adams Morgan (to the west). You can easily walk to any of these neighborhoods and their rich stock of restaurants and nightlife.

Best Places to Eat

- Macon (p191)
- Comet Ping Pong (p190)
- 2 Amys (p190)
- Buck's Fishing & Camping (p191)
- Open City (p191)

For reviews, see p190.

Best Places to Drink

- Bardeo (p192)
- St Arnold's Mussel Bar (p192)
- Nanny O'Brien's Irish Pub (p192)

For reviews, see p192.

Best Parks & Gardens

- Rock Creek Park (p188)
- Hillwood Museum & Gardens (p189)
- Kahlil Gibran Memorial Garden (p189)
- Glover Archbold Park (p190)
- Battery Kemble Park (p190)

For reviews, see p188.

Explore Upper Northwest DC

The leafy lanes of Upper Northwest have long been the place for upper-income Washingtonians to settle their families. While Georgetown houses more of the city's elite, the presence of its university and the traffic snarls have made it less appealing to folks seeking a quiet place to raise their children. The Upper Northwest's stretching serenity and supremely pleasant clumps of residential bliss do the job. It's no surprise Sidwell Friends School is here, where presidents Clinton and Obama sent their daughters.

Upper Northwest's sights could fill a day. The Washington National Cathedral and National Zoo are foremost. Rock Creek Park and Hillwood Museum (the amazing Russian art-filled manor of cereal heiress Marjorie Post) are less well known but equally worthwhile.

Some of the city's most inventive restaurants have posted up this way, attracted by a population that has disposable income to spend and an increasingly savvy attitude toward food. The nightlife scene hasn't quite caught up, but it's hardly boring either. Lots of sights and eateries cluster around Metro stops, but be prepared to bus or walk a fair distance to others.

Local Life

- **Zoo Lights** At the National Zoo in December, local businesses compete with each other to showcase elaborate Christmas-light displays fashioned to resemble animals. It's a great holiday treat to wander amid the brightness on sharp winter evenings.
- **Poetry Stars** On summer evenings, local poets read under the stars in Rock Creek Park's planetarium. The Joaquin Miller Poetry Series takes place Thursdays at 7pm in June and July.
- **Indie Cinema** The much-loved art-deco Avalon Theatre hosts family-themed weekend events and shows a wide range of films. You can also watch a film with a wine or beer in hand.

Getting There & Away

- **Metro** The Red Line is your main-vein train. Stations include Woodley Park-Zoo/Adams Morgan (for the zoo), Cleveland Park (for restaurants), Van Ness-UDC (for Hillwood Museum, bookstore, restaurants) and Tenleytown-AU (Washington National Cathedral).
- **Bus** L1, L2 and L4 buses roll along Connecticut Ave NW and pick up from the first three Metro stations mentioned above; 30-series buses run along Wisconsin Ave NW and pick up from Tenleytown-AU Metro station.

TOP SIGHT
WASHINGTON NATIONAL CATHEDRAL

This Gothic cathedral, as dramatic as its European counterparts, blends both the spiritual and the profane in its architectural treasures. The church has also played a pivotal role in the city's religious life. Presidents attend multi-faith services following their inauguration, state funerals are hosted inside and this was where Martin Luther King Jr gave his last Sunday sermon.

It took 82 years to build the edifice – Teddy Roosevelt laid the cornerstone in 1908, and construction didn't technically stop until 1990. The cathedral provoked strong opposition early on, but the multifaith character of worship helped mollify the arguments.

The building is neo-Gothic, but it's embellished by distinctive American accents. A moon rock studs one of the interior stained-glass windows, and Darth Vader's head shares space with the exterior gargoyles (bring binoculars). In the main sanctuary, chapels honor Martin Luther King Jr (in the Kellogg Bay) and Abe Lincoln. Helen Keller and Woodrow Wilson are buried in the crypt. Themed tours ($15 to $25 including admission) take in all of the above; make advance bookings online in spring and summer.

Other highlights... Take the elevator to the tower overlook for city views. Meander through the peaceful winding paths in the Bishop's Garden. The 11:15am Sunday service features choral music and a 10-bell peal of the carillon afterwards. Choristers sing Evensong at 5:30pm weekdays (and 4pm on Sundays) during the school year. There's also an excellent new cafe (p191). The 2011 earthquake damaged parts of the building. Repairs are underway, but visitors still have full access to the key areas of interest inside the cathedral.

DON'T MISS...

- Darth Vader gargoyle
- Lincoln Bay floor of pennies
- Helen Keller tomb
- Evensong
- Bishop's Garden

PRACTICALITIES

- Map p316
- 202-537-6200
- www.nationalcathedral.org
- 3101 Wisconsin Ave NW
- adult/child $10/$6, admission free Sun
- 10am-5:30pm Mon-Fri, to 8pm some days May-Sep, to 4:30pm Sat, 8am-4pm Sun
- (wi-fi)
- M Tenleytown-AU to southbound bus 31, 32, 36, 37

SIGHTS

WASHINGTON NATIONAL CATHEDRAL — CATHEDRAL

See p187.

NATIONAL ZOO — ZOO

Map p316 (www.nationalzoo.si.edu; 3001 Connecticut Ave NW; ⌚10am-6pm Apr-Oct, to 4:30pm Nov-Mar, grounds 6am-8pm daily, to 6pm Nov-Mar; Ⓜ Cleveland Park, Woodley Park-Zoo/Adams Morgan) FREE Home to over 2000 individual animals (400 different species) in natural habitats, the National Zoo is famed for its giant pandas Mei Xiang and Tian Tian, along with their cub Bao Bao (born to Mei Xiang in 2013). Other highlights include the African lion pride, Asian elephants, and dangling orangutans swinging 50ft overhead from steel cables and interconnected towers (aka the 'O Line').

This Smithsonian Institution zoo was founded in 1889 and planned by Frederick Law Olmsted, designer of New York's Central Park. The zoo's grounds follow the natural contours of a woodland canyon, and the exhibits are noted for their natural-habitat settings. The zoo is intensively involved in worldwide ecological study and species-preservation work. High points in the past decade include giant panda and lowland gorilla births – a happy change from the early 2000s, when the zoo faced controversy over mismanagement and the deaths of several animals.

Even non-zoo fans will find the National Zoo entertaining. The panda house offers fun facts on the creatures' sex lives (they only go at it three days per year – indeed Mei Xiang's pregnancy was the result of artificial insemination) and bowel production (behold the hefty replica poo). Big-cat fans will love the cheetahs' display, while the 'What's for Dinner?' feature has overly honest scales that inform you who would like to feast on you ('100lb to 150lb – you're a female warthog. A pack of lions could finish you off in an hour.') The interactive 'Think Tank' examines animal intelligence (including yours) and displays a cabinet of brains. The zoo's snack stands even sell decent beer.

The grounds are well-marked, but maps are available for $3 at the main entrance for easier navigation (or download the interactive National Zoo iPhone app for $2). Check the sign there for the day's schedule of animal feedings. Among the new attractions, is a large new, state-of-the-art, indoor-outdoor elephant habitat that opened in 2013.

EASIEST WAY TO THE ZOO

The National Zoo is pretty much equidistant between the Cleveland Park and Woodley Park-Zoo/Adams Morgan Metro stops, but the walk is downhill if you get off at Cleveland Park.

ROCK CREEK PARK — PARK

Map p316 (www.nps.gov/rocr; ⌚sunrise-sunset; Ⓜ Cleveland Park, Woodley Park-Zoo/Adams Morgan) At 1700 acres, Rock Creek is twice the size of New York's Central Park and feels much more wild. Even coyotes have settled into the wilderness (they're not dangerous, by the way). Terrific trails for hiking, biking and horseback riding extend the entire length, and the boundaries enclose Civil War forts, dense forest and wildflower-strewn fields.

Rock Creek Park begins at the Potomac's east bank near Georgetown and extends to and beyond the northern city boundaries. Narrow in its southern stretches, where it hews to the winding course of the waterway it's named for, it broadens into wide, peaceful parklands in Upper Northwest DC.

There are visitor centers at the Nature Center & Planetarium (p188) and Peirce Mill (p189) where you can pick up maps and sign up for ranger-led programs. Cell phone 'tours' are stationed around the park; when you see a dial-and-discover sign, just enter the listed number. Southwest of the Nature Center, the Soapstone Valley Park extension, off Connecticut Ave at Albemarle St NW, preserves quarries where the area's original Algonquian residents dug soapstone for shaping their cookware.

In summer, check what's on at the Carter Barron Amphitheater (p192).

NATURE CENTER & PLANETARIUM — NATURE CENTER

(www.nps.gov/rocr; 5200 Glover Rd, off Military Rd; ⌚9am-5pm Wed-Sun; Ⓜ Friendship Heights then bus E2, E3) FREE The Nature Center & Planetarium is the main visitor center for Rock Creek Park. Besides exhibits on park flora, fauna and history, it has two small nature trails, tons of information, and maps and field guides to the city. A 'touch table' is set up for kids, and rangers lead child-oriented nature walks. Free ranger-led astronomy programs happen inside the planetarium at 1pm and 4pm on Saturday and Sunday, and 4pm on Wednesday.

If you're coming via public transportation, take the E2 or E3 bus to the intersection of Military and Glover Rds; look to your left and follow the trail up to the Nature Center.

A bit further north of here, on the west side of Beach Dr, is the Joaquin Miller Cabin, a log house that once sheltered the famed nature poet.

PEIRCE MILL — HISTORIC BUILDING

Map p316 (www.nps.gov/pimi; Tilden St; ⌚10am-4pm Wed-Sun, Apr-Oct; Ⓜ Van Ness-UDC) Alongside the creek, the 1820 Peirce Mill is a beautiful fieldstone building that houses a recently restored gristmill – the last of the mills which once flourished along Rock Creek. Stop in to see it churning.

HILLWOOD MUSEUM & GARDENS — MUSEUM, GARDENS

Map p316 (www.hillwoodmuseum.org; 4155 Linnean Ave NW; suggested donation adult/child $15/5; ⌚10am-5pm Tue-Sat; Ⓜ Van Ness-UDC) Hillwood, the former estate of Marjorie Merriweather Post (of Post cereal fame) and her third husband, the ambassador to the USSR, contains the biggest collection of Russian imperial art to be found outside of Russia. Post amassed loads of Czarist swag, and her lavishly decorated mansion includes icons, paintings and a gorgeous collection of jewelry and Fabergé eggs. Post was also an avid collector of French decorative artwork, including exquisite 18th-century Sèvres porcelain, Louis XVI furniture and elaborate Beauvais tapestries.

As a bonus, the 25-acre estate incorporates some lovely gardens (which include Post's dog cemetery), a greenhouse and a museum shop. The on-site cafe serves up light fare (quiche, French onion soup, salad Niçoise) and afternoon tea. For a richer experience, join a guided tour (held at 11:30am and 1:30pm Tuesday through Saturday). It's a mile walk from the Metro to Hillwood.

US NAVAL OBSERVATORY — OBSERVATORY

Map p316 (☎202-762-1467; www.usno.navy.mil/USNO; 3450 Massachusetts Ave NW; ⌚tours by reservation 8:30pm Mon) **FREE** If you're ever late to an appointment after visiting this place, you've got no excuse, buddy: the Naval Observatory is the official source of time for the US military and by extension, the country, so you know the clocks are precise. Framed by a pair of stately white ship's anchors, the observatory, created in the 1800s, is here 'to determine the positions and motions of celestial objects, provide astronomical data, measure the Earth's rotation, and maintain the Master Clock for the US.'

Modern DC's light pollution prevents important observational work these days, but that cesium-beam atomic clock is still tickin'. Tours let you peek through telescopes and yak with astronomers, but they fill up weeks in advance, may be canceled at any time and are only offered on select Mondays at 8:30pm (7:30pm from November to February), so reserve early – check the website or phone. On observatory grounds above Massachusetts Ave NW is the official Vice President's Residence (Admiral's House), which is closed to the public. Driving is the best way to reach the observatory.

CIVIL WAR FORTS

The remains of Civil War forts that dot Rock Creek Park are among its most fascinating sites. During the war, Washington was, essentially, a massive urban armory and supply house for the Union Army. Its position near the Confederate lines made it vulnerable to attack, so forts were hastily erected on the city's high points. By spring 1865, 68 forts and 93 batteries bristled on hilltops around DC. See **Civil War Defenses of Washington** (www.nps.gov/cwdw) for more on the subject.

KAHLIL GIBRAN MEMORIAL GARDEN — GARDENS

Map p316 (3100 Massachusetts Ave NW; Ⓜ Dupont Circle) In the midst of the wooded ravine known as Normanstone Park, the Kahlil Gibran garden memorializes the arch-deity of soupy spiritual poetry. Its centerpieces are a moody bust of the Lebanese mystic and a star-shaped fountain surrounded by flowers, hedges and limestone benches engraved with various Gibranisms: 'We live only to discover beauty. All else is a form of waiting.' From a path just north of the garden, you can hop onto trails that link to Rock Creek and Glover Archbold Parks.

ISLAMIC CENTER MOSQUE

Map p316 (www.theislamiccenter.com; 2551 Massachusetts Ave NW; ⏲10am-5pm; Ⓜ Dupont Circle) Topped with a 160ft minaret, this pale limestone structure is the national mosque for American Muslims. Inside, the mosque glows with bright floral tiling, thick Persian rugs and gilt-trimmed ceilings detailed with more Quranic verse. You can enter to look around; remove your shoes, and women must bring scarves to cover their hair.

KREEGER MUSEUM MUSEUM

(☎202-337-3050; www.kreegermuseum.org; 2401 Foxhall Rd NW; adult/child $10/free; ⏲tours by reservation 10:30am & 1:30pm Tue-Thu, without reservation 10am-4pm Fri & Sat, closed Aug) One of DC's more obscure attractions, this little-known museum is tucked away in the hills northwest of Georgetown and houses a fantastic collection of 20th-century modernist art. The art – by Renoir, Picasso and Mark Rothko, among many others – represents the amassed collection of David and Carem Kreeger. Their individual taste adds a charming degree of intimacy to the experience; you feel more as if you're popping into a home than visiting a museum.

Speaking of visiting, you must do so on 90-minute, reservation-only tours unless you come for the Friday and Saturday open houses. Exhibits are constantly rotated, so you're just as likely to see Monet's dappled impressionism as Edvard Munch's dark expressionism. Head west on Reservoir Rd NW about a half-mile to Foxhall Rd; turn right and the museum is about a mile onward.

GLOVER ARCHBOLD PARK PARK

Map p316 (Ⓜ Dupont Circle then bus D1) Glover is a sinuous, winding park, extending from Van Ness St NW in Tenleytown down to the western border of Georgetown University. Its 180 tree-covered acres follow the course of little Foundry Branch Creek, along which runs a pretty nature trail.

It's a good bird-watching destination. It's also a favorite for trail runners. To make a 6-mile loop, start at the C&O Canal and run north through the park, turn west on the greenway along Edmunds St to Palisades Park, then continue south back to the canal and then east to your starting point.

BATTERY KEMBLE PARK PARK

(cnr Garfield & 49th Sts NW; Ⓜ Dupont Circle then bus D3 or D6) Skinny Battery Kemble Park, about a mile long but less than a quarter-mile wide, separates the wealthy Foxhall and Palisades neighborhoods of far northwestern DC. Managed by the National Park Service, the park preserves the site of a little two-gun battery that helped defend western DC against Confederate troops during the Civil War.

SOAPSTONE VALLEY TRAIL PARK

Map p316 (Ⓜ Van Ness-UDC) This rugged 1-mile trail follows along Soapstone Creek and makes a nice add-on to a hike in Rock Creek Park. Access the trailhead on Ablemarle St NW, about one block east of Connecticut Ave.

EATING

Restaurants cluster around the Metro stops in Cleveland Park, Tenleytown and Woodley Park-Zoo/Adams Morgan.

★COMET PING PONG PIZZA $

Map p316 (www.cometpingpong.com; 5037 Connecticut Ave NW; pizzas $12-15; ⏲5-10pm Mon-Thu, 11:30am-11pm Fri & Sat, to 10pm Sun; 👪; Ⓜ Van Ness-UDC) Proving that DC is more than a city of suits and corporate offices, Comet Ping Pong offers a fun and festive counterpoint to the marble city, with its ping pong tables, industrial chic interior and delicious thin-crust pizzas cooked up in a wood-burning oven.

Play a round on the tables in back while you wait for a seat, then feast on creative pizzas such as the Smoky, topped with smoked bacon, Gouda and mushrooms. Wash it down with a draft from Atlas Brew Works. It's possibly the most fun restaurant in the city, popular with families in the early evening and bigger kids (the 25- to 65-year-old crowd) as the night progresses. Bands take the stage from time to time.

2 AMYS PIZZA $

Map p316 (☎202-885-5700; 3715 Macomb St NW; mains $9-14; ⏲11am-11pm Tue-Sat, noon-10pm Sun; 👪; Ⓜ Tenleytown-AU to southbound bus 31, 32, 36, 37) A stone's throw from Washington National Cathedral, 2 Amys serves some of DC's best thin-crust pizzas. Pies are sprinkled with market-fresh ingredients and baked to perfection in a wood-burning oven. Avoid the weekend crowds.

A neighborhood icon, 2 Amy's hits all the right notes, drawing families early in the night, and couples and friends afterwards. Head to the back bar for local and European brews (12 or so on tap) while you wait (it's also a good spot for solo diners). Don't overlook the excellent antipasti (potato frittata, salt cod croquettes) or dessert (marsala custard, almond cake).

OPEN CITY AMERICAN $

Map p316 (☎202-332-2331; www.opencitydc.com; 2331 Calvert St NW; mains $12-16; ⏰6am-midnight; 📶; Ⓜ Woodley Park) Open City is a bedrock breakfast and brunch spot in Woodley Park, drawing a mix of hipsters, young families and old-time regulars. You'll find the usual assortment of egg and pancake-centric dishes, along with brick-oven pizzas, pot roast, sandwiches and other comfort fare. Bartenders whip up an excellent Bloody Mary. Breakfast is served all day.

Fairly quiet during the week, if you plan to brunch here on weekends, you'll need to arrive early to beat the huge crowds that begin forming by 11am.

ROCKLANDS BARBECUE SOUTHERN $

Map p316 (☎202-333-2558; www.rocklands.com; 2418 Wisconsin Ave NW; mains $8-17; ⏰11am-10pm Mon-Sat, to 9pm Sun; Ⓜ Tenleytown-AU then bus 30, 32, 34 or 36) We say Southern, but really, it's just about the barbecue here: slow smoked, red oak and hickory, no electricity, no gas, Texas-style and pretty good for the East Coast. The ribs, as you might guess, are the way to go. An expansion in 2013 means there's finally decent seating here, though you can also order at the take-out counter and get it to go.

OPEN CITY AT THE NATIONAL CATHEDRAL CAFE $

Map p316 (3101 Wisconsin Ave; sandwiches $8-10; ⏰7am-6pm; 📶; Ⓜ Tenleytown-AU to southbound bus 31, 32, 36, 37) Next to the Washington National Cathedral, this atmospheric cafe with outdoor seating serves up sweet and savory waffles, grilled sandwiches, salads, soups, pastries and well-made coffees. It's set in an octagonal building that formerly served as the baptistry, and is just to the right of the cathedral's main entrance. Despite the location beside a major tourist site, it's a much-loved local haunt.

VACE DELI ITALIAN $

Map p316 (☎202-363-1999; 3315 Connecticut Ave NW; whole pizza $9-11; ⏰9am-9pm Mon-Fri, to 8pm Sat, 10am-5pm Sun; Ⓜ Cleveland Park) If you're going on a picnic in Rock Creek Park, may we suggest getting a bit of meat, a parcel of cheese, and some bread, olives, wine and other bites from Vace, perhaps the best deli in DC? Treat yourself to some of its pizza, too; it's divine. Unfortunately, service rarely comes with a smile, but the food more than makes up for the gruffness.

★MACON FUSION $$

(☎202-248-7807; www.maconbistro.com; 5520 Connecticut Ave NW; mains $22-28; ⏰5-10pm Tue-Thu, to 11pm Fri & Sat, 10am-2pm & 5-10pm Sun; Ⓜ Friendship Heights then bus E2) Macon, Georgia, meets Mâcon, France, in this wild mash-up of delectable southern cooking with creative European accents. The space is always buzzing, as a local, well-dressed crowd come to feast on fried catfish with smoked aioli, seared chicken breast with almondine sauce, and piping hot biscuits served with pepper jelly. Creative cocktails, refreshing microbrews and an appealing all-French wine list round out the menu.

The 1925 building has loads of style, with daring wallpaper, an open kitchen and a bold flashbulb-lit sign above the 20-seat bar – which is, incidentally, a great spot for solo diners.

BUCK'S FISHING & CAMPING AMERICAN $$

Map p316 (☎202-364-0777; www.bucksfishingandcamping.com; 5031 Connecticut Ave NW; mains $15-27; ⏰5-9:30pm; Ⓜ Van Ness-UDC) We love Buck's for its vibe: haute lakeside fishing camp, complete with modern banquettes, red-and-white checked tablecloths and canoes on the walls. The menu showcases high-end comfort food at its best, with the kitchen cranking out wild sea scallops, Chesapeake rockfish and wood-grilled burgers. Make reservations on weekend evenings to avoid painfully long waits.

ARDEO INTERNATIONAL $$

Map p316 (☎202-244-6750; www.ardeobardeo.com; 3311 Connecticut Ave NW; small plates $11-13, mains $15-27; ⏰5-10:30pm daily & 11am-3pm Sat & Sun; Ⓜ Cleveland Park) Ardeo's is one of the original small plates/wine bars in the city, and still one of the best. The market- and seasonal-inspired menu showcases creative pastas, tender fish and meat selections, plus salads, sandwiches and charcuterie plates. Try the rich bouillabaisse with scallops, shrimp, mussels and salmon in a saffron broth; or the lamp chops and crispy lamb belly.

The well-curated wine list has some excellent selections to match the food menu.

ST ARNOLD'S MUSSEL BAR — BELGIAN $$

Map p316 (☎202-621-6719; 3433 Connecticut Ave NW; mains $12-20; ⊙4pm-2am Mon-Fri, 11am-2am Sat & Sun; Ⓜ Cleveland Park) This lively open-air spot in Cleveland Park makes a fine destination when you want to combine a bit of eating and drinking. Mussel lovers will love the huge selection (try mussels paella or the St Arnold's mussels with house beer sauce, carmelized shallots and duck fat). You'll also find waffles, herb-crusted salmon, and Flemish onion soup. The Belgian-heavy beer selection is outstanding.

Head to the cosy all-wood tavern downstairs for a great place to linger over a glass of Duvel, Bavik or Delirium Tremens. There's live music here on Saturday nights.

LEBANESE TAVERNA — MIDDLE EASTERN $$

Map p316 (☎202-265-8681; www.lebanesetaverna.com; 2641 Connecticut Ave NW; mains $18-24; ⊙11:30am-10pm Sun-Thu, to 11pm Fri & Sat; ; Ⓜ Woodley Park-Zoo/Adams Morgan) Lebanese Taverna has been cooking *kibbe*, *shawarma*, eggplant, lamb and other traditional dishes for more than three decades. It's pretty routine fare, but everyone we know with kids loves it for the 'little ones' menu and the staff's genuine friendliness toward the younger set. Eat in the high-ceiling, gold-hued room or outside under the shade umbrellas.

Thursday nights feature belly dancing (starting at 8:30pm or 9:30pm).

DRINKING & NIGHTLIFE

Most places tend to be of the quiet neighborhood pub variety. The exception is a cluster of rowdy Irish bars around Connecticut Ave In Cleveland Park, near the Uptown Theater. This is probably Upper Northwest's most concentrated nightlife strip, and the crowd here is young, international and determined to party.

BARDEO — WINE BAR

Map p316 (www.ardeobardeo.com; 3311 Connecticut Ave NW; Ⓜ Cleveland Park) Next door and attached to Ardeo, Bardeo is a favorite spot for starting a night out on the town thanks to its excellent vino. Sip among the menu's wine flights (three 3oz glasses) or go rogue and make your own flight.

NANNY O'BRIEN'S IRISH PUB — IRISH PUB

Map p316 (www.nannyobriens.com; 3319 Connecticut Ave NW; ⊙noon-2am Sun-Thu, to 3am Fri & Sat; Ⓜ Cleveland Park) Washington's most authentic Irish pub, Nanny O'Brien's has been a favorite with real and wannabe Irish people for decades. You won't find any cheesy shamrock schlock or shameless promotions here; no, this bar would rather concentrate on serving stiff drinks along with a good soundtrack. The place is packed and gets pretty rowdy most nights.

Plan your visit around a night of Irish music (Mondays), local bands (Fridays and Saturdays) or pub Trivia (Tuesdays). O'Brien's also throws down regular drink specials and a generous happy 'hour' daily from 4pm to 8pm.

☆ ENTERTAINMENT

CARTER BARRON AMPHITHEATER — THEATER

(☎202-895-6000; www.nps.gov/rocr; 4850 Colorado Ave NW, near 16th St NW, Rock Creek Park; ⊙box office noon-8pm show days; Ⓜ McPherson Sq then bus S2 or S4) In a lovely wooded setting inside Rock Creek Park, the 4000-seat outdoor amphitheater stages a mix of theater, dance and music (jazz, salsa, classical, reggae) on summer evenings. Some events are free; ticketed shows cost $20 to $30.

POLITICS & PROSE BOOKSTORE — LITERARY

Map p316 (www.politics-prose.com; 5015 Connecticut Ave NW; ⊙9am-10pm Mon-Sat, 10am-8pm Sun; Ⓜ Van Ness-UDC then bus L1, L2 or L4) This independent bookstore is known for hosting brain-food readings and discussions on a regular basis. If you miss your favorite author, go to the website and down load an MP3 of the reading for free. Downstairs, the Modern Times coffeehouse is a good spot for a pick-me-up; it also hosts art exhibitions, live performances and a Friday open-mike night.

THE AVALON THEATRE

When can a movie theater be more than simply a money-making enterprise? Locals faced this question when the **Avalon Theatre** (www.theavalon.org; 5612 Connecticut Ave; MFriendship Heights for bus E2) – dating from the 1920s – abruptly went out of business in 2001. Not wanting to see this historic cinema fall to the wrecking ball, the community rallied and purchased the building, then restored and reopened the art-deco movie house as a non-profit enterprise in 2003.

Today the two-screen movie house is a big source of local pride. It's DC's oldest operating cinema and shows a mix of independent, foreign and first-run features. The well-curated film selection and old-fashioned ambience – not to mention the fine cafe and snack bar (with wine, beer and fresh-baked snacks) – provides a nice alternative to the soulless multiplexes found elsewhere.

If you're traveling with kids, don't miss the weekend family matinees, featuring live music, puppet shows and movies aimed at the under-10 crowd. Check the website for upcoming events.

From the Metro, it's a one-mile walk north on Connecticut Ave, or you can take the bus from the station.

LA MAISON FRANÇAISE MUSIC, THEATER

Map p308 (202-944-6400; http://frenchculture.org/events; 4101 Reservoir Rd NW; 10am-4pm Mon-Fri; MFarragut North, then bus D6) La Maison is otherwise known as the French embassy. The beating heart of Gallic DC occupies eight elegantly landscaped acres, anchored by the marble, modernesque embassy itself. Countless cultural activities pop off here every week; check the website for listings. Reservations are required for all events.

UPTOWN THEATER CINEMA

Map p316 (www.amctheatres.com; 3426 Connecticut Ave NW; MCleveland Park) This historic one-screen theater shows first-run films near the Cleveland Park Metro. Although it opened in 1936, nothing remains of its original interior.

SHOPPING

POLITICS & PROSE BOOKSTORE BOOKS

Map p316 (www.politics-prose.com; 5015 Connecticut Ave NW; 9am-10pm Mon-Sat, 10am-8pm Sun; MVan Ness-UDC then bus L1, L2 or L4) Way up in Northwest DC is a key literary nexus and coffeehouse. This active independent has an excellent selection of literary fiction and nonfiction – it's fiercely supportive of local authors – plus it has dedicated staff, high-profile readings, steaming mugs of chai and 15 active book clubs.

It's a 1-mile walk north on Connecticut Ave from the Metro, or you can take the bus from the station.

NATIONAL ZOO SOUVENIRS

Map p316 (3001 Connecticut Ave NW; MWoodley Park-Zoo/Adams Morgan) The National Zoo has several shops on its grounds that sell toys and products featuring all manner of charismatic fauna: ostriches, seals, tigers, wolves, elephants and the inevitable pandas. (Bring home a plastic hyena for less-beloved relatives.) It also has the Zoo Bookstore, in the Education Building on the Connecticut Ave NW side, which has a decent natural-history and field-guide section.

SULLIVAN'S TOY STORE TOYS

Map p316 (www.facebook.com/sullivanstoys; 4200 Wisconsin Ave NW; 10am-6pm Mon-Sat, noon-5pm Sun; MTenleytown-AU) DC's oldest, family-owned toy store is a fun place to browse for gifts, with racks and racks of imaginative toys, crafts, puzzles, games and books that are a nice antidote to the video-game fare of many mainstream toy stores.

BARSTON'S CHILD'S PLAY TOYS

(5536 Connecticut Ave NW; 9:30am-7pm Mon-Fri, to 6pm Sat, 11:30am-5pm Sun; MFriendship Heights then bus E2) This much-loved toy shop may look small on the outside but it has a fantastic selection with all the latest kid pleasers.

MAZZA GALLERIE MALL

(www.mazzagallerie.com; 5300 Wisconsin Ave NW; 10am-8pm Mon-Fri, to 7pm Sat, noon-6pm Sun; MFriendship Heights) If you need an upscale mall, this one has the requisite Neiman-Marcus, Williams-Sonoma, Saks etc. Downstairs is a seven-screen AMC movie theater. It's right beside the Metro, a stone's throw from the Maryland border.

KRÖN CHOCOLATIER FOOD & DRINK

(www.krondc.com; 5300 Wisconsin Ave NW, Mazza Gallerie; Ⓜ Friendship Heights) This shop is known for hand-dipped truffles and amusing novelties, such as edible chocolate baskets, milk-chocolate telephones and cars.

SPORTS & ACTIVITIES

ROCK CREEK HORSE CENTER HORSEBACK RIDING

(☎202-362-0117; www.rockcreekhorsecenter.com; 5100 Glover Rd NW; guided rides $40; Ⓜ Friendship Heights then bus E2 or E3) Thirteen miles of wide dirt trails crisscross the northern part of Rock Creek Park, with an Equitation Field nearby. The Rock Creek Horse Center offers guided trail rides, lessons and pony rides. Reservations required. Weekday rides are only available during summer; weekend rides run from April to October. There are one to three rides per day; check the website for times.

FLETCHER'S BOATHOUSE WATER SPORTS

(☎202-244-0461; www.fletcherscove.com; 4940 Canal Rd NW; watercraft per hr/day from $13/25; ⏲7am-7pm Mar-Nov) This boathouse is a few miles upriver from Georgetown (accessible by bike from the C&O Canal & Towpath or by car from Canal Rd). Canoes, kayaks, rowboats, bicycles and fishing licenses are available. Take Reservoir Rd west, which merges with Canal Rd.

Northern Virginia

ARLINGTON | ALEXANDRIA

Neighborhood Top Five

❶ Walk around **Arlington National Cemetery** (p198) and you can't help but be moved: from the Tomb of the Unknowns' dignified guards; to John F Kennedy's eternal flame; to the simple white headstones sparkling out in every direction.

❷ Get lost amid sleek jets and one massive space shuttle in the mammoth hangars of the **Steven F Udvar-Hazy Center** (p200).

❸ Cycle the **Mount Vernon Trail** (p207) to Theodore Roosevelt Island, Old Town Alexandria or beyond to George Washington's estate.

❹ Take a trip through upper-crust 18th-century society on a tour through the grand **Carlyle House** (p200).

❺ Come face to face with the horrors of slavery in the **Freedom House Museum** (p201).

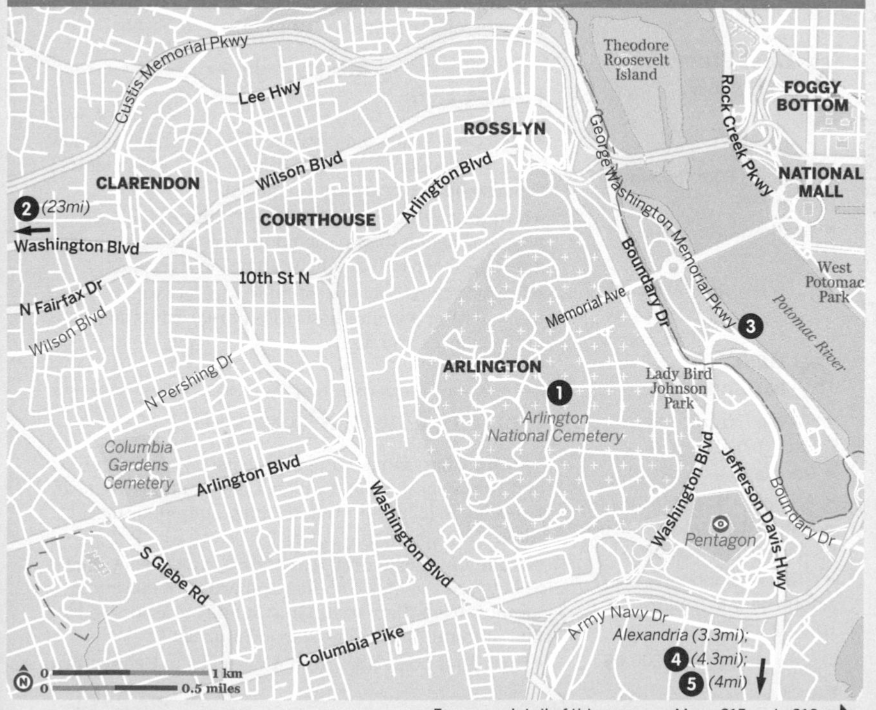

For more detail of this area, see Map p315 and p318.

Lonely Planet's Top Tip

Take a day and cycle to Mount Vernon along the eponymous trail. If you start in Alexandria, it's about 12 miles onward. The path hugs the river much of the way and you'll pedal past a lighthouse, bird-filled marsh and 19th-century fort before heading uphill to George Washington's manor. Outfitters have packages where you cycle one way and return via boat.

Best Places to Eat

- Restaurant Eve (p205)
- Caphe Banh Mi (p204)
- Del Ray Cafe (p204)
- Myanmar (p202)
- Rice Paper (p204)

For reviews, see p202.

Best Places to Drink

- PX (p205)
- Continental (p205)
- Ireland's Four Courts (p205)
- Whitlow's on Wilson (p205)

For reviews, see p205.

Best Museums

- Steven F Udvar-Hazy Center (p200)
- Carlyle House (p200)
- Arlington House (p199)
- National Inventors Hall of Fame & Museum (p202)
- Stabler-Leadbeater Apothecary Museum (p200)

For reviews, see p206.

Explore Northern Virginia

Safe, green-conscious, well-trimmed and full of surprises. Northern Virginia (NoVa) is DC's perfect neighbor, just across from the picket fence of the Potomac River. NoVa communities are basically suburbs of Washington, attached via the Metro. We concentrate on Arlington and Alexandria, which combine crucial capital sites with historic sites, cozy pubs and a buzzing food scene.

Start with Arlington. It's quite close, just a Metro stop from DC, and it holds the two main reasons to cross the border: Arlington National Cemetery and the Pentagon. Plan on a half-day for these two sights alone. Beyond Arlington you'll find the jaw-dropping Steven F Udvar-Hazy Center, aka the annex of the National Air and Space Museum, which holds three times as many jets and rockets as the Mall building. Also out this way are the Eden Center, a Saigon-style foodie emporium where the Vietnamese community clusters, and Annandale, the Korean community's hub. Unfortunately, you'll be hard-pressed to reach these places without a car.

The charming village of Alexandria is 5 miles and 250 years away from Washington. Once a salty port, Alexandria – known as 'Old Town' to locals – is today a posh collection of red-brick homes, cobblestone streets, gas lamps and a waterfront promenade. Boutiques, outdoor cafes and bars pack the main thoroughfare, making the town a fine afternoon or evening jaunt. It's also a jumping-off spot for excursions to Mount Vernon.

Local Life

- **Stay Cool** When temperatures rise, those in the know head to Theodore Roosevelt Island (p199). It's quiet too, since no bikes or cars are permitted.
- **Hangout** Whitlow's (p205) is everything a neighborhood hangout should be: boisterous, brunch-awesome, beer-rich and band-savvy on weekends.
- **Art Attack** Artisphere (p199) is a secret even to locals. The arts center hosts (often free) exhibitions, performances and films.

Getting There & Away

- **Metro** Guess what Arlington Cemetery (Blue Line) and Pentagon (Blue and Yellow Lines) stations are near? Use King St (Blue and Yellow Lines) station for most of Alexandria's sights.
- **Trolley** In Alexandria, a free trolley runs along King St between the Metro station and waterfront every 15 minutes from 10am to 10:15pm Sunday to Wednesday, and until midnight Thursday to Saturday.
- **Boat** Tour boats float from Alexandria to Georgetown.

TOP SIGHT PENTAGON

More than 23,000 people work in the massive polygon, the largest office building in the world. As the headquarters of the US Department of Defense, the Army, Navy and Air Force top brass are all here, as are the Joint Chiefs of Staff. With serious pre-planning, you can tour inside. The outdoor Pentagon Memorial is open to anyone, any time.

Just how big is the Pentagon? The entire Capitol could fit into any one of its five wedge-shaped sections. It has three times the floor space of New York's Empire State Building. The parking lots hold 8770 cars. The building's 17.5 miles of corridors hold 284 bathrooms (side note here: architects designed the building with twice the number of bathrooms needed per number of employees, because segregated Virginia required separate facilities for 'white' and 'colored' persons). The Pentagon's post office handles 1.2 million pieces of mail monthly.

Unlike other monumental federal buildings around DC, the Pentagon was built without using marble. That's because, when construction was going on during WWII, Italy – the source of marble – was an enemy country.

DON'T MISS...

- Memorial audio tour
- Flight 77 point of impact
- Memorial age lines
- Building tours (via pre-registration)
- Medal of Honor

PRACTICALITIES

- Map p318
- ☎703-697-1776
- http://pentagon-tours.osd.mil
- Arlington
- memorial 24hr, tours by appointment
- Ⓜ Pentagon

Pentagon Memorial

While the formidable edifice appears impenetrable, 184 people were killed here on September 11, 2001, when American Airlines Flight 77 crashed into the west side of the building. Just outside of the Pentagon is a tranquil **memorial** (www.pentagonmemorial.org) FREE to these victims, including passengers of flight 77. The grounds consist of 184 benches, each engraved with a victim's name, reaching over a small pool of water. The benches are arranged according to the victims' ages and where they were during the crash (Pentagon versus the airplane). The youngest victim was three-year-old Dana Falkenberg (who was on board flight 77); the oldest was John Yamnicky, 71, a Navy veteran also on the flight.

Download the audio tour from the memorial website before visiting, or access it on-site by calling ☎202-741-1004, and it will lead you through the site's features.

To reach the memorial, follow the signs from the Pentagon Metro station and go all the way through the parking lot to the end; it's about a 10-minute walk. It is OK to take photos at the memorial, but nowhere else on Pentagon grounds.

Building Tours

The Pentagon offers free, hour-long **tours** (9am-3pm Mon-Fri). During the 1.5-mile jaunt, informative guides discuss the military divisions (Army, Air Force, Navy, Marine Corps) housed here; show you the Hall of Heroes and a Medal of Honor; and take you through the Pentagon Memorial. You'll also get an eyeful of artwork and historic memorabilia in the long corridors. Tours depart from the Metro station. No electronics allowed inside.

To get in, you need to make a reservation 14 to 90 days in advance. Book online (http://pentagontours.osd.mil).

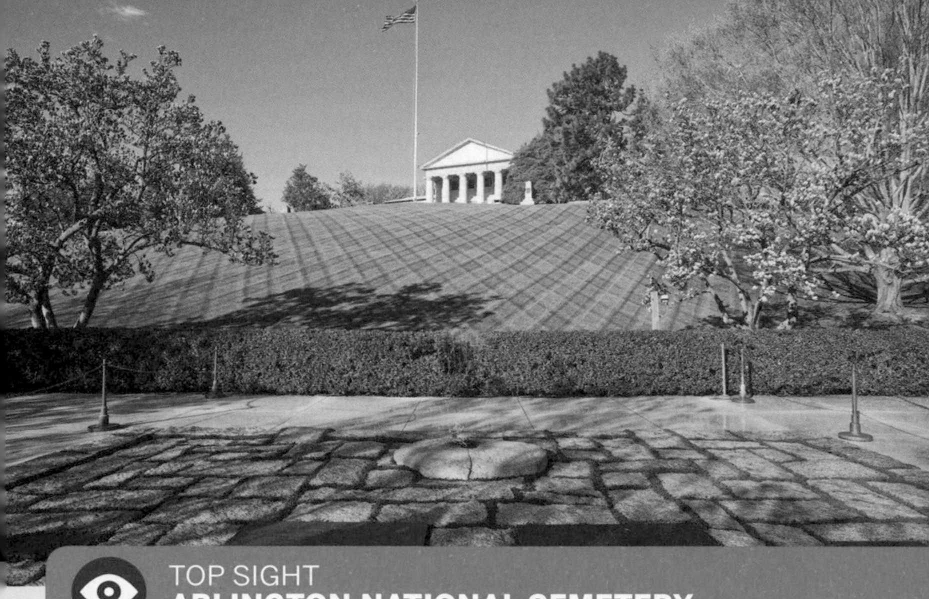

BOB STEFKO / GETTY IMAGES ©

TOP SIGHT
ARLINGTON NATIONAL CEMETERY

Washington's marble often celebrates America's victories and achievements, but this place makes an elegiac counterpoint: commemorating her losses. Simple white headstones mark the sacrifice of over 400,000 service members and their dependents. The 624-acre grounds contain the dead of every war the US has fought since the Revolution.

At the end of Memorial Dr, the first site you'll see is the **Women in Military Service for America Memorial** (www.womensmemorial.org). On the slopes above are the **Kennedy gravesites**. An eternal flame marks the grave of John F Kennedy, next to those of Jacqueline Kennedy Onassis and their two children who died in infancy. Don't forget to visit Arlington House while you're in the area.

The **Tomb of the Unknowns** contains the remains of unidentified US servicemen from both World Wars and the Korean War. Military guards maintain a round-the-clock vigil and the changing of the guard (every half-hour April through September, every hour October through March) is one of Arlington's most moving sights.

Other points of interest include the **Challenger Memorial**, the **Confederate Monument**, the **tomb of Pierre L'Enfant** and the **mast of the battleship USS Maine**. The **Iwo Jima Memorial**, displaying the famous raising of the flag over Mt Suribachi, is on the cemetery's northern fringes.

Pick up a cemetery map at the **visitors center**; the gift shop inside rents audio tours. **Bus tours** (☎202-796-2606; www.trolleytours.com; adult/child $12/6) depart out front and are an easy way to hit all the highlights. If you have a smartphone, you can also download the excellent free ANC Explorer app.

DON'T MISS...

- Kennedy graves and eternal flame
- Tomb of the Unknowns
- Iwo Jima Memorial
- Challenger Memorial
- Women in Military Service for America Memorial

PRACTICALITIES

- Map p318
- ☎877-907-8585
- www.arlington-cemetery.mil
- ⌚8am-7pm Apr-Sep, to 5pm Oct-Mar
- Ⓜ Arlington Cemetery

SIGHTS

Arlington

PENTAGON BUILDING

See p197.

ARLINGTON NATIONAL CEMETERY HISTORIC SITE

See p198.

ARLINGTON HOUSE HISTORIC SITE

Map p318 (www.nps.gov/arho; 9:30am-4:30pm, reduced hours Oct-Mar; Arlington Cemetery) FREE In one of the great spite moves of American history, thousands of Union war dead were buried in the 1100-acre grounds of Confederate General Robert E Lee's home. After the war, the Lee family sued the federal government for reimbursement: the government paid them off, and Arlington Cemetery was born. The historic house is open for public tours, and is a lovely example of Virginia grand manor architecture.

ARTISPHERE ARTS CENTER

Map p318 (703-875-1100; www.artisphere.com; 1101 Wilson Blvd; 4-11pm Wed-Fri, noon-11pm Sat, noon-5pm Sun; Rosslyn) For something completely different than memorials and museums, check out the excellent exhibits at this sleek, modern arts complex, which opened in 2011. Its several theaters host live performances (many free), including world music, film and experimental theater. There's also a cafe, restaurant and bar.

While you're here, head up to **Freedom Park** (Map p318), an elevated greenway that rests in an old road overpass running by Artisphere. It's a nice spot to sit for a while and contemplate.

GEORGE WASHINGTON MEMORIAL PARKWAY PARKWAY

Map p318 (www.nps.gov/gwmp; Arlington Cemetery) The 25-mile Virginia portion of the highway honors its namesake with recreation areas and memorials all the way south to his old estate at Mount Vernon. It's lined with remnants of George Washington's life and works, such as his old Patowmack Company canal (in Great Falls National Park) and parks that were once part of his farmlands (Riverside Park, Fort Hunt Park). The 18.5-mile-long Mount Vernon Trail parallels the parkway.

The road is a pleasant alternative to the traffic-choked highway arteries further away from the river, but you need to pull off to really appreciate the sites.

THEODORE ROOSEVELT ISLAND PARK

Map p318 (www.nps.gov/this; 6am-10pm; Rosslyn) This 91-acre wooded island, in the Potomac River off Rosslyn, is a wilderness preserve honoring the conservation-minded 26th US president. A large memorial plaza and statue of Teddy dominate the island's center, and trails and boardwalks snake around the shorelines.

The island's swampy fringes shelter birds, raccoons and other small animals. There are great views of the Kennedy Center and Georgetown University across the river. The island is accessible from the Mount Vernon Trail and is a convenient stop on a long bike ride or jog, but note bikes aren't permitted on the island itself; lock them up in the parking lot.

AIR FORCE MEMORIAL MEMORIAL

Map p318 (703-247-5805; www.airforcememorial.org; 1 Air Force Memorial Dr; Pentagon) Overlooking the Pentagon and adjacent to Arlington National Cemetery, three graceful metal arcs soar 270ft into the air. This shimmering memorial – meant to evoke the contrails of jets – pays tribute to the millions of men and women who served in the air force and its predecessor organizations.

DEA MUSEUM MUSEUM

Map p318 (United States Drug Enforcement Agency Museum; www.deamuseum.org; 7200 Army Navy Dr, entrance on S Hayes St; 10am-4pm Tue-Fri; Pentagon City) FREE The propaganda is served up with nary a chuckle at this heavy-handed museum brought to you by the Drug Enforcement Agency (DEA). Exhibits cover the last century-and-a-half of drug use, from the opium parlors of the 19th century, to 1920s cocaine-dispensing apothecaries, onto the trippy days of the 1960s, the crack epidemic of the 1980s, and more recent days of crystal-meth labs and the powder drugs favored by the 24-hour party people of today.

There are scary photos of gunned-down Latin American drug lords and coloring books for small children describing why drugs are bad. Don't miss the videos, which

WORTH A DETOUR

AIR AND SPACE MUSEUM ANNEX

The National Air and Space Museum on the Mall is so awesome they made an attic for it: the **Steven F Udvar-Hazy Center** (www.airandspace.si.edu/visit/udvar-hazy-center; 14390 Air & Space Museum Parkway; 10am-5:30pm, to 6:30pm late May-early Sep; ; MWiehle-Reston East for bus 983) FREE, in Chantilly, VA. It's three times the size of the DC museum and sprawls through massive hangars near Washington Dulles International Airport. Highlights include the SR-71 Blackbird (the fastest jet in the world), space shuttle *Discovery* (fresh from the clouds after its 2011 retirement) and the Enola Gay (the B-29 that dropped the atomic bomb on Hiroshima). Visitors can hang out in the observation tower and watch the planes take off and land at Dulles, go on a simulator (piloting a jet, taking a space walk), or catch shows at the on-site **Airbus IMAX Theater**. Free 90-minute tours through the collection are offered at 10:30am and 1pm daily.

To get out here, take the Metro Silver Line to Wiehle-Reston East station and transfer to the Fairfax Connector bus 983 one stop to the museum (you can pay $1.75 cash or use a SmarTrip card on the bus). If stopping in from Dulles airport, you can bus it (again the Fairfax Connector bus 983) or cab it (about $15). If you're driving, take I-66 West to VA 267 West, then VA 28 South, then follow the signs. Parking is $15 (free after 4pm).

feature anachronistic gems like Nancy Reagan's 'Just Say No [to drugs]' campaign. There's little nuance here, and no discussion of America's changing laws and attitudes toward cannabis.

Here the War on Drugs marches ever onward, even if the rest of the country (DC included, which voted to legalize marijuana in 2014) sees things in less black-and-white terms.

Alexandria

★CARLYLE HOUSE — HISTORIC BUILDING

Map p315 (703-549-2997; www.nvrpa.org/park/carlyle_house_historic_park; 121 N Fairfax St; admission $5; 10am-4pm Tue-Sat, noon-4pm Sun; MKing St then trolley) If you have time for just one historic house tour in Alexandria, make it this one. It dates from 1753 when merchant and city founder, John Carlyle, built the most lavish mansion in town (which in those days was little more than log cabins and muddy lanes). The Georgian Palladian–style house is packed with paintings, historic relics and period furnishings that help bring the past to life.

Free tours are given on the hour and half-hour, where you'll get a fascinating glimpse into the lives of the gentry and servant alike who lived and worked here.

GEORGE WASHINGTON MASONIC NATIONAL MEMORIAL — MONUMENT, LOOKOUT

(www.gwmemorial.org; 101 Callahan Dr at King St; admission $7, incl guided tour $10; 9am-5pm; MKing St) Alexandria's most prominent landmark features a fine view from its 333ft tower, where you can see the Capitol, Mount Vernon and the Potomac River. It is modeled after Egypt's Lighthouse of Alexandria, and honors the first president (who was initiated into the shadowy Masons in Fredericksburg in 1752 and later became Worshipful Master of Alexandria Lodge No 22).

To visit the tower, you must take a 60-minute guided tour (general admission only gets you into the 1st- and 2nd-floor exhibits). Tours depart at 9:30am, 11am, 1pm, 2:30pm and 4pm.

STABLER-LEADBEATER APOTHECARY MUSEUM — MUSEUM

Map p315 (www.alexandriava.gov/apothecary; 105-107 S Fairfax St; adult/child $5/3; 10am-5pm Tue-Sat, 1-5pm Sun & Mon; MKing St then trolley) In 1792 Edward Stabler opened up his apothecary (pharmacy) – a family business that would operate for the next 141 years, until the Depression forced the shop to close. Quite a bit of history was shut inside at that time, including over 8000 medical objects. Now the shop is a museum; its shelves are lined with 900 beautiful hand-blown apothecary bottles and strange old items such as Martha Washington's Scouring Compound.

GADSBY'S TAVERN MUSEUM MUSEUM

Map p315 (www.alexandriava.gov/GadsbysTavern; 134 N Royal St; adult/child $5/3; ⏲10am-5pm Tue-Sat, 1-5pm Sun & Mon; Ⓜ King St then trolley) Once a real tavern (operated by John Gadsby from 1796 to 1808), this building now houses a museum demonstrating the prominent role of the tavern in Alexandria during the 18th century. As the center of local political, business and social life, the tavern was frequented by anybody who was anybody, including George Washington, Thomas Jefferson and the Marquis de Lafayette. Guided tours take place at quarter to and quarter past the hour.

The rooms are restored to their 18th-century appearance, and the tavern occasionally still hosts pricey balls.

LEE-FENDALL HOUSE HISTORIC BUILDING

Map p315 (☎703-548-1789; www.leefendall-house.org; 614 Oronoco St; adult/child $5/3; ⏲10am-4pm Wed-Sat, 1-4pm Sun, tours on the hour; Ⓜ Braddock Rd) Between 1785 and 1903 generations of the storied Lee family lived in this architecturally impressive house. Guided tours show the restored house as it probably was in the 1850s and 1860s, showcasing Lee family heirlooms and personal effects, and period furniture. The Georgian-style **town house** (607 Oronoco St; ⏲closed to public) across the street was Robert E Lee's childhood home from 1810.

FREEDOM HOUSE MUSEUM MUSEUM

Map p315 (☎708-836-2858; www.nvul.org/freedomhouse; 1315 Duke St; ⏲10am-4pm Mon-Thu, to 3pm Fri; Ⓜ King St then trolley) FREE For a look at one of the darkest eras of American history, pay a visit to this small museum on Duke St. In the 1830s, this nondescript brick building housed the headquarters of the largest domestic slave-trading company in the country. Among the shackles, iron bars and low ceilings in the basement, multimedia exhibits give a glimpse of what life was like for the enslaved people held here.

Up to 150 slaves were kept in the holding pen outside (since torn down). Among those likely held here was Solomon Northup, a free black man who in 1841 was kidnapped from Washington and sold into bondage in the South. His story was portrayed in the film *Twelve Years a Slave*. There's no admission, but donations encouraged.

ALEXANDRIA BLACK HISTORY MUSEUM MUSEUM

Map p315 (www.alexblackhistory.org; 901 Wythe St; suggested donation $2; ⏲10am-4pm Tue-Sat; Ⓜ Braddock Rd) Paintings, photographs, books and other memorabilia documenting the African American experience in Alexandria, one of the nation's major slave ports, are on display at this small resource center (enter from Wythe St). Pick up a brochure for self-guided walking tours of important African American–history sites in Alexandria. In the next-door annex, the **Watson Reading Room** has a wealth of books and documents on African American topics.

Operated by the museum, the African American Heritage Park is worth a stop to see headstones from a 19th-century African American cemetery. The park is about a half-mile southeast of the King St Metro. From the station, take Reinekers Lane south, go left on Duke St, then right on Holland Lane.

TORPEDO FACTORY ART CENTER ARTS CENTER

Map p315 (www.torpedofactory.org; 105 N Union St; ⏲10am-6pm, to 9pm Thu; Ⓜ King St then trolley) FREE What do you do with a former munitions dump and arms factory? How about turn it into one of the best art spaces in the region? Three floors of artist studios and free creativity are on offer in Old Town Alexandria, as well as the opportunity to

WORTH A DETOUR

FORT WARD MUSEUM & HISTORIC SITE

Fort Ward is the best restored of the 162 Civil War forts known as the Defenses of Washington. The Northwest Bastion of the **fort** (www.alexandriava.gov/FortWard; 4301 W Braddock Rd; ⏲park 9am-dusk daily, museum 10am-5pm Tue-Sat, noon-5pm Sun) FREE has been completely restored, and the remaining earthwork walls give a good sense of the defenses' original appearance. The on-site museum features exhibits on Civil War topics. The site is about 4 miles northwest of Old Town Alexandria; take King St for 3 miles to Braddock Rd and turn left.

ALEXANDRIA VISITOR CENTER

The town's **visitor center** (Map p315; ☎703-838-5005; www.visitalexandriava.com; 221 King St; ⏰10am-5pm) issues parking permits and discount tickets to historic sights, as well as maps.

buy paintings, sculptures, glassworks, textiles and jewelry direct from their creators. The Torpedo Factory anchors Alexandria's revamped waterfront with a marina, parks, walkways, residences and restaurants.

ALEXANDRIA ARCHAEOLOGY MUSEUM MUSEUM

Map p315 (www.alexandriava.gov/archaeology; 105 N Union St; ⏰10am-3pm Tue-Fri, to 5pm Sat, 1-5pm Sun; Ⓜ King St then trolley) FREE Housed at the Torpedo Factory is the Alexandria Archaeology Museum, the laboratory where archaeologists clean up and catalog the artifacts they have unearthed at local digs. First-hand observation of the work, excavation exhibits and hands-on discovery kits allow visitors to witness and participate in the reconstruction of Alexandria's history.

CHRIST CHURCH CHURCH

Map p315 (www.historicchristchurch.org; cnr Columbus & Cameron Sts; admission by donation; ⏰9am-4pm Mon-Sat, 2-4pm Sun; Ⓜ King St then trolley) Since 1773, this red-brick Georgian-style church has welcomed worshipers from George Washington to Robert E Lee. The cemetery contains the mass grave of Confederate soldiers.

FRIENDSHIP FIREHOUSE MUSEUM MUSEUM

Map p315 (www.alexandriava.gov/friendshipfirehouse; 107 S Alfred St; admission $2; ⏰1-4pm Sat & Sun; 👪; Ⓜ King St then trolley) This 1855 Italianate firehouse displays historic firefighting gear – a great draw for kids. Local legend has it that George Washington helped found this volunteer fire company, served as its captain and even paid for a new fire engine.

NATIONAL INVENTORS HALL OF FAME & MUSEUM MUSEUM

(☎571-272-0095; www.invent.org; 600 Dulany St, Madison Bldg; ⏰11am-5pm Tue-Fri, to 3pm Sat; Ⓜ King St) FREE This museum, in the atrium of the US Patent and Trademark Office, tells the history of the United States patent. Step inside to see where the story started in 1917 in Memphis, TN, when a wholesale grocer named Clarence Saunders invented and patented what he called 'self-servicing' stores, now commonly known as supermarkets.

Incidentally, he went from rags to riches and almost back to rags again, but you'll have to visit the museum to get the rest of the story, along with displays depicting other famous and influential patents. It is about a third of a mile from the King St Metro station; take Diagonal Rd south to Dulany St.

EATING

Northern Virginia offers two kinds of eating experiences: cheap ethnic eateries, mainly in Arlington, and more upscale, traditional sit-down fare, plus pub-grub type spots, in Alexandria. Places in Old Town tend to be pricier and more tourist-oriented. For something more local in flavor, head to the Del Ray neighborhood, about 2 miles northwest of the Old Town.

Arlington

★MYANMAR BURMESE $

(☎703-289-0013; 7810 Lee Hwy, Falls Church; mains $10-14; ⏰noon-10pm; Ⓜ Dunn Loring Merrifield, then bus 2A) Myanmar's decor is barebones; the service is slow; the portions are small; and the food is delicious. This is home-cooked Burmese: curries prepared with lots of garlic, turmeric and oil, chili fish, mango salads and chicken swimming in rich gravies.

Try the *mohingar*, the Burmese take on Southeast Asian noodle soup: thin noodles, plump bits of fish and a garlicky, in-depth complexity that will have you smiling into the bottom of your soon-to-be-empty bowl. For an ethnic eating experience, it doesn't get much more authentic. It's located a bit west of Falls Church on Lee Hwy.

CAFFÉ AFICIONADO CAFE $

Map p318 (1919 N Lynn St; sandwiches around $8; ⏰7am-6pm Mon-Fri, 8am-3pm Sat; Ⓜ Rosslyn) This friendly cafe whips up excellent lattes, pastries, waffles and thick baguette-style sandwiches. The space is tiny though, so you may have to get it to go (and enjoy it at the Freedom Park or on the Mount Vernon Trail).

WEENIE BEENIE AMERICAN **$**

(2680 S Shirlington Rd; under $10; 6am-6pm; M Pentagon then bus 7F) Lovers of half-smokes will want to make a pilgrimage to this legendary food shack in Shirlington. Order that dog piled up high with spicy chili topping and onions, mustard and cheese, and let the feasting begin. It's about 4 miles southwest of Arlington National Cemetery via Arlington Blvd.

RAY'S TO THE THIRD BURGERS **$**

Map p318 (1650 Wilson Blvd; burgers $8-14; 11am-10pm Sun-Thu, to 11pm Fri & Sat; M Rosslyn) Burger buffs swoon over the juicy cheese-loaded patties, sweet-potato fries and thick milkshakes. Try the Soul Burger Number One, with bacon, Swiss cheese, sautéed mushrooms and grilled onions.

EL POLLO RICO LATIN AMERICAN **$**

Map p318 (703-522-3220; www.elpollorico-restaurant.com; 932 N Kenmore St; chicken with sides $7-14; 11:30am-8:30pm; M Clarendon, Virginia Sq-GMU) Drooling locals have flocked to this Peruvian chicken joint for decades now in search of tender, juicy, flavor-packed birds served with succulent (highly addictive) dipping sauces, crunchy fries and sloppy 'slaw. Lines form outside the door come dinnertime.

EPR is one of the first purveyors of Peruvian chicken in the metro area, and age hasn't hurt quality at one of the original kings of *polla a la brasa* (rotisserie chicken).

YECHON KOREAN **$$**

(703-914-4646; www.yechon.com; 4121 Hummer Rd, Annandale; mains $11-18; 24hr; M King St then bus 29K) Debates over who does the best Korean in the DC area have been the source of much gastronomic bickering; but Yechon is always among the front-runners. The *kalbi* (barbecue ribs) is rich, smoky and packed with flavor, and goes nicely with the complex seaweed and searing kimchi.

It's set in Annandale, a suburb on the edge of the beltway west of Arlington and Alexandria, that's the center of the Washington, DC, Korean community – and as you'd guess, the Korean culinary scene.

LOCAL KNOWLEDGE

FARMERS MARKETS

Virginia's farmland bounty is on display weekend mornings at:

Arlington Farmers' Market (Map p318; www.arlingtonparks.us/farmers-market; cnr N Courthouse Rd & N 14th St, Arlington; 8am-noon Sat Apr-Dec, from 9am Jan-Mar; M Courthouse)

Old Town Farmers' Market (Map p315; www.alexandriava.gov/farmers-market; 301 King St, Alexandria; 7am-noon Sat; M King St)

Del Ray Farmers' Market (www.alexandriava.gov/farmersmarket; 2311 Mt Vernon Ave, Alexandria; 8am-noon Sat; M Braddock Rd then bus 10A or 10B)

Yechon is open 24/7. A good thing, since nothing works off the *soju* (Korean alcoholic drink) like 3am tofu and chili.

ABAY MARKET ETHIOPIAN **$$**

(703-998-5322; 3811 S George Mason Dr, Falls Church; mains around $17; noon-9pm; M Ballston then bus 7A or 7M) Tucked into a strip mall between a bunch of hideous apartment blocks and corporate towers is the best Ethiopian food we've had in the metro area. Abay is the real deal, run by an Ethiopian former air-force officer, with clientele straight out of Addis and food that will no doubt blow your mind – if you're adventurous: Abay specializes in raw or barely cooked meat.

Alexandria

EAMONN'S DUBLIN CHIPPER PUB **$**

Map p315 (www.eamonnsdublinchipper.com; 728 King St; mains $7-10; 11:30am-11pm, to 1am Fri & Sat; M King St then trolley) You'll find no better execution of the fish and chips genre than at this upscale temple to classic pub fare. How authentic is it? It imports Batchelors baked beans from Ireland, and also serves deep-fried Mars Bars, Milky Way and Snickers. Like many resto-pubs in this part of Old Town, Eamonn's is a good place for a drink on weekend nights.

CAPHE BANH MI VIETNAMESE **$**

Map p315 (407 Cameron St; mains $6-10; ⌚11am-3pm & 5-9pm Mon-Sat, noon-9pm Sun; Ⓜ King St then trolley) Stop in this neighborhood favorite for delicious *banh mi* sandwiches, big bowls of pho, pork-belly steamed buns and other simple but well-executed Vietnamese dishes. The small but cozy space always draws a crowd, so go early to beat the dinner rush.

MOMO SUSHI & CAFE JAPANESE **$**

Map p315 (www.mymomosushi.com; 212 Queen St; sushi combos $11-16; ⌚11:30am-2:30pm & 4-10pm Mon-Fri, noon-10pm Sat, 4-9:30pm Sun; Ⓜ King St then trolley) Momo is tiny and has just 13 seats, but it serves excellent sushi. Stop in for good-value lunch specials ($7 to $9).

DEL RAY CAFE FRENCH-AMERICAN **$$**

(☎703-717-9151; www.delraycafe.com; 205 E Howell St; mains lunch $14-18, dinner $19-28; ⌚8am-3pm & 5-9pm; 📶; Ⓜ Braddock Rd then bus 10) In a beautifully restored two-story 1925 house, the Del Ray Cafe serves up excellent French and American cooking. The owner, who hails from Alsace, sources from local farms to create a tempting menu of old- and new-world comfort fare. Come for creamy eggs Benedict in the morning, softshell crab sandwiches at lunch and duck breast with fig sauce by night.

BRABO TASTING ROOM BELGIAN **$$**

(☎703-894-5252; www.braborestaurant.com; 1600 King St; mains $16-20; ⌚7:30-10:30am & 11:30am-11pm; Ⓜ King St then trolley) The inviting and sunlit Brabo Tasting Room serves its signature mussels, tasty wood-fired tarts and gourmet sandwiches, with a good beer and wine selection. In the morning, stop by for brioche French toast and Bloody Marys. Brabo restaurant, next door, is the high-end counterpart serving seasonal fare.

KING STREET BLUES SOUTHERN **$$**

Map p315 (☎703-836-8800; www.kingstreetblues.com; 112 N St Asaph St; mains $10-18; ⌚11:30am-10pm; Ⓜ King St then trolley) King Street Blues is a crazy Southern 'roadhouse' diner that serves really good baked meatloaf, country-fried steak, Southern fried catfish and other diner favorites. The interior is strewn with colorful papier-mâché figures floating across its three levels, while shiny chrome furniture and multicolored tablecloths lend a retro air. Is there blues music, you ask? Very sporadically.

GADSBY'S TAVERN RESTAURANT AMERICAN **$$$**

Map p315 (☎703-548-1288; www.gadsbystavernrestaurant.com; 138 N Royal St; mains $22-30; ⌚11:30am-3pm & 5:30-10pm; Ⓜ King St then trolley) The food isn't all that memorable, but Gadsby's scores high on novelty. Named after the Englishman who operated the tavern from 1796 to 1808 (when it was the center of Alexandria's social life), Gadsby's tries to emulate an 18th-century hostelry; it's a bit kitschy but a fun place for a meal.

Get into the spirit of things by ordering 'George Washington's Favorite,' a rich

SAIGON ON THE POTOMAC

One of Washington's most fascinating ethnic enclaves isn't technically in Washington. Instead, drive west past Arlington to Falls Church, VA. There you'll find the **Eden Center** (www.edencenter.com; 6571 Wilson Blvd, Falls Church; mains $9-15; ⌚9am-11pm; 🅿; Ⓜ East Falls Church then bus 26A), which is, basically, a bit of Saigon that got lost in America. And we mean 'Saigon' – this is a shopping center/strip mall entirely occupied and operated by South Vietnamese refugees and their descendants. You can buy Vietnamese DVDs, shop for exotic fruits (durian, star fruit, rambutan), sip bubble tea, join the crooning karoake crowd, and, of course, eat to your heart's content. It's all as fresh as a Southeast Asian street stall. Don't miss the staggering Good Fortune Supermarket, a 44,000-sq foot purvoyor of Asian ingredients that opened in 2014.

There are over a dozen restaurants here including a vegan Vietnamese restaurant (Thanh Van). Current favorite is **Rice Paper** (6775 Wilson Blvd; mains $9-15; ⌚11am-10pm), which serves up a wide range of delicacies. Whether you opt for spicy green papaya salad, crispy tofu with lemongrass, *bánh xèo* (savory crepes stuffed with shrimp and pork) or caramelized short ribs in a clay pot, this is traditional Vietnamese cooking at its very best.

glazed duck breast served with scalloped potatoes and corn pudding.

RESTAURANT EVE AMERICAN $$$

Map p315 (703-706-0450; www.restauranteve.com; 110 S Pitt St; mains $36-45, 6-course tasting menu $135; 11:30am-2:30pm Mon-Fri, 5:30-10:30pm Mon-Sat; ; King St then trolley) One of Alexandria's best (and priciest) dining rooms, Eve blends great American ingredients, precise French technique and first-rate service. Splurge here on the tasting menus, which are simply on another level of gastronomic experience.

DRINKING & NIGHTLIFE

Head to Wilson and Clarendon Blvds in Arlington or King St in Alexandria for good bar-hopping with a crowd of folks who seem to be perpetually enrolled in the University of Virginia, Virginia Tech or George Mason University.

Arlington

CONTINENTAL LOUNGE

Map p318 (www.continentalpoollounge.com; 1911 N Fort Myer Dr; 11:30am-2am Mon-Fri, 6pm-2am Sat & Sun; Rosslyn) A stone's throw from many Rosslyn hotels, this buzzing pool lounge evokes a trippy, tropical vibe with its murals of palm trees, oversized tiki heads and color-saturated bar stools. All of which sets the stage for an alternative night of shooting pool, playing ping pong or trying your hand at shuffleboard.

WHITLOW'S ON WILSON BAR

Map p318 (www.whitlows.com; 2854 Wilson Blvd; 11am-2am Mon-Fri, 9am-2am Sat & Sun; Clarendon) Occupying almost an entire block just east of Clarendon Metro, Whitlow's on Wilson has something for everyone: burgers, brunch and comfort food on the menu; happening happy hours and positive pick-up potential; plus 12 brews on tap, a pool table, jukebox, live music and an easygoing atmosphere. Head to the rooftop Tiki Bar during the warmer months.

IRELAND'S FOUR COURTS IRISH PUB

Map p318 (www.irelandsfourcourts.com; 2051 Wilson Blvd; 11am-2am; Courthouse) Buckets of Guinness lubricate the O'Connors and McDonoughs at Arlington's favorite Irish pub. The sidewalk seating draws a lunchtime crowd for shepherd's pie and fish and chips, while the verdant Irish grass-green interior attracts an evening crowd for cold drafts and live tunes (from 9pm Wednesday to Saturday).

Alexandria

PX BAR

Map p315 (www.barpx; 728 King St, entrance on S Columbus St; 6pm-midnight Wed-Thu, to 1:30am Fri & Sat; King St then trolley) This elegant, low-lit drinking den is a magical spot to linger over a cocktail or two. Jauntily attired bartenders shake up beautifully hued elixirs to a well-dressed crowd, perfectly in keeping with the speakeasy theme. True to form, there's no sign, just a blue light and a red door to mark the entrance. It's best to reserve ahead.

As expected, cocktails are in the $14 to $18 range, so sip sloooowly.

UNION STREET PUBLIC HOUSE PUB

Map p315 (www.unionstreetpublichouse.com; 121 S Union St; 11:30am-midnight Sun-Thu, to 2am Fri & Sat; King St then trolley) Gas lamps out front welcome tourists and locals into this spacious taproom for frosty brews, raw-bar delights and nightly dinner specials.

MISHA'S COFFEE ROASTER CAFE

Map p315 (www.mishascoffee.com; 102 S Patrick St; 6:30am-8pm; ; King St) Sip a lovely latte next to jars of strong-smelling beans imported from Indonesia and Ethiopia, munch on a pastry ($3 to $4), bang out your novella on your laptop (or procrastinate with the free wi-fi), check out the cute nerds at the other tables and reach caffeinated nirvana at this hip indie cafe.

PIZZERIA PARADISO BAR

Map p315 (www.eatyourpizza.com; 124 King St; from 11:30am Mon-Sat, noon Sun; King St then trolley) Sure, the focus is pizza ($13 to $20), but the beer list here is outstanding. With 14 brews on draft, 190 bottle varieties and one rotating cask selection, you won't lack for options. It's a comfy spot for hopheads to sit back and indulge in small-batch suds.

ENTERTAINMENT

Arlington

★IOTA LIVE MUSIC

Map p318 (www.iotaclubandcafe.com; 2832 Wilson Blvd; tickets $10-15; ⏲4pm-2am Mon-Thu, from 10am Fri-Sun; 📶; MClarendon) With shows almost every night of the week, Iota is the best venue for live music in Clarendon's music strip. Bands span genres; folk, reggae, traditional Irish and Southern rock are all distinct possibilities. Tickets are available at the door only (no advance sales) and this place packs 'em in (the seating is first-come, first-served).

The free open-mike Wednesdays can be lots of fun or painfully self-important, as these things are wont to be.

ARTISPHERE LIVE MUSIC

Map p318 (www.artisphere.com; 1101 Wilson Blvd; 📶; MRosslyn) The multistory arts complex hosts world music, film and experimental theater. Many performances are free; for those that have an admission price, it's generally around $20.

ARLINGTON CINEMA & DRAFTHOUSE CINEMA

Map p318 (www.arlingtondrafthouse.com; 2903 Columbia Pike; admission $6.50; MPentagon City) Ice-cold beer and second-run films at bargain prices? Count us in. You'll find comfy chairs for flick-viewing, a menu of sandwiches, pizzas and, of course, popcorn, as well as brews, wine and cocktails (this is one of the few places in DC where you can drink and catch a movie at the same time). Don't miss $2 admission on Mondays and Tuesdays.

Some nights the theater skips the movies and hosts stand-up comedy instead. There are also family-oriented programs some weekends. It's about a mile from the Metro; grab a cab or the route 16 bus from the station. You need to be at least 21 years to enter (or with a parent).

CLARENDON BALLROOM LIVE MUSIC

Map p318 (www.clarendonballroom.com; 3185 Wilson Blvd; admission $5; MClarendon) A ballroom done up to look like a big band-era dance hall, the Clarendon is a NoVa cornerstone that attracts throngs of 20- and 30-somethings to bump and grind on weekend nights. The upstairs deck is perfect for lingering over a sunset cocktail.

Alexandria

BASIN STREET LOUNGE JAZZ

Map p315 (☎703-549-1141; www.219restaurant.com; 219 King St; admission Fri & Sat $5; ⏲shows 9pm Tue-Sat; MKing St then trolley) Tortoise-shell glasses and black turtlenecks ought to be the uniform of choice at this low-key jazz venue and cigar bar, located above the 219 Restaurant. The extensive whiskey selection, amber lighting and long wooden bar make a fine backdrop to bluesy jazz performances.

BIRCHMERE LIVE MUSIC

(www.birchmere.com; 3701 Mount Vernon Ave; tickets $20-60; ⏲box office 5-9pm, shows 7:30pm; MPentagon City then bus 10A) Hailing itself as 'America's Legendary Music Hall,' this place hosts a wide range of fare, from old-time folk musicians to country, blues and R & B stars. The line-up also features the odd burlesque show, indie rock bands and the occasional one-man comedy show.

The talent that graces the stage is reason enough to come, but the venue is pretty great too: it sort of looks like a warehouse that collided with an army of LSD-savvy muralists. Located north of Old Town Alexandria off Glebe Rd.

SHOPPING

The most charming shopping here is in Alexandria, along cobbled King St in Old Town. Here you'll find craft stores and antique shops, art galleries, used booksellers and more.

TORPEDO FACTORY ART CENTER ARTS & CRAFTS

Map p315 (www.torpedofactory.org; 105 N Union St, Alexandria; MKing St then trolley) The former munitions factory today houses more than 160 artists and craftspeople who sell their creations directly from their studios. It is a distinctive setup, and there's a good chance you'll head home with a reasonably priced, one-of-a-kind painting, textile or piece of jewelry.

PRINCIPLE GALLERY ART

Map p315 (www.principlegallery.com; 208 King St, Alexandria; ⌚10am-6pm Tue-Sat, noon-5pm Sun & Mon; Ⓜ King St then trolley) One of a growing number of galleries along King St, this approachable place often assembles contemporary works of American and European realism. Even if you didn't bring the bucks, it's worth a peek inside.

FASHION CENTRE AT PENTAGON CITY MALL

Map p318 (1100 S Hayes St, Arlington; ⌚10am-9:30pm Mon-Sat, 11am-6pm Sun; Ⓜ Pentagon City) It houses 170 shops, including Macy's, Nordstrom, a cinema and a food court beneath skylights. It's your average, convenient mall – with the fun bonus of being where Monica Lewinsky got busted by Ken Starr's troopers back in '98.

POTOMAC MILLS MALL

(2700 Potomac Mills Circle, Woodbridge, VA; ⌚10am-9pm Mon-Sat, 11am-6pm Sun) A fire-breathing monster of mid-Atlantic outlet malls, just a half-hour drive south of DC, Potomac Mills features about 250 discount shops, including Ikea, Saks and Spiegel. The place now draws more tourists (about 24 million per year) and tour buses than Williamsburg or Virginia's other historic sites, which might say something about Americans' priorities. Take Exit 158-B off I-95.

SPORTS & ACTIVITIES

Despite its dense suburbs, northern Virginia is laced with hiking and cycling trails.

★MOUNT VERNON TRAIL CYCLING

Map p318 (www.nps.gov/gwmp/planyourvisit/mtvernontrail.htm; ⌚6am-10pm; Ⓜ Arlington Cemetery) The 18.5-mile-long Mount Vernon Trail is a paved riverside path that is a favorite with local cyclists. From the Francis Scott Key Bridge, it follows the Potomac River south past Roosevelt Island, Arlington National Cemetery and Ronald Reagan Washington National Airport, through Old Town Alexandria, all the way to Mount Vernon.

Groovy sights along the way include **Lady Bird Johnson Park**, which commemorates the First Lady who tried to beautify the capital via greenery-planting campaigns; tulips and daffodils go wild here in spring. **Gravelly Point**, just north of the airport, provides a vantage point for watching the planes take off and land. **Roaches Run Waterfowl Sanctuary** lets you check out naturally airborne creatures including ospreys and green herons.

The course is mostly flat, except the long climb up the hill to George Washington's house at the end. The scenery is magnificent – DC skylines and all – and the historical component is certainly unique.

WASHINGTON & OLD DOMINION TRAIL CYCLING

(W&OD; www.nvrpa.org/park/w_od_railroad; Ⓜ East Falls Church) The Washington & Old Dominion Trail starts in southern Arlington and follows the old railway bed through historic Leesburg and on to Purcellville, in the Allegheny foothills. Its 45 miles are paved and spacious, winding their way through the Virginia suburbs.

The easiest place to pick up the trail is outside the East Falls Church Metro station: exit right and turn right again onto Tuckahoe St, then follow the signs. The path allows horseback riding between Vienna and Purcellville. For the truly ambitious, it's a short jump from here to the 2000 miles of Appalachian Trail going south to Georgia and north to Maine.

BIKE & ROLL CYCLING

Map p315 (☎202-842-2453; www.bikethesites.com; One Wales Alley; hire per 2hr $12; ⌚mid-Mar–Nov; Ⓜ King St then trolley) Rent a bike and hop on the Mount Vernon Trail one block south. You'll have to call ahead, though, since bikes are available only by advance reservation (no walk-ups). Ask about package deals (including picnic provisions, admission fees and one-way boat trips) to George Washington's estate. The shop is located off Strand St.

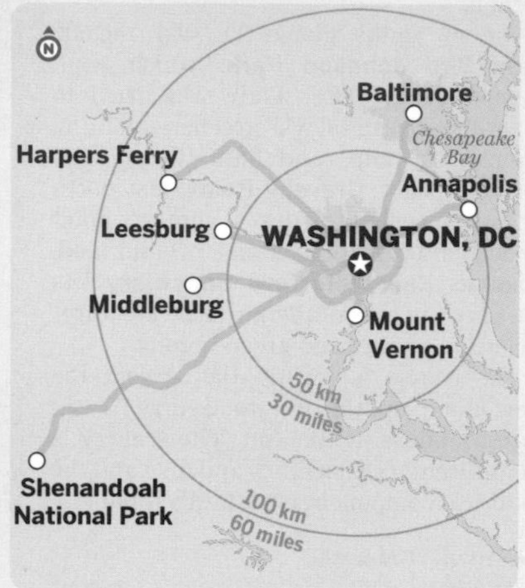

Day Trips from Washington, DC

JAAP HART / GETTY IMAGES ©

TOP SIGHT
MOUNT VERNON

A visit to George Washington's Virginia home, Mount Vernon, is an easy escape from the city – one that the president himself enjoyed. It's also a journey through history: the country estate of this quintessential gentleman has been meticulously restored and affords a glimpse of rural gentility from a time long gone.

The Setting

Above the Potomac banks, the 21-room mansion displays George and Martha's colonial tastes, while the outbuildings and slave quarters show what was needed for the functioning of the estate. At over 11,000 sq ft in size, the house was over 10 times the size of the average Virginia home when it was built. Highlights include the architecturally rich New Room, used to receive visitors; the little parlor, where the family hosted social gatherings, the study where Washington read and wrote; and a river-facing two-story piazza, which functioned as the family living room in warm weather. George and Martha are both buried on the grounds.

Ford Orientation Center

This modern center is a must-see on the grounds. It features a 20-minute film that shows Washington's courage under fire, including his pivotal crossing of the Delaware River (the do-or-die moment of the Revolutionary War).

Reynolds Museum & Education Center

These galleries and theaters gives more insight into Washington's life through interactive displays, short films and life-size models of Washington himself. The museum also features period furnishings, clothing and jewelry (Martha was quite taken with finery), and George's unusual dentures (made of human, cow and horse teeth as well as ivory).

DON'T MISS...

- The New Room
- Period clothing
- Washington's dentures
- The distillery

PRACTICALITIES

- ☎703-780-2000, 800-429-1520
- www.mountvernon.org
- 3200 Mount Vernon Memorial Hwy, Mount Vernon
- adult/child $17/9
- ⏲8am-5pm Apr-Aug, 9am-4pm Nov-Feb, to 5pm Mar, Sep & Oct, gristmill & distillery 10am-5pm Apr-Oct

Baltimore

Explore

Baltimore's dramatic and continuing redevelopment has transformed the gritty city into an exciting historical and modern destination. There's much to see here, and you could easily spend four or five days exploring without running out of things to do. If time is short, focus on the Inner Harbor, with its waterfront promenade, superb National Aquarium and sprawling Maritime Museum. It's the most touristic part of the city, but worth seeing. The upscale neighborhood of Mount Vernon lies to the north and has notable art museums (including the celebrated Walters Art Gallery), and a good selection of locally owned restaurants and bars. For nightlife, head east of the Inner Harbor to the bar-lined brick streets of Fell's Point or to Federal Hill, just south of Inner Harbor.

The Best

➡**Sight** American Visionary Art Museum (p212)

➡**Place to Eat** Woodberry Kitchen (p213)

➡**Place to Drink** Brewer's Art (p213)

Top Tip

A 10-minute drive north of downtown, Hampden is a self-consciously hip urban neighborhood that's packed with bohemian-style restaurants and kitsch-filled shops. Start exploring on the Avenue (also known as W 36th St).

Getting There & Away

➡**Car** Take I-95 or I-295 (Baltimore-Washington Parkway) north to Russell St, which terminates west of the Inner Harbor. Or take I-95 north to I-395, which spills out downtown as Howard St. Beware of this drive during rush hour; outside of peak times it should take 45 to 60 minutes.

➡**Train** Both **Amtrak** (☎800-872-7245; www.amtrak.com) and the cheaper **MARC** (mta.maryland.gov) travel daily between Washington, DC's Union Station and Baltimore's Penn Station. Buses 3 and 11 travel up Charles St past Penn Station at 1515 N Charles St.

Need to Know

➡**Area Code** ☎410

➡**Location** 45 miles northeast of Washington, DC

➡**Baltimore Area Visitor Center** (☎877-225-8466; http://baltimore.org; 401 Light St; ⊙9am-6pm May-Sep, 10am-5pm Oct-Apr)

SIGHTS

⊙ Harborplace & Inner Harbor

This is where most tourists start and, unfortunately, end their Baltimore sightseeing. The Inner Harbor is a big, gleaming waterfront renewal project of shiny glass, air-conditioned malls and flashy bars that manages to capture the maritime heart of this city, albeit in a safe-for-the-family kinda way. But it's also just the tip of Baltimore's iceberg.

NATIONAL AQUARIUM AQUARIUM

(☎410-576-3833; www.aqua.org; 501 E Pratt St, Piers 3 & 4; adult/child $35/22; ⊙9am-5pm Sun-Thu, to 8pm Fri, to 6pm Sat) Standing seven-stories high and capped by a glass pyramid, this is widely considered to be the best aquarium in America. It houses 17,000 creatures of over 750 species, a rooftop rainforest, a central ray pool and a multistory shark tank. There's also a reconstruction of the Umbrawarra Gorge in Australia's Northern Territory, complete with 35ft waterfall, rocky cliffs, and free-roaming birds and lizards.

Currently, the aquarium also has a dolphin discovery zone, where visitors can learn about aquatic mammals. These eight captive creatures, however, may soon be moved to a marine sanctuary. In an open letter written in 2014, the CEO of the National Aquarium announced that the facility was exploring the possibility of moving the animals to an open-ocean sanctuary (full reintroduction of the animals into the wild is not seen as feasible since seven of the dolphins were born in captivity and would not know how to hunt in the wild; the eighth was captured while very young). This could set a powerful new precedent for other aquariums and Seaworld-style entertainment complexes around the globe.

BALTIMORE MARITIME MUSEUM MUSEUM
(☎410-539-1797; www.historicships.org; 301 E Pratt St, Piers 3 & 5; adult 1/2/4 ships $11/14/18, child $5/6/7; ⌚10am-4:30pm) Ship-lovers can take a tour through four historic ships: a Coast Guard cutter that saw action in Pearl Harbor, a 1930 lightship, a submarine active in WWII and the **USS Constellation** – one of the last sail-powered warships built (in 1797) by the US Navy. Admission to the 1856 Seven Foot Knoll Lighthouse on Pier 5 is free.

MARYLAND SCIENCE CENTER MUSEUM
(☎410-685-2370; www.mdsci.org; 601 Light St; adult/child $19/16; ⌚10am-5pm Mon-Fri, to 6pm Sat, 11am-5pm Sun, longer hours summer) This awesome center features a three-story atrium, tons of interactive exhibits on dinosaurs, outer space and the human body, and the requisite IMAX theater ($4 extra).

PORT DISCOVERY MUSEUM
(☎410-727-8120; www.portdiscovery.org; 35 Market Pl; admission $15; ⌚10am-5pm Mon-Sat, noon-5pm Sun, reduced hours winter) Two blocks north of the harbor, Port Discovery is a converted fish market, which has a playhouse, a laboratory, a watery activity area, an artist's workshop and even Pharaoh's tomb. There are loads of special events (story times, dance and music classes, Lego building workshops, science demos); check the website to see what's on.

TOP OF THE WORLD OBSERVATION DECK LOOKOUT
(www.viewbaltimore.org; 401 E Pratt St; adult/child $6/4; ⌚10am-6pm Wed-Thu, to 7pm Fri & Sat, 11am-6pm Sun) For a bird's-eye view of Baltimore, head to the observation deck at the World Trade Center.

⊙ Downtown & Little Italy

NATIONAL GREAT BLACKS IN WAX MUSEUM MUSEUM
(☎410-563-3404; www.greatblacksinwax.org; 1601 E North Ave; adult/child $13/11; ⌚9am-6pm Tue-Sat, noon-6pm Sun, to 5pm Oct-Jan) This excellent African American history museum has exhibits on Frederick Douglass, Jackie Robinson, Martin Luther King Jr and Barack Obama, as well as lesser-known figures such as explorer Matthew Henson. The museum also covers slavery, the Jim Crow era and African leaders – all told in surreal fashion through Madame Tussaud–style figures.

JEWISH MUSEUM OF MARYLAND MUSEUM
(☎410-732-6400; www.jewishmuseummd.org; 15 Lloyd St; adult/student/child $8/4/3; ⌚10am-5pm Sun-Thu) Maryland has traditionally been home to one of the largest, most active Jewish communities in the country, and this is a fine place to explore their experience in America. It also houses two wonderfully preserved historical synagogues. Call or go online for the scheduled hours of synagogue tours.

STAR-SPANGLED BANNER FLAG HOUSE & 1812 MUSEUM MUSEUM
(☎410-837-1793; www.flaghouse.org; 844 E Pratt St; adult/child $8/6; ⌚10am-4pm Tue-Sat; 🚸) This historic home, built in 1793, is where Mary Pickersgill sewed the gigantic flag that inspired America's national anthem. Costumed interpreters and 19th-century artifacts transport visitors back in time to dark days during the War of 1812; there's also a hands-on discovery gallery for kids.

EDGAR ALLAN POE HOUSE & MUSEUM MUSEUM
(☎410-396-7932; www.poeinbaltimore.org; 203 N Amity St; adult/student/child $5/4/free; ⌚11am-4pm Sat & Sun late May-Dec) Home to Baltimore's most famous adopted son from 1832 to 1835, it was here that the macabre poet and writer first found fame after winning a $50 short-story contest. After moving around, Poe later returned to Baltimore in 1849, where he died in mysterious circumstances. His grave can be found in nearby Westminster Cemetery.

CAMDEN YARDS BASEBALL FIELD
(☎888-848-2473; baltimore.orioles.mlb.com; 333 W Camden St; tickets $10-95; ⌚box office 10am-5pm Mon-Sat, noon-5pm Sun) The Orioles' baseball park, Camden Yards, occupies an entire city block west of the Inner Harbor. It was the first 'retro' ball park, which reconciled Major League Baseball's need for more space with fans' nostalgia.

BABE RUTH MUSEUM MUSEUM
(☎410-727-1539; www.baberuthmuseum.com; 216 Emory St; adult/child $6/3, incl Sports

Legends at Camden Yards $12/5; ⌚10am-5pm, closed Mon Oct-Mar) Celebrates the Baltimore native son who happens to be the greatest baseball player in history.

SPORTS LEGENDS AT CAMDEN YARDS MUSEUM

(cnr Camden & Sharp Sts, Camden Station; adult/child $8/4, incl Babe Ruth Museum $12/5; ⌚10am-5pm, closed Mon Oct-Mar) The Sports Legends at Camden Yards honors more Maryland athletes.

LITTLE ITALY NEIGHBORHOOD

Behind the power plant is the delightful Little Italy neighborhood, packed with exquisite restaurants, a bocce ball court and a giant brick wall on the corner of High and Stiles Sts that doubles as an outdoor movie screen in summer (Friday evenings in July and August).

⊙ Mount Vernon

This elegant neighborhood has several excellent museums, a fine lookout and some good local restaurants and bars. It's a short walk from here to the harbor.

★WALTERS ART MUSEUM MUSEUM

(☎410-547-9000; www.thewalters.org; 600 N Charles St; ⌚10am-5pm Wed-Sun, to 9pm Thu) FREE Don't pass up this excellent, eclectic gallery, which spans more than 55 centuries, from ancient to contemporary, with excellent displays of Asian treasures, rare and ornate manuscripts and books, and a comprehensive French paintings collection.

MARYLAND HISTORICAL SOCIETY MUSEUM

(www.mdhs.org; 201 W Monument St; adult/child $9/6; ⌚10am-5pm Wed-Sat, noon-5pm Sun) With more than 350,000 objects and seven million books and documents, this is one of the largest collections of Americana in the world. Highlights include one of three surviving Revolutionary War officer's uniforms, photographs from the 1930s Civil Rights movement in Baltimore and Francis Scott Key's original manuscript of the 'Star-Spangled Banner.' There are often excellent temporary exhibits, exploring the role of Baltimore residents in historic events.

⊙ Fells Point & Canton

Once the center of Baltimore's shipbuilding industry, the historic cobblestoned neighborhood of Fell's Point is now a gentrified mix of 18th-century homes and restaurants, bars and shops. For bar-hopping, this is the liveliest hood in Baltimore. Further east, the slightly more sophisticated streets of Canton fan out, with its grassy square surrounded by great restaurants and bars.

⊙ Federal Hill & Around

On a bluff overlooking the harbor, **Federal Hill Park** lends its name to the comfortable neighborhood that's set around Cross St Market and comes alive after sundown.

★AMERICAN VISIONARY ART MUSEUM MUSEUM

(AVAM; ☎410-244-1900; www.avam.org; 800 Key Hwy; adult/child $16/10; ⌚10am-6pm Tue-Sun) Housing a jaw-dropping collection of self-taught (or 'outsider' art), AVAM is a celebration of unbridled creativity utterly free of arts-scene pretension. You'll find broken-mirror collages, homemade robots and flying apparatuses, elaborately sculptural works made of needlepoint, and gigantic model ships painstakingly created from matchsticks.

CROSS STREET MARKET MARKET

(1065 Cross St, btwn Light & Charles Sts; ⌚7am-7pm Mon-Sat) This well-located food emporium has tempting stalls hawking oysters, crab cakes, sushi, fresh baked goodies, rotisserie chicken, and plenty of fruit, veg and picnic fare – plus beer (big ones) near the Charles St entrance.

FORT MCHENRY NATIONAL MONUMENT & HISTORIC SHRINE HISTORIC SITE

(☎410-962-4290; 2400 E Fort Ave; adult/child $7/free; ⌚9am-5pm) On September 13 and 14, 1814, the star-shaped fort successfully repelled a British navy attack during the Battle of Baltimore. After a long night of bombs bursting in the air, Francis Scott Key, prisoner on a British ship, saw, 'by dawn's early light,' the tattered flag still waving, inspiring him to pen 'The Star-Spangled Banner' (set to the tune of a popular drinking song).

North Baltimore

★EVERGREEN MUSEUM MUSEUM

(☎410-516-0341; museums.jhu.edu; 4545 N Charles St; adult/child $8/5; ⏰11am-4pm Tue-Fri, noon-4pm Sat & Sun) Well worth the drive out, this grand 19th-century mansion provides a fascinating glimpse into upper-class Baltimore life of the 1800s. The house is packed with fine art and masterpieces of the decorative arts – including paintings by Modigliani, glass by Louis Comfort Tiffany and exquisite Asian porcelain – not to mention the astounding rare book collection, numbering some 32,000 volumes.

More impressive than the collection, however, is the compelling story of the Garrett family, who were world travellers (John W was an active diplomat for some years), astute philanthopists and lovers of the arts – if not always successful performers in their own right (though that didn't stop Alice from taking the stage – her own, which you'll see in the intimate theater below the house).

EATING & DRINKING

PAPERMOON DINER DINER $

(227 W 29th St; mains $9-17; ⏰7am-midnight Sun-Thu, to 2am Fri & Sat) This brightly colored, quintessential Baltimore diner is decorated with thousands of old toys, creepy mannequins and other quirky knickknacks. The real draw here is the anytime breakfast – fluffy buttermilk pancakes, crispy bacon and crab and artichoke heart omelets. Wash it down with a caramel and sea-salt milkshake.

★THAMES ST OYSTER HOUSE SEAFOOD $$

(☎443-449-7726; www.thamesstreetoysterhouse.com; 1728 Thames St; mains $14-29; ⏰11:30am-2:30pm Wed-Sun, 5-10pm daily, bar open til midnight) An icon of Fells Point, this vintage dining and drinking hall serves some of Baltimore's best seafood. Dine in the polished upstairs dining room with views of the waterfront, take a seat in the backyard, or plunk down at the bar in front and watch the drink makers/oyster shuckers in action.

★WOODBERRY KITCHEN AMERICAN $$$

(☎410-464-8000; www.woodberrykitchen.com; 2010 Clipper Park Rd, Woodberry; mains $24-39; ⏰5-10pm Mon-Thu, to 11pm Fri & Sat, to 9pm Sun, 10am-2pm Sat & Sun) The Woodberry takes everything the Chesapeake region has to offer, plops it into an industrial barn and creates culinary magic. The entire menu is like a playful romp through the best of local produce, seafood and meats, from Maryland rockfish with Carolina Gold grits to Shenandoah Valley lamb with collard greens, and hearty vegetable dishes plucked from nearby farms. Reserve ahead.

THE FOOD MARKET MODERN AMERICAN $$$

(☎410-366-0606; www.thefoodmarketbaltimore.com; 1017 W 36th St; mains $20-34; ⏰5-11pm daily plus 9am-3pm Fri-Sun) On Hampden's lively restaurant- and shop-lined main drag, the Food Market was an instant success when it opened back in 2012. Award-winning local chef Chad Gauss elevates American comfort fare to high art in dishes such as bread-and-butter-crusted seabass with black truffle vinaigrette, and crab cakes with lobster mac and cheese.

The setting is industrial chic, and draws a mix of bohemian neighborhood locals and foodies from far and wide.

BREWER'S ART PUB

(☎410-547-6925; 1106 N Charles St, Mount Vernon; ⏰4pm-2am) In a vintage early-20th-century mansion, Brewer's Art serves well-crafted Belgian-style microbrews to a laid-back Mount Vernon crowd. There's tasty pub fare (mac 'n' cheese, portobello wraps; $7 to $13) in the bar, and upscale American cuisine (mains $22 to $31) in the elegant back dining room. Head to the subterranean drinking den downstairs for a more raucous crowd.

During happy hour (4pm to 7pm) drafts are just $3.75.

SPORTS & ACTIVITIES

BALTIMORE GHOST TOURS WALKING TOUR

(☎410-357-1186; www.baltimoreghosttours.com; adult/child $15/10; ⏰7pm Fri & Sat Mar-Nov) Offers several walking tours exploring the spooky and bizarre side of Baltimore. The popular Fells Point ghost walk departs from

Max's on Broadway, 731 S Broadway. Book online to save $2 per ticket.

SLEEPING

★INN AT 2920 B&B $$

(☎410-342-4450; www.theinnat2920.com; 2920 Elliott St, Canton; r $185-272;) Housed in a former bordello, this boutique B&B offers five individual rooms; high-thread-count sheets; sleek, avant-garde decor; and the nightlife-charged neighborhood of Canton right outside your door. The Jacuzzi bathtubs and green sensibility of the owners add a nice touch.

HOTEL BREXTON HOTEL $$

(☎443-478-2100; www.brextonhotel.com; 868 Park Ave; r $130-240;) This red-brick 19th-century landmark building has recently been reborn as an appealing, if not overly lavish, hotel. Rooms have a mix of wood floors or carpeting, comfy mattresses, a mirrored armoire and framed art prints on the walls. It's in a good location, a short walk to Mount Vernon.

Curious historical footnote: Wallis Simpson, the woman for whom Britain's King Edward VIII abdicated the throne in order to marry, lived in this building as a young girl.

INN AT HENDERSON'S WHARF HOTEL $$$

(☎410-522-7777, 888-995-9560; www.hendersonswharf.com; 1000 Fell St; r $205-310;) Fresh flowers in the room, exposed brick walls and elegant furnishings await guests at this marvelously situated Fell's Point hotel, which began life as an 18th-century tobacco warehouse. Don't miss the complimentary evening wine reception or late-night chocolate indulgence. Consistently rated one of the city's best lodges.

Annapolis

Explore

Sailors and seafood-lovers will relish exploring the coves and waterways of the Chesapeake Bay. A day trip to endearing Annapolis is the easiest way to get a dose of both treats.

Boasting some of the tastiest seafood in the region, Maryland's capital city, Annapolis is a tribute to the Colonial era. The historic landmark is a perfectly preserved tableau of narrow lanes, brick houses and original 18th-century architecture (one of the largest concentrations of such buildings in the country).

Home of the US Naval Academy since 1845, Annapolis Harbor and its connecting tidal creeks shelter dozens of marinas where thousands of cruising and racing sailboats tie up, earning the city the title of Sailing Capital. If you have time to spare, check out the charming villages and waterfront allure of the Eastern Shore.

The Best

➡**Sight** Hammond Harwood House (p215)

➡**Outdoor Activity** Going for a sail around the Chesapeake Bay

➡**Place to Eat** Jimmy Cantler's Riverside Inn (p215)

Top Tip

Eating at a crab shack, where the dress code stops at shorts and flip-flops, is the quintessential Chesapeake Bay experience. To beat the crowds, avoid going on summer weekends.

Getting There & Away

➡**Bus** Greyhound runs buses to Washington, DC (once daily, $16). Dillon's Bus (www.dillonbus.com) has 26 weekday-only commuter buses between Annapolis and Washington, connecting with various DC metro lines.

➡**Car** Rte 50 east goes straight into downtown Annapolis. To Eastern Shore destinations, continue east over the Chesapeake Bay Bridge and head south on Rte 50.

Need to Know

➡**Area Code** ☎410

➡**Location** 35 miles east of Washington, DC

➡**Visitor Center** (☎410-280-0445; www.visitannapolis.org; 26 West St; ⏲9am-5pm)

SIGHTS

The collection of historic homes and buildings clustered on Cornhill and Fleet Sts between the State House and the harbor is extraordinary. Guided walking and bus tours abound, or you can pick up a free brochure at the Visitor Center.

HAMMOND HARWOOD HOUSE — MUSEUM

(410-263-4683; www.hammondharwoodhouse.org; 19 Maryland Ave; adult/child $10/5; noon-5pm Tue-Sun Apr-Dec) Of the many historical homes in town, the 1774 HHH is the one to visit. It has a superb collection of decorative arts, including furniture, paintings and ephemera dating to the 18th century, and is one of the finest existing British Colonial homes in America. Knowledgeable guides help bring the past to life on 50-minute house tours held at the top of the hour.

WILLIAM PACA HOUSE & GARDEN — HISTORIC SITE

(410-990-4543; www.annapolis.org; 186 Prince George St; adult/child $10/6; 10am-5pm Mon-Sat, noon-5pm Sun) Take a tour (offered hourly on the half-hour) through this Georgian mansion for insight into 18th-century life for the upper class in Maryland. Don't miss the blooming garden in spring.

BANNEKER-DOUGLASS MUSEUM — MUSEUM

(bdmuseum.maryland.gov; 84 Franklin St; 10am-4pm Tue-Sat) FREE A short stroll from the State House, this small but worthwhile museum highlights great achievements of Marylanders of African American ancestry. There are permanent exhibits on the likes of US Supreme Court justice Thurgood Marshall, explorer Matthew Henson and intellectual Frederick Douglass, as well as temporary exhibitions that often run the gamut between historical forays into the Civil Rights era, to today's crop of great African American artists, musicians and writers.

US NAVAL ACADEMY — UNIVERSITY

(www.usnabsd.com/for-visitors) The undergraduate college of the US Navy is one of the most selective universities in America. The **Armel-Leftwich visitor center** (410-293-8687; tourinfo@usna.edu; Gate 1, City Dock entrance; tours adult/child $10.50/8.50; 9am-5pm) is the place to book tours and immerse yourself in all things Academy related. Come for the formation weekdays at 12:05pm sharp, when the 4000 midshipmen and midshipwomen conduct a 20-minute military marching display in the yard. Photo ID is required for entry. If you've got a thing for American naval history, go revel in the **Naval Academy Museum** (410-293-2108; www.usna.edu/museum; 118 Maryland Ave; 9am-5pm Mon-Sat, 11am-5pm Sun) FREE.

MARYLAND STATE HOUSE — HISTORIC BUILDING

(410-946-5400; 91 State Circle; 9am-5pm) FREE The country's oldest state capitol in continuous legislative use, the grand 1772 State House also served as national capital from 1733 to 1734. The Maryland Senate is in action here from January to April. The upside-down giant acorn atop the dome stands for wisdom. Photo ID is required for entry.

EATING

49 WEST — CAFE $

(410-626-9796; 49 West St; mains $7-23; 7:30am-midnight;) This comfy art-filled coffeehouse is a good spot for coffee and light bites during the day (sandwiches, soups, salads) and heartier bistro fare by night, along with wines and cocktails. Live music some nights.

CHICK & RUTH'S DELLY — DINER $

(410-269-6737; www.chickandruths.com; 165 Main St; mains $7-14; 6:30am-11:30pm;) A cornerstone of Annapolis, the Delly is bursting with affable quirkiness and a big menu, heavy on sandwiches and breakfast fare. Patriots can relive grade-school days reciting the Pledge of Allegiance, weekdays at 8:30am (9:30am on weekends).

BOATYARD BAR & GRILL — SEAFOOD $$

(410-216-6206; www.boatyardbarandgrill.com; 400 4th St; mains $14-27; 8am-midnight;) This bright, nautically themed restaurant is an inviting spot for crab cakes, fish and chips, fish tacos and other seafood. Happy hour (3pm to 7pm) draws in the crowds with 99¢ oysters and $3 drafts. It's a short drive (or 10-minute walk) from the City Dock, across the Spa Creek Bridge.

JIMMY CANTLER'S RIVERSIDE INN — SEAFOOD $$

(www.cantlers.com; 458 Forest Beach Rd; mains $17-32; 11am-11pm Sun-Thu, to midnight Fri

WORTH A DETOUR

EASTERN SHORE

Just across the Chesapeake Bay Bridge, nondescript suburbs and jammed highways give way to unbroken miles of bird-dotted wetlands, serene waterscapes, endless cornfields, sandy beaches and friendly little villages. For the most part, the Eastern Shore retains its charm despite the growing influx of former city-dwellers and day-trippers. This area revolves around the water. Working waterfront communities still survive off Chesapeake Bay and its tributaries. Boating, fishing, crabbing and kayaking are a part of local life.

St Michaels, one of the prettiest villages on the Eastern Shore, lives up to its motto as 'The Heart & Soul of Chesapeake Bay.' It's a mix of old Victorian homes, quaint B&Bs, boutique shops and working docks, where escape artists from Washington mix with salty-dog crabbers. On weekends the village can get crowded with out-of-town boaters. During the War of 1812, inhabitants rigged up lanterns in a nearby forest and blacked out the town. British naval gunners shelled the trees, allowing St Michaels to escape destruction. The building now known as the **Cannonball House** (Mulberry St) was the only structure to have been hit.

At the lighthouse, the **Chesapeake Bay Maritime Museum** (☎410-745-2916; www.cbmm.org; 213 N Talbot St, St Michaels; adult/child $13/6; ⏰9am-5pm May-Oct, 10am-4pm Nov-Apr; 👪) delves into the deep ties between Shore folk and America's largest estuary. Narrated 60-minute cruises aboard the **Patriot** (☎410-745-3100; www.patriotcruises.com; Navy Point; adult/child $25/13) leave from the dock near the Crab Claw several times a day.

The Victorian red-brick **Parsonage Inn** (☎410-745-8383; www.parsonage-inn.com; 210 N Talbot St; r $160-225; P ❄) offers floral decadence (curtains, duvets) and brass beds, plus a friendly welcome by the hospitable innkeeper and her canine companion.

Next door to the Chesapeake Bay Maritime Museum the **Crab Claw** (☎410-745-2900; www.thecrabclaw.com; 304 Burns St, St Michaels; mains $16-30; ⏰11am-9pm mid-Mar–Oct) has a splendid open-air setting at the water's edge. Get messy eating delicious steamed crabs at picnic tables, or head upstairs for more refined seafood feasting.

At the end of the road over the Hwy 33 drawbridge, tiny **Tilghman Island** still runs a working waterfront where local captains take visitors out on graceful oyster skipjacks; the historic **Rebecca T Ruark** (☎410-829-3976; www.skipjack.org; 2hr cruise adult/child $30/15), built in 1886, is the oldest certified vessel of its kind.

Oxford is a small village with a history dating back to the 1600s and a fine spread of leafy streets and waterfront homes. Although you can drive there via US-333, it's well worth taking the old-fashioned **ferry** (☎410-745-9023; www.oxfordbellevueferry.com; Bellevue Rd near Bellevue Park; one way car/additional passenger/pedestrian $12/1/3; ⏰9am-sunset mid-Apr–mid-Nov) from Bellevue. Try to go around sunset for memorable views.

Once in Oxford, don't miss the chance to dine at the celebrated **Robert Morris Inn** (☎410-226-5111; www.robertmorrisinn.com; 314 N Morris St; mains $17-29; ⏰7:30-10am, noon-2:30pm & 5:30-9:30pm) near the ferry dock. Award-winning crab cakes, grilled local rockfish and medallions of spring lamb are nicely matched by wines and best followed by pavlova with berries and other desserts. You can also overnight in one of the inn's heritage-style rooms (from $145).

& Sat) The best crab shacks in the state is Jimmy Cantler's Riverside Inn, where eating a steamed crab has been elevated to an art form – a hands-on, messy endeavor, normally accompanied by corn on the cob and ice-cold beer.

★**VIN 909** AMERICAN **$$**

(☎410-990-1846; 909 Bay Ridge Ave; small plates $13-16; ⏰ 5:30-10pm Tue-Sun & noon-3pm Wed-Fri) Perched on a little wooded hill and boasting intimate but enjoyably casual ambience, Vin is the best thing happening in Annapolis for food. Farm-sourced goodness comes at you in the form of duck confit, BBQ sliders, and homemade pizzas with toppings such as wild mushrooms, foie gras and Spanish chorizo. There's a great wine selection, including over three dozen wines by the glass.

No reservations accepted; so go early to beat the often lengthy waits.

SPORTS & ACTIVITIES

WOODWIND CRUISE

(☎410-263-7837; www.schoonerwoodwind.com; 80 Compromise St; sunset cruise adult/child $44/27; ⊗mid-Apr–Oct) This beautiful 74ft schooner offers two-hour day and sunset cruises. Or splurge for the Woodwind 'boat & breakfast' package (rooms $305, including breakfast), one of the more unique lodging options in town.

WATERMARK CRUISES CRUISE

(www.watermarkcruises.com; City Dock; 40min cruise adult/child $15/6) The best way to explore the city's maritime heritage is on the water. Watermark, which operates the Four Centuries Walking Tour, offers a variety of cruise options, with frequent departures.

FOUR CENTURIES WALKING TOUR WALKING TOUR

(http://annapolistours.com; adult/child $18/10) A costumed docent will lead you on this great introduction to Annapolis. The 10:30am tour leaves from the Visitor Center and the 1:30pm tour leaves from the information booth at the City Dock; there's a slight variation in sights visited by each, but both cover the country's largest concentration of 18th-century buildings, influential African Americans and colonial spirits who don't want to leave.

SLEEPING

SCOTLAUR INN GUESTHOUSE $$

(☎410-268-5665; www.scotlaurinn.com; 165 Main St; r $95-140; P❄📶) The folks from Chick & Ruth's Delly offer 10 rooms, each with wrought-iron beds, floral wallpaper and private bath. The quarters are small but have a familial-like atmosphere (the guesthouse is named after the owners' children Scott and Lauren, whose photos adorn the hallways).

HISTORIC INNS OF ANNAPOLIS HOTEL $$

(☎410-263-2641; www.historicinnsofannapolis.com; 58 State Circle; r $140-200; ❄📶) The Historic Inns comprise three boutique guesthouses, each set in a heritage building in the heart of old Annapolis: the Maryland Inn, the Governor Calvert House and the Robert Johnson House. Common areas are packed with period details, and the best rooms boast antiques, a fireplace and attractive views (the cheapest are small and could use an update).

O'CALLAGHAN HOTEL HOTEL $$

(☎410-263-7700; www.ocallaghanhotels-us.com; 174 West St; r $99-180; ❄📶) This Irish chain offers attractively furnished rooms that are nicely equipped with big windows, a writing desk, brass fixtures and comfy mattresses. It's just a short stroll to a good selection of bars and restaurants, and about a 12-minute walk to the old quarter.

Harpers Ferry

Explore

History lives on in this attractive town, set with steep cobblestone streets framed by the Shenandoah Mountains and the confluence of the rushing Potomac and Shenandoah Rivers. The lower town functions as an open-air museum, with over a dozen buildings that you can wander through and get a taste of 19th-century life here. Exhibits narrate the town's role at the forefront of westward expansion, American industry and, most famously, the slavery debate. In 1859 old John Brown tried to spark a slave uprising here and was hanged for his efforts; the incident rubbed friction between North and South into the fires of Civil War.

In addition to the historic sites, there's great outdoor adventure to be had, with excellent hiking trails just steps from Harpers Ferry. Nearby are scenic spots for cycling, kayaking and rafting.

The Best

➡**Sight** John Brown Museum (p218)

➡**Outdoor Activity** Hiking up to the top of the Maryland Heights Trail

➡**Place to Eat** Canal House (p218)

Top Tip

Parking is extremely limited in Harpers Ferry. Instead head to the **Harpers Ferry National Historic Park Visitor Center** (304-535-6029; www.nps.gov/hafe; 171 Shoreline Dr; per person/vehicle $5/10; 9am-5pm) off Hwy 340, where you can park and take a free shuttle.

Getting There & Away

- **Train** Trains to Washington's Union Station are operated by Amtrak (www.amtrak.com) and MARC (mta.maryland.gov).
- **Car** From Washington take I-495 north to the I-270, which turns into I-70. Merge onto US-340 west and follow the signs for downtown Harpers Ferry. Travel time is 90 minutes.

Need to Know

- **Area Code** 540
- **Location** 66 miles northwest of Washington, DC
- **Tourist Office** (304-535-6029; www.nps.gov/hafe; 171 Shoreline Dr, off Hwy 340)

SIGHTS

JOHN BROWN MUSEUM — MUSEUM

(Shenandoah St; 9am-5pm daily) FREE Across from Arsenal Sq, this three-room gallery gives a fine overview (through videos and period relics) of the events surrounding John Brown's famous raid.

BLACK VOICES — MUSEUM

(High St; 9am-5pm daily) FREE This worthwhile, interactive exhibit has narrated stories of hardships and hard-won victories by African Americans from the times of enslavement through the Civil Rights era.

EDUCATION & THE STRUGGLE FOR EQUALITY — MUSEUM

(High St; 9am-5pm daily) FREE This small exhibit gives an overview of the groundbreaking educational center at Storer College and the Niagara movement that formed in its wake.

MASTER ARMORER'S HOUSE — HISTORIC SITE

(304-535-6029; www.nps.gov/hafe; Shenandoah St; 9am-5pm daily) FREE Among the many sites in the historic district, this 1858 house explains how rifle technology developed here revolutionized the firearms industry.

STORER COLLEGE CAMPUS — HISTORIC SITE

(www.nps.gov/hafe; Fillmore St) Storer College grew from a one-room schoolhouse for freed slaves to a respected college open to all races and creeds. It closed in 1955. You can freely wander the historic campus, reachable by taking the path to upper town, past St Peter's church, Jefferson Rock and Harper Cemetery.

JOHN BROWN WAX MUSEUM — MUSEUM

(304-535-6342; www.johnbrownwaxmuseum.com; 168 High St; adult/child $7/5; 9am-4:30pm spring & fall, 10am-5:30pm summer) Not to be confused with the National Park–run John Brown Museum, this private wax museum is a kitschy (and rather overpriced) attraction that pays tribute to the man who led an ill-conceived slave rebellion here. The exhibits are laughably old school; nothing says historical accuracy like scratchy vocals, jerky animatronics and dusty old dioramas.

EATING

BEANS IN THE BELFRY — AMERICAN $

(301-834-7178; 122 W Potomac St, Brunswick, MD; sandwiches around $7; 9am-9pm Mon-Sat, 8am-7pm Sun;) Across the river in Brunswick, MD (roughly 10 miles east), you'll find this converted red-brick church, sheltering mismatched couches and kitsch-laden walls, light fare (chili, sandwiches, quiche) and a tiny stage where live folk, blues and bluegrass bands strike up several nights a week. Sunday jazz brunch ($18) is a hit.

POTOMAC GRILLE — AMERICAN $

(186 High St; mains $10-16; noon-9pm) Serves good pub food (fish and chips, crab cakes, huge burgers) and local brews in an old-fashioned tavern atmosphere in the historic district. The outdoor patio has fine views over the train station and Maryland Heights.

CANAL HOUSE — AMERICAN $$

(1226 Washington St; mains $11-24; noon-8pm Mon, to 9pm Fri & Sat, to 6pm Sun;) Roughly 1 mile west (and uphill) from the historic district, Canal House is a perennial favorite for delicious sandwiches, locally sourced seasonal fare and friendly service in a flower-trimmed stone house. Outdoor seating. You can bring your own beer or wine.

SPORTS & ACTIVITIES

RIVER RIDERS ADVENTURE SPORTS

(☎800-326-7238; www.riverriders.com; 408 Alstadts Hill Rd) The go-to place for rafting, canoeing, tubing, kayaking and multiday cycling trips, plus cycle rental. There's even a new 1200ft zipline that opened in 2014.

O BE JOYFULL WALKING TOUR

(☎732-801-0381; www.obejoyfull.com; 175 High St; day/night tours $22/14) Offers eye-opening historical daytime walking tours (lasting three to four hours) around Harpers Ferry, as well as a spooky 90-minute evening tour.

APPALACHIAN TRAIL CONSERVANCY HIKING

(☎304-535-6331; www.appalachiantrail.org; cnr Washington & Jackson Sts; ⏲9am-5pm) The 2160-mile Appalachian Trail is headquartered here at this tremendous resource for hikers.

SLEEPING

TEAHORSE HOSTEL HOSTEL $

(☎304-535-6848; www.teahorsehostel.com; 1312 Washington St; dm/ste $33/150; P ❄ @ 📶) Popular with cyclists on the C&O Canal towpath and hikers on the Appalachian Trail, Teahorse is a welcoming place with comfy rooms and common areas (including an outdoor patio). It's located 1 mile (uphill) from the historic lower town of Harpers Ferry.

JACKSON ROSE B&B $$

(☎304-535-1528; www.thejacksonrose.com; 1167 W Washington St; r weekday/weekend $135/150; ❄ 📶) This marvelous brick 18th-century residence with stately gardens has three attractive guestrooms, including a room where Stonewall Jackson briefly lodged during the Civil War. Antique furnishings and vintage curios are sprinkled about the house, and the cooked breakfast is excellent. It's a 600m walk downhill to the historic district. No children under 12 years.

HIKING IN HARPERS FERRY

There are great hikes in the area, from three-hour (round-trip) scrambles to the scenic overlook from the Maryland Heights Trail, past Civil War fortifications on the Loudoun Heights Trail or along the Appalachian Trail – all are easily accessible from the historic district. You can also cycle or walk along the **C&O Canal towpath** (www.nps.gov/choh). The Harpers Ferry National Historic Park Visitor Center has maps and details on outfitters.

TOWN'S INN INN $$

(☎304-932-0677; www.thetownsinn.com; 179 High St; r $120-140; ❄) Spread between two neighboring pre–Civil War residences, the Town's Inn has rooms ranging from small and minimalist to charming heritage-style quarters. It's set in the middle of the historic district and has an indoor-outdoor restaurant as well.

Leesburg & Middleburg

Explore

Leesburg is one of northern Virginia's oldest towns and its colonial-era center is lined with historic sites, plus antique shops, galleries and restaurants. Leesburg sits along the Washington & Old Dominion Trail, and makes an excellent destination for cyclists.

Lying 19 miles southwest of Leesburg, smaller Middleburg is another quaint northern Virginia town, with colonial buildings that hide some enticing restaurants and shops. Either town makes a fine base for visiting the wineries in the area.

The Best

➡ **Sight** Morven Park (p221)

➡ **Place to Eat** Shoes Cup & Cork (p221)

➡ **Place to Drink** Bluemont Vineyard (p220)

Top Tip

On the first Friday of every month, you can join in **Leesburg's First Friday** (www.leesburgfirstfriday.com; ⏲6-9pm), when shops and galleries stay open till 9pm and offer drinks and special sales.

Getting There & Away

➡**Bicycle** Pick up the Washington & Old Dominion Trail just outside the East Falls Church Metro in Arlington and head west.

➡**Car** Take I-495 or Rte 66 to the Dulles Toll Rd exit (Rte 267) – look for signs to Washington Dulles International Airport. When it turns into the Dulles Greenway, continue 13 miles to the end. Exit left and take the first right exit to Leesburg Business. Follow King St to Loudoun St, the center of historic Leesburg. Middleburg is 19 miles southwest of Leesburg. Take US-15 south and turn right on US-50. Travel time is 40 minutes by car.

Need to Know

➡**Area Code** ☎703

➡**Location** Leesburg: 40 miles northwest of DC; Middleburg: 42 miles west of DC

➡**Tourist Office** (☎703-771-2170; www.visitloudoun.org; 112G South St, Market Station, Leesburg; ⏲9am-5pm)

VINEYARDS OF VIRGINIA

Back in the 1980s, when a single vineyard operated in Loudoun County, a Virginian bottle of wine was likely to earn about as much respect as a convicted felon running for office. Much has changed in the last generation, and today this rich farming area has become one of the country's fastest-growing wine regions – with more than 20 vineyards at last count. While largely unknown outside Virginia, Loudoun County wines are garnering critical attention after winning awards at international competitions.

For the traveler, going wine tasting makes a fine day's outing from DC. You can explore the rolling hills and leafy lanes of this pretty countryside, stopping at excellent restaurants and local farmers markets en route. Both Leesburg and Middleburg are fine bases to begin the viticultural journey.

For wine maps, routes and loads of other winery info, visit www.viginiawine.org.

Here are a few favorites from the wine country:

Bluemont Vineyard (☎540-554-8439; www.bluemontvineyard.com; 18755 Foggy Bottom Rd, Bluemont; tasting $5; ⏲11am-6pm Wed-Mon; 🐾) Bluemont produces ruby red Nortons and crisp Viogniers, though it's equally famous for its spectacular location – at a 950ft elevation with sweeping views over the countryside.

Breaux Vineyards (☎540-668-6299; www.breauxvineyards.com; 36888 Breaux Vineyards Lane, Hillsborough; tasting $10; ⏲11am-6pm; 🐾) One of Virginia's largest vineyards, with some 18 varietals, Breaux produces award-winning reds including an exceptional Merlot Reserve. Breaux hosts regular events, including a big Cajun festival in June.

Chrysalis Vineyards (☎540-687-8222; www.chrysaliswine.com; 23876 Champe Ford Rd, Middleburg; tasting $7-10; ⏲10am-6pm; 🐾) Proudly using the native Norton grape (which dates back to 1820), Chrysalis produces highly drinkable reds and whites – including a refreshing Viognier. The pretty estate hosts a bluegrass fest in October.

Fabbioli Cellars (☎703-771-1197; www.fabbioliwines.com; 15669 Limestone School Rd, Leesburg; tasting incl food $15; ⏲11am-5pm; 🐾) This ecofriendly winery provides an intimate but informal tasting experience, where you can learn about the wines from innovative winemaker Doug Fabbioli himself. It's open outside hours by appointment.

Tarara Vineyard (☎703-771-7100; www.tarara.com; 13648 Tarara Lane, Leesburg; tasting $10; ⏲11am-5pm) On a bluff overlooking the Potomac, this 475-acre estate provides guided tours showing the grape's journey from vine to glass. The winery has a 6000-sq-ft cave/cellar, and visitors can pick fruit in the orchard or hike the 6 miles of trails through rolling countryside. Tarara also hosts summertime Saturday-evening concerts and three major wine festivals.

SIGHTS

MORVEN PARK HISTORIC SITE

(☎703-777-2414; www.morvenpark.org; 17263 Southern Planter Lane, Leesburg; admission to grounds free, mansion tours adult/child $10/5; ⊙grounds dawn-dusk daily, tours hourly from noon-4pm Mon, Fri & Sat, 1-4pm Sun) Morven Park is a 1000-acre property that was once the home of Virginia governor Westmoreland Davis. The Greek Revival mansion, with its manicured boxwood gardens, resembles a transplanted White House, and its antique carriage museum includes more than 100 horse-drawn vehicles. Morven Park is 1 mile west of Leesburg off Rte 7 (Market St). Heading west, turn right onto Morven Park Rd and follow it to the property.

OATLANDS PLANTATION HISTORIC SITE

(☎703-777-3174; www.oatlands.org; 20850 Oatlands Plantation Lane, Leesburg; adult/child $12/8, grounds only $8; ⊙10am-5pm Mon-Sat, 1-5pm Sun Apr-Dec) Oatlands Plantation was established in 1803 by a great-grandson of Robert 'King' Carter, a wealthy pre-Revolutionary planter. The carefully restored Greek Revival mansion is surrounded by 4 acres of formal gardens and connecting terraces. It's located on US-15, about 6 miles south of Leesburg.

EATING

SHOES CUP & CORK CAFE $$

(☎703-771-7463; www.shoescupandcork.com; 17 N King St; mains lunch $8-16, dinner $15-25; ⊙7am-5pm Mon-Wed, to 9pm Thu & Fri, 9am-9pm Sat & Sun) Across from the courthouse, this antique shoe store serves up excellent fare for breakfast, lunch and dinner. Think warm brie sandwiches, kale and quinoa salads, and wild mushroom ravioli. Good drinks (coffee, microbrews, Malbecs) add to the appeal – as does the outdoor patio with bocce court.

CHIMOLE LATIN AMERICAN $$

(☎703-777-7011; 10 S King St; tapas $8-18; ⊙5-9pm Sun & Wed, to 11pm Thu-Sat) For something completely different, stop in this tapas and wine bar, serving up delicacies with Latin American accents. Try beer-battered fish tacos, Honduran-style ceviche and grilled tiger shrimp. This is also a gallery that sells pottery and paintings from Central American artists.

RED FOX INN & TAVERN AMERICAN $$$

(☎540-687-6301; 2 E Washington St; mains lunch $11-18, dinner $26-42; ⊙8am-10am, 11:30am-2:30pm & 5-8:30pm Mon-Sat, 10am-2:30pm & 5-7:30pm Sun) Set in a 1728 fieldstone dwelling, the Red Fox is an atmospheric place for a meal. Take a seat by the fireplace, beneath the hewn beam ceilings and feast on crab cakes, grilled rainbow trout and Red's famous fried chicken. The inn has elegant rooms for an overnight.

SLEEPING

WELBOURNE B&B B&B $$

(☎540-687-3201; www.welbourneinn.com; 22314 Welbourne Farm Lane, Middleburg; r $143; ❄📶🏊🐾) Located 6 miles west of Middleburg, the Welbourne is set in a historic landmark house (c 1770), surrounded by 520 acres. Guests stay in one of five heritage rooms with fireplaces. Hearty Southern-style breakfast included.

LEESBURG COLONIAL INN GUESTHOUSE $$

(☎703-777-5000; www.theleesburgcolonialinn.com; 19 S King St; d $70-150) In the center of Leesburg, this simple 10-room guesthouse has a great location and unbeatable prices. On the downside, street noise can be an issue for light sleepers, and some rooms could use a heavier hand in the housekeeping department.

Shenandoah National Park

Explore

Shenandoah National Park is easy on the eyes, set against a backdrop of the dreamy Blue Ridge Mountains, granite and metamorphic formations that are more than one billion years old. The park itself is almost 70 years old, founded in 1935 as a retreat for East Coast urban populations. It is an accessible day-trip destination from DC, but stay longer if you can. The 500 miles of hiking trails, 75 scenic overlooks,

30 fishing streams, seven picnic areas and four campgrounds are sure to keep you entertained.

The Best

- **Sight** Old Rag Mountain (p222)
- **Scenic Drive** Skyline Drive (p222)
- **Place to Stay** Big Meadows Lodge (p223)

Top Tip

To beat the crowds, avoid going on weekends – especially in the summer – when there's a lot of traffic in the park.

Getting There & Away

- **Car** From Washington, DC, take I-66 west to Rte 340. Front Royal is 3 miles south; Luray is 27 miles south. The drive to the northern entrance at Front Royal is 90 minutes.

Need to Know

- **Area Code** ☎540
- **Location** 75 miles west of Washington, DC

SIGHTS

SHENANDOAH NATIONAL PARK — NATIONAL PARK

(☎540-999-3500; www.nps.gov/shen; week pass per car $20) One of the most spectacular national parks in the country, Shenandoah is like a new smile from nature: in spring and summer the wildflowers explode, in fall the leaves burn bright red and orange, and in winter a cold, starkly beautiful hibernation period sets in. White-tailed deer are a common sight and, if you're lucky, you might spot a black bear, bobcat or wild turkey. The park lies just 75 miles west of Washington, DC.

SKYLINE DRIVE — SCENIC DRIVE

A 105-mile-long road running down the spine of the Blue Ridge Mountains, the Skyline Drive redefines the definition of 'Scenic Route.' You're constantly treated to an impressive view, but keep in mind the road is bendy, slow-going (35mph limit) and (in peak season) congested.

FRONT ROYAL — TOWN

The town of Front Royal, at the northern end of Skyline Dr, is a convenient jumping-off point for Shenandoah National Park. It's a good place to pack your picnic before heading into the wilderness.

SKYLINE CAVERNS — CAVE

(☎800-296-4545; www.skylinecaverns.com; entrance to Skyline Dr; adult/child $20/10; ⏱9am-5pm) Front Royal's claim to fame is Skyline Caverns, which boasts rare, white-spiked anthodites – mineral formations that look like sea urchins.

LURAY CAVERNS — CAVE

(☎540-743-6551; www.luraycaverns.com; Rte 211; adult/child $26/14; ⏱9am-7pm Jun-Aug, to 6pm Sep-Nov, Apr & May, to 4pm Mon-Fri Dec-Mar) If you can only fit one cavern into your itinerary, head 25 miles south from Front Royal to the world-class Luray Caverns and hear the 'Stalacpipe Organ,' hyped as the largest musical instrument on Earth.

EATING

BIG MEADOWS — MODERN AMERICAN $$

(☎800-999-4714; www.visitshenandoah.com; Skyline Dr, Mile 51.2; mains lunch $9-11, dinner $16-28; ⏱mid-May–Oct) One of several resorts in Shenandoah National Park, Big Meadows has a restaurant and tavern with nightly live music. Highlights from the wide-ranging menu include pecan-crusted trout, oven-roasted turkey and black bean burgers, with many locally sourced ingredients – all of which go nicely with Virginian wines and local microbrews.

SPORTS & ACTIVITIES

Shenandoah has more than 500 miles of hiking trails, including 101 miles of the famous Appalachian Trail. Access the trail from Skyline Dr, which roughly parallels the trail. Following are just a few of the great hikes that await, listed from north to south (horseback riding is available):

OLD RAG MOUNTAIN — HIKING

This is a tough, 8-mile circuit trail that culminates in a rocky scramble only suitable for the physically fit. Your reward is the summit of Old Rag Mountain and, along the way, some of the best views in Virginia.

SKYLAND HIKING

There are four easy trails here, none exceeding 1.6 miles, with a few steep sections throughout. Stony Man Trail gives great views for not-too-strenuous trekking.

BIG MEADOWS HIKING

A very popular area with four easy-to-medium difficulty hikes. The Lewis Falls and Rose River trails run by the park's most spectacular waterfalls, and the former accesses the Appalachian Trail.

BEARFENCE MOUNTAIN HIKING

A short trail leads to a spectacular 360-degree viewpoint. The circuit hike is only 1.2 miles, but it involves a strenuous scramble over rocks.

RIPRAP HIKING

Three trails of varying difficulty. Blackrock Trail is an easy 1-mile loop that yields fantastic views. You can either hike the moderate 3.4-mile Riprap Trail to Chimney Rock, or detour and make a fairly strenuous 9.8-mile circuit that connects with the Appalachian Trail.

SKYLAND STABLES HORSEBACK RIDING

(877-847-1919; Skyline Dr, Mile 42.5; guided group rides 1/2½hr $50/90; 9am-5pm May-Oct) Horseback riding is allowed on designated trails. Pick up your pony at Skyland Stables, near Mile 42.5.

SLEEPING

LEWIS MOUNTAIN CABINS CABIN $

(540-999-2255; www.goshenandoah.com/Lewis-Mountain-Cabins.aspx; Skyline Dr, Mile 57.6; cabins $117, campsites $15; Apr-Oct;) Lewis Mountain has several pleasantly furnished cabins complete with private bathrooms for a hot shower after a day's hiking. The complex also has a campground with a store, a laundry and showers. This is the most rustic accommodation option in the area short of camping. Bear in mind many cabins are attached, although we've never heard our neighbors here.

BIG MEADOWS LODGE LODGE $$

(540-999-2221; www.goshenandoah.com/Big-Meadows-Lodge.aspx; Skyline Dr, Mile 51.2; r $94-210; mid-May–Oct;) The historic Big Meadows Lodge has 29 cozy wood-paneled rooms and five rustic cabins. The on-site Spotswood Dining Room serves three hearty meals a day; reserve well in advance.

SKYLAND RESORT RESORT $$

(540-999-2212; www.goshenandoah.com/Skyland-Resort.aspx; Skyline Dr, Mile 41.7; r $115-210, cabins $97-235; Apr-Oct;) Founded in 1888, this beautifully set resort has fantastic views over the countryside. You'll find simple, wood-finished rooms and a full-service dining room, and you can arrange horseback rides from here.

Sleeping

DC's lodgings enjoy a scope of history other American cities have a hard time matching: when rooms here are called the 'Roosevelt suite,' it's because Teddy actually slept in them. The best digs are monuments of Victorian and jazz-era opulence. Chain hotels, B&Bs and apartments blanket the cityscape, too. But nothing comes cheap…

Seasons & Prices

The high-season apex is mid-March through April (cherry-blossom season). Crowds and rates also peak in May, June, September and October. Book well in advance if you're traveling then. Prices are lowest in January (assuming it's not an inauguration year) and February. Rates on weekends (Friday and Saturday) are typically less than on weekdays.

Hotels

There are roughly 30,000 hotel rooms in DC, seemingly rising up on every corner around downtown, the Capitol and the White House Area. All big-box chains have outposts (usually several) here. Groovy boutique hotels abound, as do uber-luxury hotels catering to presidents, prime ministers and other heads of state.

B&Bs

DC has loads of B&Bs. Set in elegant old row houses and Victorian mansions, they cluster around Dupont Circle and Adams Morgan. Many are redolent of Old Washington (in a sip-sherry-at-noon way) and are atmospheric as hell. They're generally cheaper than big hotels.

Hostels

The District has one **Hostelling International** (www.hiusa.org) property and several independent hostels that do not require membership. Browse listings at **Hostels.com** (www.hostels.com) and **Hostelworld.com** (www.hostelworld.com).

Apartments

Given all the interns, politicos and business folk who come to town for extended stays, apartment rentals are popular. They're usually great value compared to hotels. **Airbnb** (www.airbnb.com) does a booming business in the District.

Amenities

In-room wi-fi, air-conditioning and a private bathroom are standard, unless noted otherwise. Here are some other general guidelines:

TOP END

On-site concierge services, fitness and business centers, spas, restaurants, bars and white-glove room service are all par for the course. There's often a fee for wi-fi ($10 to $17). Breakfast is rarely included.

MIDRANGE

Rooms have a phone, cable TV and free wi-fi (though sometimes there's a charge for faster-speed service). Many rooms also have a mini-refrigerator, microwave and hairdryer. Often a small fitness center is on-site. Rates often include a continental breakfast.

BUDGET

Besides hostels – which provide no-frills, bunk-bed dorms – budget options are thin on the ground. Expect shared bathrooms and wi-fi that is free but may be available in common areas only.

Lonely Planet's Top Choices

Hotel Lombardy (p227) European-style, Venetian-furnished boutique catering to worldly guests.

Hotel Helix (p235) Youthful, pop-punk boutique a stumble from DC's hippest food and drink.

Tabard Inn (p231) Quirky, vintage inn with a literary bent.

Chester Arthur House (p235) B&B for those who want to explore DC beyond the norm.

Hay-Adams Hotel (p228) Heritage property awash in old-school opulence.

Best by Budget

$

Adam's Inn (p234) Twenty-six rooms to make yourself at home in a couple of Adams Morgan townhouses.

Hostelling International – Washington DC (p230) Big, amenity-laden hostel that draws a laid-back international crowd.

William Penn House (p229) Quaker-run guesthouse with garden and dorms.

Downtown Washington Hostel (p229) Good-time budget option near H St's nightlife; includes happy hours with free beer.

$$

Taft Bridge Inn (p234) Quilts and tweeds fill the rooms in this Georgian mansion B&B.

Carlyle (p232) Oft-overlooked, art-deco beauty sitting amid Dupont Circle's embassies.

Morrison-Clark Inn (p231) This 1864 mansion channels the antebellum South.

Cambria Suites at O (p235) Shiny new ecofriendly building with vast rooms near the Convention Center.

$$$

The Jefferson (p234) Luxurious, romantic, Parisian and often considered DC's top address.

Willard InterContinental Hotel (p228) When visiting heads of state come to town, they snooze in the Willard's gilded suites.

St Regis Washington (p228) Built to look like an Italian grand palace, with rooms opulent enough for nobility.

Best Contemporary Cool

Sofitel Lafayette Square (p227) Bright, airy rooms in a revamped historic building tinged with Parisian chic.

Hotel George (p230) Mod boutique near the Capitol with pop-art presidential accents.

Graham Georgetown (p229) Stately and stylish digs in the heart of Georgetown.

Best for Political Intrigue

Willard InterContinental Hotel (p228) 'The center of Washington' where the term lobbyist was coined and MLK wrote his 'Dream' speech.

Mayflower Renaissance Hotel (p228) JKF, J Edgar Hoover and Eliot Spitzer enjoyed the hotel's pleasures.

Washington Hilton (p234) Where President Reagan was shot; now a popular business hotel.

Best for Romantics

Embassy Circle Guest House (p232) French country–style home near Embassy Row that'll feed you silly.

Akwaaba (p232) Literary-minded B&B with some very sexy rooms.

NEED TO KNOW

Price Ranges

The following price ranges refer to the cost of an en suite double room in high season (excluding tax and breakfast, unless stated otherwise).

$ less than $150

$$ $150 to $350

$$$ more than $350

Tax

Washington, DC's room tax is 14.5%. Northern Virginia's tax is around 10.5% (exact amount varies by county).

Parking Costs

Figure on $35 to $55 per day for in-and-out privileges.

Tipping

- **Hotel porters** $2 per bag
- **Housekeeping staff** $2 to $5 daily (higher end of range for suites or particularly messy rooms)
- **Parking valets** At least $2 when handed back your car keys
- **Room service** 15% to 20%
- **Concierges** Nothing for simple information, up to $20 for securing last-minute restaurant reservations, sold-out show tickets etc

Check-In/Check-Out Times

Normally 3pm/noon. Many places will allow early check-in if the room is available (or will store your luggage if not).

Where to Stay

Neighborhood	For	Against
White House Area & Foggy Bottom	Central location dripping with monumental buildings and luxury lodgings where DC's powerbrokers concentrate	Expensive, not much of a neighborhood feeling
Georgetown	Lovely, leafy, moneyed neighborhood with accommodations to match	There's no Metro service, so it's not as convenient as other areas for getting around
Capitol Hill & Southeast DC	Still amid the political intrigue, but more laid-back than the White House Area; wide range of hotels, suites and hostels	Much of the area is quiet come nighttime
Downtown & Penn Quarter	Bustles with trendy bars, restaurants and theaters; near the Mall for tourists and Convention Center for business travelers	Pricey, and the scene can be a bit raucous
Dupont Circle & Kalorama	Great B&Bs and boutique hotels mix among town homes and embassies; cool shops, bistros, bars and sights at your doorstep	It is DC's most lodging-laden 'hood; main areas can be congested and rowdy at night
Adams Morgan	Young, quirky, B&B-filled area with a cache of ethnic eateries and musical nightlife	Isolated from the Metro; most properties are a 15-minute walk to the nearest station
Logan Circle, U St & Columbia Heights	Gentrifying region with fresh hotels joining scattered B&Bs and guesthouses, good for urban explorer types	Most lodgings are at least a half-mile from the Metro, and you're a haul from the Mall
Upper Northwest DC	Quiet, family-oriented residential enclave; accommodations cluster around Woodley Park, convenient to the Metro and restaurants	Far from the top-draw sights
Northern Virginia	Cheaper than the District, especially if you have a car (many places offer free parking)	Lodgings tend to be big-box chains without much character

White House Area & Foggy Bottom

Foggy Bottom tends to be cheaper than the White House Area, and has more fun boutique options.

★HOTEL LOMBARDY BOUTIQUE HOTEL **$$**

Map p296 (202-828-2600; www.hotellombardy.com; 2019 Pennsylvania Ave NW; r $180-330; P ❄ @ ; M Foggy Bottom-GWU) Done up in Venetian decor (shuttered doors, warm gold walls), and beloved by World Bank and State Department types, this European boutique hotel has multilingual staff and an international vibe – you hear French and Spanish as often as English in its halls. The attitude carries into rooms decorated with original artwork, and Chinese and European antiques.

While there is no pool on-site, guests receive passes to use an outdoor pool nearby.

SOFITEL LAFAYETTE SQUARE HOTEL **$$**

Map p296 (202-730-8800; www.sofitelwashingtondc.com; 806 15th St NW; r $220-400; P ❄ @ ; M McPherson Sq) In a fabulous corner location with lots of windows, the Sofitel's airy rooms let in loads of natural sunlight (try to reserve one of the 2nd- or 3rd-floor rooms facing 15th or H Sts; they are the brightest). The chambers have a whiff of Parisian art deco about them, with curvy wood furnishings, warm hues and downy white beds. The graceful building dates from 1880. Wi-fi costs $17 per day.

MELROSE HOTEL BOUTIQUE HOTEL **$$**

Map p296 (202-955-6400; www.melrosehoteldc.com; 2430 Pennsylvania Ave NW; r $235-340; P ❄ ; M Foggy Bottom-GWU) The Melrose got a makeover in 2012. Say hello to spiffy rooms with mod gray and white decor, accented by bursts of color (say, a lime-green couch or sky-blue pillows) and pop art (a George Washington painting or Declaration of Independence mural). The blackout curtains ensure a good night's rest. There's a tiered fee for wi-fi.

The stellar location is steps from Rock Creek Park, just over the bridge from Georgetown, and overlooking a happening span of Pennsylvania Ave.

GEORGE WASHINGTON UNIVERSITY INN HOTEL **$$**

Map p296 (202-337-6620; www.gwuinn.com; 824 New Hampshire Ave NW; r $170-300; P ❄ @ ; M Foggy Bottom-GWU) As you might guess, a lot of parents of GWU students find themselves staying in this pleasant hotel, situated on a quiet tree-lined street in the midst of tweedy academics and the occasional drunken undergrad. A little bit of colonial furnishing brightens up rooms that are fine if a bit dowdy, with lots of space and big windows.

Some on the higher floors have views out onto the Potomac. Families grab up the suites with kitchenettes and stoves. The location rocks, roughly equidistant to the Lincoln Memorial, White House and Georgetown, and amid several convenience stores and restaurants.

RIVER INN HOTEL **$$**

Map p296 (202-337-7600; www.theriverinn.com; 924 25th St NW; r $260-330; P ❄ @ ; M Foggy Bottom-GWU) Despite the name, the inn is not actually on the river, but on a quiet residential street near the Kennedy Center. The handy location provides easy access to Georgetown on one end, and the White House on the other. The sizable rooms sport mod, corporate-apartment-like decor, snug pillow-top mattresses and kitchenettes, and some have river views.

ONE WASHINGTON CIRCLE HOTEL **$$**

Map p296 (202-872-1680; www.thecirclehotel.com; 1 Washington Circle; ste $260-330; P ❄ ; M Foggy Bottom-GWU) At its eponymous address, this sleek, modern all-suite hotel has always attracted high-profile guests; for example, Nixon maintained offices here after the Watergate scandal totaled his presidency. On-site kitchens make for easy self-catering, and the rooms themselves are actually a good deal, all shimmering sheets and spaces that look like a swinging (but tasteful) '60s bachelor pad.

Bonus: each suite has a balcony. The outdoor pool opens in summer.

CLUB QUARTERS HOTEL **$$**

Map p296 (202-463-6400; www.clubquarters.com/washington-dc; 839 17th St NW; r $125-205; P ❄ @ ; M Farragut West) Club Quarters is a no muss, no fuss kind of place often used by business travelers on the go. Room are small and without views, they lack charm or quirk, but the bed is restful, the desk workable, the wi-fi fast enough and the coffee maker well stocked. Oh, and the prices are reasonable in an area where they're usually sky-high.

THE QUINCY HOTEL $$

Map p296 (202-223-4320; www.thequincy.com; 1823 L St NW; r $190-270; P ❄ @ 🛜 🐾; M Farragut North, Farragut West) The Quincy is known for its big, retro-looking rooms with kitchenette, Keurig coffeemaker and free wi-fi. The hotel likes to style itself as a chic boutique, but it's a bit too worn for that category. Still, it has a bouncy vibe and fun quirks such as a game library with Twister and Uno. Plus the price is usually quite good for the 'hood.

MAYFLOWER RENAISSANCE HOTEL HISTORIC HOTEL $$

Map p296 (202-347-3000; www.marriott.com; 1127 Connecticut Ave NW; r $280-380; P ❄ @ 🛜 🐾; M Farragut North) J Edgar Hoover lunched here daily; John F Kennedy reportedly trysted here; and NY Governor Eliot Spitzer infamously rendezvoused with a call girl here (in Room 871). Although not the exclusive enclave it once was, the Mayflower remains regal in its luxe public spaces. The contemporary guest rooms are businesslike, though they do sport marble bathrooms and posh bedding. Wi-fi costs $17 per day.

RESIDENCE INN FOGGY BOTTOM HOTEL $$

Map p296 (202-785-2000; www.marriott.com; 801 New Hampshire Ave NW; ste $145-310; P ❄ 🛜 🏊 👪 🐾; M Foggy Bottom-GWU) The Residence Inn is a good choice for families or business travelers. All the large rooms are suites, with separate living and sleeping areas and a fully equipped kitchen. So what if the decor is bland. The free hot breakfast, wi-fi, rooftop deck and outdoor pool are swell perks, and the property often shows up on discount booking websites.

★ **HAY-ADAMS HOTEL** HERITAGE HOTEL $$$

Map p296 (202-638-6600; www.hayadams.com; 800 16th St NW; r from $350; P ❄ @ 🛜 🐾; M McPherson Sq) One of the city's great heritage hotels, the Hay is a beautiful old building where 'nothing is overlooked but the White House.' The property has a palazzo-style lobby and probably the best rooms of the old-school luxury genre in the city, all puffy mattresses like clouds shaded by four-poster canopies and gold-braid tassels.

The hotel is named for two 1884 mansions that once stood on the site (owned by secretary of state John Hay and historian Henry Adams) that were the nexus of Washington's political and intellectual elite. It's also a site of scandal: in the 1980s the Hay-Adams was where Oliver North wooed contributors to his illegal contra-funding scheme.

WILLARD INTERCONTINENTAL HOTEL HISTORIC HOTEL $$$

Map p296 (202-628-9100; www.washington.intercontinental.com; 1401 Pennsylvania Ave NW; r from $400; P ❄ @ 🛜; M Metro Center) The historic Willard is where MLK wrote his 'I Have a Dream' speech; where the term 'lobbyist' was coined (by President Grant to describe political wranglers trolling the lobby); and where Lincoln, Coolidge and Harding have all lain their heads. The rooms are opulent: flowy curtains framed by potted palms, power-player views over the city and scandalously comfy beds. Wi-fi costs $11 per day.

Nathaniel Hawthorne observed that the Willard could 'much more justly [be] called the center of Washington…than either the Capitol, the White House, or the State Department.' The chandelier-hung hallways are still thick with lobbyists and corporate aristocrats buffing their loafers on the dense carpets. The presidential suites are often utilized by visiting heads of state. Upon entering the marble lobby, you'll be forgiven for expecting Jay Gatsby to stumble down the stairs clutching a bourbon. Speaking of which: the superb Round Robin bar on-site claims to be the mint julep's birthplace.

ST REGIS WASHINGTON HOTEL $$$

Map p296 (202-638-2626; www.stregiswashingtondc.com; 923 16th St NW; r from $500; P ❄ @ 🛜 🐾; M McPherson Sq) The American Institute of Architects describes the St Regis as 'indisputably one of the grandest hotels in the city.' What else can you say about a freestanding building designed to resemble nothing less than an Italian grand palace? Rooms are as gilded as you'd expect, with hand-carved armoires, double-basin marble sinks and TVs embedded in the bathroom mirrors. Wi-fi costs $13 per day.

Room 1012 is famed for being the place where Monica Lewinsky spilled details of her now infamous shenanigans with President Clinton to Ken Starr's investigators.

W HOTEL WASHINGTON HOTEL $$$

Map p296 (202-661-2400; www.wwashingtondc.com; 515 15th St NW; r from $375; P ❄ @ 🛜 🐾; M Metro Center) When one of DC's grandest dames – the 1917 beaux-arts Hotel Washington – was bought out by the W Hotel chain, eyebrows went up. Would the hip W brand do away with the property's storied sense of tradition and history? Well…now rooms are decked out in a *Mad*

Men meets *Wallpaper* magazine blend of retro-futuristic, all smooth lines and pared-down furnishings.

It's quite polished and playful, with a swank rooftop bar and sweet spa, though the accommodations tend toward the small side. In-room wi-fi costs $15 per day.

Georgetown

GRAHAM GEORGETOWN BOUTIQUE HOTEL **$$**

Map p308 (202-337-0900; www.thegrahamgeorgetown.com; 1075 Thomas Jefferson St NW; r $270-350; P ❄ @ 📶; M Foggy Bottom-GWU to DC Circulator) Set smack in the heart of Georgetown, the Graham occupies the intersection between stately tradition and modernist hip. Rooms have tasteful floral prints and duochrome furnishings with geometric accents. Even the most basic rooms have linens by Liddell Ireland and L'Occitane bath amenities, which means you'll be as fresh, clean and beautiful as the surrounding Georgetown glitterati.

GEORGETOWN SUITES HOTEL **$$**

Map p308 (202-298-7800; www.georgetownsuites.com; 1111 30th St NW; ste $275-350; P ❄ @ 📶 👪; M Foggy Bottom-GWU to DC Circulator) If you don't mind trading style for ho-hum practicality (and 1980s decor), the Georgetown Suites provide good value for the neighborhood. The most common units are 500-sq-ft studios and 800-sq-ft one-bedroom suites. It's more space than you'll get in a typical hotel room, plus all units have kitchens for self-catering. Free continental breakfast and wi-fi are included.

The property splits into a second building at 1000 29th St (a block away), which tends to be noisier. M St's shopping and dining bonanza, the waterfront and C&O Canal are within spitting distance.

GEORGETOWN INN HOTEL **$$**

Map p308 (202-333-8900; www.georgetowninn.com; 1310 Wisconsin Ave NW; r $250-350; P ❄ @ 📶; M Foggy Bottom-GWU to DC Circulator) Georgetown University alumni and parents on college weekends favor this property parked in the center of the neighborhood's action. The inn has a Revolutionary War–period look (think old Europe meets American colonial) and spreads through a collection of restored 18th-century townhouses. The stately decor (four-poster beds, furniture with feet) is aging, but undergoing renovation.

TOP PET-FRIENDLY HOTELS

A fair number of DC hotels allow pets, but the best of the bunch also provide food and water bowls, pickup bags, maps of neighborhood dog walk areas, and Milk-Bone treats. The best also do not charge for pets or have size/weight restrictions. These properties are top of the heap for Fido:

- Hotel Palomar (p232)
- Hotel Rouge (p232)
- Hotel George (p230)
- Hotel Monaco (p231)
- Hotel Helix (p235)

Capitol Hill & Southeast DC

WILLIAM PENN HOUSE HOSTEL **$**

Map p300 (202-543-5560; www.williampennhouse.org; 515 E Capitol St SE; dm $40-50; ❄ @ 👪; M Capitol South, Eastern Market) This friendly Quaker-run guesthouse with garden offers clean, well-maintained dorms, though it could use more bathrooms. There are 30 beds, including a four-bed family room ($135 per night). The facility doesn't require religious observance, but there is a religious theme throughout, and it prefers guests be active in progressive causes.

Rates include continental breakfast. The curious and spiritually minded can rise for the 7:30am worship service.

DOWNTOWN WASHINGTON HOSTEL HOSTEL **$**

Map p300 (202-370-6390; www.downtowndchostel.com; 506 H St NE; dm $25-50; ❄ @ 📶; M Union Station) This small, jolly newcomer to DC's hostel scene puts you a few blocks from H St's rollicking nightlife. The rooms, in shades of lime green, tomato red and other bright paints, have bunk beds for three to 12 people. One quibble: if the hostel is near full, waits for the bathrooms can be an issue. The free beer happy hour rocks each evening. There's a game room and big TV hooked up to cable, Netflix and Hulu for communal movie nights. Note the hostel has a no-shoe policy inside.

CAPITOL CITY HOSTEL HOSTEL **$**

(202-387-1328; 2411 Benning Rd NE; dm $20-30; ❄ @ 📶; M Union Station to bus X2) A few things to know upfront: this hostel is pretty far off the beaten path in a neighborhood that looks sketchier than it is. It's also only open to international travelers and university students. That said, it's cheap and cheerful, with great staff and management who go out of their way to make guests feel at home.

You'll have to rely on buses, but they are dependable, and you'll be fairly close to the nightlife on H St NE. From Union Station, take bus X2 going east (it'll say 'Minnesota Ave'); exit at Oklahoma Ave and Benning Rd.

HOTEL GEORGE BOUTIQUE HOTEL **$$**

Map p300 (202-347-4200; www.hotelgeorge.com; 15 E St NW; r from $300; P ❄ @ 🛜 👪 🐾; M Union Station) DC's first chic boutique hotel is still one of its best. Chrome-and-glass furniture and modern art frame the bold interior. Rooms exude a cool, creamy-white Zen. The pop-art presidential accents (paintings of American currency, artfully rearranged and diced up) are a little overdone, but that's a minor complaint about what is otherwise the hippest lodging on the Hill.

The free-wine happy hour each evening and free in-room yoga gear ice the cake (they're typical Kimpton-brand amenities). A limited number of free bicycles are also available for guests.

LIAISON HOTEL **$$**

Map p300 (202-638-1616; www.affinia.com/liaison; 415 New Jersey Ave NW; r $230-290; P ❄ @ 🛜 🏊 🐾; M Union Station) The Liason has jazzed up the accommodation options in Capitol Hill. Modernist rooms come in a stately, slate-to-earth tone color palette; they feel the right mix of corporate business and playful fun times. That said, the rooftop is all the latter: there's trippy house music and a pool that seems perpetually occupied by attractive folks. And it's all within spitting distance of the Capitol.

Wi-fi costs $10 per day (waived if you book at the hotel's website).

CAPITOL HILL HOTEL HOTEL **$$**

Map p300 (202-543-6000; www.capitolhillhotel-dc.com; 200 C St SE; r $220-300; P ❄ 🛜 👪 🐾; M Capitol South) Fresh off a whopping renovation, the hotel touts its new look as 'Federalist chic.' Dark walnut furnishings and white cushiony beds dot the spacious, clean-lined chambers. Smaller rooms have kitchenettes, while larger rooms have a full kitchen. Lots of political workers stay here, as it is the only hotel that is actually *on* the Hill. Free wi-fi and continental breakfast are included.

PHOENIX PARK HOTEL HOTEL **$$**

Map p300 (202-638-6900; www.phoenixparkhotel.com; 520 N Capitol St NW; r $170-300; P ❄ @ 🛜; M Union Station) It may look bland from the outside, but it's all Irish warmth inside. The rooms – upstairs from the Dubliner pub – have the feel of a Trinity College reading chamber that Joyce could have penned a novel in. Plus, the spot has long been home away from home for visiting Irish politicians, so when it lays on the Emerald Isle kitsch, it's genuine.

WASHINGTON COURT HOTEL HOTEL **$$**

Map p300 (202-628-2100; www.washingtoncourthotel.com; 525 New Jersey Ave NW; r $175-309; P ❄ @ 🛜 🐾; M Union Station) Washington Court is showing some wear, but the large rooms with spruce, earth-toned decor and a convenient perch next to Union Station make up for it. If you luck out, you might get a room with a view of the Capitol. Then again, you might get one with a view of a government office building. Wi-fi costs $11 per day.

Downtown & Penn Quarter

HOSTELLING INTERNATIONAL – WASHINGTON DC HOSTEL **$**

Map p302 (202-737-2333; www.hiwashingtondc.org; 1009 11th St NW; dm $33-55, r $110-150; ❄ @ 🛜; M Metro Center) Top of the budget picks, this large, friendly hostel attracts a laid-back international crowd and has loads of amenities: lounge rooms, a pool table, a 60in TV for movie nights, free tours, free continental breakfast and free wi-fi.

The dorm rooms are clean and well kept, in configurations ranging from four to 10 beds; there are a few private, en-suite rooms, too. Volunteers organize free night tours of the monuments, Dupont Circle pub crawls and the like. Reservations are recommended March to October.

CAPITAL VIEW HOSTEL HOSTEL **$**

Map p302 (202-450-3450; www.capitalhostels.com; 301 I St NW; dm from $35; ❄ @ 🛜; M Gallery Pl) Set in a red-brick house at downtown's far edge, the Capital View is a solid backpacker option. The groovy, hammock-hanging roof deck is the showpiece. The dorms – some mixed gender, others single sex, each with two to six beds in metal-frame bunks – are well kept with lots of outlets to charge electronics. The area can be a bit forlorn at night.

MORRISON-CLARK INN HISTORIC HOTEL $$
Map p302 (202-898-1200; www.morrisonclark.com; 1015 L St NW; r $150-250; P ❄ @ ; MMt Vernon Sq) Listed on the Register of Historic Places and helmed by a doting staff, the elegant Morrison-Clark comprises two 1864 Victorian residences filled with fine antiques, chandeliers, richly hued drapes and other features evocative of the pre–Civil War South. Some rooms are on the small side, but more options are coming: the inn is expanding into a church next door.

The new wing will offer larger, more modern rooms. In the interim, the ongoing renovation is prompting some excellent room rates.

HENLEY PARK HOTEL BOUTIQUE HOTEL $$
Map p302 (202-638-5200; www.henleypark.com; 926 Massachusetts Ave NW; r $170-270; P ❄ @ ; MMt Vernon Sq) The beautiful Tudor building with gargoyles and stained glass used to be an apartment building for Senators and Congressmen. The rooms – decked in tasteful plaids, paisleys and dark wood furniture – are as elegant as the edifice. It fronts a busy street so a bit of noise seeps in, but overall the historic property provides excellent value for downtown.

ELDON SUITES APARTMENT $$
Map p302 (202-540-5000; www.eldonsuites.com; 933 L St NW; apt $200-300; P ❄ ; MMt Vernon Sq) Given its location by the Convention Center, Eldon Suites puts up plenty of business folk. Families dig it, too. You get much more space than in hotel rooms in the same price bracket. Even the smallest unit has 600 sq ft, along with a big, fully equipped kitchen and separate living area. The neutral-toned decor is nothing fancy, but ah, so much room!

HOTEL HARRINGTON HOTEL $$
Map p302 (202-628-8140; www.hotel-harrington.com; 436 11th St NW; r $130-200; P ❄ @ ; MFederal Triangle) One of the most affordable options near the Mall, the aging, family-run Harrington has small, basic rooms that are clean but in definite need of an update. Helpful service and a prime location make it a great value for travelers who don't mind roughing it a bit. It's a popular crash pad for school groups, budget-minded families and international guests.

HAMPTON INN HOTEL $$
Map p302 (202-842-2500; www.washingtondc.hamptoninn.com; 901 6th St NW; r $180-300; P ❄ @ ; MGallery Pl) Cookie cutter? Yeah, well. You know what you're getting at the Hampton, and it can be a deal if you score a price at the spectrum's lower end. The 13-story property offers the requisite restful bedding, small indoor pool and hot (if spare) breakfast buffet. The location is slightly isolated, meaning you'll have to walk four blocks to reach downtown's nightlife.

HOTEL MONACO HOTEL $$$
Map p302 (202-628-7177; www.monaco-dc.com; 700 F St NW; r from $330; P ❄ @ ; MGallery Pl) Free goldfish on request and a geometric, deco-inspired interior help polish the 1930s, cool-daddy-o vibe at this marble temple to stylish glamour. The scene is set in the graceful, Corinthian-columned 1839 Tariff Building. The location works well for families: it's across the street from the Spy Museum and National Portrait Gallery, and four blocks from the Mall.

Kids stay gratis, adults sip free happy-hour wine, and active types can ride the complimentary bicycles, as per all Kimpton-brand properties.

Dupont Circle & Kalorama

WINDSOR INN HOTEL $
Map p306 (202-667-0300; www.windsor-inn-hotel-dc.com; 1842 16th St NW; r $120-160; ❄ ; MU St) The Windsor offers spare, fusty rooms. Non-fastidious travelers just looking for a place to crash at night will be fine, and grateful for the affable service and happenin' Dupont Circle/U St Corridor location. Continental breakfast costs $5. Wi-fi is free, but temperamental.

★**TABARD INN** BOUTIQUE HOTEL $$
Map p306 (202-785-1277; www.tabardinn.com; 1739 N St NW; r $195-250, without bath $135-155; ❄ @ ; MDupont Circle) Named for the inn in *The Canterbury Tales*, the Tabard spreads through a trio of Victorian-era row houses. The 40 rooms are hard to generalize: all come with vintage quirks, such as iron bed frames and wing-backed chairs, though little accents distinguish – a Matisse-like painted headboard here, Amish-looking quilts there. There are no TVs, and wi-fi can be dodgy, but the of-yore atmospherics prevail.

ACCOMMODATIONS WEBSITES

Lonely Planet (www.lonelyplanet.com/hotels) Author-recommended reviews and online booking.

Bed & Breakfast DC (www.bedandbreakfastdc.com) One-stop shop to book B&Bs and apartments.

WDCA Hotels (www.wdcahotels.com) Discounter that sorts by neighborhood, price or ecofriendliness.

Destination DC (www.washington.org) Options from the tourism office's jam-packed website.

Continental breakfast is included. Downstairs the parlor, beautiful restaurant and bar have low ceilings and old furniture, highly conducive to curling up with a vintage port and the Sunday *Post*.

EMBASSY CIRCLE GUEST HOUSE — B&B $$

Map p306 (☎202-232-7744; www.dcinns.com; 2224 R St NW; r $180-300; ; MDupont Circle) Embassies surround this 1902 French country-style home, which sits a few blocks from Dupont's nightlife hubbub. The 11 big-windowed rooms are decked out with Persian carpets and original art on the walls; they don't have TVs or radios, though they do each have wi-fi. The staff feeds you well throughout the day, with a hot organic breakfast, afternoon cookies, and an evening wine and beer soiree.

Embassy Circle's sister property – the Woodley Park Guest House (p236) in farther-flung northwest DC – is a hot spot.

CARLYLE — HOTEL $$

Map p306 (☎202-234-3200; www.carlylehoteldc.com; 1731 New Hampshire Ave NW; ste $180-320; ; MDupont Circle) In-the-know business travelers, families and couples make their way to the overlooked Carlyle. The art-deco gem offers quiet, handsomely furnished rooms with crisp white linens, luxury mattresses, 37in flat-screen TVs and kitchenettes (in some). The interior got a snazzy refresh in 2015, when the hotel became part of the Kimpton brand. Embassies and terrific restaurants surround the property.

HOTEL PALOMAR — HOTEL $$

Map p306 (☎202-448-1800; www.hotel-palomar-dc.com; 2121 P St NW; r $260-360; ; MDupont Circle) The Palomar attracts a stylish business clientele, plus a whole lot of pooches. Room decor is matter-of-fact compared to its Kimpton-chain brethren, with an emphasis on nicely powered-up work desks. Palomar's free evening wine hour is always a jam-packed scene. The outdoor pool and deck go beyond the norm. Then there's the pet-friendly vibe, which the hotel does up big time.

Not only does your dog get pampered each night with gourmet treats at turndown, he can also get a massage. If he wants to socialize, head to the Bark Bar, a three-tiered water bar for thirsty pets just outside the hotel.

AKWAABA — B&B $$

Map p306 (☎202-328-3510; www.dcakwaaba.com; 1708 16th St NW; r $185-225; ; MDupont Circle) Part of a small chain of B&Bs that emphasizes African American heritage in its properties, DC's Akwaaba outpost fills a handsome, late-19th-century mansion. Rooms are themed from abstractions ('Inspiration,' which has fine, airy ceilings and a slanting skylight) to authors ('Zora,' an all-red room that's romantic as can be). The cooked breakfast gets rave reviews, and the Dupont vibe is at your doorstep.

HOTEL MADERA — BOUTIQUE HOTEL $$

Map p306 (☎202-296-7600; www.hotelmadera.com; 1310 New Hampshire Ave NW; r $260-360; ; MDupont Circle) Cozy yet cosmopolitan, the Madera is one of DC's eight Kimpton-brand properties, the focus here being more of a small, intimate boutique than large funk-da-house hipster haunt. The airy rooms sport bright batik pillows, cushy beds and big, outlet-laden work desks; several also have balconies overlooking New Hampshire Ave. Firefly, the on-site bar, stirs romance.

A free wine happy hour, in-room yoga gear and first-come access to the hotel's loaner bicycles are also part of the package.

HOTEL ROUGE — BOUTIQUE HOTEL $$

Map p306 (☎202-232-8000; www.rougehotel.com; 1315 16th St NW; r $220-360; ; MDupont Circle) Rouge is a playful winner from the fun-loving Kimpton brand. The decor is definitively red, with bold designs, funky furniture and hip posters in the good-sized rooms. Specialty rooms have bunk beds and Xbox 360 games, while others come with kitchenettes. Rouge often shows up on hotel deal apps, where rates can be reasonable.

Free wine each evening and loaner bikes (if you can snag one) are nice perks. As funky as the hotel, Bar Rouge attracts a regular stream of locals, especially for its Thursday happy hours.

TOPAZ HOTEL BOUTIQUE HOTEL $$

Map p306 (202-393-3000; www.topazhotel.com; 1733 N St NW; r $250-360; P; Dupont Circle) Abracadabra: the door automatically swings open at the Topaz to reveal an Arabian Nights–type decor. Jewel-tone colors dominate the rooms – purple love seats, sapphire-blue drapes and pale-green lamps, all set off by satiny white beds and pillows. This is a Kimpton-brand hotel all the way, with the hip mod cons, genial service and free-flowing wine you expect.

The Topaz also provides passes to the YMCA workout facility on the next block.

SWANN HOUSE B&B $$

Map p306 (202-265-4414; www.swannhouse.com; 1808 New Hampshire Ave NW; r $240-350; Dupont Circle) A dozen rooms sprinkled throughout an exquisite 1883 Romanesque mansion, all set off enough from Dupont Circle to be quiet, but close enough to the action that it's an easy walk. The rooms are highly individualized: some are flowery and frilly while others are more subdued and contemporary (looking at you, Parisienne Suite). The backyard pool is unique for a B&B.

Staff serves the bountiful breakfast at tables in the chandeliered dining room or outside on the covered front porch. Afternoon sweets and evening sherry are also part of the package.

ST GREGORY HOTEL $$

Map p306 (202-530-3600; www.stgregoryhotelwdc.com; 2033 M St NW; r $219-309; P; Dupont Circle, Farragut North) Everyone goes ga-ga over the Marilyn Monroe statue in the lobby. It's an offbeat touch in what is otherwise a solid, business-oriented hotel. Rooms are smallish and wi-fi costs $12 per day, but that can be overlooked if you're keen on having Dupont's bars and bistros a short stroll away, and if you score a deal (the property often appears on discount booking sites).

HILTON GARDEN INN HOTEL $$

Map p306 (202-974-6010; www.hiltongardeninn.com; 2201 M St NW; r $240-400; P; Dupont Circle, Foggy Bottom) Like most trusty Hilton Garden Inns, this one caters to lots of business travelers and families. Unlike most, this one is in a glittering new Silver LEED-certified building, opened in 2014. The spacious rooms have easeful beds, a powered-up work desk, Keurig coffeemaker and fridge. The rooftop frolics with an outdoor pool and garden terrace.

The location is a trifecta of easy walking goodness between Dupont Circle, Foggy Bottom and Georgetown.

EMBASSY SUITES WASHINGTON DC HOTEL $$

Map p306 (202-857-3388; www.washingtondc.embassysuites.com; 1250 22nd St NW; ste $270-370; P; Dupont Circle) This Embassy displays the chain's typical hallmarks: all the units are two-room suites (living room with sofa bed in front, bedroom in back), there's a cooked-to-order bacon, egg and pancake breakfast each morning (often quite crowded), there's free wine each evening, and there's an indoor, kiddie-mobbed pool. The property does those basics well. Wi-fi costs $13 per day.

The location between Georgetown and Dupont Circle is handy. Families will appreciate being two blocks from Rock Creek Park, where the little ones can let off steam. Rooms on the 8th and 9th floors have views over Georgetown.

LOEWS MADISON HOTEL $$

Map p306 (202-862-1600; www.loewshotels.com; 1177 15th St NW; r $260-360; P; Farragut North, McPherson Sq) The Madison has hosted every US president since JFK. The attractive rooms are mid-sized, with silver-gray walls, fluffy white beds and wine-red accents – a color palette meant to echo DC's famed cherry blossoms. Alas, the rooms aren't very soundproof. As a side note, the Madison is supposedly the first hotel in the world to have introduced the minibar – thanks, guys.

EMBASSY INN HOTEL $$

Map p306 (202-234-7800; www.embassy-inn-hotel-dc.com; 1627 16th St NW; r $140-190; Dupont Circle) The Embassy Inn shows up on hostel booking sites, which gives you an indication of its no-frills ambience. Rooms are small and dark with thin walls, but there's a veneer of quaintness here. And the location rocks, flanked by the food and drink paradises of Dupont and Logan Circle. Continental breakfast costs $5. Wi-fi can be hit or miss.

Basically, the Embassy works in a pinch, when you turn up during a busy time and prices elsewhere are skewing sky high.

THE JEFFERSON BOUTIQUE HOTEL $$$

Map p306 (202-448-2300; www.jeffersondc.com; 1200 16th St NW; r from $450; P ❄ @ 🛜 🐾; M Farragut North) The elegant, two-winged 1923 mansion has an ornate porte cochere, beaux-arts architecture and a luxurious interior full of crystal and velvet, all meant to evoke namesake Thomas Jefferson's digs when he lived in Paris. Favored by diplomatic visitors, the hotel's antique-furnished rooms waft silk sheets, four-poster luxury, tobacco and earth tones, and Gilded Age class.

The 95-room luxury boutique regularly places near the top of Washington's best-hotel lists. The on-site cocktail bar is superb for a nightcap while listening to the gentleman piano player.

Adams Morgan

ADAM'S INN B&B $

Map p310 (202-745-3600; www.adamsinn.com; 1746 Lanier Pl NW; r $109-179, without bath $79-100; P ❄ @ 🛜 👨‍👧; M Woodley Park) Tucked on a shady residential street, the 26-room inn is known for its personalized service, fluffy linens and handy location just a few blocks from 18th St's global smorgasbord. Inviting, homey rooms sprawl through two adjacent townhouses and a carriage house. The common areas have a nice garden patio, and there's a general sense of sherry-scented chintz.

Breakfast is DIY continental style. It's a good seven blocks from the Metro, which can be problematic with lots of luggage.

TAFT BRIDGE INN B&B $$

Map p310 (202-387-2007; www.taftbridgeinn.com; 2007 Wyoming Ave NW; r $179-205, without bath $100-140; P ❄ 🛜; M Dupont Circle) Named for the bridge that leaps over Rock Creek Park just north, this beautiful 19th-century Georgian mansion is an easy walk to 18th St or Dupont Circle. The inn has a paneled drawing room, classy antiques, six fireplaces and a garden. Some of the 12 rooms have a colonial Americana theme, accentuated by Amish quilts; others are more tweedy, exuding a Euro-renaissance vibe. Breakfast is a cooked, egg-laden affair.

AMERICAN GUEST HOUSE B&B $$

Map p310 (202-588-1180; www.americanguesthouse.com; 2005 Columbia Rd NW; r $160-220; ❄ @ 🛜; M Dupont Circle) The 12-room American Guest House earns high marks for its intimate sense of service, bountiful omelet-y breakfasts and elegant, individualized rooms. Decor runs the gamut from Victorian vibe (Room 203) to New England cottage (Room 304) to colonial love nest (Room 303). Some quarters are rather small.

WASHINGTON HILTON BUSINESS HOTEL $$

Map p310 (202-483-3000; www.hilton.com; 1919 Connecticut Ave NW; r $250-325; P ❄ @ 🛜 🏊 👨‍👧 🐾; M Dupont Circle) The 1960s-style semicircular structure has all the amenities you expect at a big business hotel. The rooms are corporate blah, but considering the service you get and the nifty location near food and drink hot spots, it's not a bad deal. Wi-fi costs $13 per day.

The Hilton is famed as the site of John Hinckley's attempt to assassinate President Ronald Reagan, on March 30, 1981. Hoping to impress the actor Jodie Foster, the disturbed young man shot Reagan, his press secretary and an FBI agent near the T St NW entrance.

Logan Circle, U Street & Columbia Heights

DISTRICT HOTEL HOTEL $

Map p312 (202-232-7800; www.thedistricthotel.com; 1440 Rhode Island Ave NW; r $110-150; ❄ 🛜; M McPherson Sq) Home to some of the smallest rooms in DC, the District Hotel has spartan quarters that will work for low-maintenance budgeteers. It's in a great location within walking distance to downtown, Dupont Circle and 14th St nightlife. Wi-fi works in the common areas only. Continental breakfast costs $5.

ASANTE SANA GUEST QUARTERS GUESTHOUSE $

Map p312 (202-570-3440; www.asantesana.us; 1207 Kenyon St NW; r $135-150; ❄ 🛜 🐾; M Columbia Heights) This is a basic guesthouse with six modest rooms (all with private bath, though in some cases not en suite) and a communal kitchen for self-catering (there's a grocery store nearby). It's nothing fancy. The selling point for adventurous types is you're in a cool, off-the-beaten-path neighborhood, near ethnic eats, hipster dive bars and the Metro.

HILLTOP HOSTEL HOSTEL $
(☎202-291-9591; www.hosteldc.com; 300 Carroll St; dm $24; @📶; Ⓜ Takoma) The rough-and-ready Hilltop is in the bohemian, politically leftist neighborhood of Takoma Park, in far northeast DC. Set in a century-old Victorian mansion, it is pretty darn beat-up, but that doesn't stop international backpackers looking for cheap digs from staying here. The backyard barbecue and hammock inspire frequent impromptu parties.

Don't be put off by the hostel's distance from downtown: it's across the street from the Metro, which gets you to Capitol Hill in about 15 minutes. Besides, Takoma has its own strip of antique shops and vegetarian restaurants to explore.

★HOTEL HELIX BOUTIQUE HOTEL $$
Map p312 (☎202-462-9001; www.hotelhelix.com; 1430 Rhode Island Ave NW; r $200-300; P❄@📶; Ⓜ McPherson Sq) Modish and highlighter bright, the Helix is playfully hip – the perfect hotel for the bouncy international set that makes up the surrounding neighborhood. Little touches suggest a youthful energy (Pez dispensers in the minibar) balanced with worldly cool (like the pop-punk decor). All rooms have comfy, crisp-sheet beds and 37in flat-screen TVs.

The location next to 14th St's food and drink bounty can't be beat. Helix is a Kimpton-brand hotel – with the requisite free yoga mats, morning coffee and wine happy hour – but it's more eccentric and often cheaper than its siblings.

★CHESTER ARTHUR HOUSE B&B $$
Map p312 (☎877-893-3233; www.chesterarthurhouse.com; 23 Logan Circle NW; r $175-215; ❄📶; Ⓜ U St) Snooze in one of four rooms in this beautiful Logan Circle row house, located a stumble from the restaurant boom along P and 14th Sts. The 1883 abode is stuffed with crystal chandeliers, antique oil paintings, oriental rugs and a mahogany paneled staircase, plus ephemera from the hosts' global expeditions.

Alas, President Arthur never lived here. It's a gimmick, though the house was built by a Treasury undersecretary in Arthur's administration.

CAMBRIA SUITES AT O HOTEL $$
Map p312 (☎202-299-1188; www.cambriadc.com; 899 O St NW; r $209-309; P❄@📶; Ⓜ Mt Vernon Sq) Opened in 2014, the Cambria racks up bonus points for its vast rooms and Silver LEED-certified building design. The shiny new dove-gray and white chambers come equipped with a sofa sleeper, powered-up work desk and two flat-screen TVs in addition to a big, comfy bed or two. The 10th-floor rooftop terrace and small indoor pool are also deft touches.

Lots of business travelers stay here thanks to the Convention Center proximity. The space is great for families, too, though be aware you're a haul from the Mall and other sights. The next-door grocery store stocks good bottles of wine and snacks.

1887 INN B&B $$
Map p312 (☎877-893-3233; www.bedandbreakfastdc.com; 1309 R St NW; r without bath $140-170; P📶; Ⓜ U St) If you're looking for digs with character set a teeter away from 14th St's awesomeness, this B&B ensconced in two Victorian row houses brings it. The owner's father was a furniture maker circa 1900, and his pieces and other family heirlooms fill the place. There's a caveat though: none of the nine rooms have a private bathroom.

What's more, three rooms have a double bed versus queen bed (due to their trim confines), and most rooms are TV-less. If you can handle these facets, the property is good value for DC. The B&B also goes by the name William Lewis House.

MERIDIAN MANOR B&B $$
Map p312 (☎202-328-3510; www.meridianmanordc.com; 16th St , btwn U & V Sts NW; r $155-250, without bath $125-155; P❄📶; Ⓜ U St) Unlike in many District B&Bs, the six rooms here have a contemporary vibe. They're all decked out with designer furniture and monochrome color schemes, which stands in nice contrast to the 'manor' itself, a lovely old DC residence that blends in easily with nearby embassies. Breakfast is continental style. There's a $20 surcharge for single-night stays.

The gracious hosts can direct you to drinking and dining action in the U St Corridor (a few blocks away), 14th St in Logan Circle (about a half-mile) and 18th St in Adams Morgan (also about a half-mile away).

Upper Northwest DC

SAVOY SUITES HOTEL $$
Map p316 (☎202-337-9700; www.savoysuites.com; 2505 Wisconsin Ave NW; $130-180; P❄📶) In a tree-lined neighborhood near the Naval Observatory, the eight-story Savoy

Suites has comfortable, carpeted rooms with all the mod cons (high-end mattresses, work desks, in-room fridge and coffee maker, free wi-fi, good on-site fitness center). Book an upper-level room for good city views.

Although it's out of the action, a free shuttle takes guests to the Woodley Park Metro station and Georgetown University. In low season, prices can drop below $80 on booking sites (like Hotels.com).

WOODLEY PARK GUEST HOUSE B&B **$$**
Map p316 (202-667-0218; www.dcinns.com; 2647 Woodley Rd NW; r $180-250, without bath $135-165; P; Woodley Park-Zoo, Adams Morgan) This elegant, 1920s-era home is excellent value. Fifteen sunny rooms have antique furniture, hardwood floors and white coverlets. The front porch is a wonderful perch for a summer afternoon. The owners are incredibly friendly, and many guests are faithful regulars. Note rooms that share a bathroom have an occupancy of one person only.

Woodley Park's sister property – the Embassy Circle Guest House (p232) near Dupont Circle – is a winner.

KALORAMA GUEST HOUSE B&B **$$**
Map p316 (202-588-8188; www.kaloramaguesthouse.com; 2700 Cathedral Ave NW; r $175-249, without bath $89-115; P; Woodley Park-Zoo, Adams Morgan) Set in a cozy Victorian row house, the Kalorama offers 11 flowery, antique-furnished rooms. Nine of them have private baths; the other two rooms share a bathroom. Some rooms are in the basement, so let them know when booking if you prefer a brighter upstairs unit. Breakfast is a self-serve affair consumed at a long communal table.

In winter staff pours sherry or sangria in the evenings; in summer, it's fresh lemonade throughout the day.

OMNI SHOREHAM HOTEL HOTEL **$$**
Map p316 (202-234-0700; www.omnishorehamhotel.com; 2500 Calvert St NW; r $250-350; P; Woodley Park-Zoo, Adams Morgan) The Omni may be an 836-room behemoth swarmed by conventioneers, but we're recommending it for its family friendliness. It is a stroller's roll to the National Zoo and Rock Creek Park, and just a couple blocks to the Metro that can whisk you to DC's main sights in four stops.

Out the front door, restaurants line Connecticut Ave. Children receive backpacks with toys and games, as well as a milk-and-cookie service their first night. And you'll have a helluva time extracting them from the lovely heated outdoor pool.

Northern Virginia

Chain hotels pepper Arlington, which offers the cheapest options. Many are near the Metro and almost as convenient as staying in the District. Old Town Alexandria's lodgings are more awkward to reach Metro-wise and prices are higher, but the neighborhood is much more charming.

BEST WESTERN OLD COLONY INN MOTEL **$**
(703-739-2222; www.hotel-alexandria.com; 1101 N Washington St, Alexandria; r $112-160; P; Braddock Rd) Sure it's a chain hotel, but this place earns high marks for its good-value rooms and decent amenities. Rooms are bright, with work desks and big-screen TVs (a DVD lending library is on hand). There's also free shuttle service to Reagan airport, the Old Town (just under a mile away) and to the Metro station. Parking, breakfast and in-room wi-fi are all free.

In the low season rates can drop to $89 (and below $80 on some booking sites).

ALEXANDRIA TRAVEL LODGE MOTEL **$**
Map p315 (703-836-5100; www.travelodge.com; 700 N Washington St, Alexandria; r $90-160; P; King St) This motel – on a busy section of Washington St – is about a mile north of Old Town's historic district. It is a good bet for budget travelers who have their own car, as parking is free. Basic rooms have TV and free wi-fi. Amenities are otherwise limited.

MORRISON HOUSE BOUTIQUE HOTEL **$$**
Map p315 (703-838-8000; www.morrisonhouse.com; 116 S Alfred St, Alexandria; r from $159-279; P; King St to Old Town Shuttle) In the heart of Old Town Alexandria, Morrison House captures the neighborhood's charm with its Georgian-style building and Federal-style reproduction furniture. Rooms are beautifully decorated with a two- or four-poster bed, mahogany armoire, writing table and chairs, and some have decorative fireplaces. The on-site restaurant, including its Saturday high tea service, is well respected.

Perks include a free shuttle to Reagan airport, free pool access at a nearby sibling hotel, and a free wine happy hour each evening (a Kimpton hotel brand hallmark).

Understand Washington, DC

Washington, DC, Today

Washingtonians are feeling a new-found civic pride, fueled in part by a spate of far-reaching developments across the city. A Mall redesign (complete with an architecturally stunning new museum), an expanded Metro and more green spaces – not to mention a flurry of new restaurants and bars – are making the city more livable (if pricier) than ever before. On the downside, the battle for autonomy from the federal government continues, as Washington clamors for voting rights and the freedom to decide its own affairs.

Best on Film

All the President's Men (1976) Dramatic portrayal of two journalists who uncover the USA's biggest political scandal: Watergate.

Mr Smith Goes to Washington (1939) Frank Capra classic of idealist do-gooder (played by Jimmy Stewart) taking on the established power brokers of Washington.

Slam (1998) True-to-life portrait of a young man (and budding poet) growing up in a blight-stricken area of DC.

Best in Print

Katharine Graham's Washington (edited by Katharine Graham; 2002) Illuminating essays about the Washington experience, by presidential insiders, novelists, journalists, socialites and humorists.

Lost in the City (Edward P Jones; 1992) Critically acclaimed collection of short stories set in African American DC during the tumultuous 1960s and '70s.

Empire of Mud (JD Dickey; 2014) Eye-opening account of Washington's early days as a city of tenements, malaria, open slave-trading and political corruption.

The 51st State?

It was a new day in Washington, DC, when Muriel Bowser was sworn in as the city's mayor in early 2015. Only the second female to be elected mayor in DC's history, she wasted no time in laying out her objectives. On her first full day in office, she went to Capitol Hill to press Republican leaders to grant the city a greater role in federal government. For years, DC residents have paid billions in taxes but have had no voting representation in either house of Congress – despite having a population larger than some states (such as Vermont and Wyoming). It's no wonder that residents are proud of their license plates that brandish the slogan 'Taxation Without Representation' – and take joy in the fact that even the president's limo bears these plates.

The lack of voting representation is one of the gripes DC residents have with the federal government in their hometown. More insidious is the Fed's ability to swoop in and interfere with civic affairs after the voters have decided an issue.

Such was the case in late 2014 after voters overwhelmingly approved new legislation legalizing recreational marijuana use in the District. Congress, however, attempted to crush the measure by a spending bill. US representatives claim it is within their rights to do so, since under the Home Rule Charter of 1973, Congress must review and approve any law passed by the local government – and lawmakers can foil laws through the budgeting process. Needless to say, DC officials and democracy activists seek more autonomy for the city. The mayor laid it out quite clearly in a televised interview shortly after taking office in 2015. 'The residents of Washington, DC, deserve full democracy and statehood,' Bowser said.

Economic Downturn

After a half-decade of growth (even when other American cities struggled under the Great Recession), DC's boom days appear to be nearing an end – at least according to one major financial indicator. From 2012 to 2013, Washington's GRP (the regional equivalent for GDP) shrank by 0.8% – the only one of 15 major US metropolitan areas to see a decline.

Job growth has also made a dismal showing, with just under 20,000 jobs added between 2013 and 2014 (placing DC only slightly ahead of Detroit, but far behind 13 other major cities). The downslide has much to do with the US government's belt-tightening – federal employment fell by over 5% in the last three years while federal spending in the region has declined even more.

Capital Developments

Despite the economic downturn (which pessimists say has yet to manifest itself on the city's psyche), Washington continues to forge ahead with major development projects. The last few years have seen the laying of a new tram down H St, the inauguration of a $2.9 billion Metro line (the Silver Line), which will eventually connect the district with Washington Dulles International Airport, and massive new mixed-use spaces (condos, shopping, entertainment) popping up around town. One of the most ambitious projects is the creation of the Yards, a 42-acre development that has added residential and office space and a lush new waterfront along the Anacostia River. New restaurants, shops and one sprawling microbrewery (Bluejacket) have moved into the area, helping to reinvigorate what was once a barren corner of the city.

Elsewhere, big projects continue apace. On the Mall, the National Museum of African American History and Culture (part of the Smithsonian) will open in 2016. Expected to cost $500 million, it will be a powerful showcase of 400 years of history. If size is any indication (the building will house 350,000 sq ft of gallery space), upon completion the NMAAHC will be the world's greatest museum dedicated to the African American experience.

Nearby, the Mall itself will undergo a redesign. Situated between the National WWII Memorial and the Vietnam Veterans Memorial, Constitution Gardens will become a new recreational hub, with ice-skating, boating and a new pavilion and restaurant overlooking an expanded lake and surrounding gardens.

if Washington, DC, were 100 people

49 would be African American
37 would be White
9 would be Hispanic
3 would be Asian
2 would be persons reporting two or more races

birthplace

(% of population)

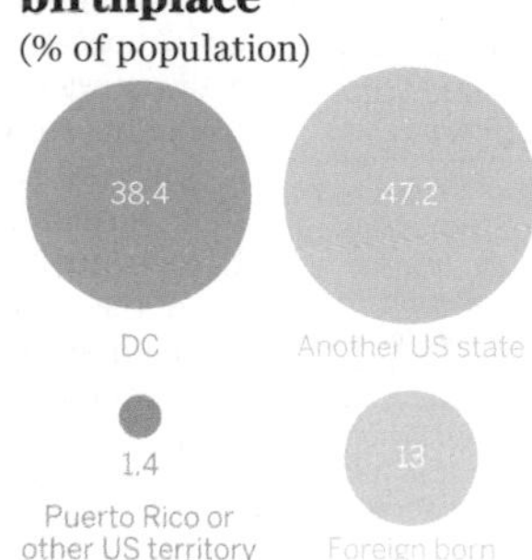

population per sq mile

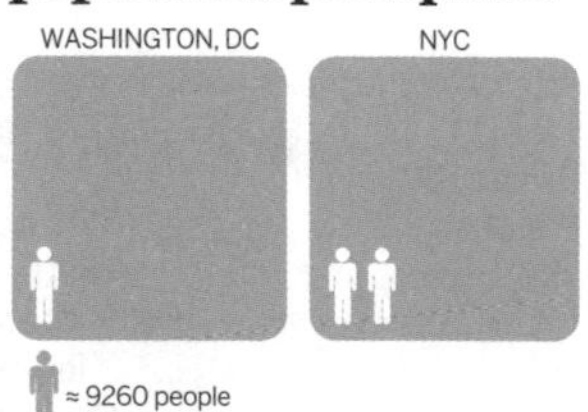

History

A compromise in a fragile new nation, Washington, DC, was built from scratch on a strategically chosen site between north and south. Following the devastating Civil War, tiny Washington grew quickly, and became a vital job creator during the Great Depression and WWII. The 20th century brought turmoil: communist witch hunts, civil rights struggles, political scandals and urban blight. By the 21st century, however, Washington's stricken neighborhoods saw revitalization, even as DC remains the focal point for America's increasingly divided political views.

Early Settlement

Historical Reads

- *A People's History of the United States (Howard Zinn)*
- *Capital Speculations: Writing and Building Washington, DC (Sarah Luria)*
- *Washington Goes to War (David Brinkley)*

Before the first European colonists sailed up from Chesapeake Bay, Native Americans, primarily the Piscataway tribe of the Algonquian language group, made their home near the confluence of the Potomac and Anacostia Rivers. The first recorded white contact with the Piscataway was in 1608 by the English captain John Smith, who set out from Jamestown colony to explore the upper Potomac.

Relations with the peaceful Piscataway were amicable at first, but soon turned ruinous for the Native Americans, who suffered from European diseases. By 1700 the few remaining Piscataway migrated out of the region to Iroquois territory in Pennsylvania and New York.

The first European settlers in the region were traders and fur trappers, who plied the woodlands beyond the Allegheny Mountains, often working with local Algonquian communities. English and Scots-Irish settlers followed, turning the forests into farmland.

By the late 1600s, expansive agricultural estates lined both sides of the Potomac. These tidewater planters became a colonial aristocracy, dominating regional affairs. Their most lucrative crop was the precious sotweed – tobacco – which was tended by African indentured servants and slaves. The river ports of Alexandria and Georgetown became famous for their prosperous commercial centers.

TIMELINE

1608

Piscataway people, who live around the Potomac and Anacostia Rivers, encounter Captain John Smith on his journey up the Potomac – a word that may mean 'trading place' in Algonquian.

1791–92

As a compromise to the growing antagonism between north and south, the site for the new federal capital is chosen. Virginia and Maryland both cede land for the 100-sq-mile territory.

1800

Congress convenes in Washington for the first time. Despite the grandeur of L'Enfant's plan, the new capital remains a sparsely populated, muddy frontier town.

Fight for Independence

In the 1770s, growing hostilities with Britain led the colonies (now calling themselves states) to draft the Declaration of Independence, severing ties with Britain. Perhaps the most empowering section of the declaration stated that Americans were 'resolved to die free men rather than live as slaves.'

At the outset of the war, the colonies faced tremendous obstacles. The colonial leaders' belief in their ultimate success was both visionary and utterly improbable. They had neither a professional army nor navy – only a ragtag group of poorly trained militiamen fighting against the most powerful army and navy on the planet. The king expected a quick suppression of the revolt.

Instead, the British faced off against George Washington, a highly skilled and charismatic military tactician whose courage under fire (in the French and Indian War) was well known. Washington was appointed commander in chief of the 20,000-odd men – a number that would swell to more than 200,000 by the war's end.

Incredibly, the war would rage on for eight years, with more soldiers dying from disease and exposure during the long bitter winters than from battle wounds. The war also brought other European powers into the fray, with France providing arms and munitions, and eventually troops and naval power.

Despite numerous losses, Washington's army prevailed. The British surrendered at Yorktown in 1783 and later ceded all formerly British-held territories to the American colonies.

FOUNDATIONS

Despite popular belief (asserted even by some congressmen), Washington, DC, was not built on a swamp. When surveying the capital, L'Enfant found fields, forests and bluffs. Some marshy areas near the river were prone to tidal fluctuations and periodic floods, but most of the new federal city was not marshy.

A Visionary New City

Following the Revolutionary War, the fledgling US Congress set up a temporary capital in Philadelphia while searching for a more permanent home. The Constitution, ratified in 1788, specified that a federal territory, no greater than 10 sq miles, should be established for the nation's capital. Northerners and Southerners both wanted the capital in their territory, and archrivals Thomas Jefferson (a Virginian) and Alexander Hamilton (a New Yorker) struck a compromise, agreeing to construct a new city on the border between north and south. The precise location was left up to the newly inaugurated and wildly popular President George Washington.

Washington chose a site some 20 miles from his own Mount Vernon estate – a place he loved and knew well. The site on the Potomac proved a strategic location for commerce and river traffic, and was politically pleasing to both Northern and Southern concerns. Maryland and Virginia agreed to cede land to the new capital.

1814

As the War of 1812 rages, British troops attack the fledgling capital, destroying many public buildings (including the White House and the Capitol). President Madison flees to Virginia.

1835

The issue of slavery is dividing the nation. The Snow Riots erupt in Washington, with white mobs attacking blacks. In response, Congress passes laws restricting blacks' economic rights.

1846

Allying more with slaveholders and Southern interests, Alexandria County residents successfully petition to return the area to Virginia. It's an indication of the north-south divide.

1860

Abraham Lincoln is elected president. The South secedes from the Union and war is declared. Washingtonians live in fear of attack from rebels, across the river in Virginia.

Over drinks at Suter's tavern in Georgetown, Washington persuaded local landowners to sell their holdings to the government for $66 an acre. In March 1791 the African American mathematician Benjamin Banneker and surveyor Andrew Ellicott mapped out a diamond-shaped territory that spanned the Potomac and Anacostia Rivers. Its four corners were at the cardinal points of the compass, and it embraced the river ports of Georgetown and Alexandria (the latter eventually returned to Virginia). Pierre Charles L'Enfant, a French officer in the Revolutionary War, sketched plans for a grand European-style capital of monumental buildings and majestic boulevards. It was named the 'Territory of Columbia' (to honor Christopher Columbus), while the federal city within would be called 'the city of Washington.'

L'Enfant, despite his great vision for the city, would be dismissed within a year. He refused to answer to anyone aside from Washington, and when he challenged the commissioning authority above him, he was eventually fired. Nevertheless, his plan for the city would play a major role in its eventual design – and no one, aside from Washington, had a greater influence upon its development. After Washington fired his planner, land speculators grabbed prized properties and buildings sprang up haphazardly along mucky lanes. In 1793 construction began on the President's House and the Capitol, the geographic center points of the city. In 1800 John Adams became the first president to occupy the still uncompleted mansion. His wife Abigail hung the family's laundry in the East Room. The city remained a half-built, sparsely populated work in progress.

City residents for their part still associated themselves with the states from which they'd come. This began to change in 1801 when DC residents lost the right to vote in Virginia and Maryland elections. According to the Constitution, Congress alone would control the federal district, which intentionally or not, disenfranchised District residents. In 1820 DC held its first mayoral and city council elections, which voters took part in – though this would not always be the case.

REVOLUTION

The miniseries *John Adams* (2008) is a riveting story, told from all sides, of the years when the American Revolution hung in the balance and fate could have swung either way.

War of 1812: Washington Burns

In the early 19th century, the young nation had yet to become a formidable force in world affairs. US merchants and seamen were regularly bullied on the high seas by the British navy. Responding to congressional hawks, President James Madison declared war in 1812. In retaliation for the razing of York (Toronto) by US troops, the British assaulted Washington. Work was barely complete on the Capitol in August 1814 when Redcoats marched into Washington and sacked and burned the city's most important buildings (but left private houses largely un-

1862

Slavery is abolished throughout DC. Washington becomes an army camp as the Civil War continues. Supply depots, warehouses and factories bring workers into the city.

1863

President Abraham Lincoln issues the Emancipation Proclamation, freeing all slaves. By the end of the Civil War, some four million African Americans will be freed.

1864

The war comes to Washington when the Confederate army attacks Fort Stevens – the only battle fought on capital soil. After a two-day skirmish, the Union army prevails.

1865

After Sherman's crippling, scorched-earth drive across the South, Confederate General Robert E Lee surrenders to Ulysses S Grant at Appomattox Court House in Virginia.

harmed). President Madison fled to the Virginia suburbs. Upon returning, the president took up temporary residence in the Octagon (now the Octagon Museum), the home of Colonel John Taylor, where he ratified the Treaty of Ghent, which ended the war. He remained there until the refurbishing of the White House was complete.

Although the British were expelled and the city rebuilt, Washington was slow to recover. A congressional initiative to abandon the dispirited capital was lost by just nine votes.

Slavery in the Federal City

When Congress first convened in Washington in 1800, the city had about 14,000 residents. It was even then a heavily African American populated town: slaves and free blacks composed 29% of the population. Free blacks lived in the port of Georgetown, where a vibrant African American community emerged. They worked alongside and socialized with the city's slaves.

Since its introduction in Jamestown colony in 1619, slave labor had become an essential part of the regional tobacco economy. In 1800 more than half of the nation's 700,000 slaves lived in Maryland and Virginia. The capital of America's slave trade at that time, Washington, DC, contained slave markets and holding pens.

The city's slave population steadily declined throughout the 19th century, while the number of free blacks rose. They migrated to the city, establishing their own churches and schools.

Washington, DC, became a front line in the intensifying conflict between the North and South over slavery. The city was a strategic stop on the clandestine Underground Railroad, shuttling fugitive slaves to freedom in the northern states. The abolitionist movement fueled further racial tensions. In 1835 the Snow Riots erupted as white mobs set loose on black Washingtonians. When the rampage subsided, legislation was passed restricting the economic rights of the city's free blacks. At last, Congress outlawed the slave trade in Washington in 1850; the District Emancipation Act abolished slavery outright in 1862.

The Civil War & its Aftermath

The 1860 election of Abraham Lincoln meant that the office of president would no longer protect Southern interests in the increasingly irreconcilable rift over slavery. Rather than abide by the electoral outcome, Southern secessionists opted to exit the Union, igniting a horrific four-year war that would leave over half a million dead. Washington was a prized target and the front lines of fighting often came quite near the capital. Indeed when the war began, city residents (including Lincoln)

History Websites

Library of Congress (www.loc.gov)

National Archives (www.archives.gov)

PBS (www.pbs.org/topics/history)

Civil Rights Special Collection (www.teachers-domain.org/special/civil)

Americans at War (http://americanhistory.si.edu/militaryhistory)

Want to read the Constitution, Emancipation Proclamation, Federalist Papers and much, much more? Peruse the National Archives at www.archives.gov or '100 Milestone Documents' at www.ourdocuments.gov.

1865

Five days after the Confederate surrender, Lincoln is shot in the head by the well-known actor John Wilkes Booth in Washington's Ford's Theatre. He dies hours later.

1865

Andrew Johnson takes office and does little to help newly freed blacks. For violating the Tenure of Office Act, he is impeached and narrowly avoids being removed from office in 1868.

1865–67

After the war Congress establishes the Freedman's Bureau to help former slaves transition to free society. In 1867 Howard University, the nation's first African American university, is founded.

1870–80

The city doubles in size during the postwar boom. Board of Public Works Alexander 'Boss' Shepherd helps modernize the city with paved streets, sewers, gaslights and parks.

FROM SLAVE TO STATESMAN: FREDERICK DOUGLASS

Born Frederick Augustus Washington Bailey in 1818 on a slave plantation along Maryland's Eastern Shore, Frederick Douglass is remembered as one of the country's most influential and outstanding black 19th-century leaders.

In 1838, at 20 years old, he escaped wretched treatment at the hands of Maryland planters and established himself as a freeman in New Bedford, MA, eventually working for abolitionist William Lloyd Garrison's antislavery paper, the *Liberator*. His years as a slave had led Douglass to a profound personal truth: 'Men are whipped oftenist who are whipped easiest.' After his escape, he took his new last name from a character in the Sir Walter Scott book, *The Lady of the Lake*. Largely self-educated, Douglass had a natural gift for eloquence. In 1841 he won the admiration of New England abolitionists with an impromptu speech at an antislavery convention, introducing himself as 'a recent graduate from the institution of slavery,' with his 'diploma' (ie whip marks on his back).

Douglass' effectiveness so angered proslavery forces that his supporters urged him to flee to England to escape seizure and punishment under the Fugitive Slave Law. He followed their advice and kept lecturing in England until admirers contributed enough money ($710.96) to enable him to purchase his freedom and return home in 1847.

Douglass then became the self-proclaimed 'station master and conductor' of the Underground Railroad in Rochester, NY, working with other famed abolitionists like Harriet Tubman and John Brown. In 1860 Douglass campaigned for Abraham Lincoln, and when the Civil War broke out, helped raise two regiments of black soldiers – the Massachusetts 54th and 55th – to fight for the Union.

After the war, Douglass went to Washington to lend his support to the 13th, 14th and 15th Constitutional Amendments, which abolished slavery, granted citizenship to former slaves and guaranteed citizens the right to vote.

In 1895 Douglass died at his Anacostia home, Cedar Hill, now the Frederick Douglass National Historic Site (p112).

remained fearful of a siege from the Confederates, whose campfires were visible just across the Potomac in Virginia. Had Maryland joined the Confederate side - and it very nearly did - the capital would have been completely isolated from the North, with disastrous results for the city and country. A ring of earthwork forts was hastily erected, but Washington saw only one battle on its soil: Confederate General Jubal Early's unsuccessful attack on Fort Stevens in northern DC, in July 1864. Nevertheless, Washingtonians lived in constant anxiety, as bloody battles raged nearby at Antietam, Gettysburg and Manassas.

As the war raged on, soldiers, volunteers, civil servants and ex-slaves flooded into the capital. Within three months of the first shots fired

1901

The McMillan Commission revives L'Enfant's original design for the rapidly growing capital, beautifying the Mall and solidifying the grandeur of Washington.

1907

The grand beaux-arts-style Union Station opens and serves as a key terminus between north and south (with 200,000 passengers a day). Today it receives over 32 million visitors annually.

1913

President Woodrow Wilson institutes a policy of segregation in federal offices (including lunchrooms and bathrooms) for the first time since 1863. Segregation continues through the 1950s.

1916–19

WWI attracts thousands of people to Washington for the administration of the war. By war's end, the city's population is over half a million.

at Fort Sumter, over 50,000 enlistees descended on the capital to join the Union Army. Throughout the war, Washington would serve as an important rearguard position for troop encampments and supply operations. Among those who spent time here were local resident Matthew Brady, whose compelling photographs provide a vivid document of the war. Poet Walt Whitman was also a Washington resident then, volunteering at a makeshift hospital in the converted Patent Office – today the National Portrait Gallery; his poem 'The Wound Dresser' is based on his experiences tending the injured and dying. This building, incidentally, also hosted President Lincoln's inauguration ball, after his re-election in 1865.

Lincoln's second term would be short-lived. One month later – and five days after Confederate General Robert E Lee surrendered to Union General Ulysses S Grant at Appomattox – Lincoln was assassinated by John Wilkes Booth in downtown Washington at Ford's Theatre (p246).

The Civil War had a lasting impact on the city. The war strengthened the power of the federal government, marking the first efforts to conscript young men into military service and to collect income tax from private households. Warfare brought new bureaucracies, workers and buildings to the capital. Between the war's start and end, the city's population nearly doubled to more than 130,000. One of the largest influxes of newcomers was freed blacks.

Vice-president Andrew Johnson, a southerner from Tennessee, assumed the presidency following Lincoln's death, but did little to help the freed African Americans; he even vetoed the first Civil Rights bill. Congress, however, did attempt to help blacks make the transition to free society, and in 1867 Howard University, the nation's first African American institute of higher learning, was founded. By this time, blacks composed nearly a quarter of the population.

Washington's economy was bolstered by a postwar boom. Although in some ways a Southern city, Washington was already part of the commercial networks of the north. The B&O Railroad connected the city via Baltimore to the industry of the northeast; while the Chesapeake and Ohio Canal opened a waterway to the agriculture of the Midwest. In 1871 President Ulysses S Grant appointed a Board of Public Works to upgrade the urban infrastructure and improve living conditions. The board was led by Alexander Shepherd, who energetically took on the assignment. He paved streets, put in sewers, installed gaslights, planted trees, filled in swamps and carved out parklands. But he also ran over budget by some $20 million and was sacked by Congress, who reclaimed responsibility for city affairs. 'Boss' Shepherd was the closest thing that DC would have to self-government for 100 years.

Civil War Onscreen

Civil War (documentary; Ken Burns)

Glory (Edward Zwick)

Gods & Generals (Ronald Maxwell)

Gettysburg (Ronald Maxwell)

Gone With the Wind (Victor Fleming)

1919

Following the armistice, decommissioned soldiers and civilians look for work, and racial tensions lead to race riots in Washington and dozens of other cities.

1920

The 19th Amendment to the Constitution grants women the right to vote. Early activists such as Susan B Anthony (1820–1906) are instrumental in its success.

1920s

The '20s see an African American cultural boom, led by Ella Fitzgerald and native son Duke Ellington; U St becomes known as the Great Black Way.

1922

The city experiences its worst natural disaster: heavy snowfall – 18in – causes the collapse of the roof of the Knickerbocker Theatre, killing nearly 100 people inside.

TRAGEDY AT FORD'S THEATRE

In 1865, just days after the Confederate Army surrendered, one of the most beloved figures in America – at least the northern part – was gunned down in cold blood. Abraham Lincoln was dead.

John Wilkes Booth – Marylander, famous actor and diehard believer in the Confederate cause – had long harbored ambitions to bring the US leadership to its knees. A plot to kidnap the president the year prior had failed. Then, on April 14, Booth learned while stopping by Ford's Theatre to retrieve his mail that the president would be attending a play that evening. He knew it was time to strike. He met with his co-conspirators later that day, and hatched a plan: Lewis Powell would kill Secretary of State William Seward at his home, while George Atzerodt killed Vice President Andrew Johnson at his residence and Booth struck Lincoln and Grant – all would happen simultaneously around 10pm. As it turns out, only Booth would succeed in his mission.

Booth, who was well known in the theater, was questioned by no one as he strolled up to Lincoln's box. He crept inside and quietly barricaded the outer door behind him (Lincoln's bodyguard had apparently headed to a nearby pub at intermission and never returned). Booth knew the play well, and waited to act until he heard the funniest line of the play – '... you sockdologizing old man-trap!' As the audience predictably erupted in laughter, Booth crept behind Lincoln and shot him in the head. The president's lifeless body slumped forward as Mary Lincoln screamed and Major Henry Rathbone, also in Lincoln's box, sprang up and tried to seize the assassin. Booth stabbed him then leaped onto the stage. His foot, however, became entangled in the flag decorating the box, and he landed badly, fracturing his leg. He stumbled to his feet and held the bloody dagger aloft, saying '*Sic semper tyrannis!*' ('Thus to all tyrants!'), which was (and remains) Virginia's state motto. Booth fled the theater, mounted his waiting horse and galloped off to meet his co-conspirators.

Lincoln never regained consciousness. He was carried across the street to the Petersen House, where he died early the next morning. In a massive manhunt, Booth was hunted down and shot to death less than two weeks later; his alleged co-conspirators, including Mary Surratt, who some claim was innocent, were also discovered, brought to trial and executed on July 7.

The aftermath was devastating for the country. Millions gathered to see the slow funeral procession that carried the president's body from Washington to New York and back to Springfield, IL, where he was buried.

Turn of the American Century

In 1900 Senator James McMillan of Michigan formed an all-star city-planning commission to make over the capital, whose population now surpassed a quarter-million. The McMillan plan effectively revived L'Enfant's vision of a resplendent capital on par with Europe's best

1931

The Great Depression devastates the country. In 1931 Hunger Marchers protest in the capital followed by encampments of 20,000 jobless WWI vets known as the Bonus Army.

1932–35

Roosevelt is elected president. His New Deal programs put people to work, and Washington sees a host of construction projects, including the National Archives and the Supreme Court.

1941–44

The expanding federal government and its wartime bureaucracy lead to another population boom. More big projects are bankrolled, including construction of the Pentagon.

1954

The Supreme Court rules that segregation in public schools is 'inherently unequal' and orders desegregation. The fight to integrate schools spurs the Civil Rights movement.

cities. The plan proposed grand public buildings in the beaux-arts style, which reconnected the city to its neoclassical republican roots, but with an eclectic flair. It was impressive, orderly and upper class. The plan entailed an extensive beautification project. It removed the scrubby trees and coal-fired locomotives that belched black smoke from the National Mall, and created the expansive lawn and reflecting pools that exist today.

The Mall became a showcase of the symbols of American ambition and power: monumental tributes to the founding fathers; the enshrinement of the Declaration of Independence and Constitution in a Greek-style temple; and the majestic Memorial Bridge leading to Arlington National Cemetery. Washington had become the nation's civic center, infused with the spirit of history, heroes and myths. The imagery was embraced by the country's budding political class.

The plan improved living conditions for middle-class public servants and professionals. New 'suburbs,' such as Woodley Park and Mt Pleasant, offered better-off residents a respite from the hot inner city, and electric trolleys crisscrossed the streets. However, the daily life of many Washingtonians was less promising. Slums like Murder Bay and Swamppoodle stood near government buildings, and about 20,000 impoverished blacks still dwelled in dirty alleyways.

Presidential Reads

- *Washington (Ron Chernow)*
- *Thomas Jefferson (RB Bernstein)*
- *Lincoln (David Herbert Donald)*
- *Mornings on Horseback (David McCullough)*
- *The Bridge (David Remnick)*

A World & a City at War

Two world wars and one Great Depression changed forever the place of Washington in American society. These events hastened a concentration of power in the federal government in general and the executive branch in particular. National security and social welfare became the high-growth sectors of public administration. City life transformed from Southern quaintness into cosmopolitan clamor.

WWI witnessed a surge of immigration. The administration of war had an unquenchable thirst for clerks, soldiers, nurses and other military support staff. By war's end, the city's population was over half a million.

The 1920s brought prosperity to Washington and other parts of the country, but the free-spending days wouldn't last. The stock market crash of 1929 heralded the dawn of the Great Depression, the severe economic downturn that had catastrophic implications for many Americans. As more and more lost their jobs and went hungry, people turned to Washington for help. Thousands gathered in Hunger Marches on Washington in 1931 and 1932; they were followed by some 40,000 protesters who set up makeshift camps throughout the city, waiting for Congress to award them cash payment for service certificates issued

1961

The states ratify an amendment to the Constitution that allows DC residents to participate (with three Electoral College votes) in presidential elections.

1963

Martin Luther King Jr leads the Civil Rights march on the National Mall. He delivers his 'I Have a Dream' speech at Lincoln Memorial before a crowd of 200,000.

1968

King is assassinated in Memphis; Washington and other cities erupt in violence. Twelve people are killed in the ensuing riots, with small businesses torched.

1969–71

As the war in Vietnam claims thousands of American lives, many citizens come to Washington to protest. Over 500,000 march in 1969, followed by many more in 1970 and 1971.

in bonds – they became known as the Bonus Army. President J Edgar Hoover ordered the US Army to evacuate them, and the troops attacked their encampments, killing several and wounding hundreds of others.

Franklin D Roosevelt's New Deal extended the reach of the federal government. Federal regulators acquired greater power to intervene in business and financial affairs. Dozens of relief agencies were created to administer the social guarantees of the nascent welfare state. In Washington, New Deal work projects included tree planting on the Mall and the construction of public buildings, notably the massive National Archives and the Supreme Court.

The Great Depression didn't really end until the arrival of WWII, when Washington again experienced enormous growth. A burgeoning organizational infrastructure supported the new national security state. The US Army's city-based civilian employee roll grew from 7000 to 41,000 in the first year of the war. The world's largest office building, the Pentagon, was built across the river as the command headquarters. National Airport (today Ronald Reagan Washington National Airport) opened in 1941.

The Fifties (1993), by David Halberstam, explores an almost schizophrenic era: TV, civil rights, McCarthyism, Elvis Presley, suburbia and more coalesced into the decade that spawned modern America.

Cold War

The Cold War defined much of US foreign – and to some degree, domestic – policy in the decades following WWII. The USA's battle with the USSR was not fought face to face, but through countries including Korea, Vietnam, Cambodia, Mozambique and Afghanistan – all pawns in a geopolitical, economic and ideological battle. Red fever swept the US, as Washington organized witch hunts, like those investigated by the House Un-American Activities Committee (HUAC), which aimed to blacklist communist subversives.

The Cuban Missile Crisis, which took place over 12 days in October 1962, brought the US and the Soviet Union perilously close to nuclear war, and some historians believe that without the effective diplomacy of John F Kennedy and Secretary of State Robert McNamara, the nation would have gone to battle.

During the Cold War, many covert battles were waged on foreign soil. Perhaps the most famous was the Iran-Contra affair in the 1980s, during Ronald Reagan's tenure as president. Staff in his administration, along with the CIA, secretly and illegally sold arms to Iran and then used the proceeds to finance the Contras, an anti-communist guerilla army in Nicaragua.

The Cold War furthered the concentration of political power in Washington-based bureaucracies, a trend that continued in the 1980s.

1974

Five burglars working for President Nixon are arrested breaking into Democratic campaign headquarters at the Watergate Hotel. The ensuing brouhaha leads to Nixon's resignation.

1975

Following the Home Rule Act passed in 1973, disenfranchised Washingtonians are finally given the right to effectively govern themselves. Voters elect Walter Washington.

1976

Metrorail opens to serve the growing suburban community. Despite intense lobbying by the automobile industry, several freeway projects through the city are never realized.

1970s–80s

Washington, like other American cities, enters a period of urban blight. Its population is falling as increased crime rates and social decay drive many residents out into the suburbs.

ESPIONAGE: A CAPITAL GAME

Near the hallowed halls of power, Washington, DC, has long played a role in the subterfuge world of intelligence operations. A few of the darker moments in cloak-and-dagger diplomacy:

On September 21, 1976, the Chilean diplomat Orlando Letelier and his American colleague Ronni Karpen Moffitt were killed by a car bombing in Sheridan Circle. Letelier served as the US ambassador appointed by President Salvador Allende before he was overthrown by General Augusto Pinochet. Several men were convicted for playing a role in the assassination, including the American Michael Townley, a former CIA operative, and Manuel Contreras, Chilean Secret Police Chief – both of whom implicated Pinochet for the role in the killing. Pinochet, who died in 2006, was never brought to justice for the assassination.

In the 1980s, the FBI and the NSA constructed a tunnel under the Russian embassy – right under their decoding room – on Wisconsin Ave. US operatives were never able to successfully eavesdrop, however, owing to a betrayal to the Soviets by FBI agent Robert Hanssen. The embassy, incidentally, is where Vitaly Yurchenko, a former high-ranking KGB operative turned CIA informant, re-defected after giving his CIA handlers the slip in a Georgetown restaurant. The KGB allegedly interrogated Yurchenko after his return, while he was under the influence of a truth serum, to ensure his return was not a CIA ploy.

Some historians suggest that Yurchenko's re-defection was really just a cover to protect one of the USSR's most important CIA informants. Aldrich Ames, a counterintelligence analyst in DC, began supplying secrets to the Soviets in 1985, and continued on a grand scale for some nine years. His betrayal led to the execution of at least 10 Soviet agents spying for the US and compromised scores of operations. In return the Soviets paid him over $4 million. The CIA slowly realized there was a mole in their organization and it took years before Ames was discovered – in part because he fooled several polygraph tests (although the $540,000 Arlington home purchased in cash was a slight tip-off). Ames, who narrowly avoided the death penalty, is serving a life sentence in a Pennsylvania penitentiary.

Segregation & the Civil Rights Movement

In the early 20th century, Washington adopted racial segregation policies, like those of the South. Its business establishments and public spaces became, in practice if not in law, 'whites only.' The 'progressive' Woodrow Wilson administration reinforced discrimination by refusing to hire African American federal employees and insisting on segregated government offices.

Following WWI, decommissioned soldiers returned en masse from the front, bringing to a head festering racial tensions in society. In

1981

Reagan survives an assassination attempt outside the Washington Hilton. The attack permanently disables press secretary James Brady, who becomes a leading advocate for gun control.

1990

In 1990 Mayor Marion Barry is arrested after being videotaped smoking crack. His arrest angers supporters, who decry the FBI 'entrapment.' Barry serves six months in prison.

1992–94

Despite serving a prison term, Marion Barry quickly rejoins Washington political life; he is elected to the city council in 1992, then re-elected as mayor (his fourth term) in 1994.

1998

The Monica Lewinsky scandal breaks, with evidence of nine sexual encounters with the president. Bill Clinton becomes the first president since Andrew Johnson (in 1868) to be impeached.

the steamy summer of 1919, the tinderbox ignited when a white mob marched through the streets attacking at random African American residents with bricks, pipes and, later, guns. In the following two days, whites and African Americans alike mobilized and the violence escalated. President Wilson called in 2000 troops to put an end to the chaos, but by then nine people had been killed (dozens more would die from their wounds) and hundreds injured. It was but a foreshadowing for more chronic race riots in the future.

In response, organized hate groups tried, without much success, to organize in the capital. In 1925 the Ku Klux Klan marched on the Mall. Nonetheless, Washington was an African American cultural capital in the early 20th century. Shaw and LeDroit Park, near Howard University, sheltered a lively African American–owned business district, and African American theater and music flourished along U St NW, which became known as the Great Black Way – Washington's own version of the Harlem Renaissance. Southern African Americans continued to move to the city in search of better economic opportunities. Citywide segregation eased somewhat with the New Deal (which brought new African American federal workers to the capital) and WWII (which brought lots more).

In 1939 the DC-based Daughters of the American Revolution barred the African American contralto Marian Anderson from singing at Constitution Hall. At Eleanor Roosevelt's insistence, Anderson instead sang at the Lincoln Memorial before an audience of 200,000. That was the beginning of the growing movement toward equality – though the process would be long with demonstrations, sit-ins, boycotts and lawsuits.

Parks and recreational facilities were legally desegregated in 1954; schools followed soon thereafter. President John F Kennedy appointed the city's first African American federal commissioner in 1961. The Home Rule Act was approved in 1973, giving the city some autonomy from its federal overseers. The 1974 popular election of Walter Washington brought the first African American mayor to office. The capital became one of the most prominent African American–governed cities in the country.

Washington hosted key events in the national Civil Rights movement. In 1963 Reverend Martin Luther King Jr led the March on Washington to lobby for passage of the Civil Rights Act. His stirring 'I Have a Dream' speech, delivered before 200,000 people on the steps of the Lincoln Memorial, was a defining moment of the campaign. The assassination of King in Memphis in 1968 sent the nation reeling. Race riots erupted in DC – and in over 100 other American cities. The city exploded in two nights of riots and arson (centered on 14th and U Sts NW in the Shaw district). Twelve people died, over 1000 were injured, and

Civil Rights on Film

King (Sidney Lumet)

Mississippi Burning (Alan Parker)

Ghosts of Mississippi (Rob Reiner)

Black Like Me (Carl Lerner)

Long Walk Home (Richard Pearce)

The Help (Tate Taylor)

1999

Barry's fourth term ends following a budgetary crisis inherited from his predecessor. A new Republican-controlled Congress overrules many of the mayor's fiscal decisions.

1999–2007

Washingtonians elect the sober, less-controversial Anthony Williams as the city's fourth mayor. During his two terms he helps restore the city's finances.

2000

Washington's real-estate boom is underway, with gentrification transforming formerly African American neighborhoods. George W Bush is elected president.

2001

Hijacked planes destroy the World Trade Center in New York and crash into the Pentagon. Another, presumed intended for the capital or the White House, crashes in Pennsylvania.

hundreds of mostly African American–owned businesses were torched. White residents fled the city en masse, and downtown Washington north of the Mall (especially the Shaw district) faded into decades of economic slump.

The legacy of segregation proved difficult to overcome. For the next quarter-century, white and African American Washington grew further apart. By 1970 the city center's population declined to 750,000, while the wealthier suburbs boomed to nearly three million. When the sleek, federally funded Metrorail system opened in 1976, it bypassed the poorer African American neighborhoods in favor of linking downtown with the largely white suburbs.

Decay & Decline

President Lyndon Johnson, until then lauded for his ambitious civil rights and social programs, sank his reputation on the disastrous war in Vietnam, which the US had entered in the 1950s. Toward the end of the 1960s hundreds of thousands of Americans had participated in protests against the continuing conflict.

The political upheaval that began in the 1960s continued unchecked into the next decade. The year 1970 marked the first time DC was granted a nonvoting delegate to the House of Representatives. Three years later the Home Rule Act paved the way for the District's first mayoral election in more than a century.

These were two rare positives in an otherwise gloomy decade. The city's most famous scandal splashed across the world's newspapers when operatives of President Richard Nixon were arrested breaking into the Democratic National Committee campaign headquarters at the Watergate Hotel. The ensuing cover-up and Nixon's disgraceful exit was not a shining moment in presidential history.

Meanwhile, life on the streets was no more glorious, as neighborhoods continued to decay; crack cocaine hit District streets with a vengeance and housing projects turned into war zones. By the late 1980s, DC had earned the tagline of 'Murder Capital of America.' In truth, urban blight was hitting most American cities.

Jimmy Carter became president in 1977. A 'malaise' marked his tenure. Gas prices, unemployment and inflation all climbed to all-time highs. The taking of American hostages in Iran in 1979, and his perceived bungling of their release, effectively ended his political career. In November 1980, Ronald Reagan, a former actor and California governor, was elected president.

SUFFRAGETTES

Iron Jawed Angels (2005), starring Hilary Swank, is a moving docu-drama about the struggles of early 20th-century suffragettes facing down the political establishment of Washington, with key events unfolding against the backdrop of Woodrow Wilson's presidency.

2001

The Bush administration oversees an invasion of Afghanistan and later Iraq. The resulting war lasts over a decade, claiming the lives of over 180,000 Iraqis and 6800 Americans.

2002–03

In the run-up to the Iraq invasion, mass protests against the planned war are held in Washington and other cities. An estimated 30 million protesters take part.

2005

As Montréal weeps, Washington receives a new professional baseball team, the Washington Nationals (and former Expos). They eventually move into a custom-built stadium in 2008.

2008–09

Barack Obama becomes the first African American president. An estimated 1.8 million people attend his inauguration.

Reagan, who was ideologically opposed to big government, nevertheless presided over enormous growth of bureaucratic Washington, particularly in the military-industrial complex.

Local politics entered an unusual period when Marion Barry, a veteran of the Civil Rights movement, was elected mayor in 1978. Combative and charismatic, he became a racially polarizing figure in the city. On January 18, 1990, Barry and companion, ex-model Hazel 'Rasheeda' Moore, were arrested in a narcotics sting at the Vista Hotel. The FBI and DC police arrested the mayor for crack-cocaine possession.

When Barry emerged from jail, his supporters, believing he'd been framed, re-elected him to a fourth and lackluster term. As city revenues fell under his term, Congress lost patience and seized control of the city, ending yet another episode in Home Rule.

RACE

In *The Souls of Black Folk* (1903), WEB Du Bois, who helped found the National Association for the Advancement of Colored People (NAACP), eloquently describes the racial dilemmas of politics and culture facing early 20th-century America.

Twenty-First Century

The 2000 presidential election went off with a history-making glitch. On election night, November 7, the media prematurely declared the winner twice, based on exit-poll speculations, before finally concluding that the Florida race outcome was too close to call. It would eventually take a month before the election was officially certified. Numerous court challenges and recounts proceeded, and the Supreme Court eventually intervened, declaring Bush the winner.

Bush's presidency unfolded during the nation's worst terrorist attacks. On September 11, 2001, 30 minutes after the attack on New York's World Trade Center, a plane departing Washington Dulles International Airport was hijacked and crashed into the Pentagon's west side, penetrating the building's third ring. Sixty-six passengers and crew, as well as 125 Pentagon personnel, were killed in the suicide attack.

In the wake of the attack, prominent media and political figures received lethal doses of anthrax in the mail. Several congressional staffers were infected and two DC postal workers died. Though unsolved, the anthrax mailings were eventually attributed to a domestic source.

Meanwhile President Bush's tenure in office was marred by controversy on many fronts. The war in Iraq – launched in 2003 to seize Iraq's (nonexistent) stockpiles of weapons of mass destruction – continued until the end of his second term, and sent the government deeply into debt. Bush was also criticized for the bungling of federal relief efforts to victims of Hurricane Katrina, which devastated New Orleans in 2005.

The 2008 election featured one of the most hotly debated presidential contests in American history. In the end, Barack Obama became the nation's first African American president. Obama had run on a platform

2008–09

The stock market crashes due to catastrophic mismanagement by major American financial institutions. The crisis spreads worldwide.

2010

Despite Congressional attempts to block it, same-sex marriage becomes legal in Washington, DC. The capital joins five other states in legalizing gay marriage.

2011

The Martin Luther King Jr Memorial opens on the Tidal Basin. It's the first memorial in the Mall area dedicated to a non-president and to an African American.

2011

A magnitude 5.8 earthquake strikes the East Coast. No one was killed, though the quake causes millions of dollars in damages to the Washington Monument and National Cathedral.

of hope and change in an era of increasingly divisive American politics. Following the financial meltdown in 2008, the Obama administration pumped money into the flailing economy. He also took on the growing crisis in Afghanistan, although his biggest challenge – an issue that some analysts say he's staked his presidency on – is the complicated issue of health-care reform.

Obama's second term saw the country emerge from the Great Recession, as the president presided over a growing economy, rock-bottom gas prices and low unemployment. However, Congress put the screws on the federal budget cutting spending and slashing jobs in the city. It also continued to meddle in Washington, DC's affairs (p239).

The film *Recount* (2008) dramatizes the events of the hotly contested 2000 US presidential election, including the issues surrounding voter fraud and disenfranchisement in Florida.

2014

Voters in Washington, DC, vote to legalize marijuana use by adults. Despite approval by 70% of the voters, Congress swoops in and blocks the law.

2014

DC's Metrorail opens its new Silver Line, an 11.7-mile stretch with five new stops, including Tysons Corner. Work continues on the line, which will eventually reach Dulles International Airport.

2015

Once a no-go area for most Washingtonians, southeast DC experiences a boom, with high-rises, restaurants, waterfront green space, a massive brewery and a ballpark fueling growth.

2016

The National Museum of African American History and Culture is scheduled to open on the Mall. The museum celebrates wide-ranging achievements and remember hard-fought struggles.

Arts & Media

Washington has made no small contribution to the American arts, courtesy of hometown musical legends like Duke Ellington, John Fahey and Marvin Gaye. In the literary world, Washington luminaries include Frederick Douglass, Henry Adams and Gore Vidal, all of whom captured a unique moment of American history. Speaking of history, DC's journalists and news organizations continue to break new ground in one of the great media capitals of the world. And for something lighter, DC's cinematic backdrop has featured prominently in disaster films, political sagas and spy thrillers.

Music

Washington Playlist

'DC Sleeps Alone Tonight' (Postal Service)

'Chocolate City' (Parliament)

'Idiot Wind' (Bob Dylan)

'Washington, DC' (Magnetic Fields)

'Rock Creek Park' (The Blackbyrds)

Only in the capital can national orchestras coexist with rebellious punk, all under the rubric of the local music scene. That military marches and soulful go-go both reached their peaks under the watchful eye (and attentive ear) of DC fans is tribute to the city's eclectic musical landscape.

In the early 20th century, segregation of entertainment venues meant that black Washington had to create its own arts scene. Jazz, big band and swing flourished at clubs and theaters around DC, particularly in the Shaw district. Greats such as Duke Ellington, Pearl Bailey, Shirley Horn, Johnny Hodges and Ben Webster all got their start in the clubs of U St NW. Today, this district has been reborn, with new clubs and theaters open in its historic buildings. After years of neglect, the renowned Bohemian Caverns reopened in 2000, and today hosts local soul-jazz music. Other venues in the area – such as the Black Cat and the 9:30 Club – have become mainstays of DC rock, blues and hip-hop.

The scene at these venues is varied, but not unique to DC. The exception is where it builds on its local roots in go-go and punk. Go-go, which stomped into the city in the 1970s, is an infectiously rhythmic dance music combining elements of funk, rap, soul and Latin percussion. These days, go-go soul blends with hip-hop and reggae's rhythm. Clubs playing 1980s dance, and lounges with mellow house and trance, are equally popular.

DC's hardcore take on punk, embodied by such bands as Fugazi and Dag Nasty, combined super-fast guitar with a socially conscious mindset and flourished at venues in the 1990s. Arlington-based Dischord Records grew out of the punk scene and remains a fierce promoter of local bands. While punk is no longer the musical force it once was, its influence on grunge and other modern genres is undeniable.

Showing off its southern roots, DC has spawned some folk and country stars of its own, too, including Emmylou Harris, Mary Chapin Carpenter and John Fahey (who named his seminal folk record label, Takoma, for Takoma Park, his boyhood home).

The immensely talented Marvin Gaye was born in Washington and delved into music early on, singing in a church choir and performing with local groups before his discovery in a DC nightclub by Bo Diddley when he was 19. He later signed on with Motown records and created some of the unsurpassed hits of the 1960s and '70s, including 'What's Going On?,' 'Let's Get It On' and 'Sexual Healing.' His tumultuous life

THE DUKE

'My road runs from Ward's Place to my grandmother's at Twentieth and R, to Seatan Street, around to 8th Street, back up to T Street, through LeDroit Park to Sherman Avenue,' wrote DC's most famous musical son, jazz immortal Edward Kennedy 'Duke' Ellington (1899–1974), describing his childhood in Washington's Shaw district. In the segregated DC of the early 20th century, Shaw hosted one of the country's finest black arts scenes – drawing famed actors, musicians and singers to perform at venues such as the Howard Theatre and Bohemian Caverns – so the Duke took root in rich soil.

As a tot, Ellington purportedly first tackled the keyboard under the tutelage of a teacher by the name of Mrs Clinkscales. He honed his chops by listening to local ragtime pianists such as Doc Perry, Louis Thomas and Louis Brown at Frank Holliday's T St poolroom. His first composition, written at 16, was the 'Soda Fountain Rag'; next came 'What You Gonna Do When the Bed Breaks Down?' The handsome, suave young Duke played hops and cabarets all over black Washington before decamping to New York in 1923.

There, Ellington started out as a Harlem stride pianist, performing at Barron's and the Hollywood Club, but he soon moved to the famed Cotton Club, where he matured into an innovative bandleader, composer and arranger. He collaborated with innumerable artists, including Louis Armstrong and Ella Fitzgerald, but his most celebrated collaboration was with composer-arranger Billy Strayhorn, who gave the Ellington Orchestra its theme, 'Take the "A" Train,' in 1941.

Ellington's big-band compositions, with their infectious melodies, harmonic sophistication and ever-present swing, made him one of the 20th century's most revered American composers. His huge volume of work – more than 1500 pieces – is preserved in its entirety at the Smithsonian Institution in his old hometown.

For more on the Duke, check out his witty memoir *Music Is My Mistress*, which details his DC childhood and later accomplishments.

led him into troubles with drugs and the IRS (he lived in Belgium for a time), and in and out of marriages. During an argument following his return home, he was shot and killed by his father one day before his 45th birthday on April 1, 1984.

Popular African American R & B and soul artist Roberta Flack was raised in Arlington, VA. Before establishing her music career, she was the first black student teacher in an all-white school in posh Chevy Chase, MD. She was discovered at a respected Capitol Hill jazz club, Mr Henry's, where the owners eventually constructed an elaborate stage for her.

Cinema

Hollywood directors can't resist the black limousines, white marble, counterintelligence subterfuges and political scandal that official Washington embodies.

One of Hollywood's favorite Washington themes involves the political naïf who stumbles into combat with corrupt capital veterans. Such is the story of the Frank Capra film *Mr Smith Goes to Washington*, in which Jimmy Stewart and his troop of 'Boy Rangers' defeat big, bad government and preserve democracy for the rest of the country. This theme reappears in the 1950 hit *Born Yesterday*, as well as in *Dave*, *Legally Blonde 2* and *Being There*.

Another popular theme for DC-based cinema is the total destruction of the nation's capital by aliens (perhaps wishful thinking on the part of certain segments of the population). Along these lines, *2012*, *Independence*, *The Day the Earth Stood Still*, the spoof *Mars Attacks!* and the Cold War–era *Earth Vs the Flying Saucers* all feature DC on the edge of destruction.

Must-See DC Cinema

- *Mr Smith Goes to Washington*
- *All the President's Men*
- *The Exorcist*
- *Good Night, and Good Luck*
- *Being There*

Not surprisingly, DC is a popular setting for political thrillers: *In the Line of Fire* (Clint Eastwood as a savvy Secret Service agent protecting the president), *Patriot Games* (Harrison Ford as a tough CIA agent battling Irish terrorists) and *No Way Out* (Kevin Costner as a Navy officer out-racing Russian spies) are entertaining stories set against – sometimes erroneously placed – DC landmarks.

The first few seasons of *The West Wing*, which starred Martin Sheen as the beneficent, liberal president ('the best president we've ever had,' fans claimed), when Alan Sorkin was writing for the show, were truly brilliant and are well worth renting on DVD.

The finest satire of the Cold War is probably Stanley Kubrick's 1964 *Dr Strangelove*. Set inside the Pentagon, the plot revolves around a power-mad general who brings the world to the brink of annihilation because he fears a communist takeover of his 'precious bodily fluids.'

Real-life intrigue has been the subject of a handful of DC films, including the 1976 *All the President's Men,* which is based on Carl Bernstein's and Bob Woodward's firsthand account of exposing the Watergate scandal (Robert Redford and Dustin Hoffman play the reporters).

In 2005 George Clooney directed and starred in *Good Night, and Good Luck*. Shot in black and white, it is a stark account of how CBS reporter Edward R Murrow and his producer Fred W Friendly took on the widely feared red-baiting American senator Joseph McCarthy.

Curiously, films featuring a character in the form of a US president typically depict him with absurd idealism: *Air Force One, The American President* and *Thirteen Days* are all rather fanciful portraits of a good, if not downright heroic, Chief Executive. Variations on the theme include *Primary Colors,* a barely disguised account of Clinton en route to the White House, and the parody *Wag the Dog,* a story of a presidential advisor (Robert De Niro) who hires a Hollywood producer (Dustin Hoffman) to 'produce' a war in order to distract voters from an unfolding sex scandal. Bizarrely, the film was released just a month before the Clinton-Lewinsky affair became headline news.

Only a select few films set in Washington, DC, are not about politics, espionage or cataclysmic destruction. The horrific highlight is undoubtedly *The Exorcist,* the cult horror flick set in Georgetown. The creepy long staircase in the movie – descending from Prospect St to M St in reality – has become known as the Exorcist Stairs. Another classic Georgetown movie is the 1980s brat-pack flick *St Elmo's Fire*. Demi Moore's and Judd Nelson's characters are supposed to be Georgetown graduates, but the college campus is actually the University of Maryland in College Park.

FILM

Slam, a 1998 docudrama, is a story about Ray Joshua, a gifted young (and jobless) MC trapped in a war-zone DC housing project known as Dodge City. Ray copes with the despair and poverty of his neighborhood by creating haunting poetry.

Film fans who want the lowdown on every movie ever shot in DC should read *DC Goes to the Movies* by Jean K Rosales and Michael R Jobe.

Over the years, DC has served as the backdrop to numerous TV series, including *House of Cards, Murphy Brown, The West Wing, Commander in Chief* and, less gloriously, *The Real Housewives of DC.*

Literature

Washington's literary legacy is, not surprisingly, deeply entwined with US political history. The city's best-known early literature consists of writings and books that hammered out the machinery of US democracy. From Thomas Jefferson's *Notes on the State of Virginia* to James Madison's *The Federalist Papers* and Abraham Lincoln's historic speeches and proclamations, this literature fascinates modern readers – not only because it is the cornerstone of the US political system, but because of the grace and beauty of its prose.

In the 19th century, Washington outsiders – who came here by circumstance, professional obligation or wanderlust – made notable contributions to the city's oeuvre. Walt Whitman's 'The Wound Dresser' and *Specimen Days* and Louisa May Alcott's *Hospital Sketches* were based on the authors' harrowing experiences as Civil War nurses at Washington's hospitals. Mark Twain had an ill-starred (and short) career as a senator's speechwriter, memorialized in *Washington in 1868*.

Frederick Douglass (1818–95), the abolitionist, editor, memoirist and former slave, is one of Washington's most respected writers. His seminal antislavery works *The Life & Times of Frederick Douglass* and *My Bondage & My Freedom* were written in DC, where Douglass lived on Capitol Hill and in Anacostia.

Henry Adams (1838–1918), grandson of President John Adams, often invited DC's literati to salons at his mansion on Lafayette Sq, which became the literary center of the day. His brilliant *Democracy* was the forerunner of many political-scandal novels of the 20th century. His later autobiography, *The Education of Henry Adams,* provides a fascinating insider's account of Washington high society during this period.

In DC, the Harlem Renaissance is sometimes called the New Negro Movement, named after the famous volume by Howard University professor Alain Locke. *The New Negro* – the bible of the Renaissance – is a collection of essays, poems and stories written by Locke and his colleagues. The writing is energetic and subversive; as a snapshot of the Renaissance and the African American experience it is invaluable.

In the early 20th century, a literary salon took root at 15th and S Sts in Shaw. Artists and writers often gathered here, at poet Georgia Douglas Johnson's home, which became the center of the Harlem Renaissance in DC. Her guests included African American poets Langston Hughes and Paul Dunbar.

Throughout the 20th century, Washington literature remained a deeply political beast, defined by works such as Carl Bernstein's and Bob Woodward's *All the President's Men* (1974).

Native Washingtonian Gore Vidal often aims his satirical pieces squarely at his hometown. His six-volume series of historical novels about the American past includes *Washington, DC* (1967), an insightful examination of the period from the New Deal to the McCarthy era from the perspective of the capital.

Advise and Consent (1959) is Allen Drury's fictional account of Alger Hiss' nomination as Secretary of State under Franklin D Roosevelt. The novel brilliantly portrays the conflicting personal and political motivations of his characters – an eye-opening revelation of what goes on inside the US Senate.

Many more purely literary writers have appeared on the scene, too. Edward P Jones does a superb job of capturing the streets, sounds and sights of DC. His collection of stories *Lost in the City* (1992) is set in inner-city DC in the 1960s and 1970s, and portrays a raw and very real city, with characters grappling with the complexities of American life.

Marita Golden writes about contemporary African American families dealing with betrayal and loss. *The Edge of Heaven* (1997) is about an accomplished 20-year-old student who must face uncomfortable truths following her mother's release from prison.

For a more frightful side of Washington, check out Tim Krepp's *Capitol Hill Haunts* (2012), which delves into tales of ghosts and specters that are believed to roam certain parts of the city.

On a less elevated note, DC has also inspired hundreds of potboilers. Tom Clancy, a northern Virginia resident and creator of innumerable right-wing thrillers, has featured Washington in books such as *Debt of Honor* (1994) and *Executive Orders* (1996). Meanwhile, Dan Brown's *The Lost Symbol* (2009) brings his Harvard 'symbologist' to the nation's capital on a suspenseful – if formulaic – journey into the secrets of DC's coded (Freemason-filled) history.

Media

Widely read and widely respected, the daily *Washington Post* is considered one of the nation's top newspapers. Its competitor, the *Washington Times,* is owned by the Unification Church and provides a more conservative perspective. The national newspaper *USA Today* is based across the Potomac in Arlington, VA. Several TV programs are

For a look at the Washington punk scene of the 1970s and '80s, check out *Banned in DC*, a colorful photo book by Cynthia Connolly.

also based in DC, including the PBS *NewsHour* with longtime host Jim Lehrer and all of the major networks' Sunday-morning news programs.

Also based in DC is National Public Radio (NPR), the most respected nonprofit, free-radio network in the nation. Popular shows include *Morning Edition, All Things Considered* and *The Diane Rehm Show*. NPR's offices are in the heart of the downtown redevelopment project. Another key Washington media organization is Politico (www.politico.com), which keeps its audience informed of breaking political stories via its free newspaper, radio show and website.

Washington has some excellent sources of independent media. The *City Paper* (www.washingtoncitypaper.com) keeps an alternative but informed eye on local politics and trends. Another valuable source for local and national events is the DC Independent Media Center (www.dcindymedia.org). Smaller rags filled with juicy Hill gossip include the *Hill* (www.hillnews.com) and *Roll Call* (www.rollcall.com).

For some amusing but decidedly left-wing political cartoon humor, check out www.markfiore.com. The Pulitzer Prize–winning artist, whose work has appeared in newspapers across the country, pens weekly animated skits that take aim at the Washington ruling elite.

Architecture

Washington's architecture and city design are the products of its founding fathers and city planners, who intended to construct a capital city befitting a powerful nation. The early architecture of Washington, DC, was shaped by two influences: Pierre Charles L'Enfant's 1791 city plan, and the infant nation's desire to prove to European powers that its capital possessed political and artistic sophistication rivaling the ancient, majestic cities of the Continent.

L'Enfant Plan & Federal Period

The L'Enfant plan imposed a street grid marked by diagonal avenues, roundabouts and grand vistas. L'Enfant had in mind the magisterial boulevards of Europe. To highlight the primacy of the city's political buildings, he intended that no building would rise higher than the Capitol. This rule rescued DC from the dark, skyscraper-filled fate of most modern American cities.

In an effort to rival European cities, Washington's early architects – many of them self-taught 'gentlemen architects' – depended heavily upon the Classic Revival and Romantic Revival styles, with their ionic columns and marble facades. Federal-style row houses dominated contemporary domestic architecture and still line the streets of Capitol Hill and Georgetown.

Design hounds shouldn't miss Architecture Week, when you can get behind-the-scenes tours of captivating buildings. It's held over 10 days in late April. Visit aiadc.com/ArchitectureWeek for more info.

Other fine examples from the Federal period are the Sewall-Belmont house and the uniquely shaped Octagon Museum. The colonnaded Treasury Building, built by Robert Mills in the mid-19th century, represented the first major divergence from the L'Enfant plan, as it blocked the visual line between the White House and the Capitol. Mills also designed the stark, simple Washington Monument, another architectural anomaly and not only because it is 555ft high, taller than the Capitol. Later, other styles would soften the lines of the cityscape, with creations such as the French-inspired Renwick Gallery, designed by James Renwick.

McMillan Plan

At the turn of the 20th century, the McMillan plan (1901–02) revived many elements of the L'Enfant plan. It restored public spaces downtown, lent formal lines to the Mall and Capitol grounds, and added more classically inspired buildings. During this period, John Russell Pope built the Scottish Rite Masonic Temple, which was modeled after the mausoleum at Halicarnassus, as well as the National Archives. Here are some of the best examples of this eclectic French-inspired design that has become so emblematic of Washingtonian architecture:

Historical Society of Washington, DC Built with funds donated by Andrew Carnegie, the former main public library of DC occupies a majestic position at the center of Mount Vernon Sq.

Corcoran Gallery of Art The Corcoran was once described by Frank Lloyd Wright as 'the best designed building in Washington, DC.' Fittingly, this grand building houses one of the nation's oldest art museums.

AMBASSADORIAL ARCHITECTURE & ANECDOTES

Some of Washington's most interesting buildings, by dint of design or history, are its embassies (p144), mainly concentrated in the Dupont Circle area and Upper Northwest DC. Note that you'll generally have to appreciate these buildings from the outside.

Indonesian Embassy (2020 Massachusetts Ave NW) The extravagant 61-room former mansion of 19th-century gold-mining baron Thomas Walsh was built in a curving neo-baroque style, and originally contained a slab of gold ore embedded in the front porch. Not one for subtlety, Walsh once threw a New Year's Eve party where 325 guests knocked back 480 quarts of champagne, 288 fifths of Scotch, 48 quarts of cocktails, 40 gallons of beer and 35 bottles of miscellaneous liqueurs (according to a piece in the *New York Times*).

Embassy of Italy Chancery (3000 Whitehaven St NW) This odd, starkly geometric structure was actually fashioned to resemble the original 10-sq-mile plan of the District itself – its layout a giant diamond cut by a glass atrium, meant to represent the curving Potomac.

Danish Embassy (3200 Whitehaven St NW) Stark and simple, this 1960 modernist building, designed by Vilhelm Lauritzen, provides a dramatic counterpoint to a city of sometimes overwrought beaux-arts design.

Finnish Embassy (3301 Massachusetts Ave NW) This sleek and modern building embodies the design principles of famed Finnish architect Alvar Aalto. Designed by Mikko Heikkinen and Markku Komonen, the constructivist, ivy-clad design features a glass wall that juts over Rock Creek Park.

Embassy of Bangladesh Chancery (3510 International Dr NW) Because water is such an important feature of the Bangladeshi landscape, the inverted roof gable atop this innovative structure is meant to resemble a water lily, while the interior, composed of different grades of slate and other materials, evokes a riverbed.

Embassy of Brunei Darussalam (3520 International Ct NW) With its post-and-beam construction and pitched roof, this deceptively modern-looking embassy is inspired by the rustic designs of traditional houses in Brunei Darussalam (a sultanate in Southeast Asia) – simple stilt structures built over water.

Meridian International Center A limestone chateau by John Russell Pope.
Willard InterContinental Hotel Grand beaux-arts hotel that has hosted high-society guests for over a century.
Union Station The archetypical example of the neoclassical beauty and grandeur of beaux arts during the age of railroads.

Conspiracy theories abound about the secret symbols planted in the nation's capital by its masonic architects. The evidence: draw lines along the avenues between major DC points and you get key Masonic symbols – the pentagram, square and compass. For more, read *The Secrets of Masonic Washington* by James Wasserman.

WWII to the Present

Classicism came to a screaming halt during and after WWII, when war workers flooded the city. Temporary offices were thrown onto the Mall and new materials that were developed during wartime enabled the construction of huge office blocks. Slum clearance after the war – particularly in southwest DC – meant the wholesale loss of old neighborhoods in favor of brutalist concrete boxes, such as the monolithic government agencies that currently dominate the ironically named L'Enfant Plaza.

Washington architecture today is of uncertain identity. Many new buildings, particularly those downtown, pay homage to their classical neighbors while striving toward a sleeker, postmodern monumentalism.

A handful of world-renowned architects have left examples of their work in the city. The National Gallery of Art is a perfect example. Franklin D Roosevelt opened the original building, designed by John Russell Pope, in March 1941. Now called the West Building, Pope's symmetrical, neoclassical gallery overwhelms the eye at first glimpse. Two wings lacking external windows stretch for 400ft on either side of the main floor's massive central rotunda, which has a sky-high dome supported by 24 black ionic columns. In the center are vaulted corridors leading off to each wing, which end with an internal skylight and fountain and a plant-speckled garden court.

The East Building of the gallery is perhaps even more spectacular. Designed in 1978 by IM Pei, the ethereal structure is all straight lines that create a triangular shape. The building design was initially difficult to conceive, as Pei was given a strange-shaped block of land between 3rd and 4th Sts. He solved the problem by making only the marble walls permanent. The rest of the internal structure can be shaped at will, according to the size of various temporary exhibitions. The design is striking, resembling the Louvre in Paris, with pyramidal skylights rising out of the ground (look up from the ground floor of the museum and you'll see a glassed-in waterfall).

Other famous buildings include Mies van der Rohe's Martin Luther King Jr Memorial Library and Eero Saarinen's Washington Dulles International Airport.

The architecture of this unique city tells much about American political ideals and their occasionally awkward application to reality. The National Mall of today is a perfect example. The western half contains a mix of sleek modern creations and neoclassical marble temples disguised as memorials. The eastern side is an entirely different story, a mishmash of sometimes awesome and sometimes appalling architecture.

One of the most successful 21st-century designs to grace the Mall is the National Museum of the American Indian, which opened in 2004. Designed by Canadian architect and Native North American Douglas Cardinal, it is a curving, almost undulating building with a rough-hewn Kasota limestone facade that references the natural wind- and rain-sculpted rock formations of the Southwest. The museum's garden has over 150 different species of plants and wildflowers that are native to the Atlantic coastal plain and the Appalachian Mountains, which add to the element of naturalism in the building and its landscape.

Other key designs on the horizon include the National Museum of African American History and Culture, a striking 374,000-sq-foot space modeled on the Yoruban aesthetic of a tripartite column or a three-tiered crown. Geometrical and bronze-clad panels give the building a dynamic quality, as does other thoughtful elements like an internal waterfall and the uplifting sculptural tilt of the roof.

Ugliest Structures in Town?

J Edgar Hoover Building (935 Pennsylvania Ave NW)

Department of Labor Building (200 Constitution Ave NW)

HUD Federal Building (451 7th St SW)

Lauinger Library (Georgetown University)

Department of Energy Building (1000 Independence Ave SW)

This Political City

It's hard to escape from politics in Washington. While LA attracts wannabe filmmakers and actors, and New York draws creative and financial types, DC draws folks wanting to be close to the corridors of power. So banter at cafes, restaurants and bars – at least downtown – tends to revolve around the latest gossip of Capitol Hill or the White House.

The Political Vortex

Even those who have no professed interest in politics can't help but follow the decisions – which often have national or even global implications – being made just up the road. (You won't find many other cities where such a large number of cab drivers listen to NPR.)

Americans vote most of their leaders into office, but not the president. Instead, they vote indirectly through the Electoral College. It is the College and its electors who actually pick the president every four years. This ensures geographically fair elections: even the small states can command election attention.

Power, it must be said, has enormous appeal, which is perhaps why Washington exerts such a palpable buzz. It draws the best and brightest, from congressional staffers and foreign diplomats to policy analysts at think tanks, NGOs and the World Bank, to name but a few of many important offices headquartered here – every one contributing to the political pageantry in all its glory and shame.

Hand in hand with power comes corruption, and Washingtonians love a good scandal (particularly if it's happening to those who belong to the other party). And there's rarely a dull news day in this town. Congressional brawls, egregious abuses of power – and, of course, the mother lode: sexual scandals – are all par for the course in the ever-changing news cycle of US politics.

Not surprisingly, the denigration of federal politicians is a widely practiced pursuit – being called a Washington insider, after all, can ruin a career. Amid the current climate of anti-government sentiment – and the scandals that help fuel the resentment – sometimes it's easy to forget the momentous events precipitated by legislators, judges and presidents. Ending slavery, creating jobs during the darkest days of the Great Depression, sending astronauts to the moon, putting an end to institutionalized racial discrimination: all the work of so-called Washington insiders. US government at work is a messy business, but at times it has brought dramatic changes for the better to the lives of its citizens.

Understanding US Politics: Separation of Powers

Everyone knows Americans do things differently – spelling, measuring, sports – and the democratic process is no exception.

'What's the difference?' The best answer probably comes from journalist HL Mencken, who summed up many Americans' feelings toward a nanny state: 'The urge to save humanity is almost always a false face for the urge to rule it.' Americans are by and large paranoid about their government. The entire country was founded by anti-authoritarian colonists, while the Civil War was fought over how much power

WASHINGTON'S SITES OF SCANDAL

Washington media loves a good takedown. Here is a list of a few ill-fated sites where some of the big stories began:

The Gate of Gates: Watergate Towering over the Potomac, this chi-chi apartment-hotel complex has lent its name to decades of political crime. It all started when Committee to Re-Elect the President operatives were found here, trying to bug Democratic National Committee headquarters; it ended with President Nixon's resignation.

Swimming for It: Tidal Basin In 1974 Wilbur Mills, 65-year-old Arkansas representative and chairman of the House Ways & Means Committee, was stopped for speeding, whereupon his companion – 38-year-old stripper Fanne Foxe, known as the 'Argentine Firecracker' – leapt into the Basin to escape. Unfortunately for Mills' political career, a TV cameraman was there to film it.

Smoking Crack with Barry: The Westin City Center (Formerly the Vista Hotel) It was in Room 727 that former DC mayor Marion Barry uttered his timeless quote: '...set up...bitch set me up!' when the FBI caught him taking a puff of crack cocaine in the company of ex-model (and police informant) Hazel 'Rasheeda' Moore. The widely broadcast FBI video of his toke horrified a city lacerated by crack violence, but didn't stop it from re-electing Barry in 1994.

Death in the Park: Fort Marcy Park The body of Vince Foster, deputy counsel to President Bill Clinton and Hillary Clinton, was found with a gunshot wound to the head in this remote McLean, VA, park in 1993. Investigations by the Park Police and the FBI determined that the death was a suicide, but conspiracy theories still proliferate among right-wing pundits.

Stool Pigeon Sushi: Pentagon City Food Court It was by the sushi bar that Monica Lewinsky awaited Linda Tripp, her lunch date (and betrayer), who led Ken Starr's agents down the mall escalators to snag her up for questioning in the nearby Ritz-Carlton Hotel in 1998.

What's Your Position, Congressman?: Capitol Steps John Jenrette was a little-known South Carolina representative until he embroiled himself in a bribery scandal. Jenrette's troubles were compounded when his ex-wife Rita revealed in a 1981 issue of *Playboy* (in which she also posed nude) that she and her erstwhile husband used to slip out during dull late-night congressional sessions for an alfresco quickie on the Capitol's hallowed marble steps. The comedy group Capitol Steps takes its name from this famous frolic.

Washington, DC, could exert over the states (among other things). Obsessed with keeping government in check, the founding fathers devised a system that disperses power through three branches that keep each other in check.

You can visit those branches starting on Capitol Hill, where the legislative branch, better known as Congress, convenes. Put simply, Congress writes laws. There are two bodies assigned to this task: the House of Representatives and the Senate. In the House, there are 435 voting representatives, which are allotted proportionally by state population – Wyoming, the least populous state, has one, and California, with the largest population, has 53. There are 100 senators: two for each state, a way of giving smaller states equal footing with more populous ones. Congress not only writes laws, it can also impeach the president, determine the jurisdictional limits of courts and vote out its own members.

Behind the Capitol dome is the Supreme Court, whose 12 justices are appointed by the president to life terms. The court's job is to determine how true to the Constitution laws are. Arguably the weakest branch, it nonetheless has a crucial role in the democratic process. While the public face of many causes in the USA are crowds of protesters, actual change is often practically effected through the courts, from the Supreme Court on down. This was the case with the Scopes Trial, which allowed evolution to be taught in public schools, the African American Civil Rights movement and the continuing bid for gay marriage.

A little way down Pennsylvania Ave sits the White House, where the president heads the executive branch. Unlike a prime minister, the president is both head of state and head of government, and possesses the power to veto (override) Congress' bills, pardon criminals, and appoint a cabinet, judges and ambassadors.

While the powers are separated, they are not isolated from each other. The founding fathers figured that each branch's ability to check its partners would generate a healthy tension. This uneasy equality makes compromise a necessity for movement on issues, and it is the true bedrock of US politics.

The Media & Washington

It's hard to imagine an area that packs so many journalists into such a small space. Politics is a game of public perception, and the gatekeepers of that opinion are the media. Politicians – even the ones who publicly lambaste journalists – must maintain a working relationship with the press corps. On the other hand, reporters must ostensibly be merciless, brutally honest and somehow removed from the politicians they cover. In reality, to gain access to the sources they require for their stories, relationships are forged between profiler and profiled.

And Washington can be a bubble. The same faces appear in the same hearings and conferences day after day, at lunches, after-work drinks and lectures. Politicians (although they'd rarely admit it) often become closer to reporters than their own constituents, and good journalism sometimes suffers as a result.

FACT CHECK

Suspicious of political factoids? So are we – particularly during political elections. Turn to bipartisan www.factcheck.org to help discern truth from 'truthiness.'

Lobbyists

'Lobbyist' is one of the dirtiest words in the American political lexicon, yet its meaning is fairly innocuous. Essentially, a lobbyist is someone who makes a living advocating special interests. This isn't Europe, where causes form their own party and seek power through a parliamentary coalition (though there are lobbyists there, too, of course). Here the agenda-pushers directly thrust their message onto elected officials.

Lobbying is traditionally dated to the late 19th century, but it took off as a vital component of US politics during the money-minded 1980s. Most politicos see lobbyists as a necessary evil, and while it's the rare politician who admits to being influenced by them, everyone understands their importance: lobbyists are the go-betweens in a city built on client-patron relationships. For better or worse, they have become a vital rung on DC's power ladder.

Labor unions and tree-huggers, gun nuts and industrialists; every group gets its say here through the work of well-paid and connected advocates. Lobbying ranks, largely based on K St (to the point that the two terms are synonymous), are swelled by those who know how to navigate the complex social webs of the capital; some watchdogs estimate as many as 40% of former congresspeople rejoin the private sector as lobbyists. In a city where getting anything done is often based on personal relationships, a lobbyist can be worth far more than, say, an embassy with rotating staff. Indeed, many countries keep embassies for ritual value and leave the real legwork of diplomacy to DC lobbying firms.

MALL OF JUSTICE

The National Mall has long provided a forum for people seeking to make their grievances heard by the government. Suffragists, veterans, peaceniks, civil-rights activists, sharecroppers and Million Mom Marchers, among many other groups, have all staged political rallies on the Mall over the years. Among the key events in history:

Bonus Army (1932) WWI veterans, left unemployed by the Great Depression, petitioned the government for an early payment of promised bonuses for their wartime service. As many as 10,000 veterans settled in for an extended protest, pitching tents on the Mall and the Capitol lawn. President Hoover dispatched Douglas MacArthur to evict the 'Bonus Army,' the violence of which helped cement Hoover's reputation as an uncaring president.

'I Have a Dream' (1963) At the zenith of the Civil Rights movement, Reverend Martin Luther King's stirring speech, delivered from the steps of the Lincoln Memorial to 200,000 supporters, remains a high point in the struggle for racial equality.

Anti-War Protests (1971) In April 1971 an estimated 500,000 Vietnam veterans and students gathered on the Mall to oppose continued hostilities. Several thousand arrests were made.

AIDS Memorial Quilt (1996) Gay and lesbian activists drew more than 300,000 supporters in a show of solidarity for equal rights under the law and to display the ever-growing AIDS quilt, which covered the entire eastern flank of the Mall from the Capitol to the Washington Monument.

Million Mom March (2000) A half-million people convened on the Mall on Mother's Day to draw attention to handgun violence and to demand that Congress pass stricter gun-ownership laws.

Bring Them Home Now Tour (2005) Led by families who lost loved ones in the war, this gathering of over 100,000 protesters demanded the withdrawal of American soldiers from Iraq.

Rally to Restore Sanity and/or Fear (2010) Comedians Jon Stewart and Stephen Colbert gathered some 200,000 to oppose the trend of radicalization in politics – and a counterpoint to Glenn Beck's conservative Rally to Restore Honor held a few months earlier.

Wining, dining, vacation packages and the art of giving all of the above without violating campaign contribution laws is a delicate dance. Every year legislation is introduced to keep lobbyists off the floor of Congress (figuratively and sometimes literally), but lobbyists are probably too ingrained in the political landscape to ever be completely removed from it.

Democracy in Action

One of the great paradoxes of US politics is how simultaneously accessible and impenetrable the system is. Visitors can walk into congressional hearings dressed in jeans and a T-shirt and address their elected representatives, in public, with minimal security screening. Mass protests have rocked the foundations of government and seared themselves on the national psyche forever. Yet most of the decisions that influence US government are made between small groups of well-connected policy wonks, lobbyists and special interests who are mainly concerned with perpetuating their own organizations.

Many Americans believe changing the system requires going to DC and coming face to face with their elected officials (there's even a cinematic subgenre devoted to the idea, from *Mr Smith Goes to Washington* to *Legally Blonde 2*). On a grand scale, the equation is partly true. Large protests, often held on the National Mall, can shift public perception a few points toward a particular cause. But smaller delegations usually require lots of money and clout to effect change.

It's maddening, but the surface of the process is surprisingly open to travelers. Check www.house.gov and www.senate.gov to get the schedules for congressional committee hearings.

Comical Political Reads

America: A Citizen's Guide to Democracy Inaction (Jon Stewart)

America Again: Re-Becoming the Greatness We Never Weren't (Stephen Colbert)

Parliament of Whores (PJ O'Rourke)

How to Fight Presidents (Daniel O'Brien)

Current Issues

US politics remains ever divided, with Republicans and Democrats rarely seeing eye to eye. The role of government is at the center of the ideological divide: those on the right believe fewer taxes, lower deficits and a smaller government will help spur economic growth, while those on the left believe government should take an active role in spending and in maintaining a social safety net.

One thing they do agree on, however, is the enormous challenges the US still faces. This despite the fact that things appeared to be on the up-and-up. The US economic crisis (the so-called Great Recession) that erupted in 2007 was largely disappearing into the distance by early 2015. Unemployment was down below 6%, the economy was growing (at a respectable 2.4% for 2014) and petrol prices were at an all-time low (below $2 per gallon in many parts of the country).

But the gulf between rich and poor was growing ever wider and for most Americans (today, the top 0.1% are now worth more than the entire bottom 90% of the US population). Wages had stagnated. Seeing little improvement in their own personal finances, many Americans remained pessimistic about the future. How to restore American confidence and address the widening chasm between the ultra-wealthy and everyone else remains one of the hot-button topics of today.

The question of health care is another pivotal talking point in Washington. Obama's health-care bill (the Affordable Care Act, nicknamed 'Obamacare'), which became law in 2010, aims to bring health care to more Americans, lower its cost and close loopholes that allowed insurance companies to deny coverage to individuals. Whether or not the bill is overturned – Congressional Republicans had launched more than 50 attempts to repeal the law since its inception – the economic pressure to improve the system is undeniable.

Other major debates in the US that are unlikely to be resolved anytime soon revolve around immigration reform, gun control and US foreign policy, particularly in the Middle East.

Survival Guide

Transportation

ARRIVING IN WASHINGTON, DC

Most visitors arrive by air. The city has two airports: Washington Dulles International Airport is larger and handles most of the international flights, as well as domestic flights, while Ronald Reagan Washington National Airport handles domestic services plus some flights to Canada. Reagan is more convenient, as it's closer to the city and has a Metro stop. Baltimore's airport is a third, often cheaper option. It's connected to DC by commuter rail, though it's not handy if you're arriving at night.

Buses are a popular means of getting to DC from nearby cities such New York, Philadelphia and Richmond, VA. Tickets are cheap, the routes are direct to the city center, and the buses usually have free wi-fi and power outlets.

It's also easy to reach Washington by train from major east-coast cities. The fast, commuter-oriented Acela train links Boston, New York and Philly to DC's Union Station.

Flights, cars and tours can be booked online at lonelyplanet.com.

Ronald Reagan Washington National Airport

Ronald Reagan Washington National Airport (DCA; www.metwashairports.com) is 4.5 miles south of downtown in Arlington, VA. There's free wi-fi, several eateries and a currency exchange (National Hall, Concourse Level). It's easy to reach.

Metro

The airport has its own **Metro** (www.wmata.com) station on the Blue and Yellow Lines, connected to the concourse level of terminals B and C. Trains (around $2.50) depart every 10 minutes or so between 5am and midnight (to 3am Friday and Saturday); they reach the city center in 20 minutes.

Bus

The **Supershuttle** (☎800-258-3826; www.supershuttle.com; ⏰5:30am-12:30am) door-to-door shared van service goes downtown for $14. It takes 10 to 30 minutes.

Taxi

Rides to the city center take 10 to 30 minutes (depending on traffic) and cost $13 to $22. Taxis queue outside the baggage-claim area at each terminal.

Washington Dulles International Airport

Washington Dulles International Airport (IAD; www.metwashairports.com) is in the Virginia suburbs 26 miles west of DC. It has free wi-fi, several currency exchanges and restaurants throughout the terminals. Famed architect Eero Saarinen designed the swooping main building. The Metro Silver Line is slated to reach Dulles in 2018, providing a transfer-free ride at long last. In the meantime, the following options are available.

Bus & Metro

Washington Flyer's (☎888-927-4359; www.washfly.com) Silver Line Express bus runs every 15 to 20 minutes from Dulles (main terminal, arrivals level door 4) to the Wiehle-Reston East Metro station between 6am and 10:40pm (from 7:45am weekends). Total time to DC's center is 60 to 75 minutes, total bus-Metro cost around $11.

Metrobus 5A (www.wmata.com) runs every 30 to 40 minutes from Dulles to Rosslyn Metro (Blue, Orange and Silver Lines) and on to central DC (L'Enfant Plaza) between 5:50am (6:30am weekends) and 11:35pm. Total time to the center is

CLIMATE CHANGE & TRAVEL

Every form of transportation that relies on carbon-based fuel generates CO_2, the main cause of human-induced climate change. Modern travel is dependent on airplanes, which might use less fuel per mile per person than most cars but travel much greater distances. The altitude at which aircraft emit gases (including CO_2) and particles also contributes to their climate change impact. Many websites offer 'carbon calculators' that allow people to estimate the carbon emissions generated by their journey and, for those who wish to do so, to offset the impact of the greenhouse gases emitted with contributions to portfolios of climate-friendly initiatives throughout the world. Lonely Planet offsets the carbon footprint of all staff and author travel.

around 60 minutes; total bus-Metro fare is about $9.

The **Supershuttle** (☎800-258-3826; www.supershuttle.com; ⏰5:30am-12:30am) door-to-door shared van service goes downtown for $29. It takes 30 to 60 minutes.

Taxi

Rides to the city center take 30 to 60 minutes (depending on traffic) and cost $62 to $73. Follow the 'Ground Transportation' or 'Taxi' signs to where they queue.

Baltimore-Washington International Airport

Baltimore-Washington International Airport (BWI; ☎410-859-7111; www.bwiairport.com) is 30 miles northeast of DC in Maryland.

Bus & Metro

Metrobus B30 (www.wmata.com) runs from BWI to the Greenbelt Metro station (last stop on the Green Line); it departs every 40 minutes from bus stops on the lower level of the international concourse and concourse A/B. The total bus-Metro fare is about $10.50. Total trip time is around 75 minutes.

The **Supershuttle** (☎800-258-3826; www.supershuttle.com; ⏰5:30am-12:30am) door-to-door shared-van service goes to downtown DC for $37. The ride takes 45 minutes to an hour.

Taxi

A taxi to DC takes 45 minutes or so and costs $90. Taxis queue outside the baggage claim area of the Marshall terminal.

Train

Both **MARC** (Maryland Rail Commuter; www.mta.maryland.gov) and **Amtrak** (☎800-872-7245; www.amtrak.com) trains travel to DC's Union Station. They depart from a terminal 1 mile from BWI; a free bus shuttles passengers there. Trains leave once or twice per hour, but there's no service after 9:30pm (and limited service on weekends). It takes 30 to 40 minutes; fares start at $6.

Union Station

Magnificent, beaux-arts **Union Station** (www.unionstationdc.com; 50 Massachusetts Ave NE) is the city's rail hub. There's a handy Metro station (Red Line) here for transportation onward in the city.

Train

- **Amtrak** (☎800-872-7245; www.amtrak.com) arrives at least once per hour from major east-coast cities.
- Northeast Regional trains are cheaper but slower (about 3½ hours between NYC and DC).
- Acela Express trains are more expensive but faster (2¾ hours between NYC and DC, 6½ hours between Boston and DC). The express trains also have bigger seats and other business-class amenities.
- **MARC** (Maryland Rail Commuter; www.mta.maryland.gov) trains arrive frequently from downtown Baltimore (one hour) and other Maryland towns, as well as Harpers Ferry, WV.

Taxi

Taxis queue outside Union Station's main entrance. A ride to downtown costs around $7, to Dupont Circle $10.

GETTING AROUND WASHINGTON, DC

The public-transportation system is a mix of Metro trains and bus. Visitors will find the Metro the most useful option.

The District Department of Transportation's **goDCgo** (www.godcgo.com) is a useful resource for cycling, bus, Metro and parking information and route planning. It even has a carbon calculator that compares different modes of local travel.

Bicycle

DC is a cycling-savvy city with its own bike-share

program. Lots of locals commute by bicycle.

➡ Riders can take bikes free of charge on Metro trains, except during rush hour (7am to 10am and 4pm to 7pm Monday to Friday) and on holidays. Bikes are not permitted to use the center door of trains or the escalator.

➡ All public buses are equipped with bike racks.

➡ The **Washington Area Bicyclists' Association** (www.waba.org) has information on recommended trails, events, bike advocacy and more.

Here are some options for rental:

Capital Bikeshare (☎877-430-2453; www.capitalbikeshare.com; membership 24hr/3 days $7/15) It has a network of 2500-plus bicycles scattered at 300-odd stations around the region, including many that fringe the Mall. To check out a bike, select the membership (one day or three days), insert your credit card, and off you go. The first 30 minutes are free; after that, rates rise fast ($2/6/14 per extra 30/60/90 minutes). Note helmets and locks are not provided.

Bike & Roll (Map p300; ☎202-962-0206; www.bikeandrolldc.com; 50 Massachusetts Ave NE; bikes per 2hr/day from $16/40; ⏲9am-7pm summer, 10am-4pm winter; Ⓜ Union Station) To rent a bicycle for longer rides, with accoutrements such as helmets and locks, this company is open year-round at Union Station, and has seasonal branches at L'Enfant Plaza and Alexandria, VA.

Big Wheel Bikes (Map p308; www.bigwheelbikes.com; 1034 33rd St NW; per 3hr/day $21/35; ⏲11am-7pm Tue-Fri, 10am-6pm Sat & Sun) A company with two-wheelers for longer rides, located in Georgetown near several great trails.

Boat

Potomac Riverboat Co (☎877-511-2628; www.potomacriverboatco.com; ⏲late Mar-Oct) water taxis toodle along the Potomac from the Mall (dock at W Basin and Ohio Drs SW) to Old Town Alexandria (dock at Cameron and Union Sts). The trip takes 30 minutes and costs $15/9 adult/child one-way. In Alexandria you can transfer to another water taxi to reach the amusements at Maryland's National Harbor for around $8 more.

Bus

DC's public bus system has two main fleets. Pay with exact change, or use a SmarTrip card. Streetcars are expected to join the action in 2015 to help serve the

USEFUL BUS STATIONS

Cheap bus services to and from Washington abound. Most charge around $25 for a one-way trip to NYC (it takes four to five hours). Many companies use Union Station as their hub; other pick-up locations are scattered around town, but are always Metro-accessible. Tickets usually need to be bought online, but can sometimes be purchased on the bus itself if there are still seats available.

BestBus (☎202-332-2691; www.bestbus.com; 20th St & Massachusetts Ave NW; 📶) Several trips to/from NYC daily. The main bus stop is by Dupont Circle; there's another at Union Station.

BoltBus (☎877-265-8287; www.boltbus.com; 50 Massachusetts Ave NE; 📶) The best of the budget options for NYC trips; it uses Union Station as its terminal.

Greyhound (☎202-589-5141; www.greyhound.com; 50 Massachusetts Ave NE) Provides nationwide service. The terminal is at Union Station.

Megabus (☎877-462-6342; http://us.megabus.com; 50 Massachusetts Ave NE; 📶) Offers the most trips to NYC (more than 20 per day), as well as other east-coast cities; arrives at and departs from Union Station.

Peter Pan Bus Lines (☎800-343-9999; www.peterpanbus.com; 50 Massachusetts Ave NE) Travels throughout the northeastern US; has its terminal at Union Station.

Vamoose Bus (☎877-393-2828; www.vamoosebus.com; 1801 N Lynn St) Service between NYC and Arlington, VA (the stop is near the Rosslyn Metro station).

Washington Deluxe (☎866-287-6932; www.washny.com; 1610 Connecticut St NW; 📶) Good express service to/from NYC. It has stops at both Dupont Circle and Union Station.

H St area of Capitol Hill; see www.dcstreetcar.com for route and fare details.

Metrobus (www.wmata.com; fare $1.75) Operates clean, efficient buses throughout the city and suburbs, typically from early morning until late evening.

DC Circulator (www.dccirculator.com; fare $1) Red Circulator buses run along handy local routes, including Union Station to/from the Mall (looping by all major museums and memorials), Union Station to/from Georgetown (via K St), Dupont Circle to/from Georgetown (via M St), and the White House area to/from Adams Morgan (via 14th St). Buses operate from roughly 7am to 9pm weekdays (midnight or so on weekends).

Car & Motorcycle

DC has some of the nation's worst traffic congestion. Bottlenecks are in the suburbs, where the Capital Beltway (I-495) meets Maryland's I-270 and I-95, and Virginia's I-66 and I-95. Avoid the beltway during early-morning and late-afternoon rush hours (about 6am to 9am and 3pm to 6pm). Clogged rush-hour streets in DC include the main access arteries from the suburbs: Massachusetts, Wisconsin, Connecticut and Georgia Aves NW, among others.

Parking

➡ Finding street parking is difficult downtown and in popular neighborhoods (Georgetown, Adams Morgan and the U St area are particular nightmares), but it's reasonably easy in less-congested districts.

➡ Note that residential areas often have a two-hour limit on street parking. If you stay longer, you run a good risk of getting ticketed.

GETTING A SMARTRIP CARD

➡ If you're going to use the Metro (p272) more than a few times, it's worth buying a rechargeable SmarTrip card, available at the machines at any station.

➡ It costs $10, with $8 of that stored for fares. You can add value as needed.

➡ Without a SmarTrip card, each ride you take is subject to a $1 surcharge for using a disposable fare card.

➡ SmarTrip cards are more convenient (they're plastic instead of flimsy paper), and they save time, since you don't have to go to a machine to buy a ticket each time you ride.

➡ The cards are also usable on all local buses (for which you'd otherwise need exact change).

➡ Parking garages in the city cost $15 to $35 per day. Some garages have early-bird specials (ie in before 8am or 10am and out by 6pm or so) that cut rates in half.

➡ **DC Parking** (www.dcparking.org) has the lowdown, with tips by neighborhood.

Road Rules

➡ Certain lanes of some major traffic arteries change direction during rush hour, and some two-way streets become one-way. Signs indicate hours of these changes, so keep your eyes peeled.

➡ Except where otherwise posted, the speed limit on DC surface streets is 25mph (15mph in alleys and school zones).

➡ You must wear your seat belt and restrain kids under eight years in child-safety seats.

Auto Association

For emergency road service and towing, members can call the **American Automobile Association** (AAA; www.aaa.com). It has a branch in the **White House Area** (☎202-481-6811; 1405 G St NW).

Car Share

Zipcar (☎866-494-7227; www.zipcar.com), with its cute, eco-friendly Priuses and parking-friendly minis, is popular in town. Weekday rates are from $8/75 hourly/daily and weekends from $10/84 hourly/daily. That includes gas and insurance and good parking spaces around town. You need to become a member first ($60 annually, plus $25 application fee).

Rental

➡ All major car-rental agencies are in DC. Rates start around $60 per day, plus tax and insurance. Gas is pricier inside the city than in Maryland and Virginia.

➡ To rent a car you typically need to be at least 25 years old, hold a valid driver's license and have a major credit card.

Unless stated otherwise, the following companies have outlets at both DC airports and Union Station:

Alamo (☎877-222-9075; www.alamo.com)

Avis (☎800-230-4898; www.avis.com)

Budget (☎800-527-0700; www.budget.com)

Enterprise (☎800-261-7331; www.enterprise.com) At the airports and downtown near McPherson Sq.

Hertz (☎800-654-3131; www.hertz.com)

National (☎877-222-9058; www.nationalcar.com)

Thrifty (☎800-847-4389; www.thrifty.com) At the airports only.

Metro

DC's modern subway network is the **Metrorail** (☎202-637-7000; www.wmata.com), commonly called Metro. It will get you to most sights, hotels and business districts, and to the Maryland and Virginia suburbs.

➡ There are six color-coded lines: Red, Orange, Blue, Green, Yellow and Silver.

➡ Trains start running at 5am Monday through Friday (from 7am on weekends); the last service is around midnight Sunday through Thursday and 3am on Friday and Saturday.

➡ Trains run every 10 minutes or so, except during weekend track maintenance, when they slow down considerably.

➡ Machines inside stations sell computerized fare cards; fares cost $1.75 to $5.90, depending on distance traveled.

➡ Fares increase slightly during morning and evening rush hour.

➡ There is a $1 surcharge for using a disposable fare card versus a rechargeable SmarTrip card (p271).

➡ Use the card to enter *and* exit station turnstiles. Upon exit, the turnstile deducts the fare and returns the card. If the value of the card is insufficient, you need to use an 'Addfare' machine to add money.

➡ Unlimited-ride Metro day passes cost $14.50, available at any station.

➡ All Metro stations have elevators, handy for travelers with strollers or mobility issues (otherwise you're relegated to escalators, which are very lengthy at some stations).

Taxi & Rideshare

➡ Taxis queue at Union Station, the main hotels and sports venues, but it's not always easy to hail one on the street.

➡ Fares are meter-based. The meter starts at $3.50, then it's $2.16 per mile thereafter.

➡ There's a $2 surcharge for telephone dispatches.

➡ The rideshare company **Uber** (www.uber.com) is extremely popular in the District. Locals say it saves time and money compared to taxis.

For those sticking with taxis, reliable companies include the following:

DC Yellow Cab (☎202-544-1212)

Diamond Cab (☎202-387-6200)

TOURS

Tours are a great way to home in on DC's attractions. Do-it-yourself types can access free walking tours from **Cultural Tourism DC** (www.culturaltourismdc.org) for 15 historic neighborhoods in the District.

Bike & Roll (www.bikeandrolldc.com; adult/child from $40/30; ⏰mid-Mar–Nov) Offers day and evening bike tours around the Mall and Capitol Hill. The 'Monuments at Night' tour is especially atmospheric. The company also arranges combo boat-bike trips to Mount Vernon.

City Segway Tours (Map p302; ☎202-626-0017; http://dc.citysegwaytours.com; 3hr tours from $75) Extremely popular way of seeing the major sites along the Mall and in Penn Quarter.

DC Metro Food Tours (☎800-979-3370; www.dcmetrofoodtours.com; per person $30-65) These walkabouts explore the culinary riches of various neighborhoods, stopping for multiple bites along the way. Offerings include Eastern Market, U Street, Little Ethiopia, Georgetown and Alexandria, VA.

DC by Foot (www.dcbyfoot.com) Guides for this pay-what-you-want walking tour offer engaging stories and historical details on different jaunts covering the National Mall, Lincoln's assassination, Georgetown's ghosts, U Street's food and many more. Most takers pay around $10 per person.

Old Town Trolley Tours (☎888-910-8687; www.trolleytours.com; adult/child $39/29) This open-sided bus offers hop-on, hop-off exploring of the major sights around the Mall, Arlington and downtown. The outfit also offers a 'Monuments by Moonlight' tour and the DC Ducks tour, via an amphibious vehicle that plunges into the Potomac. Booking online saves 10%.

Potomac Riverboat Co (☎877-511-2628; www.potomacriverboatco.com; ⏰late Mar-Oct) It offers a monuments cruise (one-way adult/child $15/9) between Georgetown (dock at 31st and K Sts, Washington Harbour) and Alexandria (dock at corner of Cameron and Union Sts). You can disembark at either location to sightsee, then return via a later cruise. From Alexandria, it also offers a Mount Vernon trip (one-way adult/child $16/9). Check the website for other themed tours.

Spirit of Mount Vernon (Map p300; ☎866-211-3811; www.cruisetomountvernon.com; adult/child $46/41) The large, flashy *Spirit of Mount Vernon* boat departs for George Washington's estate from Pier 4, at 6th & Water Sts SW in southwest DC. The day-long tour includes site admission.

Directory A–Z

Customs Regulations

For a complete list of US customs regulations, go online to **US Customs and Border Protection** (www.cbp.gov).

Duty-free allowance per person is as follows:

- 1L of liquor (provided you are at least 21 years old)
- 100 cigars and 200 cigarettes (if you are at least 18 years)
- $200 worth of gifts and purchases ($800 if a returning US citizen)
- If you arrive with $10,000 or more in US or foreign currency, it must be declared

There are heavy penalties for attempting to import illegal drugs. Note that fruit, vegetables and other food must be declared (whereby you'll undergo a time-consuming search) or left in the bins in the arrival area.

Discount Cards

The following cards can net savings (usually about 10%) on museums, accommodations and some transport (including Amtrak):

American Association of Retired Persons (AARP; www.aarp.org) For US travelers aged 50 and over.

American Automobile Association (AAA; www.aaa.com) For members of AAA or reciprocal clubs in Europe and Australia.

International Student Identity Card (ISIC; www.isic.org) For students any age and non-students under 26 years.

Student Advantage Card (www.studentadvantage.com) For US and foreign students 16 years and older.

Electricity

Emergency

Police, fire, ambulance ☎911

Gay & Lesbian Travelers

DC is one of the most gay-friendly cities in the US. It has an admirable track record of progressivism and a fair bit of scene to boot. The rainbow stereotype here consists of well-dressed professionals and activists working in politics on GLBT issues such as gay marriage (legal in DC since 2010). The community concentrates in Dupont Circle, but U Street, Shaw, Capitol Hill and Logan Circle also have gay-friendly businesses.

Capital Area Gay & Lesbian Chamber of Commerce (www.caglcc.org) Sponsors networking events.

LGBT DC (www.washington.org/topics/lgbt) The DC tourism office's portal with events, neighborhood breakdowns and a travel resource guide.

Metro Weekly (www.metroweekly.com) Free weekly news magazine. Aimed at a younger demographic.

Washington Blade (www.washingtonblade.com) Free weekly gay newspaper. Covers politics and has lots of business and nightlife listings.

Internet Access

➡ Wi-fi is common in lodgings across the price spectrum. Many properties also have an internet-connected computer for public use. Entries that appear with an internet icon @ indicate when a place has a public computer. A wi-fi icon means the property offers wireless internet access, whether free or fee-based.

➡ Many bars, cafes and museums offer free wi-fi.

➡ Outlets of the **DC Public Library** (www.dclibrary.org) offer free terminals for 15 minutes; to surf longer, you need to sign up for a free user's card.

➡ For a list of wi-fi hot spots, visit **Wi-Fi Free Spot** (www.wififreespot.com).

Legal Matters

➡ If you are arrested, never walk away from an officer. You are allowed to remain silent, and you are entitled to have access to an attorney. The legal system presumes you're innocent until proven guilty. All persons who are arrested have the right to make one phone call. If you don't have a lawyer or family member to help you, call your embassy or consulate. The police will give you the number on request.

➡ The blood-alcohol limit is 0.08%. Driving under the influence of alcohol or drugs is a serious offense, subject to stiff fines and even imprisonment.

➡ Possession of illicit drugs, including cocaine, ecstasy, LSD, heroin and hashish, is a felony potentially punishable by lengthy jail sentences.

➡ In November 2014, DC voted to legalize marijuana. The new law lets residents and visitors have up to 2oz for personal use. Selling marijuana is prohibited, as is smoking in public (so it boils down to a home-grow, home-use policy). Marijuana also is barred in about 20% of the city that is federal land.

Medical Services

Washington, DC, has no unexpected health dangers and excellent medical facilities; the only real concern is that a collision with the US medical system might injure your wallet. Remember to buy health insurance before you travel. Check the **Lonely Planet** (www.lonelyplanet.com/travel-insurance) website for more information. Recommended medical facilities:

George Washington University Hospital (☎202-715-4000; 900 23rd St NW; Ⓜ Foggy Bottom-GWU)

Travelers' Clinic (☎202-715-5100; 2150 Pennsylvania Ave NW; Ⓜ Foggy Bottom-GWU) Offers immunizations and health advice for global travels; it's part of George Washington University.

Pharmacies

The most prominent pharmacy chain is CVS, with locations all around the city. These convenient branches are open 24 hours:

CVS Dupont Circle (☎202-785-1466; 6-7 Dupont Circle; ⌚24hr; Ⓜ Dupont Circle)

CVS Thomas Circle (☎202-628-0720; 1199 Vermont Ave NW; ⌚24hr; Ⓜ McPherson Sq)

Money

The currency is the US dollar. Most locals do not carry large amounts of cash for everyday use, relying instead on credit and debit cards.

ATMs

➡ ATMs are widely available at banks, airports and convenience shops.

➡ Most ATMs link into worldwide networks (Plus, Cirrus, Exchange etc).

➡ ATMs typically charge a service fee of $3 or more per transaction.

➡ For foreign visitors, ask your bank for information about using its cards in stateside ATMs. The exchange rate is usually as good as you'll get anywhere.

Credit Cards

Major credit cards are almost universally accepted. In fact, it's next to impossible to rent a car or make hotel or ticket reservations without one. Visa and MasterCard are the most widely accepted. Contact the issuing company for lost or stolen cards:

American Express (☎800-528-4800; www.american-express.com)

MasterCard (☎800-627-8372; www.mastercard.com)

Visa (☎800-847-2911; www.visa.com)

Money Changers

Although the airports have exchange bureaus, better rates can usually be obtained at banks in the city. Another option:

Travelex (www.travelex.com; 1800 K St NW; ⌚9am-6pm Mon-Fri; Ⓜ Farragut West)

Tipping

Tipping is *not* optional. Only withhold tips in cases of outrageously bad service.

Airport & hotel porters $2 per bag, $5 minimum per cart.

Bartenders 15% per round, $1 minimum per drink.

Hotel housekeepers $2 to $5 per night.

Restaurant servers 15% to 20%, unless a gratuity is already charged on the bill.

Taxi drivers 10% to 15%, rounded up to the next dollar.

Valet parking attendants At least $2 when you're handed back the keys.

Opening Hours

Typical normal opening times in Washington, DC, are as follows:

Bars 5pm to 1am or 2am weekdays, 3am on weekends

Museums 10am to 5:30pm

Nightclubs 9pm to 1am or 2am weekdays, 3am on weekends

Offices and government agencies 9am to 5pm Monday to Friday

Restaurants Breakfast 7am or 8am to 11am; lunch 11am or 11:30am to 2:30pm or 3pm; dinner 5pm or 6pm to 10pm Sunday to Thursday, to 11pm or midnight Friday and Saturday

Shops 10am to 7pm Monday to Saturday, noon to 6pm Sunday

Post

➡ The **US Postal Service** (USPS; ☎800-275-8777; www.usps.com) is reliable and inexpensive. The postal rates for 1st-class mail within the USA are 49¢ for letters up to 1oz (21¢ for each additional ounce) and 34¢ for standard-size postcards.

➡ International airmail rates are $1.15 for a 1oz letter or postcard.

➡ For an awesome selection of stamps for sale, go to the post-office branch in the National Postal Museum (p111).

PRACTICALITIES

➡ **Newspapers & Magazines** The *Washington Post* (www.washingtonpost.com) is among the nation's top newspapers. Its tabloid-format daily *Express* is free. The *Post*'s competitor is the conservative *Washington Times* (www.washingtontimes.com). The *Washington City Paper* (www.washingtoncitypaper.com) is a free alternative weekly that scrutinizes DC politics and has great entertainment coverage. *Politico* (www.politico.com) is a free paper that covers DC's politics in-depth.

➡ **TV** The main TV channels are Channel 4 (NBC), Channel 5 (Fox), Channel 7 (ABC) and Channel 9 (CBS).

➡ **Radio** National Public Radio (NPR) is headquartered in the District. Its programs can be found on WAMU-FM88.5.

➡ **Smoking** Washington, DC, is entirely smoke-free in restaurants, bars and workplaces.

Public Holidays

Banks, schools, offices and most shops close on these days.

New Year's Day January 1

Martin Luther King Jr Day Third Monday in January

Inauguration Day January 20, every four years

Presidents' Day Third Monday in February

Memorial Day Last Monday in May

Independence Day July 4

Labor Day First Monday in September

Columbus Day Second Monday in October

Veterans Day November 11

Thanksgiving Day Fourth Thursday in November

Christmas Day December 25

Taxes & Refunds

Sales tax varies by state and county. Unless otherwise stated, prices listed in this guide don't include taxes.

DC restaurant tax 10%

DC room tax 14.5%

DC sales tax 5.75%

Maryland room tax 5% to 8%

Maryland sales tax 6%

Virginia room tax 9.5% to 10.5%

Virginia sales tax 6%

Telephone

The local phone system mixes regional service providers, competing long-distance carriers and several cell-phone companies. Overall, the system is efficient. Note that calls from a hotel phone can be expensive. Services such as **Skype** (www.skype.com) and **Google Voice** (www.google.com/voice) make calling home quite cheap. Check the websites for details.

Cell Phones

➡ Most of the USA's cell-phone systems are incompatible

with the GSM standard used throughout Europe and Asia (though some convertible phones will work).

➡ iPhones will work fine – but beware of roaming costs, especially for data. Check with your service provider about using your phone here.

➡ It might be cheaper to buy a prepaid SIM card for the USA, like those sold by AT&T or T-Mobile, which you can insert into your international cell phone to get a local phone number and voicemail.

➡ You can also buy inexpensive, no-contract (pre-paid) phones with a local number and a set number of minutes, which can be topped up at will. Virgin Mobile, T-Mobile, AT&T and other providers offer phones starting at $30, with a package of minutes starting at around $40 for 400 minutes.

➡ Electronics store chain **Best Buy** (www.bestbuy.com) sells pre-paid phones, as well as international SIM cards.

➡ Online retailer **Telestial** (www.telestial.com) also sells SIM cards and cell phones; it rents phones, too.

Phone Codes

All phone numbers within the USA consist of a three-digit area code followed by a seven-digit local number. Typically, if you are calling a number within the same area code, you only have to dial the seven-digit number. More information on dialing:

US country code ☎1

DC area code ☎202

Making international calls Dial ☎011 + country code + area code + local number.

Calling other US area codes or Canada Dial ☎1 + area code + seven-digit local number.

Calling within DC Just dial the seven-digit local number. If for some reason it doesn't work, try adding ☎1 + the area code at the beginning.

Directory assistance nationwide ☎411

Toll-free numbers ☎1+ 800 (or ☎888, 877, 866) + seven-digit number. Some toll-free numbers only work within the US.

Phonecards

Private pre-paid phonecards are available from convenience stores, supermarkets and pharmacies. AT&T sells a reliable card that is widely available.

Time

DC is on Eastern Standard Time, five hours behind Greenwich Mean Time. Daylight saving time is observed between mid-March and early November. When it's noon in DC, it's 5pm in London, 6am the next day in Sydney and 8am the next day in Auckland.

Tourist Information

Washington, DC, operates several information centers in the city to help travelers develop itineraries.

DC Chamber of Commerce Tourist Information Center (Map p302; ☎202-347-7201; www.dcchamber.org; 506 9th St NW; ⌚8:30am-5:30pm Mon-Fri; Ⓜ Gallery Pl) Offers maps, lodging brochures and coupons.

Destination DC (Map p302; ☎202-789-7000; www.washington.org) DC's official tourism site, with the mother lode of online information.

NPS Ellipse Visitor Pavilion (Map p296; ☎202-208-1631; ⌚7:30am-4pm; Ⓜ Federal Triangle) Has a staffed information desk and sells snacks; located at the northeast corner of the Ellipse, south of the White House.

Smithsonian Visitor Center (Map p294; ☎202-663-1000; www.si.edu/visit; 1000 Jefferson Dr SW; ⌚8:30am-5:30pm; 📶; Ⓜ Smithsonian) Located in the Castle, it is a great resource with a staffed information desk and everything you ever wanted to know about the museum programs.

Travelers with Disabilities

DC is well equipped for travelers with disabilities:

➡ Most museums and major sights are wheelchair accessible, as are most large hotels and restaurants.

➡ All Metro trains and buses are accessible to people in wheelchairs. All Metro stations have elevators, and guide dogs are allowed on trains and buses.

➡ All DC transit companies offer travel discounts for disabled travelers.

➡ Hindrances to wheelchair users include buckled-brick sidewalks in the historic blocks of Georgetown and Capitol Hill, but sidewalks in most other parts of DC are in good shape.

➡ All Smithsonian museums have free wheelchair loans and can arrange special tours for hearing-impaired visitors. See www.si.edu/Visit/VisitorsWithDisabilities for more.

➡ Hearing-impaired visitors should check out **Gallaudet University** (www.gallaudet.edu; 800 Florida Ave NE; Ⓜ NoMa) in northeast DC, which hosts lectures and cultural events especially for the deaf.

Visas

➡ Check with the **US State Department** (www.travel.

state.gov) for updates and details on entry requirements.

➡ The Visa Waiver Program (VWP) allows nationals from 36 countries (including most EU countries, Japan, Australia and New Zealand) to enter the US without a visa for up to 90 days.

➡ VWP visitors require a machine-readable passport and approval under the **Electronic System For Travel Authorization** (ESTA; www.cbp.gov/esta) at least three days before arrival. There is a $14 fee for processing and authorization (payable online). Once approved, the registration is valid for two years.

➡ In essence, ESTA requires that you register specific information online (name, address, passport info etc). You will receive one of three responses: 'Authorization Approved' (this usually comes within minutes; most applicants can expect to receive this response); 'Authorization Pending' (you'll need to check the status within the next 72 hours); or 'Travel not Authorized'. If this is the case, it means you will need to apply for a visa.

➡ Those who need a visa – ie anyone staying longer than 90 days, or from a non-VWP country – should apply at the US consulate in their home country.

➡ Canadians are exempt from the process. They do not need visas, though they do need a passport or document approved by the **Western Hemisphere Travel Initiative** (www.getyouhome.gov).

Behind the Scenes

SEND US YOUR FEEDBACK

We love to hear from travelers – your comments keep us on our toes and help make our books better. Our well-traveled team reads every word on what you loved or loathed about this book. Although we cannot reply individually to your submissions, we always guarantee that your feedback goes straight to the appropriate authors, in time for the next edition. Each person who sends us information is thanked in the next edition – the most useful submissions are rewarded with a selection of digital PDF chapters.

Visit **lonelyplanet.com/contact** to submit your updates and suggestions or to ask for help. Our award-winning website also features inspirational travel stories, news and discussions.

Note: We may edit, reproduce and incorporate your comments in Lonely Planet products such as guidebooks, websites and digital products, so let us know if you don't want your comments reproduced or your name acknowledged. For a copy of our privacy policy visit lonelyplanet.com/privacy.

OUR READERS

Many thanks to the travelers who used the last edition and wrote to us with helpful hints, useful advice and interesting anecdotes:

Nathaniel Bernard, Mathieu Cagnard, Carla de Beer, Eli Griffen, Pei-Chun Ko, Paul Lambert, Stephen Pickhardt, Eileen Rappoport, Mike Roberts, Mary Westley

AUTHOR THANKS

Karla Zimmerman

Thanks to Bill Brockschmidt, Amy Schwenkmeyer (and office mates!), Kate Armstrong, Rana Freedman, Kate Gibbs, Scott Berman, Yen Hoang, Melissa Walsh, Zoe Sommers and Kevin Sommers for good-heartedly answering my relentless questions. Deep appreciation to all the locals who spilled the beans on their favorite places. Thanks most of all to Eric Markowitz, the world's best partner for life, who joined me for Capital explorations and fed me during the write-up phase. You top my Best List.

Regis St Louis

Although I researched my sections during the coldest days of the year, the warmth and kindness of locals and friends more than made up for the sub-zero temperatures. Special thanks to Karla for her fine groundwork and to Dora for inviting me on board. Big thanks to Cassandra, Magda and Genevieve, who've shared the DC adventure over the years. I'm also indebted to my father, who always loved visiting DC and filled my head with wanderlust as a boy.

ACKNOWLEDGMENTS

Illustrations p64–5 and p80–1 by Javier Martinez Zarracina.

Cover photograph: Reflecting Pool and Washington Monument, Jonathan Irish/Alamy.

THIS BOOK

This 6th edition of Lonely Planet's *Washington, DC*, guidebook was researched and written by Karla Zimmerman and Regis St Louis. The previous edition was also written by Karla and Regis. This guidebook was produced by the following:

Destination Editor Dora Whitaker
Coordinating Editor Kristin Odijk
Product Editors Catherine Naghten, Martine Power
Senior Cartographer Alison Lyall
Book Designer Virginia Moreno
Assisting Editors Sarah Bailey, Gabrielle Stefanos, Jeanette Wall
Cover Researcher Naomi Parker
Thanks to Imogen Bannister, Sarah Billington, Carolyn Boicos, Daniel Corbett, Ryan Evans, Andi Jones, Kate Mathews, Wayne Murphy, Karyn Noble, Diana Saengkham, Dianne Schallmeiner, Ellie Simpson, Lauren Wellicome, Tony Wheeler

See also separate subindexes for:

Index

Sights 000
Map Pages **000**
Photo Pages **000**

Sights 000
Map Pages **000**
Photo Pages **000**

EATING

Sights 000
Map Pages **000**
Photo Pages **000**

DRINKING & NIGHTLIFE

ENTERTAINMENT

SHOPPING

Sights 000
Map Pages **000**
Photo Pages **000**

SPORTS & ACTIVITIES

SLEEPING

Washington, DC, Maps

Sights

- Beach
- Bird Sanctuary
- Buddhist
- Castle/Palace
- Christian
- Confucian
- Hindu
- Islamic
- Jain
- Jewish
- Monument
- Museum/Gallery/Historic Building
- Ruin
- Shinto
- Sikh
- Taoist
- Winery/Vineyard
- Zoo/Wildlife Sanctuary
- Other Sight

Activities, Courses & Tours

- Bodysurfing
- Diving
- Canoeing/Kayaking
- Course/Tour
- Sento Hot Baths/Onsen
- Skiing
- Snorkeling
- Surfing
- Swimming/Pool
- Walking
- Windsurfing
- Other Activity

Sleeping

- Sleeping
- Camping

Eating

- Eating

Drinking & Nightlife

- Drinking & Nightlife
- Cafe

Entertainment

- Entertainment

Shopping

- Shopping

Information

- Bank
- Embassy/Consulate
- Hospital/Medical
- Internet
- Police
- Post Office
- Telephone
- Toilet
- Tourist Information
- Other Information

Geographic

- Beach
- Hut/Shelter
- Lighthouse
- Lookout
- Mountain/Volcano
- Oasis
- Park
- Pass
- Picnic Area
- Waterfall

Population

- Capital (National)
- Capital (State/Province)
- City/Large Town
- Town/Village

Transport

- Airport
- BART station
- Border crossing
- Boston T station
- Bus
- Cable car/Funicular
- Cycling
- Ferry
- Metro/Muni station
- Monorail
- Parking
- Petrol station
- Subway/SkyTrain station
- Taxi
- Train station/Railway
- Tram
- Underground station
- Other Transport

Note: Not all symbols displayed above appear on the maps in this book

Routes

- Tollway
- Freeway
- Primary
- Secondary
- Tertiary
- Lane
- Unsealed road
- Road under construction
- Plaza/Mall
- Steps
- Tunnel
- Pedestrian overpass
- Walking Tour
- Walking Tour detour
- Path/Walking Trail

Boundaries

- International
- State/Province
- Disputed
- Regional/Suburb
- Marine Park
- Cliff
- Wall

Hydrography

- River, Creek
- Intermittent River
- Canal
- Water
- Dry/Salt/Intermittent Lake
- Reef

Areas

- Airport/Runway
- Beach/Desert
- Cemetery (Christian)
- Cemetery (Other)
- Glacier
- Mudflat
- Park/Forest
- Sight (Building)
- Sportsground
- Swamp/Mangrove

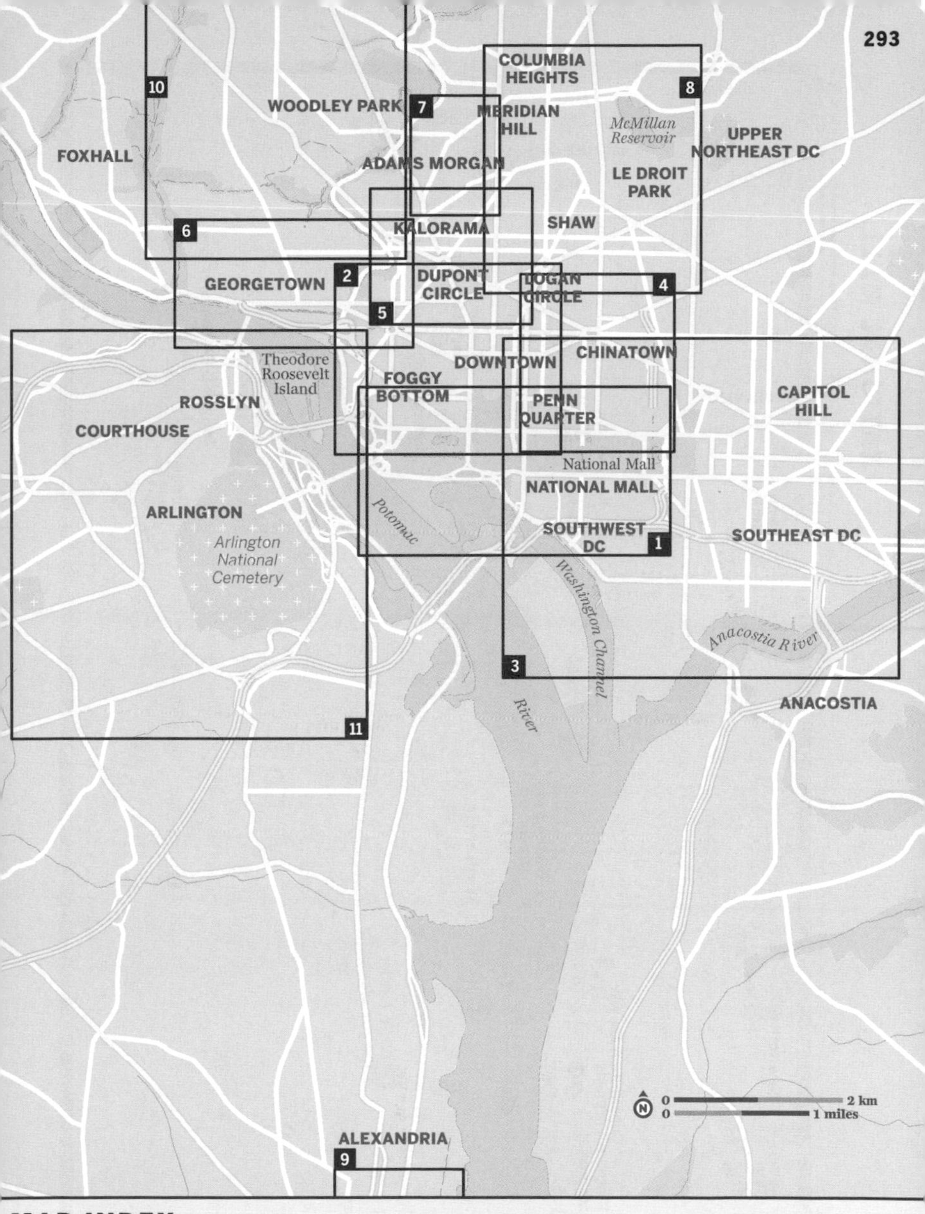

MAP INDEX

1 National Mall (p294)
2 White House Area & Foggy Bottom (p296)
3 Capitol Hill & Southeast DC (p300)
4 Downtown & Penn Quarter (p302)
5 Dupont Circle & Kalorama (p306)
6 Georgetown (p308)
7 Adams Morgan (p310)
8 Logan Circle, U Street & Columbia Heights (p312)
9 Alexandria (p315)
10 Upper Northwest DC (p316)
11 Arlington (p318)

NATIONAL MALL

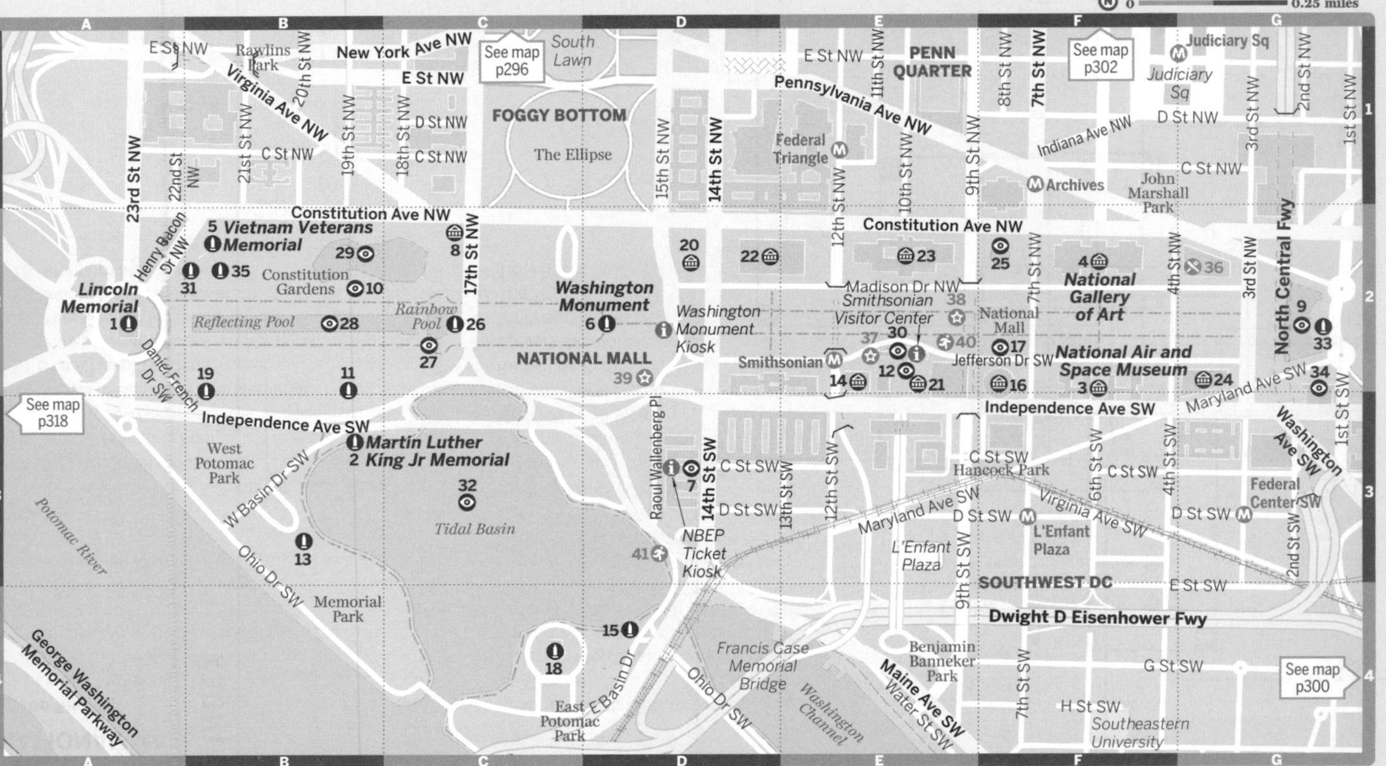

NATIONAL MALL

Top Sights **(p58)**

1 Lincoln Memorial ... A2
2 Martin Luther King Jr Memorial ... B3
3 National Air and Space Museum ... F2
4 National Gallery of Art ... F2
5 Vietnam Veterans Memorial ... B2
6 Washington Monument ... D2

Sights **(p66)**

7 Bureau of Engraving & Printing ... D3
8 C&O Canal Gatehouse ... C2
9 Capitol Reflecting Pool ... G2
10 Constitution Gardens ... B2
11 District of Columbia War Memorial ... B2
12 Enid A Haupt Garden ... E2
13 Franklin Delano Roosevelt Memorial ... B3
14 Freer-Sackler Museums of Asian Art ... E2
15 George Mason Memorial ... D4
16 Hirshhorn Museum ... F2
17 Hirshhorn Sculpture Garden ... F2
Ice Rink ... (see 25)
18 Jefferson Memorial ... C4
19 Korean War Veterans Memorial ... B2
20 National Museum of African American History and Culture ... D2
21 National Museum of African Art ... E2
22 National Museum of American History ... D2
23 National Museum of Natural History ... E2
24 National Museum of the American Indian ... G2
25 National Sculpture Garden ... F2
26 National WWII Memorial ... C2
27 National WWII Memorial Kiosk ... C2
28 Reflecting Pool ... B2
29 Signers' Memorial ... B2
30 Smithsonian Castle ... E2
31 The Three Soldiers ... B2
32 Tidal Basin ... C3
33 Ulysses S Grant Memorial ... G2
34 United States Botanic Garden ... G2
35 Women in Vietnam Memorial ... B2

Eating **(p70)**

36 Cascade Cafe ... G2
Mitsitam Native Foods Cafe ... (see 24)
Pavilion Cafe ... (see 25)

Entertainment **(p71)**

37 Discovery Theater ... E2
Jazz in the Garden ... (see 25)
38 Screen on the Green ... E2
39 Sylvan Theater ... D2

Sports & Activities **(p71)**

40 Carousel ... E2
National Gallery of Art ... (see 4)
41 Tidal Basin Boathouse ... D3

Key on p298

WHITE HOUSE AREA & FOGGY BOTTOM

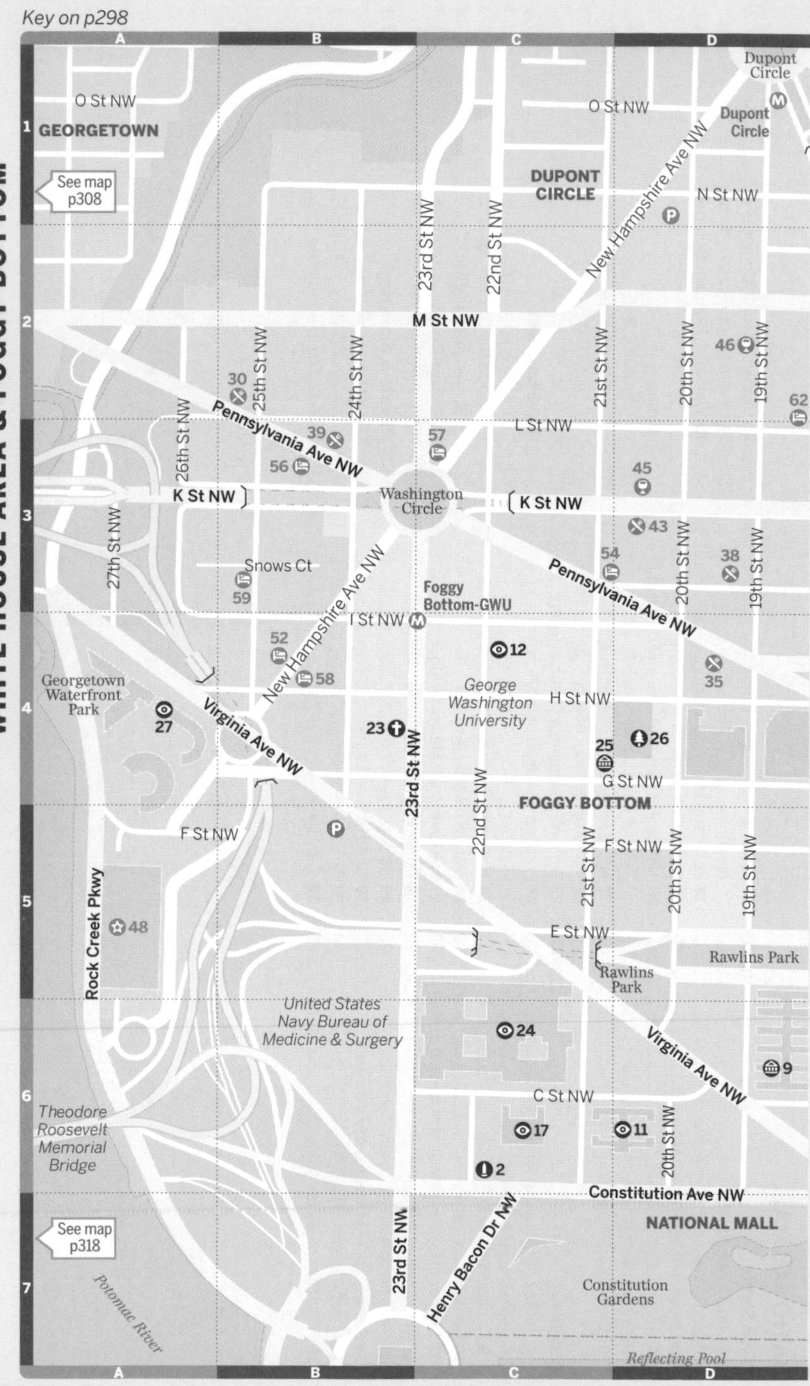

WHITE HOUSE AREA & FOGGY BOTTOM

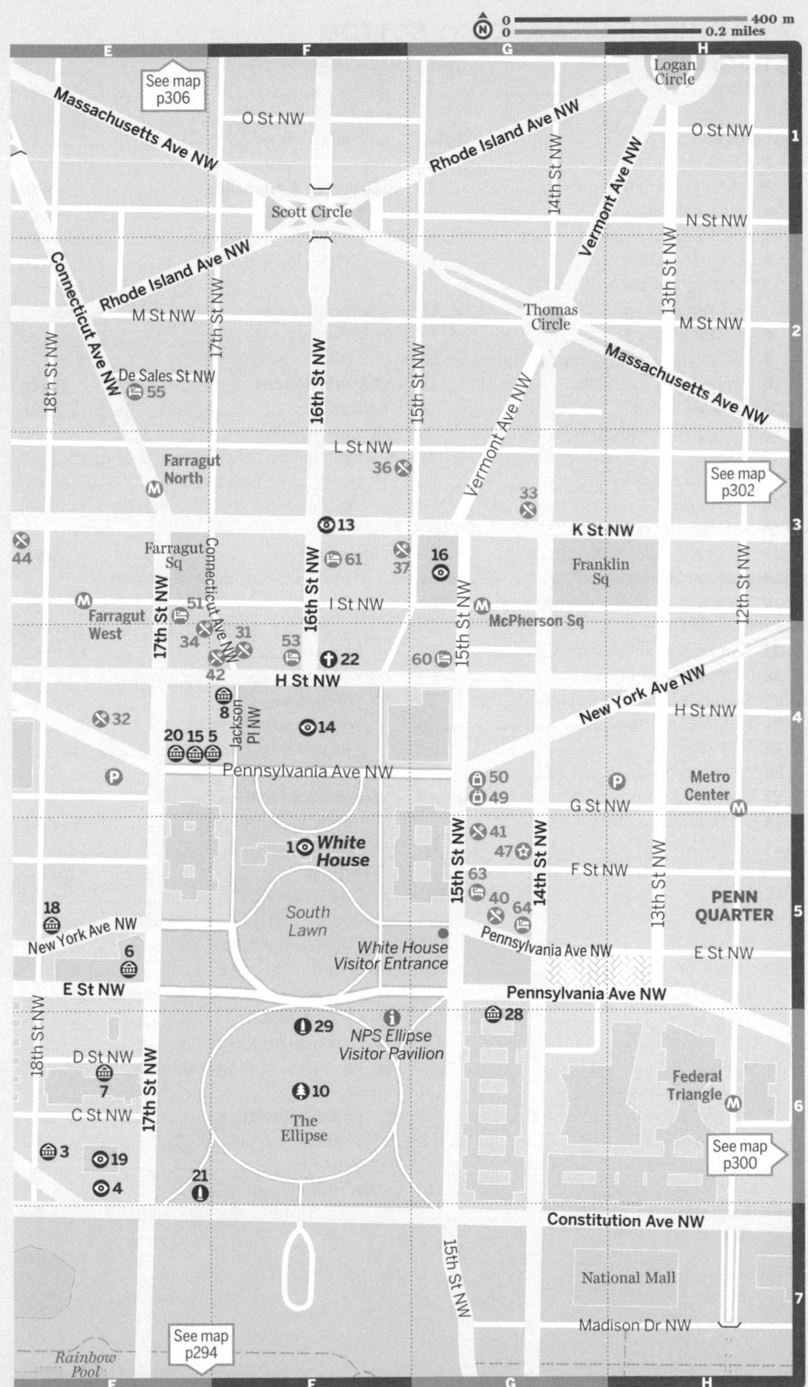

WHITE HOUSE AREA & FOGGY BOTTOM *Map on p296*

Top Sights (p78)

1 White House F5

Sights (p82)

2 Albert Einstein Memorial C6
3 Art Museum of the Americas E6
4 Aztec Gardens E6
5 Blair House F4
6 Corcoran Gallery of Art E5
7 Daughters of the American Revolution E6
8 Decatur House F4
9 Department of the Interior Museum D6
10 Ellipse F6
11 Federal Reserve D6
12 George Washington University C4
13 K Street F3
14 Lafayette Square F4
15 Lee House E4
16 McPherson Square G3
17 National Academy of Sciences C6
18 Octagon Museum E5
19 Organization of American States E6
20 Renwick Gallery E4
21 Second Division Memorial E6
22 St John's Church F4
23 St Mary's Episcopal Church B4
24 State Department C6
25 Textile Museum C4
26 University Yard D4
27 Watergate Complex A4
28 White House Visitor Center G6
29 Zero Milestone F6

Eating (p87)

30 Bayou B2
31 Bombay Club F4
32 BreadLine E4
Cafe Du Parc .... (see 64)
Circle Bistro .... (see 57)
33 DC Coast G3
34 Equinox E4
35 Founding Farmers D4
36 G Street Food F3
37 Georgia Brown's F3
38 Kaz Sushi Bistro D3
39 Marcel's B3
40 Occidental Grill G5
41 Old Ebbitt Grill G5
42 Oval Room F4
43 Prime Rib D3
44 Sichuan Pavilion E3

Drinking & Nightlife (p89)

45 Froggy Bottom Pub D3
Le Bar .... (see 60)
Off the Record .... (see 53)
POV .... (see 63)
Round Robin .... (see 64)
46 Science Club D2

Entertainment (p90)

47 Hamilton G5
48 Kennedy Center A5
National Symphony Orchestra .... (see 48)
Washington Ballet .... (see 48)
Washington National Opera .... (see 48)

Shopping (p91)

American Institute of Architects Bookstore .... (see 18)
Indian Craft Shop .... (see 9)
Renwick Gallery .... (see 20)
49 W Curtis Draper Tobacconist G4
50 White House Gifts G4
White House Historical Association Museum Shop .... (see 28)

Sports & Activities

Kennedy Center .... (see 48)

Sleeping (p227)

51 Club Quarters E3
52 George Washington University Inn B4
53 Hay-Adams Hotel F4
54 Hotel Lombardy C3
55 Mayflower Renaissance Hotel E2
56 Melrose Hotel B3
57 One Washington Circle C3
58 Residence Inn Foggy Bottom B4
59 River Inn B3
60 Sofitel Lafayette Square G4
61 St Regis Washington F3
62 The Quincy D2
63 W Hotel Washington G5
64 Willard InterContinental Hotel G5

CAPITOL HILL & SOUTHEAST DC *Map on p300*

Key on p299

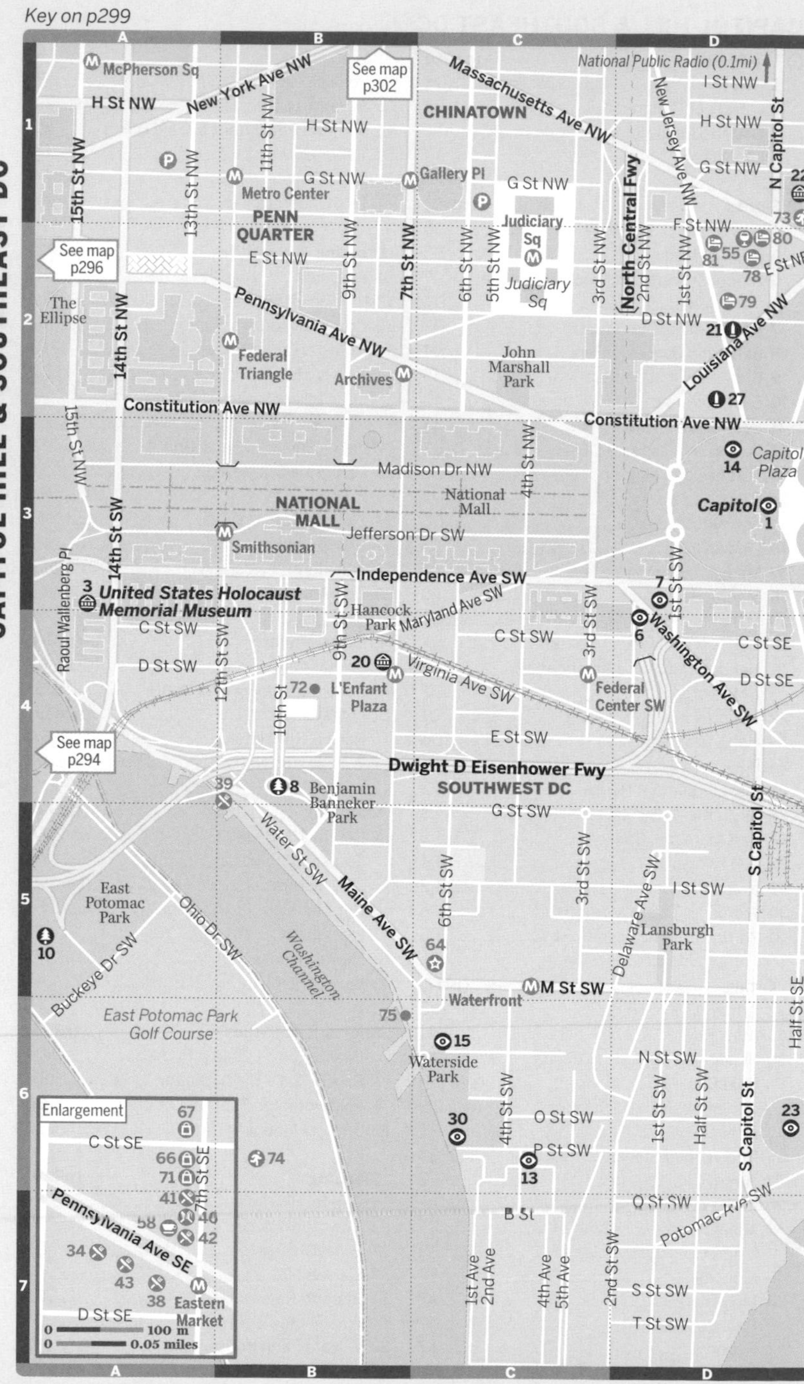

McPherson Sq
H St NW
New York Ave NW
See map p302
Massachusetts Ave NW
CHINATOWN
National Public Radio (0.1mi)
I St NW
H St NW
G St NW
N Capitol St
Metro Center
Gallery Pl
Judiciary Sq
PENN QUARTER
E St NW
F St NW
E St NE
D St NW
North Central Fwy
See map p296
The Ellipse
15th St NW
14th St NW
13th St NW
11th St NW
9th St NW
7th St NW
6th St NW
5th St NW
3rd St NW
2nd St NW
1st St NW
Pennsylvania Ave NW
Federal Triangle
Archives
John Marshall Park
Louisiana Ave NW
Constitution Ave NW
Capitol Plaza
Madison Dr NW
NATIONAL MALL
National Mall
4th St NW
Capitol
Jefferson Dr SW
Smithsonian
Independence Ave SW
United States Holocaust Memorial Museum
Raoul Wallenberg Pl
14th St SW
12th St SW
9th St SW
Hancock Park
Maryland Ave SW
C St SW
D St SW
3rd St SW
1st St SW
Washington Ave SW
C St SE
D St SE
L'Enfant Plaza
Virginia Ave SW
Federal Center SW
10th St SW
E St SW
See map p294
Dwight D Eisenhower Fwy
SOUTHWEST DC
Benjamin Banneker Park
G St SW
Water St SW
Maine Ave SW
East Potomac Park
Ohio Dr SW
Washington Channel
6th St SW
Delaware Ave SW
I St SW
S Capitol St
Lansburgh Park
Buckeye Dr SW
M St SW
Waterfront
East Potomac Park Golf Course
Half St SE
Waterside Park
N St SW
4th St SW
O St SW
P St SW
1st St SW
Half St SW
Q St SW
Potomac Ave SW
B St
1st Ave
2nd Ave
4th Ave
5th Ave
2nd St SW
S St SW
T St SW
Enlargement
C St SE
7th St SE
Pennsylvania Ave SE
Eastern Market
D St SE
0 100 m
0 0.05 miles

CAPITOL HILL & SOUTHEAST DC

DOWNTOWN & PENN QUARTER

Key on p304

DOWNTOWN & PENN QUARTER

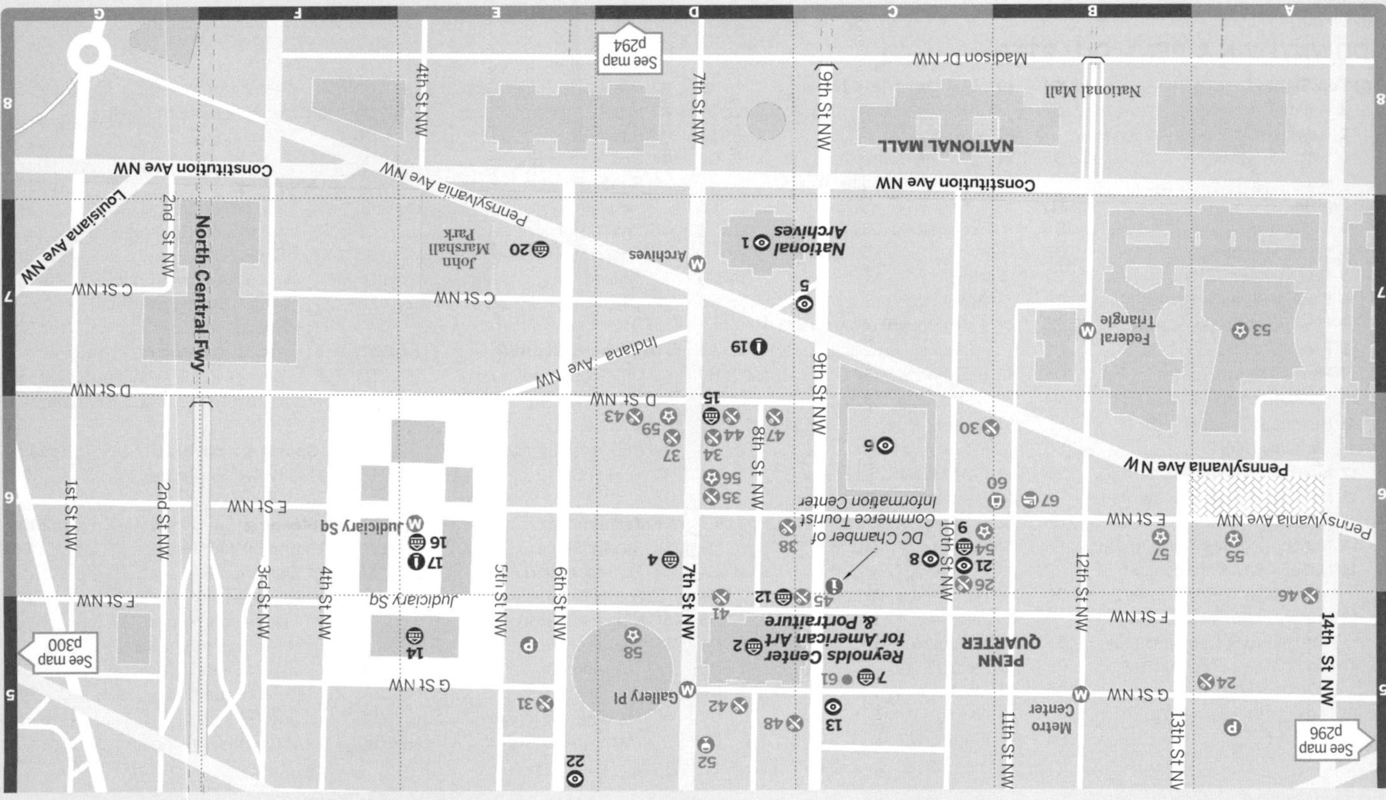

DOWNTOWN & PENN QUARTER

DOWNTOWN & PENN QUARTER *Map on p302*

Top Sights (p129)
1 National Archives ... D7
2 Reynolds Center for American Art & Portraiture ... D5

Sights (p131)
3 Chinatown ... D4
4 Crime Museum ... D6
5 FDR Memorial Stone ... C7
6 Federal Bureau of Investigation ... C6
7 Flashpoint Gallery ... C5
8 Ford's Theatre ... C6
9 Ford's Theatre Center ... C6
10 Friendship Arch ... D4
11 Historical Society of Washington, DC ... D3
12 International Spy Museum ... D5
13 Martin Luther King Jr Memorial Library ... C5
14 National Building Museum ... E5
15 National Law Enforcement Memorial Visitors Center ... D6
16 National Law Enforcement Museum (Future Site) ... E6
17 National Law Enforcement Officers Memorial ... E6
18 National Museum of Women in the Arts ... B4
19 Navy Memorial & Naval Heritage Center ... D7
20 Newseum ... E7
21 Petersen House ... C6
22 Surratt House site (Wok & Roll) ... E5
Touchstone Gallery ... (see 23)

Eating (p134)
23 Acadiana ... C3
24 Astro Doughnuts & Fried Chicken ... A5
25 Bibiana ... B4
26 Bistro D'Oc ... C6
27 Brasserie Beck ... B3
28 Busboys & Poets ... E3
29 Cafe Mozart ... A4
30 Central Michel Richard ... C6
31 Daikaya ... E5
32 Dangerously Delicious Pies ... D4
33 Full Kee ... E4
34 Hill Country Barbecue ... D6
35 Jaleo ... D6
36 Matchbox Pizza ... D4
37 Merzi ... D6
38 Minibar ... D6
39 Nando's Peri-Peri ... D4
40 Ping Pong ... D4
41 Poste ... D5
42 Proof ... D5
43 Rasika ... D6
44 Red Apron Butchery ... D6
Ronald Reagan Building Food Court ... (see 53)
45 Shake Shack ... C5
46 Shops at National Place ... A5
47 Teaism ... D6
48 Zaytinya ... D5

Drinking & Nightlife (p137)
49 City Tap House ... D4
50 Green Lantern ... A2
Poste Lounge ... (see 41)
51 RFD Washington ... D4
52 Rocket Bar ... D5

Entertainment (p138)
53 Capitol Steps ... A7
54 E Street Cinema ... C6
Ford's Theatre ... (see 8)
55 National Theatre ... A6
56 Shakespeare Theatre Company ... D6
57 Warner Theatre ... B6
58 Washington Capitals ... D5
Washington Mystics ... (see 58)
Washington Wizards ... (see 58)
59 Woolly Mammoth Theatre Company ... D6

Shopping (p139)
60 Coup de Foudre ... B6
International Spy Museum Shop ... (see 12)
National Archives Shop ... (see 1)
National Building Museum Shop ... (see 14)
National Museum of Women in the Arts Shop ... (see 18)
Teaism Shop ... (see 47)

Sports & Activities (p139)
61 City Segway Tours ... C5

Sleeping (p230)
62 Capital View Hostel ... F4
63 Eldon Suites ... C2
64 Hampton Inn ... E4
65 Henley Park Hotel ... C3
66 Hostelling International – Washington DC ... C3
67 Hotel Harrington ... B6
Hotel Monaco ... (see 41)
68 Morrison-Clark Inn ... C2

DUPONT CIRCLE & KALORAMA *Map on p306*

Key on p305

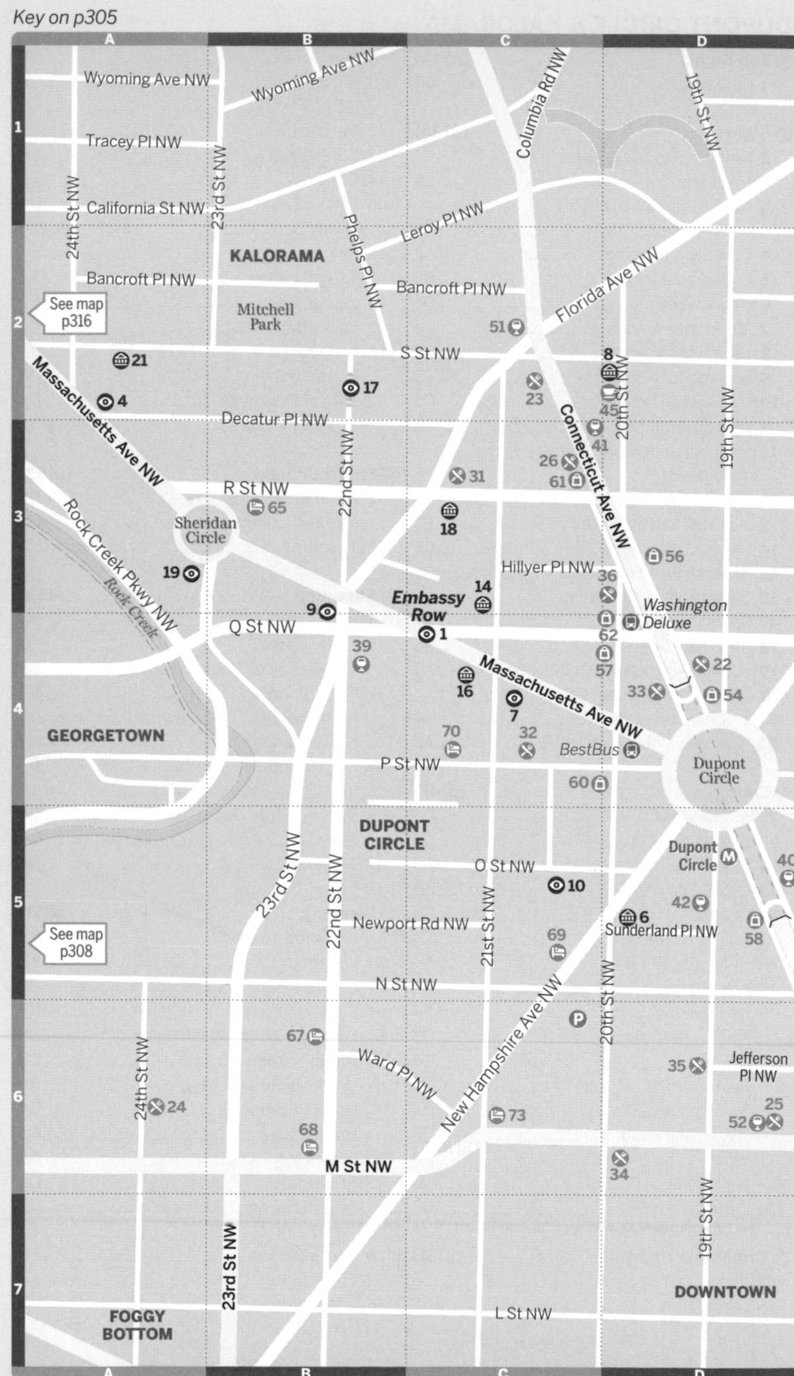

DUPONT CIRCLE & KALORAMA
A
B
C
D
1
2
3
4
5
6
7
Wyoming Ave NW
Tracey Pl NW
California St NW
24th St NW
23rd St NW
Columbia Rd NW
19th St NW
Leroy Pl NW
Phelps Pl NW
KALORAMA
Bancroft Pl NW
Mitchell Park
See map p316
Florida Ave NW
S St NW
21
17
4
8
23
45
20th St NW
Massachusetts Ave NW
Decatur Pl NW
Connecticut Ave NW
41
22nd St NW
26
31
61
R St NW
65
18
Sheridan Circle
Rock Creek Pkwy NW
Rock Creek
56
Hillyer Pl NW
19
36
14
Embassy Row
9
Washington Deluxe
Q St NW
1
62
39
57
22
16
33
54
7
GEORGETOWN
70
32
BestBus
P St NW
Dupont Circle
60
DUPONT CIRCLE
23rd St NW
O St NW
40
10
42
6
Sunderland Pl NW
58
Newport Rd NW
21st St NW
See map p308
69
N St NW
New Hampshire Ave NW
P
67
Ward Pl NW
35
Jefferson Pl NW
24th St NW
24
73
25
52
68
M St NW
34
19th St NW
DOWNTOWN
L St NW
FOGGY BOTTOM

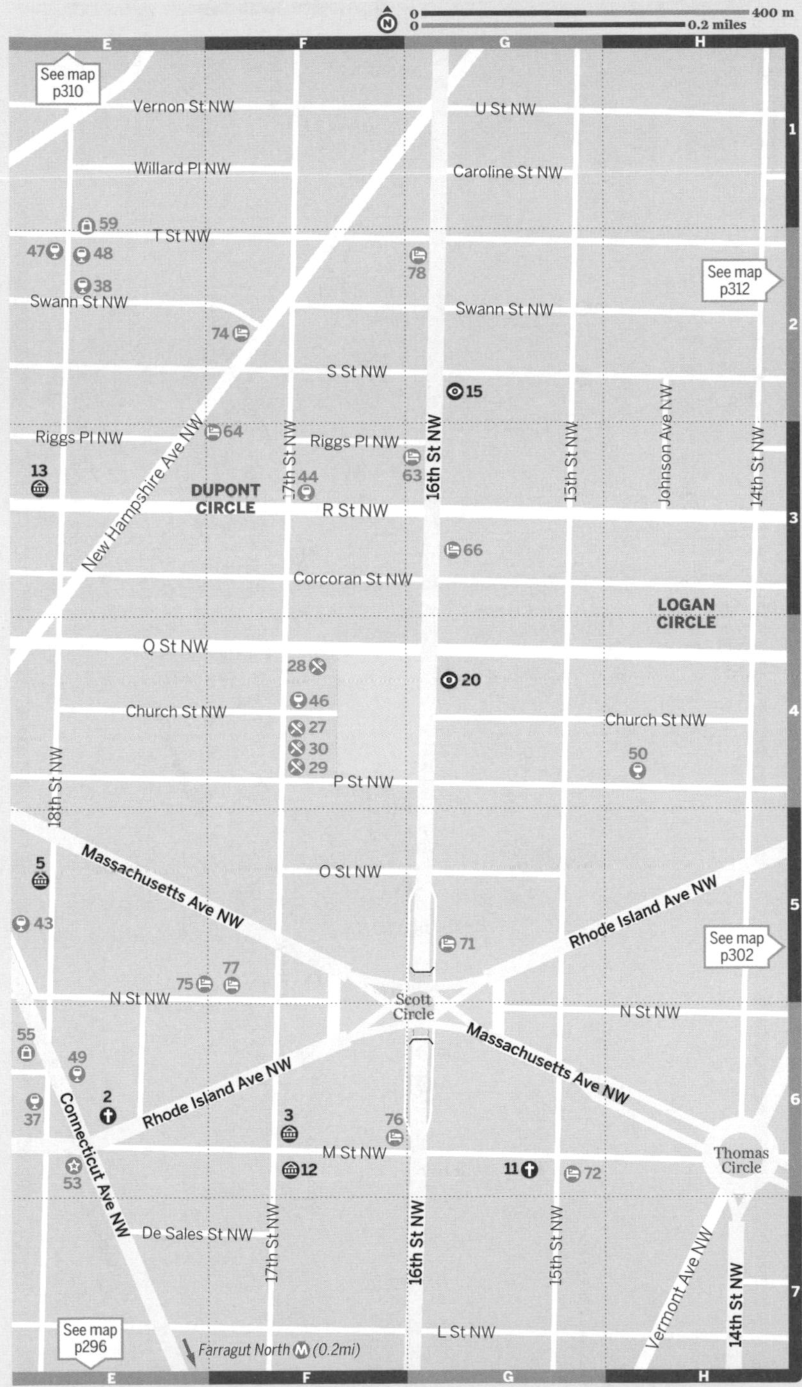
DUPONT CIRCLE & KALORAMA
400 m
0.2 miles
See map p310
See map p312
See map p302
See map p296
Vernon St NW
U St NW
Willard Pl NW
Caroline St NW
T St NW
Swann St NW
S St NW
Riggs Pl NW
R St NW
Corcoran St NW
Q St NW
Church St NW
P St NW
O St NW
N St NW
M St NW
De Sales St NW
L St NW
New Hampshire Ave NW
Massachusetts Ave NW
Rhode Island Ave NW
Connecticut Ave NW
Vermont Ave NW
Johnson Ave NW
18th St NW
17th St NW
16th St NW
15th St NW
14th St NW
DUPONT CIRCLE
LOGAN CIRCLE
Scott Circle
Thomas Circle
Farragut North (0.2mi)

GEORGETOWN

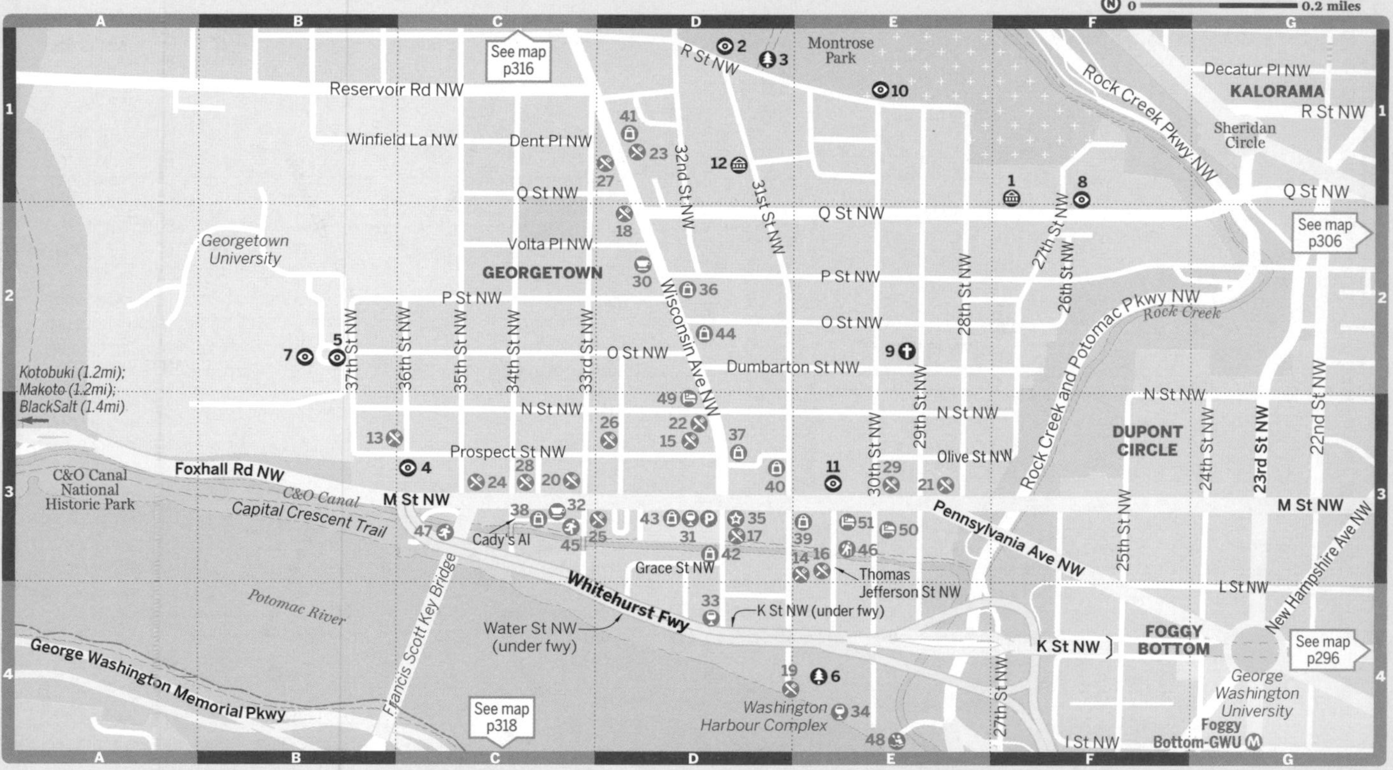

400 m
0.2 miles
See map p316
Reservoir Rd NW
Winfield La NW
Dent Pl NW
R St NW
Montrose Park
Rock Creek Pkwy NW
Decatur Pl NW
KALORAMA
R St NW
Sheridan Circle
Q St NW
32nd St NW
31st St NW
Q St NW
27th St NW
26th St NW
Q St NW
See map p306
Georgetown University
Volta Pl NW
GEORGETOWN
P St NW
P St NW
28th St NW
Rock Creek and Potomac Pkwy NW
Rock Creek
O St NW
37th St NW
36th St NW
35th St NW
34th St NW
33rd St NW
O St NW
Wisconsin Ave NW
Dumbarton St NW
Kotobuki (1.2mi); Makoto (1.2mi); BlackSalt (1.4mi)
N St NW
N St NW
N St NW
30th St NW
29th St NW
DUPONT CIRCLE
24th St NW
23rd St NW
22nd St NW
Prospect St NW
Olive St NW
C&O Canal National Historic Park
Foxhall Rd NW
C&O Canal
M St NW
M St NW
Capital Crescent Trail
Cady's Al
Pennsylvania Ave NW
25th St NW
New Hampshire Ave NW
Grace St NW
Thomas Jefferson St NW
L St NW
Potomac River
Whitehurst Fwy
K St NW (under fwy)
Water St NW (under fwy)
K St NW
FOGGY BOTTOM
See map p296
George Washington Memorial Pkwy
Francis Scott Key Bridge
See map p318
Washington Harbour Complex
27th St NW
I St NW
George Washington University
Foggy Bottom-GWU

GEORGETOWN

Sights (p94)

Dalghren Chapel .... (see 7)
1 Dumbarton House F1
2 Dumbarton Oaks D1
3 Dumbarton Oaks Park D1
4 Exorcist Stairs C3
Female Union Band Cemetery .... (see 8)
5 Georgetown University B2
6 Georgetown Waterfront Park E4
7 Healy Hall B2
8 Mt Zion Cemetery F1
9 Mt Zion United Methodist Church E2
10 Oak Hill Cemetery E1
11 Old Stone House E3
12 Tudor Place D1

Eating (p98)

13 1789 .... B3
14 Baked & Wired E3
15 Cafe Milano D3
16 Chez Billy Sud E3
17 Ching Ching Cha D3
18 Dolcezza D2
19 Fiola Mare D4
20 Georgetown Cupcake C3
21 La Chaumière E3
22 Martin's Tavern D3
23 Patisserie Poupon D1
24 Pie Sisters C3
25 Pizzeria Paradiso D3
26 Quick Pita D3
27 Simply Banh Mi D1
28 Sweetgreen C3
29 Unum E3

Drinking & Nightlife (p101)

30 Cafe Bonaparte D2
31 J Paul's D3
32 Kafe Leopold C3
33 Mr Smith's D4
34 Sequoia E4
Tombs .... (see 13)

Entertainment (p101)

35 Blues Alley D3

Shopping (p102)

36 Appalachian Spring D2
37 Apple Store D3
38 Cady's Alley C3
39 Lush E3
40 Old Print Gallery D3
41 Oliver Dunn, Moss & Co and Catharine Roberts D1
42 Patagonia D3
Relish .... (see 38)
43 Shops at Georgetown Park D3
44 Tugooh Toys D2

Sports & Activities (p103)

45 Big Wheel Bikes C3
46 C&O Canal Towpath E3
47 Capital Crescent Trail C3
Key Bridge Boathouse .... (see 47)
48 Thompson Boat Center E4

Sleeping (p229)

49 Georgetown Inn D3
50 Georgetown Suites E3
51 Graham Georgetown E3

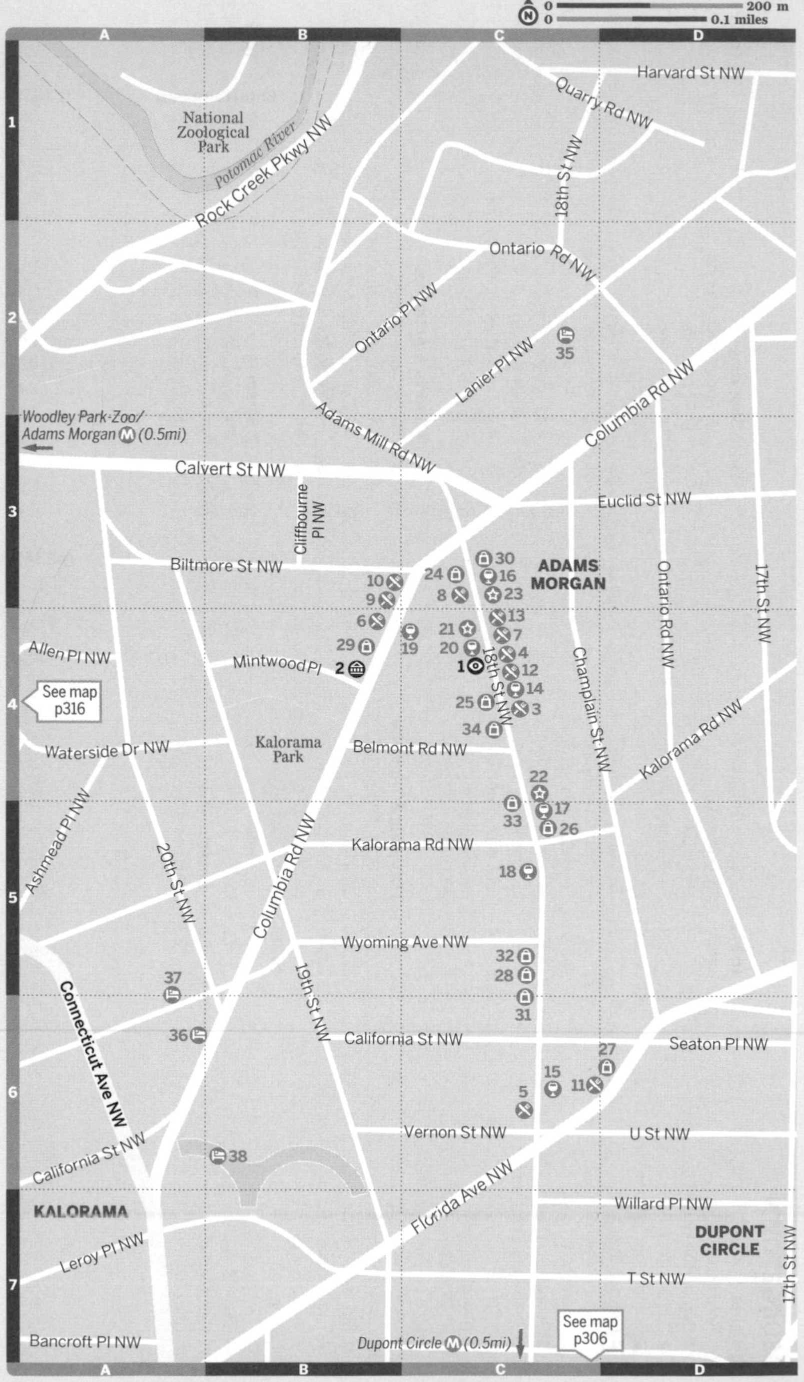

0 200 m
0 0.1 miles
A
B
C
D
1
2
3
4
5
6
7
National Zoological Park
Potomac River
Rock Creek Pkwy NW
Harvard St NW
Quarry Rd NW
18th St NW
Ontario Rd NW
Ontario Pl NW
Lanier Pl NW
Columbia Rd NW
Adams Mill Rd NW
Woodley Park-Zoo/ Adams Morgan M (0.5mi)
Calvert St NW
Cliffbourne Pl NW
Euclid St NW
Biltmore St NW
ADAMS MORGAN
Allen Pl NW
Mintwood Pl
See map p316
Champlain St NW
Ontario Rd NW
17th St NW
Waterside Dr NW
Kalorama Park
Belmont Rd NW
Kalorama Rd NW
Ashmead Pl NW
20th St NW
Kalorama Rd NW
Wyoming Ave NW
19th St NW
Connecticut Ave NW
California St NW
Seaton Pl NW
Vernon St NW
U St NW
California St NW
Florida Ave NW
Willard Pl NW
KALORAMA
DUPONT CIRCLE
Leroy Pl NW
T St NW
17th St NW
Bancroft Pl NW
Dupont Circle M (0.5mi)
See map p306
1
2
3
4
5
6
7
8
9
10
11
12
13
14
15
16
17
18
19
20
21
22
23
24
25
26
27
28
29
30
31
32
33
34
35
36
37
38

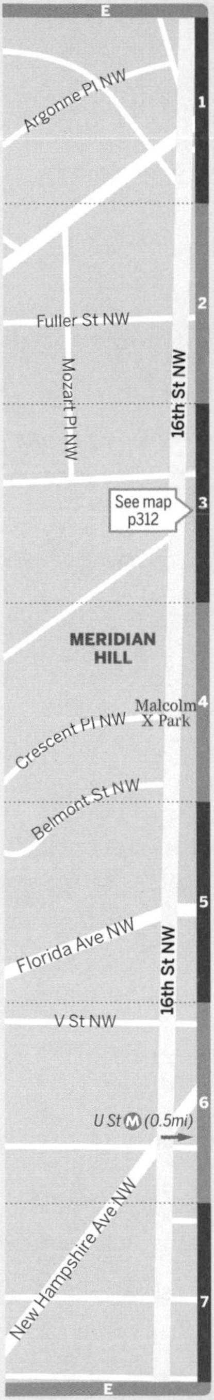

Sights (p157)

1 District of Columbia Arts Center C4
2 Hierarchy B4

Eating (p157)

3 Amsterdam Falafelshop C4
4 BUL C4
5 CakeRoom C6
6 Cashion's Eat Place B4
7 Diner C4
Donburi .... (see 1)
8 Julia's Empanadas C3
9 Mintwood Place B3
10 Perrys B3
11 Pleasant Pops C6
12 Rumba Cafe C4
13 Tryst C4

Drinking & Nightlife (p161)

14 Black Squirrel C4
15 Blaguard C6
16 Bossa C3
17 Dan's Cafe C5
18 Dr Clock's Nowhere Bar C5
19 Habana Village C4
20 Millie & Al's C4

Entertainment (p162)

21 Bukom Cafe C4
22 Columbia Station C4
23 Madam's Organ C3

Shopping (p162)

24 Adams Morgan Farmers Market C3
25 B&K Newsstand C4
26 Brass Knob C5
27 Commonwealth D6
28 Crooked Beat Records C5
29 Fleet Feet B4
30 Idle Time Books C3
31 Meeps C6
32 Skynear Designs C5
33 Smash! C5
34 Toro Mata C4

Sleeping (p234)

35 Adam's Inn C2
36 American Guest House A6
37 Taft Bridge Inn A5
38 Washington Hilton B6

LOGAN CIRCLE, U STREET & COLUMBIA HEIGHTS

Key on p314

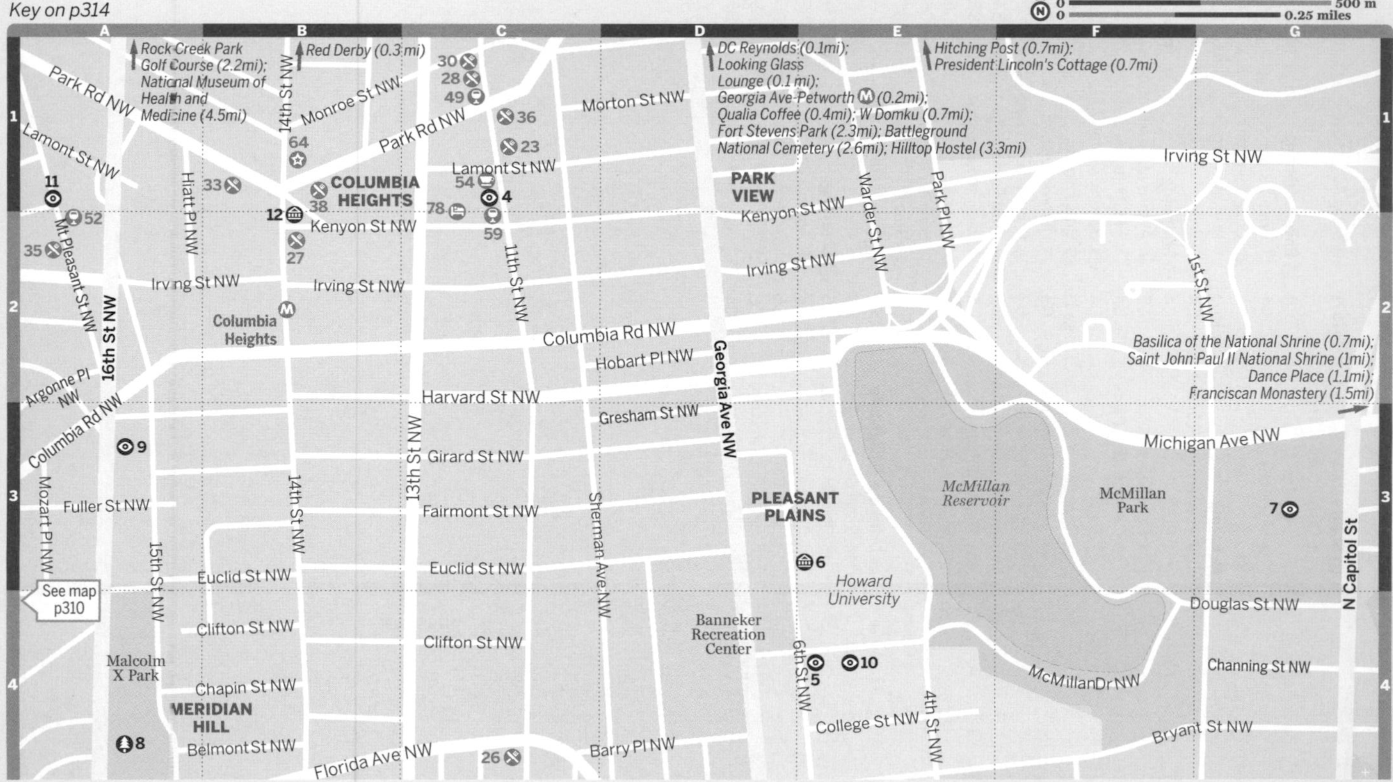

LOGAN CIRCLE, U STREET & COLUMBIA HEIGHTS

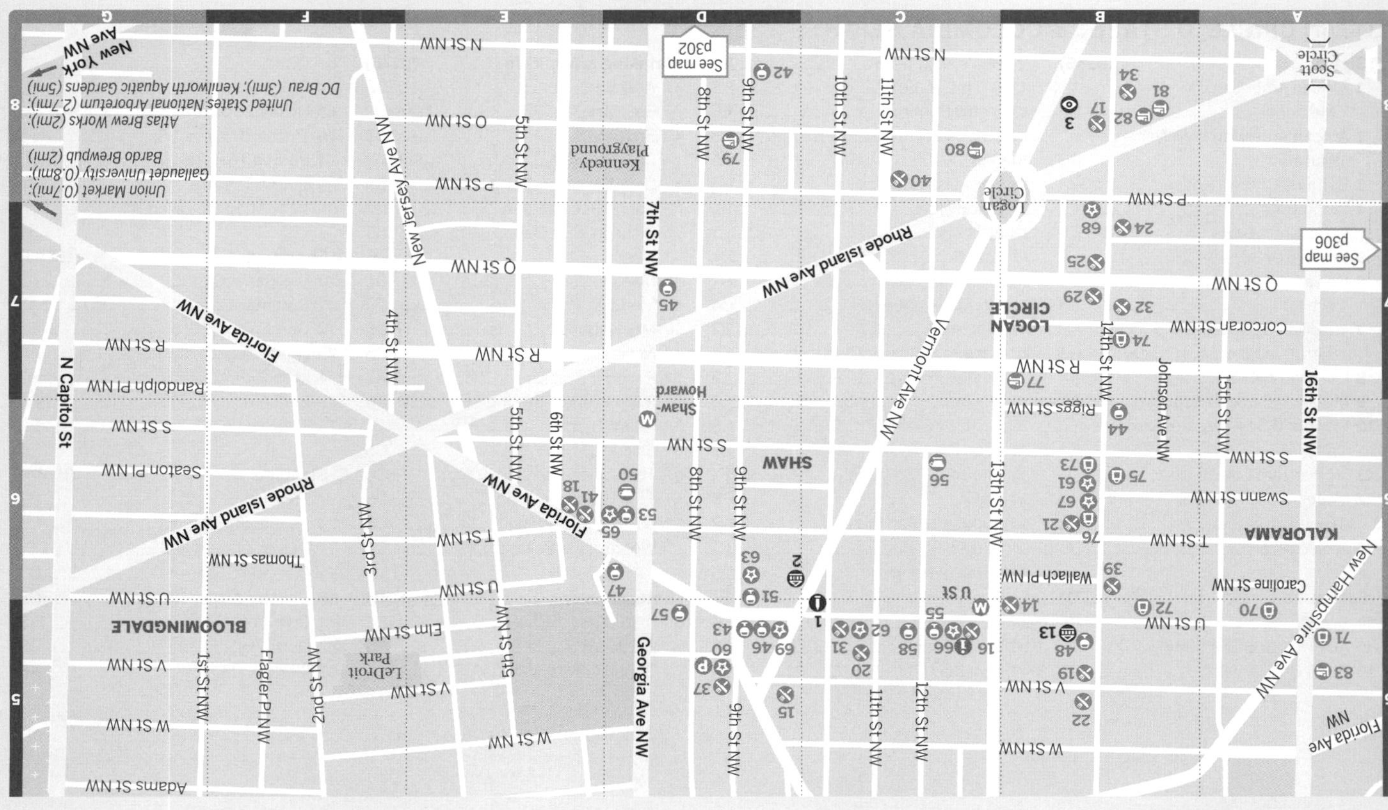

LOGAN CIRCLE, U STREET & COLUMBIA HEIGHTS *Map on p312*

Sights (p166)
1 African American Civil War Memorial ... C5
2 African American Civil War Museum ... D6
3 Bethune Council House ... B8
4 BloomBars ... C1
Founders' Library ... (see 10)
5 Howard University ... E4
6 Howard University Gallery of Art ... E3
7 McMillan Reservoir Sand Filtration Plant ... G3
8 Meridian Hill Park ... A4
9 Mexican Cultural Institute ... A3
10 Moorland-Spingarn Research Center ... E4
11 Mt Pleasant Street ... A1
12 Museum of Unnatural History ... B2
13 Project 4 ... B5

Eating (p171)
14 &pizza ... B5
15 American Ice Company ... D5
16 Ben's Chili Bowl ... C5
Ben's Next Door ... (see 16)
17 Birch & Barley ... B8
18 Bistro Bohem ... E6
19 Busboys & Poets ... B5
20 Chix ... C5
21 Compass Rose ... B6
22 Eatonville ... B5
23 El Chucho ... C1
24 Estadio ... B7
25 Etto ... B7
26 Florida Avenue Grill ... C4
27 Heights ... B2
28 Kangaroo Boxing Club ... C1
29 Le Diplomate ... B7
30 Maple ... C1
31 Oohh's & Aahh's ... C5
32 Pearl Dive Oyster Palace ... B7
33 Pho 14 ... B1
34 Pig ... B8
35 Pupuseria San Miguel ... A2
36 Red Rocks Pizzeria ... C1
37 Satellite Room ... D5
38 Sticky Fingers ... B1
39 Tico ... B6
40 Veranda on P ... C8
41 Zenebech ... E6

Drinking & Nightlife (p176)
42 A&D Bar ... D8
Bar Pilar ... (see 67)
43 Brixton ... D5
Churchkey ... (see 17)
44 Cork Wine Bar ... B6
45 Dacha Beer Garden ... D7
46 Dickson Wine Bar ... D5
47 Flash ... D6
48 Marvin ... B5
49 Meridian Pint ... C1
50 Mockingbird Hill ... D6
51 Nellie's ... D6
52 Raven ... A2
53 Right Proper Brewing Co ... D6
54 Room 11 ... C1
55 Saloon ... C5
56 The Coffee Bar ... C6
57 Town Danceboutique ... D5
58 U Street Music Hall ... C5
59 Wonderland Ballroom ... C2

Entertainment (p181)
60 9:30 Club ... D5
61 Black Cat ... B6
62 Bohemian Caverns ... C5
63 DC9 ... D6
64 Gala Hispanic Theatre ... B1
65 Howard Theatre ... D6
66 Lincoln Theatre ... C5
67 Source Theatre ... B6
68 Studio Theatre ... B7
69 Velvet Lounge ... D5

Shopping (p183)
70 Big Planet Comics ... A5
71 Caramel ... A5
72 Good Wood ... B5
73 Home Rule ... B6
74 Miss Pixie's ... B7
75 Redeem ... B6
76 Treasury ... B6

Sleeping (p234)
77 1887 Inn ... B7
78 Asante Sana Guest Quarters ... C1
79 Cambria Suites at O ... D8
80 Chester Arthur House ... C8
81 District Hotel ... B8
82 Hotel Helix ... B8
83 Meridian Manor ... A5

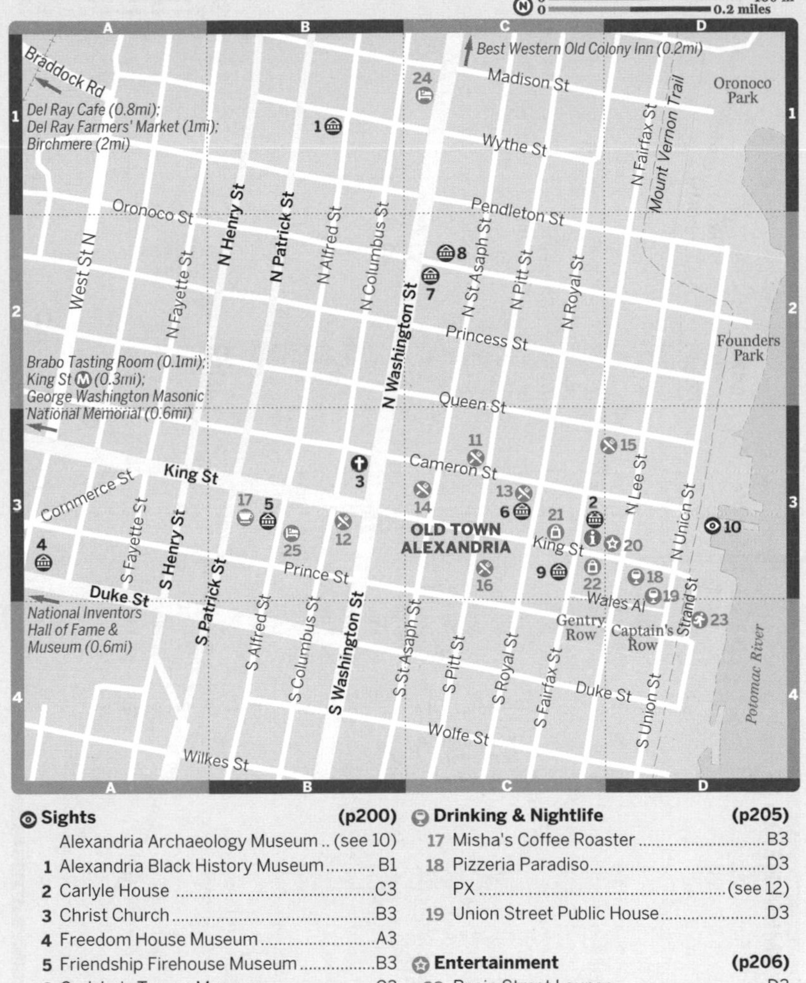

Sights (p200)

Eating (p203)

Drinking & Nightlife (p205)

Entertainment (p206)

Shopping (p206)

Sports & Activities (p207)

Sleeping (p236)

UPPER NORTHWEST DC

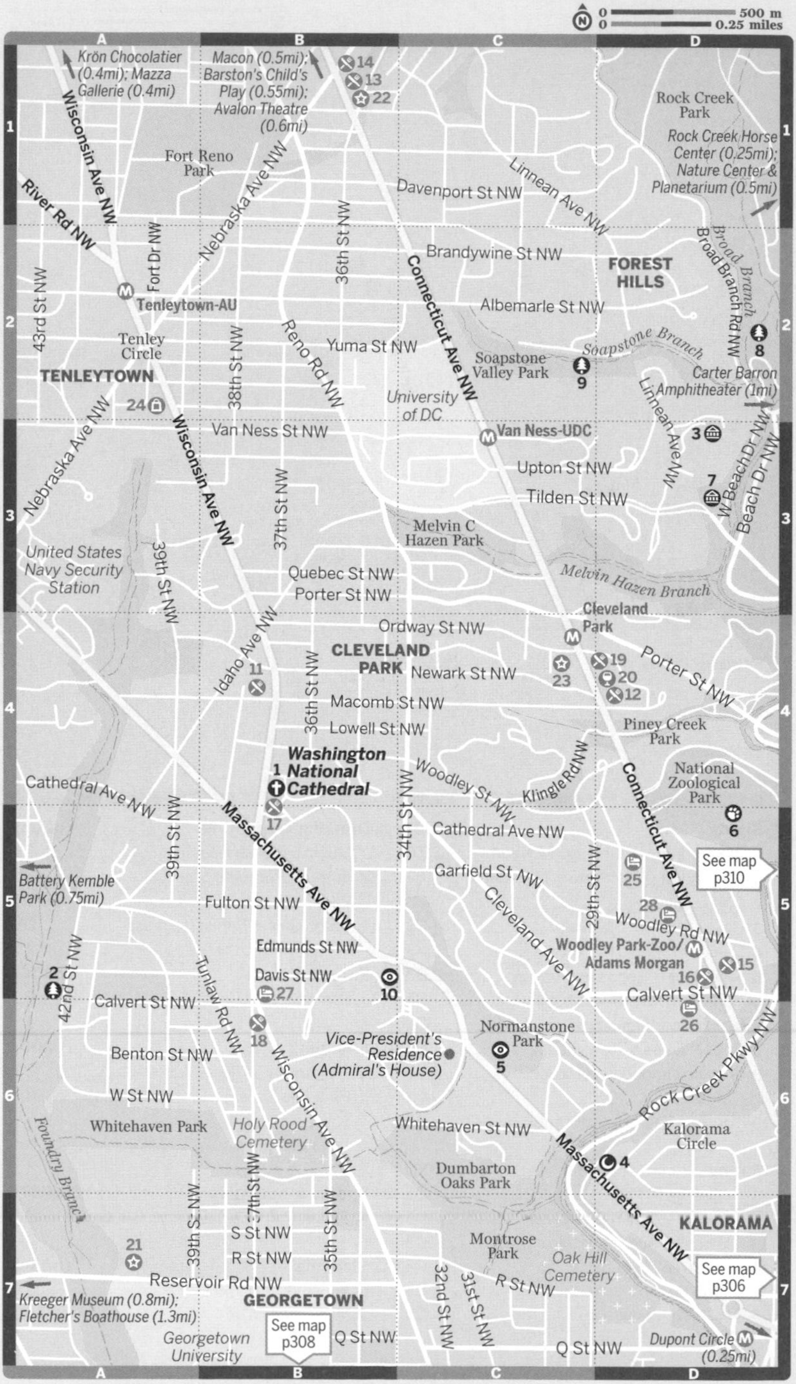

0 500 m
0 0.25 miles

Krön Chocolatier (0.4mi); Mazza Gallerie (0.4mi)
Macon (0.5mi); Barston's Child's Play (0.55mi); Avalon Theatre (0.6mi)
14
13
22
Rock Creek Park
Rock Creek Horse Center (0.25mi); Nature Center & Planetarium (0.5mi)
Wisconsin Ave NW
Fort Reno Park
Nebraska Ave NW
River Rd NW
Davenport St NW
Linnean Ave NW
Fort Dr NW
36th St NW
Connecticut Ave NW
Brandywine St NW
FOREST HILLS
Broad Branch
Broad Branch Rd NW
43rd St NW
Tenleytown-AU
Albemarle St NW
38th St NW
Reno Rd NW
Yuma St NW
Soapstone Branch
8
Tenley Circle
Soapstone Valley Park
9
Carter Barron Amphitheater (1mi)
TENLEYTOWN
University of DC
Linnean Ave NW
24
Van Ness St NW
Van Ness-UDC
3
Nebraska Ave NW
Upton St NW
W Beach Dr NW
Tilden St NW
7
Beach Dr NW
37th St NW
Melvin C Hazen Park
United States Navy Security Station
39th St NW
Quebec St NW
Porter St NW
Melvin Hazen Branch
Cleveland Park
Ordway St NW
Idaho Ave NW
CLEVELAND PARK
Newark St NW
23
19
20
12
Porter St NW
11
36th St NW
Macomb St NW
Lowell St NW
Piney Creek Park
Washington National Cathedral
1
Woodley St NW
Klingle Rd NW
National Zoological Park
Cathedral Ave NW
17
39th St NW
Massachusetts Ave NW
34th St NW
Cathedral Ave NW
6
Garfield St NW
29th St NW
25
See map p310
Battery Kemble Park (0.75mi)
Fulton St NW
Cleveland Ave NW
28
Woodley Rd NW
Edmunds St NW
Woodley Park-Zoo/ Adams Morgan
2
42nd St NW
Tunlaw Rd NW
Davis St NW
27
10
16
15
Calvert St NW
Calvert St NW
26
18
Normanstone Park
Benton St NW
Vice-President's Residence (Admiral's House)
5
Wisconsin Ave NW
Rock Creek Pkwy NW
W St NW
Whitehaven Park
Holy Rood Cemetery
Whitehaven St NW
Kalorama Circle
Foundry Branch
37th St NW
Dumbarton Oaks Park
4
Massachusetts Ave NW
39th St NW
S St NW
35th St NW
KALORAMA
21
R St NW
Montrose Park
Oak Hill Cemetery
Reservoir Rd NW
R St NW
32nd St NW
31st St NW
See map p306
Kreeger Museum (0.8mi); Fletcher's Boathouse (1.3mi)
GEORGETOWN
See map p308
Q St NW
Georgetown University
Q St NW
Dupont Circle (0.25mi)

UPPER NORTHWEST DC

Top Sights (p187)
1 Washington National Cathedral....B4

Sights (p188)
2 Glover Archbold Park....A5
3 Hillwood Museum & Gardens....D3
4 Islamic Center....D6
5 Kahlil Gibran Memorial Garden....C6
6 National Zoo....D5
7 Peirce Mill....D3
8 Rock Creek Park....D2
9 Soapstone Valley Trail....C2
10 US Naval Observatory....B5

Eating (p190)
11 2 Amys....B4
12 Ardeo....D4
13 Buck's Fishing & Camping....B1
14 Comet Ping Pong....B1
15 Lebanese Taverna....D5
16 Open City....D5
17 Open City at the National Cathedral....B5
18 Rocklands Barbecue....B6
19 St Arnold's Mussel Bar....D4
Vace Deli....(see 12)

Drinking & Nightlife (p192)
Bardeo....(see 12)
20 Nanny O'Brien's Irish Pub....D4

Entertainment (p192)
21 La Maison Française....A7
22 Politics & Prose Bookstore....B1
23 Uptown Theater....C4

Shopping (p193)
National Zoo....(see 6)
Politics & Prose Bookstore....(see 22)
24 Sullivan's Toy Store....A2

Sleeping (p235)
25 Kalorama Guest House....D5
26 Omni Shoreham Hotel....D6
27 Savoy Suites....B5
28 Woodley Park Guest House....D5

ARLINGTON

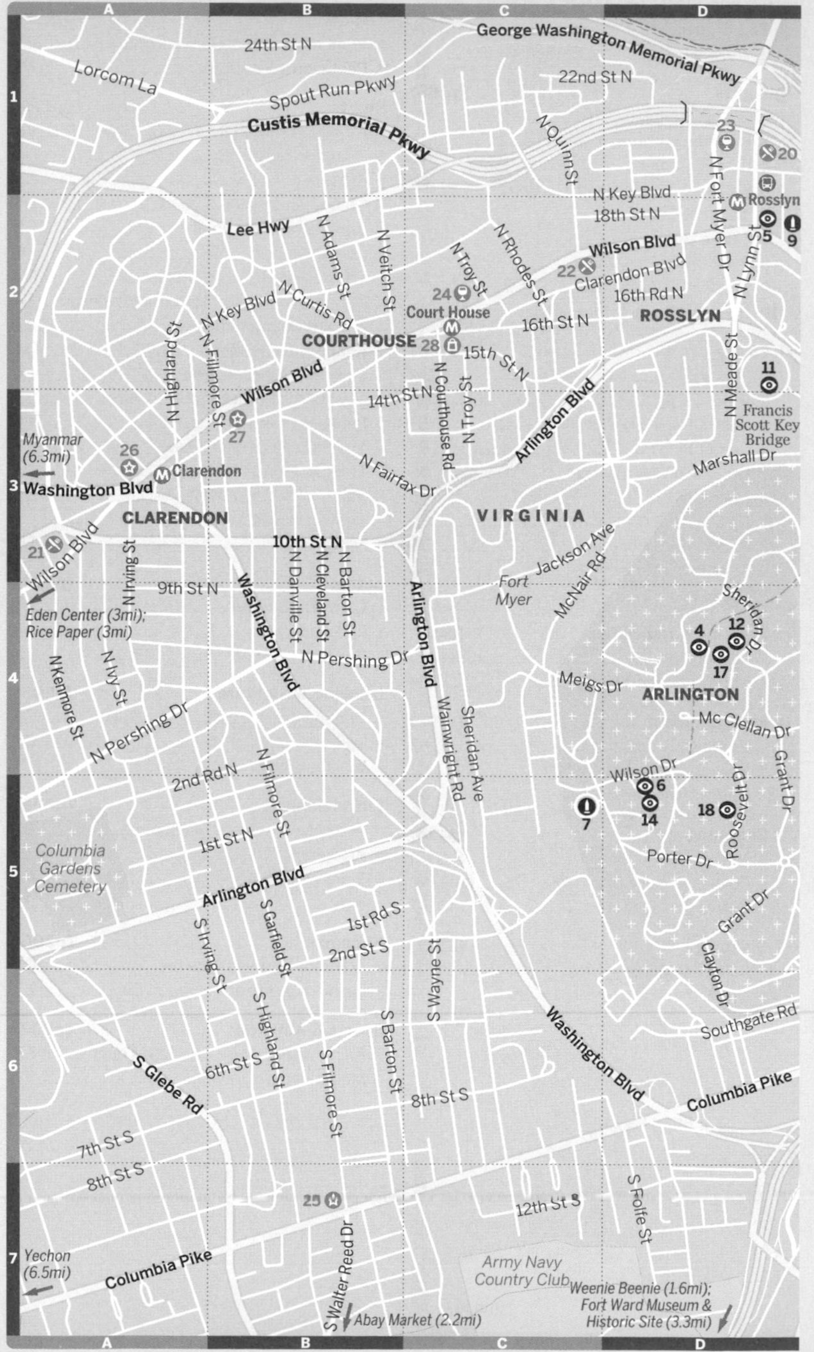

George Washington Memorial Pkwy
24th St N
Lorcom La
Spout Run Pkwy
22nd St N
Custis Memorial Pkwy
N Quinn St
N Key Blvd
18th St N
Rosslyn
Lee Hwy
N Adams St
N Veitch St
N Troy St
N Rhodes St
Wilson Blvd
Clarendon Blvd
16th Rd N
N Fort Myer Dr
N Lynn St
N Key Blvd
N Curtis Rd
Court House
COURTHOUSE
16th St N
ROSSLYN
N Highland St
N Fillmore St
15th St N
N Meade St
Wilson Blvd
14th St N
N Courthouse Rd
N Troy St
Arlington Blvd
Francis Scott Key Bridge
Myanmar (6.3mi)
Clarendon
Washington Blvd
N Fairfax Dr
Marshall Dr
CLARENDON
VIRGINIA
10th St N
Wilson Blvd
N Irving St
N Danville St
N Cleveland St
N Barton St
Jackson Ave
9th St N
Washington Blvd
Arlington Blvd
Fort Myer
McNair Rd
Eden Center (3mi); Rice Paper (3mi)
Sheridan Dr
N Pershing Dr
N Kenmore St
N Ivy St
Meigs Dr
ARLINGTON
N Pershing Dr
Wainwright Rd
Sheridan Ave
Mc Clellan Dr
2nd Rd N
N Fillmore St
Wilson Dr
Grant Dr
Roosevelt Dr
Columbia Gardens Cemetery
1st St N
Porter Dr
Arlington Blvd
S Garfield St
1st Rd S
Grant Dr
S Irving St
2nd St S
S Wayne St
Clayton Dr
S Highland St
S Barton St
Washington Blvd
Southgate Rd
S Glebe Rd
6th St S
S Filmore St
8th St S
Columbia Pike
7th St S
8th St S
12th St S
S Folfe St
Yechon (6.5mi)
Columbia Pike
S Walter Reed Dr
Army Navy Country Club
Weenie Beenie (1.6mi); Fort Ward Museum & Historic Site (3.3mi)
Abay Market (2.2mi)

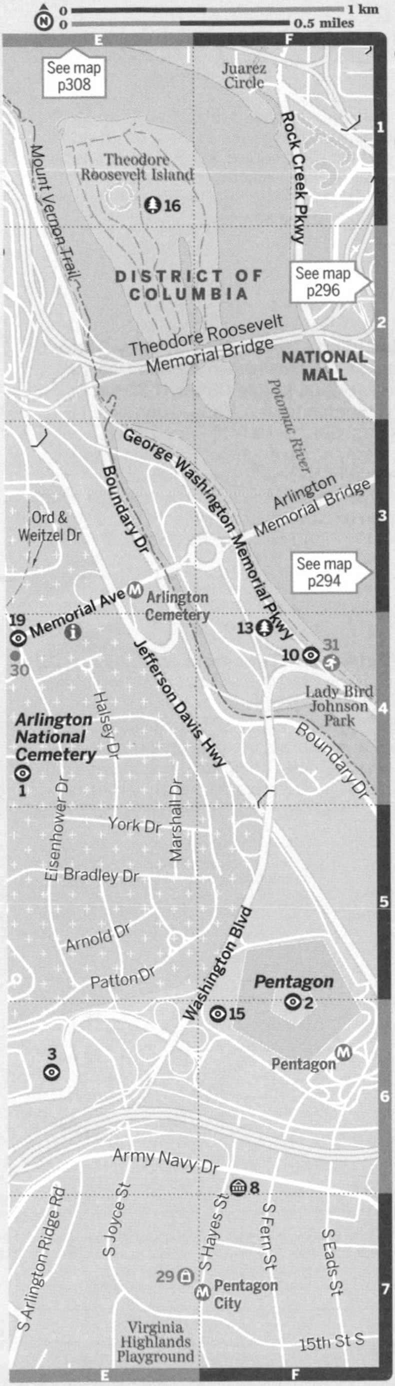

Top Sights (p197)

1 Arlington National Cemetery ... E4
2 Pentagon ... F6

Sights (p199)

3 Air Force Memorial ... E6
4 Arlington House ... D4
5 Artisphere ... D2
6 Challenger Memorial ... D5
7 Confederate Monument ... C5
8 DEA Museum ... F6
9 Freedom Park ... D2
10 George Washington Memorial Parkway ... F4
11 Iwo Jima Memorial ... D2
12 Kennedy Gravesites ... D4
13 Lady Bird Johnson Park ... F4
14 Mast of the Battleship USS Maine ... D5
15 Pentagon Memorial ... F6
16 Theodore Roosevelt Island ... E1
17 Tomb of Pierre L'Enfant ... D4
18 Tomb of the Unknowns ... D5
19 Women in Military Service for America Memorial ... E4

Eating (p202)

20 Caffé Aficionado ... D1
21 El Pollo Rico ... A3
22 Ray's to the Third ... C2

Drinking & Nightlife (p205)

23 Continental ... D1
24 Ireland's Four Courts ... C2
Whitlow's on Wilson ... (see 27)

Entertainment (p206)

25 Arlington Cinema & Drafthouse ... B7
Artisphere ... (see 5)
26 Clarendon Ballroom ... A3
27 Iota ... B3

Shopping (p206)

28 Arlington Farmers' Market ... C2
29 Fashion Centre at Pentagon City ... E7

Sports & Activities (p207)

30 Arlington National Cemetery Tours ... E4
31 Mount Vernon Trail ... F4

Our Story

A beat-up old car, a few dollars in the pocket and a sense of adventure. In 1972 that's all Tony and Maureen Wheeler needed for the trip of a lifetime – across Europe and Asia overland to Australia. It took several months, and at the end – broke but inspired – they sat at their kitchen table writing and stapling together their first travel guide, *Across Asia on the Cheap*. Within a week they'd sold 1500 copies. Lonely Planet was born.

Today, Lonely Planet has offices in Franklin, London, Melbourne, Oakland, Beijing and Delhi, with more than 600 staff and writers. We share Tony's belief that 'a great guidebook should do three things: inform, educate and amuse'.

Our Writers

Karla Zimmerman

Coordinating Author, National Mall, White House Area & Foggy Bottom, Georgetown, Capitol Hill & Southeast DC, Downtown & Penn Quarter, Dupont Circle & Kalorama, Adams Morgan, Logan Circle, U Street & Columbia Heights During her Washington travels, Karla devoured an embarrassing number of half-smokes, shook hands with Racing Abe Lincoln at Nationals Park and gaped unabashedly at the documents in the National Archives. The city will always be her first love, the one that unleashed her wanderlust. Walking up the steps of the Lincoln Memorial at night as a five year old, and seeing big ol' white-gleaming Abe, is her first magical travel memory. Karla has written for several Lonely Planet guides to the USA, Canada, Caribbean and Europe. Karla also wrote the 'Plan Your Trip' and 'Survival Guide' sections for this guide and cowrote the Sleeping chapter.

Read more about Karla at:
lonelyplanet.com/members/karlazimmerman

Regis St Louis

Upper Northwest DC, Northern Virginia, Day Trips from Washington, DC An avid news junkie and admirer of all things strange and political, Regis was destined for a long and tumultuous relationship with Washington, DC. No matter the season, he never tires of exploring the city of grand design and big ideas (if sometimes small-minded bureaucrats). A long-time travel writer, Regis has contributed to dozens of Lonely Planet titles, including the previous edition of *Washington, DC* and *USA*. When not down in the capital, he resides in Brooklyn, New York. Regis also wrote the 'Understand Washington, DC' chapters for this guide and cowrote the Sleeping chapter.

Read more about Regis at:
lonelyplanet.com/members/regisstlouis

Published by Lonely Planet Publications Pty Ltd
ABN 36 005 607 983
6th edition – Nov 2015
ISBN 978 1 74321 579 1

10 9 8 7 6 5 4 3 2 1
Printed in China